PEOPLE OF THE PEYOTE

PEOPLE

Huichol Indian History, Religion, & Survival

OF THE

EDITED BY STACY B. SCHAEFER & PETER T. FURST

PEYOTE

University of New Mexico Press *Albuquerque*

© 1996 by the
University of New Mexico Press
17 16 15 14 13 12   5 6 7 8 9 10
Paperbound ISBN-13: 978-0-8263-1905-0
Library of Congress
Cataloging-in-Publication Data
People of the peyote :
Huichol Indian history, religion,
& survival /
Edited by Stacy B. Schaefer and
Peter T. Furst.—1st ed.

p.   cm.
Includes bibliographical references
and index.
ISBN 0-8263-1684-0 (cloth)
ISBN 0-8263-1905-x
1. Huichol Indians—History.
2. Huichol Indians—Religion.
3. Huichol philosophy.
4. Peyotism—Mexico—Jalisco.
5. Shamanism—Mexico—Jalisco.
6. Ethnohistory—Mexico—Jalisco.
7. Rites and ceremonies—Mexico—Jalisco.
8. Nayarit (Mexico)—Social life and customs.
I. Schaefer, Stacy B., 1956–
II. Furst, Peter T., 1922–
F1221.H9P46   1996
972'.34004974—dc20   95-32453
CIP

Frontispiece
Temple Musicians, Santa Catarína.
(Photo by Susana Valadez.)

For the Wixárika

And the Memory of

Nicolás Carrillo de la Cruz

Santos Aguilar Carrillo

Ramón Medina Silva

and

Barbara G. Myerhoff

CONTENTS

CONCLUSION

PREFACE

The idea of putting together a multinational collection of essays on Huichol history, religion, and survival had its genesis in a fifty-year-old literary tragedy—the destruction in World War II of Konrad Theodor Preuss's manuscript of Huichol texts that Franz Boas, the "father of American anthropology," had originally planned to publish in his *International Journal of American Linguistics*. Preuss died in 1938, Boas in 1944, and the completed manuscript, never having made it to the United States, went up in flames in the bombing of Berlin. What survived of Preuss's Huichol ethnography of 1906-08 were wax cylinder recordings of sacred chants and several essays he had contributed to German journals from the field and after his return. These had never been translated into English, and a few years ago one of us (P.T.F.) decided to do so. The problem of where to put them into print remained. Jill L. McKeever Furst suggested that I join with Stacy B. Schaefer, who received her doctorate at UCLA in 1990 with a dissertation on weaving as the woman's path in Huichol culture, in making the Preuss essays the departure point for a different kind of book on the Huichols, one that would, for a healthy change, break out of the tight circle of English-speaking scholarship.

We proposed the idea to Jeffrey Grathwohl, then an editor at the University of New Mexico Press (now director of the University of Utah Press), during a meeting of the American Anthropological Association in Washington, D.C. A contract followed from a prospectus with sample chapters and a tentative list of contributors. Then came the hard work assembling and, where necessary, translating, the essays, which took several years.

The two earliest essays to arrive—from Paris—were those of the French ethnologists Denis Lemaistre, whom Schaefer knew from San Andrés, and Michel Perrin of the Collège de France. Perrin is a prominent scholar who, having previously contributed myths of the Guajiro Indians of Venezuela to a twenty-four-volume UCLA series on South American Indian mythology, was suggested to us by its senior editor, our old professor at UCLA, Johannes Wilbert. Both Lemaistre's and Perrin's essays were translated for us from the French by Wilbert's co-editor on the UCLA series, the multilingual Karin Simoneau.

From Salomón Nahmad Sittón, the Mexican anthropologist whose concern for Huichol survival dates back thirty years to his time as director of the Cora-Huichol Center of the Instituto Nacional Indigenista in Tepic, Nayarit, we received a far-ranging essay on the problems Huichols are facing in the modern world. It was translated from the Spanish by Bonnie Glass-Coffin, who wrote her own doctoral dissertation on female Peruvian shaman/healers whose practice involves *San Pedro* (*Trichocereus pachanoi*), a tall, columnar cactus chemically, though not otherwise, related to peyote.

Nahmad's contribution was augmented in the summer of 1992 with a face-to-face interview in Oaxaca, Mexico, where Nahmad is now working with indigenous people doing their own ethnographies. Guillermo Espinosa Velasco, director general of Mexico's Instituto Nacional Indigenista, dictated his recollections of the great shaman of San Andrés, Nicolás Carrillo de la Cruz, in English, which he speaks well. Maribel Carrizales, an anthropology student of Schaefer's at the University of Texas–PanAmerican, was enlisted to translate another contribution from Mexico, the ethnologist Marina Anguiano's essay on the Huichol mortuary ceremony. Yet another Mexican contribution is that on medicinal plants by Armando Casillas Romo, M.D., a physician whom Schaefer had met in the course of her field work in San Andrés.

An essay on Kiéri is authored by the Japanese scholar Masaya Yasumoto, Professor of Comparative Religion at Kyushu International University in Kitakyushu, Japan. Yasumoto is a specialist in shamanism whose fieldwork in Mexico has extended from 1979 to the present. His participation came about through a fortuitous encounter between Furst and a colleague of Yasumoto's, a Japanese ethnologist visiting the University of Pennsylvania Museum of Archeology and Anthropology in Philadelphia on his way back to Japan from studying shamanism in the Amazon. The Kiéri chapter arrived in Japanese, for which we found an able translator in Kunie Miyahara, a graduate student in psychology at West Chester University, who is as fluent in English as she is in her native tongue.

Susana Eger Valadez's essay on wolf power and wolf transformation is in a very real sense largely the work of a Huichol, a shaman named Ulu Temay (Arrow Man, or Young Arrow Person) in Huichol, and Santos in Spanish, with whom she worked for many years until his untimely recent death. Valadez is an American with an M.A. degree from UCLA who is married to a Huichol artist, Mariano Valadez.

The late Huichol artist-shaman Ramón Medina's personal recollections and philosophical musings had languished in Furst's files since the 1960s, waiting for an opportune moment to see the light of day.

The ethnohistoric look at the Huichols since the Conquest from the vantage point of Zacatecas was sent to us by anthropologist and ethnohistorian Alan R. Franz, Division Chair in the Social and Behavioral Sciences at Loyola Marymount University in Los Angeles, California. Franz's essay reinforces the unorthodox, but increasingly convincing, view that Huichols have maintained their cultural integrity not because of isolation, but as a response to almost continuous interaction with, and pressure from, the outside world.

The field work in Mexico of English ethnologist Anthony A. Shelton, Curator of Ethnology at the Royal Pavilion and Museums in Brighton, England, has focused on, among other contemporary problems, the relationship between the ideology and practice of maize cultivation in the face of change. Shelton's contribution covers that crucial topic.

Stacy B. Schaefer, in addition to her job as co-editor of this volume, has contributed two essays. The first, on the meaning of peyote to Huichols, started out as a lecture at a conference on shamanism, sacred plants, and altered states of consciousness in San Luis Potosí, Mexico, in 1992. Schaefer's second essay is on the astronomical and other functions of Huichol temple architecture. Neither essay would have been possible without the trust Schaefer has won from her Huichol friends over many field seasons since her first exposure to the culture in the late 1970s. Peter T. Furst is also a co-editor of this volume. His chapter on myth and history is the fruit of years of thinking about Huichol history and origins.

Although we did not consciously plan it that way, in the end all five comunidades indígenas that make up the Huichol territory—San Andrés, Santa Catarína, Guadalupe Ocotán, San Sebastián, and Tuxpan de Bolaños (the latter sometimes considered an annex of San Sebastián rather than an autonomous comunidad)—as well as the Huichol settlement on the lower Río Lerma, came to be represented among the various works included here. Anguiano did her research in Santa Catarína. Casillas Romo worked as physician to the Huichols and as ethnobotanist in San Andrés. Espinosa lived in San Andrés in the early 1970s. Until 1962, Ramón Medina, a multi-talented Huichol artist, musician, and ritualist with whom Furst worked from 1965 until his death in 1971, lived with his wife Guadalupe as a peasant farmer in the Huichol rural colony on the lower Río Lerma. Medina's family had moved there from the border area between Santa Catarína and San Sebastián when he was still a small boy, and his mother, the late Doña Kuka, was herself for many years a practicing shaman at Río Lerma. Lemaistre studied the ritual deer hunt and its ramifications in San Andrés, the same comunidad in which his senior compatriot Perrin collected data on the urukáme as ancestor-guardian, and where Furst was co-director of a UCLA anthropological-medical summer field school in 1967. Nahmad gained familiarity with much of the Huichol territory, its people, and its problems both as a social anthropologist and as an official of the Instituto Nacional Indigenista and the Secretaría de Educación Pública, and, most recently, as a consultant to the giant Aguamilpas dam project on the lower Río Lerma in Nayarit. Preuss collected mythology and recorded sacred chants in Santa Catarína, San Andrés, and other places, as well as among the Coras and Nahuas, in the first decade of this century. Schaefer initiated her field work in San Andrés in 1977, returned in 1983, and since January 1986 has worked there every year. Guadalupe Ocotán was where Shelton studied the ideology, practice, and contemporary problems of maize agriculture. Valadez resided for more than two years in San Andrés in the 1970s and is married to a Huichol who was born in Santa Catarína, where she travels frequently. Her shaman-consultant, the late Ulu Temay, was from La Laguna, on the border between San Andrés and Santa Catarína. The Huichol Center for Cultural Survival and the Traditional Arts, which she and her artist-husband established and have co-directed for many years in Santiago Ixcuintla, near the coast of Nayarit, and a second center they recently founded in Huejuquilla, Zacatecas, on the edge of the Sierra, are frequent hosts to Huichols from all over the Sierra. Finally, for his work on Kiéri and other topics in Huichol religion and ritual, the Japanese ethnologist of religion Masaya Yasumoto has, since 1980, made repeated and extended visits to Tuxpan de Bolaños and San Andrés, most recently in 1994.

Thus, this volume has benefited by the participation of scholars from not just the United States, but Mexico, Germany, England, France, and Japan, as well as Huichols themselves. With such a diverse group of contributors, and with representation of all parts of the Huichol territory, *People of the Peyote* really has turned out to be what we had hoped for.

Stacy B. Schaefer
Peter T. Furst

1 : INTRODUCTION

STACY B. SCHAEFER & PETER T. FURST

*If I conduct myself well, if I don't go around doing bad things, if my soul and heart
are good and clean, then the gods will look upon me well. It doesn't matter if my hat is old
and my clothes are ragged. If my heart is good then I become a reflection of the gods,
like a mirror.*
ULU TEMAY, Huichol shaman*

*Religion is to them a personal matter, not an institution, and therefore their
life is religious—from the cradle to the grave wrapped up in symbolism.*
CARL LUMHOLTZ, *Symbolism of the Huichol Indians*, 1900, p. xx

The Huichols, or, as they call themselves, Wixárika, are not among the largest of the
surviving indigenous societies of Mexico; with a population of nearly 20,000 over the
age of five, as counted by the national census of 1990, in sheer numbers they cannot
compare with contemporary speakers of Nahuatl, Mixtec, Zapotec, Maya, Huastec, or
Tarascan. In that part of eastern Mexico known as the Huasteca alone, the 1990 count
of Nahua-speakers is over 450,000!

What makes this relatively small group stand out among Mexican Indians who still
converse among themselves in their own language is thus not its size, but that, four
hundred and seventy-five years after the defeat of the Mexica, or Aztecs, of Tenochtitlan, the Huichols have maintained their pre-Christian religion without significant syncretism and with no more than nominal accommodation to the dominant Catholic
faith. It is also safe to say that—notwithstanding the addition of some Christian observances, such as Holy Week, to the annual round of communitywide ceremonies as
well as metal tools and domestic animals to the material culture and economy, and,
most recently, a degree of participation in the market economy—the majority of Huichols continue to live their everyday and ceremonial lives according to a vast body of

*In a 1984 interview with Susana Eger Valadez. (—Eds.)

practical and esoteric knowledge handed down from generation to generation by the divine ancestors. Even many of the thousands of Huichol-speakers who have migrated out of the Sierra Madre Occidental proper continue to think and feel as Huichols, and to observe at least some of the old rituals as much as possible in accordance with how they interpret the ancestral precepts. These emigrants have settled not only in such rural communities as those on the lower Río Lerma in Nayarit, but more recently also in cities like Guadalajara, Tepic, Zacatecas, Durango, and even the distant Mexican capital. In these latter settings it is obviously harder to maintain ceremonies that, being tied into the agricultural cycle in the Sierra, are now less immediately relevant to the realities of their new social and economic environment.

Nevertheless, even those Huichols most faithful to the old ways, within and outside the Sierra, do not order their lives by some strict religious dogma—and perhaps never did. There is surely a wrong way to perform the old ceremonies, but there are also many right ways, just as variations on common themes in Huichol oral tradition and sacred poetry are all "true." What this sometimes striking ideological diversity reflects, perhaps more than anything else, is not only a degree of isolation between the different communities that make up the Huichol territory, particularly between its eastern and its western halves, and the freedom of each Huichol to travel his or her own trail along the common road to the divine, but also diversity in what and who contributed in the first place to the evolution of Huichol culture as we know it today. Still, there is consensus, a certain philosophical unanimity among most members of this unique culture, that having remained Huichol through it all is something to be proud of, and that continuing to maintain that identity, even—or especially—where the forces for change and conformity seem almost irresistible, is desirable.

Huichol Political and Social Structures. Most of the mountainous Huichol territory, now measuring some 26,000 square kilometers, roughly half of what it is said to have been originally, lies within the states of Jalisco and Nayarit (Figure 1). It is bisected by the Río Chapalagana, which flows north to south through the Sierra Madre Occidental and empties into the Río Grande de Santiago, and which, when swollen by the summer rains, can be a formidable barrier to communication. Called Río Lerma along its lower reaches, including the Huichol colony established in the 1930s by refugees from the "Cristero troubles" near where the giant new hydroelectric project known as Aguamilpas was recently completed, the Santiago flows through the southern Sierra in Nayarit first to the northwest and then westward, emptying into the Pacific north of San Blas.

The rugged country the Huichols call their own is divided into several self-governing districts, or *comunidades indígenas*, that are not only independent of each other but also not always in harmonious relationship, mainly because of territorial disputes. They are not altogether independent of the outside world, however, because they fall under the jurisdictions of several different Mexican municipalities. Land is communally owned,

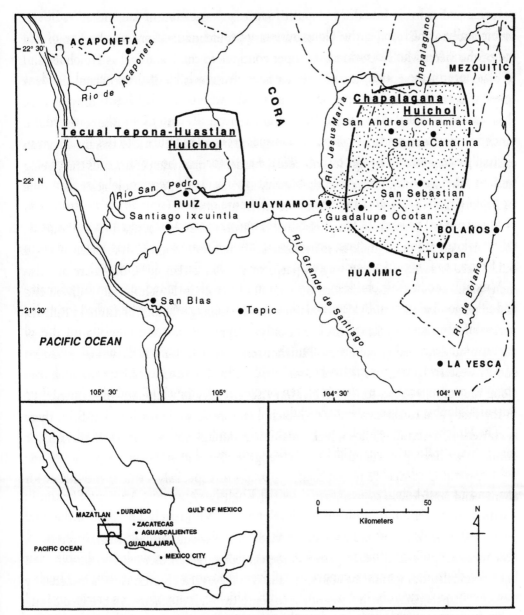

FIGURE 1. Map of the Huichol Region. (*Adapted from Grimes and Hinton* [1969:794].)

with plots assigned to individual families. This land is passed down in the family, many of which own several parcels, on which they reside in accordance with seasonal activities. This has been the practice for a very long time, and it is probably what the earliest Spanish documents referred to when they spoke of various small groups, more or less certainly identifiable as proto-Huichols, as primitive and seminomadic, part-time cultivators of the soil. There is constant encroachment on these lands from mestizos, and as a result there has been substantial alienation of traditional territory. A danger many Huichols now worry about is that these problems will be exacerbated by the federal

...proper continue to think and feel as Huichols, and

...*urukáte* (sing. *urukáme*, from *uru*,

...Huichol culture as we know it today. Still, there

...English ethnologist Anthony Shelton in Chapter 16 in relation to problems of development. With barely 3 percent of the total

maize. The several similar versions current among the Huichols give alternate names

FIGURE 2. Early Introduction to Maize. Children, especially girls, are often named for the different stages in the growth of maize. (*Photograph by Peter T. Furst.*)

for the young man whom his mother sends out in search of the first maize and who returns with Blue Maize Girl as his bride. One of these is Wáve Temay, Amaranth Boy.

Wild-growing plant foods and others that are, if not domesticated, at least managed, continue to play an important role in Huichol subsistence, especially when, as happens too frequently for comfort, last season's harvest has been depleted and government assistance is late or unavailable. Huichols love wild mushrooms and many edible species are harvested. The botanist James Bauml (1989:7), who has made Huichol ethnobotany his specialty, has listed a whole series of nutritious wild plant foods, ranging from mesquite (*Prosopis* spp.), *Manihot rhomboidea* spp. *microcarpa*, *Leucaena macrophylla*, and various tubers, as well as the fruits of manzanita (*Arctostaphylos pungens*), to the silk-cotton tree, a local variety of the *ceibas* that are so sacred to the Maya of southern Mexico and Central America. Of these, Leucaena plays a particularly important role, with Huichols eating the edible seeds as well as the tender seed pods raw and processing the dried seeds into a nourishing meal—a practice common to numerous indigenous inhabitants of the arid and semiarid zones of Mexico.[1]

Agricultural technology continues to be mainly based on the machete, the digging stick, and the hoe, although wooden plows pulled by draft animals are also employed, the lay of the land permitting (Figure 3). Traditionally, Huichols have farmed not the flat mesas but, after clearing them of trees and brush (and, in the absence of terracing, thereby exposing them to heavy erosion), the steep slopes of the barrancas. However sacred and vital to their survival Huichols consider maize to be, beset as it is by, among other limiting factors, shortage of arable land, poor soils, unreliable weather conditions, erosion, primitive technology, and continuing theft of land and damage to crops by mestizo and Huichol cattle, the maize crop is a constant source of anxiety, and much of Huichol ceremonial and individual prayer is directed toward its protection.

The natural and cultivated environment provides a good illustration of what Carl Lumholtz meant when he wrote of the impossibility of making a separation between the sacred and the ordinary in Huichol ideology, and of the fact that the whole country over which Huichols move, both within and outside the actual boundaries of their territory, is filled with "natural fetishes"—sacred rocks, water holes, lakes, groves, caves, barrancas, promontories, crossings, streams—which Huichols visit and where they leave prayers and petitions. That also includes the coastal area near San Blas, where Huichols locate the entrance to the underworld, marked by a tall offshore rock spire. There is no agreement on what this rock represents, except that it is sacred and sensate. Some Huichols identify it as Tutákame, the death god and guardian of the underworld, others as the goddess of the ocean, Tatéi (Our Mother) Haramara, still others as either another male deity or a giant candle. Whichever, this western region, where the Sun father "dies" each dusk as he descends into the sea for his journey below ground back to his birthplace in the Land of Dawn, is where the souls of Huichols travel initially after death, to join the relatives in a celebration that includes much drinking and eating peyote, before returning, again briefly, to their old community for a final farewell

FIGURE 3. On the Trail to the Coamil. (*Lithograph by Angel Bracho, Taller de Grafica Popular, Mexico City, c. 1940. $11\frac{1}{4}$" x $13\frac{3}{4}$".*)

before setting out for Wirikúta, the land of the sacred peyote cactus in the north-central desert. From there, shamans are thought to join the Sun god on his travels, first through the sky, and then guiding and protecting him on his dangerous subterranean journey back from west to east. Even though there is not complete agreement on just where the several souls each person has end up, there is a whole complex eschatological mythology connected with the journey of the soul, with numerous landmarks and animal guardians along the way. These are marked on a metaphysical map with which Huichols become familiar through the chant by which the shamans narrate its progress (see Chapters 12, 13, 14) and that is no less a part of the "natural" environment than its visible features.

Huichol mesa lands are typically covered with mixed oak and pine forest and separated by deep valleys with near-tropical vegetation cut by fast-flowing streams that served as effective natural barriers to outsiders, and even to internal communication. With the increasing shortage of land, these mesas have entered the picture, and with them, tractors. But tractors have proved a mixed blessing because they are expensive to run and keep in good repair. Also, ownership of tractors has tended to create inequalities and sometimes hard feelings. Domestic animals, except for the dog and the turkey of Old World origin, include cattle, horses, mules, burros, pigs, sheep, goats, and chickens. People sometimes go to extraordinary expense to buy a good horse for the high status it confers.

Much of the hierarchical system of elected community officials from governor on down derives from that introduced by the Franciscans in the eighteenth century. A council of *kawiteros*, usually, but not always, shamans or, at least, elders with experience and wisdom, functions as community leadership. The civil-religious hierarchy changes annually, and it is the kawiteros who, by means of dreaming and consensus, select the new governing structure. The major decisions are in the hands of the governor, *gobernador* in Spanish, *tatuani* in Huichol, a borrowing from the Nahuatl *tlatoani* (lit. "one who speaks well," an honorific also used for the Aztec ruler). He enjoys great prestige, and as his word commands respect, he often serves to arbitrate disputes within the community. He is also the religious figurehead, with his wife, who has a considerable role of her own in decision making, serving as his counterpart. Each temple district has its own commissioners, constable, judge, bilingual secretary, and police. Crimes are dealt with by fines, forced service, or jail, sometimes in the stocks. Murder, on the other hand, is dealt with by the mestizo authorities in the municipalities that have ultimate charge of the different indigenous communities.

Traditional marriage, arranged by the parents when the children are still in infancy, is bilateral, often between first cousins. In recent years the trend has been toward marriage with more distant kin, but even then people prefer that the prospective spouse be from the same temple district, or at least the same comunidad. As already indicated, children are of enormous importance. They are much indulged, they are the center of attention, and all members of the extended family help in their care. They are universally beloved, so much so that a child is sometimes considered to be "everybody's," rather than belonging only to his or her biological parents. Grandparents have a special relationship to the offspring of their own children. Often also the family shaman, the grandparent bestows, a few days after the birth, its first name on the child and presents it to the Sun Father as he comes up over the eastern horizon (Figure 4). If a child is struck by a dangerous illness, he or she will be given an additional name. New names are also bestowed at different stages of the child's maturation. Presumably because of the high infant mortality—up to 50 percent before the advent of modern medicines for epidemic childhood diseases of foreign origin, such as measles, whooping cough, scarlet fever, diphtheria, etc.—a Huichol is considered a complete human being only upon reaching the age of five. Except for those enrolled in government or mission boarding schools, children are educated informally by their parents, grandparents, or older siblings within the setting of the rancho and the annual ceremonial round, as well as during the hunt and on pilgrimages to one of the many sacred places in and around the Sierra, or to the peyote country itself. One important ceremony is focused specifically on the children: Tatéi Neixa, Dance of Our Mother, is a celebration of the first fruits

FIGURE 4. Nicholas Carrillo de la Cruz Supporting His Newborn Grandchild with His Feathered Power Arrows (Muviéris). Better known as 'Colas (d. 1974), the most respected shaman and community leader in San Andrés Cohamiata in the 1950s and 1960s, he bestows his first name on the infant and presents it to the Sun just peeking over the horizon. (*Photograph by Peter T. Furst, Spring 1967*).

FIGURE 5. Tatéi Neixa, Dance of Our Mother. This is the ceremony of the first fruits and the metaphorical flight of the youngest children to the peyote country under the guidance of the shaman and the divine messenger, Kaúyumari. The string across the crowded altar symbolizes the metaphorical journey, while the cotton balls symbolize the children whom the shaman's chant has transformed into hummingbirds. (*Photographed at Rancho El Colorín, Río Lerma Huichol colony, by Marina Anguiano Fernandez.*)

of the fields, in which the youngest children, those up to the age of five, are magically transformed into birds by the family shaman. In a lengthy chant, accompanied by a steady beat on the deerskin head of the upright, three-legged, hollow-log drum that Huichols call by the Nahuatl-derived term *tepu*, the shaman leads the children on a metaphorical flight that follows the route of the peyote pilgrimage. The transformed youngsters are represented by puffs of white cotton tied at intervals to a string, one end of which symbolizes the starting point of the magical journey, the other its destination in Wirikúta, the sacred peyote desert (Figure 5).

With children, Huichols always pay special attention to signs or portents, sometimes very subtle, that the child might become a *mara'akáme*, Huichol for shaman-singer. One way to determine this is to watch carefully the reaction from a child's first taste of peyote. The alkaloid-rich cactus is notorious for its bitter taste and acridity, and Huichols say that if a child nevertheless reacts pleasurably when his or her tongue comes in contact with it, it is likely that the child will follow the path of the shaman.

Shamans are generally male, but the vocation is open to both genders and there are also some women shaman-singers, more in some local communities than others. Children who demonstrate a desire, or a talent, for becoming shaman-singers, master musicians, or artists with the embroidery needle or on the loom, learn from family members proficient in these arts. One of us (S.B.S.) has been deeply involved for many years in the participant study of the practice and religious ideology of weaving; what S.B.S. found especially interesting was that by the time a girl reaches puberty, a rite of passage marked by cutting a lock of her hair, she has usually already mastered the basic techniques of backstrap loom-weaving, which she displays as a mark of her passage into womanhood, and that the path of becoming a true master weaver is akin to that of becoming a shaman. (The woman who taught S.B.S. the art and complex symbolism of weaving is the daughter of the female elder of S.B.S.'s long-time adopted Huichol family in San Andrés Cohamiata, who is herself a shaman-singer.)

Huichol society is basically egalitarian, but increasing participation in the market economy has inevitably created some inequalities, especially in differential access to certain economic and social advantages. Traditionally, social status is based on age, with the highest prestige and participation in community government, the important temple cargos, and the cargos in the local Catholic church accruing to the elders. Such specialists as shamans, master musicians, and those who master the arts and crafts, especially weaving, are given recognition and higher status as well.

Huichol Religion. The Huichols are unique not only because of the remarkable degree to which aboriginal religious beliefs and rituals persist among them at the end of the twentieth century, but also because their religion ties into everything else, all those subsystems that together make up a people's culture. The truth is that it is through their religion, their spirituality, and their arts and crafts, that the Huichols have captured the imagination of an outside world that has increasingly lost its own spiritual bearings. A century ago their sacred and symbolic arts drew the Norwegian Carl Lumholtz to them. His writings, in turn, inspired the German Konrad Theodor Preuss a few years later to record their rich mythology and sacred chants, in the hope that their living religious traditions, and that of their Cora neighbors, might provide clues to the religion of the ancient Central Mexicans (see Chapter 4). In the past thirty years, an increasing number of outsiders—from ethnologists, art historians, ethnobotanists, and scholars of Native American religion and sacred poetry, to New Agers and would-be Carlos Castanedas—have been drawn to the Wixárika. This is because word has spread that here more than anywhere else in contemporary Indian Mexico, conquest, conversion, and the massive socioeconomic and technological transformations since the European invasion seem to have had minimal negative effect on the indigenous religion, on the creative genius manifested in art and the sacred myths and songs, on the annual round of aboriginal ceremonies and rituals designed to assure the cycle of life, and on a connectedness with and knowledge of the natural environment disappearing from the globe as fast as are the great forests.

If this, to be sure, is an idealized image, it is nonetheless a fact that life and the old, pre-Christian religion are, for the average Huichol, and not just for the shaman as specialist in the sacred, indivisible. Every act, every symbol is a prayer and petition to higher powers that are, significantly, all called by kinship terms. What Lumholtz (1902:II, p. 15) wrote almost a century ago remains true today:

> Religious feeling pervades the thoughts of the Huichol so completely that every bit of decoration he puts on the most trivial part of his everyday garments or utensils is a request for some benefit, a prayer for protection against evil, or an expression of adoration of some deity. In other words, the people always carry prayers and devotional sentiments in visible form.

As ethnographers of Huichol intellectual culture and its relationship to everyday activities can still observe today, religion permeates all aspects of life. Most Huichols do not distinguish between the sacred and what we would regard as "secular." In truth, nothing is really "profane." Everything in the environment is alive and capable of sensation and independent action. All things are sentient, capable of feeling, action, and reaction. There is a life force, or "soul," no less in a clump of grass, a tree, a flower, a rock, a cloud, or an animal, as there is in the human being. Prayer offerings and petitions to the gods—for rain, maize, health, children, livestock, success on the hunt, and fertility of people, animals, and plants—are deposited in sacred places, usually in the form of gourd bowls decorated with beeswax, beads, and colored wool yarn, or as compound arrows with hardwood points and feather bundles attached to them, along with miniature objects representing the petitioner's desire. Tiny cut-out sandals, bottle gourds, and bows and arrows are common expressions of concern for boys, little weavings and embroideries for girls. People send the same kinds of prayer arrows to all the ancestor deities, but gourds have obvious uterine associations (just as they do among the Pueblos), and so are primarily presented to the female potencies.

Traditional religions such as that of the Huichols are often called "animistic," if not "nature worship." It would be more accurate to call them "ecological." The Huichol pantheon is a crowded one, indeed; as Preuss was told by his Huichol friends, there are as many gods as there are Huichols. Typically, these deities—a concept for which, by the way, there is no word in the Huichol language—are personifications of phenomena and forces in the natural environment. *Kakauyaríte* is one generic term Huichols use for the ancestor deities that reside in Wirikúta, the sacred peyote desert, and the Sierra. Here they manifest themselves as mountains, hills, and rocks. The meaning of kakauyaríte is uncertain; the closest the leading foreign student of the language,[2] Joseph E. Grimes, has been able to come is "Our Sandal Straps," perhaps a metaphor for "that

FIGURE 6. Yarn painting by Guadalupe de la Cruz Ríos of the hunt for the Deer-Peyote at the moment of transformation. The bird at left is a roadrunner (*Geococcyx californianus*), *üra* in Huichol, native to the southwestern United States and northern Mexican desert. Capable of inflicting the "laziness disease" (see chapter 6), this very alert bird reminds peyoteros to be swift in the hunt for the peyote. The long object between it and the peyote-deer is a shaman's *muviéri* (shaman's wand). (*Yarn painting by Guadalupe de la Cruz Ríos.*)

which ties us to the earth" (J. Grimes, personal communication). But this is admittedly not very satisfactory, and perhaps the most that can be said is that, like Wixárika, kakauyaríte is one of those archaic terms whose meaning is lost in the mists of time.

The kinship terms by which gods and goddesses are addressed become expressions of reverence by prefacing them with the word *ta*, our: Our Grandfather, Our Great-grandmother, Our Great-grandfather, Our Mother, Our Elder Brother. The deities considered to have the greatest chronological age, as well as the greatest power, are Takutsi Nakawé (Great-grandmother), the white-haired old earth goddess and engenderer who Lumholtz called "Grandmother Growth" (Figure 7), and Tatewarí, Our Grandfather Fire. With them in the top rank are the Sun god, Werikúa, meaning Eagle, who is also called Tayaupá, Our Sun Father, and Tatutsi Maxa Kwaxí, Great-grandfather Deer Tail. It was Nakawé who made the inert watery earth come to life in the first place, and it was she who also brought the environment back to life after the destruction of a previous creation by a great flood. There is no certain accounting for Nakawé, whose animal alter ego is the peccary (a curious correspondence is the Quiche

Maya origin myth recorded in the *Popol Vuh*, in which the primordial female half of the creator pair is also "Great White Peccary"); in most versions of the origin myths Nakawé simply *is*, right from the beginning of time. There is a myth of a conflict between her and two rival shamans in which she went underground, where the blood from her heart gave birth to the sacred Brazil tree (*Haematoxylum brasiletto*), from whose red-colored wood Huichols make the points of ceremonial arrows, the shaman's *muviéri* (arrows of power), and the staffs of authority carried by the community officials.

All the gods are great shamans, especially Tatewarí and Nakawé, whom some Huichols regard as the first shaman in the world, but Tatewarí has a special place as patron of the mara'akáme, who represents him and through whom he speaks or sings when curing or conducting ceremonies. Along with Takutsi Nakawé, as the oldest and greatest of the ancestor shamans, Tatewarí functions as divine patron of his human counterparts, to the point where people will actually identify an especially esteemed shaman so completely with him that they call the shaman "Tatewarí." This was the case, for example, with Nicholas Carrillo de la Cruz (d. 1974), a great old shaman and community leader in San Andrés (see Chapter 15).

In some parts of the Huichol country Tatewarí outranks Werikúa, in others the Sun is thought to be the most powerful male god. External influence, particularly from Nahuatl-speaking Central Mexican transplants, for whom the Sun god came first, help account for these differences. As in the Aztec myth, the deified Sun originated in an act of self-immolation; in the Huichol version, after throwing himself into a sacrificial fire (in another account, into a lake or the sea, which turned red with his blood) at the western horizon, the young boy who was to become the Sun traveled underground to the land of dawn, where he was reborn in a fiery eruption from a now long-extinct volcano Huichols call Re'unár. Tatewarí then led the ancestors, who in those days still had the form of animal people, to this place. The newborn Sun received his everyday name, Táu (from Turkey, who gobbled, "*táu, táu, táu*"), as his companions debated a proper sacred name. After much debate they chose Werikúa, thus giving the Sun Father the same identification with the most powerful winged predator as did the Aztecs. Meanwhile, the young solar deity, exhausted from his long and dangerous journey below ground, began to sink toward the earth. The sky vault collapsed and the terrible heat from the sun threatened to shrivel the earth and all its life. To save the earth and its life from being incinerated, Tatewarí arranged—in true Mesoamerican fashion—for four trees to be set up to support the sky at the corners, and a fifth to hold up the center, very much the same cosmic architecture as that of the Aztecs. He also ordered a little god chair to be made for the Sun so that he would not become tired and again threaten the earth with his untamed heat on his passage to the western horizon. Huichols still construct such miniature chairs for some of the gods, and full-size ones of the same design and materials for shamans and other dignitaries.

If the Sun originated in a fiery transformation, Tatewarí, the old fire god and divine patron of shamans, came into being through an act of theft when the earth was still dark, before there was a Sun to give light and warmth. It was one of the lowliest of the ancient animal people, Opossum, who, after several others of higher status had tried and failed, volunteered to descend into the underworld (in other versions, the upper world) and steal the fire away from its fiercely protective guardians. He tricked them into letting down their guard, snatched a live coal from the sacred fire with his prehensile tail, secreted it in his pouch, and made his escape up the five levels of the underworld. Because he gave fire to the people and made it possible for them to warm themselves at night and cook their food, Opossum became sacred and his flesh so taboo that if the opossum that guards the road to the underworld smells its flesh on the breath of the soul of a deceased, he will cause a deadfall trap to smash the offender before allowing him or her to proceed on the path to a happy reunion with the waiting relatives in the Otherworld.

The principal spirit helper of Tatewarí and his human counterpart, the shaman, is Our Elder Brother Kauyumári, the divine culture hero, guide, and messenger between the worlds of mortals and the deities. Tamatsi Kauyumári is also Deer, and the pairs of ceremonial arrows with pendant feather bundles Huichols sometimes wear on their heads symbolize his antlers. Real antlers represent him on the peyote pilgrimage. He is an extremely complex figure, who, in the manner of the culture hero in many Native American tales, appears in some myths of the First Times as trickster and sexual clown. This apparently anomalous condition does not in the least diminish, or interfere with, his sacred, creative, and protective functions and character (any more than the trickster aspect of, for example, Manabozho, the culture hero of Great Lakes Algonquians, interferes with that figure's sacred, creative, and protective functions).

In the symbolic and decorative arts Kauyumári is often depicted as a person with deer antlers on his head. In one myth, he receives these from Rabbit, who wears them first but turns them over to his deer companion because he finds them too heavy and is afraid they might cause him to drown while crossing a river (J. L. Furst 1989). In another story, it is the young Deer Women who take arrows Kauyumári has shot into their midst and place them on his head, where they transform into antlers. People may laugh at stories of his antics "before Great-grandmother Nakawé made him sacred," but his active participation alongside the shaman is required not only at every ceremony, communal or family, he must also be at his side when the shaman cures a human patient, or the earth, or the crops, or even the large company of the gods themselves. For they, too, can suffer illnesses that may manifest themselves, among other misfortunes, in lack of rain. Preuss gives some graphic examples of these shamanic curing rituals of people and the gods. Kauyumári, it should be noted, is also the spirit guardian and guide on the peyote hunt, when he himself, by merging with the Deer-Peyote, becomes hunter and prey at one and the same time (Figure 6).

Animals and plants have their spirit guardians, or Masters and Mistresses of the species. Rain, terrestrial water, maize, different kinds of plant life, deer and other game animals, the earth in her different aspects—all are personified, all are sacred, all have

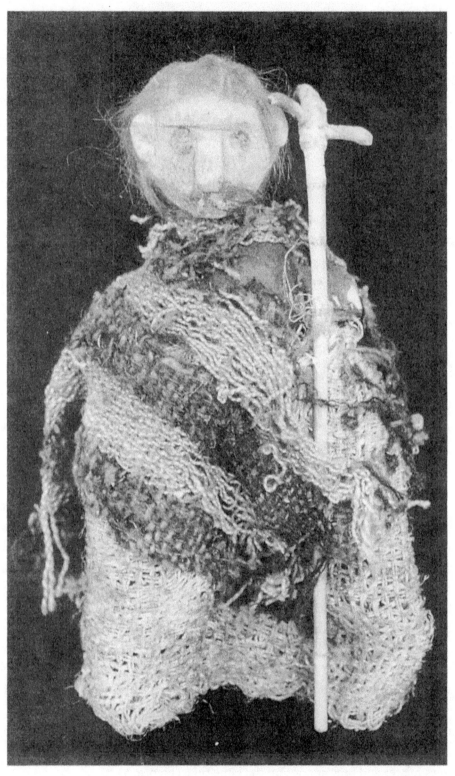

FIGURE 7. Image of the Old Earth and Creator Goddess Great-grandmother Nakawé, with Her Magical Bamboo Staff. (*Collected by Konrad Theodor Preuss in 1907 at the Santa Catarina Temple. H. 13¾". Museum für Völkerkunde, Preussischer Staatbesitz, Berlin-Dahlem.*)

power. Ancestors have the potential of doing good for their descendants, or, if offended, bringing them harm. Tools are sentient, and, if slighted—as, for example, in the ceremony of the feeding of the tools—may cut or otherwise hurt their owners to remind them of their neglected duties. Of all plants, peyote is of course the most sacred, and the one with the most ramifications. *Tutu*, flower, is its metaphor, and most of the flower designs Huichol women weave or embroider on clothing or shoulder bags in fact represent the sacred cactus. Peyote is at once itself and Deer in its manifestation as, or originator of, the divine botanical intoxicant. There is also a Mother Peyote, or Mother of Peyote, sometimes referred to as Elder Sister. Eaten whole or in liquid form, mixed with sanctified water, peyote plays a part in most observances of the annual ceremonial round, not just rituals that relate directly to the hunt for the cactus in Wirikúta.

Maize is not only the most sacred and important of the food plants, but has multiple divine personalities, appearing as the Mother of Maize, whose animal form is the dove, and as her five daughters, each a different color. In some stories, Yoáwima, Blue Maize, is the most sacred of all, just as she is among the Pueblo Indians of the American Southwest. The young Maize Goddess is also known as Niwétsika. If the maize plant is female, the individual ear is male, and both are personified as divine beings, just as they were by the Mexica, or Aztecs, of Central Mexico. There are other parallels as well that suggest relationships between Huichol and Central Mexican maize cultivation, not least the fact that much of Huichol terminology relating to maize agriculture is not indigenous but borrowed from the Nahuatl.

As Denis Lemaistre shows in his essay on the deer hunt and its place in the deer-maize-peyote symbol complex (Chapter 10), hunting is a ritual whose symbolic importance far exceeds its contribution to subsistence, the more so in that the contribution of deer to the food system is now much reduced due to shrinking indigenous lands and overhunting with firearms in place of the traditional noose. What has not disappeared is the reverential treatment of the dead deer, which is carefully laid down on a special embroidered cloth by the women, and has its hunger and thirst ceremonially stilled with offerings of its favorite grasses and water. And, of course, there is here, too, the qualitative identification of the deer with peyote.

The pantheon includes several divine patrons of the hunt, especially for the white-tailed, or Virginia, deer as the most sacred of all the game animals, and the one with the closest connection to the shaman and the ancestors. Indeed, the prominent plumelike tail characteristic of the species personifies the ancestor shaman who carries its name, Tatutsi Maxa Kwaxí, Great-grandfather Deer Tail. This ancestor god plays an especially important role in the peyote pilgrimage. He also happens to be one member of the Huichol pantheon for whom there appears to be a recognizable historic prototype (see Chapter 2).

In a very real sense, the welfare of the individual Huichol, and the extended family, lies in the hands and the mind of the mara'akáme. In the American tropics the shaman is so much jaguar that in many Indian languages both are called by the same

FIGURE 8. Huichol Shaman with His Muviéris (Shaman's Wands).
(*Photograph by P. Ernesto Loéra Ochóa.*)

name. Huichol shamans are eagles or hawks, and like these raptors are able to soar high into the sky and have vision that extends across the world. The very power objects by which they communicate with the ancestor spirits and the gods are the feathers of these birds (Figure 8). The feathers themselves are sensate and animate, capable of speech and action on their own. With the feathers tied to their power arrows, the muviéris, shamans call the soul into the body of the newborn infant. And with their feathers they accompany the life force of the deceased to the afterworld in an extended mortuary ceremony. This ceremony is described from the outside in Chapter 12 by Marina

Anguiano Fernández, a Mexican anthropologist, and from the inside in Chapter 13 by a Huichol artist and accomplished ritualist, Ramón Medina Silva. Chapter 14, by the French ethnologist Michel Perrin, analyzes the return of an ancestor from the beyond in the form of the urukáme. It is also with his magical feathers, tied to the nock end of his arrow of power, the muviéri, that the shaman, or, more correctly, Tatewarí acting through him, summons Elder Brother Kauyumári from his home at the eastern end of the world, in Wirikúta, for without Elder Brother's presence the ritual cannot take place. Tatewarí sends his feathers flying through the air to Kauyumári's home on his mountain in the east to tickle the sleeping culture hero awake. He resists, offering all manner of excuses why he cannot come. The feathers, sensate and capable of speech and action on their own, are relentless, refusing to let Kauyumári be until he is persuaded to consent. All the roles—Tatewarí; the officiating shaman; the feathers; deities, usually female; and Kauyumári—are acted out by the singing shaman alone, with two helpers by his side to repeat passages of his lengthy chant. According to Preuss, who recorded the entire drama, sometimes Tatewarí loses patience with Kauyumári's evasions and, grabbing the reluctant culture hero by his hair, drags him physically all the way to the Sierra, to the great amusement of the audience as it hears it described in the shaman's song.

In the company of Kauyumári, their principal assistant, and other helping spirits drawn from the animal world, shamans travel "out of body" to the different levels of the universe to communicate with the greater powers in behalf of their client, be it an individual or the larger community. The annual round of ceremonies is itself divided into dry season and wet season observances, with the former, which includes the peyote hunt and rituals that precede or flow from it, the more numerous. Those ceremonies centered on the harvest occur close to the fall equinox, while ritual deer hunting and the peyote pilgrimage normally take place between December and the onset of spring. Ceremonies in the *tuki*, the community temple, or the *xiriki*, the ancestor god house in the family compound, usually extend over two days and nights, with the shamans, accompanied by two assistants, singing extensive myth cycles with much repetition of individual strophes. The numerous male and female deities are called by name to participate in these rituals, and when their presence has been assured, animals may be sacrificed to provide the deities with blood, which embodies the essential life force, and which, along with the smoke of the potent *Nicotiana rustica* tobacco, is their sustenance.

We are often asked how Huichols select their shamans. The answer is, very much as in other "tribal" societies. The future Huichol shaman may receive a "call" from an ancestral shaman, often by way of an illness that proves curable only through the candidate's vow to heed the summons and begin self-training, if not at once, at least at some future time. Where the Huichol system differs is in that there is no formal apprenticeship as such. Rather, an apprentice shaman assimilates the esoteric lore and rituals in many ways: in listening to and watching experienced colleagues as they perform the chants and the rituals; by dreaming and otherwise communicating with the divine patron to whom he has made his vow to "complete"; by direct participation as assistant *cantador* (singer) in the ceremonies; and, above all, in repeated peyote pilgrimages. As elsewhere, shamanizing tends to run in families, with new shamans almost always following on the path taken previously by male forebears and relatives, or, less often, female ones. Through five to ten years of intensive self-training that includes memorizing innumerable chants of sometimes staggering length, and a minimum of five, or, preferably, ten or more journeys to Wirikúta, shamans acquire knowledge as healers, diviners, keepers of esoteric knowledge, performers of the sacred poetry, ritualists, and, inasmuch as they officiate at regular ceremonies, priests. Those shamans in charge of the temple fulfill terms of service of five or even ten years. But Huichol society is not of a type that lays down absolute rules and regulations for something so personal as an individual shaman's "path of completion." There are certain universals, but how each future shaman travels that path is up to him, or her. Most shamans or ritualists perform in the context of the extended family or the several families of a residential community. But the shaman's renown may extend beyond the immediate kin into the wider world of the comunidad indígena at large, and sometimes even beyond its boundaries. It need hardly be said that the more public service he or she renders, the greater the gifts of knowledge, memory, and performance, the more frequent and effective the diagnosis of illness and the cure, the greater also the shaman's respect, prestige, and reputation.

That the divine peyote cactus (Figure 9) stands at the center of the shaman's universe is self-evident. It functions as ally, protector, and facilitator of the ecstatic trance in which the specialists in the sacred interact directly with the gods and seek their advice in behalf of their clientele. Huichol religion thus joins the many other indigenous religions in the Americas that value the ecstatic trance experience triggered by the psychoactive alkaloids of one or another of the numerous members of the vegetal kingdom whose wondrous effects on the mind the specialists in the sacred and the healing potential of plants discovered millennia ago, and to which they ascribe the qualities and powers of the divine.

Like shamans elsewhere, Huichol specialists in the sacred use dreams to determine the causes of illness, injury, or environmental calamity, and what is to be done to counteract them. And they, but also lay people, we have found, tend to possess an impressive knowledge of medicinal plants. Among these, peyote is accorded the distinction of virtual panacea, a belief in which Huichols seem to be on to something. Some years ago, when the police made a large quantity of confiscated peyote available to researchers at the University of Arizona rather than destroying it, the latter succeeded in isolating a crystalline substance from an ethanol extract of peyote that turned out to exhibit antibiotic activity against a wide spectrum of bacteria and a species of the imperfect fungi, including strains of *Staphylococcus aureus* (McLeary et al., 1960:247–249). This is a particularly nasty bacterium responsible for septicemia (blood poisoning), pneumonia, and infections after surgery. It became resistant to penicillin within a few

FIGURE 9. Peyote Laid Out for the Ceremonies Following a Peyote Hunt. (*Photographed at the San José temple by Stacy B. Schaefer, 1987.*)

years after that miracle antibiotic came into wide use during World War II, but fortunately responded to several newer antibiotics. No more. According to an alarming cover story about the fast-approaching end of the age of antibiotics in the March 28, 1994 issue of *Newsweek*, *S. aureus* is now immune to *all* antibiotics developed by the drug industry, except one:

> If there is a lurking Andromeda Strain in all this, it is *Staphylococcus aureus*, the bacterium responsible for some pneumonias and, most worrisome, for blood poisoning in surgical wounds. Some 40 percent of staph in hospitals are resistant to every antibiotic but one, vancomycin. "We know that at some point vancomycin will succumb and the bacteria will grow and proliferate unrestrained," worries the VA's [Dr. Thomas] Beam. "It will be like the 1950s and 1960s, when we had nothing to treat this infection, and the mortality rates were as high as 80 percent." In those decades thousands of people each year died of staph infections.

We have observed Huichol *peyoteros* employing the juice of the little cactus to treat superficial wounds—to prevent them from becoming infected, Huichols will tell you, and to promote healing. There is also the reputed efficacy of peyote against intestinal ills and against the painful, and dangerous, stings of a very small but particularly nasty species of scorpion, the so-called Durango variety, that is common to both the American Southwest and northwestern Mexico. For one of us (S.B.S), the consumption of peyote during rituals several times alleviated preexisting gastrointestinal infections—

in one case quite severe—for up to five days. S.B.S. also observed her Indian friends and family eating peyote not to trigger visions but to counteract fatigue and restore vigor during ceremonies that frequently last several days and nights. Such beneficial effects were reported as early as a century ago by Lumholtz.

In any event, even if they do not know how and why it works, by experience and observation the Huichols have had, in their revered peyote, a practical means of warding off precisely those staph infections that only three decades ago killed thousands of hospital patients in the United States every year. There is thus great potential benefit for the fields of medicine and pharmaceuticals in the wisdom Huichols and other native peoples have accumulated regarding uses of wild plants to cure disease and otherwise improve health.

The Shaman as Doctor. Notwithstanding their extensive knowledge of the healing properties of plants, and other curing techniques whose apparent success often surprises skeptical outsiders, it goes without saying that modern medicine has made beneficial inroads. Indeed, more and more people, including even shamans, have come to rely on it—as did, for example, the shaman who so generously shared his firsthand knowledge of wolf power and transformation with Susana Eger Valadez (Chapter 9). Shamans are also well aware of the benefits of vaccination. Whatever might have been the situation in the past, the shaman who would reject causes other than "supernatural" ones for disease or injury is now a rarity. (For that matter, the widespread shamanic concept of sickness intrusion, i.e., illness thought to have been caused by a foreign object that was magically introduced into the patient's body, is not all that far removed from the bacterial or viral theory of disease.) Even so, shamans usually go beyond symptoms and trace the origin of such afflictions to a deity or ancestor feeling offended by, say, failure to complete ritual obligations; envious relatives; revenge by the souls of animals or plants for thoughtless or willful mistreatment when they were alive; evil winds; or the souls of deceased family members who employ "sickness vocation" to recruit a descendant into the shamanic arts.

The best kind of healing involves a combination of different techniques, some practical, others "psychosomatic." Which will prove most effective is part of the shaman's intuitive and experiential knowledge. If the healer has determined that an illness was caused by a foreign object—what Huichols call an "arrow of sickness"—shot from afar by some deity, a sorcerer, or a shaman in the employ of a human enemy, he will suck out the pathogen and "kill" the *itáuki*, a malevolent little disease-causing animal that is visible only to him. Preuss has some interesting things to say about the concept of the itáuki, which, as it happens, bears a curious resemblance to similar notions on the Northwest Coast of the United States. Sometimes the curing shaman will hurl the arrow of sickness back in the direction of an enemy. Indeed, every shaman has among his power objects several such arrows, whose painted markings and other decoration are said to identify the kind of calamity they are capable of inflicting. Where the diagnosis is soul loss, or abduction of the soul by an enemy or hostile animal, rather than by a sickness projectile, it is up to the shaman to divine the soul's location and, after retrieving it, return it to its owner. To find a lost soul the shaman resorts to a whistle language, with both he and his objective emitting a low whistling sound that, according to some Huichols, becomes louder as the healer approaches the lost spirit.

Peyote in Huichol Life and Religion. As important as anything else in his massive inventory of esoteric expertise is the shaman's grasp of the history, the sacred chants, the practical details, and the ripple effect of the annual ritual hunt for the potent little cactus that grows naturally nowhere in the world but in the arid regions of north-central Mexico and the lower Río Grande valley. The Huichols call the peyote plant *hikuli* (*Lophophora williamsii*) or, depending on the local dialect, *hikuri*. Without wishing to make its use appear to be the alpha and omega of Huichol culture, there is no question that, directly and metaphorically, peyote is the focus of much of Huichol religious emotion, the annual cycle of communal and extended family ceremonial and ritual activities, and the common intellectual culture. That includes rites intended to promote the growth of maize and other useful cultivated and wild plant life, hunting, rain, human and animal fertility, and so forth, for peyote and its effects also key into their welfare.

There is much more to be said about peyote in Huichol ethos (and there will be, in Chapter 5); here, we want to emphasize that, based on the ethnobotany and ethnology of peyote, and the ethnohistoric literature on how and to what purposes different Mexican Indian peoples employed the cactus during colonial times, we believe that Huichol communal peyote ritual today is the last intact survivor of a very old Chichimec/Desert Culture peyote complex. Divinatory, ecstatic, and medicinal uses of peyote once were the common property, with local variations, not just of Indian peoples who, like the Guachichil of San Luis Potosí or the Coahuiltecans, shared their arid hunting territories with peyote, but of other peoples who lived, as the Huichols do today, hundreds of miles from its native habitat. Even the Mexica (Aztecs) of Tenochtitlan, who laid proud claim to Chichimec ancestry, were part of this complex, at least to the degree that their shamans also employed the cactus, not exclusively or as their primary ritual "hallucinogen," but alongside other psychoactive species in curing and visionary rites. In historic times several other northwest Mexican Indian peoples—both neighbors of the Huichols, like the Coras and Tepecanos, and more distant groups, like the Raramuri (Tarahumara) of Chihuahua—not only utilized peyote in ways resembling Huichol custom but called it by the same name, hikuli or hikuri, or closely related terms, and there may have been others that have long since disappeared. Some Cora and Tarahumara shamans continue to use peyote, but today the Huichols remain the only bearers of a fully integrated range of peyote-related beliefs and customs. Among the Huichols, peyote engenders a living complex of myth and symbol and ritual behavior that they consider vital to their existence and survival as a distinct people, and that clearly has its roots in a very ancient Desert Culture substratum.

Huichols speak of the peyote they gather as the flesh of deer, and of the tap root they customarily leave in the ground as its "bones," from which new plants will grow (as indeed they do). They say things like "our game bags are full" when they have collected a sufficient number of peyote plants for the ceremonies back home, for curing and personal use, and for sale or trade to neighboring Indians. Illustrating perhaps better than anything else the conceptual identification of peyote with deer, today and in the prehistoric past, is the fact that not only do Huichol peyoteros string peyote like beads on cords for drying as though they really were the pieces of deer meat they call them, but these "peyote necklaces" look remarkably like those found in an ancient Desert Culture rock shelter (radiocarbon-dated at ca. A.D. 800) and in the peyote country on the lower Río Grande.

For all the hunting symbolism, we must not forget that for the agricultural Huichols peyote is not only deer but also maize. And so these three—deer, maize and peyote—form the central symbol complex of Huichol religious ideology, an experiential counterpart to the metaphysical Holy Trinity of a foreign faith whose attempted imposition the Huichols have so successfully resisted, or shrugged off, ever since the Spanish colonial authorities established formal control over their part of the Sierra Madre Occidental in 1722.

Natural Modeling. As is true of shamanic beliefs and practices generally, no matter the degree of their isolation in centuries past, it is doubtful that so much of the old ideological, symbolic, and ritual system would have survived among the Huichols had they not been able to validate or verify them to some degree by observation of natural phenomena and processes. Westerners tend to think of Indian people as somehow possessing the key to some eternal mystical wisdom that we have lost, and that this is reflected in their ceremonies and ritual arts. And it is quite true that in Huichol culture there is a large component of what we would call mysticism. But to the Indians themselves these are very real manifestations of historic events, experiences, and encounters of human beings with the powers of the natural world. We call these powers "supernatural," literally, something outside of, above, and greater than, nature. But for Huichols, as for other native peoples, they are *in* nature. Indeed, they *are* nature.

What the Huichols possess is a body of conscious and unconscious cultural knowledge accumulated during generations of observing, experimenting with, and utilizing the natural phenomena and resources of the environment. The Huichols express this with the concept of *iyári*, a kind of "heart memory" that encompasses everything that has come before, right back to primordial beginnings, and with which every Huichol infant comes into the world. But iyári is not static. It grows and develops as the individual accumulates experience and impressions. Iyári is limited to Huichols, and every Huichol knows that non-Huichols have no access to what in our terminology amounts almost to "genetic memory." It is possible that Huichols grant that other peoples may also possess a form of iyári, just as some of the introduced domestic animals are thought to have souls more or less comparable to those of indigenous ones. But it is not *Huichol* iyári, which is why Huichols are generally tolerant of mistakes outsiders make when attending Huichol ceremonies.

The comprehension of a natural environment from which the divine is indivisible is today only possible for people such as the Huichols, because they were born and raised in intimate association and interdependence with, and knowledge of, their natural surroundings. If they are not ultimately barred from it altogether, people not enculturated from infancy into this system, no matter how sympathetic or eager to learn from what they perceive to be a special "Indian spirituality," do not find it easy fully to participate in or even really comprehend it. This is not because Huichol spirituality is so exotic as to be utterly beyond comprehension, but, on the contrary, because it is embedded in a world view that is derived from natural modeling and directed toward the practical need of survival.

NOTES

1. For the organization of subsistence activities and wild and cultivated foodstuffs as they pertain to San Sebastián, one of the five Huichol comunidades indígenas in the Sierra, in the 1960s see Weigand 1972. A more recent review of Huichol ethnobotany is that of Los Angeles County Arboretum botanist James Bauml (1989:1–10; 1994), who has collected data and hundreds of plant samples on repeated visits to the western Huichol country since 1982.

2. The University of Guadalajara has an ongoing program to train Huichols in the transcription and translation of their own language into Spanish. Huichols thus trained are sent to the Sierra to speak to shamans and collect myths, folk tales, and other oral lore in Huichol and Spanish, so as to make them accessible both to scholars and the Huichols themselves. The program, which is administered by the Centro de Investigaciones de Lenguas Indígenas of the university's Facultad de Filosofía y Letras, has already resulted in several books, among them *Utärikayári: Antología de Narrativa Huichol*, by Paula Gómez López and Xitákame Ramírez de la Cruz.

2 : MYTH AS HISTORY, HISTORY AS MYTH

A New Look at Some Old Problems in Huichol Origins

PETER T. FURST

And they knew the qualities, the essence, of herbs, of roots. The so-called peyote was their discovery. These, when they ate peyote, esteemed it above wine or mushrooms. They assembled together somewhere on the desert; they came together; there they danced, they sang all night, all day. And on the morrow, once more they assembled together. They wept; they wept exceedingly.
FRAY BERNADINO DE SAHAGÚN, *Florentine Codex*, Book X, p. 173

Ever since the earliest Spanish days the Huichol have been regarded as connected with the extinct Guachichil far to the east of the present Huichol territory, and the fact that the latter make long journeys into former Guachichil territory to gather peyote *that does not grow in their present habitat affords ethnological corroboration of the close relationship.*
J. ALDEN MASON, "The Classification of the Sonoran Languages," (1936:191)

"Everything we write is, in the last analysis, a progress report."
WARD GOODENOUGH, University of Pennsylvania

No one who has watched Huichols on the peyote hunt greet their sacred cactus in the north–central desert of San Luis Potosí, or bid it farewell, can read Sahagún's description of a sixteenth-century Teochichimeca peyote ceremony without a sense of having been there. Like these "true," or "authentic," Chichimecs (which is what Teo-chichimeca means), Huichol peyoteros "assemble together somewhere in the desert," to dance and sing all night, all day (Figure 10). And, in the manner of the Franciscan chronicler's people of the arid north, these Huichols from the western Sierra Madre assemble again in the morning, to dance and sing some more, and to "weep exceedingly," offering their tears to the Peyote Mother and the *kakauyaríte*, the ancestor deities who,

FIGURE 10. Huichols at Encounter of First Peyote. When finding the first peyote, Huichols react strikingly like Sahagún's sixteenth-century Teochichimecas, with much ceremonial weeping and all-night and all-day dancing. (*Photograph by Peter T. Furst, December 1968.*)

in company with the divine cactus that is also deer, make their homes in that special corner of San Luis Potosí that Huichols call Wirikúta.

Nor can one ignore those many signposts on the peyote pilgrimage, and in the peyote desert itself, that point to a reverse migration to what may have been—and probably was—the original homeland of some part of the ancestral Huichols. There is much to suggest that J. Alden Mason was right in taking the peyote hunt as corroboration of an ancient connection to the Guachichil of San Luis Potosí, not least the intimate relationship they demonstrate with the ecology of the desert and the divinatory-visionary cactus, and, perhaps most persuasive, the fact that of all northwest Mexican Indian peoples that used peyote in religious ceremonies—Cora, Huichol, Tepecan, Tarahumara, and probably others now long gone—the Huichols alone continue, indeed consider it their sacred obligation, to endure hunger, thirst, salt deprivation, physical exhaustion, and harassment from private land owners, and not infrequently the police, to travel, and even walk, three hundred miles to collect a plant whose psychic effects they could easily duplicate with *Solandra, Datura,* the seeds of the morning glories *Ipomoea violacea* and *Turbina corymbosa,* or *Psilocybe* mushrooms. All of these grow wild in their present homeland. Mason would no doubt have been even more convinced had he known that Wirikúta, the sacred desert home of the peyote in San Luis Potosí, is also believed by many Huichols to be the ultimate destination of the souls of their dead, where they join the kakauyaríte in awaiting the visits of their living relatives when they come to hunt the divine cactus. Hence, participants in the peyote pilgrimages explain that the reason they slap their sandals down so hard on the desert floor when they dance in Wirikúta is to signal the spirits of their relations and invite them to join in the rituals, "so all be of one heart."

Last but not least, there is the Huichols' familiarity with the landmarks along the way that bear old Huichol place names, some of which, transposed into Spanish, even appear on maps or are in common use by local non-Indians.[1]

To gather some of the cumulative evidence—linguistic, historic, folkloric, ethnobotanical, and ethnographic—that favors the genetic connection, and to coincidentally make a proper place in Huichol ethnohistory for the least known, and least appreciated, of its pioneers, is the purpose of this essay.

The Huichol Ethnography of Léon Diguet

Modern Huichol ethnography is generally thought to have had its start with Carl Lumholtz. Actually Lumholtz was not alone. In the same decade, the 1890s, an eclectic French scientist named Léon Diguet (1859-1926) made three extended visits to what was then called the Sierra de Nayarit, that resulted in pioneering contributions to Huichol scholarship. The one with the most lasting value has to do with the contribution of myth to Huichol history. In the typically late-nineteenth-century mode of holistic natural history, Diguet's fieldwork in Mexico ranged across a whole world of science, "exact" and "soft," from chemistry and geology to natural environment; physical anthropology, ethnology, ethnohistory, archaeology, botany, zoology, linguistics, economics, and more. He covered so much ground, geographically and across the disciplines, that he deserves a more prominent place than he has been awarded in the history of anthropology and the natural sciences in both France and Mexico (Jáuregui 1992:7-49).

Born in Le Havre on July 25, 1859, Diguet, who died in Paris on August 31, 1926, arrived in Mexico in 1889 under contract to the House of Rothschild in Paris. He passed the next four years as an industrial chemist, geologist, and metallurgist at the Rothschilds' El Boléo copper mine, near Santa Rosalía, Baja California, then the most important source of copper in Mexico. During those four years he conducted extensive, and often pathbreaking, explorations of Baja California geology, zoology, botany, rock art, archaeology, and ethnology. He went back to France with major scientific collections from this then still barely known peninsula (as he also did from the Huichol country), and returned to Mexico five more times during the following decade on various scientific missions: to Baja California again in 1893-94; to Jalisco and the territory of Tepic in 1896-98; to Puebla and Oaxaca, including the Isthmus of Tehuantepec, as well as southernmost Baja California and the offshore islands (1901-04); and to Michoacan, Jalisco, and Baja California once more in 1911-13 (Jáuregui 1992:7-8).

Between 1895 and 1896 he spent nine months in Huichol and Cora territory (Jáuregui 1992:26), returning twice more to the Huichols, in 1898 and in 1905, when he also visited the Tepehuanos. Though his Huichol observations are somewhat superficial, especially compared to Lumholtz, Diguet had respect for mythology and its possibilities for occasionally establishing history, especially if there was supporting evidence. Thus, he assumed that when Huichol shamans sang about a legendary culture hero named "Majakuagy," meaning Deer Tail, who led his followers from the homeland of the Guachichil in the peyote desert of San Luis Potosí into the Sierra Madre Occidental, they were talking history. Students of Huichol culture and religion will recognize this legendary culture hero as the prototype for the ancestor deity Huichols call Tatutsi Maxa Kwaxí.

If Diguet was right, and I believe he was, it helps explain a great many things, not least why some Huichols credit Maxa Kwaxí, Great-grandfather Deer Tail, with having revived the traditional hunt for peyote when he led the divine ancestors to Wirikúta, whereas other versions of the peyote tradition award that honor to Tatewarí, the old fire god and patron of shamans (cf. Furst 1972; Myerhoff 1974). But even in those versions of the mythic charter for the pilgrimage in which it was Tatewarí who prescribed the first peyote hunt as a cure for ills afflicting the divine ancestors, Maxa Kwaxí is Tatewarí's chief assistant and second in responsibility for the safety of the peyoteros and the success of the sacred enterprise. Either way, in the modern reenactment of the primordial pilgrimage, Great-grandfather Deer Tail is right there in the lead.

As both geologist and geographer Diguet was first of all concerned with the environment—climate, the lay of the land, vegetation, natural resources, mountains, and barrancas. But it is clear from the amount of space he devoted to the Huichols and their Cora neighbors, that what really caught his interest was the indigenous peoples. In 1899 he published "Contribution à l'Étude Ethnographique des Races Primitives du Mexique. La Sierra de Nayarit et ses Indigènes," a lengthy essay that included numerous ethnographic observations on the Coras and the Huichols, but with considerably more attention to the latter. Diguet was obviously taken with the Huichols and the remarkable degree to which they had managed to preserve their indigenous religious beliefs and rituals, in contrast to the Coras, who seemed more acculturated and Catholicized. He followed this with two more papers on Huichol topics alone, "Le 'peyote' et son usage rituel chez les Indiens du Nayarit" (1907:21–29), and "Idiome Huichol. Contribution à l'Étude des langues mexicaines" (1911:23–54). The latter was the first scholarly attempt to dissect and comprehend the structure of the Huichol language. Both appeared in the *Journal de la Société des Américanistes de Paris*.

As the more prolific writer, Lumholtz was destined to become far better known as a Huichol scholar than Diguet, especially to English-speaking readers. Lumholtz was also extremely fortunate to have had a young bilingual shaman of wide-ranging knowledge and many contacts named Pablo de la Cruz as his companion and chief consultant on symbolism and religion, on whom he depended for much of his information. His first American Museum monograph, on symbolic art, appeared in 1900, followed by a second, in 1904, on the "decorative" arts. Between these two scholarly works came *Unknown Mexico* (1902), a popular and widely read account in two volumes of five years of travel and exploration among the Tarahumara, Tepehuan, Cora, Huichol, and other indigenous peoples of northwestern Mexico. While Lumholtz, a Norwegian, wrote in English, Diguet published in French, which is not the first language for Mesoamericanists. Of the forty or so titles in Diguet's bibliography on Mexican topics, prior to 1992, when at long last a collection of Diguet's works was published in Spanish translation in Mexico under the editorship of Jesús Jáuregui and Jean Meyer, only two appeared in Spanish, one on the ethnobotany, technology, and economics of maguey cultivation in Tequila, Jaliso (1902), the other a monograph on Baja California (1911).

In any event, whether because of language difficulties, or bias, or some other reasons, the fact is that in the United States not even the most interesting and challenging of Diguet's ideas about the Huichols have received the attention they clearly deserve. Except for Mason, who never doubted the Huichol-Guachichil connection, where Diguet's writings are mentioned at all they have more often than not been so garbled by mistranslation and the omission of crucial details as to bear little resemblance to the original. Myopia, bias, or language difficulties, Diguet deserves better, and so do the Huichols.

This is not to say that Diguet could not also be wrong, and sometimes very wrong indeed. But that should hardly surprise us. Who among us is not sometimes wrong—and with far less excuse than a pioneer like Diguet? In 1899, Diguet did not even have Lumholtz's first monograph against which to check some of his own observations, and *Unknown Mexico* was still three years off. Even if the conclusions he drew from measurements and observations about who and what went into the origins of the modern Huichol population had more than a little validity, there is obviously more to Huichol ancestry than just the blending of an older brachycephalic population and a more recent dolichocephalic admixture out of a northern desert homeland, as Diguet assumed. A great many different groups and individuals—including Indians of diverse cultural affiliations, Africans fleeing slavery, and probably a few Filipinos from the Manila galleons—sought refuge in the rugged mountains of the Sierra Madre Occidental, many settling in and around the Huichol country in the wake of the bloodletting and brutality that marked the *entrada* of the unspeakable Nuño de Guzmán into the western provinces in 1530, the defeat of the pan-Indian rebellion of 1540-41 known as the Mixton War, the Tepehuan rebellion of 1616, and innumerable other failed uprisings, large and small, against colonial oppression and exploitation. The areas through which Nuño de Guzmán's army rampaged, including a portion of the Huichols' own territory just north of the Río Grande de Santiago (Río Lerma) in Nayarit, suffered enormous demographic calamities. Thousands of Indians were killed, thousands more died of disease and starvation, thousands were deported from their highland homes to sicken and die in the hot and humid coastal lowlands. According to historian Peter Gerhard (1982:49), when the Spanish arrived, the *tierra caliente* had an indigenous population of perhaps 320,000; thirty years later fewer than 20,000 were left. In the aftermath of the Mixton rebellion in 1541, thousands of Indians in the highlands above Guadalajara, most of them Cazcan, were slaughtered, and equal numbers starved to death or were carried off in chains to work in the silver mines. A few survivors fled into the safety of the mountains, while their wives and children were enslaved on Spanish farms and *haciendas*. A plague in 1545–48 killed off more than half of the surviving highland Indians. In the west, in the same tragic decade,

> many of the mountain-dwelling Tecoxquines and Huicholes were forced to move to the coastal plain, while others retreated to the more inaccessible parts of the sierra (Gerhard 1982:49).[2]

Thus, during these turbulent times of intensive culture contact and mixing just before and just after the Spanish invasion, there must have been a constant process of syncretism, during which Huichol, or proto-Huichol, intellectual culture, including the inventory of ceremonial objects, became enriched by accretions from non-Huichol sources, even as these, in turn, assimilated elements of a symbol complex that by the very nature of its core, the peyote cactus, could, by any reasonable measure, only have evolved not in the western Sierra, where the sacred cactus does not grow, but in the distant desert to which it is native. And, surely, notwithstanding their well-known aversion to mating with non-Huichols, some of these new arrivals in their midst made their contribution also to the Huichol gene pool. Both genetically and culturally, then, the Huichols, as Diguet saw them in the 1890s, were considerably more than just a mixture of an established older population and the carriers of a peyote tradition from San Luis Potosí.

Finally, modern studies of Uto-Aztecan languages, and of Huichol, have taken us considerably beyond Diguet's somewhat primitive, idiosyncratic, and often inconsistent orthography. Yet there is not complete agreement even now on how to write Huichol words so that their pronunciation is reasonably clear to the non-linguist reader, the more so in that pronunciation varies from one part of the Huichol country to another. If Diguet's orthography seems old-fashioned now, and sometimes downright mystifying, it must be remembered that he was writing in French, for French-speaking readers, so that French pronunciation also influenced how he chose to set down Huichol words. Certainly, no modern linguist would render the Huichol word for "Deer Tail" as "Majakuagy." "Maxa Kwaxí," with the "x" pronounced, as it would be in Nahuatl, like a soft "sh," comes closer.

But these are relatively minor quibbles. It is surely past time to acknowledge that, however cursory his observations sometimes appear in comparison to those of Lumholtz, there is much of lasting value in this pioneering French scholar's remarks on religion, social organization, ritual, language, sacred places and their aboriginal names, foodstuffs, the peyote pilgrimage, and sacred and domestic architecture. In fact, it is to Diguet that we owe one clue to the origin of the circular shape of the indigenous

Huichol temple, called *tuki* in Huichol, or *calihuey*, a Nahuatl borrowing (from *calli* = house, *uey* = big), when Huichols speak Spanish to outsiders. Since the turn of the century, Huichol houses have all become rectangular, but in Santa Catarina in the 1890s Diguet still found dwellings that were of the same round form as the tuki. Thus, we see among the Huichols the same replication in sacred architecture of an older domestic architecture as in the American Southwest, where the circular Anasazi *kiva*, of which the Great Kivas of Chaco Canyon are the most spectacular examples, evolved from the semisubterranean pit house (Nabokov and Easton, 1989:357). Just as the kiva was the old domestic dwelling writ large, so then, was the Huichol temple, both house and sacred space being models of the cosmos, in whose exterior and interior spatial arrangements not only human beings but their ancestors and deities had to feel at home (see Chapter 11, this volume, for the Huichol temple as, among other things, solar observatory). Very much the same evolutionary phenomenon from domestic to sacred architecture, from round nuclear family dwelling to the ceremonial roundhouse, even long after domestic architecture had shifted to right angles, can of course be observed in many other places.[3]

But Diguet's premier contribution to Huichol scholarship lies in the realm of myth and history. In the late nineteenth century astral interpretation of mythology was the fashion of the day. It is thus very much to Diguet's credit that when he heard the chant of "Majakuagy," he assumed, correctly, that it was not phenomena in the night sky the Huichols were singing about, but a piece of their history, framed in the language and imagery of myth and magic: the story of a real-life, charismatic Guachichil shaman-chief, idealized, to be sure, as a great civilizer and religious reformer, who had led a band of his followers on a 300-mile migration from San Luis Potosí into the Sierra Madre Occidental, along a route retraced (insofar as this is still possible) ever since by Huichol peyoteros, and, after overcoming the resistance of the people he found there, introduced to them a new religion that had as its sacred focus a powerful little psychoactive cactus native not to the Sierra Madre Occidental but distant Wirikúta. (It is a mark of the heterogeneity of Huichol historical mythology that another legend, cited by Lemaistre in Chapter 9, has Maxa Kwaxí's sisters be the ones who brought peyote to the Sierra.)

Even granting that portions of the chant may be poetic imagination, its importance for the ethnohistory of the area is beyond question. As López Austin (1991:152–157) has wisely pointed out, even the most fabulous and imaginative events, may, when additional documents become available, reveal themselves to be histories with the details omitted. And there is the additional tasty morsel for the historian of religion: the transmogrification, in the not-so-distant past, of a real-life, charismatic shaman-chief named Deer Tail into a divine culture hero and major deity (Figure 11). As such, beyond his place in the topography of the sacred as a great ancestral shaman, patron of the ceremonial deer hunt, religious innovator, legislator, unifier, and successful prose-

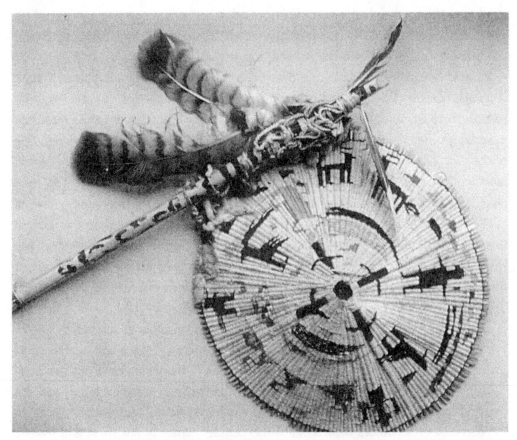

FIGURE 11. Shaman's Arrow (Muviéri) and Niérika of Tatutsi Maxa Kwaxí, Great-grandfather Deer Tail. (*Collected by Konrad Theodor Preuss in 1907 at Santa Gertrudis rancho temple. Diameter of niérika 11¾". Museum für Völkerkunde, Preussischer Kulturbesitz, Berlin-Dahlem. Photograph by Peter T. Furst.*)

lytizer for his own traditional peyote-centered religion, he functions not only as one of the leading ancestor deities in the so-called "dry season" round—that is, the desert and peyote-oriented ceremonial cycle—but, in company with the old fire god Tatewarí, the aged creator and fertility goddess Nakawé, and Werikúa, Eagle, the ritual term for the deified sun, as one of the four most important members of the crowded pantheon of Huichol nature and ancestor deities.

Anthropometry and Myth. I will begin with Diguet's foray into Huichol physical anthropology (problems and all), and the fit he perceived between it and the legend of Majakuagy/Maxa Kwaxí. It is unfortunate that, except for a few fragments, the legend appears to have been largely forgotten in the course of this century. I say "appears" because its loss is possibly more apparent than real. Perhaps it is only a matter of the right questions not having been asked of the "right" Huichols, that is, those who could be expected to have preserved a memory of such matters. Fortunately, much potentially helpful ethnological and ethnohistoric information has been accumulated by historians and other scholars since Diguet's time against which to consider the Majakuagy legend and some of Diguet's ethnohistorical and linguistic assumptions.

From their physical appearance and his own measurements, Diguet wrote in 1899, it is evident that the Huichols consist of at least two different ancestral populations. Both men and women, he observed, exhibit the distinctive physical traits of one of these two parental groups, which must have come together and merged at some unknown time in the past. Diguet assumed this to have occurred at some time prior to the Spanish invasion; more recent writers, notably Mason, the premier student of the Tepecano neighbors of the Huichols in the nearby Bolaños Valley, place the migration westward of the Guachichil component of Huichol ancestry at about, or just after, the Spanish Conquest. One recent German ethnographer of the Huichols, Christina Hell (1989), has even suggested that "Majakuagy" of legend might have been a leader of one of the early pan-Indian uprisings against the Spanish, such as the Mixton War and the Tepehuan Rebellion.

Diguet defined one of these two recognizable physical types as relatively short of stature, heavy-set, with rather large feet and hands, and markedly brachycephalic cranial measurements. The second, which he assumed to be descended from the Guachichil, was taller, long-headed, with more delicate features and extremities. On the basis of a comparison of two brachycephalic skulls from an old Huichol burial cave in the barranca of Rhaïmota with skulls found decades earlier in burials in San Andrés del Teul, that is, in Tepecan country, and studied by French scientists at the time of the short-lived reign of Maximilian, he suggested that the brachycephalic population was the earlier and more "primitive" one, sharing characteristics with the Chichimec "indios barbaros" that formerly inhabited the fringes of the Sierra, and who were known as Teules or Teules–Chichimecos, names under which they appear on Orozco y Berra's ethnographic and linguistic map of 1864 (Diguet 1992:122–123).

In that connection, it is interesting that the burials excavated by Hrdlička at Totoáte, in the Bolaños valley, contained individuals belonging to a "subbrachy- to brachycephalic people of not very large stature" (Hrdlička 1903:395). Hrdlička also noted that the Tepecanos he saw in the village of Azqueltán "are the shortest in stature and the most brachycephalic of all the Mexican tribes north of latitude 21" (ibid., p. 415). Could the people upon whom "Majakuagy" and his Guachichil migrants imposed themselves, to whom they introduced their own peyote traditions when they settled in the Sierra, and with whom the ancestral Huichols came to exchange and share certain cultural traits in the process of acculturation, have been Tepehuan/Tepecano? That distinct possibility is also suggested by a tradition of the Tepecanos themselves, first reported by Hrdlička (1903), and expanded by Mason (1918:344–345), that a part of the country where the Huichols now live was originally theirs, and by an early missionary's query to his superiors whether the language of instruction to the Indians in the mountains had still to be Tepecano or some other local tongues, or could now be "Mexican," that is, Nahuatl. In Mason's view, the fact that parts of the Huichol country were originally Tepecan was

further evidence for the proposition, already suggested by Orozco y Berra, that the Huicholes are the descendants of the former Guachichiles, of the state of San Luis Potosí, who retreated to their present homeland shortly after the Conquest.

To recapitulate: in Diguet's opinion the original inhabitants of the Sierra were short-statured and brachycephalic, meaning broadheaded, while the Guachichil migrants from the peyote country in San Luis Potosí were both taller in stature and dolicho-cephalic, that is, long-headed. So there is at least an implication that if not throughout what is now Huichol country, at least the region around Santa Catarína was origi-nally settled by the Southern Tepehuan/Tepecan, and that this branch of the Piman-speaking Teules-Chichimecos supported itself by hunting, fishing, and foraging, not horticulture, which, according to this legend, was introduced by Majakuagy.

Perhaps so. But whereas in Diguet's day physical anthropologists put a great deal of trust in anthropometry, especially head form, since the early 1960s reliance on head shape or physical type to differentiate populations, or draw evolutionary conclusions, has fortunately gone out of style. For one thing, head shape has long been known to be elastic, responding to factors ranging from nutrition to environment, an argument advanced already a century and a half ago by the German Theodore Waitz (1858/1872). That makes it a dubious marker indeed for evolutionary purposes. More to the point, even if such measurements have some limited utility, not much can be made of them in the absence of blood group markers, a modern technique not available to Diguet and his contemporaries. In his fascination with cranial measurements and body shape, then, Diguet was only following scientific fashion that was the near-universal dogma of the time. But he was too eclectic a scientist, and too curious, to rely on overt physi-cal characteristics and his calipers alone to draw conclusions about Huichol ancestry. What struck him was the apparent overlap between physical characters he had per-sonally observed, the measurements of the pair of skulls from old burials, and a living tradition among the Huichols of Santa Catarína about their own historical past. Here, he thought, was a case where physical anthropology not only coincided with mythic history, but where the one could be used to validate the other.

The legend has several versions that differ in minor detail, but basically the story went like this:

The ancestral Huichols were still living in the peyote country in San Luis Potosí when a man who supposedly was light of skin, and who had the personal name of "Majakuagy," meaning Deer Tail, was sent to earth from the heavens by the supreme sky god and creator, called Tahuehuiakame, with instructions that he teach the people new ways and a new and more humane code of laws. "I, engendered by no one," so goes the opening passage of Diguet's translation of an invocation to the deified culture hero, "I the son of Tahuehuiakame, I Majakuagy, who was sent by Tahuehuiakame to govern in this world." Majakuagy convinced many people of his message, but he also made many enemies, which is why he decided to leave in search of a new home that would be secure from enemies, so that he and his followers might live in peace (Diguet 1899:571-574; 1992:110-112).

But when he assembled his people at a place called Rhaitomuany, which Diguet placed between Real de Catorce and the city of San Luis Potosí, they were attacked. The victors smashed the gourds in which Deer Tail's people had planned to carry the water they needed on the journey and scattered the broken pieces over the desert. They also broke everything else the people required to sustain themselves on their migration. Seeing this the gods were moved by pity and transformed the broken fragments into plants with magical properties to stave off hunger and thirst. This enabled the travelers to face and overcome the obstacles that lay in their path, without concerning themselves with the necessities of life (Diguet 1992:145, 155). The marvelous lifesaving plant was peyote, *Lophophora williamsii*, which does indeed suppress hunger and restore energy, and for which Huichols go to their beloved Wirikúta.

Diguet (1992:156) gives the meaning of this place name as "In back of the Goddess of Peyote." One of the divine Mothers (*tatéima*, sing. *tatéi*, lit. Our Aunt, Our Mother in Santa Catarina), she is also referred to as Elder Sister. Collectively, the male and female ancestor and nature deities are known as the *kakauyaríte*, or *kakauyarixi*, an archaic term for which we have no precise translation, although the linguist Joseph E. Grimes (personal communication) suggests "our sandal straps" as a literal translation, perhaps as metaphor for "those who connect us physically to the earth." The ancestor deities in general manifest themselves in the phenomena of the weather and the natural environment—clouds, fire, water, sun, wind, deer, and so forth; the kakauyaríte, in particular, are embodied in the sacred mountains, hills, and rocks in the peyote country. The sacred peyote itself, notwithstanding its qualitative equation with a male deer, particularly in the context of the peyote hunt, is conceived as female.

The legend is not specific about the identity of the enemies of Majakuagy. They might have been other Guachichiles, but it is also possible that they were the same Huastecs whose archaeological remains are found over much of San Luis Potosí, and who also left evidence of their former presence in Wirikúta/Real de Catorce in the form of a sizable circular ceremonial structure that was identified by archaeologists not long ago close to where the Huichols go to gather peyote (Patricio Dávila Cabrera and Diana Zaragoza Ocaña, 1992, personal communication). Mexican colleagues in San Luis Potosí tell me they see certain similarities in Huichol and Huastec religion, and it is certainly not inconceivable that the Guachichil who once inhabited this area had assimilated traits from their Huastec neighbors by the time they began their own westward movement into Zacatecas and northern Jalisco.

It took the legendary Majakuagy and his Guachichiles five years of walking and many hardships to reach their goal. Diguet says that the exact route they followed is now almost impossible to reconstruct, but that the Huichols remember, and recite, by name each of the places at which the ancestors stopped and rested along the way. He obtained a list of fifteen of these, together with the meaning of their Huichol names (Diguet 1992:155-156). These are the sacred places that Huichol peyote pilgrims acknowledge with prayers and offerings, either directly or at a distance. Once in the safety of the Sierra, the travelers found people already living there, whose initial resistance they had to overcome. But the culture they brought proved superior, they knew the arts and how to grow food rather than merely collect it, and in time Majakuagy succeeded in his civilizing mission. He imposed a new code of laws and a pantheistic religion with a cult to the Sun and Fire, with thirty-seven principal deities that had charge of the actions and destinies of human beings, and, of course, the peyote ceremonies, with their annual reenactment of the original migration. The Sun was called "Our Father," Fire "Our Grandfather," as they are to this day. As though to anticipate his own eventual transmogrification into a deity, the legend also mentioned a god called Tatutsi, Great-grandfather. This is the ritual kinship term by which Huichols address Maxa Kwaxí (Majakuagy). In time Majakuagy unified the Huichols, Coras, and Tepehuan/Tepecano into what Diguet understood to have been a "theocratic state," which controlled a territory much larger than it is today.

When Majakuagy died, his devout followers made him into a god and placed his remains in a burial cave, tied in seated position as though alive in a chair (Figure 12). The location of Majakuagy's cave was said to have been made known to only a handful of Indians. But elsewhere Diguet notes that one of the most sacred cave shrines in Teakáta, near Santa Catarína, is dedicated specifically to Great-grandfather Deer Tail. (In that connection, it is interesting that a Huichol companion of T. J. Knab, during a visit to Teakáta some twenty-five years ago, told him that one of the hidden caves in this, the most sacred locale in the Huichol territory, was where long ago the *antepasados* ["those who came before"] put the mortal remains of Tatutsi Maxa Kwaxí [T. J. Knab, personal communication].) But Diguet also heard that only fifteen years before his own visit to Santa Catarína, Maxa Kwaxí's funerary bundle was seen in a cave in a place called Tzinata, near Pochotita, a Huichol community on the banks of the Río Chapalagana.

Following the death of Majakuagy, so concludes the legend, his confederation broke apart and was soon rent by civil war, with Huichols, Coras, and Tepehuanes continually fighting one another for supremacy. This rivalry was never resolved and only came to an end with the arrival of what were said to be Nahua-speakers, who took control of the area and established a temple and sacrificial altar at El Teúl (Diguet 1992:111-112). That the Deer Tail legend owes a few details to both Central Mexican mythology and the New Testament is self-evident. Most likely, they derive from the same source: the semi-Christianized Nahuatl-speaking Tlaxcaltecans and other Central Mexicans whom the Spanish transplanted to western Mexico to guard against incursions by the so-called *indios barbaros*. (The first of these Tarascan- and Nahuatl-speakers actually arrived as early as 1530 with the army of Nuño de Guzmán.) Majakuagy, as a white man,

FIGURE 12. Sacred Bundle with Effigy of Tatutsi Maxa Kwaxí, Great-grandfather Deer Tail, in Miniature Shaman's Chair, Adorned with Prayer Arrows, Thread Crosses, and Archaeological Mace. The arrows have lost their feathers to insects. (*Collected by Konrad Theodor Preuss in 1907 at Rancho Santa Barbara. H. 28¼". Museum für Völkerkunde, Berlin-Dahlem. Photograph by Peter T. Furst.*)

recalls the half-historical, half-mystical Çe Acatl Topiltzin Quetzalcóatl (1 Reed Prince Quetzalcóatl) of Tula, the Toltec–Aztec culture hero. He, too, is described as a light-skinned man who descended from the heavens to introduce the arts and agriculture, a new code of laws, and a more humane religion, only to be forced into exile by his enemies through the machinations of his rival, the sorcerer Tezcatlipoca. The Maja-kuagy myth also reminded the Mexican historian Wigberto Jiménez Moreno (1943) of Mixcóatl (Cloud Serpent, a Nahuatl metaphor for the Milky Way), the legendary founder of the Toltec Empire, and celestial father of Quetzalcóatl. True, the historic Mixcóatl (assuming there was such a personage) dates back to the tenth century A.D. But there is no reason why fragments of an older tradition should not have merged with a later one. Central Mexican concepts might also have merged with Christian teach-ings, in the name Tahuehuikame for a Supreme Deity. This, according to T. J. Knab (personal communication) becomes a direct analog for one of the names of Tezcatli-poca, *Titlahuan*, "maker of what is made." And there is surely something of *Jesucristo* in Majakuagy proclaiming himself as the magically engendered son of the Supreme Deity. Nevertheless, the basic tale reveals itself as an indigenous historical tradition framed in, and embellished by, the imagery of magic, myth, and symbolism.

Huicholes and Guachichiles

Doctor Hrdlička . . . states that the most intelligent man among the Huichol told him that Guachichil was the ancient name of his tribe.
CYRUS THOMAS, Indian Languages of Mexico and Central America (1911:41)

To put the Majakuagy story in ethnohistorical perspective, we need to look at what is documented about Guachichil penetration into areas not originally their homeland, that is, as far west as Zacatecas and northern Jalisco. Driving north into Zacatecas in search of silver mines, a Spanish party led by Pedro Almíndez Chirinos, who previously, during the exceptionally brutal Spanish invasion of western Mexico in 1530, had taken one part of the army and some of its Central Mexican and Tarascan Indian retainers directly across Huichol country to meet up with Nuño de Guzmán's men at Tepic, encountered a band of five hundred "Guachiles" (Guachichiles) living in circular huts in an oak forest near the present city of Zacatecas. There was no clash of arms and the Chichimec Guachichiles fed the hungry Spaniards on acorn meal (Gerhard 1982). But there are other accounts, as well, of a Guachichil presence in places immediately adja-cent to, or in close contact with, people more or less certainly identifiable as ancestral Huichols. Citing Orozco y Berra, Cyrus Thomas (1911:40–41) included in Guachichil territory at the time of European contact parts of San Luis Potosí, Nuevo León, Coa-huila, and Zacatecas, and notes that Orozco y Berra also "appears to bring together the Cazcan and the Guachichile as pertaining to the 'Teules Chichimecas.'"

Missionary activity in the Nayarit sierra began in 1580, with the first description of the Indian peoples of this mountainous region, that of Commissioner-General Fray

Alonso Ponce, dating to 1587 (Sauer 1934). Ponce's report "is notable for its systematic observations on Indian languages and customs" (ibid., p. 7). In the heart of the mountains he found the province of "Vaynamota" (Huaynamota). This became his point of reference. North of it was the province of Vazamota, to its south were about six hundred Zayabeco bowmen, allegedly cannibalistic; to the southwest were the Cora, who shared a language with natives on the coastal plain; in the eastern mountains was the sterile country of the Uzare (one of several names applied to Huichols, others being Alica, Usulique, Guisare, Vitzurita, and Guisol)[4]; and to the west "he found the great province of Tepeque (Tepic), who favored the Chichimeca (i.e., wild) Guachichil and joined them on plundering expeditions" (ibid., p.7). "In this, the earliest account," writes Sauer (1934:14), Ponce "notes their connection with the Guachichil." Sauer (p. 9) also mentions that in seventeenth-century documents "relating to the Guachichil there is mention of an uprising of Tepeo and Usilique in the mountains near San Andrés del Teul and Colotlán, Santoscoy considering, I think correctly, the latter people to have been Huichol."

In his 1899 essay Diguet identified the Huichol language with that of the Guachichil, or directly descended from it. Linkage, or identity, between Huichol and Guachichil has ever since been generally accepted as a given or possibility by most linguists, as, indeed, it was earlier by Orozco y Berra. So, for example, in his classic work, *Indian Languages of Mexico and Central America* (1911:22–23), Cyrus Thomas wrote of the Huichols and their language that, though closely related to and formerly classified as a division of Cora,

> recent investigation, chiefly by Hrdlička, have led to the conclusion that they are more closely related to the Guachichile than to the Cora, and are apparently an offshoot of that tribe.

Both Sauer (1934) and Kroeber (1934) took Huichol and Guachichil to be either the same or closely connected, the latter writing (p. 8) that "Huichol–Guachichil" might, with further knowledge, "easily prove a connecting link between Sonoran and Nahuan." In the more recent literature on Mesoamerican and Utonahuan (Uto–Aztecan) languages Huichol is also often linked with Guachichil. So, for example, Guachichil is followed by the notation "a variety of Huichol?" in Campbell's list of forty-eight extinct or near-extinct Uto–Aztecan languages of Mexico (Campbell 1979:911). Commenting on extinct languages in his survey of Uto–Aztecan in Vol. 10 of the *Handbook of Middle American Indians*, Miller (1983:122) also aligns Guachichil, as well as Tecual, with Huichol.

Diguet expanded his Huichol–Guachichil hypothesis in an essay published in 1911 that also provided more details than the earlier paper of the prayer chant dedicated to Magakuagy/Maxa Kwaxí. The Huichol language, he writes,

> is used today by a small indigenous population in the Sierra de Nayarit. There are at most five thousand speakers today, but according to native tradition the popu-

lation was far more extensive before the Spanish Conquest. This is the language spoken by numerous nomadic and primitive groups known as the Guachichiles, who once occupied a major portion of the immense territory north of the Central Mexican plateau, a region that today includes the states of San Luis Potosí and parts of Zacatecas and Coahuila. The Guachichiles, who are considered to be the ancestors of the present-day Huichol Indians, were gradually exterminated during the time of Spanish colonization. Their language has survived, and comes down to us today thanks to a small fraction of the tribe that, before the Conquest, established itself in the Sierra Nayarit under the leadership of a powerful chief called Majakuagy, who founded an independent sedentary state along with the Cora and Tepehuan tribes

In the early documents, he continued, the Huichols are mentioned under various names, but in more recent works, such as those of Mota Padilla (1855 [1742]) and Frejes (1878), "the terms Huichol, Guichol and Guachichil are used interchangeably," with Guachichil being occasionally "reserved exclusively for the Huichols." As noted earlier, in the account of Almíndez Chirinos's search for silver mines in Zacateca and Guachichil territory in the 1530s the Guachichil are called "Guachila" by their Zacateco neighbors. "Guachil" sounds even more like "Huichol" than does Guachichil, a Nahuatl name said to mean "redheads" (from *quaitl* = head, *chichiltic* = red) for their custom of painting their faces red, Diguet noting that this same custom was still practiced by the Huichols (as, indeed, it is today). Yet he also notes that "according to the more erudite Huichols, the term Guachichil, sometimes spelled Huachichil by different authors, could only be a corruption of Wicharika," the name by which the Huichols call themselves. The meaning of Wixárika, or, as it is also spelled in the early colonial accounts, Vitsarika or Vitsurika, is uncertain. Diguet was told it meant "cultivators," to distinguish Majakuagy's band from those Guachichiles relying exclusively on hunting and foraging. Lumholtz translated it as "doctors," for the large number of shamans among the Huichols, while a recent Mexican writer rendered it as "people from the region of spiny plants" (Schneider 1993), though on what authority is not known.

However the name came to be, the Guachichil were Chichimecs, speakers of a Utonahuan language (Swadesh 1968:79–83), and prime candidates for the "Teochichimeca," the "true" or "real" Chichimecs whom Sahagún's Nahuatl-speaking informants credited with the discovery of the intoxicating peyote cactus. For Jiménez Moreno (1943:129), "Teochichimeca" meant essentially those Chichimec peoples that had best preserved the characteristic nomadic lifeway of northern desert hunter-gatherers, among them the Guamares, Guachichiles, and "some of the peoples of southern Zacatecas and the Sierra de Nayarit." It is conceivable, however, that at least some of these groups were nomadic only in the sense of adjusting their movements to the times when the major wild plants on which they relied as staples were ready to be harvested. The vast forest of tree-sized tuna, or prickly pear, cactus in San Luis Potosí, known as El Tunal, which also sheltered a variety of game, including deer, peccary, rabbit, prairie dog, and other rodents, and which in the sixteenth and seventeenth centuries served Guachichil Chichimec warriors preying on Spanish caravans as an almost impenetrable redoubt, could easily have sustained relatively large populations without need for maize or other cultigens. In fact, as permanent refuge for one of the divine ancestors, Rabbit Person (a reference, perhaps, to a Rabbit Clan?), El Tunal plays a role in the charter myth of the peyote pilgrimage. With the old forests long gone and lake beds dry, the contemporary environment is misleading, for early accounts mention large forests of mixed pine and oak, especially in the higher elevations (Gerhard 1982), where little now grows but mesquite, varieties of cacti whose fruits have long been important in indigenous nutrition, as well as yucca, tree-sized members of the lily family with highly nutritious seeds and fruit.

One should also not discount the possibility—suggested already in the legend of Majakuagy—that where the environment allowed it, even some Guachichil and other desert hunter-gatherers might have had kitchen garden horticulture, perhaps growing amaranth, which is far more resistant to drought than maize, or perhaps even some hardy variety of the latter, with much the same technique of dry desert farming that one can still observe among the Hopis and the Navajos. Cultivation, or management, of the maguey cactus is another possibility; as Susan Evans (1990:117-132) has demonstrated in a significant recent paper, the maguey and its cultivation contributed mightily to the Central Mexican food system.

The designation "Guachichil" may have been applied across the board to what were really independent, small-scale societies organized on the level of simple bands that shared a common lifeway as, primarily, hunters and collectors of wild foods, and spoke related dialects of an Aztecoidan language, but still considered themselves distinct from their neighbors. As Jiménez Moreno (1943) has pointed out, there were even Guachichil groups with a much more complex social organization, to the point where, at the time of European contact, they had established incipient local states led by powerful and charismatic chieftains capable of putting up a fierce and sustained resistance to Spanish incursions. Frederick Johnson, in his commentary to the *Linguistic Map of Mexico and Central America* he published in 1944, notes the difficulties with fixing the geographical limits of Guachichil, but argues that

> [i]n spite of the fact that so little is known of it, there seems to be little doubt but what some language related to the Aztecoidan Family was spoken in the vast region to which this name has been applied. The extent has varied greatly during the different periods in its history, and a demarcation of the boundaries is but a guess, probably a bad one.

One reason is that these boundaries were in constant flux even before European contact. As already noted, when the Spaniards made their first forays into what later became the *reales*, from which they extracted enormous riches in silver, they came upon a strong Guachichil presence not only in San Luis Potosí and Coahuila, but also in Zacatecas,

Jalisco, and Durango. In other words, assuming that the Majakuagy myth embodies factual history, the band of Guachichiles he is credited with leading into the security of the Sierra Madre Occidental was but one of many that had, under whatever compulsion, migrated out of their heartland hundreds of miles westward into Zacatecas and northern Jalisco, without necessarily losing their former allegiance to peyote as divinatory-visionary sacrament and the panacea it still is today for Huichols, and even introducing it, and its rituals and lore, to other indigenous populations. That would help account for the rapid spread of peyote use through northwestern Mexico in comparatively recent times. The arid region around Nieves, for example, consisting of what is now northwestern Zacatecas, with a small slice of Durango, was mostly occupied at contact time "by rancherías of Zacatenco-speaking Chichimecs, but there was a frontier with the Guachichiles in the east" (Gerhard 1982:115). The corner of Zacatecas known as Los Altos de Jalisco was almost completely occupied by "Chichimec hunter-gatherers, probably Guachichiles with a sprinkling of Guamares in the east" (ibid., p. 104). The Jeréz region was explored by Spaniards in the 1550s and 1560s, and by 1569 there was a small settlement of Spaniards at Jerez, entirely surrounded by Chichimecs, "probably Zacatenco-speakers, although there may have been Guachichiles in the vicinity" (ibid., p. 89) (Figure 13).

Perhaps most pertinent to our speculations is the *alcaldía mayor* of Charcas, a large slice of territory that extended all the way from northern Jalisco to the northwestern part of San Luis Potosí, and that also included Wirikúta (Real de Catorce), the peyote country the Huichols consider their own. Charcas seems to have been wholly Guachichil country, with a population estimated at 25,000. Based on the early Spanish documents, the historian Peter Gerhard (1982:81, 83) describes the large territory nominally administered from the small Spanish outpost at Charcas as consisting of what is now the northwest corner of the state of San Luis Potosí, along with a part of modern Zacatecas. This vast, arid highland, he writes, forms part of the Mesa del Norte, a region of *bolsones* (interior drainage basins, often with salt flats) at 1,300–2,200 m, separated by limestone ranges reaching 3,000 m. With very slight rainfall of an average of 300–450 mm yearly, the area supports desert scrub, but "there were pine-oak forests, not many of which survive, in the higher mountains." Gerhard estimates that the entire alcadía mayor of Charcas was probably occupied at contact by Guachichil hunter-gatherers.

There are two additional observations to be made here. One is that it is precisely parts of this formerly entirely Guachichil territory that the Huichols have traditionally traversed on the pilgrimage to Wirikúta and back. Wirikúta is identified with the silver mining district called Real de Catorce, the northernmost extension of the Charcas alcaldía. The Guachichil were renowned among the Spaniards as fierce defenders of their territory against all foreign intruders. Assuming that the peyote pilgrimage dates back to the earliest days of Spanish colonization, is it likely that the Guachichil inhabitants of the Charcas region would have allowed armed groups of other Indians

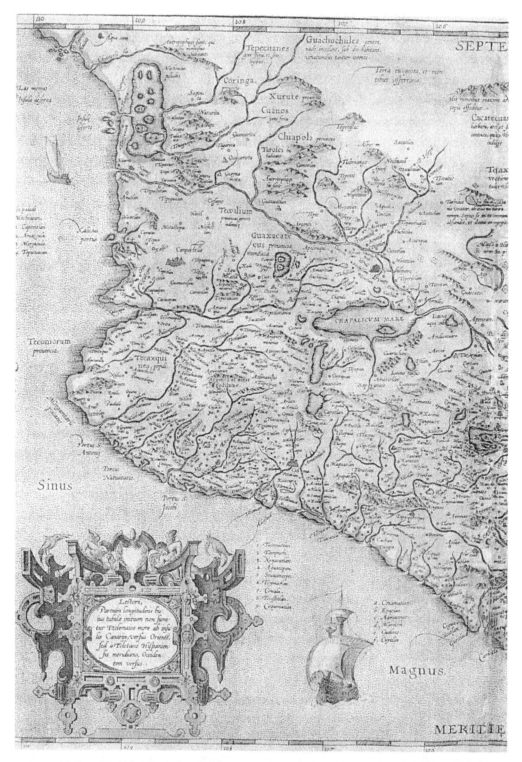

FIGURE 13. Detail of Abraham Ortelius' 1559 Map of Mexico. This section shows Guachichiles (*top*) as neighbors of the Tepehuanes, far to the west of their original homeland in San Luis Potosí.

to travel unhindered for hundreds of miles through their country?* Probably not, un-less, of course, these strangers were not properly strangers at all, but their own cultural cousins, speaking the same language and following religious traditions with which they were themselves familiar.

The evidence that Huichols first started going to Wirikúta after the Spanish invasion is admittedly circumstantial. According to the version of the charter myth of the peyote pilgrimage one hears most often, Tatewarí, the old fire god and patron of shamans (or, if not Tatewarí, Maxa Kwaxí, Great-grandfather Deer Tail) prescribed the resumption of the ancestral hunt for the peyote as a cure for ailments they were suffering because, for unstated reasons, they had not done "as the ancestors did"—that is, they had not been following the ancestral custom of gathering and ritually consuming the sacred peyote. Whichever version one prefers, they all contain implicit or explicit statements that these first peyoteros, who were to become the ancestor gods, had to evade dangers posed by the Spanish occupation at the height of the silver boom, with its mass en-slavement of Indians to extract the precious metal from deep mines in northern Jalisco, Zacatecas, and San Luis Potosí. That would locate this important event in the Huichol past not long after the Spanish invasion. It also helps place the semimythical migration of "Majakuagy" in the context of the history of Spanish colonization. In the version of the charter myth of the pilgrimage Ramón Medina related to Myerhoff and me, the ancestors are warned by Tatewarí to be careful and travel by night, lest they be captured by Spanish slave raiders, presumably as forced labor for the silver mines. The dangers faced by these ancestral peyote hunters were, and continue to be, very much on the Huichols' mind, for they come up in several mythological contexts. Not only is there the explicit admonition to the ancestral peyoteros by Tatewarí, but there is also—in the children's ceremony Lumholtz called "First Fruits"—Great-grandfather Maxa Kwaxí's admonition to the little ones who are about to "fly" transformed into birds to Wirikúta and the land where the Sun Father was born:

"In this pueblo live bad Spaniards, avoid it." "Here they must not see you, they might try to capture you, do not light a fire." (Furst 1972:149)

The implication is almost always one of clear and present danger, not something that happened in the distant past. That this should be so is not surprising. In the peyote hunt past becomes present, the peyoteros their own ancestors, walking silently single file, carrying their bows as the old ones did, bundles of arrows sheathed in deer skin quivers that now have no other use. The silver mines took a fearful toll of Indian people in the first two centuries after the Conquest. How many of those who set out for Wirikúta in those terrible times never returned?

---

*Bows and arrows in deerskin quivers remain even today an indispensable part of the parapher-nalia of Huichol peyoteros, even though these weapons no longer have practical use.

Huichols and Tepecanos

The last problem I want to consider is the historical relationship between the Huichols and the southernmost branch of the Southern Tepehuan known as the Tepecanos. The proper place to start is clearly with J. Alden Mason, the prolific University of Pennsylvania Museum ethnologist and archaeologist who was their premier student. In 1912-13, when he carried out field research in the Tepecano village of Azqueltán in the Bolaños river valley, most of its indigenous inhabitants already conversed exclusively in Spanish, but there were still enough native speakers for him to consider questions, and come to some important conclusions, about the relationship of these southernmost survivors of the Southern Tepehuan to those living farther north, whose aboriginal language exhibited only very slight differences, mainly in the pronunciation of some words, from that of the Tepecano. Mason thought that the Huichols, or, more correctly, their Guachichil antecedents, could conceivably have been responsible for the break of ninety or so miles separating the Tepecanos from their Southern Tepehuan cousins. He was much concerned with the uncritical way in which, with the single exception of Lumholtz, writers on western Mexico were then tending to ignore the considerable differences in language and culture between these Southern Tepehuan and the Northern, treating them as though they were a single culture, with data from one applicable to the other, when in fact the Southern and Northern Tepehuan have few cultural traits in common.

> This consistent lack of differentiation between the Northern and Southern Tepehuan in spite of the linguistic difference, while the linguistically similar Southern Tepehuan and Tepecano were distinguished—although some chroniclers mention the practical identity—poses some problems and suggests some interesting explanations. Were the Tepehuan of history the Northern group only, who have gradually retired to the northernmost and most isolated part of their former habitat, while the Southern Tepehuan represent the descendants of the Tepecano (who term themselves today Tepehuan) who migrated northward? Or were the Tepecano a Southern Tepehuan group that migrated southward, as stated in a legend recorded by Hrdlička?
>
> Was the region of the Southern Tepehuan and Tepecano once coterminous or continuous until separated, possibly, by a westward migration of the Guachichil-Huichol? The linguistic differentiation is so slight that the separation must have been relatively recent, of the order of a few centuries. (Mason 1952:37-38)

Linguists have calculated that mutual intelligibility is gradually reduced through time and ceases altogether after 500 years of separation between two populations that started out speaking the same language. Mason based his conclusion of relatively recent separation on the fact that when residents of Azqueltán visited the Southern Tepehuan, they found that language to be virtually identical to their own. Experience shows that this would not be the case had they become isolated from one another much longer ago than a few hundred years. Although there are fewer and fewer native Tepehuan speakers left, other writers since Mason have found the same thing.

It is generally assumed that the hearth of the Utonahuan (Uto-Aztecan) languages was the region of the upper Gila or northern Sierra Madre, with separation of the different branches from the common ancestor beginning as early as 5500 B.C. Miller (1983:118, Figure 2) estimates the Sonoran branch of Southern Uto-Aztecan to have separated from that leading to Classic Nahuatl (Aztec) and related Nahuatlan languages, including Pipil and Pochutec, as early as 4700 B.C. In addition to Huichol and Cora, the Sonoran family also includes Upper Piman (Pima-Papago), Northern Tepehuan, Southern Tepehuan and the closely related Tepecano dialect, Mayo, Yaqui, Guarijío, Tarahumara (still spoken by some 50,000 Indian people in southwestern Chihuahua), and such extinct languages as Totorame (aligned with Cora) and Tecual and Guachichil (aligned with Huichol), and, to the east, Zacatec, Concho, Lagunero, Suma and others (Miller 1983:122). In any event, writes Miller (ibid., p. 123), the "division between the two branches of Southern Uto-Aztecan, Sonoran and Aztec, is profound, going back almost to the time of Proto-Uto-Aztecan." That Cora and Huichol share "some similarities with the Aztecan languages" may indicate "that they probably were the ones closest to the Aztecan languages in the old Sonoran dialect chain" (Miller ibid., p. 121). Such an ancient connection going back many millennia should not, of course, be mistaken for any sort of close relationship in recent times between Cora or Huichol and, say, sixteenth century Classic Nahuatl (Aztec) or its descendants, the several Nahua and Nahuat(l) dialects spoken today in central Mexico, Guerrero, and the highlands of Puebla and Veracruz. Indeed, in contrast to the Nahuatlan languages, Cora and Huichol (usually grouped together as "Corachol" by linguists), as well as the other Sonoran languages, are syntactically, morphologically and, except for some vestigial forms, grammatically, very distant from Classic Nahuatl, or Aztec.

The one Indian language of the Sierra Madre Occidental that really is close to Aztec is the Nahua spoken in San Pedro Jícora, Durango, known as "Mexicano" in Preuss's time, i.e., the first decade of the twentieth century. But Mexicano, like Classic Nahuatl, belongs to the Nahuatlan group, not the Sonoran, which is why Preuss, having studied Nahuatl in Berlin under Eduard Seler, found it relatively easy to acquire fluency in the native language of this small and relatively isolated Indian community to the north of Cora territory.

Over time, speakers of Uto-Aztecan languages would be found as far west as California and the Great Basin, as far north as southwestern Wyoming, and as far south as Nicaragua and El Salvador, not to mention large areas of Mexico. As the most divergent of the Sonoran languages, Pima-Papago-Tepehuan is thought to have been the first to separate, an assessment, according to Romney (1971:230-31), that agrees "with previous inferences of Kroeber and Whorf on phonological grounds." It also agrees with Miller's above-mentioned family tree diagram showing relationships in the Uto-Aztecan family. Mason (1950:5) characterized Piman as

> the most aberrant of the Utoaztecan families, with relatively few subdivisions. The component languages are slightly differentiated, less so, probably, than Italian and Spanish. This is most remarkable since nearly a thousand miles separate the Pima at the north from the Tepecano in the south.

Whatever can be inferred from the language situation, it is self-evident that (1) Tepecan and Southern Tepehuan are to all intents and purposes identical, (2) the relationship between Huichol and Tepecan is a very distant one, indeed, with all mutual intelligibility between the two branches of Uto-Aztecan to which they belong, Aztecoidan and Piman, already gone several millennia ago, and (3) there is an obvious fit between Mason's conclusion about Huichol origins and Diguet's Majakuagy tradition, as well as with other ethnohistoric data. The Tepecano migration story to which he refers was told to Hrdlička in 1898 by an old and, he says, highly respected resident of Askeltán: The ancestors came a long time ago

> from the north, from a *Rio Colorado*, and were of the same people as the *barbaros* there and continued as "barbaros" after their arrival. (Hrdlička 1903:409–410)

"Barbaros," barbarians, was the pejorative used for people subsisting on the collection and hunting of wild foods rather than on agriculture. Askeltán (Azqueltán), Temastian, Acapulco, Huila (Huilacatlan), Santa Catarína, and Nostic were all once part of the territory of the Tepecano ancestors, who themselves were originally "Mecos," meaning Chichimecos. Except for Santa Catarína, situated in Huichol country only about 8 leagues slightly northwest of Azqueltán, all the mentioned settlements are located on or close to the Río Bolaños. According to Hrdlička (ibid., pp. 409–410), when he visited Santa Catarína in 1902, he

> came across a number of old petroglyphs, such as are found in the ruins a little north of Azkeltan, for which the Huichols could offer no explanation except that they were made by "other people."

Hrdlička did not put a name to these "other people," but presumably they were the same "Tewi" who Huichols say lived in the Sierra before they did, and to whom they ascribe the crude figurines, stone tools, arrowheads, and other archaeological remains they occasionally find in caves or in the ground (Tewi is a Cora term meaning "people" or "persons"). There is also an interesting Hewi or Tewi origin myth, partly shared with the Coras, that has a decidedly Southwestern flavor, including emergence from a *sipapu*-like hole in the center of the earth and a Grandmother Spider-like or Spider Mother-like earth and creator goddess (Furst 1974). Although there is not room here to consider it in depth, it may well be that the subject of Chapter 9, wolves as power sources for a certain class of Huichol shamans and, with it, wolf transformation, is ultimately a syncretistic survival from a Tepecan, and hence Southwestern, substratum. The fact is that the wolf appears never to have played an important role in Mesoamerican symbolism, in contrast to North America, where he is almost everywhere a major power animal and spirit ally of Indians. In the Puebloan Southwest, where the wolf plays a major role in myth and ritual, he is also one of the four animal guardian deities of the cardinal directions, his being the all important east (Tyler 1975). Most directly pertinent, perhaps, is the fact that by Hrdlička's and Mason's time some Tepecanos still retained something of a tradition of wolves as guardians.

Mason also heard that Santa Catarína and some other places where Huichols now live were once Tepecan. What impresses me is that nowhere, not in Huichol myths, nor in the traditions of the Tepecanos, is there anything to suggest a Tepehuan/Tepecano conquest and subjugation of the Huichols.[5] The cumulative evidence, rather, suggests that when the ancestral Southern Tepehuan/Tepecano reached the end of their thousand-mile migration from the north, they settled not only the barranca of the Bolaños, but the adjacent mountains and valleys, including places that became Huichol only later, with the former occupants either adapting to, and culturally and genetically blending with, the newcomers, or moving elsewhere.

That the Tepecan, who according to Lumholtz (1902:123) called themselves simply *Xumátcam*, "the people," were regarded as true mountain folk is implicit in the very name by which they became known, "Tepehuan" or "Tepecan" being almost certainly derived from the Nahuatl *tepetl* = mountain. There is a long list of words with this root in Remi Simeon's *Dictionaire de la Langue Nahuatl*, including a deity named *Tepeua* or *Tepehua*, meaning "Master of the Mountains"; with the postposition *can* this becomes *tepeuacan*, from the mountains.

This is not to say that when the Tepecanos arrived they necessarily found the mountains and barrancas empty of people, only that there is no evidence that if they had predecessors there, they did not have to have been the people we now call "Huichols." In any event, there is much to suggest that the Tewi or Hewi of Huichol mythology may very well have been the Piman-speaking Tepecanos, whose surviving aboriginal religious beliefs and customs Mason judged to be a blend of Southwestern, Chichimec, and Mexican traits.

Earlier I made reference to Mason's observation, in his 1950 monograph on Papago (itself a dialect of Pima), that the Piman languages are only slightly differentiated from one another. The extraordinary thing is that this remarkably versatile scholar and more recent linguists have calculated the separation of Southern Tepehuan/Tepecan from Pima in southern Arizona at less than seven centuries. Other things being equal, this implies that the Tepecanos might have arrived in northern Jalisco as late as the thirteenth to fourteenth century A.D., suggesting that what drove them out of Arizona and the northern Sierra Madre and sent them southward in the first place was the sustained drought that also devastated the Anasazi and forced the abandonment of such major sites as Chaco, Mesa Verde, and Bandelier.

This, in turn, has implications for the dating, or the cultural affiliation, of certain archaeological sites within Tepecan territory, such as Totoáte. In any event, at some point the Bolaños valley and the adjacent Sierra Madre Occidental came to form the southernmost extension of a continuous, relatively narrow, strip of mountainous country along the eastern side of the Sierra Madre Occidental inhabited by speakers of Tepiman (Pima–Papago–Tepehuan) languages, extending from southern Arizona and Chihuahua southward for a thousand miles to northern Jalisco (Mason 1952:38). Not only linguistically but also culturally this entire band of related Piman languages had, and intermittently continues to have, in the words of Carroll L. Riley (1994, personal communication), something of a "Southwestern flavor." This finds its most immediately apparent expression in ceremonial objects that resemble, in construction and use, those of the Hopis and other Southwestern peoples, and that the Huichols, and also the Coras, share with the Southern Tepehuan/Tepecan. No doubt the Tepiman linguistic corridor also facilitated cultural exchanges between northwestern Mexico and the American Southwest in the colonial period, but there is little question that some traits Huichols, Coras, and Tepecanos share with the Pueblos predate the Spanish invasion.

Just how and why the Southern Tepehuan of Azqueltán came to be differentiated from their closest relatives to their north as "Tepecano" is not clear, the more so in that Mason reported in 1912 that "this name is absolutely unknown to the natives of Azqueltán, who speak of themselves as Tepehuán." According to Mason:

> One of the few references, found in the Franciscan Relations, and quoted by Orozco y Berra, is to the effect that the Franciscan monasteries of Colotlán, Nostic and Chimaltitlan were founded in the territory of the Teules-Chichimecos, who spoke a language known as Tepecano. A further note of the Franciscans gives Tepecano as one dialect of the Teul-Chichimec group, the others being Cazcan and Tecuexe. . . . Tradition among the present Indians, as well as a few words found by Dr. Boas to the south in the region of San Juan del Teul, tends to corroborate the testimony of the early missionaries. This tradition is to the effect that at the time of the Conquest, the Tepecanos, as they have always been termed, occupied a considerable territory in Jalisco and Zacatecas, north of Guadalajara, reaching to the Rio Santiago and the pueblo of Teul on the south, and to Colotlán on the east. Hrdlička notes also the tradition that a part, at least, of the country of the Huicholes, the nearest neighbors of the Tepecano, *was originally theirs, which is further evidence for the proposition, already suggested by Orozco y Berra, that the Huicholes are the descendants of the former Guachichiles, of the state of San Luis Potosí, who retreated to their present home shortly after the Conquest* (emphasis added). (Mason 1912:344–345)

With the Spanish conquest of the Southern Tepehuan territory in 1530, so goes the tradition cited by Mason, the majority of the Tepecan left, a part going to join the Southern Tepehuan to the north, and another part migrating even further north, "to a Rio Colorado, which Hrdlička identified as a river in the country of the Northern Tepehuane," and the remainder withdrawing to the country around the pueblo of Azqueltán, in the barranca of the Río Bolaños. Their former lands were occupied by Nahuatl-speaking Tlaxcaltecs, who were transferred to the western frontier by the Spaniards for protection, "and possibly also by Huicholes" (ibid., p. 345).

Tepecan and Huichol Religion. Although aboriginal Tepecan religion was already obscured by a heavy overlay of Christianity in Hrdlička's and Mason's day, it is still possible to reconstruct something of its core from their writings, and those of Lumholtz. When Mason died in November 1967 he left behind a manuscript on Tepecan beliefs and ritual he had planned to complete with a comparison to Southwestern ceremonialism. Before he died he gave a copy to George Agogino, suggesting that the latter publish it, if possible with new data from Azqueltán. Agogino did so, in 1972, in the form of a small monograph, with photographs and additional data on the village of Asqueltán as it appeared more than fifty years after Mason's stay there. Equally essential is Mason's collection of thirty-seven Tepecano prayers, in the native language and translation, which he published in 1918 in the first volume of the Franz Boas's *International Journal of American Linguistics.* In his Introduction to Mason's essay on Tepecan ceremonialism Agogino noted Mason's unhappiness that only slight attention had been paid to his collection of prayers, despite its considerable ethnographic interest as showing "a blend of Mexican and Southwest U.S. religious traits" of the sort that "Chichimec and other invaders from the north" may also have carried into the valley of Mexico (Agogino 1972:8). Notwithstanding the extent of Christian conversion and echoes of the Trinity in the way some of the Tepecano deities are addressed, Mason himself felt that the content of the prayers, *perdones* in Spanish, was much less affected by Christianity than appeared at first sight.

My impression of Mason's data is that, beyond certain fundamentals to which all the indigenous peoples of the Sierra Madre Occidental subscribe and that, as Mason himself pointed out, are shared in their general outlines by Native American religions from the Southwest to southern South America, Huichol and Tepecano religion are quite distinct from one another. The two things they do share are several kinds of sacred objects used in the ceremonies, and, up to a point, peyote ceremonialism. With respect to the former, it should be noted that (1) these also resemble, in form and function, those of the Puebloan Southwest, and (2) that, as Hrdlička (1903) pointed out, the Huichol and Tepecano prayer sticks, and also the *chimales*, from the Nahuatl *chimalli* = shields, which are made by spiraling yarn around crossed sticks, differ in several respects, such as the use of colors and materials, those of the Tepecanos generally being made of white cotton and the Huichol ones of colored wool.

Most striking seems to me to be the difference between their respective deities. Like many other native peoples, Huichols and Tepecanos have a Sun god, referred to as Father. But beyond that I find no overlap in the identities, functions, genders, associations, and names of divine beings that have charge of natural phenomena and, by extension, the affairs of human beings. Tepecanos and Huichols both venerate mountains in their respective environments and personify them as deities to whom offerings are made and petitions and prayers for favors addressed. But this is true as well of Mesoamerican Indians generally, past and present, as it is of many other Native American peoples, North and South. In the case of the Huichols, in addition to the mountains, hills, and other natural formations in the Sierra Madre Occidental, those in the distant peyote country hold a special place in their hearts, for these are manifestations of the kakauyaríte, the divine ancestors.

The Tepecanos, but not the Huichols, had a female deity with lunar associations who is the wife of the Sun god. And there is no indication in what remained of Tepecano belief in Mason's day of a counterpart to Great-grandmother Nakawé (Lumholtz's "Grandmother Growth"), the white-haired old earth and creator goddess of the Huichols, nor of the many other female members of the multitude of ancestor and nature deities that make up the Huichol pantheon. Nakawé may have a lunar connection, but not explicitly so. Conspicuous by his absence from the Tepecano pantheon is a direct analog to the aged fire god and patron of shamans, whom the Huichols address as Tatewarí, Our Grandfather, and who presides, in the person of the mara'akáme, the shaman-singer (Spanish *cantador*), at every ceremony and ritual. There is a Tepecan fire god, but he is the younger of the two sons of the Sun god, the elder being the all-important Morning Star. As the father of Maize Girl, the Tepecano sun god is also the father-in-law of her husband, the personified *toloache* (*Datura*), to whom Tepecanos addressed *perdones* for riches and other benefits.

Peyote Ceremonialism. The importance of peyote to the Tepecanos, and analogies between Tepecano and Huichol peyote ceremonialism, have long been accepted as givens. It is on closer scrutiny that we begin to see differences that make the supposed analogies seem more like echoes. Granting that our information is limited, by every reasonable measure it appears to me that Tepecano peyotism is essentially a reflection of the Huichol prototype (or, if we will, the Guachichil), and not, as suggested in some of the recent anthropological literature on the Huichols, the other way round.

I can think of no more poignant and convincing an affirmation of what peyote means to "being Huichol," of how deeply the little psychoactive cactus is embedded in Huichol intellectual culture and religious ideology, historical tradition, mythology, ethnic consciousness, spirituality, the annual ceremonial round, and economic well-being (for even the beloved maize and the other crops will not grow without it), than that which ethnographer Stacy B. Schaefer heard from a peyotero from San Andrés Cohamiata:

> Peyote is everything, it is the crossing of the souls, it is everything there is. Without peyote nothing would exist. (See Schaefer, Chapter 5, this volume.)

In the world view of committed Huichols, then, peyote constitutes the very soul of the religious culture: peyote as visionary sacrament, pathway to the realm of the ancestor deities, and the hunt for it in Wirikúta as sacred mandates passed down from the ancestor gods through the generations and reaffirmed over and over in poetry and ritual, in artistic creativity, in expenditure of religious emotion and economic and physical sacrifice.

Here, in full, is Mason's description of Tepecano peyote ceremonialism:

Peyote (*Lophophora williamsii* or *echinocactus*) is most important in Tepecan religion, as in all the religions of the natives of the Sierra Madre Occidental. Also termed "maize," it is a god and a protector of the Indians, and helps to bring rain. It relieves tiredness and aids the memory. "Rosaries" of peyote buttons are worn at some ceremonies.

Probably at the time of assuming office, each Cantador Mayor is supposed to go (at least once) on the search for peyote, which does not grow in the Tepecan region. Thereafter, he may purchase it, presumably from the Huichol. Rito de la Cruz made the journey about 12 years before my visit to Asqueltán, or about the year 1900.

The nearest place where peyote is securable is near Cerro del Venado y las Camuzas, about eight days journey east of Zacatecas. The round trip requires just a month, including five days hunting and the return journey. The trip is made about the middle of September. No food is eaten during the entire trip, and bathing is also forbidden. No water is taken until mid-afternoon.

On arriving in the peyote region, payments are left. Peyote bought from the Huichols is purchased with money, but payment for growing line peyote is, of course, of a ceremonial nature. The latter is paid for with jicaras, with beads, small mirrors, etc. The jicara is said to be peyote. A large jicara is placed on the ground, with beads and other payments in front of it. A prayer which is no longer remembered was recited facing the east. The hunter sees a figure of a deer, but it is peyote and not a deer. They hunt for five days, each day in a different direction, and a prayer is recited each afternoon. A final prayer is said upon departure.

On return to Asqueltán, about October 24, a Peyote Fiesta is held immediately in one of the patios, where peyote is given to everyone present. The usual ceremonial singing and dancing lasts all night. The next morning the Cantador may have his first meal and bathe, but after that he must fast for another 20 days to give thanks. Peyote, generally regarded as an infusion, plays a very prominent part in Tepecan religious ceremony. It is usually at all the calendrical ceremonies and probably in many less formal activities. At the ceremonies participants are sprinkled with peyote water. (Mason, in Mason and Agogino, 1972:19-20)

Assuredly, there are analogies here to Huichol practice: offerings and prayers to peyote, all-night dancing and singing, identification of peyote with maize and deer, harvesting for five days, restrictions on food and bathing, the peyote fiesta—all these and more are familiar components of peyote ritual among the Huichols. But what strikes me as at least as significant as the similarities are the differences. First and foremost of these is one that Mason does not mention but that can be found in Lumholtz, who did not visit the Tepecanos personally, but obtained information on their culture from three visitors from Asqueltán:

> The sacred cactus hikuli is used by them and called by this name. As recently as three years ago the Tepecanos themselves went for the plants, but now they buy them from the Huichols. A form of common hemp called *mariguana* or *rosa maria* (*Cannabis sativa*) sometimes takes the place of hikuli. (Lumholtz 1902:125)

Both Lumholtz and Mason observed that once the Tepecano cantador has fulfilled his one obligatory journey to the peyote desert, purchased peyote will do as well. Huichols would find this unacceptable. Moreover, to be recognized as a shaman, or cantador, in the first place, a Huichol has to have completed a minimum of five peyote pilgrimages, and preferably ten. In fact, some older Huichol shamans can look back on twenty, thirty and even more, to hunt and partake of the sacred cactus in its native habitat and to return with sufficient quantities for the many ceremonies requiring its use and for sale or trade to other Indian peoples. But if purchased peyote is not acceptable, the idea of substituting some other psychoactive species when hikuli is not available is anathema—even one of indigenous origin rather than a foreign import like marijuana. Huichols are, of course, well aware of other plants that will affect consciousness and trigger visions, but that is not the point. It is, rather, that peyote is special, it is the gift of the ancestors, and in return it would be unthinkable to attempt to approach them by any other pathway. Not even peyote that could still be freely purchased in the 1960s and '70s from herbal stalls in the public markets of Guadalajara, Zacatecas, or Tepic would do. For Huichols, peyote is embedded in a whole complex of history and myth and symbol, of observation and experience, of the merging of past and present and future, and no other species, not the *Psilocybe* mushrooms or morning glory seeds that were so important in the divinatory-visionary rituals of the Mexica and other Meso-american peoples, and assuredly not *Cannabis sativa*, carry these meanings for them. In fact, the only other psychoactive substance that bears a direct ideological relationship to peyote is the potent native tobacco, *Nicotiana rustica*, which peyoteros smoke in the form of cornhusk cigarettes to increase receptivity to the peyote experience.

One could go down the line and point to other discrepancies that clearly mark Tepecano peyotism, however vibrant and important it clearly was in former times, as derivative, a secondary and not a primary religious phenomenon. I cannot emphasize this too strongly, because the recent anthropological literature contains a revisionist model of the origins of Huichol religion according to which the profound emotional involvement of Huichols with peyote and the peyote hunt may not be aboriginal at all, but only a borrowing from the Tepecanos:

Taking into account the presence of the peyote rituals and the extremely elaborate ceremonial compounds in the Bolaños valley, it is possible that much of what we regard as Huichol ceremonialism was developed and formalized in the Bolaños valley. I think that the cultural relationships between the eastern Huichol districts and the archaeological and Tepecan Bolaños tradition are extremely close. . . . The peyote emphasis . . . may indicate *that it was the Bolaños valley, not the Chapalagana, that served as the aboriginal hearth of the southern Sierra Madre peyote/peyotero complex* (emphasis added). (Weigand 1981:11)

Respect for the Huichols and their right to their own version of history should, even in the absence of ethnohistoric and ethnographic corroboration, give anthropologists pause before committing themselves in print to personal opinions to which knowledgeable Huichols themselves could hardly subscribe. Some recent literature also contains the dubious proposition that the circular form of the Huichol temple was copied from archaeological ruins in the Bolaños valley—as though sacred architecture had nothing to do with indigenous conceptions of the cosmos. As for peyote, the idea that the Tepecanos, and not the Huichols themselves, or their lineal ancestors, were the originators of what is the very heart of Huichol spirituality seems to me wrong on virtually every count—linguistics, history, ethnography, geography, ethnobotany, archaeology, comparative religion, and, let it be said, just plain common sense. First of all, the ultimate homeland of the Piman Tepehuan/Tepecan is the Southwest, specifically southern Arizona. Ethnographically and ethnobotanically, the Southwest, including California, is "*Datura* country," in the sense that most, if not all, of its indigenous peoples, the Pima included, employed *D. inoxia*, for which California Indians adopted the Nahuatl-derived term *toloache* during the early Mission period, in divinatory, initiatory, and therapeutic ritual. So did both the Northern and Southern Tepehuan. The Tepecanos themselves addressed prayers for riches and good fortune to *toloache*, the Sun's son-in-law.[6]

The Piman peoples have no history of involvement with peyote prior to the establishment of the syncretistic Native American Church,[7] whose pan-Indian adherents have, for more than a century now, employed the cactus as sacrament. Peyote, as we know, is native to the arid north-central region of Mexico and the lower Río Grande Valley. If any place is the real hearth of the complex of beliefs and rituals that revolve around peyote, it would surely have to have been precisely where Huichols still go to collect it, and not a valley inhabited by Piman-speakers hundreds of miles west of where it grows, and even less so "the lake area to the south" of the Bolaños valley, as Weigand (1979b:26) has proposed.

At the time of European contact, peyote was widely employed for visionary and divinatory purposes, and also as medicine, by native peoples within and also at some considerable distance from its native range, including the shamans, priests, and doctors of the Mexica of Tenochtitlan. From archaeological excavations in the painted rock shelters of the Trans-Pecos region we know that Desert Culture people in southern

Texas and adjacent northern Mexico used it alongside the red and black, beanlike seeds of *Sophora secundiflora*, which though hallucinogenic, are also dangerously toxic. The earliest radiocarbon date we now have for peyote in these shelters is 5,000 B.C. (Furst 1976; 1989a). In colonial New Mexico, some Spaniards were put on trial in the early 1600's by the Inquisition for taking peyote to locate lost or stolen property and strayed spouses (Scholes 1935). That seems to be about as far west as peyote was traded in colonial times. The ultimate homeland of the Piman-speakers of northwestern Mexico and Arizona is nearly a thousand miles from the nearest natural occurrence of peyote. That there is no evidence for Pima use of peyote in precontact times does not, of course, rule it out, but if they did, they would have had to obtain it, directly or indirectly, by long-distance trade from those who had direct access to it, that is, such Chichimec peoples as the Guachichil.

Given the historical, geographical, and botanical situation, where, when, and from whom, other than the Huichol/Guachichil, are the Tepecano, relatively recent immigrants into northwestern Mexico from southern Arizona with no peyote tradition of their own, supposed to have acquired it as divinatory/ecstatic sacrament and panacea in place of *Datura*, the customary Southwestern visionary plant? And not just the sacred cactus itself, but everything that goes with it—the great complex of beliefs, behaviors, ancestor veneration, origin myths, song, symbolic meanings, associations, transformations, the healing arts, public and private ritual, sacred geography, environmental and ethnobotanical wisdom, and all the rest that are an integral part of peyote use among the Huichols?

But even without specific objections, it is surely only common sense to look for the origin of a trait where it is most elaborated and remains most firmly and prominently embedded in the cultural matrix. In the case of "peyote ceremonialism," so-called, that is surely the Huichols and not a people for whom, even before the end of the last century, the sacred cactus had so paled in significance that when none was available, marijuana was an acceptable substitute.

Some Concluding Thoughts

The thrust of this essay has been that the cultural and genetic heritage of the Huichols probably includes a substantial Guachichil-Chichimec contribution. Exactly when this occurred is uncertain, but about five hundred years ago is not a bad guess. The most dramatic living expression of this ancient Guachichil component is, of course, the ritual and symbol complex that has the peyote cactus as its heart and soul. Myerhoff (1974) saw in the strong vestiges of a hunting and gathering ideology in Huichol religion and ritual, from hunting arrows to carry prayers and petitions to the gods or illness to enemies, to the explicit characterization of the peyote pilgrimage as a hunt, and it, in turn, as a necessary prerequisite to agricultural success, an "incomplete transition" from the older way of life to full-scale reliance on maize and other cultigens. It is probably more appropriate to see it as what one might call "situational syncretism," an ongoing dialectic in which, depending on the season, the circumstances and felt needs, sometimes the older predominates, sometimes the newer. However "traditional" Huichol culture may seem to us, it is not a fossil frozen in time but a dynamic process in which all manner of phenomena, material and ideological, old and new, even "myth" and "history"—and Huichols make no distinction between these—are constantly being adopted, rejected, or reworked and, where deemed useful, brought into harmony with one another. Huichols are always stressing the need for harmony, for everything and everyone being "of one heart" to assure the continuation of life. That is why there is no conflict or gap between hunting and cultivating. For Huichols, having sprung, or been transformed, from its tracks, its antlers, and its flesh, the sacred intoxicating cactus is a function of the great sacred deer of the time of the ancestors. Maize, the sacred cultigen, may have been relatively late in breaking into, and becoming integral to, the conceptual unity of deer and peyote. But as things stand today, and presumably have for centuries, peyote is so much maize and maize peyote that without the hunt for the latter in the distant desert home of the ancestors the sacred crop will not flourish in the Sierra.

To us a maize plant appears to have absolutely nothing in common with a cactus like peyote. But I suggest that for Huichols they share, among others, this important characteristic: both are capable of triggering altered states of consciousness. For maize is consumed not only in the form of tamales or tortillas, but also as a native beer, a fermented ceremonial beverage made of the sprouted kernels that Huichols call *nawá*, or by the Nahuatl-derived term *tejuíno* (*tesguíno*), and which is consumed in prodigious quantities in the religious festivities. Moreover, it somewhat resembles the ground-up and liquified form in which peyote is customarily consumed at these ceremonies.

The effects of eating or drinking peyote are, of course, considerably more powerful, and carry meanings that are far more profound. But perhaps there is a thread connecting the one experience to the other. One might also speculate that what Solomon Katz (1988) has suggested for the domestication of grain in the ancient Near East—that its original impetus was not bread but beer—applies as well to maize, not just among the Huichols, but from the very beginning of the domestication of its wild ancestor, perhaps five thousand years ago.

While much of the Huichol past endures, especially in religious ideology, world view, sacred poetry, ritual, and shamanic techniques, much that has proved valid and valuable for the preservation of their cultural and physical integrity is increasingly under assault, including even the peyote pilgrimage, which Myerhoff rightly called the Huichols' sacred journey, a journey back into their own ancient past. The number of converts to evangelical fundamentalism among them is increasing. Their long semi-autonomy, if not isolation, behind the protective shield of their rugged mountains and barrancas, breached until a few years ago only by the occasional light plane, has come to an end with the opening of what are optimistically described as all-weather roads. And roads mean not only lumber and other natural resources going out, but beer trucks coming in.

Like the Mayas of Chiapas, the Huichols are a people under siege. To be sure, reconfirming a part of their historical past, even one as central to their very existence as a people as the indigenous origins of the complex of symbols, rituals, and spirituality the nucleus of which is the psychoactive hikuli, will not improve the Huichols' present lot. It will not protect their lands against mestizo encroachment or the potentially disastrous effects of changes in agrarian law; it will not insulate their traditional religion, and especially the time-honored use of peyote and the peyote pilgrimage, which Huichols take to be their sacred birthright as a mandate from the ancestors, against missionary or drug enforcement zealotry, or, finally, their bodies against toxic chemicals—some so virulent they are banned in the United States—to which the hundreds of Huichol men, women, and children who annually migrate to the coast to work in the tobacco harvest are exposed.

But it still seems a worthy goal.

The aim of this exercise has been just that, by looking at whatever data, from whatever source, in whatever discipline, that might with the greatest degree of probability and good sense contribute to the reaffirmation of Huichol religion, especially the peyote symbol complex, as the work of their own, and not somebody else's, ancestors. The caveat is that, as my colleague Ward Goodenough used to tell his graduate students when they were about to start on their dissertations, everything we write is, in the final analysis, a progress report, a work in progress. This essay is thus as much subject to future correction and revision as to confirmation.

NOTES

1. An example of this is La Puerta, which means Doorway or Entrance, the Spanish toponym for a wide, V-shaped pass with sloping sides covered by cactus and other desert vegetation located on the western edge of Wirikúta, the sacred terminus of the pilgrimage route. The Huichols call this place Va'cúlii kiitenyi (Wakuri kiteni), a tentative reading for which would be, "Doorway of Elder Sister in her Proper Place" (va [wa]= in her proper place, cúlii [cúrii, kuri] = elder sister, kiiténie [kiteni] = doorway, entry, passage [Grimes et al., 1982:212, 248]). The obvious implication is that the European newcomers simply took the old indigenous name and translated it into Spanish, perhaps in ignorance of exactly what this place was supposed to be a "doorway" to.

Some Huichols explain the aboriginal name as meaning that here one enters the vagina of the Peyote Mother, the divine being who watches over the peyote plants in Wirikúta. Another version speaks of Wakuri as a particular female deity who went to Wirikúta in the First Times, when the ancestral goddesses were scouting the proper route to the sacred peyote country, and remained there as guardian of this vital passageway.

This is probably the place Lumholtz's informants were talking about when they told him of a mountain called "Wákuli" near the peyote country. Lumholtz (1902:II, p. 123) assumed this to be the same name as that by which Huichols call the Tepehuan, perhaps because he did not fully appreciate how radically the meaning of a Huichol term can change when stress is shifted from one syllable to another (e.g., *téiwari* = neighbor, mestizo, and *tewarí* = grandfather). According to Lumholtz, Huichols call this hill or mountain "Elder Brother." Inasmuch as *Va'cúli* appears to refer to the Mother of Peyote, it is hardly likely that her hill would have been called "Elder Brother." There is, however, a hill in Wirikúta which Huichols refer to as Our Elder Brother, but that is the sacred mountain where Kauyumári has his abode. In accounting for the origin of Wirikúta as the name for the sacred peyote country, Stacy Schaefer's consultants have also given the peyote goddess' name as Wiri Uvi in place of Wakuri.

Finally, it should be noted that in one of Zingg's unpublished myths, Wákuli is given as the name of one of two deer-related deities of the First Times—the other being the hunting god Pálikata—who ask permission to place their "rancherías" near that of the culture hero and Deer Person Kauyumári (Zingg n.d., p. 96). As noted, in the sacred geography of the Huichols, Kauyumári has his permanent abode in Wirikúta. Zingg's story of the placement of the deities in the First Times by the old goddess Takutsi and the Sun Father thus fits nicely with the physical location of "Wákuli's Doorway" on the western approach to the sacred peyote country and almost within sight of Kauyumári's Hill.

2. An early colonial mention of a forced resettlement of sierra Huichols to the coast is interesting, because to this day Huichol shamans and their followers travel west on pilgrimages to San Blas, on the Nayarit coast, to make offerings, including fresh water from sacred springs in the interior, to Tatéi Haramara, who sends rain clouds to the Huichol country. In return they take sea water, shells, sand, bits of seaweed, and feathers shed by gulls and other shore birds as gifts to the Mothers of the terrestrial and celestial waters in the interior. On one level this can be interpreted as a kind of world renewal ceremony, in which the Pacific Ocean, as the largest remnant of the cosmic sea that once covered all the earth, before Nakawé moved the rain deities from the waters into the sky and caused dry land to appear, is reunited with its smaller remains, represented by the springs, water holes, lakes and swamps in and outside the Huichol territory.

More to the point here, as the place where the Sun goes down, to begin his subterranean journey back to the east, the west is also the direction in which the souls of the dead travel to the underworld, whose entrance Huichols locate near San Blas. Some Huichols explain heavy rains accompanied by thunder and lightning as the clash of the clouds—i.e., the rain serpents—that come from west to east with those that personify the rain goddesses of the other cardinal directions, especially the east. There is thus far more to Huichol interest in the Pacific coast than meets the eye.

3. What Peter J. Wilson (1988:66) says about architectural evolution in the rest of the "domesticated world" applies as well to the Huichols:

> The house, and often the village, serves not simply as a dwelling, shelter, and spatial arrangement of activities but also as a central instrument through which people record and express their thoughts. Furthermore, it, or its derivatives, embodies the spiritual beliefs of people and contributes the setting, and sometimes the text, of their religious lives. . . . It makes its own contribution to expressive culture *and has evolved from the multipurpose dwelling to the exclusive sacredness of the temple* . . . (emphasis added)

Also to be noted—without, however, necessarily implying historical connections—is the striking resemblance between the interior arrangement, or floor plan, of the Huichol temple and the Great Kivas in Chaco Canyon and the circular ceremonial chambers at other Anasazi sites.

These resemblances have not been lost on Huichol visitors to Anasazi sites in the Southwest (cf. Furst 1989). Also to be mentioned is that circular ceremonial buildings are a hallmark of Huastec architecture. San Luis Potosí itself is full of Huastec sites with round ceremonial complexes and circular buildings (Meade 1942; Cabrera Ipiña 1991). Remains of a round Huastec temple were identified not long ago even in Real de Catorce, close to the Huichol peyote gathering grounds (Patricio Dávila Cabrera and Diana Zaragoza Ocaña, 1992, personal communication). The San Luis Potosí archaeologist Joaquín Meade (1953) has discussed Huastec relations with areas to the west, and another Mexican archaeologist, José Corona Nuñez (1953), has even proposed a Huastec penetration as far as Nayarit, with the circular temple at Ixtlán del Río as one striking example of Huastec, or Huastec-influenced, ceremonial architecture in early post-Classic northwestern Mexico.

4. Among the "Uzare," that is, Huichols, Fray Alonso Ponce apparently saw none of the large circular local temples or any sign of the well-developed, temple-based, communitywide ceremonialism and temple cargo system that are of such great religious and sociopolitical importance among the Huichols today, and that Stacy B. Schaefer discusses in Chapter 11. The earliest Spanish observations among the neighboring Coras do speak of native temples, which they call *calihueys*, a borrowing from the Nahuatl (*cali* = house, *uey* = great, large). In contrast, of Uzare, that is, Huichol, religious practices, the sixteenth-century friar reports that they had no "*adoración comun*," each, rather, choosing whichever "*idolo*" suited him best (Ponce in Rojas 1992:24).

5. It is not that Tepehuan/Tepecan conquest of other peoples in the course of their southward migration is unthinkable, but rather that there is no ethnohistoric, archaeological, mythological or folkloric support for such an event in Huichol history.

6. Mason (1918) identified it as *Datura*, but his description of it as having "a thick trunk of nine inches in diameter" and "growing on the bare rock," with long branches extending to "the cardinal points and to the heavens," sounds less like the shrubby *Datura inoxia* than its close relative in the Solanaceae, the viney *Solandra guttata*, which Huichols call Kiéri and which shares some of the same chemistry with the Daturas. (See Chapter 8, this volume.)

7. The single exception is a small population of Mountain Pima, located between Sonora and Chihuahua, on the edge of the territory of the Raramuri (Tarahumara), whose use of *híkuri* (peyote) is well-documented. It is almost certainly from these Tarahumara neighbors that the Mountain Pima adopted the intoxicating cactus, along with *híkuri*, its Tarahumara name (David L. Shaul, personal communication). The Huichols employ the same term, but not the Cora, who call peyote *wátari*.

ACKNOWLEDGMENTS

I am indebted to Carroll L. Riley for drawing my attention to the 1935 article by France Scholes on the Inquisition in early colonial New Mexico, and for his generosity in sharing his long experience with the Tepehuan and northwest Mexican prehistory; and to T. J. Knab for clarifying problems in Diguet's work on the Huichol language and in Nahuatl and Huichol linguistics. The responsibility for any errors is, of course, exclusively mine.

INTRODUCTION TO CHAPTER 3

Most Huichols today live within the states of Jalisco and Nayarit, with a few others in Durango and Zacatecas. Nevertheless, Zacatecas played a considerable role in Huichol ethnohistory, politically as well as culturally. Various campaigns to subdue the Sierra Indians had their inception in Zacatecas territory; the Bishop of Zacatecas exerted a powerful influence over the Sierra Madre Occidental; parts of sixteenth-century Zacatecas were home to numerous Guachichiles, a Chichimec people with whom some Huichols, if not all, shared a common ancestry, culture, and, probably, language; and it was through Zacatecas that Huichol peyoteros traveled between their homes in the Sierra and the sacred peyote desert in San Luis Potosí, as they still do today. In fact, the hill just outside the city of Zacatecas, topped by a colonial church that draws thousands of devout pilgrims every year hoping for miracle cures or other beneficence from the Virgin, is also one of the important way stations for peyoteros, not because of the Catholic shrine but because the divine ancestors rested near this hill on the first journey to Wirikúta (Figure 14).

It is therefore right and proper that Huichol ethnohistory since the Spanish invasion be considered not only from the point of view of Jalisco and Nayarit, but also Zacatecas. The following essay by anthropologist and ethnohistorian Allen Franz is based on fifteen months of field work in Zacatecas in the 1970s, including visits to the Huichol communities of Santa Catarína and San Sebastián, and several years more of archival and library research in Mexico, at the University of California, and in the Library of Congress. Unfortunately, the state archives of Zacatecas were destroyed by fire in 1975; still, says Franz, there are many sources, from missionary and administrative reports to the journals of early travelers, from which to extract a picture of the distinctive position the Huichols occupied within the broader cultural history of colonial and postcolonial western Mexico.

Stacy B. Schaefer and Peter T. Furst

FIGURE 14. Convento de Guadalupe. It was from here, the third Franciscan monastery established in the Americas, that monks were educated as missionaries and sent into colonial northern Mexico, including the Huichol region, and the southwestern United States. Note the young Huichol mother and child in the foreground: Huichols have been coming here for many years to sell beadwork and other folk art, and peyoteros from the Sierra stop here on their way to Wirikúta to commemorate the pilgrimage of the ancestor gods. (*Photograph by Peter T. Furst.*)

3 : HUICHOL ETHNOHISTORY

The View from Zacatecas

ALLEN R. FRANZ

Although modern commercial aircraft crisscross the skies overhead, single and twin-engine planes make periodic landings on mesa-top airstrips, and beer trucks lumber up new roads into the Huichol country, despite the fact that the majority are now bilingual, own transistor radios and other modern goods, and many of them travel extensively in the outside world, Huichols insistently remain "traditional" Indian people in a jet age world. This chapter explores the interrelations between the Huichol Indians and neighboring indigenous and immigrant groups from the vantage point of Zacatecas, in an effort to explain the Huichols' remarkable sociocultural and religious integrity. At the same time, it is a study of the numerous factors that have influenced acculturation and assimilation, however minimal. The Huichols are indeed an ethnic group, in that, whatever the differences between the several local territorial units, or *comunidades indígenas*, in pronunciation or dialect, or in emphasis in aspects of religion, myth, and ceremony, especially between the eastern half of the territory and the western, they can be seen as a collectivity sharing a common language, a common religion, and a common heritage among themselves, all the while interacting with outside groups.

With few exceptions, ethnographic studies of the Huichols from the time of Carl Lumholtz, in the last decade of the nineteenth century, have dealt primarily with contemporary sociocultural patterns, especially their remarkably elaborate and well-preserved religion and its expression in art, myth, and ritual. It has generally been assumed, implicitly or explicitly, that the Huichols' minimal degree of acculturation to outside standards has been the result of their isolation from Spanish and mestizo influences. I will argue instead that the strength and cohesion of the Huichol sociocultural system exist despite—or, in a sense, because of—their interrelations with other groups, indigenous as well as immigrant, for their ethnohistory as a discrete group is inextricably bound up with the broader history of western Mexico.

Many significant aspects of Huichol culture are inexplicable within a purely synchronic framework; their very existence is something of a fluke when considered historically. They present something of an enigma to the ethnologist; along with indigenous neighbors, the Coras, Tepecanos, and Mexicaneros—all of whom have acculturated to a greater degree than the Huichols—they are a remarkable exception to the rule of Hispanicization and *mestizaje* ("miscegenation," or race mixture, the term Mexicans use for the genetic blending of peoples, mainly European and Indian, that began with the Spanish invasion) that otherwise characterizes most of western and northern Mexico. The process of race mixture and acculturation has generally been more thorough in these regions than elsewhere in Mexico, and yet the Huichols stand out conspicuously as one of the least-changed peoples in all of the New World.

At the time of contact, the Huichols were not culturally unique to nearly the degree they are today. They were simply one among many in a continuum of interrelated groups organized in relatively simple bands, horticultural villages, and incipient chiefdoms; all of these groups shared a cultural complex retaining elements from a hunting-gathering past with more recent horticultural practices, which can be traced in western Mexico and on the northern plateau to the first millennium B.C. Thus, the survival of the Huichols as a distinctive ethnic group becomes an even more perplexing historical problem, considering the modification and elimination of their kindred Utonahuan (Uto-Aztecan) neighbors. If all of these groups had shared a very similar cultural inventory—which should have provided all with comparable capacities for preserving their sociocultural integrity—how or why did only the Huichols survive in such relatively pristine form? This is an historical question, and can only be answered in historical terms.

Relatively little is known for certain about the prehistory or history of the Huichols; in the nineteenth century the Mexican historiographer Orozco y Berra even asserted that they had been completely unknown to the civilized world until quite recently. While the written record is undeniably slim, nevertheless there do exist some passing references to them, though these are often obscured by the tentative spellings used: the Huichols' self-referent Wizrarika or Wixárika, has been variously rendered by different writers as Huisare, Uzare, Guisare, Visalika, Usilique, Alica, Ahelita, etc. Early on, too, they and their language were also linked with the Chichimec Guachichiles (see Chapter 1). In addition, many early writers explicitly or implicitly lumped them together with the Nayares, or Nayaritas—a political term sometimes applied more exclusively to the Coras—or with the Tecual, or Xamuca, with whom they were closely associated at the time of European contact.

For our purposes, the ethnohistory of the Huichols falls into five periods:
Spanish Aggression, 1530–1620
Recession and Withdrawal, 1620–1700
Spanish Domination, 1700–1810

Mestizo Aggression, 1810-1930

Modern, 1930-Present

Different aspects of their distinctive complex of economic, political, social, and religious patterns during these historical periods can be gleaned from a variety of sources that provide consistent pictures and tend to corroborate one another; a variety of clues can be gathered and compared with contemporary observations and accounts to expand our knowledge of the Huichols and develop a generative model of sociocultural phenomena.

Spanish Aggression, 1530-1620

The Huichols apparently occupied more or less the same lands at the time of European contact as they do today, although the earliest documents also place Huichol bands, generally characterized as "primitive" semisedentary, part-time farmers, some distance outside their present territory (cf. Gerhard 1982). At contact time they were bordered by closely related Tecual and Tecuexe nations to the south and west, and Tepehuanes to the north; in addition, they shared close ties with the Guachichiles of Mexico's northern plateau. According to Diguet, the Huichols' term for themselves, Wizrarika, derives from the Guachichil word for *agricultor*, planter, suggesting that "Huichol" may have originally designated those Guachichiles who moved into the agriculturally more favorably-endowed canyons of the southern Sierras. All these groups were descendants of the Utonahuan-speaking peoples who had migrated into western Mexico beginning two or three millennia earlier; all occupied similar or interdependent geographical niches and shared a common sociocultural substratum.

The conquering Spaniards did not turn their attention to western Mexico until 1530, eleven years after Hernan Cortés's landing on the Mexican Gulf Coast, and nine since his subjugation of the mighty Mexica (Aztecs) of México-Tenochtitlan. Cortés's nephew Francisco Cortés de Buenaventura had made a preliminary foray to the west in 1524, but it was not until the infamous Nuño de Guzmán set out in 1530 that a full-fledged conquest of the Indian nations north of the Río Grande de Santiago was attempted.

As the Spaniards had been advised by their Indian allies, the natives to the north and west of central Mexico were more primitive and intractable, and possessed fewer of the easily exploitable riches craved by the plundering Spaniards; that the west, especially Zacatecas, possessed great below-ground riches in silver was not discovered until some years later.

The Indians north of the Río Grande de Santiago, known collectively as Chichimecs, were especially renowned for their ferocity, so Nuño de Guzmán was just the man for the task of subduing them. This *conquistador* had earned an ugly reputation as a slave raider in the Panuco province on the Gulf Coast, and as a cruel and self-serving administrator while president of the first *audiencia* of Mexico; as a result of these and other activities, he was one of the few conquistadors with the personal wealth to finance an extended undertaking such as the conquest of western Mexico. It was the policy of the Crown, whenever possible, to avoid government expenditures in a conquest through private financing, to be compensated by the granting of titles or tribute prerogatives. By the terms of his commission, Nuño de Guzmán, in return for his services to the Crown, was made independent of the Audiencia, the colonial administration in Mexico City, leaving him virtually free from meddlesome higher authorities while raging through the west with a cruelty virtually unparalleled in the history of the European conquest of the Americas.

Nuño de Guzmán's conquest of western Mexico began rather easily, as the Indians of Tonalá, an ancient pottery-making center just east of present-day Guadalajara, surrendered without a fight. The Spaniards did not have to wait long, however, to discover what they were up against; the neighboring Tecuaxe Indians attacked the Tonalatecans for betraying their common cause by submitting to the invaders without a fight. Nuño de Guzmán's army then set out to conquer the Tecuexes and Cazcans, to the immediate north of the Río Grande. The Spanish and Indian auxiliary troops (the latter consisting largely of Tarascans and Nahuatl-speaking central Mexicans) were then divided among his lieutenants, who engaged in independent maneuvers so as to cover more ground. At least one of these, under the direction of Pedro Almíndez de Chirinos, passed through and nominally subjugated the Sierras of Tepeque, Xora, Cora, Huainamota, and perhaps Huazamota, on the periphery of the Huichol–Tecual territory. By virtue of their remoteness and the rather superficial nature of the initial conquest, the territories of the Huichols were apparently not touched, and many of their neighbors were only superficially affected; it appears that Almíndez de Chirinos ran into more difficulties with the rugged terrain than with the natives, who had probably heard of the Spaniards' bloody tactics and avoided confrontation.

Eager to establish an administrative center from which to coordinate Spanish operations and interests, Nuño de Guzmán elected to locate Guadalajara, the capital of his province of Nueva Galicia (names derived from his homeland in northeastern Spain, the city of Guadalajara in the province of Galicia), near the site of the present-day Nochistlan, Zacatecas. The decision was allegedly based on the site's difficulty of access from the authorities in Mexico City (it lay across the Río Grande de Santiago), as well as upon the need to closely monitor the unruly Indians of the region. It soon became clear, however, that the Chichimecs in the vicinity were too dangerous; those of Teul, towards the Sierra from Nochistlan, rebelled in 1531, massacring the local Spanish garrison as well as the reinforcements dispatched to subdue them, before submitting to a larger Spanish reprisal. By 1533 Nuño de Guzmán was forced to withdraw his capital to the more easily defensible site of Tlacotes, and eventually to three more sites, before finally settling on its present location on the more secure south side of the Río Grande, where it flourished to become, in time, Mexico's second-largest city.

To reward the soldiers who had assisted in the conquest, Nuño de Guzmán in 1535 granted *encomiendas*—rights to exact labor or other forms of tribute, coupled with the obligation to provide for the religious education of the natives by sponsoring missionary efforts—over many native communities in Nueva Galicia. The Cazcanes, Tecuexes, and Zacatecas, many of whose communities had been placed under encomiendas, rebelled within a year, and the Teultecs rebelled for the second time in 1536. So serious was the Indian menace that the acting governor of the province, Diego Pérez de la Torre, was himself killed while fighting the rebels. The Spaniards in Nueva Galicia stubbornly ignored the repeated warnings from the Crown and the Council of the Indies, which oversaw Spain's colonial interests, to curtail their enslavement of natives and other provocations, and as a result tensions between the Spanish and the native communities continued to build.

When, in 1540, the new governor of the province, Francisco Vásquez de Coronado, set out on his ill-fated quest for the fabled—and utterly fictitious—seven cities of gold (Cíbola), he took with him most of the available troops; the Indians quickly took advantage of the opportunity to launch a rebellion of major proportions. In the opinion of historian Leslie Bird Simpson (1971:57), this rebellion represented "the most dangerous uprising the Spaniards had to face in three hundred years." The revolt began when the Indians of Huainamota and Huazamota, inspired by an old shaman, killed their *encomendero* Juan de Arce; within a few days all of the Indian nations from Culiacan to Guadalajara rose in revolt. The Indians refused to pay their tribute or provide free labor, destroyed churches and other Spanish properties, and rampaged through the entire province. For two years they had the Spaniards of Nueva Galicia fighting for their lives, at one point holding even the capital of Guadalajara under siege.

The rebellion, which came to be known as the Mixton War (after the Indian stronghold where the natives were finally defeated), represented an alliance of numerous tribes. In 1542 Viceroy Mendoza arrived from Mexico City with a large army of Indian auxiliaries, capturing a large concentration of the rebel Indians in the Juchila valley; many were either tortured or enslaved and many others blinded, but a large number escaped into the rugged Sierras to the west.

The Mixton War made the Spaniards in Nueva Galicia painfully aware of the vulnerability of their small numbers. To remedy this problem and, it was hoped, bring a measure of peace and prosperity, missionary efforts were redoubled and both Spaniards and civilized Indians were encouraged to immigrate into the province. Cristobal de Oñate, who served as governor after Coronado's departure (the luckless Coronado himself died after his return of injuries received when his horse fell on him) expended considerable wealth to attract settlers; he stimulated livestock herding and other enterprises in the area, and in 1543 opened the silver mines of Huachinango, Etzatlan, Culiacan, Xaltepec, Espiritu Santo, and Xocotlan. This brought a rush of settlers to the area, and gave a renewed impetus to exploration. In 1543 the Crown also granted provincial officials the authority to occupy and distribute lands, and approved the capture and enslavement of Zacateca and other "savage" Indians who rebelled against the Catholic faith.

The year 1546 brought a new silver strike that was to have profound consequences for the province, and indeed for the entire colonial empire. A party of Zacatec Indians led prospector Joánes de Tolosa, a lieutenant of Governor Oñate, to some of the mineral outcroppings in the *serranía* of Zacatecas, two hundred miles north of Guadalajara. By 1548 a major new silver rush was on, quickly flooding the area with Spanish treasure-seekers and Indians eager for the high wages offered by the miners. This major strike stimulated extensive new prospecting explorations along the eastern foothills of the Sierra Madre Occidental as well as in the desert country to the north and east, where the Spaniards were once again confronted by hostile and intractable natives determined to keep the strangers out; nevertheless, within the next fifteen years European friars, soldiers, and explorers had discovered and settled over a dozen mining communities as far north as Chihuahua.

The rather sudden intrusion of the Spaniards into the mountains and deserts of northern Mexico, involving the rapidly expanding livestock herds as well as miners, quickly precipitated a reaction from the natives. As the Indians — if not the Spaniards — were keenly aware, the mining outposts were at first isolated islands of Europeans on the otherwise unfamiliar and hostile landscape of the barren northern plateau.

Understandably antagonized by the Spaniards' practice of enslaving the natives to provide labor for their mines, the Chichimecs of the area began to attack wagon trains that brought supplies to the mines and carried away the precious bars of silver; in their assaults they killed both Europeans and their Indian allies, carrying off their clothing and livestock, and occasionally also women and children — either as booty or for trade with neighboring tribes. The Indian raids served as a pretext for further slave-taking, and a vicious cycle of retaliations was set off; since the Spanish soldiers were generally underpaid and could make substantial money selling slaves, they often indiscriminately rounded up any Indians they could, whether friendly, neutral, or hostile. Understandably, this only further aggravated the Indians and triggered renewed raiding against European convoys, herds, and settlements.

By 1561 the various Chichimec tribes had formed a general alliance against the Spaniards and escalated to direct attacks on Spanish *ranchos* and mining settlements. Through their native informants, the Spaniards learned of plans to drive the Spaniards off the plateau with a series of major attacks, beginning with the mining town of San Martín. The Spaniards hastily organized troops and were able to surprise and scatter the Chichimecs, but for some time the situation was desperate.

The prolonged sequence of attacks and reprisals led to the militarization of Spanish society in the north; military *presidios* and defensive settlements were established on the plateau and around the sierras. The presidios provided escorts to protect supply convoys, patrolled against the Chichimecs, and also prospected for mine sites; the important mines at Mazapil, for example, were located during maneuvers against the Guachichiles of the region.

The Chichimec War is often treated by historians as a plateau affair, but in fact the Indians of the Sierras played a role, raiding ranchos and convoys along the routes between Guadalajara and Zacatecas, to within eight leagues of Guadalajara. The mountains from Nochistlan and Jerez in the east to Acaponeta in the west were in *tierra de guerra* throughout the Chichimec War. The Indians of Huainamota, in Cora territory, and Huazamota took up arms on hearing of Diego de Ibarra's mine explorations in the area, and he was unable to work a strike located by his agents because of the hostility of the Indians. The secretary of Franciscan inspector Fray Alonso Ponce (1968:69) was informed in 1587 of a close relationship existing between the Guachichil Chichimecs of the desert and a sierra tribe, possibly Huichol or Tecual:

> They are allies of the Chichimec Guachichiles, in whose troops they go by order of their *principales* to carry out assaults; the Guachichiles offer their spoils of clothing to the principales to propitiate them so that they will supply warriors when they are needed; a Guachichil Indian comes to captain them, conducting to and from the raiding targets as many warriors as he requests.

Fray Ponce was dissuaded from visiting the Franciscan convents in Juchipila and Teul because of the Chichimec danger north of the Río Grande de Santiago; nevertheless, he traveled to a number of towns along the coastal plain in present-day Jalisco and Nayarit. In Ponce's travels he frequently encountered "Chichimecas de la Sierra," a fact that suggests close ties between the Sierra Indians and those of both the coast and the interior plateau. His journal offers valuable comments on the dress and ritual offerings of the lowland Indians as well as of the "Chichimecas de la Sierra," revealing striking similarities to the modern Huichols. His account also contains the earliest reference to the Huichols—rendered as "Uzares" by Ponce's secretary. His informants clearly locate the Huichols in their present territory, commenting on the remoteness and sterility of their lands and the poverty of their agriculture; they also referred to their individualistic patterns of worship, saying that each chose whatever idol best suited his natural inclinations. The journal further mentions that the Huichols and their neighbors to the west, the Huainamotecas, traveled regularly to Acaponeta and Centicpac near the coast, to trade for salt and fish.[1]

By 1590 the Spaniards had more or less pacified the plateau area between the towns of Zacatecas, San Luis Potosí, Saltillo, and Durango; as they learned the Indians' habitat and developed an effective military policy, they exterminated and enslaved many of the Chichimecs and drove many others into the more remote sierras and deserts to the west and north; many were also absorbed into mission settlements. In 1591 the Spaniards imported several hundred families of civilized and converted Tlaxcaltecan Indians from central Mexico, whom they settled at a number of strategic locations adjacent to

Chichimec settlements; it was hoped that they would set a good behavioral example for the more primitive Chichimecs and teach them sedentary life, agriculture, and other productive skills. This event is usually regarded as the termination of the Chichimec War, but in fact resistance to the Spaniards remained strong, particularly in the Sierras, where many of the rebels had taken refuge.

In 1585 the Huainamotecas, just east of Huichol country, had rebelled against the mission system, killing two Spanish friars and their native assistants and desecrating church relics, which they offered to their own deities and then distributed among their allies. The Spanish quickly retaliated with force, marching to Huainamota where they overcame native resistance, executing the leaders and enslaving or dismembering over a thousand Indians. Another attack came in 1592—after the war on the plateau had drawn to a close—when a defensive settlement of Tlaxcaltecan Indians at San Andrés del Teul on the northeastern Sierra frontier was attacked by local Tepehuan and Huichol warriors; the natives massacred most of the Tlaxcaltecans as well as a friar and several other Europeans, and the survivors of the settlement had to be relocated to Chalchihuites, a larger town farther from the Sierras. That same year another friar was killed near Huejucar, to the southeast, and the small Spanish settlement at Aguascalientes was wiped out by Indian raiders in 1593. While the Spanish mining interests might have been thus secured, resistance to them was far from extinguished.

The last major conflict of the initial phase of Spanish-Indian contact in western Mexico was the Tepehuan revolt, a bloody affair lasting from 1616 to 1618. Led by native shamans, the Tepehuanes and their allies in the Sierra rebelled and fought off the Spaniards until 1618, when they were finally dispersed by a major Spanish counteroffensive. This campaign entered and nominally conquered the Sierras, marking the last important Spanish military *entrada* until the following century. When peace treaties were ratified in 1620 and 1621, the initial phase of culture contact had drawn to a close.

Throughout this entire period of Spanish aggression, the natives of the Sierra were also subjected to Christian missionary pressure. By 1540 Spanish outposts had apparently been established at Huainamota and Huazamota, both deep in the mountains only a few leagues from the Huichol territories. Both locations were isolated and unsafe, though, being over forty leagues from the nearest Spanish town, so neither became a permanent settlement. After the assassination of their encomendero in 1540, Huainamota was used only sporadically as a missionary post—with little success—and Huazamota only became a mission vanguard after 1582. It was not until the 1580s that the friars began systematic efforts to settle and convert the hostile Sierra tribes, who had killed or expelled the few friars who had earlier ventured among them. The Franciscan order was given control of Indians in the province of Nueva Galicia—including the Huichols, Coras, Tecuals, and Cazcans—while the Jesuit *frailes* worked the territory of the Tepehuanes and other natives of Nueva Viscaya to the immediate north.

The missionary efforts around the periphery of the Sierra continued to meet strong opposition and aroused further antagonism by their techniques and attitudes; for example, after the Spanish reprisal for the Huainamota uprising of 1585, a number of the captives were taken to Guadalajara in the hope that they could be persuaded to convert and then be used to help the Spaniards establish a foothold in the Sierras; all, however, suffered torture and eventual execution rather than betray the deities of their people.

This incident was by no means unique among Spanish efforts to control and convert the Indians. A friar at Mazapil had helped to solve these problems, as well as the labor shortage in the local mines, by directing the capture of native Guachichiles and then locking them inside the mines. In the Sierra de Xora immediately south of Huichol lands, the friar Pedro del Monte burned the local Indian fields wherever he could find them, and then brought in a supply of maize from the towns of Teul and Jerez to induce the desperate Indians to settle around his makeshift chapel. Yet despite these efforts, at the close of the initial period of Spanish aggression the Indians of the same area were still hostile to the Europeans, adhering to their traditional beliefs and customs. Thus in 1620 the Indians of Amatlan de Xora abandoned their settlement village; the friars Antonio Tello and Diego Rivera were only able to resettle them by luring a handful of their leaders into the chapel, then holding them as hostages to force the remainder of the community to return and accept their preaching.

By the end of the period the friars had still made only modest inroads among the Coras, Tepehuans, and Huichols. A number of Huichols had been settled in Huajimic in 1610 and 1611 by Fray Francisco Barrios and Fray Pedro Gutiérrez, but they rebelled several times and burned down their church within the first decade. On the whole, then, traditional patterns in the Sierra had not been significantly altered by the initial phase of Spanish aggression.

The motive force behind the Spanish conquest throughout this period had been the search for riches—especially precious metals; the natives were a relatively secondary consideration. Nevertheless, they loomed large both politically and economically—as obstacles to effective Spanish control, on the one hand, and on the other hand as the labor force with which the Spaniards hoped to exploit the natural resources of the territory. The survival of the indigenous sociocultural systems in western Mexico had depended, to a large degree, on the resources of each region and on the manner in which they had been incorporated into the Spanish polity.

In the valleys to the south of the Sierra, where there were few important mines, the major resource was the land itself, and the labor of the natives. For the most part, these areas were distributed among the conquistadores, who were allotted encomienda or *repartimiento* (assessment) rights over the native communities. A few communities of Central Mexican Indian allies also settled in this area following the initial conquest and each of the subsequent pacifications, and a few Spaniards operated ranchos and *estancias*, but Domingo Lazaro de Arregui's 1621 account makes it clear that they represented only a small minority when compared to the remaining indigenous population.

After pacification, many of the native villages had been granted communal lands and left more or less intact and self-governing; many even enjoyed relative prosperity supplying maize and other produce to the mining centers, but especially to the south and west many were ruthlessly exploited by their encomenderos, an ultimately counter-productive situation on which a royal decree directed to the administrators of Nueva Galicia commented as follows:

> We are informed that in this province the native Indians are dying out because of the bad treatment received at the hands of the encomenderos, who have so diminished the Indians that in some communities more than a third of the population has been lost, yet the remainder have to bear the full community tribute obligations, and are treated worse than slaves. . . . These Indians have developed a great hatred for the word Christian and take Spaniards for villains, not believing anything they are taught, so that nothing is achieved except by force. (Mendizabal 1946:197-198)

On the plateau, in stark contrast to the southern valleys, fundamental changes were wrought—primarily as a consequence of the much-coveted mines that dotted the area. Here, the seminomadic natives were either driven off, exterminated, killed by disease, enslaved, or absorbed; their traditionally loosely organized bands were not able to survive the transition to settled villages, and they quickly disappeared as distinctive sociocultural entities. As the Spaniards expanded across the plateau, much of the arid countryside was quickly exploited for livestock pastorage; blacks and *mulattos* became the earliest *vaqueros* of the north, and along with poor Spaniards also began farming in more favorable niches to take advantage of the food and fodder needs of the mine centers.

To replace the native Indians of the plateau, the Spaniards brought in slaves and civilized Indians from central Mexico; many of these originally came to the north as auxiliaries in the conquest, while others came to escape epidemics, burdensome tribute, or the loss of their traditional communal lands to Spanish estates. Often the different nations of civilized Indians formed separate *barrios*, or even entire villages, which helped to preserve their traditional languages and cultures. Thus, as early as 1561 the mining towns of San Martín had settlements not only of local Chichimecs but also of immigrant Cazcans, Tlaxcaltecas, Tarascans, Cholultecans, and Otomis. By the turn of the century, the city of Zacatecas—which by then had grown to become the third largest city in all of New Spain, after Mexico City and Puebla—counted over two hundred Spaniards, eighty *criollos*, a dozen Italians and Portuguese, over eight hundred blacks and mulattos (both slaves and freemen), and probably more than two thousand Indians. Several hundred Indian mine workers were boarded at the mine *haciendas* where they worked, and another thousand to fifteen hundred lived in the city's Indian barrios, each of which had its own internal government.

The inherent instability of mining operations left its mark on the Indians who had worked the mines; most were free laborers and could move wherever the rewards were greatest, the result of which was a high rate of mobility. As Bishop de la Mota y Escobar wrote in 1605:

Even though all the Indians are settled, it is impossible to know the population of any *pueblo* because of the frequency with which they move from one province to another or go to work for the Spaniards in the mines, on cattle ranches, in wagon trains, or in industrial sweatshops. Also, it is hard to determine their numbers because of the contagious diseases which sometimes afflict them (1968:21).

Although the maintenance of tribal barrios limited assimilation, nevertheless the mobility of the Indians inevitably led to a breakdown of community sanctions and emulation of the dominant Spaniards. De la Mota y Escobar remarked:

The Indians who presently live among or near Spaniards act very differently, imitating the Spaniards as much as possible in their dress and comportment, . . . in their meals, in their production and consumption habits, and in riding horses and owning mule teams. (Ibid.:20)

The Sierras constituted still a third major political and economic region within the province of Nueva Galicia. There were no major mines or large arable expanses in the Sierras, so aside from the friars, few Spaniards were willing to take the risk of entering the hostile Sierras. The natives were generally able to retreat into the labyrinth of *barrancas* to avoid confrontation with the Spaniards, whose troops could not maneuver in the precipitous mountain passes, and as a result they remained free throughout the period. The nominal conquest of the Sierras in 1618 that concluded the initial phase of Spanish aggression had little lasting effect on the natives, who continued to remain independent.

This does not mean, however, that the Sierra Indians, the Huichols among them, were isolated from Spanish social and cultural influences. The *serrano* tribes interacted with outside communities in a variety of frameworks, and incorporated a number of European goods and practices. Spanish clothing, livestock, and even captured women and children were absorbed as booty during the wars, and the Sierra tribes also gave refuge to a number of runaway slaves and fugitive Spaniards. In addition, the Huichols and other Sierra natives often traveled outside the Sierra for trade, or to seek work seasonally on Spanish agricultural estates around Valparaiso and in the Poana and Suchil Valleys to the northeast, and probably also toward the Pacific coast. Settled Indians in communities near the Sierra frontier such as Jerez and Colotlán, and along the coast, were reported to maintain close ties with the *serranos*, suggesting a fair degree of interchange among these different groups.

The Franciscan and Jesuit friars, of whose enterprise and courage there is no doubt, comprised still another point of contact, although they were bitterly opposed by most of the Sierra natives. Even in instances where they were forced or enticed into mission settlements, the Sierra Indians' resistance to the teachings of the Church remained strong; for example, the settled and nominally converted Coanos, to the south of the Huichols and Tecuales, were still practicing their rites in secret in the 1600s. In 1592 the foremost Indian leader in the Sierras, Naye, or Nayarit—namesake of the modern state of Nayarit—actually voluntarily sought religious instruction at the Franciscan convent in Juchipila, but apparently was not too impressed, because he evidently instructed his followers to reject the Catholic church and maintain their traditional beliefs and rituals.

Recession and Withdrawal, 1620–1700

The second major period in the interaction between the Spaniards and the Huichols and other Sierra Indians, from 1620 to 1700, was one of relative inactivity. The zeal and idealism of earlier generations of missionaries and conquistadores had waned, and in addition Spain and her colonies were in the throes of serious political and economic problems (in large part the inflationary legacy of the huge silver strikes). The Zacatecas mines, along with many others, went into a marked decline in productivity from the 1620s until the end of the century. This pulled the rug out from under the rest of the colonial economy, and as a result the period was one of local and regional withdrawal; commerce slowed and many rural areas shifted from market to subsistence production. Society became—at least formally—more rigid and castelike, as crown authorities launched a series of restrictions to protect Spanish interests and limit racial mixture; Indians, blacks and *castas*—the various hybridizations of European, African, and American genes—were separated and distinguished with increasing detail. Among other things, sumptuary restrictions were imposed forbidding Indians to wear Spanish clothing or jewelry, bear arms, or ride horseback; furthermore, they could be compelled to work to pay off their debts—setting the legal basis for debt peonage.

Yet, despite the Crown's efforts to separate and stratify colonial society on the basis of racial and ethnic criteria, social and cultural interchange continued apace during this period. In urbanized mining and commercial centers such as Zacatecas assimilation and acculturation had, by 1700, proceeded to the point that no pure-blooded Indians remained, although at least four of the old Indian barrios continued to function as distinct sociopolitical entities. Furthermore, as European-derived epidemics ravaged the countryside and the Spaniards and their criollo offspring continued to increase in numbers, basic demographic conditions changed; more whites began filtering out of the urban centers into niches such as agriculture and ranching, which they had earlier disdained.

In many rural areas and in the Sierras, most local Indian communities maintained their sociocultural integrity for well over a century after their nominal subjugation and conversion—a fact that irritated the Church, if not the secular authorities, because of the stubborn adherence to pagan cults, even in communities supposedly incorporated by the colonial regime. Although they had made progress during the period in settling a few Huichols and other serrenos, their frontier settlements such as Huejuquilla, Tenzompa, Mezquitic, Huajimic, and Ixcatlan remained crude and heathen. Thus, around mid-century Fray Arias de Saavedra wrote somewhat piquedly that many lowland communities still sent offerings to pagan temples in the mountains for first fruit rituals; they were difficult to control and convert because of the proximity of refuge in the Sierras. A *padre* in Teocaltiche complained that the ritual and medicinal use of the psychoactive peyote cactus was still widespread throughout the Cazcan territory.[2] Native beliefs and practices were thus apparently able to withstand the disapproval of the friars. Records of the Holy Inquisition in Mexico indicate that peyote use was now also widespread among the civilized castas, who learned its use from the natives, and was popular through central and western Mexico, with its distribution centering around Zacatecas.[3]

The Sierra Indians, meanwhile, continued to interact with the outside world for economic purposes and to adjust to ongoing changes beyond their boundaries. By mid-century it was reported that although the serranos spoke Cora, Tepehuan, and Huichol among themselves, many also knew some Spanish from travel and work in the Zacatecas mines and on agricultural estates. These contact situations did not involve directed efforts at cultural change, so assimilation and acculturation proceeded in a spontaneous and integral manner; gradually, the situation was transforming into one of systematically interacting—albeit still mutually antagonistic—ethnic groups, within an increasingly integrated sociopolitical macrosystem.

Spanish Domination, 1700–1810

The third major phase in the relationship between the Spaniards and the Huichols and other serrano Indians, beginning around 1700, coincided with a renaissance of Spanish and colonial culture; on a more material plane, it also coincided with a marked recovery in mine productivity and a consequent resurgence of commerce. As part of this renaissance, colonial authorities reasserted their dominance and took the offensive in relations to the remaining pockets of political and religious nonconformity, finally establishing formal sovereignty in the Sierras of western Mexico.

Beyond the gradual but inexorable assimilation and acculturation of subjected groups to the dominant Spanish polity, and the continuing spread of mestizaje, no major sociocultural turning points developed in those areas around the Sierras that had already been incorporated by the colonial system. Indian communities protected by legal charters and preserving communal lands generally persevered, especially in more remote areas. The settled and nominally converted Indians of the Sierra frontiers remained wild and idolatrous, resistant to Catholic propaganda, and generally preserved their traditional tribal or ethnic affiliations, even while their social and cultural content gradually changed. Those native communities that had been more directly harnessed by the colonial system, too, seem in many cases to have retained their ethnic identity and integrity during this period. The Indians of the Cazcana continued to prosper as the principal breadbasket of the Zacatecas mines. The Indian community which had occupied San Pedro Piedra Corda, slightly southeast of Zacatecas, persevered despite being removed to San José de la Ysla in the rugged hills south of Zacatecas; these Indians adapted to a special niche as woodcutters, supplying charcoal and firewood to the refineries of Zacatecas. Even in the city itself, with its high levels of mobility, mestizaje, and public disorders, the old Indian barrios continued to function until at least 1732.

But while things remained relatively stable in incorporated areas, the eighteenth century brought to an abrupt end the phase of peaceful coexistence in the Sierras. The Crown was again in a position to flex its muscles, so it finally sought to redress the fact that it was being defied by a handful of "barbarians," such as the Huichols, living outside the law and without the benefits of the true faith; the result was a major turning point in affairs in the Sierras.

The Crown's new policy was initiated in 1701, when the title of Protector del Gran Nayar was bestowed upon Francisco Brocamonte in exchange for his services in directing and financing the conquest of the Sierras. Brocamonte organized troops and sent emissaries to parlay with the Indians, but they were informed that the Indians did not wish to be Christians, and wanted no laws but their own; the natives told the emissaries that the best demonstration of Christian love that the Spanish troops could give would be to leave. The reply of Brocamonte's troops was to burn some frontier Indian ranchos and advance into the Sierras, where the expedition came to an abrupt ending when all save one were massacred.

The following year, 1702, the Indians of the Sierra de Tepec went on a rampage, marauding through Spanish settlements and making off with livestock. On one occasion they even attacked the town of Acaponeta, killing two Spaniards, in order to free an Indian imprisoned in the town jail. During this revolt, the Indians of Nayarit not only sent warriors to join the Tepec rebels, but also promised refuge in the event of reprisals. Difficulties continued when the Indians of Nostic and Colotlán rebelled again in 1704, but the trouble there was quickly controlled.

In 1705 the colonial authorities determined once again to attempt the pacification of the Sierras; the Audiencia in Guadalajara financed two entradas, but both were repulsed. Around the same time Captain Antonio Escobedo, who enjoyed friendly relations with serrano Indians who worked on his agricultural estates, mounted two expeditions to the Sierra from the north, but he, too, was unable to penetrate cultural and territorial barriers. To put more pressure on the natives, the Spaniards cut off the Indians' important salt routes to the coast, thereby triggering increased raiding.

Realizing that little headway was being made, the Crown in 1709 finally agreed to finance the conquest of the Sierra with government funds, to be drawn from the royal treasury in Zacatecas. At the same time, missionary efforts in the mountains were accelerated. A group of friars from the Huainamota outpost attempted to enter the Huichol territory, but were prevented from crossing the Río Chapalagana by a party of warriors; the friars began preaching on the spot, but the Indians drowned them out and drove them away by shouting back the values of liberty and of their own religion. In

1711 two more missionary entradas were attempted. Padre Margipari entered the Cora lands from the south, but was turned back by Indian insistence that their first king, Nayarit, had admonished them not to convert or accept the friars. Fray Margil de Jesús approached the Sierra from Zacatecas with the hope of negotiating with the natives, but his proposals were rejected by the Indian elders and his advance was blocked; he solemnly advised the Crown authorities that only force could break them down.

The first Spanish success of any significance came in 1715, when the Audiencia in Guadalajara commissioned Gregorio Matías de Mendiola, owner of some haciendas in the Suchil Valley, to parlay with the Indians. Mendiola enjoyed good relations with the serrenos because of his fair treatment of those who worked on his estates, and he and his entourage were led some distance into the Sierra to a mesa—probably the Mesa del Nayar—where they were received with considerable pomp and display by an assembly of shamans, elders, and warriors. Mendiola finally induced the natives to recognize the sovereignty of the Spanish monarch, but they could not be persuaded to embrace the Catholic faith. According to a Jesuit father who belonged to Mendiola's party, their reason for not converting or admitting missionaries was

> so as not to offend the Sun, whom they and their ancestors had always worshipped, because they feared arousing his anger and incurring retributions, adding further that it would be very hard for them to abandon their rites and customs of their ancestors. (Ortéga 1887:84)

The agreement reached by Mendiola, however, was not implemented successfully, as difficulties continued. The salt route remained blocked, and a number of Indians were imprisoned in outside towns. The Indians' resistance to conversion was evidently the issue preventing peace, so the natives apparently sent emissaries to Guadalajara, agreeing to admit Christian missionaries—but only Jesuits, not the Franciscans in whose domain they lay. This engendered resentment from the Franciscans, who had spent over a century in missionary efforts in the Sierra and endured numerous martyrdoms; no response was made to the proposal.

The Indians of the Sierra next approached a friendly landowner, Juan de la Torre Valdéz y Gamboa of Jerez, asking if he would mediate negotiations with Crown officials. After writing to the king, the viceroy, and the Audiencia of Guadalajara, he was commissioned to organize negotiations and granted the title of Capitán Protector del Nayar. Tonatí, the Cora *cacique* of the Mesa del Nayar, came to Jerez with an escort of warriors, and de la Torre Valdéz accompanied them to Zacatecas and then to Mexico City to confer and negotiate with colonial and ecclesiastical representatives. Although the resultant treaty ultimately had little import, its terms offer some insight into Spanish and Indian interests. On behalf of the Indians, Tonatí demanded the opening of the salt routes to Acaponeta and Mezcaltitlan, without fee, and the liberation of Indians imprisoned in Colotlán and Guadalajara; in addition, he obtained exemption from tributary obligations. While the Indians of the Sierra would be forced to concede the sovereignty of the Crown, they were to be subject not to the Audiencia in Guadalajara, but to the viceroy in far-off Mexico City; this left them more or less independent of local authorities. The colonial negotiators demanded admittance of missionaries into the Sierra, but Tonatí insisted that they be Jesuits, not Franciscans. Also of interest in the treaty was the Spanish intent to install Tonatí and his successors as sole rulers of the Sierras, with Spanish military backing, rather than dealing with the existing system of local caciques.

On the return trip to Zacatecas and the Sierra, Tonatí became increasingly agitated by doubts as to whether the Spanish conditions would be acceptable to the other Indian leaders. Tonatí had a dream in which his deity spoke to him opposing the treaty; the angry supernatural warned him that the Spanish soldiers and missionaries would kill many Indians, take away their belongings, deprive them of their liberties, and ban traditional practices such as polygyny, drinking rites, and vengeance, and destroy their temples and sacred idols, "the only recourse they had to ensure that the rains were not withheld" (Ortéga 1887:115). Tonatí attempted to back out of the agreement, relating his dream to the Spaniards, but they would not allow it.

The Spanish troops, accompanied by missionaries and many Indian auxiliaries impressed from nearby settlements, waited at the frontier while Tonatí and his entourage returned to the Sierra to try to persuade the other caciques to accept the treaty. As it turned out, though, many of the leaders did oppose it, and it was decided instead to ambush the Spanish troops if they would not leave. A group of Indian elders went to meet the Spanish contingent and demanded that they depart and return home,

> because the Nayares, in spite of whatever Tonati and other badly informed persons might assert in Mexico City, were devoted lovers and worshippers of their own great deity and faithful observers of his rites and religion, which they had received from their ancestors; they did not wish to subject themselves to a foreign yoke or admit any other religion or adore any god but their own, who always favored them with such great providence that they had no need to go to foreign lands to sustain themselves. (Ortéga 1887:129)

The last remark quoted was undoubtedly meant as a jibe at the Spanish colonial system, and the Indians concluded their visit by threatening to kill the Spaniards if they did not leave immediately.

The Spaniards, in the meantime, had already determined to advance. The Indians set an ambush, but it was repelled with only minor losses. A second parley was arranged between Spanish and Indian leaders, but this time the Spaniards seized the Indian elders and then advanced again. On January 16, 1722, a small party of Spanish troops stormed the Mesa del Nayar, meeting little resistance, and the conquest was proclaimed. They quickly rounded up many natives and began organizing nucleated settlements and establishing military and missionary outposts in the country of the Coras. The prophecy of Tonatí's god had come to pass: the Spaniards killed a number of natives, confiscated much of their livestock and other goods, deprived them of their liberties, and destroyed their temples and idols, sending to Mexico City the bejeweled mummy of their former leader Nayarit, which had become a sacred oracle.

While victory over the Coras is usually regarded as a more or less definitive conquest, in fact resistance remained strong in many areas. Many of the dissidents fled to the south and west, where they took refuge in Huichol, Tecual, and other Cora communities, including Tonalisco and Huajimic, as well as in San Blas on the Pacific coast, where the natives were also hostile toward the Spaniards. Nevertheless, by the end of 1723 most of the Coras had been rounded up and congregated in eleven communities, under Jesuit authorities, while Franciscan outposts had been established in the three northernmost Huichol territories—San Andrés, Santa Catarína, and San Sebastián; both the Cora and Huichol land titles date from this period, despite the fact that the Huichols were not settled into villages as were their Cora neighbors.

By the end of 1723 most of the soldiers had been sent home, thinking that the area was secure, but in early 1724 a *junta* of Indian leaders was held and the Indians abandoned their settlements; two of the new missions were burned and their religious paraphernalia destroyed, and the converted cacique of one settlement was killed. Their attack on a remaining garrison of troops was unsuccessful, however, and Spanish reinforcements quickly dispersed the rebels; by 1725 the communities had been resettled. To discourage further insurrections, the Spanish authorities ruled that no Indians could leave the Sierra without a permit from the friars. This effort at forced confinement must not have been too effective, though, inasmuch as the Sierra Indians continued to work seasonally and to carry on trade with the coast as well as with mining centers, trading salt, wax, honey, fruits, feathers, songbirds, and other goods. In addition, they continued to carry on local trade in seeds, fruits, and the like with their settled compatriots in Tenzompa, La Soledad, San Nicolas, and other villages on the frontier.

The Jesuit father José Ortéga, who labored for many years among the Coras, was very confident and optimistic about the effectiveness of the missionaries in changing the "barbarian" ways of the natives, although even he admitted that as late as 1750 their drinking rites and the resulting disorders were a continuing problem for the friars. A more clear-eyed appraisal suggests that the natives simply learned to accommodate the missionaries in certain details, without abandoning their ancestral customs. Resistance to Church teachings remained strong in many areas of the Sierra; a secret new temple to the sun was discovered in 1730, and dozens of others were located from time to time in the remote barrancas. The Franciscan padre José Arlegui, who served in the town of Huejuquilla on the Huichol frontier around 1730, remarked on the wildness and idolatry of the Indians and on their opposition to religious conversion. He also noted that near the settled pueblo of Tenzompa a fellow friar had located a temple containing a mummy oracle and a variety of ritual offerings. Even the settled Indians in Huejuquilla and throughout the region still practiced polygyny and the medical and ritual use of peyote, and animistic "superstitions" persisted. Arlegui sadly acknowledged that

> the greatest torment suffered by our brethren in this and other convents in the Sierras . . . is to learn from experience that when they most struggle for the salvation of souls, then they discover new temples in the vast and rugged expanse of the mountains, in which even those who appear to be the best Christians give reverent adoration to the devil and his idols. (Arlegui 1737:87)[4]

The efforts of the friars to reshape serreno society and culture were limited both by their small numbers and also by their short tenure. The Jesuits were expelled from the Spanish colonies in 1767, as the Crown became envious of their extensive tax-free properties and angered by the occasional abuses of their privileges and authority. Seven of the Jesuit missions were taken over by the Franciscans, but their order was also on the wane; by 1798 only a dozen missionaries remained in the Nayarit Sierras.

The very arrival of troops and missionaries in the Sierra was a significant event in the history of the area; nevertheless, despite their concerted efforts to reorganize native customs and engineer social and cultural changes, their long-term impact was relatively minor in many respects. The Huichols were apparently the least affected of all the Sierra tribes, since they were never congregated into nucleated mission settlements. If we may take the accounts of Ortéga and Arlegui at face value, as representative of real differences between their respective Cora and Huichol congregations, then the Huichols probably retained a greater degree of autonomy, even openly flaunting their traditional customs, during this period of final Spanish domination in the Sierras.

Mestizo Aggression, 1810–1930

The period from the outbreak of the War of Independence from Spain until at least the third decade of the present century was one marked by recurrent turmoil and conflict. Like the preceding period, it marked a significant change in the position of the serrano Indians and a turning point in their relationship with the outside world; the buffer of semiwild Indian communities that had previously sheltered them from direct confrontations with the rapidly growing mestizo society was rent by the endemic political unrest of the age and by the collapse of the colonial casta system that had provided a legal basis for their separation.

In western Mexico, as throughout most of the country, popular support for the War of Independence came from two distinct sources, with quite distinct interests and incentives. On the one hand was the growing class of mestizos, who occupied a powerless and immobile limbo status in a society still controlled by *peninsulares* and their criollo underlings. On the other hand were the Indians, who wished to throw off the restrictive laws, the onerous tributes and taxes, the intolerant padres and frailes, the degrading social rank to which they were consigned, and their manipulation by forces outside of their own communities.

With the first news of Morelos' and Hidalgo's initial revolt, the military garrisons near the Sierra frontier at Colotlán, Jerez, and Fresnillo were recalled to Zacatecas to protect the treasury mint, the mines, and other wealth concentrated there. The Indians of the Sierra from Nayarit to Colotlán and even Juchipila quickly rose in revolt; an Indian named Mascara de Oro (Golden Mask) led rebels near Tepic and in the Cora highlands, seeking to reestablish the Indian empire of Mocetuzoma ("Montezuma"). The Indians of Colotlán and Huejucar defeated a royalist contingent in the *cañones* of southern Zacatecas, and soon a rebel clergyman had organized an army of over eight thousand Indians from the Juchipila, Tlaltenango, and Colotlán valleys and the adjacent Sierras. Although this force was eventually defeated by the royalist army of General Negrete, the entire area remained a rebel stronghold. Royalist troops had to be dispatched to the area on numerous occasions to disperse rebel concentrations; the troops took out their wrath on the rebel sympathizers by raiding and stealing maize, livestock, and other provisions.

The termination of the War of Independence in 1821 did not bring about the establishment of political stability and security; neither did the fall of the colonial regime lead to a renewed isolation of the Sierras from all secular or ecclesiastical pressure. With the withdrawal of Spanish power, local *caudillos* contested with one another for supremacy or local autonomy, while the *intendencias*—the redistricted provinces—squabbled with one another and with the various national governments that succeeded each other throughout the period. Western Mexico experienced near-constant political unrest because of the repeated conflict between liberal and conservative forces; for a few years in the 1830s Zacatecas even declared and defended a claim to being a free and independent nation. Taking advantage of the political instability of the era, still-wild nomadic Indians from the deserts of northern Mexico began raiding and overrunning northern and central Zacatecas, while bands of lawless brigands preyed on unwary travelers and even small communities. The governor of the state gloomily noted in 1871 that nearly the entire state budget was spent in simply trying to maintain public order.

Along with the breakdown of the colonial system of social stratification came radical changes in land tenure laws. Since the fleeing Spaniards had managed to carry off most of the wealth of their former colony as well as their virtual monopoly on leadership and technical skills, the new Mexican nation was compelled to seek financial and managerial assistance from abroad in order to reconstruct the economy. Under the favorable terms conceded by the government, many foreign interests invested in Mexican mines, and later also in lands and in industries processing agricultural and mineral raw materials. This initiated a second great age of the hacienda, as investors acquired extensive lands and other properties—over which the resident laboring populace had no more claim than before the War of Independence. With the ascendance of Juárez and his fellow liberals, a series of land tenure reforms was enacted, immediately throwing the country back into turmoil. Although intended to promote a more flexible and equitable distribution of land by removing the legal basis for corporate land holdings such as Church properties, the new laws also undercut the communal lands that were the basic source of security for most surviving indigenous communities.

Local rebellions again broke out in many parts of western Mexico. In the Sierras, one Manuel Lozada, known as "el Tigre de Alica," formed a largely Indian army with the goal—once again—of reestablishing the old Aztec empire of Mocetuzoma. Lozada's carefully reasoned program centered around a demand for the return of usurped Indian lands; when his ultimatums were not respected by the *hacendados* encroaching on the Sierras, his troops attacked and the lands were distributed among the warriors. Lozada and his army, which included many Cora, Huichol, and Tepehuan warriors, marauded in and around the Sierras of southern Zacatecas, northwestern Jalisco, and Nayarit for nearly two decades, at one point even holding the city of Guadalajara under siege (shades of the Mixton War!). Finally, in 1873 federal armies pursued him to his refuge in the Sierra, in the process occupying many of the Cora communities, and then capturing and executing Lozada himself in the Huichol comunidad of San Andrés Cohamiata.

The turmoil in and around the Sierras continued, nevertheless, as the government sought to impose its land tenure changes. The "Pax Porfiriata" of the Díaz dictatorship around the end of the nineteenth century ushered in a lull in the conflict, but only at the price of repressive measures.

The continuing rapid growth of foreign-owned estates accentuated outside pressures on remaining Indian lands; although few haciendas encroached as far as the Huichol territories (a notable exception being a hacienda right in the middle of Santa Catarína), they displaced many other communities whose members often attempted to relocate deeper in the Sierras, thereby increasing pressure on the Indians. Most remaining communal lands outside of the Sierra proper, in the Cazcana and to the southwest, were eliminated, and increasing numbers of whites and mestizos moved into the area. Furthermore, the alienation of lands led to a dramatic increase in the landless labor supply, causing wages to fall. At the same time, since many of the new estates were geared to export production, the supply of domestic foodstuffs and other goods declined, while prices rose. In reaction to this sequence of events, abortive revolts sprang up at the turn of the century in the Teul—Bolaños region, and around Acaponeta and Compostela; they were, however, quickly suppressed by the Díaz regime.

The early anthropologist Carl Gustav Lumholtz, who traveled extensively in the Sierras in the 1890s, found the Huichols and other tribes extremely anxious over the fate of their lands (as they indeed still are today). With good reason: for example, in 1912 the Bishop of Zacatecas negotiated a pact with a North American railroad and development company that would have meant construction of a railroad across the Sierra Huichol from Jerez to Tepic, along with the commercial exploitation of forests, agriculture, and livestock in the region; in return the Huichols were to receive new homes in urbanized residential centers to be constructed in the Sierras.

Happily for the Huichols, this scheme was never set in action because of the outbreak of the Mexican Revolution; however, the Revolution and the ensuing Cristero Revolt brought renewed armed conflict in the Sierras. Many Huichols were forced to flee to the south or to more secure towns, such as Colotlán and Jerez; but in the meantime many of their lands were taken over by mestizos. It was not until at least the 1930s that relative peace and tranquility returned to the area.

The political and economic turmoil that characterized much of the period from 1810 to 1930 took its toll on social patterns in the immediate area outside the Sierras, as we have already alluded to. Already by 1826 there were no longer any pure Indians in the city of Zacatecas; only whites, mestizos, and a few blacks were to be found in the city or for many leagues in the surrounding countryside. Around the old Indian settlement of Colotlán, on the Sierra frontier, intact communities of Chichimecas de Soyatitan and Techopa Tepehuanes still survived and preserved their native tongues in 1826, but the town itself was white and mestizo, and Spanish was the lingua franca. Particularly after the alienation of communal landholdings, with very few exceptions Indian society and culture across the country went into a tailspin. Whites and mestizos continued to spread into more remote areas, displacing Indians as their communal lands became alienated. By the 1880s only a quarter of the population of the Cazcan valley of Tlaltenango remained Indian; another quarter of the population was white, and the remaining half mestizo. In the adjacent valley of Juchipila whites outnumbered the remaining Indians by more than two to one and the few remaining pure-blooded Indians were indistinguishable from mestizos, since they had lost their native language and much of their distinctive culture. Remnants of Indian communities still existed, for instance at Juchipila, Apozol, Amoxochil, Mezquituta, Cuzpala, and Mecatabasco in the Juchipila valley, and in the Jerez valley at Sustizacan, El Chiquihante, Juancho Rey, and Lirios, but they were racked by internal conflicts as the members, anticipating the subdivision of their remaining communal lands, squabbled over the allocation of fields and other properties. By 1892 pure Indians reportedly existed only in a few scattered and remote pockets of the state of Zacatecas, while the Indian populations of Jalisco, Nayarit, and Durango had also declined to a few thousand apiece. When Lumholtz met visitors from Azqueltan, a Tepecano settlement near the southeast frontier of the Sierra in the Bolaños valley, he learned that mestizos were gradually infiltrating the community; they had destroyed the Tepecan religious idols and forced traditional religious observances by the remaining Tepecanos to go underground. Hrdlička (1903) was able to locate two surviving Teultec villages, Tepatitlan and Tepicoak, in the rugged mountains farther south. But in the former Tepecan village of Azqueltan, he found that participation in traditional rites had dropped sharply as a result of acculturative pressures from the mestizos. Hrdlička also had the dubious fortune to meet the last surviving pure Indians in both Nostic and Huejucar.

So far as the Indians of the Sierra proper are concerned, the national census of 1910 listed 4,303 Coras, 3,011 Tepehuanes, and 4,154 Huichols in the Sierras of Jalisco, Nayarit, Durango, and Zacatecas; the latter number corresponds closely with Lumholtz's estimates of 4,000 Huichols.

Despite growing pressures from mestizo society throughout this phase of their history, the Huichols more than anyone else stubbornly retained their traditional sociocultural integrity. At the same time they also maintained accustomed patterns of interaction with the outside world, from seasonal labor and trade to ritual pilgrimages. In 1826 the British mine official Captain G. F. Lyon met a party of twenty Huichols who had come to the mining town of Bolaños for market day, selling salt carried from the coast. He also mentioned that a certain Captain Basil Hall had met a party of Huichols in Tepic, an area to which Huichols had long and close ties.[5] In the 1880s parties of Huichols were mentioned as frequent visitors to nearby towns such as Colotlán, Jerez, and Tlaltenango to sell pitch pine from the Sierra; around the same period they were also reported to visit these towns, as well as Valparaiso and Fresnillo, to sell copal incense, cumin seeds, pine, and gum. Lumholtz noted the sale of pitch pine and cheeses in Mezquitic, and remarked that it was customary for Huichol men to carry sacks of maize weighing a *fanega* (120 pounds) from Mezquitic to Santa Catarína—a distance of 50 kilometers over often precipitous terrain—in just three days. Lumholtz also wrote that Huichol parties often worked in the cotton and maize plantations of the *tierra caliente* (i.e., the coastal lowlands) during the dry season. Lumholtz was quite impressed by their knowledge of the outside world and of current events, "almost as if they had newspapers or telegraphs" (1902:111).

In addition to these continuous economic interrelations with the outside world, many Huichols were at times forced to take refuge outside of the Sierra. Conversely, they also apparently continued to incorporate occasional outsiders into their own society. Thus, Lumholtz encountered several mestizos who had married into and been accepted by Huichol communities, and a half-Tepecan, half-Nahuan man from Azqueltan who had been adopted by the Huichols as a boy.

Despite the Church's declining political influence during this period, it too remained active in the Sierra; missionaries continued making token visits to the former Huichol missions, as well as those of other Sierra tribes, to attempt the conversion of the natives. Captain Lyon in 1826 reported that a padre or friar made annual tours of the Huichol territories to perform marriages and baptisms; at the end of the century Lumholtz found that a padre from the Hacienda de San Antonio to the north made similar annual rounds through San Andrés and Santa Catarína; in 1870 the Bishop of Zacatecas had himself made a formal visit to the Huichols. Church representatives were none too popular, though, as on one occasion a padre had destroyed several presumably sacred idols at the cave shrine of Teakata.[6]

Accounts by Ing. Roseando Corona in 1888, and by Lumholtz in the 1890s, are as similar to those described by Sahagún in the sixteenth century as to those witnessed in the 1960s by Benítez, Furst, and Myerhoff, and by others since. It follows that the overall impact of the Church during this period was relatively negligible.

Modern, 1930—Present

The present state of the Huichols and the problems they face are adequately dealt with elsewhere in these pages, but some observations on these last sixty years in Huichol history are in order here. The modern period begins, to all intents and purposes, in the 1930s. Now for the first time church and state were effectively separated at all levels of government. The mestizo, the "*raza cosmica*," has become the man of the hour in Mexico, the Spaniards and their criollo offspring having either left or been absorbed, while the remaining Indians, whose number has actually increased with the advent of modern medicine, have nevertheless been rationalized away by many Mexicans as the romantic, though clearly degenerate, remnants of a once great people. Yet despite— or because of—the fact that Indians continue to occupy a subordinate rank, belong to the poorest stratum of the national society, and continue a struggle for the most basic rights that began with the Spanish invasion, this most recent period has seen the emergence of powerful segments of the larger society, including many Mexican anthropologists and government functionaries, that are concerned with their human and constitutional condition. In recent years, too, cultural and ethnic pluralism has more and more come to be seen as a viable resolution of many of the serious problems facing modern Mexico.

Rights to their lands and security from its alienation by outside interests are the one big problem that I see troubling the Huichols today. There are others, too, but without arable land there can be no life as Huichols, for it is their traditional territories—much smaller now than they once were, and with many more mouths to feed—that provide the basis for self-determination and sociocultural and religious autonomy. Ironically, not only is there the persistent problem of invasions by mestizo farmers hungry for land and the continuing alienation of large sections of arable land and pastorage by powerful outside interests such as the big cattle owners, in recent decades there have also been land disputes between the Huichols and bordering pueblos, such as Tenzompa and Huajimic, that were originally Huichol settlements. The fact is that with an increasing shortage of usable land in the face of rapid population growth, roughly half of all Huichols now live outside the formally constituted territories of the comunidades indígenas, some in rural colonies, like that established during the Cristero revolt on the north bank of the lower Río Lerma (Río Grande de Santiago), in territory that at the time of the invasion of Nuño de Guzmán was also Huichol, others in cities like Zacatecas, Guadalajara, Tepic, and even the distant Mexican capital. At the same time, Huichols continue to travel periodically in the outside world—for trade, employment, religious pilgrimages, or simply *para conocer,* to learn about the world around them, even as more and more mestizo *comerciantes* visit them in their mountains to buy and sell livestock, tools, seeds, manufactured goods, and, unfortunately, beer and hard liquor.

Through it all, however, the Huichols remain clearly, and proudly, Huichol, just as in the days of their ancestors, preserving traditional beliefs and customs and finding satisfaction within the framework of their own religious beliefs and their own social and cultural ways. They are indeed a remarkable people.

NOTES

1. The one crucial thing for which we have no colonial records at all from this entire period is the Huichol peyote pilgrimage, which, if it was going on in these turbulent times, would of course also have maintained contact with other native groups, such as the Zacatecas and Guachichiles, whose territory lay astride the route through Zacatecas to San Luis Potosí. (—Eds.)

2. Inasmuch as peyote is not native to the Sierra or its environs, this suggests that notwithstanding the dangers, Huichols, and perhaps also other Indians, were in fact traveling regularly to San Luis Potosí to hunt peyote.(—Eds.)

3. Use of the cactus by Spaniards also spread to the Spanish colony in New Mexico. The editors are grateful to Carroll Riley for drawing our attention to a 1935 article by France V. Scholes in the *New Mexico Historical Review* (1935:219-220), citing references to peyote use in sworn declarations before the Inquisition by three individuals, two of them women and the other a man, on March 25, 1631, and May 25 and September 21, 1632, respectively:

> In the first place, it [peyote] was recommended as a potion to give a bewitched person for it would enable such a person to have a vision in which the identity of the sorcerer would be revealed, following which the health of the bewitched person would be restored. It was also stated that in the visions induced by taking peyote a person could tell just what person might be on the way from New Spain.

Juan Anton, a mulatto, also admitted using peyote in New Spain to discover the location of property stolen from him.(—Eds.)

4. Judging from the record of a lengthy investigation and trial for idolatry of several Cora men in 1789, Huichols helped their Cora neighbors in Jesús María to continue to practice their traditional rituals by supplying them secretly with ceremonial objects that had been outlawed by the friars. In exchange, the Huichols received maize. This previously unknown document was recently discovered by William Merrill while searching the West Mexican archives for Tarahumara materials and shared by him with our English colleague Anthony Shelton, who in turn sent it to us.

Even at this relatively late time, the Huichols themselves were evidently still primarily hunters and foragers, with only a little horticulture. Beatríz Rojas's recently published collection of historical documents relating to the Huichols includes a lengthy account of observations in San Andrés, Santa Catarína, San Sebastián, etc., by a Spanish colonel, Felix Calleja. The Huichols, Calleja reported, planted very little and lived by hunting and fishing, trading salt, and the spoils of frequent raiding, especially for cattle (Rojas 1992:101-107).(—Eds.)

5. This goes back at least to the early years of Nueva Galicia. Gerhard (1982:49) writes that in the 1540s "Nahuatl-speaking colonists from Tlaxcala and the Valley of Mexico settled in Tepecano country to serve as a frontier militia and civilizing influence, *while some of the mountain tribes in the west (Huicholes, Tepehuances) were induced to form colonies in the vicinity of Tepic and Acaponeta*" (emphasis added). In the same decade, the Spaniards also forced "many of the mountain-dwelling Tecoxquines and Huicholes . . . to move down to the coastal plain." (—Eds.)

6. They were still none too popular even in the 1960s. A Franciscan priest from the Basilica

of Zapópan, Father Loera Ochóa, for example, told one of the editors (P.T.F.) of an unpleasant experience when he visited San Andrés. Though in civilian clothes, he was recognized as a priest when Huichols saw a mestizo woman kneel before him and kiss his ring. Within moments he found himself surrounded by men armed with machetes, who escorted him to the airstrip and did not leave his side until the arrival of a mission plane to take him out.(— Eds.)

INTRODUCTION TO CHAPTER 4

For the student of Huichol religion and sacred literature it is hard to imagine a greater loss than the destruction in World War II of Konrad Theodor Preuss's manuscript of sixty-nine lengthy Huichol ritual orations or chants, complete with translations into German. This immeasurable—and never to be duplicated—treasure of Huichol sacred poetry was recorded in longhand, in part also on wax cylinders, along with numerous sacred chants, in Santa Catarína, San Andrés Cohamiata, and various Huichol settlements and *ranchos* during Preuss's nine months among the Huichols of the Sierra Madre Occidental as part of his Nayarit Expedition of 1905-07. Sad to say, both the original and the only carbon were destroyed, the former with the offices of B. G. Teubner, his Leipzig publisher, who in 1912 had brought out his monograph on the religion of the Cora, the latter when Preuss's old home in Berlin-Friedenau fell victim to a bombing raid in March 1944. The pioneer student of the rich oral poetry of the Indian peoples of the Sierra Madre Occidental himself had died in 1938, a year before the Nazi invasion of Poland set off World War II.

However, all is not gone of Preuss' Huichol legacy. From the Sierra Madre he contributed two long essays on his travels and experiences among the Huichols to *Globus*, a geographical journal, and a third, in 1908, a few months after his return to Berlin from Mexico, to *Archiv für Religionswissenschaft*, a periodical devoted to comparative religion. He also published a discussion of style and content in Huichol sacred songs in French, and a paper comparing the dialogues in the *Rigveda* with those chanted by the officiating shaman-singer in Cora and Huichol ritual (Preuss 1909:41-46).

Preuss's early schooling had been in religion; in fact, after graduation from gymnasium he first enrolled in a seminary. But then he turned to ethnology and linguistics, and after graduation joined the staff of the Museum für Völkerkunde in Berlin. Although his first appointment was in its Oceanic and African Section, he became more and more interested in the indigenous religions of the New World, especially Mexico. The great pioneer of Mesoamerican studies, Eduard Seler, was then the head of the museum's American Section, and once Preuss was transferred to it, it was inevitable that he would immerse himself in some of Seler's favorite topics, in particular the religion and language of the Mexica, or Aztecs, and the pre-Hispanic and early post-Conquest Central Mexican pictorial codices.

That, in turn, sparked an interest in possible survivals of pre-Hispanic religion, ritual, and oral traditions among Mexican Indians. In 1898 the American Museum of Natural History in New York had published Carl Lumholtz's first article on the Huichols of the Sierra Madre Occidental, followed in 1900 by his monograph, *Symbolism of the Huichol Indians*. Lumholtz's *Unknown Mexico*, a popular two-volume account of five years of travel among Indian peoples of northwestern Mexico, appeared in 1902. In 1899 there had been an article on the Huichols, with interesting speculations on their probable relationship to the Guachichil-Chichimecs, by the French scholar León Diguet. Seler published a long discussion on Huichol culture in 1901, in which, among other things, he was the first to draw attention to the striking similarity between Huichol ritual behavior regarding peyote and that described for the Teochichimeca, or True Chichimecs, by Fray Bernadino de Sahagún in Volume 10 of his monumental *Florentine Codex* (Seler 1901:138–163).

In 1903 Preuss published a long essay on the nature and functions of the Aztec fire deities as a possible key to unlocking the larger puzzle of Aztec religion (Preuss 1903:130–233). But what he was clearly hoping for was an opportunity to follow in Lumholtz's footsteps, travel to western Mexico, and look for, record, and translate into German the sacred oral poetry he felt Lumholtz had unfortunately neglected by focusing almost exclusively on art and symbolism.

What Preuss wanted to determine above all was whether the religious beliefs, rituals, and mythologies of the Coras, Huichols, and Nahua-speaking "Mexicanos" living in the mountains of southern Durango might contain clues to the ancient religion of the Aztecs. Seler supported the idea, having himself stressed the need for a study along these lines in the concluding passages of his 1901 Huichol essay. An opportunity to study the indigenous peoples and languages of the Sierra Madre Occidental firsthand came at last in 1905, when the Prussian government awarded Preuss a grant from the foundation established for Americanist research by the Duke of Loubat, which also supported Seler's work in Mexico. En route to the Sierra Madre Occidental, Preuss stopped off in New York for a courtesy call on Franz Boas. The "father of American anthropology" was himself a veteran of Berlin's Museum für Völkerkunde, and he and his wife had Seler's assistant to their home for dinner. Preuss never forgot their generous hospitality and professional encouragement. Immediately after his return to Germany nearly two years later, in 1908, he wrote Boas to explain that lack of funds and illness had forced him to return to Germany directly, so that he was unable to tell Boas personally about his treasure trove of Cora, Huichol and Mexicano texts, and his plans for their translation and eventual publication.

Preuss reached Tepic, in what was then the Territory of Nayarit, on December 25, 1905. Six long, exhausting days on foot and muleback brought him to Jesús María, in the heart of Cora country. Language was for Preuss the gateway into a people's soul and culture. Hence, wherever his ethnographic forays led him, he first sought to acquire fluency in the native tongue. Already well versed in Nahuatl, which he had studied in Berlin under Seler, he was to have little difficulty with the related Nahua dialect of the Mexicanos of San Pedro Jícora, Durango. As a result, once he had worked with the Coras and the Huichols, he found the final three months of his Nayarit Expedition to be sufficient for gathering an enormous body of texts. But Cora was then still virtually unknown, even though Padre José Ortega had published a short Cora word list in 1722. What Preuss accomplished in three months among the Mexicanos had required twice the time among the Coras. Lumholtz published a short word list of Huichol in 1900, but even less was known of that language. Diguet, who, like Lumholtz, had visited the Huichols in the 1890s, suggested in 1899 that Huichol was a survival of Guachichil, a Chichimec language thought to have become extinct, but his larger study of Huichol was not to appear until 1911, leaving Preuss without any signposts into the Huichol tongue. As much for this as for any other reason Preuss reserved his longest single period of field work, more than nine months, for the Huichols, through whose rugged country he traveled widely on foot and by mule, settling down in his tent or in some Huichol dwelling or temple to record texts in longhand and on wax cylinders, make interlinear translations on the spot with the assistance of Huichols conversant in Spanish, and, incidentally, gather a considerable collection of Huichol art and material culture, especially ceremonial objects, for the Museum für Völkerkunde. This valuable collection has fortunately survived World War II, as has a portion of the numerous wax cylinder recordings he brought back from Mexico.

Shortly after his return to Berlin the museum promoted Preuss to Curator, and in 1912 he succeeded Seler as head of the North and Middle American Departments. In that year he also published *Die Nayarit-Expedition*, Vol. 1: *Religion der Cora-Indianer*, a work that reproduces a great number of sacred texts and myths in Cora and German and that has never been surpassed for its wealth of sacred poetry of contemporary Mexican Indians in its larger ceremonial context and religious belief and ritual. A second volume was to be devoted to the Huichols, and a third to the Mexicanos. But there were numerous unavoidable interruptions, including a South American sojourn, mainly in Colombia, that was to last, through no fault of his own, for six years. When he went to Colombia in 1913 he presumably expected to remain no more than a few months. But World War I broke out in 1914 and kept him in enforced exile in South America for the next four years, with an additional year's residence following the armistice. Like Malinowski in the Trobriands, Preuss made good use of this unexpected gift of time, studying not only the living religions of such peoples as the Witoto and Kágaba, but also the spectacular monumental art and archaeology of the upper Río Magdalena, famous for its great stone sculptures (Preuss 1920-21, 1929). Eventually, in addition to his museum position, he received an appointment to the faculty of the University of Berlin, with the rank of Reader, or Lecturer, in Ethnology. But Preuss was clearly first and foremost a museum man, who, his erudition notwithstanding, never attracted many students. Two of these, however, were Elsa Ziehm and Gerdt Kutscher, who decades later were to play crucial roles in making Preuss's Nahua texts available to the scholarly world. If not a notable teacher, Preuss was certainly a highly productive scholar: at the time of his sudden death, on June 6, 1938 at the age of 68, his bibliography had 148 entries. Though ready for publication, missing from it were the Huichol texts and their translations into German. These Boas had offered to publish, as he previously had Preuss's Cora grammar and a Cora–German dictionary, in his *International Journal of American Linguistics*, but, for whatever reason, these plans fell through and the manuscript never left Germany. Still awaiting Preuss's linguistic and analytical talents when he died was a veritable mountain of Nahua material. In the confusion and hardships of the early postwar period in Berlin no one knew its whereabouts, or even whether it had survived the destruction of Preuss's home. Then one day, by a fortunate coincidence, Kutscher, the director of the Ibero–American Institute in Berlin, happened to be leafing through a publishers' magazine when he saw the name Werner Preuss mentioned as author of one of the winning entries in a literary contest. The rest, as they say, is history: not only did Herr Preuss turn out to be the grandson of Kutscher's old teacher, but he informed Kutscher that on January 3, 1944, during a Christmas leave from the front, he had visited Preuss's old home in Berlin-Friedenau. Here he had come across four thick diaries and notebooks numbering hundreds of pages, each filled with closely spaced writing. On the spur of the moment he had taken these with him to his home in Treysa—a fortunate decision indeed, for three months later the Preuss house was no more. He told Kutscher he would be happy if they turned out to be of some use to science. When Kutscher saw them, he was ecstatic: three of the "diaries," numbering two hundred pages each, were filled with unpublished Nahua texts with Spanish translations from San Pedro Jícora (the fourth diary contained already published Cora material), while the notebooks pertained to Preuss's work in Colombia. It took another five years before Kutscher found someone qualified to undertake the difficult task of deciphering Preuss's idiosyncratic shorthand, translating the texts into German, and writing a commentary to make them accessible to the reader: Preuss's former student, Elsa Ziehm. Ziehm went twice to San Pedro herself for clarifications and to check the accuracy of her translations before entrusting them to print in three volumes published by the Ibero-American Institute, the first in 1968 and the last in 1976. Her work also includes an ethnomusicological analysis of those of the Huichol chants and songs Preuss had recorded on wax cylinders that survived the war and that are part of the Preuss Archive and ethnographic collection at the Museum für Völkerkunde in Berlin-Dahlem.

How much has been lost to Huichol studies with the destruction of Preuss's original texts and German translations becomes all the more evident when we read in his essays synopses of, or allusions to, myths and oral traditions that must have been part of his vanished collection. Fortunately, the essays also include important observations on Huichol social and family life, polygyny, religion and ritual, the curing of gods, earth, and people, language, shamanism, the journey of the soul to the land of the dead in the west, the sacred deer person Kauyumári as culture hero-cum-trickster, messenger of the gods, and indispensable assistant to the old fire god and first shaman Tatewarí, and so on.

Like that other giant of Americanist studies of the early twentieth century, Leonhard Schultze Jena, Preuss seems also to have been one of that all-too-small band of pre–World War II German anthropologists who did not wholly capitulate to the Nazi madness. The evidence for this is indirect but persuasive: an exchange of letters between Franz Boas in New York and Preuss in Berlin, correspondence that began with the latter's return to Berlin from his West Mexican expedition and that continued into the early years of the Nazi regime. The letters, copies of which are preserved in the Boas Archive in the library of the American Philosophical Society in Philadelphia, are overtly—perhaps even determinedly—non-political in content: the political statement lies in the fact that they were written at all. For once the Nazis were in power, any German who kept up an active international correspondence with a Jewish intellectual whom the Nazis had declared persona non grata in Germany, and whose works had been publicly burned, was putting himself at risk. Worse, Boas sent, and Preuss accepted, modest funding from New York to assist in the translation of the Huichol texts and the preparation of the manuscript for Boas's journal.

For a short time after Hitler's rise to power Preuss held on to his position at the museum, while it was increasingly undergoing "ethnic cleansing" (for which the Nazis coined the euphemism *Gleichgeschaltung*, meaning ensuring "racial" and political conformity through the removal from their jobs of "non-Aryans" and anti-Nazis). By one reliable account, either before or after his retirement, Preuss's house was raided and searched by the Gestapo, reportedly on the instigation of a Nazi colleague, who may or may not have been the noted Mesoamericanist Walter Krickeberg. No wonder Paul Kirchhoff, a determined anti-Nazi who had emigrated to Mexico after the Nazi ascent to power, publicly turned his back when Krickeberg, in Mexico City to participate in an international congress after World War II, tried to shake his hand!

Preuss was by all accounts not what one would call a political man. He was an erudite, rather formal, multilingual scholar of the old school, a student and interpreter of American Indian religions, past and present. To a degree, he was captive to the astral interpretation of mythology so popular at the beginning of the twentieth century; indeed, occasionally he was one of its leading exponents. (Though often dismissed as old-fashioned, looking to the sky and its phenomena for explanations of certain myths and artistic representations may, in retrospect, not have been all that wrong, as indicated by recent Maya studies.)

Those who have sniped at Preuss for allegedly having "Aztecized" the Huichols are victims of their own ignorance of German. First, if Preuss drew attention to parallels between the Huichols and the Central Mexicans, it was because these parallels existed. Second, one might as well speak of "Huicholizing" the Aztecs, because, like the Huichols, they occasionally became their own ancestors, went on communal rabbit hunts, and made miniature offerings to their gods. Preuss did perceive similarities, certainly, and he saw natural history as the foundation of major aspects of the indigenous religions of both the Sierra Madre and Central Mexico. But he never regarded the Huichols as "primitive Aztecs," or as ancestors to them. Steeped as he was in Aztec religion, ritual, language, and calendrics before he ever went to the Sierra Madre, he was alert to analogies. He demonstrated that the Uto–Aztecan-speaking peoples of the Sierra Madre Occidental shared ideas with one another and with the dominant Mesoamerican civilization of the late pre-Conquest period. He must also have been aware that some of these conceptions might, like Nahuatl loan words in their language, probably have come late to the Huichols, after the Conquest, when the Spanish settled Nahuatl-speaking Tlaxcalans and other Central Mexican Indians nominally converted to Christianity on the western frontier of New Spain as buffers against the "uncivilized" (meaning as yet unconquered) inhabitants of the Sierra Madre Occidental.

With all the shortcomings of the state of knowledge in his time, Preuss was bold in his thinking and a true pioneer. Not only for the high regard he demonstrated over a lifetime for the integrity of the languages, ideologies, and sacred poetry of Native peoples, but as a scholar in the great humanist traditions of German social and natural science, he deserves our respect.

Peter T. Furst

4 : KONRAD THEODOR PREUSS (1869–1938)

ON THE HUICHOLS

Translated from the German by PETER T. FURST

Translator's Note: Brief excerpts from Preuss's writings on the Huichols were used in an essay on the role of the first fruits ceremony in the enculturation of Huichol children, which the Mexican anthropologist Marina Anguiano and I published in English in 1976, and which was subsequently translated into Spanish and published as a monograph by the Instituto Nacional Indigenista in Mexico (Anguiano and Furst 1979, 1988). Except for this and other occasional references, Preuss's significant and interesting surviving commentaries on the Huichols, a total of some 20,000 words, remained untranslated into English and, until the present volume, virtually unknown to English-speaking readers.

I.

The Marriage of Maize and Other Traditions of the Huichol Indians

From *Globus*, Vol. 91 (1907), pp. 185–192.

San Isidro, October 14, 1906.

In the Sierra it is the coming of the rains that sparks the same sensations and emotions that spring and summer generate in our people at home. To be sure, the trees have already begun to change their appearance. But this has not happened all at once: some are in full bloom, and in the last months before the rains there is already an abundance of fruit: tunas, the fruits of the nopal cactus; pitayas; ciruelas (plums); mesquites and guamuchiles. The sun in its northward passages passes through the zenith in May, and already by March the heat in the valleys is positively oppressive. And yet all this time the Sierra conveys a feeling of hibernation, even of old age. The sun moves across the sky with numbing monotony, not even a single cloudlet affording relief from its burning rays, from dawn to dusk the jagged ridges of the mountains are sharply etched against the sky, most streams and creeks having long since dried up—not even a tenth of the broad boulder-strewn riverbeds is covered by water, for lack of water many of the ranchos lie deserted, and the meadows with their tall zacate grass are grey and dry. There are no crops and no harvest. Now and then the traveler, rocking half asleep on his *mula* uphill and down, is briefly startled into consciousness by a loud crackling sound like rifle shots when one of the *arrieros* sets the dry grass on fire with a carelessly tossed match or the glowing butt of a cigarette. Especially at night one frequently sees whole mountain tops aglow with fires that have been deliberately set. Later, in May, the country is aflame with innumerable coamil fires, when the brush that was cut in November to clear the land for planting is burned.

That is how the Sierra appeared to me during the half year, from the end of December 1905 to the end of June 1906, I spent with the Cora Indians, who live some six days' travel north of Tepic. Although with every passing day new stories and sacred chants enriched my collection of texts, I had to call a halt when the Río Santa María started to rise, threatening to cut me off from the Huichol Indians, to whom I was planning to devote the next six months of my stay. The great planting dances the Cora call mitotes were done with, the gods were sufficiently moved to respond with rain and the proper growth of maize, and all around me the people who provided me with data for my research were far too busy with planting to have time for me.

And so there I sat with my two Mexican factotums in my rented rancho of San Isídro, about four hours east of Jesús María near the border of the state of Jalisco, my little hut stuffed to the rafters with supplies of maize, rice, beans, coffee, sugar, tobacco, etc., that were supposed to last the whole rainy season until October, all my trade goods, in particular the white cotton called manta, wool yarn (*estambre*), white and blue beads (*chaquíra*), colorful bandannas, and so forth, the saddles and aparéjos for my six animals and all the many other things that are required for an expedition of this sort. Added to all this were all the objects I had been collecting, strung up everywhere to facilitate comparison and description.

In the meantime the mountains had become covered with fresh, dark green vegetation, spotted here and there along the slopes with the lighter green of the new maize plantations that in three months' time were to furnish sustenance for the entire year. For this aspect of the Sierra the Huichols have the peculiar name *natikari*, "their (the gods') night," an expression that recurs frequently in their religious songs; accordingly, *tikaripa*, "in the night," also means "in the rainy season," "en las aguas," as the Mexicans call this season to distinguish it from "las lluvias," the occasional rains that punctuate the dry season without accompanying thunderstorms.

In this time of the longest days of the year it almost seems as though the earth was being blanketed with the darkness of midwinter. The Huichols also call the bamboo dance staffs that are decorated with cloud designs in black, as well as the small black-painted wooden sticks that are given to the gods as offerings for rain, *yuaitsu*, meaning "blue (in place of black) staff."

But this is the kind of night that only fills the Indian's heart with joy. It is not an object of dread, like the night that begins over there, in the west, at the mountain called Autarika, half a day's journey west of the Mesa de Nayarit, from where one can look over the ocean with its dangerous snakes and the realm of the dead. Anyone who crosses this mountain for the first time on the way to Santiago has his face covered by two companions, who take him under the arms and pull him at the double up hill and back down again behind the protective escarpment. Only then can he cross the summit without danger.

While Indians stop walking with nightfall, not even the strongest downpours, nor the fiercest thunderstorms that customarily accompany the rains in the wet season, keep them from essential errands. Of course their clothing consists solely of a shirt, hat and sash, and when it rains they use a breechcloth in place of the former. Almost certainly one can ascribe the feeling of joy that makes Huichols come alive in the rainy season to the beckoning ears of maize that will put an end to the chronic food shortage in the weeks before the harvest. At the same time it is certain that the play of clouds and lightning across the mountain peaks and the grey-black sheets of rain, for which they have a multitude of names, that drift across the landscape are capable all by themselves of stirring the most pleasant feelings—just as they do in the traveler, however vexed he may be by the problems of the rainy season. Only in the morning is it possible to move with any expectation of dry weather, and only where there are no larger streams to cross. The two rivers that slice from north to south through the center of the Cora and Huichol territory, respectively, and that drain into the Río Grande or Río Santiago, the Río de Jesús María and its tributary, the Chapalagana, easily forded in the dry season, can be crossed in the rainy season only by dugout canoe, a questionable mode of transport to which it is impossible to entrust valuable luggage. And of such canoes there is only a single one in the pueblo of Jesus Maria, and another at the mouth of the Chapalagana. The risk of crashing headlong on the rain-soaked path is the greater in that the mules are customarily shod only in front and hence walk with unsteady gait. Meanwhile uninterrupted rains that last several days are so rare that one of four days' duration may already awaken fears of a new Deluge among the Huichols.

All around my rancho there were only scattered settlements of Huichols, with whom I soon established friendly relations. They are far more trusting than the Cora, who, apart from the people of the pueblo San Francisco, want nothing to do with strangers or who can be persuaded to part with objects or knowledge only against substantial payment. Usually, when I step out of the door early in the morning there are already several Huichols waiting for me outside, either in expectation of beans and tortillas or the sale of crafts and stories, or the possibility of acquiring trade goods. Others pass by the rancho from distant parts on matters of business, to buy maize, for example, or catch deer for the fiesta of the elotes (young ears of maize), or simply driven by a natural propensity for visiting, places a whole day's walk away being considered nearby. To be sure, Huichols walk twice as fast as a mule and can follow far more difficult trails.

On the other hand, one cannot assume that these visitors will immediately provide useful data, especially when one has to begin then and there to learn a language of which next to nothing is known. So for the moment they can really serve only for observing behavior, winning their trust and spreading it among their fellow tribesmen, as a starting point for questions to the interpreter about their personal lives, and so forth.

To make the most of the time available, a Huichol fluent in Spanish as interpreter is an absolute necessity if one wants to get further than the usual questions about the native names of body parts, objects, etc. Even in Santa Maria I made every effort to do just that, and was extremely fortunate to have been able to start working with José Maria Carrillo, who was related by blood or marriage to several leading cantadores and curers and also knew many myths himself, on the very day I finished my Cora translations. Moreover, he was serving as an auxiliary judge and, though only 23, commanded sufficient respect to get people to come to my rancho. True, his Spanish was not as good as that of my Cora interpreter, Molina. But that was more than offset by the fact that unlike the latter, who alone among his fellow tribesmen disdained the old religion, he was so totally committed to the old beliefs and rituals that as our friendship grew he shared with me everything he thought and did in accordance with the Indian world view. On the other hand, he was quite willing—so long as we were alone—to "sell" me all sorts of votive offerings from the innumerable god houses that are put up for individual deities beside the temples that are meant for all the gods. But before doing so he always greeted them three times, "Texe, texe, texe," meaning "Good day." He even sold me the souls of his grandparents and parents in the form of small stones that make their appearance soon after death or following the ceremony of the toasted maize, and which the shaman either catches in mid-air or directs into a bowl of fermented maize beer, where, being still soft, they gradually harden.

Whereas among the Cora it took me a month just to find a "man of knowledge," here I could start immediately with recording myths and chants. Also, the daily wage was only about a fourth of what I was used to paying among the Cora, about six to eight reales, equivalent to one and a half to two German marks, a substantial sum for Huichols accustomed to earning only two reales for a day's labor in the fields. By paying only after several days of uninterrupted work and a bonus if they remained overnight I was also able to keep Carrillo, as well as the others, coming on a regular basis, if not actually bedding down in my hut. And if they nevertheless failed to show up at least by 8 a.m., I sent my mozo to look for them and bring them, however unwillingly, back. Of course in that event the whole morning was lost. Promises of showing up alone are just not enough, neither among the Cora nor the Huichol.

Worse still for the traveler, to be sure, the Indians may be inclined to tell pointless fibs, for which the motive seems to be just the fun of having fooled the "gringo." One day a group of Indians arriving from Santa Gertrudis, a rancho a day's trip to the south near the Rio Chapalagana, told of a rainmaking ceremony that was going to be held in their temple in three days' time. They said they had already purchased a cow to sacrifice and were now on their way to the nearby pueblo of Santa Rosa to buy maize for the ceremony. So for me there was nothing more urgent than to set out the following morning for Santa Gertrudis, because with all the rain we had already had there would surely be no other opportunity of observing such a ceremony. Not only did we find the rancho completely deserted, because everybody had moved to the maize fields and no one was giving any thought whatever to any kind of ceremony, but they kept us there for eight days in expectation that there might be one—while at the same time ardently wishing us to go away. Had I not taken the precaution of taking along my Cora interpreter, all this would have been a waste of time. As it was, living as we did in the Santa Gertrudis temple, I was able to refine my Cora texts. The same thing happened when I traveled for five hours to a rancho for the ceremony of the calabashes and found no one there either, notwithstanding the fact that Carrillo himself had taken care to make several inquiries beforehand.

Accompanying this proclivity for telling fibs is a certain gullibility on the part of the Huichols—one after the other, almost all of my regular visitors had charges filed against them by their own people for alleged cattle theft, and were dragged off to face the judge in Santa Rosa, arbitrary acts that were possible only because Huichols have great respect for the authorities. For me these cases were very annoying, because I was never able to dissuade Carrillo from his zeal for such unpaid police work and so lost his services for days at a time.

As a rule the recording to Huichol texts took place in the midst of a multitude of Indians, and despite all the conversation even the arrival of new visitors hardly interrupted our work. Everyone squatted or rested on the ground, the tobacco pouches and corn husk for wrapping cigarettes were passed from hand to hand, everyone coughed and spat—as is customary also among the Mexicans—and chatted and laughed. One of my mozos would search through the shoulder bags of the visitors for things to purchase for my collection, inspect the wide sashes with their beautifully woven designs— of which some men wore as many as four or five—or the patterns in the headbands, ear ornaments and armbands, and so forth, and hold cash or things to be traded for the desired article as temptingly as possible before the owner's eyes. So I could devote myself entirely to my own studies, especially the texts. Once it had been determined that I had not yet recorded, or had set down incorrectly, a certain myth, the Huichol concerned patiently dictated while I repeated every word, Carrillo functioning as middleman to correct faulty pronunciation. Almost every one of the visitors proved capable of using this technique. Immediately afterwards, with Carrillo's help, we made interlinear translations, which of course were initially very rough. Their only purpose was to determine whether Carrillo had understood everything correctly, and to give me the opportunity to question the story teller about the meaning of the content of the story. Everything of a linguistic nature was held over for later study with Carrillo. The similarity of many words and the whole structure of the language to that of the Cora made the work considerably easier. Further east, for example in Santa Catarína, because of the change of consonants—l for r and r for x (sh)—the language sounds less like Cora.

The transcription of the religious chants presented considerable difficulties. The Cora cantadores always dictated their chants at a brisk pace. But here it always took a long time before the three singers available to me were moved to give me a word for word text. First they would waste much time and effort on an extract, with numerous addenda. But these tended to be so aphoristic that there was little content beyond a list of deities and objects. And then it was impossible to convince them to repeat the same chant with nothing left out. Only after several false starts—and with two of the three of them it never did come to this point—was I able to get a word for word dictation, from beginning to end.

And now to my horror it suddenly became clear why the other two could not be persuaded to do this. The fact is that here, in contrast to the Cora, the chants do not repeat themselves at the different ceremonies. Nor are there individual chants with specific content. Instead a single chant goes on all through the night, and another the whole following day, if the ceremony lasts that long. This is possible through constant elaboration of every individual idea and its application to the numerous deities of all the four to six directions. However, the repetitions are not identical, so that to understand the meaning always requires the complete text. In this way the chants become truly monstrous in length, only slightly shortened by the fact that each phrase is immediately repeated in chorus, thus taking up half of the time available, allegedly to keep the singer from tiring.

To listen to this chorus, whose members sit or lie every which way around the fire, is not always an aesthetic experience, because with everybody singing for himself, without much regard for anyone else, it often all sounds more like howling than singing. Also, the singer's intonation always remains the same the whole night through. And yet to listen to some of them gave me much pleasure. At some ceremonies there is no musical accompaniment to the songs, at others the singer beats steadily with both hands on the drum, which resembles the ahuehuetl of the ancient Mexicans.

The content of the songs consists mainly of a dialogue of the gods with the messenger of the fire god Tatewarí, the roguish trickster Kauyumári, who is deer, and who seems to represent starlight, or with Tatewarí himself. Objects speak, and their deeds are recounted, the feathers of birds, arrows and other ceremonial objects—in short, it is a magical universe that to this day is alive in Huichol ideology.

To mention only one example, and that only briefly, the chant that is sung by daylight at the ceremony of the young calabashes and the tender maize cobs narrates their journey from west to east to the end of the world and back to the temple. All the gods come from the west, and also all the fruits of the fields, and the young ears of maize are specifically named for a little bird with yellow feathers that lives on the coast. Its name is *Uaínu*, and the young maize cobs are accordingly called *teuainuríxe*, the affix *té* meaning Mother. In the ceremony they are represented by festively attired boys and girls aged one through five. In the sowing ceremony the maize goddess Niwetsika says farewell to all the gods, because she is about to die and hence is the principal speaker.

How much work awaits me here is easy to imagine when one considers that there are about ten of these ceremonies—up to the present I have seen the sowing ceremony (more correctly, the "Husking of the Maize"), the ceremony of the Clearing of the Fields ("Washing of the Jícaras"), and the ceremonies of the calabazas and elotes and the cooking of the elotes—and that, in the case of a curing ritual or a death, the singing shamans are capable of working at least one whole night through. Other than taking a few samples, it will not be possible in the time remaining to record the same chants in other places in Huichol country, where, as in the different pueblos of the Cora, there is almost certainly an abundance of variations. In addition to portions of other ceremonial chants, up to now I have taken down the feast of sowing, of the clearing of the fields, of the calling of the dead, and one called "Cow," the latter intended to bring rain. The death chant, in which Kauyumári brings the deceased back from the land of the dead for a final visit to his house, is sung for five nights following death, and the things that happen to the deceased on his journey to the land of the dead in the west are narrated with real drama. But I will not here deal in greater detail with Huichol religion, in part already for the simple reason that an overview over the hundreds of deities that appear in the songs, and over the different kinds of ceremonies, will be possible only when my research has been concluded. Many ceremonies as well as ceremonial paraphernalia are the same as those of the Cora, and I have no doubt that the underlying religious ideology is also similar, despite the paucity of named deities among the Cora and not-withstanding the bewildering multiplicity of paraphernalia and dramatic actions among the Huichols . . .

The several legends whose translation follows below seem to be some distance re-moved from religion. And yet in their case, too, I need to add a few words at the end about how Huichols conceive of nature, and so also about their religion. Up to now my collection includes some forty myths, a quarter of them exhibiting similarities to those of the Cora. I am certain, however, that many more will be added, inasmuch as I intend, in light of the exceptionally rich harvest, to spend altogether about eight to nine months among the Huichols, the last three in Santa Catarína and other Huichol pueblos.

The Marriage of Maize

There was a terrible famine. "I am hungry (said the man) and will ask the people." "Where do you buy (maize)," he asked them. "Over there is maize, let's go and buy." They set out together. "Here we will spend the night." They lay down. When he woke up there was no one there, and he no longer had hair. He was bald. "What am I going to do, I am hungry." (Sitting) on a ridge he saw a dove approach with *masa* (maize dough) in her beak. "Can I come to your rancho?" he asked. He set off and came to the rancho. "Is there maize to buy? I came here (because) (people) invited me. Where did they disappear to? They shaved me. They told me there was maize here. Where did they disappear to? I come alone and want to buy maize." "Good," said the owner of the rancho, an old woman, "good, if you want it and your mother (wants) it, I give you a girl." She opened (the door and called out): "Come, yellow maize; red maize, come; black maize, come; multicolored maize, come; white maize, come; come, squash flower; come, *uaute* (amaranth). You go (with him), yellow maize." "No." "Red maize, you go." "No." "Black maize, you go." "I won't go."

"Multi-colored maize, you go." "I do not go. Tomorrow or the day after he scolds me. I go very slowly." "Squash flower, you go." "No. One cuts me with the knife." "Red uaute (amaranth) you go." "No, one throws me away." "White maize, you go." "Yes, I go."

"Construct five maize bins and build a beautiful house. For five days put red cempoal flowers (marigolds) in the south end (of the house), yellow cempoal flowers in the north, betonicas (hedge nettles) in the east, tempranillas (early grapes) in the west, and in the center put down corpus flowers. For five days light a candle at night. Do not scold her, keep her in the house and sweep it clean."

He set out. Five days later (the girl) arrived. Seeing maize heaped up in his house he ate. (But) his mother reproached her: "Prepare (the meal). You are a woman and not a man, to give you food," she said to her. She began to grind the maize. Blood flowed from her hands. Weeping she ground (the maize). She burned her hands. (Finally) she disappeared. Finally there was (no longer) any maize in the house.

"What do I eat?" asked the old woman. "Bring her back, she ran away to her rancho." The man went. He arrived and asked: "I lost her; did she come (back here)?" "I told you, you scolded her. I do not give her (back). She came (here). Her hands were completely burned. You go alone. You do not understand how to eat." He went. Having arrived at his rancho he reproached his mother: "You scolded her. For that reason she left and we will die of hunger."

The meaning of the story becomes clear as soon as one learns that the people who cut off all the protagonist's hair are ants (arrieras). The hero is the sprouting ear of maize (jilote) on which no kernels have yet formed. Long columns of arrieras are notorious for carrying off the maize. In my own rancho it was daily warfare with firebrands against them. In the milpa they also devour the corn silk on the young ears, which the Mexicans call *cabellito* and the Huichols likewise call *kupáixa* (*kupá*, hair), causing the ear to wither. Inasmuch as the ants cut off our hero's hair while he is looking for maize, his death from starvation is preordained and he is unable to keep the maize girl that was given to him permanently in his rancho. With the exception of white maize all the other varieties ripen very slowly, which is why they refuse to accompany him: "I go very slowly." The squash is cut, the uaute has such small seeds that many are lost during harvesting: "One throws me away." The ceremonies of welcome correspond to the preparations for the harvest in the rancho.

Finally, five is the sacred number of the Huichols and the Cora. The meaning of the story was lost to the Huichols, as it was for the Cora, among whom I recorded a long variant of the same narrative. Among both the Cora and the Huichols the dove is the animal of the earth and maize goddess. In one song I recorded the Huichols explicitly refer to maize as "dove."

How the Cloud Came to Be

He married. Then they had a child that cried constantly. They did not like their son and threw him out. "Why do you cry? We kill you." The mother threw him behind the house and herself remained inside. His older brother was not present. In the afternoon he came and asked about his younger brother. "I threw him out she (his mother) told his brother. "Why did you did you do that, why remove him?" He looked for him but there was no one there. "Where did you leave my younger brother?" He wept. Only traces of his playing were left. He did not find him. The mother looked for him but failed to find him. "What happened to him?" Because the brother did not find him he sat down. (Then) he set out, always following his tracks, until he came upon him in a lake. Then he spoke to him: "Brother, I search for you, here you are, come, brother, why did you go so far?" "(The mother) threw me out. I will not go. They scolded me. No, I won't go. You go by yourself, brother." Then the other wept. (The other) did not want to go. Weeping he arrived at his house. "Where is your brother?" the mother asked. "He went away and does not want to come. I asked him to, (but) he won't come. They scolded me and threw me out." Again he went on his way: "I go to look for him." Where he had found him there was no one. All the time he followed the tracks he had left while playing, and found him playing in a lake. "Now you come (home), brother, I don't want to stay far away, let us, I won't scold you, come." "I do not go, I went away. Now make me my chair, my jícara, my arrow, my sandals and my bracelet," he said. "Then await me, one, two, three, four, five nights. I (will) appear white on the mountain peak." On his day he appeared as a cloud. Father, mother and brother set up candles and awaited him. He rose into the sky and thundered, came to his parents and addressed them. "We don't understand what you say," they said. He fell on them and killed them, killed his mother and his father. The brother alone did not die. "Now they are dead," he said. "Here Our Mother is raining."

There is more of this story. That is why lightning strikes the fir tree and the oak, his food. He could not pull out the (*uaikuxa*) plant. Here the story ends. It (the hair on the head) continues.

The concluding phrases explain the story. Oaks and pines, which grow at the higher altitudes in the Sierra, are often hit by lightning. They are the parents of the cloud child, the uaikuxa is his brother. That is also how the interpretation of Carrillo, who dictated the story to me. The conception of the mountain and rain gods as children alone is Aztec. The Huichols attribute rain to the rain goddesses of the four directions, especially Tatéi (Our Mother) Nariwáme, who lives in the east. The child is so little that it can crawl only on all fours, although of course like all objects in the myths it has the power of speech. The infants who were sacrificed in large numbers in Mexico as representatives of the little mountain and rain gods were of the same age. If they cried a great deal before the sacrifice it signified a heavy rainfall—the very same conception that is expressed in the weeping cloud child in the myth. The candles and other offer-, ings to the clouds are ceremonial objects dedicated to all the Huichol deities. The final phrase means that the story teller will lose his hair if he fails to say, "It continues."

Traditions of this kind, which simply recount a constantly repeating natural cycle, form by far the largest part of both Huichol and Cora mythology. Flowers, trees, clouds and the like are the protagonists. Represented most often, however, is the annual cycle between preeminence of starlight and sunlight, whose brother is the rain, because the rainy season and the preeminence of the sun coincide. To test this I give the following example:

(A turtle) was unable to cross a rocky hillside and called, "Deer!" He came. "I don't want you," he said. (This was repeated five times.) He called. Then came a large deer. "You I want, help me across, I cannot cross the rocky hillside, put me down in the creek." She climbed up. After he had walked a little distance, then he said, "Give me a stone." He handed him one. "Another sharper one," she said. He gave it to him. Further on they came to the creek. He hit him with the stone so that he fell down. He climbed off, removed his skin, cut wood and threw it in a pit (an earth oven). While he was throwing it in (a wolf) came. "Here you are, brother-in-law," (he said). "Yes." "I go now." "Since I am steaming meat we eat, (then) you go." "No, I am going to Tetamuyewie to have some maize roasted (to eat with the meat), I come at once," he said.

Shortly thereafter arrived (the squirrel). "Here you are, brother-in-law." "Yes." What are you doing?" "I killed a deer and am steaming him." "Good, who came by here? Here are his tracks." "Yes, a man came by, he left (again). It seems he said he goes to have maize roasted." "Well, he goes not to roast maize, he devours you," said (the squirrel), "he goes to fetch his companions. I will take out (the meat), I make a nest." He climbed a fir tree and broke off (branches). When it was done, he climbed down again and took up the meat. "There we eat," he said, "brother-in-law, hold on to my tail." He jumped, and they sat down.

No sooner had they arrived than (a wolf) appeared. "Brother-in-law, I told you." They came to the pit, searched, and found nothing. An old one put her son down beneath their hiding place. There they searched. They found nothing. The turtle dropped a bone. It fell on the head (of the child). He started to cry. "Who threw?" said (the mother). She came and took hold of her son. "Search," she said to her companions. Then the child said: "What is that? It is a neck" (the long neck of the turtle). "Where?" "There he is." "As a matter of fact, we want to knock him down, bring an axe."

They brought one and starting hitting. They gave one blow and a second. Then the axe broke. "Well, bring (another one)." One brought it. They started hitting. He falls. "Well, brother-in-law, he falls, let's jump, take hold of my tail." (The squirrel) jumped to another tree. (This is repeated five times). They sat down. "There he is," said the child. They came and started hitting. "Take hold of the top of my tail, brother-in-law, don't let go, we jump (far), there is a creek."

When (the tree) was falling, they jumped. (The turtle) came as far as the middle, let go and fell down. The creek resounded. He alone fell into the creek. Then they searched for him. "Where did you fall in?" they (the wolves) said. They searched and were unable to find (him). They grew tired. Then the raven said: "There he is." "Where? Did he say?" they spoke. He pulled him along the ground and called, "Here!" They came and ate him. "Go fetch water, boys, we want to drink." They went to the water hole; when they arrived it was dry. They came: "There is nothing there, it is dry." "Go to the river for water, there it is not dried up." When they arrived it was dry. They returned: "There is none." "Go to the creek for water, there it is not dried up." "There is only mud there." They found nothing. All the boys died of thirst.

While they were dying, because he was a man the squirrel bathed in the creek and threw a bit of water in the air. "Throw, throw it to us, we want to drink," they said to him. He threw a little, (the water) stayed there. "Die," he said, "you ate the water, you know how to make water, drink the water." They all died of thirst. Afterwards he said to them—two were left—"surrender." They surrendered. "Now sew the turtle together and stuff it with cotton." They did so. "Some water," they said to it. A little came out. They licked it up. "Why?" said (the squirrel) to them. "Let it go to the river, then drink." Then he said to them, "Now drink. Never do this again (or) I (will) punish you." They drank the water by throwing themselves down and so they remained for a long time. Then they arose and laid down in the same place.

While they were lying down, one burst open and water leaped out. Then the other also burst open. Now they died. This is what they did. Now the turtle consists of pieces that are put together. That is how far the story goes.

The Cora, among whom I recorded a variant of the same story, still believe that the stars are deer. This is also evident in the ceremonies of the Cora, as in those of the Huichols. A Cora told me, "The turtle causes water to flow." Of the numerous species of squirrel in the Sierra the one called *teaku* in the myth is the animal of the sun or, respectively, the sun itself. Just as I was unequivocally informed, for example, that the *tacuache* (*yauúxu*, opossum) is the animal of the fire god, that is, the fire itself. Inasmuch as squirrel (sun) and turtle (water) are here associated in a most original manner, the connection to the same fate of sun and water in nature is unmistakable: the rainy season is already under way in the time of the northernmost position of the sun, and the rains end soon after the autumnal equinox.

In many other stories the sun appears as the liberator of his brother water. In others still both suffer the same fate, it goes badly with both, and their adversary is Tutákame, "the nocturnal one," the god of death, that is, the night, which rules during the dry season. So he kills the turtle, that is, the rainy season, the largest deer, the stars. While they and the squirrel, the sun, are busy with the preparation and consumption of meat, the stars already slowly return, as is in fact the case immediately following the sun's victory after the solstice, that is, in the form of a wolf, who, significantly, summons his companions from the south, the place called Tetamuyéwie ("where the stone hangs"), located south of Guadalupe Ocotán in the southernmost part of Huichol country.

II.
Travels Through the Land of the Huichol Indians of the Mexican Sierra Madre

(*Globus* 92 [10] pp. 167–71)

San Pedro, May 1, 1907

To a certain degree traveling becomes the ethnologist's nemesis from the moment he begins his work among tribal peoples. Not only does moving from place to place itself consume a great deal of valuable time, but one has to start over and over again to win the trust of the indigenous people, and repeatedly make a fresh start in the collection and integration of useful data in these new settings. In consideration of the time remaining and the virtually endless number of sacred songs still to be recorded I decided to stay put at Rancho San Isidro, where I had spent the rainy season of 1906, and continue working there with my Huichol informants. Otherwise I could not be certain that my material on the annual ceremonial cycle was complete. But come October and the beginning of the dry season and the new round of harvest ceremonies, my Huichol friends were less and less enthusiastic about working with me, and I myself wanted to see to what extent the ceremonies in other places differed from those nearby. My hope that along the way we might finish up with the recording of some texts already begun was dashed when only five days later my interpreter as well as the *cantador*, the knowledgeable shaman-singer who had been dictating the texts, quietly removed themselves. What they wanted to avoid was having to introduce me to their own people, which is also why they had resisted accompanying me in the first place, behavior that nevertheless did not prevent resumption of our collaboration following my return.

It was my intention to visit one by one all the main centers in the Huichol country, beginning on this initial excursion with the southwestern region.

I was told that a ceremony was to be held in the temple of Santa Gertrudis, a day's travel to the south. During my first visit in the rainy season the path there was completely deserted, but now I met groups of Huichols, their faces covered with bright red ceremonial paint and their hats decorated all over with flowers and feathers. Occasionally a particular kind of shrill call or a trumpetlike blast from a meter-long hollow wooden tube heralds the presence of bands of Indians on the move in connection with the ceremonies, to purchase food for themselves and for the fiestas, to prepare *vino*, and so on. From them I learned that first there was to be a ceremony at Guastita, an extensive ranchería in a western valley leading off the Río Chapalagana. And so the following day, just before reaching Santa Gertrudis we turned east.

Our previous southerly direction had taken us roughly along the border between the state of Jalisco and the territory of Tepic, between and parallel to the Rio de Jesús in the west and the Rio Chapalagana in the east. The former generally marks the boundary between the Cora and Huichol Indians, but in such a way that in between, flanking the eastern shore, there are several villages of Spanish-speaking Mexican *vecinos*, villages that were formerly inhabited by speakers of Cora or Nahua, respectively. The Chapalagana, on the other hand, cuts north-south almost through the very center of Huichol country and then flows, in a slightly westerly direction, into the Río Jesús María, about three days' travel above its confluence with the Rio Grande, which flows from west to east. Inasmuch as the mountain chains run primarily in a southerly direction, we had relatively smooth going on our way to Santa Gertrudis, at least once we had climbed to the top from the lower elevation of San Isídro. Especially toward the west for quite a while we had a particularly fine view across the lower mountains on the near side of the Rio de Jesús María to the high ranges from which one descends to the coast, for example to Toákamuta, which bounds the Mesa de Nayarit, flat as a table and rich in myth, with its numerous caves of the Cora and Huichol deities, to the notoriously frigid Sierra de Santa Terésa, the northernmost Cora pueblo, and to the even more elevated range of the Sierra de los Tepehuanes, which frames the view toward the north.

Turning eastward also meant surmounting the north-south mountain ranges. The whole region was extremely lonely and isolated: there were few distant views, and I encountered neither people nor ranchos, nor milpas, during a seven-hour-long ride, everywhere only large-leaved oaks and tall pines. Then the vista suddenly opened to the mountains bordering the Chapalagana, and before us lay the ranchería of Tierra Blanca, comprising some 20 households and already belonging to Guastita, which is more spread out and lies at a lower elevation. As luck would have it, when I started setting up my camp in front of the temple structure I found myself in the middle of a ceremony—the roasting of the *elotes*, the young maize cobs, which is usually appended to the preceding ceremony of the squashes and the cooking of the elotes.

This is not to be confused with the big ceremony of the esquites, the toasted maize, in March, although both feature the same chant and the same kind of dance around the fire. At this ceremony there are few rituals. However, for purposes of preventing illness it was combined with a ceremony for the rain goddess of the south, Tatéi Xapawiyemáka, Our Mother the Rain-giving Zaláte (an imposing and beautiful tree of the Sierra valleys), in whose honor a young bull had been sacrificed shortly before our arrival.

Evidently at this time of the year such curing ceremonies are more frequently held for the southern deities, because then the sun tarries in the south and is characterized in the myths as ill. In December in the temple of Santa Gertrudis I witnessed such an annually recurring curing ceremony for Tayáu, "Our Father," i.e. the Sun, and for Tamáts Haiwiyéme, Our Elder Brother, the Rain-giving Cloud, likewise a southern deity. The customary curing chant was sung all night long. A bull was sacrificed at dawn to each of the two deities, and while the meat soup was placed on the altar for the two gods the women threw maize dough balls, called *táuri*, sun, from east to west and north to south and back again across the altar of the Sun. One can imagine what a pleasure it was for me to find here too a kind of ball game that emulated the path of the Sun, inasmuch as the ancient Mexican ball game can be traced back to the same source.

First, before the beginning of the chant in Tierras Blancas, the deer meat soup, which had been bubbling in the big cooking pots all afternoon, was ceremoniously poured into the long row of jícaras and consumed. The beef soup was ready only after midnight. For it all the gods, some fifty in number, were invited in a lengthy prayer, each being named separately, with the constant repetition "*náite, náite*," meaning "all, all," because it was impossible to name every single one of the hundreds of different deities. Although, as mentioned, the ceremony was dedicated only to the one female deity, the jícaras with the meat and the tortillas were initially meant for all the gods and were displayed until dawn on the eastward-facing altar. To notify the gods a Huichol wearing the tail and horns of the sacrificed bull bellowed in the four directions in imitation of the bull at the place of sacrifice and at the altar. A clown wielding the horned staff of the old earth goddess and the penis of the bull carried on all night long, waking up those who had fallen asleep and by his own example calling on them to dance. Sometimes he wears a mask with long, white hair, which also associates him with the old goddess Takutsi Nakawé, Our Grandmother (Earth) the Growing One. In fact, the only mask I saw among the Huichols was one representing this goddess in Santa Catarína.

However, the *sikuáki's*, or clown's, summons to dance related less to the dance around the cantador and the fire that belongs to the ceremony of the roasting of the maize than to the hopping up and down in place to the rhythm of the native tunes of the violin and guitar, which are especially indispensable in observances for the saints or in the sacrifices of cattle, but which can also be found on other occasions, often in close proximity to the cantador. At the conclusion of ceremonies all the participants often dance in this style, their ceremonial objects in hand, and yet these pieces of music are completely secular inasmuch as they include a considerable repertoire of unmistakable love songs—I recorded fifteen of these—and the same melodies are also played at any hour of the day. Many a Huichol no more allows himself to be separated from his homemade violin than from his bow and arrows, and when they came to visit me in San Isidro I sometimes knew of their arrival from the sound of the violins, which they didn't stop playing even along the way.

The nightly processions around the fire with bundles of maize cobs attached to canes were over, the maize was ceremoniously offered to Tatewarí, Our Grandfather, and the sun was greeted. Now alcohol, in part in the form of a home brew distilled from *sotol*, a species of cactus related to the maguey, in part commercial liquor, came even more into its own. Already as the night wore on the mighty bass of the grizzled cantador, whose long white hair hung down over the shoulders, was becoming more and more animated under the influence of liquor. During the dances it was only with great effort was he able to keep himself on his feet. But this was the case with everybody. People danced with bottle in hand. The women too received their portion, because there was a lot of liquor around, and very soon the mood among them changed from one of easy amiability to overly loud demeanor. It all became a tangled confusion of the more than one hundred participants, and finally it came to blows that continued all the way back to their houses. Men and women were rolling on the ground, their hands buried in the long hair of their adversaries. Clothes were torn, bodies exposed.

And yet none of this put a halt even for a moment to the high spirits of those not directly involved. No weapons came into play. Everything was in keeping with the easily excitable, but harmless temperament of the Indians. If someone hit too hard he was tied to a tree, as I observed it during the following ceremony in Las Guasimas. The tethered hero, who incidentally had become stark naked, wept bitter tears and when he finally succeeded in freeing himself slunk home. In fact tears are very much the order of the day in the prayers during the ceremonies, and the easy excitability of the Huichols is also evident in the fact that some momentary agitation may be followed by suicide through hanging. In general, however, brawling does not conclude every ceremonial. For instance, I never saw anything like it during the many major ceremonies I witnessed in Santa Catarína, despite the prevailing drunkenness.

However, the gods themselves indulge in this infamous method of grabbing the adversary by the hair to bring him to his senses. In every chant at the beginning of night the fire god first summons Kauyumári, who personifies the deer and the stars, and who as divine messenger is supposed to deal with all the gods for whose sake the ceremony is being conducted. He always comes unwillingly, and then the fire god grabs him by the hair and drags him along the ground, whereupon he carries out his duties with all the formality and diligence that sometimes drives me to distraction in trying to set it down on paper. Just so, for example, wife No. 2, having first emerged as victor in a bout with the legitimate wife, only to lose a romp on the ground with the husband, was busy at work again a few hours later roasting squash seeds in her capacity as housewife. Because she was young and by Huichol standards pretty she could easily have gone to someone else, as indeed occurs almost daily without any further consequences.

Only late in the evening of the second day was I able to take a well-earned rest. The following morning it was up again and back along the same route to Santa Gertrudis, and because the promised ceremony was to take place only after another one in the Rancho las Guasimas had been completed, from there four hours westward straight down into a deep valley, where the high and dense crowns of guasima trees shaded a stream of considerable depth whose waters rushed downward over rocky ledges. Close by the four widely spaced little houses, along the steep slopes and, virtually springing from the rock itself, yellow maize stalks almost twice a man's height rustled softly in the wind. In vain did I look for the almost never missing hut for the gods, where the ceremonial paraphernalia and the souls of the dead are kept in the form of little stones. But my doubts whether any kind of ceremony would in fact be held here were soon dispelled by the arrival of the participants. One was carrying a box with a rolled-up image of the Virgin of Guadalupe, which nevertheless was never uncovered during the entire ceremony. They made do instead with a primitive wooden framework for an altar, which, by the way, later collapsed when people started fighting, and now for two nights running came the *danzantes*, a religious fraternity from the comunidad of San Andrés, whom the reader already got to know in the same get-up, complete with rattle, palm leaf and tall blue heron feather crown, in my report about the Cora Indians (cf. *Globus*, Vol. 90, p. 165). There they were identified as cloud beings, their leader, who wears a mask, being specifically credited in San Francisco with outstanding importance for the welfare of the pueblo. Among the Huichols, and also the Nahuat-speakers of San Pedro, where I saw the same characters, their meaning has been forgotten. The latter, however, wear paper crowns similar to those worn by gods and rulers among the Aztecs.

Here for the first time since my arrival among the Huichols I encountered hostility, evidently because my looking for a sacred structure was taken for prospecting for mines, and my photographing the landscape was likewise construed as a means of finding mines. By looking into the camera one was supposed to be able to discover mines. All Huichols are afraid that their lands will be taken from them, and for that reason greatly dislike seeing foreigners come into their country. Convinced of their rights to their land and used to serving and following the orders of their own elected authorities in the wider context of communal affairs, they also hold quite erroneous ideas about the power of their officials over strangers. So they wanted to prevent me from moving freely about or photographing the landscape, charge me one peso, equivalent to 2.12 German marks, for every day of my stay, and so on and so forth. That is the less surprising in that during this excursion the judge of Huajimic, a pueblo inhabited solely by *vecinos*, wanted to put me in jail because I photographed the church and because my purpose, the study of language and customs, appeared too bizarre. In this last case I did not have my letter of recommendation at hand because I had not intended to come so far. But for the native people, too, a recommendation from the government is often decisive, especially inasmuch as even among the Huichols there are two individuals who are able to read a little, one in Guadalupe Ocotán and one in Santa Catarína. In Las

Guasimas it was sufficient to suggest that one was sent "by the government" to cause those grumbling the loudest to make a special effort at the next ceremony in Santa Gertrudis, where the same people came together, to demonstrate their friendship, e.g. with gifts of tamales, etc.

A striking aspect of the ceremony was the large number of people blind from birth. There were no fewer than six of these men, and in one rancho we passed along the way there, there were three who were blind, meaning that of the approximately fifteen inhabitants that made up the rancho, twenty percent were without sight. Despite the steepness of the trail all six came down to the ceremony, and because of the surplus of women all six were married. Before a child is born the Huichols frequently make an offering of a jícara decorated with wax figures to their bat deity Katsi. These are meant to convey the wish that the new infant not be born blind.

Except for the absence of a bull sacrifice, the ceremony in Santa Gertrudis was identical to that in Tierras Blancas. Very few people showed up for it, despite the fact that here there is a large—and virtually solitary—temple. So I could finally continue my journey to the pueblo of Guadalupe Ocotán on the other side of the Rio Chapalagana. The trail now led further to the south. There beyond the river a broad valley now opened up with ever less steep and jagged mountain ranges: the way to Huajimic and further to Tepic. In contrast in the north on this side of the river there is the extensive high plateau of San Andrés, bounded in the south by a deep fissure running in an east-west direction. Around noon we descended to the river, where in place of oaks and pines we were suddenly engulfed by the same sort of mixed arboreal vegetation to which I had become accustomed in the broiling heat of the valley of the Río de Jesús María during my half year among the Cora. There is nothing so surprising for the traveler as this contrast between the frigid highlands, where the daytime temperature in winter fluctuates between +2 degrees and +20 degrees centigrade in the shade, and the hot river valley with 20 to 35 degrees centigrade, a contrast experienced during the descent in the course of little more than an hour. Because the rainy season had ended less than a month before, we found the trail so overgrown with woody vegetation that it required constant use of the machete, but the river itself, which in every rainy season claims its victims among the Huichols, had already fallen so low that the mules were in water only to the knee, although in all seasons there was enough space for sizeable crocodilians in the many shallows at the foot of perpendicular cliffs. We forded the river a few hours above its confluence with the Río de Jesús María. Everywhere its bed looked the same as I'd experienced it at other crossings: a deeply cut, narrow canyon, strewn with gigantic boulders, as different as could be from the broad valley of the Río de Jesús María.

Only by late evening did we reach the highlands again, and as often happened after river crossings, now we saw Santa Gertrudis, which we had left in the morning, lie there before us almost close enough to touch. After a quiet night in a rancho in front of the god house—only the second one we had seen all day—early the next morning we reached Guastita. Around a dozen widely scattered houses and an adobe church, but no temple, only gathering places for the festivities. Like their large and usually solitary temples, the pueblos of the Huichols are only ceremonial centers. Otherwise the ranchos are located near where people work, especially where the maize is planted. And like the temple, the church, like all churches in Cora and Huichol country, presumably constructed by the Jesuits at the time of the Conquest, some 200 years ago, was renovated in the eighteen fifties. Of the inhabitants, whom the only Huichol present called together, some were already dressed like Mexicans (vecinos). In any case, I managed to secure the services of the one literate Huichol living here with whom I might later practice my Huichol grammar.

But for now I felt real pressure to get back to the work I had started in San Isidro, especially inasmuch as I wanted to visit several places on the way back, and only the lack of rice, next to beans the most essential of my provisions, caused me to continue southward to Huajimic. My Mexican guide assured me it was only four hours away, but it took us all day to get there. The trail followed a broad valley, beside which a few scattered Huichol ranchos can also be found here in the gradually retreating and ever lower mountain chains. But after about three hours the last sizable settlement is left behind; instead of scattered milpas on the steep slopes one now sees broad fields worked with the plow, and instead of the occasional Huichol walking by himself, one meets up with numerous riders, because many horses and mules are raised here on the farms. Even the cattle nearest the settlements are here herded on horseback.

The whole year long I had never been so close to civilization as in Huajimic, located only three days' travel from Tepic. Then another day brought me close to Guadalupe, where we found a large ranchería, but—because of the harvest—again deserted. So it went all the way to the river; many of the houses had all their household goods and stores of maize, a sign that the inhabitants weren't far away. The narrow doorways were barred with spiny branches to keep cattle out, with cattle dung piled up to show if anyone had entered in the meantime.

We forded the river further north, above the former crossing, and then four hours later reached the heavily settled valley of Guastita, perhaps the richest region in the whole Huichol country, where we found many people busy harvesting in the maize fields. Some still had twine strung to protect the maize against the ravens. Everywhere beside the huts there were great mounds of pumpkins, and huge cylindrical containers of giant bamboo were filled to the brim with maize cobs. Later the maize will be shelled and stored in elevated circular bins of stone and clay roofed with zacate and supported by a low frame of wooden poles. Everywhere there is hustle and bustle. A number of Mexicans are tenaciously waiting for an opportunity to trade cattle.

I set up my tent at a rancho of two acquaintances from the ceremony at Tierras Blancas, which though higher up belongs more or less to Guastita. The two were brothers in their early twenties and married to two sisters. Each had his little house. Such sororal marriages in close proximity is common among the Huichols, just as the inhabitants of a rancho tend to be closely related to one another. But there can be tragedy even in such idyllic arrangements. In one rancho in Santa Catarína one brother murdered the other because he envied him for a few cows his wife had brought as dowry: his own wife's cattle the killer had wasted, while those of his brother were growing in number. The former was a shaman named Pablo, the same one who some years back had performed valuable services for Carl Lumholtz. At the moment he was in prison, and so I was unable to work with him, as I had hoped.

As luck would have it, during the night there was a curing ceremony in the rancho. I already knew the shaman from a visit in San Isidro. I asked in vain who was sick. "We are all sick," was the usual reply. It was a question of one of the general curing ceremonies that are more often held during the winter months. Here it consisted only of a curing chant within the immediate family circle, without any larger effort, such as a cattle sacrifice. Although there are curanderos who cure without singing, only by sucking all sorts of foreign objects from the body of the patient, most curing is done with a night-long chant by the shaman who sings at the ceremonies. I have recorded six of these curing chants:

1. The common curing song in which the divine messenger Kauyumári, Deer and Morning Star, in a manner of speaking determines by questioning all the gods that there is no illness. In other words, mainly a prophylactic measure.
2. The song for a serious illness, in which the gods reveal who sent the sickness and what sacrifice is required for the cure.
3. The curing of people and livestock after the death of an elder. It is assumed of such an individual that, out of spite, before expiring he called into being an *itáuki*, a disease-causing animal.
4. The curing of the earth when it fails to bring forth sufficient fruit. This takes place especially at the onset of the rainy season.
5. The curing of rain; this is done during the rainy season with the purpose of bringing down the waters.
6. The curing of the gods, conducted especially when they fail to provide sufficient rain, and only after several years have passed.

Most of these involve the killing of the above-named mythological animal, the itáuki, which can be seen only by the singer; afterwards it is shown to ordinary mortals only in the form of maize kernels, a hair of a cow, and suchlike. The killing is done by hurling a feathered arrow symbolizing an arrow shot from a bow. This is an arduous undertaking, in which the singer falls shaking and vomiting to the ground, at least in the song. This act was demonstrated for me repeatedly out of sheer pleasure, even by a shaman. In this case the singer acts as proxy of the god Xuráwetamai, the "Star Boy" who is the best shooter and who evidently is the Morning Star, because when the sun comes up he also slays the deer, that is, the other stars, just as I described it earlier from the Cora.

During the curing ceremony in Guastita just before dawn the shaman spat all around the darkened patio, stroked the different household objects, especially the maize storage containers of bamboo, with his ceremonial arrow, and, while singing, hurled it in the different directions, after which he picked it up again without discovering anything or killing it. Afterwards my Huichols from San Isidro said that nothing like this is ever done among them. In the half-light of dawn he then began to suck on the different people who had come to lie down where he was singing. Otherwise he never moved from his place in the patio, always facing east, interrupting his chant each time I came near him with a most good-natured, "Give me a cigarette!"

The day before I looked in vain for the two large temples reported by Lumholtz, who also notes two Guastitas close together. There were only different private god houses and the ruins of a chapel that was established thirty or forty years ago from the direction of Guadalupe. However, a temple with the name Kiéremanáwe was said to be located higher up, and the following day I did indeed find it after a ride of about an hour. Like most it stood completely alone and there was little to be found here. So I made do without a visit to the only other temple, in Popotita, that was of interest to me, and two days later reached San Isidro by the familiar route.

My second three-week excursion to the northwestern part of the Huichol country, particularly to San Andrés, had very different purposes from the first. It was January and at this time no ceremonies were to be expected. As was the case already for the past three years, the only ceremony, the transfer of offices to the new officials, proceeded solely with a drinking bout among the few officials to show up. Instead I was hoping to remain in San Andrés for some time so as to record some texts and, through systematic study of the surrounding temples and god houses, become familiar with the ceremonial paraphernalia of the gods and the many sacrificial offerings and acquire them for my collection (Figures 15–20). The fact is that there are usually some little huts dedicated to specific deities beside the temples, and in part also quite distant but still part of the same complex, filled with votive arrows, chairs, jícaras, resting places called tepári, beds (itári), things for "seeing" and "countenances" (niérika), with crosses and the related tsikuri, with the woven rods used to prevent evil, and so forth. All these objects the gods brought with them when they, like those of the Aztecs, emerged from the underworld in the west and set out toward the east. The gods require all these things for the maintenance of the world, and it is up to human beings to renew it. In addition the efficacy of the gods and the desires of people find expression through the embellishment of these objects with images of wax, beads and wool, etc. On the other hand, things that are required for the ceremonies are often stored in the temples or else in the little god houses of the rancho in front of which the ceremonies are performed.

This time I was accompanied by Ramón, a young Huichol nineteen years of age, who spoke tolerable Spanish. He was already the "real" father of a child that in the meantime had died from a scorpion sting—"real" because with husband and wife fre-

FIGURE 15. Wooden Stepped Pyramidlike Model of "Stairway of the Sun." Located in a steep canyon within the *comunidad indígena* of Santa Catarína, Teakáta, the most sacred place in the Huichol sierra, is the site of numerous cave shrines and god houses dedicated to the major deities. Huichols readily part with such offerings once they have served their purpose. (*Collected by Konrad Theodor Preuss in 1907 at Teakáta. H. 5½". Museum für Völkerkunde, Berlin-Dahlem. Photograph by Peter T. Furst.*)

quently so very young, the first child is often fathered by somebody else—and I owed his company largely to the fact that he was getting a daily beating from his fifteen-year-old better half. Already on the occasion of a ceremony in Santa Barbara I was startled to see the young wife, lustily swinging a big stick, pursuing him at top speed round and round the house that was their home. But it took her grabbing him by the hair during the dance inside the temple and his complaining to me about his troubles for me to understand the situation. Apart from this he was actually braver than his fellows, in that on several occasions he got me people to take me to the temples, god houses and caves and in company with them sold me objects that came from them. This sort of business really became fully legitimate only during my third visit to Santa Gertrudis,

FIGURE 16. Niérika. This object, woven of thin sticks and wool yarn, serves as a kind of portal to the Otherworld. (*Collected by Konrad Theodor Preuss at San José from the god house of the Sun. Photograph by Peter T. Furst.*)

where the two highest temple officers, those serving the fire god Tatewarí and the sun god Tayaupá, took me, with the complete acquiescence of the governing officials of the comunidad, and after I had distributed gratuities to everyone, to the many places of the gods, and allowed me to come away with far more than I had ever dared hope. The fact was, of course, that the real owners of the objects were the many people who had made pilgrimages to these sacred places. Fortunately, once offerings have been given to the gods the Huichols themselves no longer put much value or meaning on them, so that I never got into any serious conflict with them on this account.

I was especially interested in two ceremonial huts in the neighborhood of San Andrés, because I knew about them from the chant that was sung during the ceremony of the roasting of the elotes. As I mentioned in my earlier report, the young ears of maize are portrayed as tewainuríxe by young boys and girls two to five or six years old and led by the divine messenger to where the sun comes up, clearly in reenactment of the first journey of the gods from the underworld to the dawn. On this journey they pass all the important places where the gods rested on their way to the east. The chant places special importance on the hut that is jointly dedicated to the messengers of the gods Kauyumári and Párikuta Muyéka ("he who wanders about at the end of the

FIGURE 17. Temple Offerings Representing the Wooden Box. In the Huichol version of the deluge myth, the Great-grandmother Nakawé saved Watákame (Clearer of Fields), his female dog companion, and the seeds of beans and the five colors of maize from the cataclysmic flood that drowned a previous creation. The spirals represent the swirling waters and the circular peregrinations of Nakawé paddling Watákame's craft. (*Purchased by Konrad Theodor Preuss at the temple of Santa Catarína. L. of box 8⅝". Museum für Völkerkunde, Berlin-Dahlem. Photograph by Peter T. Furst.*)

night", i.e. the Morning Star). These two deities are one and the same, except that the first is venerated more in the west and the second more in the east in Santa Catarína. The other is the god house of the Sun. Although they stand in complete isolation, I was successful in locating both, and I was able to obtain many things from them. But I also brought many things home from the other structures—four temples and some thirty god houses—even though most of them turned out to be completely empty.

This time in San Andrés counts among my most pleasant memories of the Huichol Sierra. The pueblo is located on a high plateau, and it is possible to ride for many hours north as well as south without having to scale any great heights. It is only to the south that one soon comes up against the deep east to west rift in which the temple of Las Guayabas is located, and toward the east the terrain slowly descends toward the Río Chapalagana, whose canyon one reaches in about three hours. Lofty oaks and pine trees soar park-like to the sky, and between them swaying zacate grass so high that in the rainy season the mules disappear in it. Here and there quietly browsing deer come into view, flocks of the large, loudly cawing, iridescent red and blue guacamayos fly overhead, and when one sets out in the morning the little birds the Huichols call *situi* give their incessant call, "túi, túi," which in Aztec means, "let's go, let's go!" No sooner is the sun above the horizon than its rays fall on this strip of earth as though to indemnify it for the cold of night, less severe in the valleys but also slower to depart.

East-northeast from my rancho San Isidro one reaches the top of San Andrés already

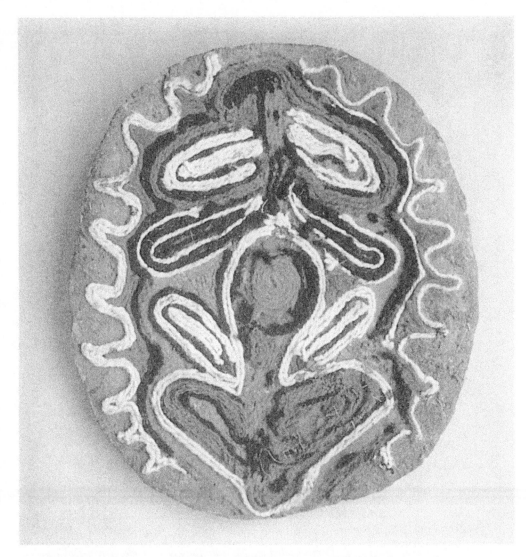

FIGURE 18. Wooden Niérika Decorated with Wool Yarn Design of Birds Pressed into Beeswax. Ceremonial objects such as this are the forerunners of the modern Huichol yarn painting. (*Collected by Konrad Theodor Preuss in 1907 from the cave shrine of Tatewarí, Grandfather Fire, at Teakáta. D. 8⅝". Museum für Völkerkunde, Berlin-Dahlem. Photograph by Peter T. Furst.*)

in more or less the middle of an eleven-hour ride; here, too, is the watershed between the Río de Jesús María and the Chapalagana. On the right hand one sees the volcano Ceboruco, across whose lava flow the *coche* took me in November 1905 from San Martin, the last railway station, to Tepic, towering threateningly over the entire Sierra.

San Andrés itself has a temple that stands within the pueblo. The two in the north, Coameata and San José, as well as the temple of Las Guayabas in the south, stand all alone. The temple of San José, the largest in the whole Huichol country, was struck by lightning every year for five years, and each time the roof was constructed anew following the rainy season. Both the diameter of the circular substructure, unusual for being made of adobe, and the overall height are more than twelve meters. From there

the emergence and entry holes of the gods in the temple. This disk was collected from the temple at Santa Catarína. (*D. 7⅞". Preuss Collection, Museum für Völkerkunde, Berlin-Dahlem. Photograph by Peter T. Furst.*)

northward it takes only about four hours to get to the Río Chapalagana, where way down the above-mentioned god house of the Sun is located, and four hours is also the distance from San José to San Andrés. On the way to the god house of the Sun one also passes the place where the Earth Mother Takutsi, who here, as in Aztec Mexico, is at the same time the Moon, was slain by the Kakauyárite, the mountains and ancestors of the people—these are at one and the same time the gods and also the stars: a transparent lunar myth. A stone yoke symbolizes the goddess, another, elongated, rock is her staff and a hole in it the place where her heart, which was not found in the body of the goddess, was extracted. At this place too the Huichols have deposited some offerings. Having arrived at the gradient of the river, diagonally across from where the temple of Pochotita stands on the uplands of the other shore, in the afternoon, I started the precipitous descent in the company of my three Huichols in the first grey light of dawn, so

FIGURE 20. Prayer Offerings in the Form of Miniature *Uwénis*. These shaman's chairs also serve the deities, particularly the Sun, for whom the great shaman, Grandfather Fire, made such a chair to carry the Sun across the sky after his first appearance from a mountain in Wirikúta. *Left*, a tiny model chair Preuss collected at Teakáta, the most sacred place in the Sierra; *right*, a sixteen-inch-high miniature uwéni, from the temple at Las Guyabas, in the territory of San Andrés. (*Museum für Völkerkunde, Preussischer Kulturbesitz, Berlin-Dahlem. Photograph by Peter T. Furst.*)

as to be able, if at all possible, to begin my work down below before the sun had risen very high into the sky. I reached the hut with shaking knees, but a quick look revealed that I had attained my real goal, namely to find a large number of the large disks of woven rods called nierikas, some twenty to forty centimeters in diameter. These are the specialty of this ceremonial house; elsewhere one finds them only in ones or twos. True, I did see some very beautiful ones in the Sierra de Nayarit in a cave of the western rain goddess Kiewimúka, but under the watchful eyes of the much more critical Cora Indians it was impossible to take any of them away with me. Farther down below, but relatively close by, is a cave of the Sun, but it contains few objects. In four hours' time we were back on top and were able to get back to San Andrés by nightfall.

The trail to the temple of Las Guayabas leads past the place where in former times the Huichols used to tie criminals together and roll them down into the abyss. But with a mule it is possible to get down into the valley. There lived the richest man among the Huichols, the owner of several hundred head of cattle . . . From his sons alone I purchased about a hundred marks' worth of decorated sashes, bags, armbands, etc., in which the Huichols are so very rich. But this wealthiest of men also had the most outstanding harem, namely six young women in addition to the legitimate one. All lived peacefully together, which is all the more remarkable in that polygamy is by no means common practice among the Huichols, to whom, on the contrary, the songs promise many cattle as reward for abstaining from other women for five years—their sacred number. Drinking and carrying on with women are essentially the only transgressions which the Huichols, like the Aztecs, consider to be sinful.

In San Andrés, as earlier in Jesús María, I made my home with the priest in the convent of the church; generally speaking I owe much of my success to having made contact with the padres. Among the Huichols at the moment there are two padres, who have already lived there for six years, one in San Andrés and one in San Sebastian. They belong to the Order of the Josefinos in Zacatécas, although politically the Sierra Huichol lies almost exclusively in the state of Jalisco. San Andrés is the only place where I can judge the effectiveness of the church, which up to the present time is equivalent to nil, though admittedly only for the casual observer. For the moment the padre has wrested the church from them, because they deal with the building, along with Christ and the saints, exactly as they do with their temples and their gods. It is almost impossible to imagine the hullabaloo that filled the church of Santa Catarína during the so-called Pachita observances.

This is because the Huichols have a relationship of real intimacy with their gods. They devote a truly enormous part of their lives to them, and they take great pride in this relationship. The gods developed from the basic idea that there are at least of them as many as there are people. A different name immediately signifies another deity. I was even told that even a deity of the same name need not always mean the same god, because as among people, the same name crops up again and again among the gods. No wonder that each Cristo, each María, each image of a saint has his or her special name, that jícaras and votive arrows are made for each, that bulls are sacrificed for each, and that there are individual chants for each. Even before the Sun has been created, Christ, going by the name Tewari Yuráme, roams over the Sierra as a culture hero, pursued by Jews. Similarly everything they know of the saints has been completely reworked to make it fit into their own world view. Only with time, when Mexicans have settled everywhere among them and they have become more accustomed to the latter's beliefs and the customs of the church, can one expect any real transformation. Already there are five Mexican families in the pueblo and two in the vicinity, whereas in Santa Catarína only the teacher is a Mexican. His efforts, by the way, are to all intents and purposes in vain.

III.

Sacred Songs and Myths of Some Tribal Peoples of the Mexican Sierra Madre

From *Archiv für Religionswissenschaft*, Vol. XI, pp. 369–398, 1908.

Translator's Note: The opening passages of the following essay have been condensed and slightly rearranged to eliminate repetition, and a lengthy section relating Sierra Morning Star mythology to the myth of Quetzalcóatl of Tollan (Tula) abbreviated to conserve space.

In the course of my residence in the Sierra Madre Occidental between 1905 and 1907 I recorded a total of 296 myths, legends and stories, all in the native languages—49 from the Coras, 69 Huichol and 178 Mexicano.

Singing goes on virtually without interruption during all the native ceremonies, most of which last all night and sometimes part of the following day. I was privileged to observe twenty complete pagan ceremonies and was actually able to record, in the original language, the chants of all those that take place in the pueblos and ranchos. This does not include ceremonial practices connected with the Catholic Church; besides, for the most part these do not involve singing. I will therefore not deal with them and in the following pages limit myself to the presentation of the ceremonies and with it, by way of the songs and prayers, the Indian religion itself. The myths themselves are eminently suited to give us some understanding of belief, inasmuch as the nature deities and their naming is a prime concern of a major part of them, just as many chants also contain mythic elements. For this reason I will refer to some of them.

The degree to which not only the sacred chants but also the myths and tales have remained untouched is nothing short of amazing, considering that by 1722 the Cora country was already conquered by the Spaniards, followed by the entry of the Jesuits and the construction of churches. To be sure, there was no consistent missionary activity thereafter, and in recent times, too, there has been only sporadic and halfhearted missionizing. Even the few myths of saints and Christ have been completely swamped by pagan concepts, and it would be a great loss for the study of religion if the only Huichol chant devoted to the saints, conducted as it is completely in the style of the rest of the pagan ceremonial chants, were left out. It is only among the Mexicano that a few mythic motifs of European origin have become widely disseminated.

However much they may differ in the performance of ceremonies, and also their number, the three tribal peoples, Cora, Huichol and Mexicano, constitute, among themselves and also with the Aztecs, an ideological unity, so that rather than racking his brain when something puzzles him in the ceremony of one group, the investigator is better off looking for explanations in the comparable ceremony of another. In the interest of space, however, I will here have to limit myself to one group, the Huichols, with only an occasional reference to explanatory material from the other two peoples.

During the ceremonies of the Huichols the singer is always seated facing east. On his right and left, respectively, sit two assistants who, together but without waiting for one another, repeat each phrase whenever the singer makes a pause. So it goes all night long, from about 8 p.m. to sunup, virtually without interruption and without division of the chant into sections. It is not a series of individual songs but a single chant, or rather for the most part a sort of melodious recitation, without the singer, however, adhering strictly to the text. The monotony is the greater in that, with the exception of the ceremony of the peyote or the esquite in March, there is no dance step to the songs and, with the exception of the mentioned rituals, also no dancing. Only at the ceremony of the squashes in October, effectively the harvest ritual, is there rythmless dancing around the fire, a few steps forward and then again, without turning, a few steps slightly sideways and backward. In the ceremony in June called Haxári Kuáixa (eating of cakes made of coarse maize), and the sowing ritual that follows it closely, there is relaxed dancing, or more accurately, walking, around the fire. The rhythm of the song simply doesn't tempt one to dance. During these three ceremonies the singer pounds the indigenous skin drum, which resembles the Aztec *huehuetl*, with his hand, producing a monotonous beat, and in the harvest ceremony of the squashes the young children who impersonate the tender squashes carry rattles. Otherwise the singer chants without musical accompaniment.

Let us now turn to the content of the songs, which also tells us most clearly what is going on in the rituals. With the exception of that of the sowing ritual, which begins in the morning, all of the songs begin with a summons to Kauyumári, the deer and divine messenger—as we will see, evidently the Morning Star—to come from his house at the eastern end of the world. This begins with a dialogue about the impending cere-mony between the singer and the fire burning in the center of the temple, that is, with its manifestation as the old fire god Tatewarí, Our Grandfather, who ordinarily lives in the earth beneath the hearth. But Tatewarí (speaking through the shaman-singer) declares that he cannot do it alone, and dispatches two feathers, that is, two muviéri, the feathered ceremonial arrows or staffs. The feathered messengers find Kauyumári asleep in a darkened room enclosed by magic feathers, guarded by jaguars, mountain lions and poisonous snakes. The feathers touch him on the feet. But he is not at all disposed to heed the summons to the ceremony, pleading indisposition as his excuse, which may be malaria, or a head cold, or pain in his feet. His wife further reinforces his determination to stay home. When he finally does decide to go he can't find his ceremonial arrows. His wife fusses over him and fits him out with everything he needs for the journey, all the while admonishing him not to take up with other women.

Following these domestic scenes, which, to the great delight of the Huichol audience the singer always embellishes further, after passing several way stations he arrives in the temple. There he immediately takes a firm hand in bargaining with the gods, calling them in, presenting them with the case at hand, and negotiating with them on how best to remedy whatever needs putting to rights. He is also the last to leave the scene of action. But this he must do before sunup, because he fears the Sun, and if the ceremony takes longer, he has to ask him for permission. All this takes place solely in the form of the chant, for neither does one see the god, nor are there more than a few inconspicuous ritual gestures, such as lifting the feather wands, turning to the cardinal directions, and the like. Among the Cora it is also the Morning Star, called Hatsikán, "Elder Brother," represented by a small boy, who brings off the ceremonies, the Coras being very much aware that the god is Deer and at the same the Morning Star. There, too, the concluding ceremony is the dance of a deer that hurries back to its house in the mountains before the sun comes up. But among the Cora, who make this explicit, and also among the Huichols, deer are the likenesses of stars, and Kauyumári, as mentioned, is also deer.

The last of the annual ceremonies is the sowing ritual, which accounts for its name, Hewásiixe, meaning "the last." Then at the end of June or in early July the rainy season begins, and with it in a certain sense the new year, manifested in the sprouting of the new maize on which human existence depends. The next concern now is for plenty of rain, because the water quickly drains away from the maize fields and down the rocky slopes, and the young crops can easily wither in the sun. This is why rain ceremonies are held as needed, to call up the rain. At such a ritual the gods appear at Kauyumári's summons and, and at once make known what they want to be done for them before they are ready to provide rain. Not only do they require offerings of food, the soup or meat of a bull, or maize beer, but even more do they expect the magical objects they need for their functions or that in and of themselves have magical powers. These include prayer arrows; gourd bowls with sacred symbols; paraphernalia for seeing (nieríkas), consisting of starlike symbols woven of rods and wool with a hole in the center; candles and the like, or, finally, animals and plants that are sacred to the respective deities and with which they are occasionally identified.

The eastern rain goddess Tatéi (Our Mother) Naariwáme, for example, desires the image of a mythical monster that lives in the sea and that is said to resemble a steer. Of a terrible thunderstorm it is said that the Hakayuka animal is turning up the ground and making mischief. The maize goddess Utuanáka wants a catfish that is conceived as a snake and that corresponds to the prototype of the goddess as the water snake Háiku. The earth mother Takutsi Nakawé (Our Grandmother, the growing one), who is at the same time the Moon, demands a small species of agave cactus that grows among the rocks, a jicama or camote root; a lizard; a peccary, and an image of the ark in which the only man to survive the deluge saved himself. It was this goddess who at that time announced the flood and guided the canoe through the waters, which is why such an offering is still regarded to this day as capable of bringing rain. The Sun, from which in the last analysis all rain is thought to come, evidently because the rainy season begins with the summer solstice, requires among other things a god house at the place of his birth, the place of dawn (many deities have their own special god houses outside the larger communal temple throughout the Huichol country).

One is now under the impression that the song is ended, that everyone's wishes have been assured of fulfillment, and Tamatsi Ékatewári, "Our Elder Brother Wind," who resides in the east in company with the rain mother Naariwáme, has promised to stay no longer "in front of his mother" and thus prevent her from coming up. Then suddenly the goddess herself speaks: I am afraid of the rainbow, I cannot go. Before my door in the mountains a sorcerer has covered up the waters. He has planted an arrow in the north, another in the south and another in the center. And despite his promise, Ékatewári, the wind who scatters the cloud of Naariwáme, is here. Kauyumári sets out for the place of the harmful arrows and does away with them by shooting at them with his own magical feathered arrow. He tames the wind by pouring *tumári*, maize meal mixed with water. When he returns Kauyumári hears a noise. It comes from an *itáuki*, a magical creature that emerges from the fire. It impedes the rain-making work of the gods and makes them and people sick.

The itáuki, a term signifying only something hidden, is also the work of the sorcerer. It roars like a lion, can fly buzzing through the air, and is killed by sticking arrows in the ground all around the fire and slowly moving them closer and closer to the flames. Kauyumári asks Xuráwetámai, Star Boy, who, like the Morning Star Boy of the Coras, is an expert bowman, for his arrows, that is, his feathered staffs, and slays the itáuki. But the hunt is a tremendous strain, the marksman falls to the ground and water is poured over his head. This scene is in fact played out in reality, except that the cantador (singing shaman) takes the role of Kauyumári, who is no more visible to the naked eye than is Xuráwetámai. While alive the itáuki manifests itself only to the singer, but afterwards it is shown also to the others in the form of wax candles, hairs, maize, arrows, and the like.

This is also the time of private rituals to free the fields from magic spells that have impeded the growth of the crops. These also have their lengthy chants. The fire god explains a sorcerer has thrown maize at him—i.e., the flames. Here, too, the magic must be removed by killing the itáuki in the manner described above. The goddess

Yurienáka, the moist earth, is ill and is cured in the same way through the killing of the itáuki.

The most remarkable thing, however, is that at certain long intervals, let's say every ten years or so, at the onset of the rainy season, or shortly thereafter, it is the entire enormous company of the gods that becomes the object of a curing ritual. Their illness manifests itself in their not giving sufficient rain, and, as usual, the drawn-out all-night chant that is sung for this purpose explains the process of healing. In the main it differs little from the usual curing rituals. The fire god Tatewarí blows smoke from his tobacco pipe over the god who has just laid himself down for the cure, and his assistant Kauyumári sucks the foreign object that caused the illness, a stone, for example, from his body. As a rule there is again also the killing of the itáuki, which sometimes seems itself to have entered the patient's body. In this song it is said of the gods that they are praying.

Inasmuch as there is actually no formal prayer as such, one can see how much power is attributed to words alone. The chant also has to replace a great many actions to which in the song there are only allusions, and that hence are in and of themselves imbued with magical power. Actions mentioned in the chant are frequently without corresponding rituals, even some of the offerings may be presented in word alone rather than in fact, and it is very likely that this is not all that different from the way it used to be in the past.

The corresponding ceremony to this curing of the gods in Aztec times is the ritual of the dumplings cooked in water (*atamal qualiztli*), which was observed every eight years in October, and in which the foodstuffs, meaning all the deities, rested through strict fasting, the desired effect being rain. This is underscored by the fact that despite the presence of all the deities, the principal participants in this ceremony were the rain deity Tlaloc and the little mountain and rain gods.

These three ceremonies, the rain ritual, the curing of the earth, and the healing of the gods, are, as stated, not absolutely essential. Rather, the first ceremony of the year is celebrated at the time of the clearing of the fields, its proper name being the Washing of the Gourd Bowls, the sacred jícaras. I think it is actually not the clearing of the fields of weeds and brush that determines the timing of this ceremony, but rather the sprouting of the seeds. The gods are awaiting their maize. Its renewal creates the impression that all the ceremonial objects, especially votive arrows and gourd bowls, have to be made anew. The gods require this and they want their maize, because they were the owners of all these things when they came from the west, from the underworld; they left them to human beings and the latter bear the responsibility for their renewal.

It is said that when people make such sacred objects the deity is giving them its own property. Not only are such offerings deposited in the houses, caves and other sacred places of the gods, but each rancho owns one or more gourd bowls, arrows, etc., for specific deities, especially Tatei Niwétsika, Our Mother Maize. The jícaras are not newly made, however, but only washed, which is done in the morning following the night-long singing, and, sunlight notwithstanding, by the light of candles. It is this that gives the whole ceremony its name. There are many allusions in the chant to washing off the "earth," meaning dirt, and I was told that the earth is the transgression through which the jícara became soiled, specifically sexual transgression, apart from which there really are no others. These are ideas that correspond completely to those of the Aztecs. Perhaps not coincidentally, the jícaras symbolize the vagina, just as it is the women in whose care they are during the ceremony.

The harvest rituals begin in the first days of October. The most important one is that of the squashes, preceded by five days by the ceremony of the earth goddess Takutsi Nakawé and followed five days later by that of the elotes, the tender maize cobs. The earth goddess is the first to receive her tribute of young squash plants and *jilotes*, the maize cobs on which the kernels have not yet formed. On the whole, however, what is expressed in the two last chants is only the pleasure of the gods at the endeavors having been crowned with success, and about their harmonious collaboration in the coming of rain.

Some unusual ideas manifest themselves in the harvest ceremony of the squashes. By way of exception it is celebrated during the day from sunup to sundown. This is then followed from nightfall to dawn by a second chant that in the main repeats that sung during daylight. Very probably the change to daytime was done out of practical considerations, because the young squashes are represented by little children aged one to six who must continually shake their rattles. They sit in the hot sun on both sides of the cantador who, facing east, beats the drum with his hand. At the eastern end of the plaza stands a post with a belt called *uíwa* hanging from it, beneath which, in addition to the offerings and magical arrows, the new fruits of the field have been placed with their slender end facing east, their number corresponding to that of the children. The idea behind this is that these fruits or, more correctly, the children, are traveling to the place of dawn, Paríyakutsie, "the end of the night," or Taurúnita, the "land of light," to show themselves to the innumerable deities who during their primordial journey from the underworld in the west to the east took up their abodes everywhere in the whole world in the form of mountains (Kakauyárite), etc. . . .

In the chant that is sung at their harvest ritual, the contemporary Mexicanos whom I visited say that the maize cobs, Our Mother (Tonantsi), ascend weeping to the sky. In the corresponding song of the Cora, (in cooking) the fire kills the maize, the son of Our Mother (Itaté Yaura). In the chant that follows, the Evening Star, Sáutari, appears in the sky and informs all the gods that he did not die after all. The Aztecs also conceived of the maize god as a star in the sky, in a cyclical drama of the vegetation deity's springtime descent from the sky in the form of a star, and the celestial ascent of the maize goddess in the fall that I treated elsewhere in some detail (cf. K. T. Preuss, "Der dämoniscvhe Ursprung des griechischen Dramas," *Ilbergs Jahrbuch*, Vol. XVIII, pp. 165 ff.). Now, the Huichol songs sometimes allude to the fire spirit Timuxáwe, the god who planted the first milpa. In the mythology, this god marries a young earthly woman, prepares an enormous maize field that yields a rich harvest, even though the only thing he had to sow was chaff. His mother-in-law is nonetheless dissatisfied with him for no reason at all, so that he returns once more into the sky. The Mexicanos have the same myth, in which the hero is even explicitly called Morning Star, who, to the sound of weeping from the people, ascends as evening star from the ceremonial plaza into the sky during the ritual of the elotes. So the hero is not only the fire that causes maize to sprout, but maize itself, just as in the Cora song. As his helpers the chant names the deer, that is, the rest of the stars, whom all three peoples conceive as deer.

Our tewainuríxe, that is, the squashes, will no doubt now also start out on their flight through the sky to the east, even though the chant describes at great length how they visit the gods one after the other in their terrestrial places. The sash that hangs down from the post is the special symbol of the celestial journey of the tewainuríxe, standing as it does for the path along which they travel. The sash was a gift of the Sun, just as their entire outfit came from the solar deity. Dressed as an eagle he speaks to the tewainuríxe, and two eagles, represented by two men, accompany them on their journey. But their guide is the "yellow arrow (urú muxáure)," allegedly so called because the maize stalks become yellow, or—in another community—Tatutsí Máxa Kwaxí, Great-grandfather Deer Tail, another fire god, the personification of the sacred deer tail. He puts them all in a jícara, which "swims" eastward, stopping everywhere at the places of the gods.

Unfortunately we are unable to accompany them on their adventurous journey, nor even listen to the myths that are sung about the gods they visit, or how the water became red when the sky goddess Wáxe Uimári, the "pretty maiden," had her first menstruation, or how the rain goddess of the east, Tatéi Naariwáme, transformed into a cloud. Instead I must turn to the singular rituals of the peyote pilgrims, which commence soon after the harvest rituals, toward the end of October, and continue until the peyote ceremony or the ritual of the esquite, respectively—the latter also a kind of harvest rite—around March. I will also only touch briefly on the ceremonies that fall in between, the cooking of the maize cobs and the ceremony of the Sun, because at the former the same chant is sung as at the feast of the esquite, and at the latter a curing chant that actually has little to do with the sun and with which I will deal later, along with others of the same kind.

It is likely that there is much illness especially during the winter months and that the Sun itself seems weakened, so that one must come to its assistance through offerings and magical actions. For example, at this time the women throw little balls of corn dough called táuri, Sun, from north to south and east to west and back again across the altar of the Sun. This certainly supports the suggestion in the pictorial manuscripts that the ancient Mesoamerican ballgame reenacts the course of the sun and not that of the moon. It is also during this ceremony that the rising of the sun is formally celebrated and extolled in a chant that tells how the Sun god called forth the yellow rattlesnake (dawn), how he loosed his arrow among the deer (the stars), and, after traveling across the sky, will be received by the western solar deity Sakaimúka and, finally, by Tatei Haramára, "Our Mother the Ocean." This apparently is also already a kind of magical spell for the coming spring, just as the Aztecs also performed the bloody battle between Sun and stars in November during the feast of Panquetzaliztli.

The rituals of the peyote hunt are set forth above all in a narrative that has the form of a chant, consisting mainly of a series of dialogues—one might even characterize them in part as prayers—that occupy the entire journey from departure to return. The relatively short song that is sung at the destination and following the return also contains much of interest. Each temple district sends some twelve or more men on a six-week journey far off into the eastern desert, to the vicinity of the town called Catorce, where they collect the cactus known as peyote, whose effect is both invigorating and intoxicating. They are led by the old fire god, Tatewarí, Our Grandfather, who is joined by three other gods, in Santa Catarína, for example, (principally) the Sun god. Remaining behind in the temple is the *itáuri*, a man who represents the sacred staff, *itáuri*, of the gods, and who day by day unties one of the 42 to 43 knots in a cord, each representing one day. The leader of the pilgrims carries an identical knotted cord which he similarly unties.

In accord with the sacredness of the entire ceremony, the participants must observe the strictest ritual purity. This is achieved through much fasting, abstention from washing and bathing, and abstention from sex. More than that, along the way they must name each and every one of all the women and girls—true, these are mostly younger men—with whom they have had sex. For each so named a knot is made in a cord representing the individual concerned, and all these cords are burned at the end of the confession. It is said that this sometimes involves beatings and food deprivation—perhaps now less so than in former times—when someone refuses to tell the truth. In addition he is punished with death by the gods, who cause him to become confused while eating peyote, leading him off to die miserably, something that may indeed happen in reality.

Before I became aware of these ways of achieving ritual purity, I did not completely understand why my Indians regarded sexual transgressions as the only sin and did not include murder or robbery, for example, in this category. The Huichols are anything but chaste, and yet their chants frequently allude to the need of limiting themselves to one wife, with the expectation that this might bring great wealth in cattle. When all is said and done, sexual continence is supposed to guarantee success, in other words, confer special powers. The whole idea is sometimes expressed with great humor in myths in which, just before a difficult undertaking, a goddess beds herself down completely naked in front of the men, who are certain they will triumph if they can endure looking at her without betraying their emotions.

The peyote seekers are now ready to fulfill their task in the land of light, Taurúnita, or of dawn, Paríya kutsiyé. The first peyote appears to the four leading gods in the form of a deer and is slain by them with arrows that are fired from the four directions. Afterwards each goes searching by himself. They decorate their hats all over with the feathers of the wild turkey or the tails of squirrels, both magical animals of the Sun, and on the return journey paint their faces with yellow symbols representing the gods. In short, it is the sacred deer hunt of the gods that is here reenacted on the peyote hunt, and this deer hunt in the land of peyote, the place where the sun comes up, is repeated again in different forms during the ritual of the toasting of the maize in March, and again in June during the Haxári kuáixa ritual, the eating of cakes of coarse maize. People representing deer are chased into noose traps right there on the dance ground, or the Sun god Tayáu, Our Father, and a variation of the fire god Tatutsí Máxa Kwaxí, Great-Grandfather Deer Tail, track the deer impersonator to Paríyakutsiyé, the place of the rising sun, or there is a footrace for the feathers of the blue cuckoo or for deer tails, again to the above-mentioned place, feathers being only a metaphor for deer antlers, and so on.

Why this astonishing expenditure of energy in the performance of always the very same magical acts, with which the real slaying of many deer as sacrifices for the ceremonies is closely connected? Without catching deer and without spattering the maize and the sacred objects with deer blood there will be no rain, no maize, and no health, the three things on which all Huichol endeavor is focused. But the real explanation for how such ideas came about is that the deer are seen as the embodiments of the stars which the Sun or his assistant, the Morning Star, slays or chases off each day, but especially in the spring, at the time when the sun really does win out over the night. Then, toward the end of June and the summer solstice, it actually does begin to rain, which is why, as mentioned, the sun is regarded as the principal bringer of rain. The deer live in the underworld in the west, where, as in ancient Mexican thought, all growth originates and where they guard the maize.

To clarify this core of Huichol religion as much as possible, I recorded the chant of the deer hunt of the gods from four singing shamans in four different settlements, whereas—apart from the important chant of the ritual of squashes, which I recorded twice—the enormous length of the other chants enabled me to fully master only one from beginning to end. The four chants of the hunt, each differing considerably from the others, are in part recited around noontime of the esquite ceremony, in part they are woven into the long chant of the same ritual. The deer hunt of the gods is said to be the principal subject even of the chant that is sung in June during the ritual feast of the tamales of coarse maize. The myth also deals with a part of this event.

With his arrows, Kauyumári, or Párikuta muyéka, respectively, "he who travels before daybreak," wounds several deer who then transform into women and, because he wants his arrows back, entice him ever further west all the way into the underworld, Tatiápa, the House of their mother, Muiníma. There, by partaking of their food, he himself becomes deer. He receives his feathers, that is, the antlers, and it is really this that makes the deer hunt of the gods possible. The deer and Párikuta muyéka are brought in some mysterious way to the circular temple, which symbolizes the cosmos. But they manage to escape, while Muiníma instructs a rat to extinguish by its magic the fire burning in the center of the temple.

Now begins the hunt, in which Xuráwetámai, Star Boy, and Kúkatámai, Bead Boy, who is Vulture, play a special role. Xuráwetámai hits Párikuta muyéka with his arrow, but Vulture, who is also one of the hunters, fools his companions by attracting the wounded deer to himself, pulling out the arrow, covering the wound with one of his feathers, and allowing him to escape to the east. But then Párikuta muyéka shoots himself, or, respectively, allows himself to be hit. He teaches the gods how they are to hunt the deer with noose traps, and he is the first to strangle himself in such a noose. He also causes Háutsitámai, the "Boy of the Falling Dew," who is Rabbit (tátsiu), the Moon, to stick his head in the noose. But the latter fails, succeeding only in breaking off his own antlers.[1]

Despite the obscurity of individual passages, whose consideration I must at this point deny myself, the image of the Morning Star, Párikuta muyéka, as hunter (precursor of the Sun) and hunted (brother of the astral deer) emerges clearly. Where he himself is slain he is replaced by Xuráwetámai, Star Boy, who, as we saw, assists Kauyumári-Párikuta muyéka with his arrows. The Morning Star also manifests himself as culture hero, who makes the first milpa appear with the seeds of his sprouting bow, who completes the arrangement of the world, consorts with the gods, and introduces and participates in all the sacred ceremonies and rituals, precisely as in the songs of the Coras. Inevitably, this brings to mind the story of the priest-king of Tollan, Quetzalcóatl, whom Tezozomoc's *Cronica mexicana* turns into the ruler of a specific people, the Toltecs, but who is nothing else than the Morning Star in the land of the Sun, god of an age of high culture, penitent, the faster who draws blood from his own body—just as the Morning Star of the Huichols also sacrifices his own body.

On the peyote pilgrimage the Huichols only think of success in the year ahead; by the time of the feast of peyote or the esquite, respectively, in March, the field must have been cleared for the next sowing. Shortly before, the field is readied for the fire god himself by everyone encircling the temple for about an hour, making the motions of cutting down the trees, the grass, and the brush. In the ceremony itself the participants dance with bamboo staffs that are painted with cloud and lightning designs. In the chant the maize goddess settles accounts with those deities that have not sufficiently rained, and finally the sun has its own "game," the hunt of the deer impersonator into the noose traps mentioned earlier. In general, during the big dance all the participants in this feast of the toasted maize, or, as the case may be, peyote, hold deer tails in their hands, thereby identifying themselves as the deer that are the guardians of the maize for the coming harvest. The rhythmic dance has to stir up enormous clouds of dust, in order to do justice to the constantly repeated words of the Yumuánita chant ("In the Dust"), because Tumuánita is said to be the place in the west where the deer leap back and forth in order to stir up the dust.

As soon as a sufficient number of deer have been killed for the feast, a preliminary ceremony is organized. Around midnight the skins are laid out around the fire and tamales placed on them for the deer. Then there commences a brief dance during which each of several dancers rub two notched shoulder blades of the slain animals against each other. The song that accompanies this is called Karatsíki. It describes the success of the hunt and the ceremonies of the feast, in which the gods again are considered to be participants. This, however, is only a brief chant. But, on the other hand, should the hunt have been unsuccessful, the singing goes on all night, with the usual attempt to determine which of the deities are angry and what kind of offerings might induce them to grant deer.

I have already drawn attention to the fact that the Haxári kuáixa or Karuánime feast in June, though differently elaborated, in the main expresses the same ideas as the feast of the esquite. In June there is still a deer hunt in the early hours of the morning, because there is symbolic value in catching a deer precisely at this time. Probably because this is nowadays too difficult, in Santa Catarína I saw the sun god Tayáu and the fire deity Maxa Kwaxí pursue a man disguised as a deer to "the place of dawn" and chase him back to the temple. For that reason the chant is first of all mainly concerned with the question whether the gods will grant a deer, for which all sorts of omens are put to the test, for example, whether a deer hair falls out of the air into a jícara. Here the earth goddess Takutsi appears wearing a mask. Further, at this feast only cakes of coarse maize are eaten that are supposedly cooked in the earth beneath the hearth, i.e., the place of the old fire god Tatewarí; however, in Santa Catarína, where I witnessed this feast, this was not the case. There are three kinds of these cakes—*tamíwari*, a large cake of which everyone gets a piece, the small *karwánime*, and *haxári*, which has the form of a rooster that stands atop a mountain in the east. This is an animal of the sun, and if it does not receive it, the sun bars the way to the eastern rain mother Naarwáme, that is, it blocks all rain.

To partake of the karwánime, at noon all the gods are invited by name in an especially solemn and ceremonious manner, although it is the image of the sun god that stands in the center of the heaped-up karwánime cakes, as it does generally on the altar of this feast. In the morning there follows a notably brief chant, called *tsikári*, thorn or spine, because in it the words of Tsikári támai, Thorn Boy, are communicated at the places, each mentioned by name, where the gods reside. He is the leader of the hunt, a representative of the fire god, which is why in his bag he carries a little tobacco that is secured with five spines of the nopal cactus. Because of the sacred tobacco he is commonly called Yakwawáme.* With his two companions (*ukwáwame*), the leaders of the hunt on the right and the left, he dances around the fire.

Several new and fundamental concepts are introduced with the final ceremony of the year, although I do not have space to deal with them here in detail. Every par-

---

*ya=tobacco, *Nicotiana rustica*. *Ya* is also used for *N. tabacum*. (—Eds.)

ticipant brings five unhusked ears of maize that are decorated with beaded armbands, woven bands and the like and tied together into a bundle that is dressed in female clothing, carried five times around the fire, and presented, to the accompaniment of prayers whose wording corresponds to the content of the chant as a whole, to the gods of the five directions. The maize goddess herself takes leave of the gods: here they come already, they who remove my husk and burn me. The cantador sings: "See where the smoke is traveling." What is meant by this is that the husks are being burned in the east, all the maize is consumed in the fire, and takes its leave in the direction of the smoke.

While the brief chant, haríme or yuríme, is being sung, men and women engage in the same sort of foot race for the feathers of the blue cuckoo and the deer tails I witnessed in Santa Catarína during the ritual of the roasting of the maize. The Huichols say both symbolize antlers or deer, respectively. With these the participants spear small breads baked of uáute (wawé, amaranth) that are called kakaí, sandals, and that lie on little house models about seventy-five centimeters high. Chasing the runners and urging them on is an old man carrying a banner with five shelled ears of maize. Everybody then eats the "sandals." Because they symbolize the maize goddess Utuanáka, one can assume that by this magic the goddess is to return, together with the rain, because hawíme and yuwíme mean drenched or soaked. According to a myth I cited in a previous report (see above, pp. 103-4), the turtle, who among the Coras is the one "who makes the water flow," slays the deer (the stars) with a stone. She is then pursued by the wolves, who also represent stars, and protected for a long while by the squirrel, the animal of the sun—in other words, the Sun itself—but is finally devoured by them. Thereupon all waters dry up and the wolves die of thirst, until Squirrel instructs the surviving pair to vomit up the remains and sew them back together again. Expressed in the inverse of this myth is how the capture of the deer also brings forth the water, the domain of Turtle, because the rainy season and the summer solstice, which coincide, slay the stars.

At noon during the same ceremony there is a second characteristic ritual, accompanied by the chant called ipinári. This name refers to a post that "reaches to the sky." Hanging down vertically from this pole are beautifully patterned woven sashes like those worn by the Huichols, their number corresponding to that of the temple officers. The latter, dressed as women, take hold of the belts and perform a dance. One man, the húna, steadies the post to keep it from falling over. Húna, however, refers to a tiny flying insect, the barrillo, that bites ferociously from sunup to sundown. He carries a bagful of tamales on his back, suspended from a headstrap. Another man, called hará-pai, because he represents the harápai, a small aquatic animal that hides beneath stones in the river, also supports the tree, but he carries a drum, suspended from a shoulder strap, that is beaten by the shaman-singer who stands behind him. But the principal role is that of an old man (because young men refuse to take it on), the yuhunáme, who runs around with penis exposed and acts out sexual intercourse with the dancers disguised as women. The general idea underlying a ritual held such a short time before the harvest is too obvious to require elaboration here.[2]

This, all too briefly, constitutes the corpus of the chants of the annual ceremonies, among which, nonetheless, the song of the Christian "gods," that is, Christ and the saints, has to be reckoned as well. This chant, which is sung in the ceremonial centers, but not in the ranchos, during Easter and Christmas, is important because what it enumerates is the customs and offices created under the influence of the Church, in such a way as to suggest that they originated in primordial times, even though the saints have been completely assimilated into the pagan ideology, their origins and functions so completely reworked to conform with the Indian ethos that it is exceedingly difficult to identify even a few Christian traces. Nevertheless, insofar as they are not mentioned at all alongside the other gods in the rest of the sacred repertoire, they occupy a special place. Among the things that do emerge quite clearly in this chant of the saints is that the sacrifice of cattle is preeminently dedicated to them, and that they are in fact the real Masters of livestock.

That is also why the saints are invoked in rituals intended to break a spell that has been cast over cattle, a concept that is otherwise completely indigenous. This too requires an all-night chant, as does the removal of a spell from people. However, for the latter no saints are invoked. This happens at any time about a year after the death of an old man or an old woman, but only when someone falls ill, the cows fail to calve, or suffer in some other way. It is thought that just before expiring, while invoking the gods of the west, they pointed a candle, maize or hairs against people meant to be bewitched, or cast a spell on cattle with a blue or red stone that they solicited from the kakáyarite, the mountain deities. They showed these things to the itáuki, the already mentioned mythological animal, and it is the latter that now activates the illness, infertility, and the like, in those against whom the spell has been cast. This animal is killed by the singing shaman in the manner already described, in which he slowly approaches the human patient or the animal from the front to hurl his feathered muviéri over them. In the chant it is once again Kauyumári, Deer, who, assisted by Xuráwetamái, Star Boy, is the actual performer.

Apart from this the Huichols have two other all-night curing chants. One is distinguished by the fact that it is sung for the common welfare, as something on a regular basis. And the time in which this is done is, as noted earlier, winter, which is when I heard it among other chants during the ritual of the sun. All the gods are invoked, ask for and receive their offerings, in reciprocal exchange for which they remove whatever illnesses may have arisen.

If someone is seriously ill, the chant has a very different content. Then the first task is to determine whether the soul is still being kept at the zenith, the fifth direction directly above us in the heavens, by Wérika Uimári, Eagle Girl, or whether its equivalent, the *táuka*, which remained in the earth at birth, might have shriveled up. Because, as in ancient Mexico, when children are born they come down from the sky, and it is to the heavens that the souls go back at death, until they are snatched from the air by the shaman-singers in the form of five little stones of which their relatives take custody.

If the táuka has shriveled up, all hope for recovery is lost and the song is broken off. Or else the chant inquires among the gods about the cause of the illness, and now we hear of the highly interesting conception that it is dangerous to make arrows and the sacred objects to ask for something from the deities—deer, for example, or maize, or the art of singing and knowledge of the sacred chants. If the petition is not answered within a certain time, one not only has to deal with the disappointment, but frequently also with the effects of the magical objects in the form of illness. "He took hold of my arrow," says the god, meaning that the person had made one. If, for example, someone takes Tatéi Yurianáka, Our Mother the Moist Earth, from some sacred place to his milpa, it is assuredly a good thing for the field itself, but just by passing by her she can also have a negative effect on the individual. Likewise, intercourse with women is often the cause of illness. The vulva is very dangerous, is the way the Indian puts it, the conception being that it makes him unable to perform certain tasks and directly causes illness. By this he does not mean some venereal disease, which in fact does not exist among them, but any old physical ill whatever. Finally, the deities give instructions for the kind of offering the patient is to give, Kauyumári and Tatewarí, the fire god, remove the pathogen by sucking—that is, the shaman-singer does it in their place—the patient is sprinkled with sacred water, and after five days, during which the patient is to abstain from salt, the same chant is repeated.

To round this out, there is also the all-night death chant, which is sung five days after a demise. It is on this night that the deceased returns once more to his home, is fed and finally driven off by magical means. Especially effective for this are, among other things, branches of the *zapote* tree, a species of burr, and lampblack, which the participants smear on their cheeks, hands and feet. In other words, the color of mourning as a prophylactic! The soul has ascended to the sky, to be taken hold of by Wérika Uimári. But where is the deceased? Kauyumári is dispatched to look for him, his physical self has journeyed to the west, and Kauyumári now inquires of all the Kakayárite (the mountains, etc.) along the way whether he had passed by. They tell him that a puff of air, *haikúri*, passed this way. Might that have been him? Finally he comes to the five vats into which the deceased was dunked and from which he emerged again as a kind of fly. Then the deceased arrives at the huge *zalate*,* the mighty tree of the earth goddess that stands at the entrance to the land of the dead, throws the vulvas of his female relatives—represented by jícaras—five times at the fruits for which the dead are waiting, and, having been received by the rain goddess of the west, Kiewimúka, of whose water he drinks, joins with them in a dance. But now comes Kauyumári, flings a burr at him and, thus caught, drags him back to his former home. At the entrance to the courtyard he is frightened by the magical prophylactics. To enable him to speak

---

*From the Nahuatl *zalatl*, wild fig, genus *Ficus*. (—Eds.)

once more with his relatives his soul is returned to him one more time. The deceased makes some long speeches, and then he is told: "Now go."

And with those words Kauyumári takes him away.

Translator's Note: Preuss did not specify where exactly Kauyumari and the soul of the deceased are headed after the latter's return from his or her visit to the underworld for a final farewell to the relatives in his or her old rancho. The culture hero and personified Deer has his home on, in, and as a hill located in the center of Wirikúta, and it is Wirikúta (or alternately, the sky above it) that is said to be the final destination of the Huichol dead. Here they join, and merge with, the rocks, hills, mountains and other power spots in which the ancestor deities, the kakauyaríte, are embodied. Deceased persons held in special regard for their wisdom, in particular those who were shamans in life, may eventually return to give counsel and protection to their descendants, having manifested themselves to the shaman as rock crystals (see Chapter 14). Shamans are also said to accompany the Sun on his daily round through the heavens and the underworld, a conceptualization of the fate of certain elite deceased that recalls similar beliefs among the ancient Aztecs.

Although the three essays in these pages represent the bulk of Preuss's surviving observations on the Huichols, a later article by him compares the style of Huichol ritual dialogues to that of the Rg or Rig Veda, the great Indo-European epic dating to the second millennium B.C. (Preuss 1909). That essay features the verbatim transcription, in German translation, of the performance by the officiating shaman as he sends magical messengers to Kauyumári to summon the culture hero from his home in the east, i.e., his hill in Wirikúta, to the Huichol sierra.

Nowadays Huichol peyote pilgrims make use of various means of public and private transport—cars, trucks, wagons, railroad—for at least part of the three-hundred mile trek to Wirikúta. This adaptation to the modern world has also made it a great deal easier for foreign guests of the Huichols to accept the honor—and it is an honor—of being invited to come along. In Preuss's time the pilgrimage was done on foot, taking weeks each way. Whether he was invited or not we do not know. Perhaps not—Huichols were not so used to inquisitive foreigners as they are today. In any event, he was not able to go on the arduous journey and though he seems not to have been excluded from any ceremony, including those connected with the hunt and the consumption of the sacred psychoactive cactus, and was well aware of the intense emotional attachment of the people to the distant home of the Deer-Peyote and the kakauyaríte, the ancestor gods, he never had the modern investigator's advantage of experiencing it firsthand.

NOTES

1. For the natural history model for the horned rabbit in Huichol myth see Jill L. Furst, "Natural History and Myth in West Mexico," *Journal of Latin American Lore*, Vol. 15.1, pp. 137–149. (—Eds.)

2. The analogy to the ictyphallic Kokopelli, the hump-backed flute player, of the Puebloan Southwest is self-evident, as it is also to an Aztec ceremony in which sexual intercourse is similarly parodied. (—Eds.)

INTRODUCTION TO CHAPTER 5

"Peyote serves as an enculturating force, echoing religious tenets and reoccurring themes that are transcended to visions, the spoken word, through myths and songs, actions and rituals and ceremonies, and beliefs that permeate all levels of individual and collective Huichol consciousness."

So writes Stacy B. Schaefer, the author of the following essay and co-editor of this volume. Schaefer's essay shows why, although there is, of course, much more to Huichol ideology, it is peyote, the peyote experience, and its ramifications that in a very real sense contain the essence of "being Huichol"—why, indeed, though other Mexican Indians also used, and continue to use, the visionary cactus, at the end of the twentieth century it is the Huichols who are indeed "People of the Peyote."

In the peyote experience it is, for Huichols, not just a matter of trusting in the myths they have heard from infancy, or in the kinship they have been told they have with the divine in nature and the ancestors. When Huichols partake of the sacred plant in the rituals and feel its wondrous effects, the ordinary boundaries between past and present vanish, the gods, the ancestors, the events of Huichol mythic history, become physical and emotional reality. Some Huichols, however few, may never eat peyote in all their lives. For, although there may be expectation (especially in the cargo roles, be they community-, temple-, or rancho-based), there is no requirement that they do so. But even they are so enveloped by myth, ritual, and their vicarious participation through family members and friends in the peyote pilgrimage and its attendant rituals, that peyote becomes for them, too, almost as much of a reality.

But beyond that, the extensive and deep-going practical knowledge Huichols have of the plant itself and its micro-environments, the perception of its morphology, growth habits, the meanings applied to its colors, changes during maturation, and differential effects from the ingestion of different varieties and hues, virtually presupposes lifelong familiarity with the cactus in its native habitat, if not firsthand, then perhaps handed down through the generations from a past in which seeing peyote grow was not an occasional experience but part of everyday life.

For their present homeland affords no such opportunity. The cactus is not native to the Sierra Madre Occidental, and even though some peyoteros plant quantities they bring back from the sacred hunt, to keep them fresh at least for Hikuri Neixa, the Dance of the Peyote that is held between May and July, the combination of wrong soil conditions, too much rain, theft, and grazing animals, especially goats, more often than not dooms these attempts to failure.

Whatever the implications one wishes to read into this in terms of Huichol ethno-history, peyote has been, and will probably continue to be, a vital force that enables Huichols to take changes in the world around them and, more than merely accept and live with them, "Huicholize" and integrate them into the dynamics of their traditional culture.

Peter T. Furst

5 : THE CROSSING OF THE SOULS

Peyote, Perception, and Meaning among the Huichol Indians

STACY B. SCHAEFER

It was an early March morning in 1988. I was at the Tepic airport, waiting for the plane to take me once again into the Sierra, when I ran into some of the Huichols who had been my companions on a pilgrimage from San Andrés Cohamiata to the peyote country in San Luis Potosí. I was surprised and pleased to see them because I had brought copies of photographs from the journey to give to them. Sharing my pictures with the peyoteros had been one of their conditions for allowing me to record the event with my camera. Along the way they even directed my attention to scenes, objects, people, and actions they thought were important for me to capture on film. Now they stood around, photos in hand, laughing at their own images and pointing out details.

Minutes later, another Huichol whom I knew from the community approached our little group, took a look at a photo of some pilgrims collecting peyote and became a bit agitated. "You people take photographs," he said to me. "You come with us on the pilgrimage and even partake of the peyote. But you never ask 'why' to the peyote. You never ask. Well, I'm going to tell you: peyote is everything, it is the crossing of the souls, it is everything that is. Without peyote nothing would exist, but you people never ask why."

At first I was somewhat taken aback at his reaction. In retrospect, however, I owe him a debt of thanks. At the very least, his reproach was a humbling experience for me, and a constructive reminder that, as ethnographer, I should never be deceived into thinking that I fully understand Huichol culture. Regardless of how many years I have now been doing field work, or of the fact that I have gone with the Huichols on their sacred pilgrimage, I must constantly remind myself that there will always be so much more that I do not know and still have to learn—indeed, that there is much I will probably never know or understand. Concerning peyote and its meaning to Huichols, this one man's words posed a challenge: look for answers to his question, "Why?" What did he mean when he said peyote is the "crossing of the souls"? These questions inevitably led to others. There is an abundance of recent literature on peyote use and symbolism among the Huichols; Furst (1972, 1976), Myerhoff (1974, 1978a, 1978b), Valadéz (1978, 1986b), Benítez (1968a,1968b), Mata Torres (1976, 1980), and Negrín (1975,1977, 1985) have all written on the subject. But I wanted to go further and learn firsthand, not what westerners think about the sacred cactus, but what Huichols themselves know and believe—about the botany of this powerful little plant; about what kinds of experiences they have; about what meanings they place on a psychoactive succulent that, not being native to the Huichol country of the Sierra Madre Occidental, requires them to make long and arduous journeys to collect it in the high desert hundreds of miles to the east.

Since that chance meeting in 1988, another milepost in my professional and personal life has steered me in this direction of inquiry. In 1989–90, with Ph.D. in hand and field work among the Huichols ongoing, but now at last beyond the dissertation stage, it was time to look for academic employment. The job market for anthropologists has not been good for several years, but as luck would have it, a tenure-track position did open up for someone with my qualifications and interests—at, of all possible places, the University of Texas-Pan American. As it happens, the campus is situated in the lower Río Grande Valley in South Texas, the only region north of Mexico where peyote grows naturally. And, sure enough, in my first year there I actually entertained Huichol visitors who had heard of peyote growing north of the Río Bravo (the Mexican name for the river we know as the Rio Grande) and who were eager to see it for themselves. They had traveled to Texas in the company of Susana and Mariano Valadéz, old friends of mine who are co-directors of the Huichol Center for Cultural Survival and the Traditional Arts in Santiago Ixcuintla, Nayarit. Mariano is Huichol, a renowned yarn painter; Susana is a U.S. citizen with an M.A. degree from my own alma mater, UCLA, who has spent years working with Huichols, including a two-year residence in the Huichol *comunidad* of San Andrés Cohamiata. By this time I had already become familiar with some of the places north of the border where peyote grows wild, and it is there that I took my visitors. Although it was not their revered Wirikúta, the Huichols were visibly touched by the sight of so many peyote plants (Figure 21). Most important for me, they were moved to talk about things connected with the sacred cactus I had not known before.

Rich though this experience was for me, most of my contact with Huichols has been with families living in and near San Andrés. I have worked there since the 1970s, and over the years have had the chance to develop close relations with a number of individuals. They, in turn, have become valued consultants for my work as ethnographer. My major consultants are men and women who are *mara'akámes*, shamans, and/or have been raised in a traditional environment and are thus well versed in Huichol religious beliefs, rituals, and ideology. All have participated in the pilgrimage, some as many as five times, others ten times or more.

I do not claim that what I have learned about peyote from these people applies

FIGURE 21. Peyote in the Lower Río Grande Valley. (*Photograph by Peter T. Furst.*)

across the board to the beliefs and practices of all Huichols. Regional and individual variations concerning the sacred cactus, its use, and rituals that revolve around it can be found from community to community, a phenomenon to which scholars who have accompanied Huichols on the pilgrimage can attest. At best, I would call the following essay a progress report—information that I hope and intend to build upon over the years. For I, too, see myself as a pilgrim, on an endless path seeking knowledge over time and through experience.

Since peyote is such an integral part of Huichol culture, and its ethnobotany and pharmacology such a complex subject, I have organized this essay into discrete, though obviously interdependent, sections. The first two concern Huichol ethnobotanical knowledge about peyote and its preparation and consumption. Native-grown tobacco of the species *Nicotiana rustica* being integral to Huichol use of the potent little cactus and its effects on the central nervous system, I will next explore the pharmacological aspects of both peyote and tobacco, and the relationship between these two otherwise very different and unrelated psychoactive agents in Huichol beliefs and ceremonies. The next section contains firsthand descriptions by some Huichols of their own peyote visions. These experiences, and various aspects of their mythology and the rituals themselves, lead into a discussion of the meanings Huichols place on the sacred cactus. This, finally, takes us into a consideration of the place of peyote as a unifying force in ideology and society, and its crucial role for Huichols in their determination to maintain and continue their distinct cultural integrity.

Ethnobotanical Knowledge

Peyote has a very long cultural history in Mesoamerica. The Spanish invaders found it being used by the Mexica (Aztecs) of Central Mexico, and there is good information on the subject in the writings of the sixteenth- and seventeenth-century chroniclers, notably Fray Bernadino de Sahagún (1950-1963), Diego Durán (1971), Hernando Ruíz de Alarcón (1984 [1629]); Jacinto de la Serna (1656), and Francisco Hernández (1651). Sahagún credited the discovery of peyote, which the Mexica, or Aztecs, also used in divinatory ritual, to northern desert hunter-gatherers he called Teochichimeca, "true Chichimecs." But there is much evidence that peyote was known and used in Mexico long before the Mexica: it is depicted, for example, in 2,000-year-old funerary sculptures from western Mexico (Furst 1974) (Figure 22). The earliest evidence for peyote use comes from Desert Culture rock shelter sites in northernmost Mexico and the trans-Pecos region of southern Texas. These were occupied as early as 10,500 B.C. and as recently as A.D. 1000. Peyote has been found in several, often in association with the psychoactive but also highly toxic beanlike seeds of a small flowering tree known to botanists as *Sophora secundiflora* (Furst 1976). From one of these sites in northern Mexico, archaeologists recovered a "necklace" of peyotes strung beadlike on a fiber cord that yielded a radiocarbon date equivalent to A.D. 800 (Adovasio and Fry 1976).[1] The Huichols still string dried peyote, which they equate with the flesh of the deer, in this way on the peyote pilgrimage, just as they do with venison.

Impressive as the 1,200-year-old date for the peyote string is, recent assays by the UCLA radiocarbon laboratory of two peyote plants excavated in a Texas Desert Culture site, and since stored at the Witte Museum in San Antonio, have pushed the use of the cactus as far back as the year 5,000 B.C. (Furst 1989). Peyote thus joins *Sophora* and tobacco as the three most ancient psychedelic species employed in the Americas— at least according to our present state of knowledge.

The term peyote derives from the Nahuatl word *péyutl*.[2] The Huichols, however, call it *hikuri*, a name also used by the Tarahumara, Cora, and Tepehuan. Since peyote first came under the scrutiny of western botanists and psychopharmacologists, it has gone through a series of name changes, until science finally settled on *Lophophora* for the genus and *williamsii* and *diffusa* for the two species of peyote that have been positively identified (Anderson 1969, 1980).

The powerful little cactus grows in a series of special ecological zones commonly referred to as Chihuahuan desert scrub environment. The latitudinal distribution of peyote within this large desert area spans about 1,200 kilometers within southern Texas and northern Mexico. *Lophophora williamsii* is native to the high desert region of San

FIGURE 22. Hollow Redware Figurine of an Androgynous Hump-Backed Dwarf Holding a Pair of Peyotes, Colima, Western Mexico, 200 B.C.–A.D. 100.

Luis Potosí, which the Huichols call Wirikúta, as well as parts of the Mexican states of Zacatecas and Coahuila, and the south Texas plains along the Lower Río Grande. *Lophophora diffusa*, on the other hand, has only been observed growing in a small desert zone in the Mexican state of Querétaro (Anderson 1969:299–302).

Huichols have their own system of plant taxonomy. One species they recognize under the classification of peyote is *tsuwíri*, which some Huichols say is capable of causing madness or even death, for which reason it is known as "the false peyote." Several phenylethylamine alkaloids have been isolated from this rosette-shaped cactus, identified botanically as *Ariocarpus retusus*, which the Tarahumara are said to consider "stronger" than *Lophophora williamsii* (Schultes and Hofmann 1992:35, 70; Furst 1971;

1972:178–179). Another kind of peyote, called *yáwei hikuri*, is recognized by Huichols as the peyote of Kauyumári (Our Elder Brother Deer), as well as of wolves and coyotes. According to Huichol lore collected in San Andrés Cohamiata, these animals also go on the pilgrimage to Wirikúta, and yáwei hikuri is the peyote they eat.[3] It is said to resemble the *pitaya* cactus, and to have a strong effect upon anyone who ingests it. Another cactus, *aikutsi*, is also said to be a form of peyote, but not the "true peyote." Botanist James Bauml of the Los Angeles County Arboretum identifies it as a species of barrel cactus, possibly *Echinocactus visnaga*. A mara'akáme with whom Susana Valadéz has worked for several years told Bauml that "they take candles and arrows, a lot of offerings (to the aikutsi). In the middle they stick it with a feathered wand, juice comes out which they mix with peyote. It is eaten so that one does not become too *empeyotado* (intoxicated with peyote)" (J. Bauml, personal communication). In Huichol myths, aikutsi was born when Kauyumári arrived in the desert and spent the night sleeping atop a hill in the center of Wirikúta. In the morning he woke up to find what he thought were tamales, but what were really peyote. He put the peyote into a gourd bowl and out of this bowl sprouted the aikutsi.

Peyote grows in various shapes. Age and size determine the number of ribs on a peyote plant. Younger specimens have up to five ribs, while mature ones may have as many as fourteen. Some may not have any ribs at all (Anderson 1969:302). Huichols have their own well-developed classification system for differently shaped peyote plants. Women visually document these kinds of peyote in the designs they weave and embroider (Figures 23, 24).

Although I have not collected an exhaustive sampling of these designs, or a list of peyote types based on shape and form, my Huichol consultants have given me the following information.

First, there are the individual peyotes. The smaller peyotes with five ribs, or those that form a starlike shape from the outer ribs to the center, are called *niérika*. Niérika refers to a sacred design that serves as a portal, a doorway into other worlds. Several Huichols commented that these little peyotes are very bitter, unlike the larger peyotes, which are said to be more palatable and to have a better flavor. One kind of peyote has a crown shaped into individual sections, like kernels, and hence is called *iku*, meaning maize.

Another, more mature, form of peyote is called *kiéri*. It gets its name from a highly toxic psychoactive plant of the genus *Solandra* that is used with great care by certain Huichol shamans and that is also associated with sorcery (see Yasumoto, this volume; see also Knab 1977, Furst 1989). The ribs on this peyote fan out into a swirling formation that covers the crown and continues part way down the base toward the root. One other form of peyote, known as *maxa*, deer, has evenly divided ribs, with prominent white tufts on each that are said to resemble the tail of the common white-tailed Virginia deer of Mexico and the United States. Both kiéri and maxa are especially strong

FIGURE 23. Peyote-in-Flower Motif in Embroidered Shoulder Bag.
(*Photograph by Stacy B. Schaefer.*)

and are considered to be the peyote of the *mara'akáme*, the shaman. Further research by botanists and psychopharmcologists may confirm that there is a correspondence between the shape and/or age of a peyote plant and the potency of its alkaloids.

Huichols also classify peyote by the way it grows in clusters. Some peyote plants grow from a single rootstock that burrows deep into the ground. If an individual peyote is injured or harvested with part of the root remaining in the soil, numerous new peyotes sprout from the base of the original plant (Figure 25). Huichols are well aware of the generative nature of peyote and take great care when harvesting it by cutting it with a knife or machete several inches below the soil line, leaving the taproot in place. Huichols are so attuned to the way peyote generates itself that women illustrate the growth stages of peyote in some of their artistic designs. The production of art in this manner is one major way in which women not only visually express but also transmit cultural knowledge about their natural world.

Peyote can also reproduce from seed and oftentimes young plants can be found growing around the parent plant. Given enough time, undisturbed by humans or animals, peyote can grow in clusters, some of which have very distinct formations. When Huichols go looking for peyote, they hope to come upon one of these clusters of the sacred cactus. If a pilgrim encounters an unusual formation, it is considered to be a sacred message from the deities, who have thereby sent special blessings to the individual. Some of these groupings are described as taking the form of votive gourd bowls,

FIGURE 24. Embroidered Bag Depicting Mature Peyotes. The artist, Guadalupe de la Cruz Ríos, wove in the "Mother Peyote" in the upper right corner. (*Photograph by Peter T. Furst.*)

plaited shamans' baskets (*takwátsi*), and crosses. Others appear like serpents, the animal form of the rain goddesses and the rattlesnake, *raye*, the animal ally of the sun and guardian of the peyote. The latter forms were described to me by a consultant who had recently returned from Wirikúta: "One can distinguish the forms; sometimes they are serpents. If they are serpents, then they are in places where there is nothing but peyotes. Sometimes one can find a peyote formation like this with a real snake lying to one side of it. This means that it is part of the serpents."

This same idea was also brought to my attention by an older shaman, a brother of the yarn painter Mariano Valadéz, who lives in the *comunidad indígena* of Santa Catarina and who came to South Texas in the company of Mariano and Susana. I took them to the home of a local man with whom I have been working and who is licensed to sell peyote to members of the Native American Church of North America. For the use of his Native American clients he has constructed an altar in his backyard with different

FIGURE 25. A Clump of Peyotes. These specimens grew from a single root stock left in the ground—a phenomenon botanists call cloning. Huichols give great respect to such clumps, which may be especially sacred because people see in some the shape of a deer or the Mother of Peyote. Peyoteros customarily leave portions of the root of each peyote they harvest in the ground so that its "bones" can give birth to new growth. (*Photograph by Peter T. Furst.*)

clusters of peyote he found in the countryside and brought home to transplant. One grouping had a most unusual shape. When the Huichol shaman spotted this he immediately squatted down, prayed over the peyote, and placed some Mexican coins on the plants as an offering. He told me this peyote was especially powerful because it is the sacred snake one finds in Wirikúta.[4]

From the various descriptions I have collected, of all the formations of peyote one can encounter, the most prized manifests itself to Huichols in the shape of a deer. That is because when Huichols collect peyote, they say they are hunting deer; or, conversely, they speak of themselves as hunting deer when they are in fact harvesting peyote, for peyote is deer and deer peyote.[5]

When I accompanied a temple group on the pilgrimage, the high point of the ceremony in Wirikúta occurred when we followed the leading mara'akáme to a large cluster of peyote he identified as "the Mother of Peyote." All the pilgrims placed their votive arrows, gourd bowls, and other offerings around the cluster, exactly as they do around the deer after it has been hunted. One consultant remarked that a person is very fortunate "when he is looking and arrives where there are deer tracks. The same form is made by the peyote; it can be deer tracks. Then, afterwards, one can arrive at a place that is formed with hikuri; it is the same as the deer. Its antlers, its entire form. This means that the person has truly encountered something sacred for himself." After the deer that is peyote is killed, Ramón Medina, a completing shaman, told Furst (1972:175, 1976) that the soul, the life essence of the animal, its *kupúri*, rises from its head in the colors of a brilliant rainbow, to escape to the top of the sacred mountains.

Peyote grows in subtly varying shades. Anderson (1980:179-181 and personal communication) lists these colors as blue-green, yellow-green, and reddish-green, and in part attributes the color variations to environmental conditions. Blue-green, he says, reflects ideal conditions, where the plant is partially shaded. Yellow results from stress due to intense solar radiation, and red is the response of young plants to protect chlorophyll. These naturally occurring phenomena fit well with the Huichol model that ties peyote and maize together into the same entity. In Huichol lore, the maize goddess Niwétsika was treated badly by her mother-in-law and in consequence fled to Wirikúta, where she turned into peyote.[6] One female shaman gave me a more complete explanation of this relationship. "Yes," she said, "there are five colors of hikuri. They are the same as the five colors of maize. There in Wirikúta sometimes one can see many colors. One might think they are the same but they aren't. They are different colors in the different places where the gods live. For example, there is a place in Wirikúta that is called Paritsika Manáve. There is peyote over there, but it is pure yellow. In every place there are names, for example; one place where there are white peyotes is called Hái mutiyo, which means white peyote. In Kuanamayéipa, close to Kauyumaritzie, Kauyumari's Hill, they are blue-colored. In the very center of Wirikúta there is peyote of all the colors, yellow, white, blue, red and spotted, like the maize."

According to several Huichols, the colors of peyote do not contribute to stronger or weaker visions. Others claim that blue peyote is stronger. Some tell me that peyote with a reddish tinge is no good because it is old.

Another important part in peyote anatomy is the flowers. In the center of each peyote is an areola-bearing tuft of soft yellowish or whitish trichomes. Flowers arise from the center of the peyote anywhere from March through September (Anderson 1980:179-180). Flowering peyote in the north is usually pink, and occasionally pure white. In the south the flowers rarely show any red pigment and are for the most part either white or greenish-white (Anderson 1970). Huichol consultants report that the color of the peyote flowers changes with age. Some are varying degrees of pink, others are "speckled," but none are pure white. The color of the flower is not a reflection of the potency of the plant. Once again the analogy of maize and peyote was made, this time by a man in describing the significance of the flowers: "The flowers represent when one plants maize. After five days the plants begin to grow a little, but it is difficult to see. This means that when one goes to Wirikúta sometimes it is not so easy to find peyote when it is not flowering. If one finds a few with flowers he is very lucky."

On the pilgrimage in which I participated, one of the *kawitéros*, who are usually wise old shamans, taught me how to look for peyote. He harvested a cluster of nine peyotes

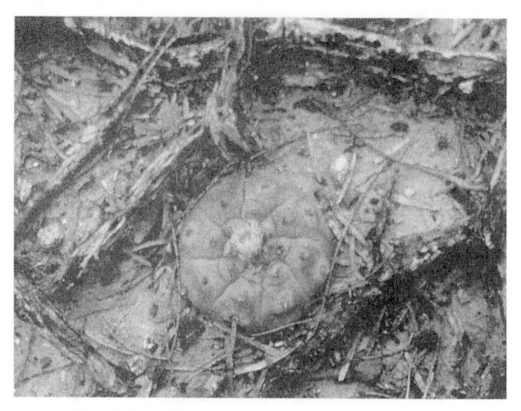

FIGURE 26. Peyote in Flower. (*Photograph by Peter T. Furst.*)

from their common root stock, as usual taking care to leave the bottom part of the root in the ground. One of these had a little pinkish-lavender flower blooming on top (Figure 26). He picked the flower, pressed it to my eyes, put it in my mouth and told me in a soft but sure voice, "Eat this flower of the peyote. We are not allowed to eat peyote yet, it is not time. But if you eat this peyote flower it will help you, it will guide you to find many, many beautiful peyotes." I ate the flower and began to look. It was uncanny but within minutes I found clusters of peyote all around me. When I called the kawitéro over to tell him about this, he calmly replied with a smile, "I told you the truth, I do not tell lies. I know these things, that's why I am a kawitéro."

Preparation and Consumption of Peyote

The preparation and consumption of peyote is almost always done within a strictly ceremonial context.[7] Eating peyote, as pointed out by Furst (1972:76, 1976:125–127), is a highly ritualized activity likened to the partaking of sacramental food. The optimal manner of ingesting peyote is in Wirikúta when it is freshly harvested. Peyote cannot be eaten until all of the ritual obligations are performed by the pilgrims. The peyotéros must first stalk and hunt it like deer in Wirikúta. Afterwards, the pilgrims collect peyote in the surrounding area in their woven baskets, known as *kiliwei*. No peyote is eaten until the shaman indicates that the time is right to do so. On the pilgrimage in

FIGURE 27. Kauyumari's Hill in the Center of Wirikúta. (*Felt-pen drawing by Estela Hernández. Photograph by Stacy B. Schaefer.*)

which I participated, the blessing and eating of peyote commenced on top of Kauyu-maritzie. This hill in the center of Wirikúta is the home of Elder Brother Kauyumári, from where the shamans summon him to participate in the ceremonies (Figure 27). It is covered with scrub cactus and on the summit there is some flowering sage. Everyone sat on the rocks crowning the summit, positioning themselves so as to face east. All of the ritual objects were taken out and blessed by the leading shaman with sacred water. Candles and copal incense were lit and while the shaman pointed his plumed wand to the five directions everyone prayed. Votive bowls were taken out and fresh peyote placed inside them. The shaman purified everyone with his feather wand and sacred water and touched the peyote to their cheeks, throat and wrists. The white tufts on the peyote were removed and placed with the offerings. Then the peyotéros peeled the tough skin at the base of the cactus and consumed small amounts of the first peyote of the pilgrimage. That done, everyone hiked down the hill to our encampment.[8]

Back in camp, the sacred fire was kindled and that night the shaman, with the help of his assistants, sang. Throughout the night all the pilgrims circled the area five times. Five is the sacred number for Huichols and all the members consumed peyote five times during the night. At the first rays of dawn, they painted designs on the faces of their ritual companions, *compañeros* in Spanish, with the ground-up yellow root of a desert shrub known as *uxa* (Figure 28) (Bauml, Voss, and Collings 1990). They also exchanged

FIGURE 28. A young Peyote Pilgrim, with Uxa Face Paint, on a Peyote Pilgrimage. (*Photograph by Stacy B. Schaefer, 1987.*)

peyote they had selected especially, each giving some to all the others and receiving some in turn from everyone else, a custom also observed by Furst (1972; 1976:128). Then it was time to hunt "the Mother of Peyote," the peyote cluster whose form resembles a lifesize deer. When the "deer" was found, some of its constituent plants were skewered onto votive arrows. Sacred gourd bowls were unwrapped and fresh peyote was put inside them. Candles and copal were lit. The leading shaman called each family to the site and blessed everyone with sacred water and peyote. One large peyote in the cluster represented the heart of the deer. The mara'akáme divided this up into slivers. He sandwiched the slivers into peyote buttons that had been opened and cleaned, and placed one each inside the mouths of the pilgrims. Upon completing this ritual, and having spent the night consuming peyote at regular intervals, the pilgrims had reached the state in which they were journeying inwards, caught up in their own visions, their own communications with the divine Huichol entities.

Although Huichols prefer to consume peyote fresh, the pilgrims also dry peyote in the desert in order to store it better. This is done by trimming the roots of the plants, opening the buttons so that all the ribbed sections are exposed to the sun, and removing the white tufts in the very center of the cactus (Figure 29). As noted earlier, later they may be strung on a special twined maguey cactus fiber string and carried

FIGURE 29. Peyotero Couple Slicing Peyote for Drying in Wirikúta. Peyote is transported dry or fresh for use in the ceremonies. (*Photograph by Stacy B. Schaefer.*)

back to the Sierra, where they will be used in future ceremonies such as Hikuri Neixa (Peyote Dance).

During this latter ceremony a woman is specially selected to grind the dried peyote on her metate. She adds water to the pulverized peyote, making it into a white frothy drink for the participants. The leading shaman stirs the drink with the point of a prayer arrow and people are anointed on the head with the foam from the peyote. In some instances, cattle are also anointed on their heads and horns, as are bags of offerings. The celebration of Hikuri Neixa lasts two days and nights. During this time, the pilgrims and their compañeros dance five times around the temple compound. Five spots are demarcated with pine trees to indicate the cardinal directions and the sacred center. At each location, the participants drink cupfuls of the liquified peyote and offer the same to their companions. Some Huichols say that the potency of the peyote does not diminish when dried. In fact, when drinking peyote one may ingest more than when eating it fresh, because it is easier to consume greater amounts more quickly in liquid form. I was told by one Huichol about a relative of his who came across some dried peyote he had been saving for the last two years. He was getting ready to prepare his land for planting and took the peyote with him. He ground the cactus, consecrated the soil with the powder, added water to the rest, and drank the mixture so that he would have more energy to complete the task of clearing his field. Even though the peyote was over two years old, it was stronger than he expected and he ended up "wandering lost" in his field until the effects wore off.

To return to the pilgrimage, there are two important people who serve as guides for the pilgrims. One is the leading shaman, known as Saulizika, the other is the "Keeper of the Peyote," called Nauxa (pron. nauzrra). Saulizika presides over all of the rituals, and when he sings he travels beyond his immediate surroundings of the circle of the pilgrims around the fire in Wirikúta, by calling upon all of the gods to come join them on their journey. His song becomes a road that transports both pilgrims and divine entities. Nauxa has the major responsibility of making sure that the pilgrims are able to travel along this path. He fills a basket with peyote that his fellow pilgrims have gathered for the ceremony. When the fire is lit and burning and all the necessary prayers are made to Tatewarí, Grandfather Fire, Nauxa first blesses the Saulizika and Urukuakáme, the Keeper of the Temple. He then circles the fire and blesses each pilgrim in turn. In completion of this ritual, Nauxa circles the fire again, walks some distance away, blows on the bull's horn trumpet that is also used for the deer hunt, and returns to the group.

By this time the pilgrims, seated around the fire, have selected a certain quantity of fresh peyote which they place in front of themselves. Nauxa blesses the peyote with his *muviéri*, his plumed wand, and gives each pilgrim the number of peyote they themselves have indicated they plan to consume at this time. Everyone eats his or her peyote and the mara'akáme begins the chanting that will continue through the entire night. While the mara'akáme carries the souls of the pilgrims along the journey of his song, Nauxa makes certain that the pilgrims are in the physical and mental states that facilitate their out-of-body travel along this path. Five times during the night, when the pilgrims must circle the fire after a cycle is completed in the mara'akáme's song, Nauxa places the same amount of peyote as originally consumed in front of each pilgrim. If an individual started the ceremony eating five peyotes, he or she would eat five more peyotes after each cycle in the shaman's song. By the time the night is over, that individual would thus have consumed twenty-five peyote plants. What this means is that although the individual participants decide ahead of time on the dosage they plan to take, it is Nauxa who distributes the peyote and who, in doing so, keeps the road open for all the pilgrims to travel.

This ceremony is replicated later in the Sierra upon the pilgrims' return to the temple and their awaiting families (Figure 30). It is Nauxa who is the vital link between the pilgrims and those members of their families who stayed behind. He goes ahead of the pilgrims to the temple and announces their arrival. Slung across his shoulders he carries bags filled with votive gourds and peyote that have been given him by the pilgrims. On this night Saulizika sits outside and sings the entire night. Nauxa blesses and distributes the peyote on five separate occasions to the families inside of the temple. As one of my consultants explained, "Afterwards, at dawn, the pilgrims begin to arrive

FIGURE 30. Return of the Pilgrims to the San José Temple. (*Photograph by Stacy B. Schaefer, 1987.*)

at the temple. They give blessed water to their women, their mothers, to all of their family. But the family members are 'lost,' they are in another realm, at least those who ate a lot of peyote. Only Nauxa and Saulizika know what is happening there and who is traveling with the peyote. They know this because of the singing and because of the center of the fire. Nauxa knows what is being sung and what is happening in the temple."

When the temple ceremony has been completed, the pilgrims return to their *ranchos* and repeat the peyote rituals with their family members. This time, the family ancestor-god house, *xiriki*, serves as the temple, the place where the offerings are deposited and the peyote distributed. The pilgrims present their close kin, young and old, with peyote they have selected especially for each, as well as with thinly sliced pieces of the "heart of the Mother of peyote" originally gathered in Wirikúta. In the past, the family rancho was structured similarly to the temple cargo system. Everyone in the extended family had a special cargo that changed every five years. At the present time, only some of the cargos continue to be assigned to individuals. The family members who have gone to Wirikúta and the shaman, or shamans, in the family preside over this ceremony to celebrate the successful pilgrimage. The family members who partake of the peyote usually spend the night around the fire insulated from the external world while embarked on a journey within their own personal realms.

Tobacco and Peyote

Another sacred plant integral to peyote and the pilgrimage is a special tobacco called *makutse*, *Nicotiana rustica*. This species contains the highest nicotine levels recorded to date, measuring 18.76% + 2.6% (Siegel, Collings, and Diaz 1977:22; Wilbert 1987). Well aware of the potency of this tobacco, Huichols cultivate it strictly for ritual use. Makutse is smoked in rolled corn husk cigarettes or in clay pipes during ceremonies that revolve around deer hunting and the peyote pilgrimage. Miniature makutse cigarettes are tied to children's rattles during the Tatéi Neixa ceremony, in which the mara'akáme, through the medium of his chant and the rhythmic beating of the drum, leads the children on a metaphysical pilgrimage to the peyote desert. On the actual pilgrimage older men and experienced peyotéros carry the tobacco in sacred gourds with wartlike formations, or in smooth-skinned gourds that are sometimes covered with deer scrotum skin (Furst 1972:176-177, Myerhoff 1974:126). A special bag, *wainúri*, is woven to contain the first seasonal cuttings of makutse. Safely bound within a special weaving, the wainúri holds the spiritual essence, the heart-memory, of the Huichol gods. Makutse is considered part of Tatewarí, Grandfather Fire. According to some Huichols, the tobacco bag is the single most important ritual object carried on the pilgrimage to guide the pilgrims (Schaefer 1990:268-284).

The idea of an extremely potent tobacco guiding the peyote pilgrims on their journey can be perceived on various levels. On one level, this is ritually acted out with the tobacco bag carried in the front of the line of travelers. The wainúri is the first gift for the ceremonial kindling of Grandfather Fire at every stopping place, a rite that signifies warmth and safety along the perilous journey. On another, pharmacological level, the smoking of the tobacco in conjunction with the eating of peyote may in fact facilitate (a better term might be enhance) the transition from the physical to the metaphysical worlds traveled by the pilgrims.

In pharmacological terms, there are some interesting links between peyote and tobacco and the neurochemical reactions that occur in the body with their ingestion. The chemical constitution of peyote is very complex. Fifty-six naturally occurring alkaloids, alkaloidal amides, and amino acids have been isolated from the cactus (Anderson 1980). Over half of these chemical components are classified as types of phenethylamine or tetrahydroisoquinoline alkaloids. The greatest amount of research has focused on mescaline, 3, 4, 5-trimethoxy-β-phenethylamine, as the main constituent that triggers visual effects (Schultes and Hofmann 1992:75). Other alkaloids, less well studied but associated with peyote intoxication, are known to induce tactile, auditory, olfactory, and gustatory effects (Schultes 1972:15). Nicotine, the active agent in tobacco, can cause "hallucinations" and even catatonia if consumed in large enough doses (Wilbert 1987:150-160). Both nicotine and mescaline are able to function like neurotransmitters produced by the brain itself. Depending on dosage, nicotine or mescaline can activate, inhibit, or block the transmission at synaptic receptor sites in the central nervous system. This, in turn, affects the transmission in neurons to the brain and how the brain perceives these signals. Norepinephrine is a neurotransmitter that is chemically related to mescaline. Both mescaline and norepinephrine are derivatives of phenylethylamine (Schultes and Hofmann 1992). Nicotine is also able to trigger the release of norepinephrine, which can produce such effects as tenseness, excitement, restlessness, wakefulness, and in some cases anxiety, fear, weakness, and dizziness (Wilbert 1987:148).

Another neurotransmitter, serotonin, is structurally similar to the "hallucinogens" psilocybin and psilocin, the principal psychoactive constituents of the sacred *Psilocybe* mushrooms of the Mazatecs and other indigenous groups, and can be released with the correct concentration of nicotine (Wilbert:ibid.). One effect of the release of serotonin, which comes from the amino acid tryptophan, is to control excitement. The serotonin system is linked to depression and may regulate the inhibiting influences of repeated stimulation, or habituation. There is much evidence to support the idea that mescaline may also interact with the serotonin system. Rather than creating the feeling of sameness and boredom, mescaline may actually inhibit the perceptual adaptation to psychological habituation. This response may be expressed in feelings of renewal and revitalization, experiences which Huichols time and time again convey in their conversations about the beauty of peyote and Wirikúta (Mandell 1978:78, Furst 1972:183-184, Myerhoff 1974:164-166).

While scientists have found links on a molecular level between mescaline, which is present in peyote, nicotine in tobacco, and naturally occurring hormones in the central nervous system, Huichols also recognize a definite link between tobacco and peyote within the structure of their symbolic associations and the ritual consumption of these mind-manifesting substances. Huichols tell me that Kauyumári "formed" the sacred tobacco, and they smoke it because it is part of the gods. Peyote is also deer. When the pilgrims hunt and eat peyote they are eating the substance of the gods in order to be able to communicate with them and, however briefly, become one with them. According to some of my consultants, in the past the smoking of makutse throughout the peyote ceremony was highly ritualized and carried on at regular intervals. At the turn of the century, Lumholtz (1900:127) writes, each of the pilgrims carried up to five special gourds holding tobacco along the journey. Presently, Huichols say that the group is only required to smoke makutse when the peyote is hunted and right before it is ingested. One man who had just completed his third pilgrimage within five years explained that the tobacco is to "help one feel the peyote." Most women do not smoke makutse, and those who do, smoke it sparingly.[9] On the pilgrimage I attended, my weaving teacher, who is also my *comadre*, told me that it was the first time she had ever smoked the sacred tobacco. She said that with the combination of tobacco and peyote, she definitely felt the effects of the peyote differently. She said that the tobacco made her feel better and may have played some part in allowing her to reach greater depths in her visionary experiences.

Peyote Visions

Upon the ingestion of peyote an individual can expect to experience brilliantly colored visions in fluid motion. Before these visionary effects manifest themselves, the body, as it breaks down and absorbs the plant alkaloids, undergoes a period of "contentment and hypersensitivity followed by calm and muscular sluggishness." The individual "sees flashes of color across the field of vision, the depth and saturation of the colors (which always precede the visions) defying description" (Schultes 1972:15). Within three hours after ingestion, endlessly repeated geometric patterns such as mandalas and latticework designs, as well as more complex imagery of elements such as flowers, animals, people, and scenery, appear in vibrant colors. These are typical designs that arise from stimulation of the central nervous system discharging neurons into structures of the eye (Siegel 1977:139). The designs perceived are phosphene patterns and are intimately related to the geometry of the eye, the visual pathway and the temporal cortex (Oster 1970:83). Phosphene imagery, first analyzed by Heinrich Klüver (1926, 1928, 1942, 1966), appears in constant patterns that are characterized by varied and saturated colors of intense brightness, giving the impression of having textures and symmetrical configurations. Given the right conditions, any human can perceive these patterns. The luminosity and fluidity of such designs can vary with the dosage taken. Huichols consider these designs to be a form of communication with the gods, and individuals actively strive to receive these visions (Siegel and Jarvik 1975:138-139). Since peyote-induced phosphene images are constant, Huichols have integrated these designs into their cultural worldview and have endowed them with special meaning and significance.

Phosphenes induced by psychoactive chemicals appear in two stages. The first involves brightly colored geometric imagery in motion, called *nieríka* by Huichols, in reference to sacred designs that serve as portals to other worlds. Many take the form of pulsating mandalas (Figure 31). The Huichol shaman interviewed by Eger Valadez (1978:41) describes these as follows: "The peyote niérika are very colorful and pass by often, many of them. They just go passing by, passing by, all moving, getting bigger and smaller all of the time. Many animals and beautiful snakes also appear and pass by, without any explanation." I have received various descriptions of snake imagery. One woman told me: "I saw some animals that looked like snakes of many colors, some were striped. They filled the room. I turned and saw up above it was filled with snakes. Wherever I turned there were snakes all over." Elements in the natural environment can become incorporated into this psychedelic imagery. Numerous Huichols reflect upon their visions of the sun as a brightly glowing sphere that shines like a mirror. One consultant describes what he saw when looking into the fire: "I felt I saw the fire turn into tissue paper. . . . The form of the fire disappeared and I saw only tissue paper in the glowing form of flowers like the ones we make when we are going to sacrifice a calf. There were many colors of this flowerlike tissue paper" (Figure 32). Huichol women experience the same kinds of phosphene designs and consider them to be sacred

FIGURE 31. Mandala-like Vision in Early Stages of Peyote Intoxication. (*Yarn painting by Ramón Medina, 1966. Fowler Museum of Cultural History, University of California at Los Angeles.*)

gifts from the gods. They feel it is their duty to record these psychedelic patterns in their weaving and embroidery designs after they have returned home. Failure to do so may result in serious hardships and illness sent by the gods for not having shared these divine communications with their family and community (Schaefer 1990, 1993; Eger 1978; Eger Valadez 1986b).

Some pass from this first phase of phosphene imagery into a second phase where figural representations appear that for the most part are culturally determined. Reichel Dolmatoff (1978:47) notes that while the more geometric phosphene patterns are already present within the structure of the eye, the figurative images are projections of preexisting models that are culturally determined. During the second phase of phosphene perception, Huichols say they have direct communication with various gods. The link from the first to the second phase of psychedelic images is sometimes likened

FIGURE 32. Peyote Vision of Grandfather Fire, Flanked by Peyotes, Exploding Below- and Aboveground in a Cascade of Shimmering and Constantly Changing Colors. (*Yarn painting by Ramón Medina, 1967. Fowler Museum of Cultural History, University of California at Los Angeles.*)

to going through a tunnel, following a path through the darkness, and entering through a doorway or passage to reach what lies ahead. My consultant who told me of his vision of the fire goes on to describe this experience: "Then in the very center of the fire I saw in the distance a person; afterwards the mara'akáme told me it was Tatewarí, Grandfather Fire. I saw the entrance to the temple, even though we were in Wirikúta, and I entered the temple. I saw the vines that hang from the rafters in the temple roof to mark the four directions. From there, in the very center I saw Haramara (the goddess of the Pacific Ocean) in motion; then I saw Chapala (a large lake south of Guadalajara where the goddess Rapauwieyéme lives) in motion."

My comadre related to me part of the visions she had when we were in Wirikúta: "I saw a large plant where we had left offerings for the Mother of Peyote. Rays of light like ribbons were coming from this plant. On one side there was a lit candle. This same candle had roots. There was a deer where the peyote was. The deer acted like it was drunk. Then white foam started to come from its mouth, the kind of foam that comes from grinding peyote. It was coming out of its mouth. The foam looked like soap, like when the hikuri is killed. That's how it was pouring out. But the deer was talking to me. I didn't hear her very well until she saw me and we looked each other right in the eye."

The figurative images that come from this second phase of psychedelic phosphenes are interpreted as actual representations of the Huichol gods, and play a special part in the visions of shamans. One mara'akáme explains it as follows:

> If I eat peyote at sunset, then I will feel this way about midnight. I will begin to see beings that look like people, but they aren't people; they are gods, messengers of the gods, who are beautiful. They have beautiful clothes on, their faces are painted, they wear lots of feathers. Then they begin to speak to me and reveal many things about themselves, how they came to be, and what things I must do. (Valadez 1986a:21)

In addition to visual effects, the mescaline in peyote can bring on olfactory, tactile, gustatory, and auditory sensations. I have not recorded any olfactory ones, but with respect to gustatory experiences I have heard from several Huichols that after eating the first peyote, which tastes extremely bitter, the next ones taste much sweeter and are easier to chew and swallow. This was also reported by Furst (1972:177), who quotes Ramón Medina as telling a pilgrim to "Chew well, chew well, for it is sweet, it is delicious to the taste." Although Furst attributed Ramón's instruction to the youth as a ritual reversal of words and meaning, there may in fact be some validity to this in cases where gustatory sensations are also involved.

As for tactile experiences, the only one that was related to me was that of my comadre's son. At the time, he was twelve years old. He and his sisters had eaten the peyote their parents had brought them from Wirikúta. He retreated inside his house and lay down on the pallet, completely covered with a blanket. I went in to talk to him and touched him on the back. He recoiled and I heard him take a deep breath. His sister told me that he was "lost, traveling with the peyote." I later found out he was having a vision of snakes all over the room. They were completely covering him, he could feel them slithering back and forth, and curling around his body.

Many Huichols with whom I spoke talked of auditory sensations. The wind and its different sounds are often described. One woman told me that when she was deep within the peyote a man came to visit her. It was the god of the wind Eka Tewari (Wind Person). He spoke to her and told her she had to remember his song. He began to sing for her and repeated the song until she knew it well. In the morning she related this to the mara'akáme, who told her she must sing the song for the whole temple group. Once she sang it out loud for everyone she knew she had it memorized. She says that it is now a part of her forever.

On one occasion I was attending the Hikuri Neixa ceremony. It was the wee hours of the morning and, having stayed up two days and nights straight, most of the members were sleeping in the temple, myself included. I awoke to hear the woman who shared the cargo of Tatewarí with her husband break into a spontaneous song. She sang on and off for close to an hour. Later, I asked my comadre about this and she said it was the peyote that brought her the songs.

Receiving these songs is a sign of good luck and that the gods are pleased. During a Hikuri Neixa ceremony I attended in 1992, one of my compadres was completing his tenth year with the role of Nauxa. He sang and sang with great emotion, all the while dancing in step to the beat. Other temple members followed him, and the violin and guitar player who held cargo in the temple improvised to accompany him and his songs. A fellow temple member recorded the singing on his tape recorder. The next day my compadre told me that he didn't "make up these songs"; rather, they were songs the peyote had given him.

The mara'akáme interviewed by Valadez (1989a:21) explains how the music comes to him when he is *empeyotado* (inebriated with peyote):

> For about the first hour I don't feel anything. Then my voice will start to feel strange and I won't understand very well what people are speaking. Then I will have a very strong urge to play music, so I will play my violin. I will listen to music coming out of the air, pure air. Then I'll be feeling that the air is coming down, like a cloud that is being lowered onto the earth. Soon I'll be able to hear everything very close and clear, but I'll hear things differently than they normally sound.

Not all Huichols achieve this state of going beyond the geometric designs to seeing figures, scenes, or animated objects. Not everyone is able to hear the gods and converse with them. Those who strive to reach these levels will eat many peyote plants over a long period of time. Even then, such deep visions are never assured.

Peyote visions, as explained by one shaman, differ depending on the level of spiritual awareness an individual has achieved on his or her life's path:

> . . . when mara'akámes who have reached a very high level look into the fire they will see Tatewarí—Grandfather Fire—as a person, an old, old man with grey hair and a wrinkled face. He speaks to the mara'akámes and they listen to him. . . . The mara'akámes use their mirrors and their muviéris (feathered wands) to understand him better. The other people, the ones who aren't as far along on their 'path', don't see this old man in the fire. They will only see rattlesnakes, speckled lizards (relatives of the Gila Monster), and mountain lions, who are the special messengers of this god—his representatives. (Valadez 1989a:20)

Huichol shamans incorporate the visionary and other effects they experience into the ceremonies they are performing, as well as in healing and divining rituals. An older female shaman with whom I have a close friendship, will sit with her family in a circle around the fire. After eating peyote, she wraps herself from head to toe in her blanket and waits until the peyote takes effect. At intervals in the night she sings songs that are meant for specific family members. She has attuned herself to the peyote to such a fine degree that even when not intoxicated, she can hold peyote, or merely be in its presence, and break into song. She tells me she sings what the peyote are saying. The peyote also enables her to dream better so that she can heal people.

The mara'akámes, being experienced travelers who have sought knowledge from the teachings of peyote, interpret the visions that other pilgrims have received:

> They have to reveal it to the mara'akáme, because they see important things in their visions. They receive directions from the gods. . . . So all the people speak of their visions together . . . everything appears in a person's visions, and so he talks of it. He reveals everything except for the special messages of the gods that pertain only to his own life and shamanic path. Those special instructions pertain to him and only him, and he won't explain any of this. (Valadez 1989a:21–22)

Levels of Meaning

Peyote and the peyote pilgrimage are integrating elements that reinforce Huichol cosmology and the beliefs and traditions that revolve around their culturally shared worldview. Peyote serves as an enculturating force, echoing religious tenets in recurring themes that are transcended to visions, the spoken word through myths and songs, actions in rituals and ceremonies, and beliefs that permeate all levels of individual and collective Huichol consciousness. Having visions of a sacred deer appearing out of a large peyote cluster, as did my comadre, and feeling it look you right in the eye and talk directly to you, is bound to have a profound effect on any individual. Within the context of Huichol culture, believing in the myths, rituals, even the entire religious system, is no longer a matter of passive acceptance of one's indoctrination but of truly interacting with all they contain, and experiencing them as realities and as truths about the nature of the world and humanity at large.

Huichols, like participants in any society, begin learning about their culture at birth. The fact that they are introduced to peyote, first while in the mother's womb, then through her milk, and finally by actually ingesting the sacred cactus, has a definite effect on how children see the world, and how they learn to interpret these phenomena. I have noticed a marked change in the behavior of children after they have received small doses of peyote via their mother's milk. They become very calm, smiling often, and occasionally grabbing into the air at what I believe must be imaginary objects and colors. Several women confirmed my observations, stating that the disposition of their children does indeed change if they nurse at a time when they have been consuming peyote.

Huichol children, even before they reach the age where they will eat enough peyote to dramatically change their conscious state of mind, are well clued-in to what they can anticipate to experience (Eger 1978:41-43). They learn about this when family members talk of their peyote experiences, or when they hear temple members give accounts of their inner experiences before the leading mara'akáme. Brilliant peyote-induced phosphene designs surround them in their daily life in woven and embroidered clothing, belts, and bags—even in the yarn and bead art work Huichols make to sell. The fact that they actually see many of these same phosphene images under the influence of peyote gives credence to the worldview that Huichols have constructed around the peyote. Combined with this is the peyote pilgrimage itself. Mothers who are still nursing or have children two years or under, prefer to take them along wherever they go. This includes the journey to Wirikúta, where children, like all members, become pilgrims and actively participate in the sacred rituals. Another ceremony, Tatéi Neixa, which celebrates the first maize and green squashes, is also held especially for all children five and under. The shaman, through his song, metaphorically transforms the children into hummingbirds, eagles, or other birds and takes them on the pilgrimage to Wirikúta, an event that has been discussed in great detail by Furst and Anguiano (1976).

Peyote and the pilgrimage to Wirikúta have a powerful influence on unifying the family as well as the temple community and all of its members. Huichol conceptions of family have been explained to me by various consultants as resembling the growth of a vine. One woman said: "Do you know a plant that we have which grows and makes new buds that turn into branches? This is the way we see the family. If you have family, and if you are a plant, then you grow. At one point a branch grows as if it were your hand, and another like your legs. And it gives off more branches on this side and that. I think that the gods see us this way when we are a family. The gods know us because we grow this way."

Families share the same *iyári*, heart-memory. From the descriptions I have received about this, the concept of iyári seems to refer to a kind of genetic memory that comes from past and present family members. This same woman told me, "Although we were born without a single thought, a single memory, it was there for us, it came from my mother and father, they gave this memory to us from before." Even after someone in the family has died, he or she is still physically present in the form of a rock crystal captured by the shaman in a special ceremony to bring the deceased back to the family. The *urukáme* lives in the family shrine, upon the altar, and is brought out for all the rituals (Furst 1967; see also Michel Perrin, Chapter 14, this volume).

With these concepts of family in mind, it is no wonder that when some of the family go on the pilgrimage, those who are left behind at the rancho follow their loved ones along the journey in their thoughts and in the rituals they must perform to ensure their safety on this dangerous passage. They, too, observe many of the same restrictions, fast until late afternoon, do not eat salt, and abstain from sex. They make the ritual fire every day and pray for the pilgrims. At night they dream with them, and from these dreams the elders usually predict where they are on the pilgrimage and what has happened to them. Upon the return of the pilgrims, each family member in the rancho is blessed with sacred water and given peyote chosen especially for them so that they may also share the visions and other experiences. If a family member has not been truthful in naming all of the people with whom he or she has had sexual relations, aside from the spouse, the consequences may be devastating when it comes to eating the peyote. In one rancho where I attended the ceremony marking the return of the pilgrims, the eldest daughter and her husband retreated into their bamboo house after eating the peyote. Several hours later the rest of the family, myself included, were sitting around the fire in the patio and could hear her thrashing around, moaning, and occasionally screaming. I was concerned about her, but her mother told me to leave her be, that the peyote was punishing her because she had not confessed completely. The mother and grandmother had tears in their eyes, and the next morning it was a very emotional scene when they talked to the young woman and convinced her to tell all before the mara'akáme so that they all would be clean and purified.[10] This was the first time I had ever seen someone have a "bad trip" with peyote. Everyone I talked to, however, had a story or two to tell about someone they knew who had a negative experience. Other reasons for such an adverse reaction to the sacred plant are that the person has not fully completed ritual obligations with a god, or has not been truthful in his or her dealings with others. Thus, peyote also reinforces the importance of properly following the traditions as well as the moral code, which, in turn, brings families closer together in a unified whole.

The temple members are united on the pilgrimage.[11] When the group sets out on the journey, its members also undergo a purification ritual that involves confessing any sexual transgressions. Afterwards, the shaman ties knots in a special string, with each knot representing a pilgrim and the uniting of the souls of all participants. They are thus both physically and symbolically tied together for the entire pilgrimage, as well as afterwards, up to and including the completion of Hikuri Neixa, months later, when in one of the concluding rituals the knots are untied.

I witnessed the importance of this concept and the degree to which all the members vehemently acted this out when we stopped in Zacatecas before reaching Wirikúta. We were traveling in the trucks and van of several mestizo friends and acquaintances of the temple group. One Huichol man had a very sick little daughter. Before leaving San Andrés on the pilgrimage, the medical doctor of the clinic, Armando Casillas Romo, had supplied the family with a mixture of water and glucose to administer orally to the little girl. Emaciated from debilitating diarrhea, she had also developed a severe cough that racked her frail body. Since the child's mother was in a ritual fast, her breast milk had dried up. The mestizo companions were very concerned, and with the best of intentions made a detour to take them to the emergency room in the city hospital. The doctor there insisted that the only way the child could recover would be to leave her in the hospital for several days or more; the mother could stay with her. All of the

Huichols rejected this, and those most adamant were the child's father and the leading mara'akáme. They insisted that she was part of the pilgrim group, that the group was all joined together, and that we could not be separated. Everyone contributed to pay for antibiotics, glucose solution to be given orally, and powdered milk. Despite the unbearable heat in the day, the freezing nights, and lack of purified water, the little girl made it through the pilgrimage and is now a healthy eleven-year-old. Father and shaman attributed this miraculous recovery to the help of the gods and the offerings left for them in their sacred peyote homeland.

Perhaps the most poignant example of the enculturating forces at work in the consumption of peyote and the rituals of the pilgrimage was brought to my attention with a Huichol woman I have known for more than eight years. I first met her in the mestizo town of Santiago Ixcuintla, Nayarit, near the Pacific coast. She had come to visit the Huichol Center there, and I began to get to know her.

At first I thought she was a mestizo because she wore the typical western dress of a mestizo woman and because her Spanish was excellent. But it turned out that her family was from San Andrés Cohamiata, where she had also been born and raised. At a very young age, she had been taken to the Franciscan boarding school at the mission of Santa Clara, about two hours away, whether by her parents' choice or by force is not clear to me. I have gathered some accounts from Huichols who were fellow students at the mission school. Some of them had indeed been compelled to go, under threat that otherwise the nuns would not help the sick who had come for medical aid. The arrangement was that in exchange for the nuns' medical services, one of the children had to stay behind and attend the school. The woman in question completed the sixth grade, married a Huichol who also had attended the school, and they had moved down from the Sierra to live near Tepic, the capital of Nayarit. She rarely went to the Sierra to visit her family and did not actively participate in any of the religious ceremonies.

The national economic crisis in the 1980s affected everyone, and, no longer able to afford to live in the city, a few years ago she and her husband decided to move back to San Andrés Cohamiata. After some years living there, they were given a cargo in the community government, and at this writing have just received a major temple cargo. In 1992 they joined the temple group on the peyote pilgrimage. For both of them it was the first time they had assumed so great a responsibility, and it was also the first time they had ever eaten peyote. I talked to this woman after their return from the pilgrimage. Both she and her husband were elated, praising the sacredness of the peyote and the beauty it brought to them in their visions and experiences. Now, they are active members in the temple and eagerly look forward to the next pilgrimage the group will make. The woman also took me aside and confided something very special. She told me that for years she and her husband had been trying to have a second child. After consulting a mara'akáme, and with his guidance leaving special prayers and offerings in Wirikúta, she has just become pregnant. With a warm, broad smile on her face she told me that what the shamans say is true—that what the peyote tells you is true, that you must follow these teachings with your heart and the gods will look after you.

Conclusion

Having sought answers to why peyote is "the crossing of the souls," and what it is that Huichols know about the sacred cactus, and having collected firsthand descriptions of inner experiences with peyote, I am only too well aware how much remains for me to learn about the multiple meanings that for Huichols revolve around peyote. From the perspective of an ethnographer, I would say that peyote is meaningful because it unifies family and community members; and that it serves an enculturative purpose, instilling and reinforcing the importance of cultural beliefs and values, as well as a collectively shared worldview. However, speaking from a more personal point of view, from the intimate conversations I have had with Huichols about peyote, and from the experiences that I, myself, have had with these people and their sacred plant, I am led to think that it is much more than this. As one Huichol put it, "Peyote is for learning; those with strong hearts will receive messages from the gods." Peyote enables a person to tap into other dimensions, other ways of seeing, feeling, hearing, and sensing the world. With their carefully structured cosmology that includes a belief system constructed around peyote and nature, the Huichols are provided with a cultural framework in which to place the information received and interpret the things they experience. The door is thereby opened for one to develop and evolve a more profound sense of self as well as family and community. Experiences such as these make one contemplate life, mortality, the metaphysical world, and the requirements involved in following a spiritual path to reach higher levels of awareness. As the twentieth century draws to a close, Huichols are experiencing greater pressures than ever from the outside world and are challenged more than ever to maintain their own cultural integrity. The peyote experiences are an essential way for Huichols to reaffirm their cultural identity and yet step beyond this cultural threshold to understand and become part of a greater whole, of an increasingly multicultural world where cultures transcend political boundaries.

And yes, the words of that Huichol man are engraved in my memory: "Peyote is the crossing of the souls, it is everything that is. Without peyote nothing would exist."

Nevertheless, because of antidrug agitation and federal and local police action, many Huichols now have great fear of running into problems with the authorities in the states through which they pass on their way to Wirikúta. There have, in fact, been detentions of pilgrims for possessing peyote, for the use of peyote, even among Huichols, is still not legal under Mexican federal law. A great deal of ambiguity exists in this body of legislation. The Supreme Law, which defines general normative principles of the Mexican federal law, contains nothing that would suggest peyote prohibition. The regulatory laws, codes and regulations, however, forbid the use of peyote. Classified as a psychotropic substance, it falls under the most stringently regulated category of narcotics. (Ari Rajsbaum 1995, personal communication).

The other thing Huichols fear is that overharvesting by people other than themselves will one day exhaust the peyote supply. This concern is real and well founded. Ari Rajsbaum, an INI official working in the Procuraduría de Justicia (Justice Department of Indian Affairs), told me in the fall of 1995 that clandestine harvesting in Wirikúta by non-Huichols has escalated to the point of jeopardizing the quantity, supply, and well-being of the peyote population as a whole, especially old-growth peyote. Rajsbaum reports that the plants are ripped from the ground, root and all, leaving no possibility for the peyote to regenerate. As a result, where there once used to be areas filled with larger clusters of peyote, only a scattering of small immature plants now remain, if any at all.

But protecting peyote and its ritual use has implications beyond allowing some indigenous cultures to practice their religious traditions. The quest for peyote among the Huichols is also a quest for the self. In that sense, the peyote hunt is part and parcel of a universal quest for society and the sacred that transcends cultural boundaries and unites humankind in its ultimate search for its own humanity. No doubt, not all Huichols are conscious of these meanings beyond their own society. But some are. It is worth quoting what a Huichol shaman said to me during the closing peyote ceremony before the coming of the rains. He was telling me that the neighboring mestizos think that Huichols are lazy, that they don't work hard because they have so many ceremonies. He went on to say: "Yes, it's true that we have many ceremonies to ask our gods for luck, health, that the maize grows well, that there are many deer and cattle, that our families are healthy. What these people don't understand is that we do not have these ceremonies just for ourselves alone. We have them to ask the gods to care for all the people, everywhere, so that the world will keep going, so that life (in the world) will continue to exist."

NOTES

1. One of the federally licensed Hispanic peyote distributors with whom I work in the lower Rio Grande valley showed me a necklace of obviously great age that was strung with shells. He told me he had found it out in the peyote fields and that next to it was an old strand of dried peyote buttons strung on a fiber cord. Unfortunately, he was unable to relocate it later so that it might be dated.

2. Anderson (1980:138) discusses the various theories of the etymology of the word, the most widely accepted being that it derives from the Nahuatl *péyutl*. Molina's *Dictionary* gives its Spanish meaning as *"capullo de seda, o de gusano"* ("silk cocoon or caterpillar cocoon"). Anderson suggests the "silk" may be the wooly white tufts on the cactus. Remi Simeon's *Dictionnaire de la Langue Nahuatl ou Mexicaine* (1963:336) gives the following meanings for péyutl or péyotl: "plant whose root is made into a beverage that is used in place of wine; silk worm cocoon; outer covering of the heart."

3. See Valadéz, Chapter 9, this volume, and Fikes (1985) for a description of the wolves that go on a peyote pilgrimage.

4. This particular peyote growth formation is commonly known as cresting and occurs when the crown of the plant loses control of its growth regulation process; instead of growing upwards, the peyote begins spreading laterally. Anderson (personal communication 1994) informs me that cresting is the result of peyote being infected with a virus, which, to his knowledge, does not harm the plant. Further studies may indicate that the alkaloid content of cresting peyote is altered and hence different from normal growth peyote.

5. The several films that have been made of the peyote pilgrimage document the metaphorical hunting of peyote as though it were deer.

6. For the origin of the maize myth, see both Preuss and Shelton, this volume.

7. Outside of ritual, peyote is consumed only to restore energy, stay awake, ward off hunger and pain, and alleviate intestinal disorders.

8. Although not occurring on this particular pilgrimage, in some instances a peyotéro may spend the entire night on the summit of Kauyumári's hill in the hope of receiving a special message from the deities.

9. Wilbert, in his comprehensive work on tobacco and shamanism in South America (1987), describes cultures in which "woman tobacco" is widely used.

Since writing this chapter I have learned that the only women who are allowed to smoke ma-kutse are shamans or those training to be shamans. Women tend to be much more secretive in these matters, compared to their male counterparts who are publicly recognized as specialists in healing and esoteric knowledge. Women shamans keep a low profile because they are more likely to be accused of hexing or evil doing and fear the reprisals they might suffer in consequence of such allegations.

10. Lumholtz (1902:156) describes the effect of peyote on one Huichol man, who, based on his behavior, was said to have violated the rule of sexual abstinence during the deer hunting rituals:

> The attack lasts only a few minutes, and subsides as suddenly as it came on, though a person may become very violent, tear off his clothes, and run against the others with threatening gestures and wild, loud talking. In that case he is seized and tied hand and foot until he regains his senses.

The importance of confessing sexual transgressions during the purification rituals of the peyote pilgrimage is made clear in Myerhoff's account of the 1966 pilgrimage she and Furst attended (Myerhoff 1974:135-136). One of the young women participants was very reluctant to name her sexual partners and was sharply berated for it by her companions. According to Myerhoff,

> Ramón explained that her action had jeopardized the entire journey, that had she not at last relented, the trip could not have been undertaken that year, for "all must be of one heart, there must be complete unity among us."

11. The interrelationship among temple members is a very complex one. See Schaefer, Chapter 11.

ACKNOWLEDGMENTS

I am grateful for the research support of a Fulbright Fellowship, Organization of American States Fellowship, Programs on Mexico Grant from the University of California at Los Angeles, Faculty Research Grants from the University of Texas–Pan American, and from Mr. and Mrs. Vernon and Lysbeth Anderson. I also wish to thank Edward Anderson of the Desert Botanical Garden in Phoenix, Arizona, for his instructive comments; Johannes Wilbert, who will always be my teacher and advisor as he was during my years at UCLA, for drawing my attention to the connection between peyote and tobacco and to the ramifications of this link; and to Ari Rajsbaum for keeping me up to date on Mexican peyote legislation and its effect on Huichols and their way of life.

INTRODUCTION TO CHAPTER 6

In the course of the six years during which Barbara G. Myerhoff and I worked on and off with the Huichol artist and shaman Ramón Medina Silva and his life's companion, Guadalupe de la Cruz Ríos ("Lupe" for short) (Figure 33), we recorded a great number of what, for want of a better term, we call "myths." For Ramón and Lupe, these were the true chronicles of the Huichol people. They insisted that what Ramón was telling us was, in the Spanish they both spoke well, "nuestras historias," our histories, the true histories of the Huichol people.*

Ramón's command of Huichol narratives was impressive. Of course, his voice was only one of many. In Huichol oral poetry, as in that of other indigenous peoples, there is not one truth but many. The stories shift in detail and emphasis and vary in the telling, not only from *comunidad* to *comunidad*, but also within the same community. That the myths Robert M. Zingg (1938) collected in Tuxpan de Bolaños in the 1930s are very different from everyone else's does not make them wrong or false, only different. Not even the sacred chants and invocations, with their elliptical or shorthand recounting of the doings of ancestors and gods, are constant, as Preuss discovered in 1907 when each of four shaman-singers from the same comunidad gave him a different version of the same song. There is thus no "right" or "wrong" way of telling the stories. There are many versions and all have their own validity.

But there are overlap and agreement as well. The narratives of Ramón, who from early childhood absorbed the traditions of both San Sebastián and Santa Catarína from his mother and other relatives, have many similarities with those from other parts of the Huichol country. There are myths that are not just pan-Huichol, but pan-Sierra. For example, Ramón's version of the tale of the boy who joined the ant people to search

---

*Ramón's Huichol name was Uru (Ulu) Temay, Guadalupe's is Matsuawima. She gives the meaning of the former as Newly Made Arrow, the latter as Bracelet with Power. Uru (or Ulu) Temay can also mean Young Arrow Man or Arrow Youth. By conicidence, two other Huichols who figure prominently in this book also had this popular male name: Santos Aguilar Carrillo (Chapter 9), and Nicholas Carrillo de la Cruz.

FIGURES 33. Lupe and Ramón in Wirikúta, December 1968. She watches intently as he slices the first peyotes for commununal consumption. (*Photograph by Peter T. Furst.*)

for maize and returned to his mother's *rancho* with the daughter of the Maize Goddess as his wife, only to lose her again—and with her the maize itself—when his mother fails to respect her sanctity, is strikingly similar to the maize origin myths Preuss collected among the Coras and the Nahua-speaking "Mexicanos" of San Pedro Jícora, Durango. (Indeed, the latter may well have been the source for this widely shared and sorrowful sacred story, which for Huichols provides both the mystical and the historic rationale for their reverence for maize as *the* sacred foodstuff, and for the rituals and symbols thought to be indispensable to its thriving and use [cf. Furst 1994; Shelton, this volume]).

Not surprisingly, Ramón himself was sure that his were the "authentic" Huichol histories. So is every other storyteller. But it is a mark of the extensive command Ramón had of Huichol myth and ritual, what one might call his literary genius, that with all the stories he shared with us, there is little duplication between them and the considerable repertory he dictated to Fernando Benítez (Figures 34–36). Ramón gave us enough material for a book, yet there was enough left over to fill more than a hundred pages of Volume 2 of the five volumes on Mexican Indians published between 1968 and 1980 by that well-known Mexican writer, journalist, historian and, most recently, diplomat. Ramón started working with us on a fairly regular basis in 1965. Toward the end of 1967 he took time out to accompany Benítez, on the recommendation of the latter's friend, the Mexican social anthropologist and Indian service official Salomón Nahmad (see Chapter 17), on an extended trip through the Huichol sierra as guide, translator, and consultant on Huichol myth and ritual. Ramón's all-too-human frailties and inner torment notwithstanding, Benítez came away with an unequivocal impression of him as not only a gifted, multitalented artist and storyteller, but *"un aprendiz de cantador excepcional,"* an outstanding apprentice shaman (Benítez 1968:382). Nor was this peasant farmer-turned-artist and future shaman at all shy about voicing his opinions publicly: according to Benítez (1968:358), soon after Ramón moved from his milpa on the Lerma to Guadalajara in 1962, he appeared several times on the radio, becoming "admired and looked up to" among his recent fellow Lerma colonists for his vigorous advocacy and outspoken defense of the Huichol cause. Years later, in the fifth and final volume of his popular ethnography of Mexican Indians, Benítez wrote with sadness of the violent end in 1971 of this talented and innovative artist and exceptional apprentice *cantador* (shaman-singer), likening Ramón's violent death to the suicide of another much-conflicted Indian shaman, a Tepehuan, he had known and admired (Benítez 1980). Ramón was born in the Huichol sierra on the borderline between the indigenous communities of San Sebastián Teponahuaxtlan and Santa Catarína. Lupe's birthplace was San Miguel de Zapóta, in the Sierra de Nayar, where her family, led by her paternal shaman-grandfather, Ignacio de la Cruz, had emigrated during the bloody conflicts of the Cristero Revolt that in the 1930s set mestizos against Huichols and Huichol against Huichol.

Ramón's native San Sebastián was itself practically emptied of its indigenous inhabi-

FIGURES 34, 35, 36. Ramón, Shaman Storyteller. Shamans are often consummate actors who make their narratives come alive for their audience. Ramón frequently inhabited all the major

players in his stories, laughing, crying, even "dying" with them. In telling the myth of an epic struggle between the culture hero, Kauyumari, and his adversary, the sorcerer Kiéri, he acted out both their parts: Kauyumari, who vanquishes his enemy with the aid of peyote and the fifth of five magical arrows; and Kiéri, who, in dying, transforms into his plant form as "Tree of the Wind" (cf. chapter 7). (*Photographs by Peter T. Furst.*)

tants during these troubles. His family fled from its rancho and maize plantings, along with hundreds of other Huichols, to Nayarit and the safety of the lower Río Lerma, an area that, judging from early colonial documents, had actually been Huichol at the time of the Spanish invasion in 1530. Along this part of the river, which is also called the Río Grande de Santiago, the refugees established small farming settlements and ejidos and continued to live, as much as possible, traditional Huichol lives, though obviously without the solidifying benefit of the traditional temple organizations and communitywide annual ceremonial round in the Sierra.

Ramón did not much like to speak of that time, preferring the present, when things were better. What came out loud and clear was that the poverty on the Lerma was grinding, especially after his father deserted the family. (Years later, when his father, then very sick, suddenly reappeared, Ramón, having forgiven him, helped support him and stood by him during his final illness.) Left to themselves, life became even harder for Ramón's mother, whose name was Kuka, and her children. Every year, children and adults migrated to the coast to work for starvation wages harvesting maize and tobacco on Mexican farms. Though blinded by cataracts, Doña Kuka, who came from a family of shamans, trained as a *mara'akáme*, a shaman-singer and curer (Benítez 1968:355). After she grew up, Ramón's older sister Concha followed in her mother's footsteps. Ramón learned much from his mother; in fact, even after he and Lupe moved to the Guadalajara area in the early sixties, and during the time we knew him, he would sometimes take off by bus to Tepic to return, most of the way on foot, to the Lerma colony to help his mother and sister conduct ceremonies, or clear brush to plant maize.

It was during one of the annual migrations to the coast that Ramón, then just eighteen years old, met Guadalupe (Figure 37). Like him, she was working on the same Mexican farm, harvesting maize for pennies a day. Twelve years his senior and a recent widow, she, too, came from a family of shamans; in fact, by all accounts, hers seems to have been much more important. Not only was her paternal grandfather, Ignacio de la Cruz, a wise and respected mara'akáme and *"un gran sabio,"* a man of much knowledge and spiritual power, in his native Santa Catarína, but her maternal grandfather, too, was a shaman. Not as wise as her other *abuelito* and hence not as respected, she told me recently, but still a man of knowledge and wisdom.

As Ramón tells it in one of the narratives below, it took some doing to convince her that, though compared to this experienced woman he was only a boy, nevertheless he would one day amount to something and that, though so much older and better versed in life, she should agree to live with him as his wife. Although to their mutual disappointment, for both loved children greatly, Lupe was unable to conceive, their close cooperation on many levels lasted until his violent death in 1971, albeit with ups and downs. In the last years of his life, Ramón took a young, and singularly untalented, woman as his second wife, and although polygyny is accepted, Lupe temporarily moved out. She moved back in, however, when the young woman gave birth to a baby boy, unceremoniously appropriating the infant as though he were her own (Figure 38), all the while berating the unhappy biological mother as lazy, stupid, without talent for embroidery or weaving, unable even to make good tortillas, and, to top it off, for not being faithful to Ramón.[1]

By the early 1960s, Ramón, a man of many talents and considerable intelligence and curiosity, had become increasingly frustrated by the limitations and hardships of life as a poor Huichol peasant farmer on the lower Río Lerma. Lupe, herself talented in all the arts common to Huichol women, and a fine singer and traditional dancer besides, told me she came more and more to share his frustrations and, despite her attachment

FIGURE 37. Lupe on the 1966 Peyote Pilgrimage. She is praying over the *tostadas*, toasted tortillas, that are used as offerings to the sacred deer. Tostadas are the only nourishment peyoteros permit themselves on the pilgrimage. (*Photograph by Peter T. Furst.*)

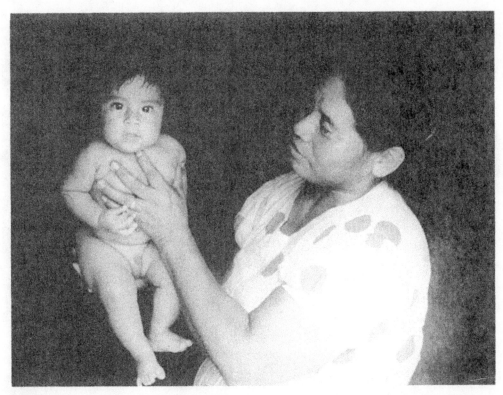

FIGURE 38. Lupe in Tepic, Nayarit. She proudly displays, as though he were her own offspring, the baby borne by Ramón's second wife in their short-lived union. (*Photograph by Peter T. Furst.*)

to her uncle José Ríos, the shaman-elder of a nearby extended family rancho called El Colorín (coral tree, *Erythrina* sp.), and she wanted a better life elsewhere. Finally, having heard that Padre Ernesto Loera Ochóa, a Franciscan priest at the Basilica de Zapópan, near Guadalajara, was giving Huichols a helping hand in establishing a new life by buying their arts and crafts, Ramón and Lupe left his mother and sister behind to try their luck in Mexico's second largest city.

The work of clearing fields and planting maize in the rough and arid country along the lower Lerma was backbreaking. Even with the addition of wages from day labor on the coast, Ramón and Lupe never moved beyond bare subsistence, but this clearly had no effect on the emotional bond that tied these two Huichols to the soil and, especially, to the sacred maize. Instead of joining other Huichols in the urban slums, they found themselves a patch of unused land with a stand of castor bean plants and tuna cactus on the northern outskirts, just off the highway to Zacatécas. They cleared it by themselves of brush, weeds, stones, and trash, using machete, ax, and hoe, and then planted the traditional mixed crop of maize, beans, squash, tomatoes, and a few chile peppers (Figures 39, 40). They constructed a ramada of four posts and palm thatch, and from found materials built themselves a small, spare but sturdy, windowless little dwelling.

The castor beans and prickly pear cactus they left standing, because Ramón knew

FIGURE 39. Dawn on Lupe's and Ramón's Rancho and Milpa on the Outskirts of Guadalajara, August 1966. *Right*, the ramada stands with the hearthstones for the cooking fire. (*Photograph by Peter T. Furst.*)

how to make medicines from the seeds of the former, while both the fruit and joints of the latter are popular foods in Mexico. Their miniature urban rancho quickly became a magnet for Huichols traveling between the city and the Sierra. For them, the self-assured Ramón was a culture broker—an intermediary between the familiar traditional world of the Sierra and the mysterious ways of urban life and governmental bureaucracy.

I was pointed in Ramón's direction in 1965 by the cultural affairs officer of the American Consulate in Guadalajara. He told me that the large and colorful Huichol yarn painting hanging over his desk had been made by "a very intelligent aspiring witch doctor" named Ramón, that Ramón and his wife grew maize on a postage stamp-sized farm on the outskirts, that they sold their yarn art to Padre Ernesto in Zapopan, and that the priest would know where to find them. As it turned out, the good padre, who had gone to college in the United States, did not know exactly where they lived, but he told me that Ramón came every few days with his and his wife's art works to sell—Lupe was truly superb at embroidery and weaving on the backstrap loom—and that if I came often enough I'd be sure to meet him.

Ramón did show up the following day with a packet of two-foot by two-foot yarn paintings on masonite and a bagful of his wife's weavings. I bought them all for the

FIGURE 40. Ramón Singing to the First Elotes (Tender Young Ears of Maize) from His and Lupe's Own Coamil (Milpa). (*Photograph by Peter T. Furst.*)

UCLA ethnic arts collection, and over the following weeks we established what I like to think was a relationship of mutual trust. Not long afterwards, Barbara G. Myerhoff, a friend and fellow anthropology graduate student at UCLA, who had a long-standing interest in Native American religion and shamanism, and with whom I had worked briefly on the Luiseño Indian Reservation near San Diego, arrived in Guadalajara in search of a topic for her doctoral dissertation. I introduced her to Ramón and Lupe. The following year, 1966, Ramón insisted that without having eaten some peyote we would never understand his culture, and he invited us to come along on a peyote pilgrimage that December, the third of five he had pledged toward his "completion" as a shaman to Tatewarí, the old fire god, and Werikúa, Eagle, the Sun Father.

The rest, as they say, is history. The 1966 peyote hunt (which, being organized outside the traditional temple organization, as is customary in the Sierra, was rancho- and extended family-based, but still very much within the ancestral traditions), was the first to be witnessed by anthropologists. It became the subject of Myerhoff's Ph.D. thesis and her subsequent book, *Peyote Hunt: The Sacred Journey of the Huichol Indians* (1974), a classic of its kind. As for Ramón the artist, though his yarn paintings were always beautifully balanced—he insisted on symmetry—and technically of high quality, like the one I saw at the American Consulate, Ramón himself always described them as "*puros adornos,*" only decorations, and thus without symbolic content. One day in 1965, after he had begun dictating myths, I asked if he had ever thought of illustrating his *historias* with yarn paintings. He had not, but he would try. And so was born the story-telling yarn painting, of which he was the pioneer and which has long since become the standard of Huichol art production (Figure 41).

Among the narratives Ramón dictated to us were serious and funny ones, and also some of the most important in the Huichol repertoire. These included the previously mentioned origin story of the sacred maize and its loss because the people failed to treat it with reverence; the journey of the soul after death; the epic of Kiéri, a sola-naceous plant personified as a sorcerer, and his war for supremacy with the culture hero, the sacred Deer Person Kauyumári, and peyote; the tale of Kauyumári in his aspect as trickster and sexual clown in a primordial time when, as Ramón put it, he was—like Ramón himself at times—"half-bad"; the story of the primordial hunt by the *kakauyaríte*, the ancestors as deified mountains; and the stories of the sacred Deer who was peyote; of the birth of the Sun and the theft of Fire from its guardians in the underworld; of the magical flight of the children transformed into hummingbirds to the land of dawn and peyote; of Great-grandmother Nakawé, Watákame ("Clearer of Fields") and the deluge that drowned a previous world; of the origin of the Huichols as children of Dog Woman; of the Bee People; of peccary, or javelina, the compan-ion animal and animal manifestation of Great-grandmother Nakawé; and on and on—hours and hours of this gifted storyteller's interpretations of Huichol sacred poetry (cf. Furst and Myerhoff 1966; Furst 1967, 1990, 1992; Benítez 1968; Myerhoff 1974; Furst and Anguiano 1977).

For the most part, we conducted our taping sessions under the thatch-roofed ramada in Ramón's and Lupe's little rancho. At other times, we drove out into the countryside to do the recording away from the noise and distractions of passing traffic and Huichols stopping by for hours, or days, on their way into or out of the city.

These were two people with a foot in both worlds who nevertheless were never in any doubt as to their own identity and their pride in being Huichol. Inevitably, they taught the Mexican and North American anthropologists who came to know them that our old definitions of "acculturation," of who and what is an "Indian," were, for the most part—and certainly in this instance—wrong-headed, patronizing, and inappropriate. Indians, so went one hoary theory, cease being "real" Indians when they leave their traditional communities. Physically, Ramón and Lupe had done just that, of course. But it was self-evident that neither they, nor other so-called "urban" Huichols we met, had thereby stopped being Indians. On the contrary, for Ramón and Lupe, and other Huichols like them, daily confrontation with "the other," the dominant society, seemed to reinforce, rather than weaken, their pride in being Huichol, and their determination to remain so.

This pride also came through loud and clear during their first experience outside Mexico, when, in the spring of 1971, they traveled to California at the invitation of the Los Angeles County Museum of Natural History, which had earlier given Ramón's

FIGURE 41. Narrative Yarn Painting Depicting the Myth of the Origin of the Dangerous Scorpion. The Master of Animals, *lower right*, gave Vulture a closed basket, similar to those in which shamans stow their power objects, and ordered him to carry it to a distant hidden place, where it would be safe from prying eyes and hands. Under no circumstances was Vulture to look inside. After Vulture flew away with the box, he, like Pandora, could not contain his curiosity. When he pried off the lid, he found the inside crawling with scorpions. The stings of some were mild; the poison of others was deadly. By the time he could close the basket, the scorpions had escaped to all parts of the world, where they hid behind peeling bark and under stones and waited to inflict their painful stings on unwary people. (*Yarn painting by Ramón Medina. Fowler Museum of Cultural History, University of California at Los Angeles.*)

yarn paintings in the UCLA museum collection a major exhibition. When a Spanish-speaking reporter sent to interview Ramón by the *Los Angeles Times* asked him why— one hallucinogenic drug being, after all, "just as good as another" for tripping out— Huichols didn't just buy LSD instead of traveling hundreds of miles for peyote, he was given a stern lecture on what it means to be Huichol. And as for drugs, *"Aspirina es droga,"* said Ramón. *"Peyote es sagrado."* Ramón was pleased but not overawed when

I took him to meet Dr. Franklin Murphy, the UCLA Chancellor who told him how much he liked Huichol art, complimented him on the quality of his yarn paintings, and asked informed and sympathetic questions about the Huichols and their condition, and that of Indian people generally, in modern Mexico.

Perhaps had Ramón been literate and realized he was meeting a famous cult figure and the author of a bestseller, he might have been more impressed when Barbara Myerhoff, who was putting Lupe and Ramón up in her San Fernando Valley home for a second week's stay in the U.S., brought her former fellow student Carlos Castaneda home with her so that he could at long last meet the Huichol shaman-artist who had figured so prominently in her dissertation, and about whom she had told him so much over the years. Castaneda had been asking Myerhoff for an introduction to her Indian friend ever since she returned from the 1966 peyote pilgrimage, in which we had both participated, under Ramón's guidance, but the opportunity had not presented itself until Ramón's and Lupe's Los Angeles visit in April 1971. (Castaneda could, of course, have gone to Mexico to meet Ramón on his own, but it is to his credit that he respected Myerhoff's prior claim and waited for a personal introduction.) It is surely the case that, as the psychologist Richard de Mille (1976, 1980) has documented, some elements of Myerhoff's and my early writings about Ramón found their way into Castaneda's descriptions of the "Yaqui sorcerer" he called Don Juan Matús, in what some of us had come increasingly to suspect by the early 1970s was fiction, not ethnography. But the fact is that there was already in 1962-63—three years before either Myerhoff or I had ever laid eyes on Ramón—a manuscript by Carlos in which his professed adventures and conversations with "Don Juan" are recounted in very much the same words as in his later bestsellers. It was this early paper that over the next several years was to evolve into the book, the first of seven, that brought him fame and fortune.

Guadalupe told me years later that during their first and only encounter in Los Angeles, just two months before Ramón's tragic death, her husband and Carlos had hit it off splendidly, telling jokes in Spanish and practically splitting their sides with laughter all through a Mexican meal. Presumably, each—the Huichol artist-shaman and the Peruvian-born doctoral student in anthropology and gifted raconteur—recognized in the other something of his own trickster personality. True to form, Ramón invited Carlos to come and visit him in Mexico, even to accompany him on a peyote hunt. But they were never to see each other again, though Lupe told me Castaneda did come to visit her once in Tepic a year or so after Ramón's death and asked her to tell him about the circumstances of her husband's murder.

Guadalupe was then, as she is today—nearly thirty years after I first met her and Ramón—a woman of great strength, dignity, and talent. She was certainly no less committed to Huichol religion and ritual than Ramón. And if she was not as fluent in the mythology as he was, she knew a lot, and she was no less adamant than he that the stories told what really happened. That was so when I knew them in the 1960s and it remains the case today, even as she carries with her on her travels a paper image of her

FIGURE 42. Lupe Conducting Ceremony, 1988. The drum, *tepu* in Huichol, a word of Nahuatl origin, is a hollowed-out, three-legged log with a deerskin head. The images carved into the front of the drum are the culture hero, Kauyumari, in his deer guise and the drum's own spirit, whose booming voice is heard through the hole. The instrument is female, addressed as "Our Mother (the) Drum." (*Photograph by Peter T. Furst.*)

FIGURE 43. Propitiating the Sorcerer, *Datura*, Bandelier National Monument, August 17, 1989. (*Photograph by Peter T. Furst.*)

divine namesake, the Virgin of Guadalupe (whom some Huichols, in any case, consider to be one of their own). Ramón died from bullet wounds he received in July 1971 in an argument with a cousin over a woman that suddenly turned violent. The altercation occurred—as violence so often does—after much drinking, during a ceremony marking the clearing of brush for a new *coamil* (maize field) Ramón was planning to cultivate near his mother's rancho.

After she buried Ramón, Lupe did not enter into another permanent relationship, though from all accounts she certainly did not shun male companionship. At this writing, she is in her late seventies, and though commanding considerable esoteric knowledge and occasionally conducting ceremonies for family and friends (Figure 42), she does not consider herself more than in training to become a mara'akáme, a vocation her husband held from the day he completed his fifth peyote hunt in December 1968 to the time of his death. The last time we got together, in August of 1993, she said that she still had much left to "complete"—that is, to fulfill her vow to become a shaman—and that she was not sure that her health would permit her to make the peyote pilgrimages of her own, as distinct from the six or seven on which she accompanied Ramón, she felt she still needed "for learning." In the meantime, she has come to love traveling, seeing new places and meeting new people. A few years ago, during a visit to Santa

Fe, New Mexico, she asked me to show her "where the ancient, ancient Indians lived," the forefathers of the Indian governor who on an earlier visit had invited her and her extended family to his pueblo. I took her to Bandelier National Monument and she insisted on bringing chocolate, cigarettes, candles, and some feathers to leave as gifts of respect to the Old Ones that lived there. For much of her life she has been suffering from rheumatoid arthritis in both knees, and though walking was difficult and painful, she insisted on seeing everything. When we came upon a large *Datura inoxia* in full flower just below the trail past the Long House ruin, she stopped dead in her tracks and clapped her hands. She asked us to wait, while she stepped off the path and circled the *Datura*, a sister species of those found in the Huichol country whose potential for harm Huichols treat with respect and fear. She was obviously scolding it, shaking her finger at it and muttering invocations in rapid-fire Huichol that she later explained told the sorcerer not to move from there and not to harm us and others (Figure 43).[2]

Though her eyes are dimming and she is often in considerable discomfort, and, what is most worrisome, was recently diagnosed with congestive heart failure, over the past several years Lupe has earned enough money with her art work, and collected more from friends and admirers, to purchase a piece of well-watered land near Santa María del Oro in Nayarit for members of the large extended family, several of them also talented artists and artisans, of which she is the elder and for whose welfare she feels herself responsible. Some people might regret that in recent years she has also become favorite "medicine woman" to some New Agers. But they also give her and her family help, and if that suits her and brings her benefits, more power to her. And seeing her with her new prescription eyeglasses and full set of uppers and lowers (with which she, who had lost most of her natural teeth years ago, was fitted just this past year by a generous Santa Fe dentist), and hearing about the fruit trees and the little stream on her newly acquired piece of land in Nayarit, who could doubt that it does?

Peter T. Furst

6 : "HOW ONE GOES BEING HUICHOL . . ."

RAMÓN MEDINA SILVA (ca. 1925–1971)

Editor's Note: In the years during which Barbara Myerhoff and I were privileged to hear Ramón tell and sing the ancient stories, and watched him illustrate them with colored yarns pressed into beeswax, he occasionally lapsed into personal reminiscence and philosophical rumination about his own life and the meaning of being Huichol. As graduate students we had to read Paul Radin's classic, Primitive Man as Philosopher (1927). That is what the best of the shamans are—philosophers—and that is assuredly how the always convivial Ramón impressed us—with all his weaknesses, his tendency to squander money he earned from his art on occasional binge drinking with friends and strangers alike, and the inner torments all Indian people must feel who are daily confronted with the dominant culture. In the all-too-short time that we knew him he philosophized about many things—relations between Huichols and representatives of the dominant culture, whom he, who insisted that Huichols were the true, the authentic, Mexicans, would sometimes characterize disdainfully as foreigners, even as gachupines, *a less than flattering term for Spaniards; about the importance and sacredness of maize and deer; about the ancestor gods; the meaning of fire; about peyote; the theft of Huichol lands; the threat from sorcerers; his becoming a mara'akáme; the proper way of thinking and acting when preparing the field in accordance with the rules of life laid down by the divine ancestors; and on and on. Sometimes, when he talked in this way he made me turn my tape recorder off. More often, he insisted I have it on to make certain his words would not disappear into thin air, watching all the while to make sure the tape was not running out or slowing down because of weak batteries.*

The narratives and thoughts that follow were mainly dictated in 1966 and 1967. Ramón conveyed these thoughts mostly in Spanish, in which he was quite fluent, partly in Huichol. Some were dictated in snatches, over a period of several days, to be pieced together later. In rendering them into English, passages relating to the same topic but recorded at different times were combined and words or sentences rearranged for the sake of clarity and flow. Always, however, care was taken to preserve the flavor of the original as much as possible.[3]

I.
"More or Less My Age Is Forty . . ."

More or less my age is forty, as I am speaking to you here. I am close to forty, perhaps. When my mother brought me into this world, there in San Sebastián Teponahuaxtlan, I came, I don't know from where. But once I started growing up—I must have been five or six years old—my father left us alone. Alone he left us, to make do for ourselves. My mother brought us up according to how one must do such things, as Tayaupá,[*] as Tatewarí[†] gave her the ability, as he gave her the will, the love.

From then we started working. A very hard life, very hard. Growing up without a father. I remember we used to braid, when I was a small boy, making braided strips of palm in order to support ourselves. That with which one makes hats. In order to put on clothes, in order to eat. I remember I ran around without pants, without shirt, without anything. I was cold, often I was cold. Later I would go and work for some people. In the afternoon I would return, very tired, without a thing. All that work, herding goats, cleaning maize, doing all those things. Six *centavos* they paid, a *centavo* a day. If one paid in maize, one paid one liter of maize a day for all our family. One liter! There was much hunger then.

Early in the morning my mother would say, "Hurry son, it is time to go to work." To earn six centavos! What are six centavos? To be able to eat, to be able to dress— what do six centavos come to? We would stay there from six in the morning until six in the evening. Until the crickets commenced their calling. Only then the *patrón* would let us go home. Those rich ones, those *vecinos*, those Spaniards, owners of *haciendas* who had much money, much food, many clothes, much maize. Here we were children, small, hungry, working as best we could to make money for food. When we returned, sometimes it rained. Then we arrived all wet and we had no clothes to change into. Nothing into which to change so that we could be dry and warm. That is how we slept. In that cold, poor ones without anything.

Well, then one night it happened that Tayaupá spoke to me. He said, "Look, son, do not worry. You must grow up a little more so you can go out and become wise, so that you can support yourself." He said, Tayaupá said, "Do not worry son. It will be good with you one day."

Since then I had these dreams. Sometimes it would happen when I was asleep, dreaming. Then sometimes when I was awake, when it was day. When I was working there, so hard. I heard everything, I saw my life. And then I would be very happy.

I was still a small boy. Five, six, seven years old. Then I would become happy. I would wake up happy, because Tayaupá would say to me, "Look, you will be able to support yourself well. You are going to do this, that and the other." From that time on

[*]Lit. "Our Father," an alternate name for the sun god Werikúa (Eagle). (—Eds.)
[†]Our Grandfather, the old fire god and First Shaman. (—Eds.)

they started to say that one day I would be a mara'akáme. They would say that one day I would do these things which I make nowadays. I would be told, "You will make fine things, you will make these designs one day and everyone will like you."

In those days I did not think of anything. Oh, in all that time I did not speak one word of Spanish. Nothing. Not one word. There was no one to explain things to me. No school, no one to tell me and explain this word, or that. There we were all alone, sleeping, working, and sometimes going without food for two days, for three days. Because we had nowhere to go and we had no money with which to buy food. We were really poor!

Ah yes, at this time my father was very thoughtless. He did not think of us. He is dead now and his soul is there with Díos Sol. But at that time he was thoughtless. He went to enjoy his life. And we remained there with our mother, the one who brought me up at her breast. Who gave me nourishment, everything. Well, in those years I was believing everything, knowing little. But I reflected, I reflected on this and that, listening to all that which Díos Sol said, all that which Tatewarí said. They said, "You are going to be this way and that, it is for this you were born. It is for this that we are telling you everything, this way and the other."

Very well. At first I was frightened by this. I did not know. And with time I began to reflect on this, knowing everything, learning everything. Listening to them when they sang that which is our history. Well, I started to think, "Oh, this is what they told me, that I was going to become a mara'akáme. That I was to be this way and that."

When I was older, some years older, I began to clear some land. I cleared this land, I cut the brush, I burned it with the help of Tatewarí. I began to plant there so that I could support my mother. But there was little land and many people. I started to work as it should be in order to support ourselves. But when there is little land, what can one do? I tried and tried but it did not work out well.

And then some people said, "Ah, what is that boy going to be good for? He will never be able to help us in anything. Always he goes alone, always he reflects. There he is by himself, always reflecting on these things." They wanted to reject me, my cousins, everybody. They saw I was sad, all alone. I would be embarrassed, but what is one to do?

That is how I was, always alone. And I would think to myself, "Whatever those great ones say, whatever Tatewarí says, whatever Díos Sol says, that is the correct thing. If one does it that way it will come out well." That is how I did it, learning this way and that, how one cures, how one goes to Wirikúta, how one learns all those stories of ours which are our history. How one makes those sacred things, the offerings. All that. It takes many years to do such things, much work, much sacrifice.

Now I see that I grew up well. I have learned what there is to learn. And who is it who does these things for his relatives now? Who would do it, if not I? If they had seen these things when I was small it would not have been as it was for me. They would not have said these things about me. Now, when something happens, some sickness, some business with the government, when one has need of this or that, they go to Ramón.

When I was born, that is a very big thing, something that we are not able to comprehend. My poor mother sacrificed herself, she sacrificed much. Day and night she worked, day and night all of us worked, braiding the palm fiber in order to sell it all those days. Herding, working at everything. For that is all we could do to support ourselves.

But now it is well. It is that I have learned much. Have I not learned much? We know how to support ourselves. How to give to those others, those poor ones, so that they will not go hungry.

I have learned how to speak with the vecinos. How to cure. How to make these things that are our symbols, those adornments people buy for their pleasure. And my wife, she makes beautiful embroidery, she weaves well. And it is that I have learned how to make all the chants and all the stories which are ours, which are the stories of the indigenous Huichols of Mexico.

So that nothing will be forgotten. So that we Huicholes, indigenous Mexicans of this state of Jalisco, will continue to exist in this world.

II.
"I Am Torn and Need to be Mended . . ."

You ask how I met my wife.

Well, at that time I was already grown. I was eighteen, almost nineteen years old, perhaps. I was going to work there, every day. I was clearing fields, weeding, all that which one does to support oneself. Cutting the brush, burning, planting. Then the harvest. It was hard, hard. Always hungry, tired, tired.

And here (the Huichol colony on the lower Río Lerma), here also I lacked something. I lacked someone at my side, for always. I went down to the coast, in Nayarit. I went to a small village, which they call Pimientillo. I went there to work in the maize harvest. Many Huichols, many, many, they go there when they are hungry. Every year they leave, they leave the Sierra and go down to the coast, to earn a few centavos, in the maize fields, in the tobacco fields. Then they return, poor ones, with sickness, others tired, worn out.

Well, there I went. This one who is now my wife, she also, she came down there to work. She came down from where she was born and she went to where I was, working. And two cousins came, two first cousins of mine. They knew her. And I, still young, still alone. I see this woman there, all alone. Ah yes, I think, that is good, for I do not have anyone to make my tortillas. And I am cold. I am cold and I need something to warm me up a little, no? I am all alone. And I, well, with fear and courage, all the time being afraid, I had much good will towards her. Much affection.

But she, no. She did not like me at all. Who knows about such things? There is no understanding it, is there?

And then one of my first cousins said to me, "Let us go where she is. Let us go there a little." We went to where she was, to a little rancho. There we went and we saw them there, roasting ears of maize on a fire. I was hungry. I said to my cousin, "Tell her to give me a little piece. Ask her for a little piece of *elóte*, if she happens to have any such thing."

She gave it to my cousin and my cousin gave it to me. I ate it. And she saw this. She was looking at us and she saw how he gave it to me and I ate it. Oh, she was so angry! She said, "Why did you give it to him? Why did you give it to him? I gave it to you and you gave it to him!" She was very angry, that one. You see? She did not like me at all. Not one little bit.

Well, then I said to them over at that rancho, "We came to work but there is no work to support us anywhere." They said, "Yes, there is. There is work for you for one week or two." No more than that, just two weeks. Well, we said, let's see how it comes out. So we went to work there. I went playing the violin, to see what she would say. I returned again about eleven o'clock in the night, playing the violin. She was already asleep.

Well, I took my blanket. I went to a tree to sleep. A companion, my first cousin, and I, we stretched out there under that tree and went to sleep. We slept until about three or four in the morning. Oh, that night! I was dreaming. I was dreaming about her.

Then, early, very early, I saw her pass by that tree. Going to draw water. On her return I was waiting for her. I grabbed her. I told her my feelings. I said, "Be my wife." But she, no. She said, "No, you have another over there." I told her, "No, I am all alone. I do not have anyone else. I do not have another woman, I do not have a wife."

She said, "Who knows if you do?" I said, "I am as I am. You can see I need someone to make my tortillas to eat." And then, "Look, I am torn and need to be mended. I need to be washed and ironed and everything." But no, she did not like me. That is what I thought.

But when one wants to be a mara'akáme, one must be astute in everything. Is that not so? I told her about my promise, my vow. I said to her, "I will be a mara'akáme. I have made that promise, I have made that vow. And I want you to be my wife. To help me always." That is what I said to her. I thought, perhaps she thinks I am crazy. And I said, "I want us to support ourselves always, so that we can live as we should, you and I." I thought, now let us see whether she likes me or not. And then, after one or two hours, she speaks: "Yes, if that is how it is." She told me yes.

Then we went together. And she brought her things, those poor things she had, her clothes, her blanket. That is all she owned. We were very poor, both of us were very poor. She came to where I was, bringing her things. And I told her, "For all my life you are going to do." And she said, "Yes."

And I said to her, "For all your life, for all my life, we are never going to do less." And she said, "I think so also." And I told her, "And you will be much in my heart." And she said, "Yes. And you also in the same way."

"Penitinacayeri," one says. It is as if one says, "I love you." Then she responds: *"Hei natsanacayeri."* The woman says, "You, I love you too."

One hour. Two hours.

Good. In that way we were united.

And that was the way in which we have loved each other always, until right now. More than nineteen years we have been together. That is the way it has been. That is the way we are with each other, all this time.

III.
How One Should Go Working in One's Field

I will tell you now how it is with us Huichols. I tell you this so that you will take note of everything that is Huichol, here in the state of Jalisco. How we should clear the fields. That is our custom, to go and clear the *coamil*, which is our field. Because the Huichol cannot live without working.

Let us say he has a wife in his house. Of course he has a wife. Because how can one live without one's wife? Then one says to her, "Look, little daughter, let's get up early so that you can make me some tortillas. Some *atole* (maize gruel), too. Because I am going to work."

He gets up early, that Huichol. He begins to sharpen his machete. He will take with him his sharpening stone, his machete, his ax, his gourd full of water. She says to him, his wife speaks, "Have you finished sharpening your machete?" "Yes, it is ready." She says, "Good. Then come and eat your food. Your food is ready so that you can eat."

Then he eats. He eats his breakfast and is content. He says, "Ah, that one up there, Díos Sol, he has given us light on this day, on every day." Then he says to his wife, "I have told you this, my wife. That as long as we live we must work to support ourselves. So that we will have food to eat. You have your beans, you have your maize, you have everything. From this we get our food, we get our clothing, we get everything."

She answers, "That is very true, little father." She calls him father as it is he who supports her. He is giving her food, everything. She says, "Yes, it is true, as you say it. That is why I am so happy living with you."

He says to her, "Very well, little daughter, I am going now." He leaves. He takes his machete. He takes his ax. He takes his gourd filled with water. He takes his little bag of tortillas. She has made them into tacos, with beans inside them. He leaves.

She walks with him part of the way. She says, "Be careful, do not hurt yourself. There are many trees out in that coamil that can strike you and hit you. Only Tatewarí knows. Only Tayaupá knows. They will help you." He says, "That is how it is." She says to him, "What do you think? Shall I bring you something to eat at noon?" He says, "No, that is not necessary. You have made me tortillas. You have made me tacos. At noon I can heat them." She says, "Yes. But it is not the same." He says to her, "That does not matter. Do not worry, wife, I will return in the afternoon."

Well. He leaves. He arrives. The first thing he says is, "Only Tayaupá knows. Only Tatewarí knows. Tatéi 'Utuanáka* she knows. The kakauyaríte,† they are the ones who will watch over me."

He arrives there. He says, "This field has to be cleared." So he begins clearing. But first he collects some wood and makes a little fire. He has a piece of brazilwood, the red wood of the brazil tree. That is the sacred food of Tatewarí. The fire is Tatewarí, so that he can watch over him. All day he feeds Tatewarí, so that he will not go out, so that he will guard him always. And he makes an offering, a candle, perhaps, a little sacred *xucúri*,‡ some flowers, a little chocolate. As it should be done.

He works all day. Soon he feels hungry. He says, "Ah, when one is out working one gets very hungry. That is true." He has a fire and starts to eat his food. He eats his tortillas. Then he rests a while. Very tired, perspiring. Perspiring so heavily that all his clothes are damp. From so much work, using his machete, using his ax. For it is hard work, very hard.

He returns to his work in the afternoon, to chop up all he has cleared. In the morning only he clears the brush. In the afternoon he chops up all that which he has cleared. Then he says, "Now I can go. I have done it well today. I can be happy with what I have accomplished here. Tomorrow is another day."

Then he leaves. The last thing he does before leaving is to take a piece of brazilwood, which is sacred there. He takes it home from his field. This he must take to Tatewarí, because he is the one who has watched over him, the one who gives light in the night. Then he goes, that Huichol, walking back to his home.

His wife is ready there, waiting for him. She is looking toward the path he will take. Then she sees him and says, "Here comes my husband. I must go to meet him." She goes inside the little house which is the *xiriki*. She lights a candle. After she had lit the candle she walks out, taking her little cape. Now she is ready to receive the ax and the machete in her cape. The ax, the machete, they are alive, they have a soul. Her husband comes forward with his arms outstretched. He says, "Here, take them, little daughter. I have arrived safely and happily, with the help of Tatewarí, with the help of Tayaupá, with the help of all those great ones."

He gives them to her. Then she turns and walks into the xiriki. There she leaves them, the machete and the ax. Then she brings food for the machete, for the ax. She brings them special food, a special *pinole*, which is sacred. She gives it to them, to the machete, to the ax.

Then she gives something of this sacred food to her husband, so that he can eat. She says to him, "I have not eaten. I have not eaten because I have been waiting for you. I have had no nourishment, waiting for you." Then she gives him some water to drink.

*The goddess who personifies the earth moistened and ready for planting. (—Eds.)
†Ancestor deities. (—Eds.)
‡Gourd bowl. (—Eds.)

He drinks it and says, "Oh, I feel very content now. Now I can go and rest." She puts out the sacred candle inside the xiriki. Then she tells her husband, "Now I have hot food for you. Tortillas. Fat little *gorditas** Hot beans. This thing and the other."

Then they eat. Having eaten, they go to bed, if they have a bed. Or on the floor or however it may be. Then he gives her advice. "You see, have I not told you we must work so we can eat and support ourselves?" She says to him, "Certainly it is that I must take this advice. We must live so that others may come and be pleased by the example we set."

She says, "More or less we should not wander to and fro, because if we do that we will have nothing to eat." He says, "That is how it must be. This advice I have given to you we must follow from the first to the last in order that we may live happily."

That is how it should be when one is Huichol.

IV.
On Thinking Bad Thoughts While Clearing the Field

Ah, one ought not to go thinking bad thoughts.

Because when one goes with evil thoughts, when one goes thinking bad thoughts while clearing the fields, what then? One says, "Ehhhh, I am walking clearing the fields. When am I going to harvest? What if it does not rain, what if I do not clear the fields well—ahhh, I do not have maize with which to eat, with which to manage to exist. Ahh, we are lacking this and that, what if this, what if the other?"

If one goes thinking in this manner, that one clearing his coamil, then one says, Watákame says, "No, do not be thinking about this. You work and I will help you."

Only then when he is going with bad thoughts, when he goes thinking bad thoughts, then one is censured. Ahhh—a machete cuts your foot, eh? In this life one does not go lacking for something with which to get stuck in the eye. A piece of grass, a stake, it is the same. No, that is not lacking.

It is through Watákame, he is the one who makes and unmakes.[†] For this reason there are Huichols here, here in Jalisco, who have gone using their machetes and cut their feet. They have given themselves blows as they went clearing their fields. When they were walking with bad thoughts. They were thinking bad thoughts. One ought not to do this.

---

*Gorditas are made by adding mashed or ground beans surrounded by *masa* (maize dough) to the center of a tortilla and cooking it on the comal. Gorditas should not be confused with tamales. Tamales, which presumably also date back long before the Spanish invasion, are made by adding ground beans to the center of the flattened masa, which is then rolled into the form of a sausage, tied in corn husk and boiled. (—Eds.)

*In other words, has shamanic powers of transformation.(—Eds.)

Think of him who helps us. That one who is called Clearer of the Fields, Watákame. While one is clearing the brush one should think how long ago he worked. How he was accomplishing it. How he did this when the little old white-haired one, Nakawé, remade the world. With axes of stone, with machetes of stone. How with his power he cleared everything for us, so that we could learn. That is good.

No, one ought not to go thinking bad thoughts.

v.

On The Sacredness of Fire

Why do we honor the one who is and is not of this world, whom we call Tatewarí, the one who is called The Fire? We have him because we believe in him in this form. In this form we see him. *Tai*, that is fire, only fire, flames. Tai came out of the wood, the wood contained him and he came out when it was rubbed. Tatewarí, Our Grandfather, that is The Fire. That is the Mara'akáme from ancient times, the one who warms us, who burns the brush, who cooks our food, who hunted the Deer who is Peyote, that one who is [together] with Káuyumari. We believe in this. Without him, where would we get warmth? How would we cook? All would be cold.

Imagine. One is in the Sierra, there where the Huichols live. One walks, one follows one's path. Then it becomes dark. Darker and darker. One is alone there walking. One sees less, less, less. Then one sees nothing. What is it there in the dark? One hears something? It is not to be seen. All is black. All is cold. Then one makes camp there. One gathers a little wood, food for Tatewarí. One strikes a light. One brings out Tatewarí. Ah, what a fine thing! What warmth! What light! The darkness disappears. It is light there, warm, fine. One feels well, contented, safe. Tatewarí is there to protect one.

Far away, another walks. He sees it. There he is, walking, all alone in the darkness, afraid perhaps. Then he sees it from afar, that light, that friendly light. A friendly thing there in the dark. He says, "I am not alone. There is another Huichol. There is someone. Perhaps he has a place for me there, a little warmth."

So he speaks. Tatewarí is there in the dark, making it light, making one warm, guarding one. Is it possible to live without such a thing, without Tatewarí? No, it is not possible.

Or if it is a matter of clearing the brush, how is it then? One works hard. One works with machetes, with axes, one gives one's strength, all one's will. Why? For the purpose of having maize, squash, beans, melons, everything the earth produces. But is it enough, this effort? Is one's machete enough? Is one's will enough? No, they are not enough. None of these things, none of that which we need for our sustenance, can be gained only by cutting the brush, by clearing the land of trees, of undergrowth. For that we need Tatewarí.

We clear the land, we knock down the big trees, the small trees. The branches and everything. Then, when the month of May comes, all our people, all our brothers are assembled. Then we say, "Look, it is time now to burn the field clean. To place Tatewarí there, because with his power he will burn the tree trunks, the branches, everything we have cut, all the brush, all the weeds."

Then we say, "Come, let us do this thing." We hold a ceremony, we make our offerings to him, to ask him to help us. And some who have already thought of this make a line so that only the cleared field will burn, so that Tatewarí does not burn too much, there where the *barranca* is, where it is too steep to go there quickly to put out the flames. We make this line, which is as though to say to Tatewarí, as if to plead with him, "Look, do not burn too much, do not burn more than the cleared field, because it will harm us." If one does not do this, if one does not make the proper offerings, then he will burn more than we wish, more than we need.

Because Tatewarí, with his power, burns everything—sticks, tree trunks, grass, weeds, everything. He cleans the coamil for us. Because if we only cut the brush, without his aid, if we did not burn the trunks and the branches, how could we plant? How could we harvest? How could we have maize? How could we obtain melons, squash, everything? He burns away everything as he burns away our transgressions. When he has burned the fields, when he has cleaned everything with his power, with his heat, then Tatewarí says to Díos Sol, to Werikúa, "Come, let us work together now, you and I, to give these Huichols their sustenance." They say this, Our Father who is the sun, Our Grandfather who is fire, Our Mothers who are the rain and the water, Our Mother 'Utuanáka, they all say, "Let us work together now so that what they have planted will truly sprout, that it will grow, that they will have life."

Then it comes up, the new maize, the young maize plants. Oh, so green, so beautiful! So beautiful, the young field that there is nothing in all the world more beautiful to us.

But Tatewarí comes first. Before one can plant one must burn. Before one can eat, one must cook. Oh yes, one does not to eat anything raw. There may be some in this world who have no need for food, who need nothing warm, nothing cooked. But I believe that cannot be so. I believe that all have him, that all have fire. How else could one live? What is there which one would wish to eat raw? Not much. Not that which gives us our nourishment. Not meat, not maize, not beans. How could one make tortillas without Tatewarí? If one has a wife, and even if she is not one's wife, she wishes to cook for one. How can one satisfy one's hunger with a pot of raw beans? With raw maize? It does not satisfy. But give these things into the hands of Tatewarí, let them be warmed by the flower of his flames, then it is well.

In ancient times he was transformed. When the ancient ones brought him out, he came out as Mara'akáme, transformed, so that all could see him as he was. So that he could embrace Our Sun Father when he was born. So that he could lead those ancient, ancient ones to hunt the deer, to hunt the peyote.

So that Kauyumári and he became companions, so that our life, our customs could be established there from ancient times.

VI.

On Sorcerers

You and I, we are in accord. That is why I can tell you these things. Things which are our life, which are our secrets. But not to some other persons. There one must guard it well. Because one cannot know if that other person is a sorcerer or not. Because if he is a sorcerer, he can take all that away from you, that which one knows. Because they are very envious, those sorcerers. If you want to keep that which you know for yourself, some knowledge, something you have that gives you power, and you tell a sorcerer, he can take that away from you. Then you will have nothing left. You will be left as if you had known nothing.

It is possible to recognize a sorcerer. But only if you have had training. If one has spent some years learning these things. Then you can say to yourself, "Ah, that one, he is a sorcerer." Then he can do you no harm, because you can protect yourself. Only the mara'akáme knows who is a sorcerer. L.* tried to learn to be a sorcerer. That is why he is ill now. He is ill because of this. Tauyapá is punishing him. Because once he said he wanted to be a mara'akáme, but he did not finish. He lacked this balance. He must first be able to do things well. If he cannot, he might try to be a sorcerer.

In what way are sorcerers different from other people? In their hearts. They are known. This sorcerer, that sorcerer looks at me. He passes his bad thoughts to me. They come right away. I see them. Other people might not know what he is. He might be a good person to them. He might be a bad person. It is possible for one to be a good person on the outside but bad inside.

Yes, a person who appears like a good person to others can be a sorcerer. Only the mara'akáme knows. Who is good inside there, who is bad. Who comes thinking bad thoughts. There are sorcerers who know what they are. They do things this way and that. There are sorcerers also who do not know what they are. They are good on the outside. They think they are good inside, in their hearts. They do not know they have this power. They do not know themselves. They are different. One must know why that person did these things. A sorcerer does and a sorcerer thinks. That is how he can do evil.

Now that one who was here yesterday! That one you met here in my house. That old man, he started to become a mara'akáme. He got that power. Then he became a sorcerer. He went to the Kiéri. Yet in all ways we are friends. I am not afraid of him. It is a shame that he is teaching himself. It is a shame. And he so old. Imagine! One can talk with him. I can talk with him. We can be friends. As long as they do not begin to play with their things, so long as he does not use his *takwátsi*† with one, eh? He wanted

*A Huichol of our acquaintance. (—Ed.)
†Elongated lidded basket containing power objects.(—Eds.)

very much to be a mara'akáme, that one. Now he is old, he is weary. He will have to remain no more than a sorcerer.

It is as I say. It is a shame.

VII.
On Huichol-Mestizo Differences

Some Huichols are still afraid of the Spaniards.[4]

They are so afraid they run off when they see strangers. They live far, far away in the barrancas because they are afraid. So that when one nears their home, they go away, they leave their houses and run away. From fear.

It is because of the bad times long ago. First, when the Spaniards came they came looking for gold. Then later came the Villistas. That was during the Revolution. People do not remember about the Spaniards when they came long ago, when the Indian people fought them. But we lost. That is what they say. Well, people do not remember much about that time. But they knew about the Villistas and the Cristeros and all those who fought in those times. In my country there are still old people who lived during that bad time. People came up there who shot the Huichols. They looked for money, for livestock, for maize. They killed the Indians, they hung them up, poor things. Because if in those days a Huichol had many cows, or even one, they took them. They took everything they could find. Since then they have been afraid.

Well, today the Spaniards and the Huichols do not mix much with each other. The Mexican who is a Spaniard lives in one place and the Mexican who is a Huichol lives in another. They live in a different manner.

The Spaniard cannot mix well with the Huichols because he cannot speak Huichol. Why is this so? Perhaps he does not know how to learn it. Why is this so? Perhaps he does not know how to learn it but perhaps he does not wish to. But the Huichols learn this new language. Nevertheless, it is not the same. The Huichol cannot translate everything he thinks. He cannot say all he wishes to say, as he does in his own language. And that is the reason why the Spaniards and the Huichols do not come together. They do not understand each other.

The vecino is not supposed to go into our country. But he does so anyway. He takes our land and when he does, he is mean about it. He is not allowed to do this, yet he does. It is that the Mexican who is a Spaniard can do as he pleases in our land. Yet he cannot do this where he belongs. I think the Spaniard must be mean all the time because people are always making him do this or that. They say to him, "You cannot do this. This you can do. Go here. Go there. This must be done another way. If you do not do it this way you will be in prison." So they tell him. They have many laws, much government, those vecinos. They cannot do as they wish. Their customs, their life, are different. They wish us to be as they are, to do as they do. So that we also cannot be free. That is why the Huichol cannot admit the vecino.

The Huichol lives as he wishes. He lives there freely in the Sierra. Out in the wind, everywhere. We work as we wish, we go as we please. And the Spaniard? He cannot do this. The Huichol is different because he is free to come and go as he wishes. But the vecino must do as the government says. The government has him in this way. The Huichol has government, too, but it is not the same. It does not tell us that we cannot do this and that and the other thing.

So the Huichols are gayer. They are more pleased with life. They like their life even when it is hard. They are happiest of all in their own land, even when it is hard. In the cities, no. In the cities many Huichols are silent. They are not gay and happy. That is because they do not know how to express it well. They remain quiet, those poor ones. In the Sierra they can say what they wish. But in the cities, no. That is not their land and the Spaniard can be mean. But in their own land, on their own rancho, there it is different.

If the vecinos come up there and make it as it is in their cities, who knows how it will be?

VIII.
On Eating Peyote

Look here. The good peyote comes from over there, where we go to hunt it, from Wirikúta Pariyekutsie.

That is hard, very hard, that journey. One goes there to find our life. Some people buy it at the market, but these are not Huichols who do this. That one is not good. One eats only that which comes from Wirikúta.

One does not buy it because one does not know whether it is good or not, because you know they bring it cut in any manner whatever, in any manner they want to. And so it is not sacred in the way in which we hunt it and bring it back.

That other peyote, that which one buys, it did not reveal itself in the Huichol manner. One did not hunt it properly, one did not make offerings to it over there. That is why it is not good for us.

When we bring it back we plant it at home, in a little earth. Any amount you bring back you can plant near your house so that it lives. In the dry season one plants it, one waters it a little with care and there it is. Then one has it whenever one wants it. The following year, when one goes to Wirikúta, one brings some more and one eats some and one plants some.

Sometimes one eats it cut into little pieces. One chews it well and then one swallows it. Sometimes one grinds it up and mixes it with a little water, and then one drinks it.

At the first ceremony after one returns from over there, when one cleanses everything, then one grinds it up in the *metate* with sacred water from Tatéi Matiniéri. At the ceremony of the *xaqui** it is also eaten ground up, but then it is mixed with water from the *arroyos* in the Sierra. And at the ceremony of the bull, when the bull is sacrificed, it is eaten in little pieces and the water one uses is also from the arroyos or the river.

The first time one puts peyote into one's mouth, one feels it going down into the stomach. It feels very cold, like ice. And the inside of one's mouth becomes dry, very dry. And then it becomes wet, very wet. One has much saliva then. And then, a while later, one feels as if one were fainting. The body begins to feel weak, it begins to feel faint. And one begins to yawn, to feel very, very tired. And after a while one feels very light. The whole body begins to feel light, without sleep, without anything.

And then, when one takes enough of this, one looks upward and what does one see? One sees darkness. Only darkness. It is very, very dark, very black. And one feels drunk with the peyote, very drunk. And when one looks up again it is total darkness except for a little bit of light, a tiny bit of light, brilliant yellow. It comes there, a brilliant yellow. And one looks into the fire. One sits there, looking into the fire, which is Tatewarí. One sees the fire in colors, very many colors, five colors, different colors. The flames divide into colors.

It is not yellow, that flame, it is not red, that flame. It is many colors, all brilliant, very brilliant and beautiful. The beauty is very great, very great. It is a beauty as one never sees it without the peyote. The flames come up, they shoot up, and each flame divides into those colors, and each color is multicolored. Blue, green, yellow, all those colors. The yellow appears on the tip of the flames as the flame shoots upward. And on the tips one can see little sparks in many colors coming out.

And the smoke which rises from the fire, it also looks more and more yellow, more and more brilliant. Then the fire turns to yellow, a brilliant, brilliant yellow, very bright. One sees the offerings there, many arrows with feathers and they are full of color, shimmering, shimmering.

That is what one sees, many things like that. And one sees Tatewarí, if one is mara'akáme, if one is the chief of those who go to hunt the peyote, then one sees Tatewarí. And one sees Tayaupá, one sees the Sun. One sees the mara'akáme venerating the Fire and one hears those prayers, like music. One hears praying and singing and chanting.

All this is to understand, to comprehend, to have one's life. So that we can understand what Tatewarí lets go from his heart, what the Fire lets go from his heart. One goes understanding all that which he lets go from his heart.

That is when we understand all that, when we find our life over there.

But many do not take good care. That is why they understand nothing. That is why

---

**Esquite*, parched maize. (—Eds.)

they do not understand anything. One must be attentive so that one understands that which the Fire and the Sun, and all those others, are saying. That is why one sits like that, to listen and to see all of that, so that we can understand it.

During the first ceremony after one has hunted the peyote, when they are eating the peyote, then they cannot eat anything. They can eat later, but not together with the peyote. They can eat after they have returned to where they are sleeping, that day, or the next day. But it must not be while they are eating the peyote.

That which one feels when one eats the peyote lasts from four to five hours. That is the most and during that time one does not eat. It depends on the amount one takes. If one takes two little pieces only, it is only about half an hour. But if one takes more, if one takes several pieces, four, five, it may last for three hours. In order to have a real effect one must take an entire peyote. One feels better with a larger amount. One sees more. With two or three pieces, little pieces, no, one does not see much. With a whole one, yes. One may feel sleepy, with two pieces or three. All it does is put you to sleep if one eats just two or three pieces. But it is not real sleep, it is that you are sleeping but you can still hear and see things.

And afterwards, after one has eaten a whole peyote and has seen many things and heard many things, one remembers everything. One remembers everything one has seen and heard. You keep it in your heart, what one hears and what one sees. It is kept in one's heart. Only oneself. Only oneself knows everything, oneself alone knows it all. It is a very personal thing. It is a very personal experience. It is like a secret, because others have not heard the same thing, others have not seen the same thing.

And later, during the rest of the year, one eats it when one wants to. If one has planted some peyotes, there by one's house, one eats it. One eats it at the ceremonies or one eats it when one wants to. If you want to eat it, you eat it. And if you do not want to eat you don't. And if someone asks you for some you give it to him if he wants to do it. If you have it to give you give it. If you don't, you don't.

One eats it like medicine or for whatever purpose one wants to eat it. If one feels weak, if one feels tired, if one feels ill, if one needs strength, then one eats it.

As I tell you, if one has the desire to eat one does so. That is how it is: if you have it you eat it, if not, then not.

Thank you very much.

IX.
On the Needs of the Huichol People

Well, here among our people, in our country which is a part of Jalisco and Nayarit, we have a problem. Year after year we have a problem. Year after year we have not been able to organize ourselves well. We have not been able to arrange things well, as they were in ancient times.

This I believe. I believe in ancient times things were very well arranged. All our people, our lands, all that was well arranged. That is what I cannot fully understand, that is what I cannot stop thinking about. I do not know in what manner it was so well ordered. But I know that it was. Years ago, our people got along well. But now, who knows why, in many areas it seems that people want to steal our lands. It seems that the government lets this happen. Only recently they have taken away ten thousand hectares. And that is not as it should be.

Of course, the Huichols name some governors, who are called *tatuán* in our language. Many of them are placed there because one thinks they know, they understand. But no. Those poor ones, they do not know. They do not comprehend. They do not understand. Poor ones, one tells them anything, one lies to them. Look, in this world there is much politics. But they are trusting. They come and tell them, this way and that. Poor little Huichol, he does not know what a plan is, what a title is, what a map is. He says, "Ah, this is our land. This has been the land of our ancestors. It is ours." But no. That is not enough.

So that is why much land, our land, is already in *ejidos*, as one calls them. There is now an ejido called de los Amotes. Those settlers, they have already taken possession of it. They are not Huichols. Yet they have taken it away, they have taken it over from the people of San Sebastián Teponahuaxtlan, from our Huichol *comunidad*. That is what happened. But when they name a governor, they say he is there to arrange things, to defend us. The whole community says, "Ah, this Huichol knows things very well, this way and the other, let's name him governor. He will defend us. He will do it well." But he cannot. That is not the reality. Because he knows little, poor man. He does not even know how to speak Spanish. Often he does not know one word. He does not know how to read.

Well, in such a case I believe that our land, our customs, our history, they will go. I think that in the manner in which we are going, as quickly as these things are now happening, we will be robbed even of this, of our customs, of our history, of our stories. And that should not be so.

Is it that I am telling you a story? No, it is not. But these things I believe, that the government should arrange these things properly, as they should be arranged. So that we can live in peace, so that we can live well, so that we can follow our customs. Why? Because that is our right. It is because we are authentic Huichols who live in the Sierra.

Take note of this. We must take heed, we must know how to understand. How to comprehend, how to learn these things well. We must learn these things, about titles, about land. And also we must venerate it well. We must follow our customs, our history, as you have seen it. Is it not that we walked pure, cleansed, following our ancient stories? But one must teach us those other things, so that one can help the governor of San Sebastián, of Santa Catarína, of San Andrés Cohamiata, so that they can defend our customs, our history, our life. So that we may be Huichols, tomorrow and the day after tomorrow.

But no, that is not how it is. On the contrary. In San Andrés Cohamiata, what is it they say? What is it they (the missionaries and other agents of change) tell them? Instead of telling them to follow their stories, to live pure lives as Huichols, to be in unity with everything, they say, "Be like the vecinos." They compare us with the vecinos. The padre wants them all to be the same. He wants all of us to be the same! No, I believe that is not right. It should not be this way. On the contrary, he should help them. He should do these things as they should be, so that the Huichol can be an authentic Huichol.

Should they build hotels, as they are saying? No, they should not speak of such things. That is not the right thing. That does not belong there. Hotels for tourists, that is for the cities, that is for Guadalajara, for Tepic. For them, yes. But over there, in our country, that does not belong there. In our country, among our people, they should help us to understand things, to understand about titles, about plans, about land. They should not try to take that away which is ours, our stories, our customs, our history. They should watch over us, they should aid us. So that we can learn. So that tomorrow, or the day after, we may have from our land that which one needs to maintain himself. That can only be when one knows how to venerate well.

Some speak to us of bringing tractors. They want us to cultivate with tractors. But no, we do not need that.[5] We work clearing the land with machetes. As they did in ancient times, we clear it with machetes and with axes. We venerate it well. We make the offerings. They are our friends. We do not need those machines. It is that we need our land. In order to work and support oneself. If one does not have land, one does not even need machetes. I think that we must wake up a little bit, to become a unity, so that we can guard out history, our customs. Our life.

You have seen how it is when we walk for the peyote. How we go, not eating, not drinking, with much hunger, with much thirst. With much will. All of one heart, of one will. How one goes being Huichol. That is our unity, our life. That is what we must defend.

How is that I say this? It is that we do not know how to guard it well. It is that we do not know how to defend ourselves a little bit, we do not know how to guard it well. Because our governors, they do not know. So that any person can come up there, and have his way. He can come up and take this piece of land. Another takes another. Another comes and takes another piece. And we are there at the edge, with nothing. Before we know it we are without land.

We are ancient Huichols. You have seen how we are. We are indigenous Mexicans. Because that is what we are, Mexicans of the purest blood, pure black blood. The Huichol is the real Mexican Indian. But as we are not a people that fights, a people that kills, a people that robs things, that is why one does these things [to us].

Nowadays there are Huichols who know a little how to write, how to read. Some even are teachers. Some even are secretaries. What is their head good for? Why learn to read? Why learn to write? Why these things if not to defend our customs, our history, our land? If not to be able to know, to get hold of things well? But no. Many prefer to know nothing. Many prefer to go getting drunk. Some leave our land, they leave the Sierra. They come to the city. They prefer to throw themselves away on this vice and that, to run around knowing nothing. No, that is not right. If they have learned how to read, how to write, it should be to defend [our people]. Because our lands are our Mexican country. This is the Mexican earth, it is our land. We must defend that. We must follow our history, our customs, our stories.

I do not know these things well. But I know that it is not as some say to us, that we must be like everyone. Why should all be the same? That we should not follow our history, our customs, with a good heart, with a pure heart? That is what I cannot fully understand.

I think it is enough for us that we should have our land, our place, so that we can maintain ourselves, so that we can have this unity of ours which you have seen. To go on with this unity.

No, I do not think it is a bad thing being Huichol.

Thank you very much.

—By Ramón Medina Silva, indigenous Mexican, pure Huichol of black blood, from San Sebastián Teponahuaxtlán, Jalisco.

NOTES

1. Not surprisingly, in 1970 the biological mother took Ramón's baby and ran off with another Huichol.(—Eds.)

2. On this visit, as on previous and subsequent occasions, Lupe was the guest of Ada Browne, production coordinator of the *Santa Fe Catalogue*. Ms. Browne's long-time concern for the health and well-being of Lupe and, through her, the large extended family in Nayarit, for whose members Lupe considers herself spiritually and economically responsible, deserves recognition. (—Eds.)

3. What Benítez (1968:389–390) says about Ramón's style of narrating the myths duplicates our experience. Ramón, writes Benítez, dictated myths to him in Spanish over a period of several weeks, and in doing so, he made some slight modifications in the conjugation of verbs so as to avoid monotony. He also introduced a certain syntactical order, without which the texts would have been incomprehensible. Nevertheless, Benítez continues, Ramón remained entirely faithful to the spirit as well as the form of the narratives, in contrast to other versions Benítez collected that were greatly schematized. Every shaman, Benítez concludes, "is an artist who leaves his own imprint on the myths."(—Eds.)

4. Ramón's occasional use of "Spaniard" in place of *vecino*, neighbor (Huichol *teiwari*), the usual term Huichols use for non-Indians, probably came from his contact with professors from the University of Guadalajara, who, having heard about him from Padre Ernesto Loera Ochóa, invited him to perform Huichol music and recite sacred songs in their classes, and possibly also from the Padre himself. At the Basilica of Zapopan Padre Ernesto maintained a small Huichol museum and crafts store and even a replica of a Huichol rancho temple, with all its customary sacred contents, including wooden images of some of the principal Huichol gods carved for him by Ramón and other artists.

5. Things have changed greatly since this was recorded. Roads have been constructed into some of the indigenous communities in the Sierra, allowing, among other things, both negative and positive exploitation of forest resources by lumber interests, as well as large-scale importation of beer and soft drinks. As a result, consumption of alcohol has greatly increased, and so has domestic violence. When I stayed in San Andrés in 1967, I was told that wife-beating, though known, was extremely rare. It isn't anymore. Binge drinking of hard commercial liquor—as distinct from the much milder native maize beer—during the ceremonies, or socially, was then rare to nonexistent. It is no longer. Tractors have long since ceased being curiosities. But tractors and plows are expensive to acquire and costly to maintain. And they hasten erosion. Meanwhile, on the lower Río Lerma, the giant new Aguamilpas Dam of the Comisíon Federal de Electricidad (Federal Power Commission) has created an enormous lake that compelled the resettlement of many Huichols to higher ground. Thanks to the intervention of Mexican anthropologists and protests from the Huichols themselves, the Comisión Federal was forced to abandon an elaborate plan for new villages of one-family houses that utterly ignored traditional Indian settlement patterns. Old-style extended family ranchos on a series of artificial terraces above the new lake, each with its *xiriki* (ancestor-god house), replaced this well-intentioned but misguided plan. The Comisión Federal also furnished the Indians with building materials superior to those previously available to them. In addition, Huichols slated for resettlement were compensated financially for the loss of low-lying lands.

The Comisión Federal has also provided a motorized barge that allows Huichols improved access to the market by shipping their cattle directly across the water to a new road to the Nayarit capital of Tepic. Previously, the river could be crossed only by dugout canoe and cattle had to be driven long distances along a difficult overland trail, entailing many losses. Some Huichols have adapted with surprising speed and enthusiasm to their new lacustrian environment, acquiring outboard motors and the skills—and cash—to maintain them, for fishing and transporting goods and animals. I am told by the noted photographer Justin Kerr that a huge metal sculpture by the well-known Mexico City sculptor Alejandro Prieto, erected in celebration of the dam's completion, was designed so precisely by him that on the solstice the sun shines through a circular hole in its center to a specific point on the ground, in the same way that it does in the traditional temple (see Chapter 11)—a fact that, of course, did not escape the Huichols. All in all, life promises to be better for the colonists.

On what most of us would consider the negative side, evangelical Protestantism of what traditional Huichols derisively call the "alleluia" variety has made considerable inroads into at least two of the lower Lerma settlements. "Alleluias" are also active in San Andrés and other indigenous comunidades in the Sierra, resulting, as might be expected, in factionalism and intra-community tensions. On the other hand, it has somewhat reduced the problem of heavy drinking, and the domestic violence associated with it, which women converts say has, along with various sorts of handouts, attracted them to the new religion.

Unaffected by the new lake were Ramón's maternal rancho and his former land, along with a traditional temple (*tuki*) not far away that was constructed in the 1970s with the financial assistance of the famous Huichol yarn painter José Benítez.(—Eds.)

ACKNOWLEDGEMENTS

I am happy to acknowledge the invaluable help we received in 1965 and 1966 from the linguist-missionary Joseph E. Grimes and his wife Barbara of the Summer Institute of Linguistics. Expert in the Huichol language, they took many hours and days out of their busy lives to translate Huichol passages in these and other texts we had recorded. Grimes told me at the time that he was impressed that, except for having to make the sacred songs comprehensible to us, when Ramón spoke in Spanish he hewed so closely to the typical Huichol style that he somehow managed to make even the translations sound Huichol. Most of the transcribing and translating of the Ramón Medina tapes was done by Elena Herskovitz, secretary from 1965 to 1967 of the UCLA Latin American Center's office in Guadalajara. For her patience, forbearance and bilingual skills, I take this opportunity to offer her my heartfelt thanks.(— P.T.F.)

INTRODUCTION TO CHAPTER 7

The author of the following essay, Armando Casillas Romo, M.D., is a young Mexican doctor who first came to the Sierra Madre Occidental to do the year of social service required of graduates of Mexican medical schools in exchange for their education. He stayed on for another two years, treating illness and gradually assimilating, with his associate Carlos Chávez, some of the extensive medical understanding possessed by the specialists in the sacred, the shamans. Though not himself a doctor, Chávez, now the director of AJAGI (Asociación Jalisciense de Apoyos a Grupos Indígenas), is well versed in medicinal botany. Together they observed the manner by which Huichol shamans classify diseases, how they determine a disease's origins and its most efficacious treatment, and how they apply both practical and supernatural means to restore their clients to health. Among other things, they discovered that the Huichols employ specialized suffixes in their medical terminology, and they learned these, too. They found that, like other native peoples, the Huichols have acquired extensive knowledge of the therapeutic properties of plants in their mountainous environment. Dr. Casillas Romo was able to identify 115 of these. No doubt many others remain to be studied. What, for example, are the plants some Huichols insist work effectively as contraceptives, and what species do they employ against lockjaw? Dr. Casillas Romo is not a botanist but a medical doctor; that he and his co-worker were able to match the Huichol names of most of these plants to the Linnean system of classification and, in many cases, to identify the names under which some of them are known also in Mexican folk medicine, as well as gather considerable information on the manner of their use by the Huichols, is no mean achievement.

The real achievement, of course, is that of traditional Huichol medicine, a holistic system of curing reinforced by centuries of exploration of the environment, experimentation, close observation, and experience. Who, to cite one dramatic example in Dr. Casillas Romo's study, could have imagined that at some unknown point in the past, and in the absence of doctors armed with vaccine, a Huichol shaman should himself have hit upon a "primitive" but effective form of smallpox vaccination, providing his patients with a form of immunity against this dreaded scourge? And that, when his method was shown to be effective, it should have become generalized among other healers?

As Casillas Romo would be the first to concede, not every traditional method of treatment is effective, and not every medicinal plant does the job that is claimed for it. But others apparently do, and it will be up to the "hard" sciences to determine, among the Huichols and other indigenous groups, which these are and why they work. That job cannot be done solely in the sterile environment of the laboratory, but requires input from the native healers themselves. And, that, in turn, presupposes respect for their knowledge and experience.

Not surprisingly, Huichols spend a lot of time thinking about and trying to explain, as well as cure, the terrible diseases that were unknown before the coming of the Europeans. Casillas Romo begins his essay with a myth that accounts for the origin of those terrible foreign illnesses that wiped out much of the indigenous population over large areas of Mesoamerica within the first century or two of the European invasion. The intriguing thing about this myth is that it links the first appearance of these Old World scourges among the Huichol ancestors to the appearance also of the first maize. In light of the historical fact that it was as much smallpox as military prowess that brought the Spaniards their victory over the Mexica, or Aztecs, it is interesting that the San Andrés Huichols tell of one of their own shamans who, when their community was last afflicted with *etsá*, smallpox, made a pilgrimage to Popocatépetl, the great snow-covered extinct volcano near Mexico City that was sacred to Central Mexican peoples, to placate the spirit of etsá. It must have worked, for according to the myth, after he returned to San Andrés smallpox never again afflicted that community.

Stacy B. Schaefer and Peter T. Furst

7 : THE SHAMAN WHO DEFEATED ETSÁ SICKNESS (SMALLPOX)

Traditional Huichol Medicine in the Twentieth Century

ARMANDO CASILLAS ROMO, M.D.,

in collaboration with CARLOS CHÁVEZ

How Disease Came into the World: A Huichol Myth

In the beginning of the world, while all was still in darkness, there was a gathering of the *kakauyári*, the ancient ancestor gods. They were waiting for the maize to arrive, and when it came, they placed the first ear into the fire to roast.

While it was being roasted, they saw something like smoke come out of the red-hot coals in one corner of the fire. But this smoke was really *irüváriya* [whooping cough], and it made one of the kakauyári ill.

When the sun rose for the first time in Teúpa, which is one of the most sacred places the Huichols have, other diseases were born in the four winds (the four cardinal points) and in the fifth direction, which is the center.

The first of these to appear was *xuriya-cuitayári* [dysentery]. It emerged in the west. The second to appear was *tápacuíniya* [pneumonia]. It arose in the east. The third illness was *tawaiya* [bubonic plague], which appeared in the south. The fourth disease, *tsipüriquiyá* [rubella] emerged in the north. Appearing in the fifth place were *etsá* [smallpox] and *sarampión* [a Spanish term meaning measles, which was also unknown in the Americas in pre-Columbian times].

Both of these arose in the center.

Afterwards, the kakauyári made a votive gourd bowl [*xukúri*] and an arrow. This was done to "cover up" the diseases. Later they fed them. The foods they offered were *cucu* [a small chili pepper], *wáve* [amaranth], *taatsi* [a sweet cane, similar to sorghum], *harrits* [a long white ceremonial grass], and *yeeri* [a wild edible tuber called *camote del cerro*, mountain yam, in Mexican Spanish].

Then Takutsi Nakawé [Our Great-grandmother] was born. After that Nauku [Our Elder Grandmother, a rain goddess] was born.

Afterwards, the disease asked for a deer [*maxa*]. The sun ate it. Then the disease asked for a peccary [*tuíxu*]. Nakawé ate it.[1] Later on it asked for Utuanáka, Our Mother [the Earth], who is also the goddess of fishes. Then the disease asked for *mikürí* [owl].

Afterwards, the arrows appeared and the gods asked for *mayé* [a mythical feline most Huichols call *león*, lion, when speaking Spanish]. Later it [the disease] asked for *uráwee* [wolf]. Then *tepári* [a circular stone disk carved with sacred symbols] appeared. Then it asked for *cauxi* [fox].

After this first group of diseases appeared, the others emerged. Seriekáme Maxa Kwaxí [Great-grandfather Deer Tail] was responsible for sending each disease in a different direction. In each of these places there is now a *xiriki* [godhouse]. Each disease has its *kakauyári* [deity] and its *xiriki*, even those not considered as significant, for instance colds.

One finds these sacred places both inside and outside our Huichol country.
—Narrated by the shaman Daniél Villa, San Andrés Cohamiata

In trying to determine how Huichols classify disease and what therapeutics they employ in conjunction with, and to reinforce, the familiar traditional "psychosomatic" methods of the shaman, we found that we had to learn a whole new branch of Huichol linguistics, a specialized medical terminology. Huichols, we discovered, have suffixes as well as prefixes that convey specific states, be they physical, mental, or spiritual. These are used in conjunction with words identifying the nature or origin of the illness.

Thus, the suffixes *cuiniya* and *xíya* indicate a state of malaise or illness. As a rule, the part of the word preceding the suffix points to the symptoms of the illness or its origin. For example, *maxaxiyá* is "deer disease," an illness that comes from deer, *maxa*. *Üra* is the name of a certain disease and also of a deity; *üracuiniya* is "Üra's disease," or "disease caused by Üra."

The suffix *xiya* is more common than the suffix *cuiniya*, but occasionally the two are used interchangeably. For example, the disease caused by a *tepári*, the stone disk in the temple engraved and painted with sacred designs, can be called either *tepariíxiya* or *teparicuíniya*.

In the special terminology of Huichol herbal medicine, a common suffix is *huayéya*, a term meaning something like "medicine for" or "that which heals." For example, *cuitsi-huayéya*, from *cuitsi*, pinworm, means something like "that which cures cuitsi" or "medicine for cuitsi"; *teparíxiya huayéya* translates as "that which cures tepári sickness."

With that brief introduction we can now turn to an inside view (with an occasional aside from modern medicine) of the principal illnesses that afflict Huichols and the practical therapeutics Huichol shamans employ against them, always remembering that shamanic doctoring is a holistic system that treats the mind as much as the body, with the direct participation of the gods, the ancestors, the members of the patient's family, the patient him- or herself, and places and objects to which power is ascribed.

Disorders of the Digestive Tract

I. NETÜÁRICÁ

From *netü*, that which sprouts or gushes. For Huichols this is one of the most frequent and important of all ills. It manifests itself in the form of a swelling that starts at the edge of the rib cage and may involve the spleen, the liver, and the epigastrium, or all of these in combination, with a sensation "as if they were spider legs." There is considerable pain in the affected area that precedes the swelling by approximately two months and that sometimes manifests itself also in the chest. There is often fever and sometimes diarrhea and vomiting. One informant mentioned that the fevers come every other day and last for approximately twelve hours, accompanied by chills that last almost an hour. The patient suffers from headache and from general malaise. Sometimes there is swelling of the eyelids (palpebral edema) and of the feet, and an itching of the hands. People say that it is especially while running or riding a horse that the swelling comes and goes, and that for that reason one should avoid these activities during bouts of the disease. It is also said that if the swelling descends to the lower abdomen, the patient will die. I have been told that *mestizos* also suffer from this disease, which may strike at any age, and that its Spanish name is *bazo*, meaning spleen.

So what is the disease in our terminology? Without any doubt, it is primarily malaria, an illness with a high incidence in the Huichol country. It is also probable that other diseases fall into this same native classification, including typhoid fever, infectious hepatitis, and amoebic liver abscess.

The most common healing method involves the use of the two kinds of plants that are known to the Huichols by the generic name *netüáricá-huayéya*. The difference between them is that one—the species most often employed—is "hot," and the other "cold." Both are applied as poultices to the affected area. The "cold" one is often applied, usually twice, from 1 p.m. until the following morning. The "hot" one is applied for 15 to 30 minutes. The classifications of "hot" and "cold" in Latin American folk medicine are usually unrelated to temperature or spiciness, but here the "hot" plant is just that, strongly irritating the skin and even scarring and hyperpigmenting the area to which it is applied. It is because it does not have these effects that the cold plant poultice is usually the more popular one. But because not many shamans know enough about it, its actual use is limited (those shamans familiar with this species, as well as other plants with medicinal properties, do not readily share their knowledge).

Other, less frequently used, treatments for *netüáricá* include:

a. one cuts bark in the shape of *huarache* (sandal) from the tree known to Huichols as *haüri* and to mestizos as *capomo* (*Brossimum alicastrum*) and drinks five drops of the sap diluted in a small amount of water;

FIGURE 44. The Nopal Cactus Functions as a Virtual Tree of Life for Huichols. Its leaves as well as its fruits are edible; the whole plant yields medicine; and it shares a parallel destiny with children whose umbilicus and afterbirth are buried beneath it. (*Photograph by Peter T. Furst.*)

b. one cuts a piece of nopal cactus in the shape of a *huarache*, removes the spines and rubs the affected portion of the patient's body with it for about half an hour. Then one hangs the cactus up and leaves it hanging for several days until it dries. The same is said to be happening to the disease (Figure 44);

c. one drinks two handfuls of urine;

d. one pushes the swelling upward with the hand to keep it from descending to the lower abdomen and thereby killing the patient.

2. *AIXÍYA*

From *ai*, cloud. Its symptoms are very similar to *netüáricá*. There is the same sort of swelling and pain of the spleen and liver, or in the epigastrium, or a combination of all of them, but with the important exception that the swelling occurs from the beginning, rather than being preceded by pain. There are high fevers and there is often also diarrhea and violent vomiting. This appears to be typhoid fever, or possibly some form of salmonella-induced gastroenteritis. One of the treatments is a poultice of the plant known as *aixíya-huayéya* (*Ipomoea* spp., Convolvulaceae family) to the affected region.

3. NAMÁXIYA

From *nama*, to obstruct, close, or hide. The name derives from the belief that this disease, which may strike at any age, obstructs the passage of food. It resembles *netüárícá* in that there is pain in the same regions, but with the important difference that there is no swelling. There are palpitations accompanied by considerable pain, and frequent episodes of slight fever. Occasionally, there is diarrhea. Very probably this is an amoebic liver abscess, or else amoebic colitis, irritated bowel, or dysmenorrhea. Treatment consists of a poultice made from the root of the *wequíxa* plant, well ground and placed once or twice on the abdomen.

4. WEKIÜXÍYA

From *wekiüxí*, the tail motion of a fish. In this disease it is said that the there is a fish tail inside the patient and that it is this that causes the illness. There is pain from the mid-thorax down to the mesogastrium. The patient often suffers some weight loss. There is occasionally diarrhea. In our terms, this may be gastric ulcer, but aclasis of the esophagus and esophagus cysts cannot be ruled out.

5. TEPARÍXIYA

This illness, another of the important and common of Huichol diseases, is also called *teparicuíniya*, from *tepári*, the circular stone covered with symbols dedicated to the deities.

In this disease a "ball" forms under the umbilicus, manifesting itself as a hardening of that region, accompanied by localized pain and a throbbing (actually an increase of the normal pulsations of the abdominal aortic vein). This is usually accompanied by fever, diarrhea, vomiting, and morning chills. The pain increases after strenuous exertion and it radiates to the lumbar region. It is said that all the Huichols suffer from *teparíxiya* but that only a few develop symptoms severe enough to require attention from a shaman.

Teparíxiya is almost an exact equivalent of what is commonly known in Mexican folk medicine by the Spanish term *latido*, throbbing, and several Huichols have told me the same thing. Considerable research has been done in Mexico on this disease, but apparently it has no scientific medical equivalent. I have observed, however, that when there is marked loss of weight, the pulsations of the abdominal aorta are more perceptible and a few people end up believing that they are suffering from *latido*.

One of the treatments consists of drinking a tea made from the plant known as *teparíxiya-huayéya* for several days, until the symptoms disappear. Another treatment is with a poultice made from a plant with the same Huichol name of *teparíxiya-huayéya* (*Cosmos* spp., Compositae family), well ground and placed on the abdomen.

6. ÜQUIXIYA

From *üqui*, sweet maize cane considered sacred that is cut for certain ceremonies. The disease, therefore, is one that "comes from the maize." Symptoms include weakness and lethargy. There is strong pain that runs in more or less a straight line from the thorax down to the hypogastrium. There are periods of high fever, anorexia, and memory lapses, but there is no diarrhea or vomiting. This seems to be brucellosis, but the same condition could also indicate typhoid fever, malaria, or chronic tuberculosis. There being no herbal medicine for this illness, treatment is limited to intervention by the shaman with the gods and the familiar shamanic treatments.

7. CUCUINIYA YURIÉPA

From *cucuiniya*, pain, and *yuriépa*, stomach. This is the term used for stomach ache or stomach discomfort. Treatment consists of poultices of the root of *aüxiya-wequíxa*, known in Spanish as *matarique* (*Odontricum pachyphyllum*, Compositae family).

8. ICÚ PEPÁYEYETSÁ OR ICUXIYA

From *icú*, maize. Huichols explain this disease as one caused by eating too much maize over a long period of time. It is supposed that maize has become trapped or stuck in the abdomen and in the head. Symptoms are difficulty in digesting food, abdominal pain, a little diarrhea, and occasional vomiting. The cause seems to be mainly helminthiasis (intestinal parasitic worms) or amoebiasis. Treatment consists of a shamanic sucking cure in which the *mara'akáme* removes maize kernels from the head and the abdomen (Figure 45).

9. HIKURICUINIYA

From *híkuri* (*hikuli*), the Huichol term for peyote (*Lophophora williamsii*). Huichols believe that, as in the previous case, eating peyote for a long period of time causes its fuzz to "get stuck" in the head and abdomen. The symptoms are the same as those for *icú pepáyeyetsá*, the maize disease; treatment is also the same, with the shaman sucking fuzz out of the head and abdomen (Figures 46, 47).

It is also believed that if a pregnant woman eats too much peyote for too long a time, the fuzz of the cactus will become trapped and cause her to have a miscarriage.

10. ITÉÜRIXIYA

From *itéüri*, big ceremonial candle. Supposedly, in this disease one has a candle trapped in the abdomen and in the head. The symptoms are the same as in the two previous diseases. Treatment consists of having the shaman suck fragments of a candle from the abdomen and head.

Because the three diseases above share the same symptoms, their diagnoses are not based on physical aspects but on magical ones.

FIGURE 45. Yarn Painting of Maize Stalks with a Votive Gourd Attached to the Center. Ramón Medina explained this depiction as a full-size version of an offering to cure "maize disease," which is described in Chapter 6 by Dr. Casillas Romo. (*Yarn painting by Ramón Medina. Fowler Museum of Cultural History, University of California at Los Angeles.*)

FIGURES 46, 47. Peyote Sectioned and Drying in Wirikúta for Later Ceremonial Use. Conceptually united in a symbol complex with deer, maize and peyote are valued as essential sustenance for body and spirit. Peyote, dried as here or kept fresh by planting it in the Sierra, also has an important place in the Huichol *materia medica*. The other side of the coin is that too much of a good thing can bring on disease. According to Casillas Romo's consultants, pregnant women especially should not eat too much peyote over too long a period, lest the fuzz on the cactus cause miscarriage, whereas eating or drinking it ground up and mixed with consecrated water in the ceremonies entails no risk. (*Photos by Stacy B. Schaefer.*)

11. ACUITSI

This illness is also called *acuichi*, the term used for diarrhea. One of the treatments for diarrhea is drinking a tea made from the plant the Huichols call *acuitsi-huayéya*, known in Spanish as *janajuana* (*Helianthemum glomeratum*, Cistaceae family).

12. XURIYA-CUITAYÁRI

From *xuriya*, blood, and *cuitayári*, stool. This refers to dysentery, evidently from any cause. Due to the high incidence of amoebiasis in the Huichol region, this disease is almost certainly associated in the main with amoebic dysentery. Treatment consists of drinking a tea brewed from one of three plants: *xuriya-cuitayári huayéya*, known in Spanish as *vara de San Francisco* (*Vernonia steetzil*, var. *aristifera*, Compositae family); *utú uxavi* (species name unknown); or the fruit of the *cuaxuari*, Spanish *colorín* (*Erythrina leguminosa* or *E. corraloides*).

13. CUÍTSI

Also known as *cuíchi*. This refers to oxyuriasis or infestation with pinworms. Treatment consists of drinking a tea brewed from the plant known in Huichol as *cuitsi-huayéya* and in Mexican Spanish as *cuomecate* (*Antigonum reptopus*, Polygonaceae family).

14. ARECÚXI

The term for this illness derives from *arecú* or *harecú*, the nematode worm known to medical science as *Ascaris lumbricoides*. The disease is ascariasis, an infestation of the nematode worm. Treatment consists of the oral administration of one of several diarrhetic plants. Among these is one called *weriya-huayéya*, whose root, chewed in small quantities, triggers intense diarrhea.

With respect to the digestive system, there are several other Huichol terms that are important for rural health workers to know: *puta-eva*, meaning vomiting; *panacaxüni* or *panacayüná*, dehydration; *tamé-cuiniya* (from *tamé*, tooth, and *cuiniya*, disease, malaise, or pain, and thus literally toothache).

Diseases of the Respiratory Tract

15. CUQUÍYA

Cough. There are several treatments for this in traditional Huichol medicine. One consists of drinking a tea brewed from the flower the Huichols call *nauxi*, *rosa de San Juan* in Spanish (*Macrosiphonia hypoleuca*, Aposynaceae family). A soothing tea may also be made from the plant called *cuquíya-huayéya* (species unknown).

16. TSUCÁXIYÁ

This is also known as *sumé* or *chumé*, mucus. The name derives almost certainly from the excessive amount of mucus discharged by one suffering from this respiratory illness.

17. TÁPACUÍNIYA

From *tápa*, the word used for either side of the thorax. This illness, which may strike people at any age, consists mainly of a strong thoracic pain "as though a spear had gone through the chest" that "doesn't let you breathe"—in other words, shortness of breath. Huichols say it feels "as though a belt was tightened in the chest." The pain is accompanied by fever, coughing, and fatigue, and sometimes blood in the sputum. Occasionally, sufferers die after only one or two days. This appears to be pneumonia, mainly of bacterial origin. Treatment consists of the use of *ütsa*, *palo de Brasil* in Spanish (*Haemotoxilon brasiletto*, Leguminosae family). This is the same reddish wood that is used to make the staffs of power and the wooden foreshafts of ceremonial arrows and shaman's wands.

18. IRÜCÁRIYÁ

Whooping cough. Huichols treat this disease with a tea made from the succulent called *irücáriyá-huayéya* (*Euphorbia* spp., Euphorbiaceae family), and with the ground-up root of another plant, *Triumfetta* spp., known in Spanish as *lampozo*. Because of its use to treat whooping cough, this plant, though from an entirely different family, the Tilaceae, is also called *irücáriyá*; another name for it is *nari muxa*.

Whooping cough is a serious problem, especially for children, so it is not surprising that its appearance among the Huichols should be accounted for not just in the myth that introduces this essay but in other stories as well, including the following:

Irücáriyá first appeared in Upayaküha, which is a rocky area near the Chapala-gana River. The *héwixi* [ancient ones] were gathered there. They invited *üpá* [skunk], *xüye* [armadillo], and *xiri* [mouse] to Tatéi Néixa [Dance of Our Mother, usually held in October], which was about to be celebrated. Their wives were just beginning to weave the shirts that each would wear to the festivity. Because it was about to begin, the husbands started hurrying their wives to finish. Because of this haste, the shirts did not come out well. Despite this they put on the shirts not fully finished. This is why the suit the skunk wears is striped, and that of the armadillo [its shell] very small.

In the festivity there was a beautiful girl who had the name of Amaima. She was the sister-in-law of skunk and she was in love with him. She would ask herself, "How will I make the skunk fall in love with me? He is very cute. I really like that skunk. I think I am going to dance with him tonight."

When the dance began, the girl invited the skunk to take part in it. He accepted. While they were dancing, she gave him *pinole* [a drink made from finely ground roasted maize, sweetened with honey or brown sugar]. While he was eating it she began to tickle him. This made him start to choke. He could not breathe and he started to urinate on everybody. The guests started to cough, because they were already sick with the whooping cough.

The shamans got together to see what could be done to alleviate the situation, because everybody was already sick. That is why in former days, when whooping cough was very common, when it would come from Tepic [the capital city of Nayarit], the shamans would get together and take offerings to Upayakūha, where this illness emerged, so it wouldn't affect the Huichols.

19. QUETSÜXÍYA

"Fish disease," from *quetsü*, fish. As in the disease called *netüáricá*, in this illness there is swelling at the edge of the rib cage. The principal symptom is severe coughing, sometimes of such intensity that patients are kept awake all night. Occasionally, bloody sputum is coughed up. There is also frequent fever. With this disease—evidently tuberculosis—Huichols say "people die little by little." No plants were mentioned for treatment of this disease.

Skin Diseases

20. HAIYÁ

This is a disease whose symptoms consist of "large lumps" that sometimes appear in different areas of the body. These lumps are red, they hurt badly, and frequently burst open after a time. Evidently these are abscesses. Huichols also appear to use the same term for any extreme swellings.

21. TEMUITSI

Impetigo. For this disease Huichol healers employ parts of the sacred psychotropic plant known as *kiéri-nánari* (Spanish *Floripondio [Solandra]* spp., Solanaceae family). (For more on *Solandra*, see Nos. 22 and 34 below and Chapter 8.)

22. NERÜITSI

Scabies. There are several herbal remedies for this disease, among them the above-mentioned *kiéri-nánari*, *aiyéxa*, *natüüxa*, and the bark of the tree known in Spanish as *caevananchi*.

23. TSIPURIQUIYÁ

Probably rubella. This is an exanthematic disease that afflicts mainly children. However, it occurs only once in a lifetime. Symptoms are skin eruptions with red spots smaller than those characteristic of measles, preceded by fever that lasts a maximum of seven days. A few days after the fever the skin eruptions show up, first on the face and then on the chest, arms and legs. These last a maximum of one week.

Huichol healers advise that the little patient be placed on a fresh banana leaf and that the parents confess their "sins"—that is, extramarital sexual relations—to the *mara'akáme*, the shaman, who ties a knot for each transgression in a palm leaf string that is subsequently burned. If one "prays completely," meaning that if every transgression is openly proclaimed, the patient will get well. If not, it is likely that the illness will worsen considerably.[2]

In addition, the shaman also prescribes herbal treatment with the root of *tsipúriquiyáhuayéya* (*Kosteletzya tubiflora*, Malraceae family). The root is taken internally, preferably ground.

24. ETSÁ

This is the dreaded smallpox. The people of San Andrés Cohamiata say that no one in this area has had this disease for a long time, as long as fifty years.

The extraordinary thing is that to ward off this scourge in the absence of medical help from the outside, Huichol shamans developed their own technique of immunization. We were told that the *mara'akáte* (pl. of *mara'akáme*) would use the thorns of the plant known as *huizache*, a thorny shrub found over much of Mexico, to pierce the skin eruptions of people already suffering from smallpox and extract the liquid from them. With the permission of the parents, they would then inoculate the arms of healthy children with this liquid. The cure also involved the same "confession" rite as that prescribed for rubella.

Several Huichols told us that *etsá* disappeared from their community thanks to a famous *mara'akáme* named Carrillo, who died several decades ago.[3] It is said that to "cover up"—that is, calm—the disease he made a pilgrimage to Haixáripá, a sacred place on the slopes of Popocatépetl, the great snow-covered dormant volcano near Mexico City, where Huichol mythology says smallpox made its first appearance. His efforts were successful and smallpox never again bothered the people of San Andrés.

25. SARAMPIÓN

Measles, of course, came in with the Spanish, and Huichols employ the Spanish term, *sarampión*, for this disease, pronouncing it somewhat like "sarampió." The healing rite is identical to that for rubella and smallpox.

26. ATÉTSI

Atétsi is the plural for *até*, louse. Some Huichols are said to know of plant remedies for fighting these parasites, but these remain to be investigated.

27. TUXARÍYA (DANDRUFF)

This is a common affliction among the Huichols. One initial treatment, not commonly known to many Indians, consists of washing the hair and scalp with an infusion of the bark of the walnut tree, *cariu* in Huichol (*Julgans regia*, Junglandaceae family). Another is more radical: all the hair is cut off and a poultice made of ground walnut bark is applied to the scalp.

FIGURE 48. Yarn Painting of Flowering *Datura* with Its Characteristic Spiny Seed Pods. (*Yarn painting by Ramón Medina. Southwest Museum, Los Angeles, California.*)

Urinary Disorders

28. *TATEWARIXÍYA*

This is the disease of Tatewarí, Our Grandfather (Fire). As in many other cases, there is both a shamanic aspect—sucking a small piece of charcoal from the patient's abdomen—and a practical one—drinking a tea made from the stalk and root of a plant called *tsítsicayacuai*.

29. *YAKUAIXIYA (YAKUARRIYA)*

From yacuai (*yakwéi*), the gourd in which the sacred *macuche* tobacco (*Nicotiana rustica*) is stored (Figure 48). This species, which has a nicotine content many times higher than commercial tobacco, is smoked mainly by the *mara'akáte*, the shamans. Herbal treatment for the illness sent by the tobacco consists, as above, of an infusion of the stalk and root of the *tsítsicayacuai* herb.[4]

30. *NAXIXÍYA*

From *naxi*, white ash. The term for this illness derives from the ash obtained from burning twelve small wooden sticks made of oak, a very small bag of tobacco, and a tiny rope in a ceremony related to the pilgrimage to Wirikúta, the sacred peyote desert in San Luis Potosí. These objects are burned during the festivity called Híkuri Neixa (or Híkuri Neixa), literally Dance of the Peyote, held around June. To heal this illness, a tea is brewed from one large root, or two or three small roots, of *naxipúri* (*Senecio* spp., Compositae family) ground on a stone and administered for several days, until the disease disappears.

31. *KÜPIERIXÍYA*

A urinary infection, from *küpieri*, a tree trunk used to feed the ceremonial fire.

32. *IXITÁRI*

This term is used both for this illness—presumably kidney stones—and for the terminal part of deer intestines, which, circular in shape, resemble a coiled snake. Urination is said to be normal, but there is intense pain in the kidneys and slightly elevated temperature. The practical part of the treatment includes placing slices of the tall *Cereus* cactus called *pitayo* in Spanish and *maara* in Huichol on the affected area. Huichols claim that doing this twice is usually sufficient.

Behavioral Disorders

The following are illnesses considered to be of a spiritual nature, or illnesses that have no physical symptoms but manifest themselves as marked changes in behavior.

33. *NIÉRIKÁXIYÁ*

This is the disease of the *niérika*, an object that gives the shaman the power of supernatural vision. The disease is caused by a spell cast by the *itáuki*, a dangerous little spirit animal visible only to the shaman. The ailment manifests itself as sadness and aversion to other people. The patient believes that everyone but he himself is crazy. In our terms, we would call this depression or perhaps paranoia.

34. *KIERÍXIYÁ*

Possession by *kiéri*, a psychotropic plant related to the Daturas that is known in Spanish as *copa de oro*. Huichols also call *kiéri* "*arbol del viento*" ("tree of the wind") (*Solandra guttata* or *S. brevicalyx* Standl., Solanaceae family). Many Huichols attribute evil powers to this plant. *Kiéri* possession illness appears to be endemic mainly among female adolescents. The "possessed" go through periods of hysteria and afterwards lose consciousness. The same name may be applied to the consequences of ingesting the plant.

Next to peyote, *kiéri* is of great importance in Huichol culture. According to mythology, Kiéri tried to maintain supremacy over peyote, the little cactus Huichols consider divine. There is a belief that if certain offerings are made to the *kiéri* plant it will grant powers or privileges in the performances of particular activities, such as violin playing, embroidering, or weaving, the latter two specialties of women. Occasionally, people will bed down beneath the *kiéri* plant so as to obtain enlightening dreams. Some people also cut off the tip of the plant and carry it so as to have its aid.

Several Huichols, including a few shamans, occasionally abandon the use of peyote in favor of *kiéri*. There is also the belief that if those who pledge themselves to *kiéri* do not fulfil their duties to the plant spirit they will go insane—precisely the condition identified as *kieríxiya*. Dr. José Juan Ramírez, a physician with the Mexican Ministry of Health in the Huichol community of San Miguel Huaixtita, Jalisco, where the *kieríxiya* disease is said to be endemic, told me of a man suffering from this ailment who withdrew completely to live alone in the mountains. Occasionally, he would appear naked in the village and eventually he fell into a precipice and was killed (see also Chapter 8).

35. *ÜRÜXIYA*

This is a disease caused by the *ürükáme* of a dead relative (see Chapter 14). *Ürü (ülü)* is the Huichol word for arrow, but it also refers to a certain spot in the lumbar region.

The *ürükáme* is the manifestation of the soul of a relative in the form of a small stone or rock crystal that is recovered by the shaman and tied to an arrow; hence, the name of the illness could be rendered as "wounded by an arrow."

Some Huichols believe that the ailment appears if the relatives of the deceased have failed to observe the ceremony usually conducted on the fifth day, or the fifth year, after death, or did not conduct it to the satisfaction of the deceased. It is said that the disease manifests itself as an early morning fever. The patient has an intense desire to be among deer, as though they were sending him telepathic messages to come and join them. This is the way the *ürükáme* tells the relatives that it wants them to go deer hunting.

All these things are taken as signs that the soul of the dead relative is in the process of crystallization. Interestingly enough, the illness is said to strike mostly people of middle or advanced age.[5]

The typically shamanic treatment includes recovery by the shaman of the crystallized soul and the making of the arrow and the little bundle that will be its new home and that will assure it a place near its beloved deer.[6]

36. NIWEMAMA MEPUCAXÚRI

The term literally means "his/her children fell." In Huichol belief, the *kúpuri*, the human soul or life force, resides in the superior-posterior part of the head. It is identified with the so-called cowlick, the tuft of hair that grows in a different direction from the rest of the hair and will not lie flat. The *kúpuri* is made up of five "children" that are usually in harmony. A shaman can see these five children as five small clouds. If, for example, a person falls and hits his head, the five children come into disharmony, they become dispersed, requiring a *mara'akáme's* intervention to bring them back into harmony with his *muviéri*, his feathered power arrows.

37. KUPÜRIPIYA OR KUPÜRICUÍNIYA

This is a form of soul loss, in which the *kupüri* of a person has been stolen by an *itáuki*, the dangerous little spirit animal mentioned above. The *mara'akáme* visualizes the stolen *kupüri* in a small drop of water which he places on the patient's head. If this is not done, the patient dies.

Nutritional Disorders

The ailments in this section are *maixíya*, *tetsuxíya*, *wavexíya*, *xaríxiyá*, *temuxíya*, *atacuaixíya*, *maxaxiyá*, and *üracuíniya*. The first five of these disorders, according to Huichol belief, appear between the first and third year of life. Some common aspects shared by these five illnesses are: protruding abdomens and inability to walk when, chronologically, they should already be able to do so; or losing that ability after they had started walking. Several of these disorders are undoubtedly *kwashiorkor*.* As in other kinds of illnesses, in order to distinguish one from another Huichol healers usually employ magical-religious criteria.

38. MAIXÍYA

This derives from *mai*, the century plant (*Agave* spp.) used in Mexico for making mezcal and other popular alcoholic beverages, and whose heart and seeds are used as food. The child cannot walk and its abdomen becomes protruded. There is no visible emaciation. The cause appears to be severe malnutrition, but not to the extreme of kwashiorkor. Very likely there is helminthic infestation (intestinal worms). Treatment consists of a shamanic healing, in which the *mara'akáme*, using a stick, gently knocks the child to the ground in apparent imitation of the way in which Huichols knock down century plants.

---

*A nutritional disease affecting mainly infants and children, caused by severe lack of protein.

39. *TETSUXÍYA*

In this disease the child is also unable to walk and its abdomen becomes protruded, without emaciation. The name derives from *tetsu*, the Huichol word for tamale. It is called the "tamale disease" because the body of the child afflicted with this illness is said to somewhat resemble this sacred food. This too appears to be severe malnutrition, but not to the extent of kwashiorkor, probably with helminthic infestation.

Treatment consists of the following: During the Híkuri Neixa, the Dance of the Peyote, large tamales are made to be eaten in the afternoon. The shaman takes one of these and cuts it four times, symbolizing the four world quarters. Any child in the community suffering this disease should be restored to health by means of this ritual.

40. *WAVEXÍYA*

From *wave* (*huave*,) amaranth, a sacred food for the Huichols, which is considered to be the cause of this illness. The afflicted child cannot walk, has a protruded abdomen, is emaciated, and is sometimes very irritable. Sometimes the child victim has invisible pimples throughout the body, which only a shaman can see. This is almost certainly kwashiorkor. Treatment consists of a ritual in which the shaman uses a piece of cloth to remove amaranth—visible only to him—from the patient's body.

41. *XARÍXIYÁ*

This illness has the same symptoms as those just mentioned, but, in addition, the child's head is larger than usual (or so it is said), and its skin becomes darker (hyperpigmentation). The name comes from *xari*, the term for the big clay *olla* in which *nawá*, the maize beer that is indispensable in most Huichol ceremonies, is fermented.

The curing ritual consists of the *mara'akáme* placing the child's head inside such an *olla*, which is then broken.

42. *TEMUXÍYA*

From *temu*, toad. In this illness the child also has a protruded stomach, which Huichols say resembles the body of a toad. Children suffering from this ailment are usually anorexic, are very weak, and have severe diarrhea. It is believed that the disorder is caused by playing with tadpoles or having killed toads. This too seems to be severe malnutrition, but not to the extreme of kwashiorkor. For treatment a plant called in Huichol *temuxíya-huayeyári* is ground and applied for five to ten days to the abdomen.

43. *ATACUAIXÍYA*

From *atacuai*, a small lizard that is usually found on the trunks of trees. People with this disorder usually suffer from fatigue, fever, diarrhea, and dehydration. This also appears to be a form of malnutrition, with the possible addition of gastrointestinal infection.

44. MAXAXIYÁ

From *maxa*, deer. This is "deer disease," or "disease of the deer." The illness is thought to emanate from the soul of a deer. The patient becomes emaciated and has a very protruded abdomen, usually accompanied by considerable apathy. The affliction appears mainly during childhood, but could occur at any age. To us it appeared to be a classical case of kwashiorkor.

The cure involves a very complex and prolonged ritual that is performed over two days and nights, in which the *mara'akáme* "kills" the soul of the deer from which the illness came.

If the shaman has diagnosed *maxaxiyá*, a series of requirements must be fulfilled before the actual shamanic healing can begin: a string trap or noose for catching the deer—the usual method before the introduction of rifles; ceremonial arrows or prayer arrows; a muviéri, the feathered power arrow employed by shamans for curing; two small branches of *uupári*, a small shrub whose leaves are believed to be a favorite food of deer; and finally, a large quantity of grass. After all these essentials have been gathered, a bonfire is lit in the afternoon of the day before the curing ritual begins. The grass is placed on the ground beside the fire, along with the other articles.

On the following day, during the actual curing rite, the patient approaches the fire. After gently knocking the patient to the ground onto the bed of grass, the *mara'akáme* performs the motions of a deer sacrifice on him or her. In the course of this ritual the soul of the deer that is supposed to be the cause of the disease dies and becomes trapped in the net. Finally, the shaman pretends to skin the patient, in the same way that a deer is skinned. This is done by first placing the patient on his or her back, and then on the stomach.

This curing ritual is performed only during Tatéi Neixa (lit. "Dance of Our Mother") or Hikuri Neixa, the peyote dance. That for the Huichols *maxaxiyá* is a very important disease is surely due to the divine nature attributed to deer.

45. ÜRACUÍNIYA

This is the "disease of *üra*," the Huichol name for the common roadrunner (*Geococcyx californianus*), a native of the southwestern United States and northern Mexican desert. It is said to be "the disease of laziness," but it seems to include not only people perpetually idle but also those suffering from chronic fatigue due to malnutrition. Treatment is purely shamanic, with the *mara'akáme* sucking a wing feather from this bird from the patient's abdomen.

The following myth, accounting for the origin of the "laziness disease," was narrated by a young mara'akáme named Gregorio Carrillo. It is usually told to children and adolescents as a kind of morality tale.

There was a man once who had two daughters, one chubby and the other thin. Without first obtaining their consent, as used to be customary among the Huichols, he tried to arrange a marriage for each of them with two well-known adolescents. One was named Üra and the other Tumuxávi. Üra was thin, extroverted, very talkative and very funny. Tumuxávi was a little plump, serious, and introverted. The man wanted his slender daughter to marry the thin Üra, and his fleshy daughter to marry Tumuxávi. But the four adolescents did not agree with this arrangement and decided to change things around. Üra ended up with the chubby girl and Tumaxávi with the slender one.

The father-in-law much preferred Üra. He mistook Tumuxávi being introverted for laziness and thought that Üra was hardworking for being extroverted. Besides, Üra was always boasting of being a hard worker. But the truth was the opposite, as the man would later discover for himself.

As used to be the custom, the man gave both sons-in-law a piece of land to sow, and also the tools for working the land. From his *iqui* [storage house] he took maize, amaranth, squash and beans for Üra to sow in the *coamil* [milpa, maize plot]. Because he considered him to be a loafer, the man did not give Tumuxávi any seeds. Üra burned the brush to clear his coamil and sowed his seeds. Then Tumuxávi burned a plot of land much larger than Üra's. Seeing so much smoke, the father-in-law went to find out where it was coming from. When he saw what Tumuxávi was doing he was much surprised, in part because Tumuxávi's plot of land was so much larger than Üra's, in part because he had not given Tumuxávi any seeds and yet this son-in-law was preparing land. Then Tumuxávi planted his land with seeds he found on the ground.

Instead of sowing, Üra, who was truly the idle one, went to a cave to cook the seeds his father-in-law had given to him to sow, intending to eat them. He had completely betrayed the man. While he was thus cooking, his mother-in-law climbed up the cliff above the cave. Üra was inside. She did not know where he was. While squatting on the cliff she urinated. The urine ran all the way down to the entrance of the cave. Seeing the urine, Üra thought it was raining. He peeked out of the cave to see if it was really raining. While doing so, he was seen by his father-in-law, who by chance was near the entrance of the cave. Then he realized what Üra was doing. The man became very upset and began to beat him. Üra fled and was transformed into a bird [the roadrunner]. The kind of bird he turned into is also called Üra to remind us of him. Since then, every time these birds speak, they say "Üra, Üra, Üra."

Some time later Tumuxávi took his father-in-law to see his *coamil*, which was beautiful, with many crops. There were many people working there. The man was very pleased and excited and told Tumuxávi that he was going to bring food for all those who were working there. He left. But when he returned with the food, there were no people there. They had all turned into different kinds of animals. Tumuxávi, too, had become a bird. Since then, the kind of bird he turned into is also called by his name, in remembrance of him.

Since then, Üra, the idler who had turned into a bird, has been the cause of the "laziness disease."

Obstetrical-Gynecological Ailments

46. CANIWEWE

This is the name given to female infertility. It is sometimes believed that a woman with this disorder has her uterus "backwards" due to *nanaimari* (a curse from a *mara'akáme*). There is a corresponding disorder in men called *canuaríve*.

47. METSÁXIYÁ

From *métsa*, moon. This is the name given to menstruation. It is also called *puxüre*. Although of course menstruation is not a "disease," in Huichol culture it is called "the disease of the moon." In Huichol thought menstruation and pregnancy (*paye-ucá*) are intimately related and influenced by lunar cycles. It is believed, for example, that a lunar eclipse can cause congenital malformations.

48. PANYÉ-IWETSI

This is the term employed for miscarriages and premature births. It is believed that the main cause is a curse from the soul of a deer. Another cause may be, as mentioned earlier, the ingestion of too much peyote during pregnancy, because its fuzz is supposed to adhere to the abdomen and head of a woman during gestation (the disease known as *híkuricuiniya*).

49. YUCAMÁ-PEYEMÍE

The name given to breech deliveries (delivery of the fetus with the feet or buttocks appearing first). The cause is sometimes believed to be an *ürükáme* (the crystallized soul of a deceased relative).

50. IPAÜXÍYA

This is the disorder of the *ipaü*. Both men and women have an *ipaü*. In men its concept is vague, but in women it seems to be equivalent to the uterus. It is said that when men or women suffer from *ipaüxíya* they experience pain in both iliac fossae, and that while palpating these two regions a somewhat creaky sound is produced that is very similar to that obtained from squeezing a lung. Sometimes there is vomiting and diarrhea. Specifically in women, there is pain in the mesogastrium and a "ball" that protrudes out of the vagina. This usually occurs shortly after giving birth. Sometimes there is dysuria (painful urination) and/or oliguria (insufficiency in the amount of urine produced). It seems to be a uterine prolapse. It is also very probable that it is a cystocele (a protrusion of the urinary bladder into the vagina), and possibly a rectocele (the protrusion of the posterior wall of the vagina with the anterior wall of the rectum into the vagina), or else enterocele (posterior vaginal hernia).

Miscellaneous Disorders

51. HEÜYÁ

Term employed for fever. One of its treatments consists of the use of the flower known in Huichol as *tutuwari* and in Spanish as *Guadalajarita del campo* or *yerba de San Pedro* (*Zinnia augustifolia*, Compositae family). The term *xüríxiyá (rrürixiya)* is for a high temperature in a specific part of the body.

52. MU-ÚCUINÍYA

From *mu-u*, head. This is the name given to headaches. One of the plants used to counteract this affliction is *tüpina-ukí*, known in Spanish as *espionosilla* (*Loeselia mexicana*, Polemoneaceae family). The plant is ground, a small amount of water is added, and this preparation in placed on the head. Another treatment is with *yeuca xavari* (leaves from the avocado tree, *Persea americana*, Lauraceae family). An infusion made from boiling the leaves is rubbed on the head.

53. TAI

Burns, from *tai*, fire. One treatment is with the leaves of the plant called *küxauri nanári*, the *guaje* of the mestizos (*Lagenaria siceria*, Cucurbitaceae family). The leaves are burned and the ash is combined with a small amount of water and spread on the burned area.

54. ÜXICUINÍYA

From *üxi*, eye. This seems to apply only to conjunctivitis. One treatment involves the flower called *tutú-yuyuavi* (*Cuphea* spp., Lytracea family). Several flowers are gathered and tightly squeezed with the fingers until they yield a "juice." This liquid is applied for several days to the ailing eye until it is healed. There is a belief that this illness is caused mainly by maize pollen. So as to prevent this, a votive gourd bowl, *xukúri*, is offered to the deities and a ceremony performed.

55. UMÉ-MANUMURI

Fractures. Although several species of plants are applied to the affected area, Huichols agree that they are not effective and frequently seek help from mestizo *sobraderes* or *hueseros*, traditional healers specializing in curing bone injuries.

56. CUITSITERI OR CUISTERI

Literally, this means "worms." Apparently, it refers to venereal disease of any kind. It is believed that there are six kinds of worms of different colors that cause venereal diseases and that are visible only to the shamans. It is said that if a person dies of a venereal disease he or she expels a "ball of worms." Treatment includes confessing the identity of one's sexual partner (other than husband or wife) to the *mara'akáme*, making offerings to the deities, and doing some penance. In addition, a tea brewed from the *cuitseri-huayéya* plant (*Calea* spp., Compositae family) is drunk in the morning for two days, followed by a three-day waiting period to see if the patient responds. If there is no improvement, it is drunk for three more days.

57. HURIÉCATE

This is the name given to arthritic and rheumatic ailments and paralysis. *Huriécate* are small insects resembling spiders that are visible only to the shaman. The insects protect houses and orchards from theft by weaving a long rope around them. Following a special ritual, the *huriécate* climb up a tree in order to reach this protective rope, but if the insects go past the rope or if anything has been taken from the house or fruit trees, illness ensues.

58. TAWAIYA

This is a disease that comes from the sun, *táu*. Many years ago, it is said, it was a very common disease that killed many people. Its main symptoms are headaches and dizzy spells that make the patient "feel drunk." People suffering from this ailment would have frequent fevers and vomit often. They would be prostrate. All this sounds like bubonic plague, one of the diseases that in the myth sprang magically from the fire in which the first maize was roasting. The word *tawaiya* is also used for simple dizzy spells due to low blood pressure or low blood sugar levels (hypoglycemia).

One of the treatments for *tawaiya* is placing the wet leaves of the tree called *Nakawé-küye*, known in Spanish as *zorrillo* or pinacatillo (*Ptelea trifoliata*, Rutaceae family) on the head, and covering it with a hat. A small branch may also be soaked in water and then used to wet the patient's head.

As has happened in other cases, it was the dream of a shaman, Atanasio de la Cruz, that revealed the efficacy of this plant for the *tawaiya* disease. This is his story, as recorded by Carlos Chávez-Reyes:

> I began having *tawaiya*—dizzy spells, feeling drunk, nauseous, vomiting. This happened because Tatewarí [Our Grandfather, the old fire god] sent it to me. A *tekü* [squirrel, an animal whose form is sometimes taken by this god] was in a pine tree and made an acorn drop on my head. I then started getting sick. Then I dreamed Tatewarí, and he told me: "Kill the *tekü*." I looked for it, but I couldn't kill it. Then Nakawé [the white-haired old goddess of the earth and growth] came and she showed me this plant. She placed a wet one on my head, like this, under my hat [he demonstrated this to us], and she left another one soaking in water. And with that I got healed.

59. TAWEKÁME (ALCOHOLISM)

Tawekáme is also the *kakauyári* (deity) of drunkenness. Alcoholism is a punishment from this deity. If the *tatoani* (governor) or the shamans do not fulfil their obligation, alcoholism will come as a punishment to the people as a whole. Huichols know of a plant whose root, brewed into a tea, is used to treat alcoholism. Its effect is said to last from three to five years.

60. CUITAPURÍXIYÁ

Epilepsy. Apparently, this also includes any kind of convulsive seizure. Its name derives from *cuitapuri*, a large green flying beetle known in Mexican Spanish as *mayate*. In Huichol belief, there is a close relationship between *mayates* and epilepsy. This is so because, it is said, during a convulsive seizure the victim moves in the same fashion as a *mayate* does when it is placed on its back and tries to get back on its feet. If a Huichol child suffers from epilepsy, it is because its father, or a grandfather, has not fulfilled his obligation to observe the old customs (*costumbre*, as they say in Spanish). Whenever there is a convulsive seizure it is because Nariwáme, a goddess of water who is also responsible for epilepsy, is upset.

Healing consists of a shamanic ritual in which the *mara'akáme* extracts with his hand a *mayate* beetle from the patient's head, but only where the duration of the illness is brief (four to five seizures maximum, and not lasting more than a year). An offering is also taken to a sacred place called Chinamekuta.

A relatively young *mara'akáme* told me how his grandfather, also a *mara'akáme*, cured his small son from an attack of cuitapuríxiyá of relatively brief duration—two or three seizures. He took a *mayate* beetle out of the child's head by means of a curing ritual. Since then the child has never suffered another seizure and is now a teenager.

We were also told a brief myth about how epilepsy first came to the Huichols:

> There was once a boy who with his family lived in Arawámata, near the region the Huichols call Tuapari [Santa Catarina in Spanish]. The child was ill-tempered and a crybaby. Once, on a very rainy day, he was weeping. His mother got fed up with his crying. She threw him out of the house, leaving him out in the rain.
>
> The boy began walking away from the house. Later that day his family decided to look for him. First his sister tried, but she did not succeed. Then the woman tried and she too did not have any luck.
>
> The reason they were not able to find the child was that he had gone all the way to Chinamekuta, a place near Wirikúta, the sacred land of the peyote. At Chinamekuta he became a kakauyári [one of the divine beings]. He became Nariwáme, the goddess of the waters.
>
> Since then, when someone has an epileptic seizure, it is because Nariwáme is upset. To calm Nariwáme's anger, one must take offerings to Chinamekuta.[7]

NOTES

1. The peccary is Nakawé's animal companion and, in some accounts, also her animal alter ego and transformation.(—Eds.)

2. This is identical to the purification ceremony at the beginning of the peyote pilgrimage, when all the participants, as well as the relatives who remain behind, proclaim every act of adultery and other sexual "sins." The transgressions are symbolized by knots which the officiating shaman ties in a cactus fiber string. After "confessing," the *peyoteros* are purified with the shaman's plume (*muviéri*) and the knotted string is burned in the fire, the personification of the old fire god and First Mara'akáme Tatewarí, Our Grandfather (Myerhoff 1974; Furst 1976:116).(—Eds.)

3. The Carrillo lineage is a good example of Huichol shamanism running in families. The name Carrillo keeps recurring in stories about San Andrés shamans—for example, in Yasumoto's and Espinosa's essays in these pages.(—Eds.)

4. *Tzitzic* is a Nahuatl borrowing. A medicinal herb called *tzitzicton*, little *tzitzic*, is illustrated in the sixteenth century Aztec herbal known as the *Codex Badianus*, Plates 46 and 64, with the notation by the translator, Emily Walcott Emmart (1940:251), that although the root of the word is unknown, "the plant is definitely a yellow rayed member of the *Compositae*," whose juice Aztec physicians used with other ingredients "to anoint the chest to relieve pain."(—Eds.)

5. According to other Huichol informants, the *ürükáme* sometimes manifests his or her desire to return by sending an illness to a child.(—Eds.)

6. The *ürükáme* may be housed in a specially constructed *xiriki* (god-house) or in an already existing one; what is probably meant here is that the *ürükáme* will be living in close proximity with sacred objects symbolizing his "beloved deer," such as deer antlers, deer snares, shaman's plume fashioned from a deer tail, or even a mask made from the deer's facial skin.(—Eds.)

7. Ramón Medina dictated a legend to Furst, clearly related to this one, in which a human couple, fed up with the constant wailing and weeping of their ill-tempered newborn infant, throw it out of the house. The child crawls far away, and the Mother of Maize comes to its rescue. After a time, the baby's parents, no longer hearing it cry outside, regret their impatience and search for it. But the baby has disappeared and transformed into a rain cloud. A version of the weeping baby that transforms into a rain cloud was also recorded by Preuss (Chapter 4). One is inevitably reminded here of Aztec rituals in which the tears of children chosen for sacrifice to the rain god symbolized the hoped-for rains.(—Eds.)

INTRODUCTION TO CHAPTER 8

The following chapter by the Japanese scholar Masaya Yasumoto, Professor of Comparative Religion at Kyushu International University, is both the newest and most far-ranging study of what is in many ways an apparent anomaly among people as focused as are the Huichols on a cactus as the ecstatic/divinatory sacrament willed to them by the ancestors: the persistence, in uneasy coexistence with the divine cactus, of a minority "cult" centered on a very different psychoactive species, a potent member of the Solanaceae. This plant is called Kiéri, personified as Kiéri Tewiyari, Kiéri Person, who has a certain following as power source and benefactor among some Huichols, but whom the majority views with ambivalence and even fears as a dangerous sorcerer who is to be propitiated lest he inflict harm (Knab 1977). But, as most, if not all, phenomena contain within them their complementary opposite, and nothing is unequivocally bad or good, even some of the latter grant that dangerous as he certainly is, Kiéri can be asked for, and bestow, some benefits as well.

Thirty years ago Ramón Medina dictated a lengthy myth to Furst and Myerhoff (1966:3–39) describing a bitter contest for supremacy between the culture hero, Elder Brother Kauyumári, the personification of Deer, whose ally and spirit "co-essence" is peyote, and Kiéri Tewiyari, also called "Tree of the Wind." Zingg (1938), the first ethnographer to write about Kiéri, identified him as *Datura meteloides*, since renamed *inoxia*.

Zingg's taxonomy stood until it was corrected in the 1970s to *Solandra*, a close relative of *Datura* (Furst 1976; Knab 1977; Schultes and Hofmann 1979). Ten years later the widow of Ramón Medina, Guadalupe de la Cruz Ríos, added important details to Ramón's version that also demonstrated anew how much of Huichol animal and plant symbolism is rooted in natural history observation (Furst 1989).

However, even with the shift from *Datura* to *Solandra* (a discovery for which the credit belongs largely to an amateur botanist, Colette Lilly, who first recognized that with its size and shape, and trumpet-shaped blossoms yellow in color, rather than white, the plant Huichols identify as the "true Kiéri" was not a *Datura* but a close solanaceous relative), and the subsequent identification of the species involved as either *S. brevicalyx* or *guttata*, or both, the taxonomy of Kiéri is not nearly so straightforward as previously thought. As Professor Yasumoto learned in the field, although they recognize certain Kiéri plants as the "true" ones, Huichols apply the name not just to specific *Solandra* specimens, but also to *Datura* and even an introduced member of the Solanaceae formerly known as "tree datura" but now placed in a separate genus, *Brugmansia*. All three share similar chemical constituents and all have showy flowers of similar trumpet shape.

Ramón's 1966 narrative unequivocally characterizes Kiéri as an evil sorcerer who only pretends to the beneficial powers of a true shaman. Nevertheless, with his songs, his violin, and his juices he has seduced people into becoming his followers. In the end, though, his powers prove inferior to those of peyote, which is Kauyumári's spirit ally and secret weapon. After spying on Kiéri to learn his secrets and tricks, and protecting himself with peyote, he fires five arrows into his enemy. The fifth hits him in the heart and Kiéri falls as though dead. But he does not truly die. Instead his spirit flies off to a rocky cliff, where he transforms into a tree "with five branches." Thus revived he has continued to this day to deceive some Huichols into intoxicating themselves with the powers of sweet words and his juices. Those who follow him are not true shamans, however, but only "sorcerers." Ramón's epic concludes as follows:

> For the mara'akáme who is a true Huichol there is only the hikuri, peyote. The mara'akáme does not have anything to do with kiéri. Peyote is the heart, the heart of the deer, the heart of the maize. . . . It has more power. Elder Brother Kauyumári killed Kiéri Tewiyari, that Tree of the Wind Person. He fought him with peyote. He could not resist. (Furst and Myerhoff 1966:23)

Kiéri thus survived the ancient struggle to play a continuing role, not just in what Ramón and other Huichols insist is purely nefarious activity, but in some positive aspects of Huichol ceremonialism as well. Certain Kiéri plants are sacred shrines to which people bring offerings and petitions for wealth, luck in deer hunting and other pursuits, and the acquisition of such skills as playing the violin. There is even a kind of "Kiéri shamanism," in the sense that one may become a shaman by committing to Kiéri instead of participating in the minimum of five peyote pilgrimages, and, preferably ten or more, that are ordinarily expected of a future mara'akáme. It is nevertheless beyond question that, as Knab confirmed on two visits to Santa Catarina, many Huichols regard Kiéri as essentially an evil thing, a patron of sorcerers, and few would grant someone who only pledged himself to Kiéri the same standing as one who followed the path of the ancestors to Wirikúta.

The use by the religious specialists of the same culture of different species capable of triggering the desired "state of altered consciousness" for divination, curing, or contacting the gods is not unusual: depending on context and availability, Aztec priests and shamans, for example, used sacred mushrooms, morning glory seeds, *Datura*, *Solandra*, and other psychoactive plants. Even contemporary Mazatec curers in the mountains of Oaxaca employ not only their sacred *Psilocybe* mushrooms, which they identify with

Christ, but also the seeds of the morning glory *Ipomoea violacea*, which contain alkaloids closely related to LSD. The Huichol case differs in that, for most Huichols, any "hallucinogenic" plant other than the beloved peyote, which is at the same time deer and maize, is simply unthinkable as a pathway to the divine.

So why does a rival species persist, especially one whose use is, in contrast to peyote, fraught with real danger to mental health and even life? In our 1966 paper Myerhoff and I proposed that Ramón's Kiéri legend could be read as history, that it seemed to phrase in the language and imagery of myth and magic a real event in the Huichol past: the displacement, if not the complete suppression, of beliefs and rituals centered on *Datura* by a tradition whose heart and soul is peyote.

But when would that have happened? *Datura*, called *toloache*, from the Nahuatl *toloatzin*, in Mexico and also in Indian California, was, and in many places still is, the ritual intoxicant of choice among native peoples of the Southwest and northwestern Mexico, including the Tepehuan. But toloache is not always or exclusively *Datura*. It is worth noting that a description by Mason (1918:551-52) of the toloache to whom Tepecanos addressed prayers or petitions for wealth and other good fortune, sounds, like that of Ramón for the revived Kiéri, more like the tall and rangy *Solandra* than it does the shrubby *Datura*:

> It is said to have a thick trunk of nine inches diameter and no roots, growing on bare rock. Its five branches extend to the cardinal points and to heaven.

Ramón also described the "tree of the wind" into which Kauyumári's adversary transformed himself as having five branches and growing on rocks. In contrast to Huichol attitudes, however, there is no indication that the Tepecanos regarded toloache, who is thought to be the son-in-law of the Sun god, as anything but a source of good, provided he was properly approached and propitiated.

When one faith supplants another, the losing side is often banished to the realm of sorcerery and witchcraft. Could the solanaceous "Kiéri cult" and its present association with sorcery be a remnant of a greater Southwestern pre-peyote substratum? And if so, is the myth of Kiéri's defeat by peyote, though credited to Kauyumári, whose home is Wirikúta, really about Deer Tail, the Guachichil shaman-chief who, according to the legend recorded by Diguet and discussed in Chapter 2, brought his own ancestral peyote-oriented religion from San Luis Potosí into the Huichol sierra?

Peter T. Furst

8 : THE PSYCHOTROPIC KIÉRI

IN HUICHOL CULTURE

MASAYA YASUMOTO

Translated from the Japanese by KUNIE MIYAHARA

I have been studying aspects of Huichol society and culture, especially religion and ideology, since 1980. At the center of Huichol religion is the peyote-deer-maize symbol complex, in which the sacred psychotropic cactus, the deer, and the agricultural staple are intimately associated and even equated with one another. Peyote—*hikuri* in the Huichol language—itself and the sacred deer and the maize are conceived as one and the same, for it is said that they walk along the same path, that is, they belong to or depend on one and the same source (Yasumoto 1986). The altered state of consciousness triggered by psychotropic plants has long been recognized by students of comparative religion as a central aspect of the shamanistic religions of the New World (La Barre 1970:368-373; Furst 1976). The particular study of the role of peyote among the Huichols is therefore clearly of great value to the field of comparative religion, shamanism, and ethnology. I am convinced, however, that defining the characteristics of a particular culture should logically, as well as methologically, precede comparison. This paper represents an extension of earlier attempts on my part to extract patterns of thought that distinguish the Huichols from other people whose religions are also shamanistic, and who likewise value the ecstatic experience—in short, to try and illuminate what makes the Huichols unique.

Having discussed Huichol beliefs and rituals concerning peyote elsewhere (Yasumoto 1986, 1987a, 1987b, 1989a), my purpose here is to elucidate the place of another psychotropic plant, the one they call Kiéri, in the belief system of the Huichols, especially in shamanic ideology and practice. The specific problems to be examined in these pages are how the phenomena associated with Kiéri are experienced by Huichol people, and further, to what extent these experiences are related to Kiéri's pharmacological and psychotropic effects.

To these ends, let us first place the problem into context. In terms of numbers, the Huichols are one of the smaller indigenous populations in Mexico. What makes them especially interesting and significant to Mesoamerican ethnology is, among other phenomena, that their aboriginal religion, ritual, and mythology are still relatively intact, that is, remarkably unaffected by the Catholic religion introduced by the Spanish.

The Huichol population has been estimated at about 12,000 individuals,[1] many of them spread out in small local residential units over a territory of 4107.5 square kilometers in the rugged Sierra Madre Occidental, mostly in the states of Jalisco and Nayarit but spilling over into neighboring Zacatecas and Durango. The other half of the population has moved to various cities and to the Huichol colony on the lower Río Lerma, also known as the Río Santiago. In the Sierra the basic unit is the extended family *rancho*, consisting of a cluster of dwellings and one or more *xirikis*, the Huichol word for the family temple or oratory that Lumholtz called "god-house." Outwardly, these god-houses closely resemble the ordinary dwelling; within, they contain the family's sacred objects and images.

There are no firm rules of residence after marriage, and polygyny is permitted (Yasumoto 1989b). Maize, squash, and beans are cultivated by the slash-and-burn method on the slopes of mountains and in the valleys. Despite the existence of sizable mesas, large level land planted to maize is rare. The agricultural and grazing land is jointly owned by the *comunidad indígena*. The right to farm individual holdings is inherited from father to son or, where there are no sons, to daughter. Cattle, goats, and sheep, all Spanish introductions, are raised on pasture land.

The region where the Huichols and their neighbors, the Coras, make their homes is, with its high mountains, precipitous escarpments, and deep gorges, a natural fortress that successfully barred entry to outsiders for many years, even after the fall of Mexico-Tenochtitlan. The Aztec empire was conquered in 1521, but it was not until 1722 that the Sierra de Nayar, which included both the Coras and Huichols, was brought under Spanish control. New comunidades and churches were constructed in the region of the Coras by the Spanish military and clergy, who tried hard to suppress traditional Cora religion centering on the deified Sun. Traditional shrines constructed of stones and adobe and roofed with straw were destroyed and burned, but some of the old belief system continued to maintain itself (Yasumoto 1988).

The Huichols were less affected by the conquest. The Spanish divided the Huichol country into three comunidades—San Andrés, Santa Catarina, and San Sebastián, which grew into five with the addition of Guadalupe Ocotán and Tuxpan de Bolaños. The Franciscans had charge of propagating Christianity, to which end they constructed churches, called *teyupani* in Huichol, in the ceremonial centers of the newly established comunidades. Nevertheless, most of the nearly twenty indigenous *tuki* (temples), which the missionaries called (as they did those of the Coras) by the borrowed Nahuatl word *calihuey* (from *uei* = large, *calli* = house), escaped destruction. It is on these traditional temples, and their organization of elected temple officers, that the traditional communitywide non-Christian ceremonies, such as those for clearing the fields, the cultivation of maize and other basic staples, the sowing of seeds, the harvest, and the increase of livestock, are centered. The comunidades are governed by a rotating civil-religious hierarchy, usually elected for one-year terms, headed by a governor, called *tatuani*, an honorific of Nahuatl (Aztec) origin, and including *mayordomos* who have charge of the Catholic church, the icons of Jesus Christ, the Virgin of Guadalupe, and various saints. These governing structures, introduced by the Spanish in the early eighteenth century, are still maintained today.

Each ceremonial center has its *casa real*, literally "royal house," that serves as head-quarters of the civil-religious hierarchy, as court to adjudicate disputes and conduct trials, and as a place of deliberation of community affairs. Various events, such as the change of government in January, the day of the national flag in February, Semana Santa (Holy Week) in spring, St. Francis Day on October 4, and the fiesta of the Virgin of Guadalupe, take place in the ceremonial center. Their overall purpose is to pray for and celebrate the security and prosperity of the comunidad as a whole, with all its constituent ranchos, rancherías, and districts. It is clear, then, that however gentle the Franciscans might have been in their efforts to restructure and reorient the indigenous society, especially in comparison to what occurred in other places, the Huichols were under compulsion to accept and integrate the foreign system of government and to tolerate, if not give themselves over to, the religion of the outsiders. Though there is evidence that the missionaries maintained a presence among the Huichols for some years, by the nineteenth century the churches seem to have been taken over by the Huichols themselves.

Whatever the efforts of the Franciscans, the gods of the traditional religion have maintained themselves in full strength. For the most part they are the deified natural phenomena, such as fire, sun, earth, the food plants, game animals—especially deer—and rain, as well as deified ancestors in the broad sense. The sacred deer, and the equally sacred peyote cactus (which is not native to the Sierra) are, as noted, especially impor-tant. In contrast to the Christian deities in the church, the indigenous gods are not enshrined on altars in the tuki, although images of some, carved of wood or stone, exist and are honored with sacrifices. Huichol gods are embodied in decorated gourd bowls called *jícaras* in Mexican Spanish (from the Nahuatl *xicalli*), and *xukúri* in Huichol. The Keepers of the Votive Gourds are elected to serve this cargo, as are the tuki officials. Within the tukis and the xirikis, and in the aboriginal rituals, the Sacred Deer Person Kauyumári, who is the chief assistant to the old fire god Tatewarí and chief helper of shamans, is most often represented by a pair of antlers. Tuki officials are chosen for five-year terms by the people living in the various extended family ranchos within a certain distance; the number of these temple officers varies, but, depending on the size and importance of the tuki, may exceed thirty.

In contrast to the old Huichol male and female ancestor and nature deities, the nu-merous Catholic supernaturals classified by the Huichols as gods, including Christ, the

Virgin of Guadalupe, San José, San Andrés (in the comunidad that bears his name), and other saints, are recognized as of recent origin. Virtually everything that came in with the Europeans, from the comunidades themselves and their system of government, to metal tools, the Mexican flag, and money, is believed to be the creation of these foreign gods. In contrast to other Mexican Indian peoples, the Huichols have not substituted the names and personalities of these foreign deities for their own, although there is some overlap between one or two of them (e.g., the Virgin with a sky goddess known as Our Mother Young Eagle Girl).

The peyote pilgrimages and the peyote rituals that follow them are perhaps at heart intended as petitions for the successful cultivation of maize. But by including the pilgrims in the functions of the ceremonial center, the church, and the casa real, they contribute to the overall prosperity of the comunidad as a whole. This is a crucial factor in the continuation of Huichol society and culture.

The survival of the distinctive Huichol culture is unthinkable without the mara'akáme. Because so many functions and concepts are subsumed under "mara'akáme" there is no exact equivalent to this term in our languages, but "shaman-priest" or "shaman-singer" perhaps comes closest to the core meaning. The mara'akáme is the repository of the sacred chants, the histories of the ancestor deities, and the guardian of the accumulated knowledge that has been handed down through the generations. There are very few female shamans. It is the shaman-singer who has access to the gods, officiates at the communitywide celebrations, performs the sacred songs and orations, deals directly with the ancestor gods, makes offerings to them, leads the peyote pilgrimages and is responsible for the safety of the participants, and has knowledge of diseases and their cures. He even sings what Zingg (1938) called the "Christian myth cycle." He may make sacrifices for the whole community in the tuki, the temple of the traditional religion, and the sacred space around it, including god-houses for individual deities as well as special maize plantings, or in connection with the xiriki of the extended family rancho. It may take five, six, even seven hours to complete a single chant with all its repetitive phrases, its prayers and petitions to the gods, its lessons on morality, and its histories of the Huichol world. To learn them takes many years.

Mara'akámes are nevertheless not conscious of having memorized their chants—at least they do not credit their ability to perform them well to a good memory. When questioned they will tell you that while singing they hear the voices of the ancestor gods, male and female, and are merely repeating what they hear. Even in his role as diagnostician and curer of illness, a shaman will say that in his curing song he is only repeating the voices of the divine beings, and that in treating sickness he is merely following their direction. On the other hand, shamans also possess an extensive empirical knowledge of the healing properties of plants, although they seldom use them in their treatment.

The minimum requirement for a future shaman is to remain celibate, or, if married, monogamous, for the five years following a vow to "complete" as a mara'akáme.

Coupled with this are successful pilgrimages, to sacred caves in the mountains, to a great rock, and to other sanctified places within and outside the mountainous homeland of the Huichols. Above all, one must go to Wirikúta, the home of the peyote. Wirikúta is located in the high desert of the state of San Luis Potosí, about 300 miles northeast of the Huichol country. Peyote pilgrimages take place once a year, in the dry season. Five of these arduous undertakings are a necessary requirement for future shamans.

Future shamans teach and train themselves, by observation and participation, and it is only after he has completed his self-training, made five peyote pilgrimages, and deposited offerings at the prescribed sacred places, that the novice is given recognition as a mara'akáme by his group.

Huichols say there is a way to get around some of these obligations, that one may become a shaman even without the pilgrimage to Wirikúta. If one wants to be just a shaman, it is said, one can do it faster by taking one's vow to Kiéri, the "Tree of the Wind."

Kiéri, Tree of the Wind

Huichols associate wind, particularly whirlwinds, cyclones, or tornados, with souls of the dead or the gods. Such a wind, they say, is the harbinger of illness and other misfortunes. Most feared among the whirlwinds is one bearing the name of Taweakáme. However, Taweakáme is not the whirlwind itself. Taweakáme is the Huichol term for drunkard. To specify wind as a whirlwind, it is called E'éka Taweakáme,[2] meaning Wind of Taweakáme, because such a wind transforms everyone into a drunkard just like Taweakáme.

> "It walks like a drunkard, but it isn't really drunk. So it can change others into drunks. For example, it would carry you off, blow you away so far. Yet you do not feel anything, you see nothing. You are senseless for a time, and when you recover consciousness, you do not remember anything." (Leocadio López Carrillo)

As the term indicates, it is Taweakáme that makes the whirlwind into E'eka Taweakáme, the drunken wind. But when they think or hear the expression E'éka Taweakáme, Huichols almost unconsciously associate it with Kiéri—not just with a plant of that name, but with its personification as Kíeri Tewíyari, Kiéri Person, and Kiéritáwe, the drunken Kiéri.

As a plant, Kiéri can be found in several locations in the mountains of the Huichol country. But the Kiéri of mythology was once a *kakauyári*, the word used for unknown being or ancestor deity in general, and thus a mysterious and supernatural being. In mythic times, when there was no difference between human beings, animals, and plants, when gods could appear as men and women or as animals, this kakauyári was a mara'akáme, a shaman who could sing and treat illnesses. There are different versions of the Kiéri myths; in some, the Sacred Deer Person Kauyumári (the culture hero)

FIGURE 49. Kiéri Tewíyari's Defeat by Culture Hero Kauyumari (with Deer Antlers) Aided by Peyote and His Transformation into the "Tree of the Wind." (*Yarn painting by Ramón Medina, 1966. Fowler Museum of Cultural History, University of California at Los Angeles.*)

discovered that Kiéri was a sorcerer, and with the help of Tatewarí, the old fire god and first Mara'akáme, challenged him to a battle and killed him.[3] However, being a kakauyári this Kiéri did not really die. Instead he transformed himself into a Kiéri tree, and is still feared as one who performs sorcery on people. It is the kakauyári transformed into a Kiéri tree who was called Kiéri Tewíyari, Kiéri Person (Figure 48). But not all Kiéri plants are Kiéri Tewíyari.

For example, there is a story about a place called Ratumuyéve in a gorge near Pueblo Nuevo. One time a group of hunters from the Las Guayabas district of the comunidad of San Andrés went there to hunt deer so they could make their offering. They found a deer and shot an arrow at it. Though it was hit, the deer escaped. Following its footprints, they came upon a Kiéri tree. They saw that the arrow that had been shot into the deer had pierced clear through the tree. So the mara'akáme sang to it, and in singing found out that this Kiéri was a kakauyári. And they named the Kiéri and promised to offer it candles, a votive gourd bowl (*jícara, xukúri*), and arrows. This Kiéri is one that brings luck, and it is said that if you take some water home from a nearby stream and anoint your livestock with it, cows will bear calves every year (Benítez 1968:283-284). Thus, a specific Kiéri plant at a specified location where people go to give offerings is Kiéri Tewíyari, Kiéri Person. The cave called Nakuta, near Santa Terésa in the territory of the Coras, is famed among Huichols for this kind of Kiéri.

There are also some Kiéris that are too *delicado* and *bravo*, so that no one any longer goes to them to give offerings. The terminology employed here, "delicado" and "bravo," is, of course, Spanish rather than Huichol, although both are used as though they were in fact Huichol words. But the meanings the Huichols apply to them are not those in the dictionary. Delicado is not "subtle, elegant, or delicate," or "hard to handle," but, rather, "dangerous, sacred." Similarly, bravo has the meaning of "difficult, out of control, fierce."

When praying to and petitioning the deities, one must arrange for the offerings demanded by them. After the request has been granted, one has to make these sacrifices on a regular basis. Knowledge of what the particular deity expects from you comes through the medium of the mara'akáme, and the petition to the gods takes the form of a pledge or contract. In Latin America, the word *manda* is used to mean a pledge to a deity or saint, as in "Dear God, I have a wish. If you can grant my wish, I will offer (or perform) such and such a manda in return." Huichols also use "manda" as though it were a Huichol word, meaning an offering. The gods punish those who commit a breach of such a pledge or contract by sending a disease. But Kiéri Tewíyari is even more unforgiving, causing madness and even death for the transgressor. Hence he is "delicado" and "bravo."

But regardless of whether or not a particular Kiéri is Kiéri Tewíyari, Kiéri in general is feared. It is believed that the pollen of Kiéri flowers makes birds and insects faint, and causes honey bees to lose their sense of direction. The fragrance of its flowers can intoxicate people. There is the account of one individual who, having been deluded into believing he could fly through the sky, fell off a cliff and died. Another received a direct hit from the energy flowing out of a branch and was blown far away. It is quite possible for such accidents to befall one in the mountains. Whatever other explanations there might be, being "spirited away" is often blamed on Kiéri. For example, there is the story of a woman who, having gone out into the wilds with her baby on her back, did not return home for a month. She herself had no idea what had happened to her. When she regained her senses, she found herself at the top of a rocky mountain, and her baby dead. Weeping, she buried the little corpse among the rocks. But then she again lost consciousness. By the time she was herself again she had reached home. But her husband, suspecting that she had spent the time with another man, angrily demanded to know where she had been. Remembering nothing and thus unable to explain anything to her husband, the woman despaired and hanged herself. This sad tale has become one of the Kiéri legends of the comunidad of Tuxpan de Bolaños.

But is it really possible for such things to occur? Did the kakauyári who transformed into a Kiéri tree use magic on her, as the people say he did? Or was her disorientation and loss of consciousness due to her having actually eaten the flowers or the leaves of a Kiéri plant? Are there other examples of incidents that might be blamed not on the magical powers ascribed to Kiéri but on its actual effects?

To answer these questions, we must first consider who and what plant the Huichols have known as Kiéri, and what it actually is, in what we would call the "real," rather than the mythic, world.

Botany and Pharmacology of Kiéri

When you ask Huichols to translate "Kiéri" into Spanish, they will tell you that it means *el arbol del viento*, "the tree of the wind" (Furst and Myerhoff 1966; Nuñez Franco 1982). The scholar who first showed interest in the mythology and botany of Kiéri was Robert Mowry Zingg, who in 1934 conducted anthropological field work in the comunidad of Tuxpan. Zingg recorded tales of the evil shaman Kíeli Tewíali, whom he called *Datura*-Man, and his good adversary, the culture hero Kauymali (Kauyumári) (Zingg 1938 and undated ms.) (Figure 49). Unfortunately, Zingg did not identify which species of *Datura* was meant.

The genus *Datura*, with some ten to twelve species, belongs to the Solanaceae (Schultes 1972:46-50; Schultes and Hofmann 1979:41-42, 106-111; Ott 1979:68). The Aztecs employed several of these species not just for their psychoactive effects but therapeutically in the treatment of illness. Species of *Datura* were also used as anesthetics in medicine and, apparently, in sacrificial rites, to deaden the pain of the victims. The Nahuatl names *toloatzin* and *tolohuaxihuitl* apparently applied to several species, although the former is generally believed to pertain to *Datura inoxia* (formerly *meteloides*) (Figures 50, 51). The Aztec toloatzin has passed into Mexican Spanish as *toloache*, and it is as such that it still plays a role in folk medicine, as a remedy for the pain and swelling associated with rheumatism and other complaints. Generally, however, people tend to associate the use of toloache with sorcery, for example, as effective love magic, as a means of controlling a violent husband or adulterous wife, or, in extreme cases, to poison an enemy or drive him or her into insanity.

Members of the genus *Datura*, like certain other solanaceous plants such as belladonna (*Atropa belladonna*), henbane (*Hyoscyamus niger*), or mandrake (*Mandragora officinarum*), contain the tropane alkaloids scopolamine, hyoscyamine, and atropine. All these tropanes block neurotransmission in the parasympathetic nervous system and produce rapid heart rate, dilated pupils, flushing, heat, dryness of the skin and mouth, constipation, and difficulty in swallowing. Atropine is well known to medicine, and so is scopolamine. The former, among other uses, is often applied for stomach pain due to excessive digestive acid and to dilate the pupils. Scopolamine has similar effects as atropine, but its action in the suppression of the nerve center is different. Because it can

FIGURE 50. *Datura inoxia. (Photograph by Peter T. Furst.)*

FIGURE 51. The Spiny Seed Pods from Which *Datura* Got the Popular Name "Thorn Apple." (*Photograph by Peter T. Furst.*)

strengthen the anesthetic property of morphine, scopolamine is used as a pre-treatment for general anesthesia. It is also used by itself as an analgesic and antispasmodic in ailments of the digestive system (Kimura and Kimura 1981:200). Specialists uniformly warn of the danger of death due to overdoses (Ott 1979:66, 68, 72). They can "produce fever, delirium, convulsions, and collapse. Death may occur in children, the elderly, the debilitated, and any person usually sensitive to the antiparasympathetic effects" (Weil 1980:168), or, to cite an authoritative Japanese source, "With a large quantity, it (scopolamine) paralyzes the central nervous system" and, "in the end, causes death due to heart failure after frenzied madness" (*Sekai Daihyakka Jiten* 1988, vol. 28:603).

"After frenzied madness" seems to describe the psychological aspect of the pharmacological effect of scopolamine. Andrew Weil, a medical doctor as well as ethnopharmacologist, believes that the psychotropic effect of solanaceous plants such as *Datura* is due to scopolamine rather than hyoscyamine, and that therefore these solanaceous plants should be regarded as deliriants rather than psychedelics or hallucinogens. Delirium is a mentally impaired state characterized by confusion and disorientation. Scopolamine's "mental effects are equally dramatic: restlessness, disorientation, and other symptoms of delirium, including vivid hallucinations that may seem so real that people lose all contact with ordinary reality. Because scopolamine usually leaves you with some amnesia, it is often hard to remember these hallucinations clearly when the drug wears off. Going into other worlds is fascinating, but the worlds datura takes people to can be frightening, populated by monsters and devils and filled with violent, frenzied energy" (Weil and Rosen 1983:132).

However, diverse native peoples of North America had a profound knowledge of the dangerous effects of these plants, and employed them with great care in medicine (as an analgesic, for example), and in collective rituals, or individual divination, for communication with the deities. For example, among the Zuni Indians of New Mexico, members of the Rain Priest Fraternity ate the roots of *Datura inoxia* (Ott 1979:70; Schultes and Hofmann 1979:110). This is significant, because the root contains a very low level of scopolamine and is thus the safest part of the plant. Indian peoples in Southern California also employed *Datura inoxia*, and Algonquian-speakers in the East used the eastern species, *Datura stramonium*, in their initiation ceremonies (Furst 1976:141–142; Ott 1979:72). Most daturas have white trumpet-shaped flowers, but there is also one, *D. tatula* L., that has light purple blossoms.[4] It is the eastern species, *D. stramonium*, that acquired the name Jamestown Weed, later contracted to Jimsonweed during the days of the English colonies (Furst 1976:141). Generally speaking, in North America "jimsonweed," *D. stramonium*, pertains to the east, toloache, *D. inoxia*, to the west.

But to which of these different species does Zingg's Kiéri belong? Or is it really a plant of the genus *Datura*? These were questions that in the 1960s, when Furst and Myerhoff published a myth in which Kiéri is *Datura* and a much-feared sorcerer, were still very much up in the air. At the time Furst recorded this myth, no scientific botany had been done on Kiéri, or, for that matter, on any other plants in the Huichol environment, so that, in the absence of information contradicting Zingg, their paper assumed Kiéri to be *Datura*. By the early seventies the situation had changed, Kiéri having now been identified for the first time as a species not of *Datura* but the related solanaceous genus, *Solandra* (Knab 1977:80–86) (Figure 52). Commenting on verbal information from T. J. Knab that in the area where he had done research (the comunidad of Santa Catarina), Kiéri was definitely identified, not as a *Datura*, but as *Solandra*, Furst (1976:136) speculated that there might be different Kiéris, associated with different members of the Solanaceae. My research shows that to be the case.

Datura, Solandra, and Brugmansia

In their book, *Plants of the Gods: Origins of Hallucinogenic Use* (1992), Richard Evans Schultes and Albert Hofmann, the former the ranking authority on New World plant hallucinogens, and the latter the discoverer of LSD, included a paragraph on *Solandra* (*S. brevicalyx* Standl.), with Kieli (Kiéri), Hueipatl, and Tecomaxochitl given as its Huichol and Aztec names. The authors also mention, without identifying their source, that Huichols distinguish between *Datura inoxia* as kieritsa, rendered as the bad kieri, and *Solandra* as the good, or true kiéri (Schultes and Hofmann 1979:73). In fact, what Huichols mean by the suffix -tsa or -xra is that the plant to which it is applied resembles, or is similar, to the real or true Kiéri, that is, *Solandra*, rather than that it is a bad manifestation of the supernatural called Kiéri and of his botanical form. What is correct, and where I agree with Schultes and his colleagues, is that the Huichols recognize a close relationship among plants of three solanaceous genera, *Solandra*, *Datura*, and *Brugmansia*.

I have not heard *Datura inoxia* (i.e., toloache) being called the "bad Kiéri," at least not in the comunidades of San Andrés and Tuxpan. What Huichols there say is that it is "similar" to Kiéri—that is, that it is "Kiéri-tsa." Although I am not sure whether *Solandra* is called "True Kiéri" in San Andrés, it is unmistakably Kiéri. At a place called Kukatawíye, located on a cliff on the southwestern plateau, there is a small xiriki, a shrine or god-house, for the Kiéri. The Kiéri growing here is *Solandra*. In Tuxpan, some people call *Solandra* "True Kiéri," because *Datura* is a shrub, whereas *Solandra* is truly a tree and thus fits the definition of "Tree of the Wind." Of course, *Brugmansia*, formerly called "tree datura," is also a tree, but I will deal with *Brugmansia* later, as also with yet another vexing problem—the existence of a Kiéri that so far has defied botanical identification.

The genus *Solandra* consists of some ten species that are closely related to both *Datura* and *Brugmansia*. All contain tropane alkaloids, including hyoscyamine, scopolamine, and nortropine. In Mexico, where they are cultivated as ornamentals, the *Solandras* are popularly known as *copa de oro*, cup of gold. In the city of Guadalajara, they measure about fifteen feet in height at maturity, with large, fragrant, trumpet-shaped yellow or cream-colored flowers. In addition to their role as ornamentals, they

FIGURE 52. Blossom of *Solandra guttata*, Called Kiéri by Huichols, Near San Andrés Cohamiata. (*Photograph by James A. Bauml.*)

also function in contemporary folk medicine: a tea made from boiling water poured over a single flower is said to be an effective cough medicine. On the other hand, decoctions are said to be dangerous.

In contrast to the treelike ornamental variety, the copa de oro growing in the comunidad of Tuxpan and elsewhere in the Sierra, that is, the one the Huichols know as Kiéri, grows on steep slopes and rocky cliffsides strewn with loose stones of volcanic origin. With its roots spreading out among the stones, this type of *Solandra* barely reaches six feet in height and its trumpet-shaped flowers are considerably smaller. Constantly struggling against the strong mountain winds, the plants seem unable to grow vertically and so branch out among the rocks like vines. However, craggy cliffs of this sort are not common.

To reach Tuxpan overland one must traverse steep mountains more than 6,000 feet above sea level, along trails that twist and turn before descending more than 3,500 feet to the main center of Tuxpan. Looking back from the little pueblo one sees the mountains forming a range on the east that separates the Huichol territory from its neighbors. One mountain, somewhat higher than its neighbors in the range, is called in Spanish El Cerro de Saucillo.[5] It is a long distance from Tuxpan and both ascent and descent are steep and dangerous. Hence, it is not a place that people visit under ordinary circumstances. But people are aware that considerable stands of *Solandra*, that is, Kiéri, are to be found there.

While *Solandra*'s identity with the plant spirit Kiéri is thus firmly established, it is nevertheless a fact that some Huichols believe that *floripondio* is also Kiéri (Nuñez Franco 1982:67). Floripondio is one of the Spanish names for the nine known species of the genus *Brugmansia*, the so-called tree daturas native to South America that were introduced into Mexico by the Spaniards as ornamentals. In July of 1986 I took an eleven-hour ride on muleback in the company of some Huichol youths from San Andrés to the little community of Huaistita. The Kiéri I saw there was unmistakably *floripondio*, that is, a species of *Brugmansia*, probably *B. aurea* Lagerh. It was in full flower, its yellow blossoms emitting a nearly overwhelming perfume (Figure 53).

For a year starting in September 1988, Armando Casillas Romo, M.D., a medical doctor from the Guadalajara State University Medical School, conducted research on traditional medicine and medicinal plants in the region of San Andrés. He identifies Kiéri as copa de oro, that is, *Solandra brevicalyx* Standl., and refers to floripondio as Kiéri-nánari, meaning "root of kiéri" (Casillas Romo 1990:134–135; see Chapter 7).[6] In Huichol folk medicine, the roots of floripondio are used to treat itchiness and impetigo, but the Huichols of my acquaintance do not refer to floripondio itself as Kiéri-nanári. Rather, so far as I could ascertain, in San Andrés Kiéri-nánari signifies the Kiéri with long, vinelike branches.

The floripondio I saw in 1986 was wild-growing, but others appear to be a cultivated variety. The situation here seems to be similar to that in its original South American habitat: "In parts of Colombia, Ecuador, and Peru a profusion of these strange and

FIGURE 53. *Brugmansia*. In shape if not in color, the showy yellow flowers of *Brugmansia*, once called "tree datura," resemble those of its close solanaceous relative, *Datura*. (*Photograph by Peter T. Furst.*)

beautiful trees around a dwelling virtually advertises the residence of a witch doctor" (Weil 1980:173). As noted, floripondio was once thought to belong to the genus *Datura*, and the varieties used by South American Indians were accordingly identified as tree daturas. More recent studies have determined that the "tree daturas" need to be reclassified as members of the genus *Brugmansia* (Schultes and Hofmann 1979:36). The same authors note that all species of *Brugmansia*, a genus "closely related to *Datura*," have probably been used psychotropically for millennia, and that they are all cultigens unknown in the wild.

Use of different species of *Brugmansia* is widespread among South American Indians, as far apart as the Mapuche of Chile, the Chibcha of Colombia, and various Amazonian peoples, usually "in the form of powdered seeds added to fermented drinks, or as a tea made from the leaves" (Schultes and Hofmann 1979:68–69). The genus, said to be "biologically very complex," occurs in the warm tropical lowlands, especially western Amazonia, but "most of the species . . . prefer the cool, wet highlands above 6,000 feet (ibid., p. 36).

In the city of Guadalajara floripondio can be found as a short tree a little over six feet in height. In Japan, some families in northern Kyushu cultivate floripondio for the sheer beauty of its flowers. But in fact it is also an important medicinal plant that also goes under the name of "Angels' Trumpet," yielding the raw material for hydrobromic scopolamine, which so far has not proved amenable to synthesis (Kimura and Kimura 1981:200). In Mexico there is a runaway underground bestseller, entitled *Donde no hay Doctor: Una guía para los campesinos que viven lejos de los centros médicos* (*Where There Is No Doctor: A Handbook for Peasant Farmers Living Far from a Clinic*. First published in 1973, by 1989 it had gone through twenty printings. It recommends four medicinal plants, and one of these is floripondio:

> Floripondio (*Datura arborea*). The leaves contain an element to lessen pains of the twisted intestines, the side and the gallbladder. Mash one or two leaves and soak them in seven spoonfuls (100 ml.) of water for a day. Then administer ten to fifteen drops of this every four hours (adults only). Floripondio is poisonous if more than an appropriate dose is ingested, so it is better to use a regular antispasmodic when possible. (Werner 1973:12)

Schultes and Hofmann (1979:69) also warn against the dangers entailed in uncontrolled use of floripondio:

> All species of *Brugmansia* are chemically similar, with scopolamine as their principal psychoactive constituent. Content of lesser alkaloids is also similar. A dangerous hallucinogen, *Brugmansia* brings on an intoxication often so violent that physical restraint is necessary before the onset of a deep stupor, during which visions are experienced.

In medieval Europe solanaceous plants were closely linked to belief in witchcraft. The comments of ethnologist Michael Harner (1973a, 1973b) on this question, backed by his own observations of the solanaceous *Brugmansia* among the Jivaro of Ecuador, are especially useful here. It was widely believed that witches smeared ointments on their bodies and flew through the air on their brooms to attend the Devil's sabbath. The plants mentioned as having been employed for these purposes are all members of the Solanaceae, principally *Atropa belladonna*, *Hyoscyamus* (henbane), and *Mandragora*, or mandrake, sometimes with *Datura* added. Witches were said to smear the ointment made from these plants on the absorbent parts of their bodies, upon which they fell into a state of hallucination and delirium. "Solanaceous hallucinogens are so powerful," writes Harner (1973b:146),

> that it is essentially impossible for the user to control his mind and body sufficiently to perform ritual activity at the same time. In addition, the state of extended sleep following the period of initial excitation, sleep which can extend for three or four days, together with the typical amnesia, made this hardly a convenient method for daily practice of witchcraft. Furthermore, there is some ethnographical evidence that too frequent use of the solanaceous drugs can permanently derange the mind.

Harner continues that the very real differences between witchcraft and shamanism lie in part in the fundamental differences in the nature, functions and effects of the hallucinogens employed.

> I arrived at this particular insight . . . during my fieldwork among the Jivaro Indians (*untsuri šuara*) of eastern Ecuador, who use both the solanaceous plant, *Datura* [since reclassified as *Brugmansia*, Eds.], and non-solanaceous hallucinogens. They utilize the solanaceous plant in the vision quest, simply to encounter the supernatural, but do not use it in shamanism because it is "too strong," and prevents the shaman from being able to operate in both worlds simultaneously. (Harner 1973b:146)

About the Huichols and the Solanaceae, it can be said with certainty that Kiéri is never consumed in cases of treatment of illness by a shaman, or in group rituals. There is nevertheless a phenomenon which the Huichols construe as having been brought on by Kiéri. They experience it as such, and their experience ought to be positioned within the framework of collective symbolism. For that reason, I will examine some "abnormal" experiences they say they have had with Kiéri, and in doing so I hope to contribute to our understanding of Huichol culture.

LEARNING TO PLAY THE VIOLIN

In general it can be said that most Huichols stay away from Kiéri. Many Huichols are not even aware that *Datura inoxia*, which is not a "tree," can also be Kiéri, and that it is potentially both a poison *and* a medicine. As for the "Tree of the Wind," that is, *Solandra*, many are not conscious of its pharmacological properties, their fear of it

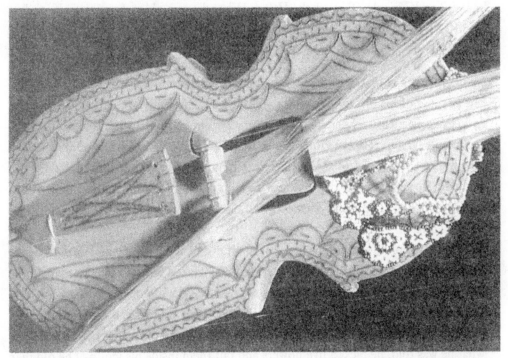

FIGURE 54. Ramón Medina's Homemade Violin and Horsehair Bow, Decorated with Hot Knife Engraving and Beadwork. (*Southwest Museum, Los Angeles. Photograph by Peter T. Furst.*)

being based, rather, on the belief that it is a transformed kakauyári (ancestor deity) possessing abnormal power. The Tree of the Wind readily grants your wishes, yet is too "bravo," and hence should not be approached. Such traditions have been transmitted from generation to generation. Mentioned among the wishes Kiéri may grant are to become a mara'akáme without going through five peyote pilgrimages, to play the violin like an expert in a short time, and to be successful in hunting a deer for an offering to the ancestor deities.

Huichol men play small, homemade three-string violins, as well as homemade guitars (Figure 54). They learn to play these stringed instruments, which were introduced into Mexico by the Spaniards in early colonial times, by following the example of others. Those who play well are elected to serve for terms of five years as musicians with the other members of the temple group. They also receive invitations from neighboring communities to perform in their ceremonies. There is something very moving in watching young people practicing alone on their instruments, in the hope of attaining superior skill. But across all the comunidades there is a belief—and many stories to support that belief—that mastering the violin can be done incredibly fast by learning from Kiéri.

When Juan Ríos, an accomplished "yarn painter" born in 1930, was nine, he told his father of his desire to become a master violinist who served in the ceremonies. His father took him on a peyote pilgrimage to Wirikúta, and also on a pilgrimage to offer a "manda" to Kiéri, the Tree of the Wind. When he was older, Juan himself made a vow to Kiéri, and as a result became known as a master of the violin (Negrín 1977:54). Another story, dictated to Benítez by Ramón Medina:

There was a young man who loved to listen to the music of the violin. When he saw a friend of his playing the violin and the guitar exceedingly well at a ceremony, he became suspicious. Then he heard from someone about the wind tree Kiéri teaching people how to play the violin. So he made himself a violin and went alone to the cliff where the Tree of the Wind grew, thinking he would spend a night there. At midnight he awakened to the sound of a violin playing far away. He thought it must be Kiéri playing. The sound seemed to get closer and closer. But the wind tree made him fall asleep.

While asleep, he saw a lightning bolt flash out of the Tree of the Wind like fireworks. A young girl approached him calling his name. Then an old man playing the violin appeared and said, "Follow me. Let's eat some white tortillas at my rancho." Leaping from rock to rock on the edge of a cliff, the old man led him to the center of a rocky mountain. There was a tree there with flowers of various colors. Obeying what he was told, he picked five flowers and put them inside his violin. The old man showed him how to hold the violin and bow. After trying this he told the old man that he could not play. "Remember the songs I taught you," the old man told him. "For the next five days, play by yourself. You must play thinking about the Tree of the Wind. The five flowers you picked are five songs. You must fast and sleep by yourself for five days. Now I will take you home. Your family must be wondering if you have fallen down a cliff or been eaten by a wild animal."

In the morning he was awakened by a cold wind and went home. Though his wife asked what had happened he did not answer. Following the old man's instructions he fasted and slept alone for five days. By the end of five days he was able to play the violin. The five days of fasting were over so he could again have salt. He went to the fireplace and threw salt into the fire. It made a crackling sound, which indicates Grandfather Fire was eating the salt. "Grandfather Fire, thank you for blessing the salt. Tree of the Wind, Kiéri, I thank you for transforming yourself into a man, and making me play and sing beautiful songs so well." At the very next festival he performed with his violin in front of others. He was so happy to see many of his friends in the audience. Everyone wondered and said, "Where did he learn to play so well, so fast?" (Benítez 1968:285–286).

The above tradition originates in Santa Catarina and San Sebastián. Benítez heard a comparable, though somewhat different, story in San Andrés from a Huichol grade school teacher named José Carrillo:

There was a bad Kiéri up from the community of Las Guayabas who was known to teach the violin. One night a mara'akáme named Hilario was lying asleep in a banana planting, when about midnight he heard the sound of a violin. In the morning he found a Kiéri near the bananas. That evening he attended a fiesta and said to a group of young men who happened to be there, "I heard Kiéri playing the violin very well last night. Why don't you go and see if the story about it is true." One of the young men who heard Hilario's advice fasted for five days and then went to the Kiéri. At midnight a child appeared from the Kiéri, took a violin and, surrounded by yellow powder, played it for a long time. The young man broke off a branch from the Kiéri, put it inside the violin, and went home.

In less than a year, he could play very skillfully, and was invited to the fiestas. But during the third year a woman came into his life, and they had fun together. In other words, they were united. This was a terrible thing, because in exchange for learning from the Kiéri to play the violin, he had taken a vow not to have relations with women, and he was two years short of fulfilling it. (Benítez 1968:284)

The Hilario of this story was the most prestigious mara'akáme in the comunidad of San Andrés when I did field work there. His sons serve as *kawitéros*, elders. When I accompanied a peyote pilgrimage in 1985, Hilario and his sons came as well. He passed away in 1986 at age 86.

Hilario did not learn to play the violin from Kiéri. The young man, however, went mad and in the end died. Not much is said about his condition of madness. What the story emphasizes, rather, is that you must know the dangers of Kiéri before expecting to gain some power from it.

In these two stories of the violin, the first Kiéri is undoubtedly copa de oro, *Solandra*, inasmuch as it grows in rocky terrain. It cannot be either *Datura* or *Brugmansia*. The second Kiéri is also certainly not *Datura*, although at this point I cannot decide whether it is *Brugmansia* or *Solandra*. In either instance, we can assume that the perfume of the Kiéri flowers acted as an anesthetic. Nevertheless, learning to play the violin from Kiéri has nothing to do with the perfume of its flowers, or with eating the flowers or leaves. It is not the intention of the Huichols to put themselves under the influence of Kiéri's pharmacology. Generally speaking, they are not necessarily even aware of such an effect.

VOWS

To become a mara'akáme, one has to train for at least five years. A peyote pilgrimage to the sacred land of Wirikúta must be accomplished once a year for a total of five times. As noted earlier, however, there is also a belief that if one makes a vow to Kiéri, the knowledge and power necessary for a mara'akáme will be granted without going through the peyote pilgrimages.

The artist Guadalupe González Ríos, a well-known maker of wool yarn paintings, who was born in 1920 and whose father was a mara'akáme, hoped to become one himself. He had faith in Kiéri, and by visiting it from time to time, he deepened his knowledge of Huichol traditions. He also interpreted dreams. He continued to practice after his marriage. He went through the required fasting, that is, abstaining from salt, and he trained all night on the summit of a rocky mountain. But his wife, who had always accompanied him, went insane. It took another mara'akáme nine months to treat her. Kiéri is the most jealous and quick-tempered among the ancestors, the kakauyári (pl. kakauyaríte) and bringing a wife to a pilgrimage like that was a violation of the rule. His training to become a mara'akáme failed, and so he went to Tepic, the capital of Nayarit, to make his living as an artist. He had practiced his faith in Kiéri in the hope of becoming a mara'akáme, but because of his wife's illness his training was wasted. In spite of this, Guadalupe began to do it all over again. He resumed his meditations atop the rocky mountain, and he decided to go on pilgrimages to the sacred land of Wirikúta, the place where the peyote grows (Negrín 1977:54).

Like Guadalupe, the aforementioned Juan Ríos also wanted to be a mara'akáme. I do not know whether either Guadalupe's or Juan's wishes were eventually fulfilled. What I did wonder about, however, were the circumstances of Guadalupe's wife going insane. Did she become temporarily deranged, or only intermittently so? Was she aware of herself and did she recognize her husband? Anyone who trains to become a mara'akáme should certainly know about the toxic effects of scopolamine. The flowers, leaves, or seeds of *Datura*, *Brugmansia*, or *Solandra* plants should never be eaten. Even in cases of making a vow directly to Kiéri, one just takes offerings. Then what happened to Guadalupe and others? It is possible to become intoxicated by the perfume of its flowers if one stays too long under the Kiéri tree. But according to the story, nothing had befallen Guadalupe, even though he meditated directly under the Tree of the Wind, and it was his wife who had gone mad instead.

The Huichols explain it this way: Wanting to become a mara'akáme by making a vow to Kiéri is easy but dangerous not only to yourself. People who became mara'akámes in this manner are more adept at using sorcery to make others ill than at treating illness. Moreover, "It is a bad thing to go to Kiéri. Why, it fixes the length of the period (of a contract)!"

Wishing to a Kiéri means making a contract. The minimum requirements in the contract are abstaining from salt and sexual intercourse. The Kiéri indicates the required length of the taboo by appearing in a dream as an old man or a child, and handing out small balls that look like *queso*, cheese. One ball represents a month. The contract is concluded when one accepts the balls. If five balls are received, one must abstain for five months. Moreover, one must undergo various trials during these five months, such as meeting (but resisting) beautiful women. The Kiéri can kill people as well. Thus, making such a contract with Kiéri implies your own or a family member's death sooner or later. As the Huichols say, we cannot win over Kiéri. To make a contract with Kiéri is to submit to its extremely dangerous control.

It is possible to murder people with Kiéri, but does that suggest the use of Kiéri as a poison?

Like the goddess Aramara of the western sea, Kiéri, the Tree of the Wind, renders assistance to those who try to kill others by placing a curse on them. For example, if a man who was betrayed by a woman wants to kill her, he would first gather one each of her hair, hairs from maize, deer, and her livestock, and place them, wrapped in a small cloth, inside the hollow shaft of a ceremonial arrow. The shaft is made from the reed Mexicans call *carrizo*. Pollen from Kiéri flowers is also added. He would then make an effigy of his wife from beeswax, tie it to the arrow, and hang it from a Kiéri branch. And he would fast (i.e., abstain from salt) for several days afterwards. Soon the woman would begin to feel ill, lose weight, and die. Even a mara'akáme cannot heal her. He himself would only faint or fall ill himself (Palafox 145–146).

It must be emphasized that in black magic of this sort no component from the Kiéri's pharmacological properties is used to harm individuals. Aside from putting the pollen in the arrow shaft and hanging it from a branch, the magic really has nothing directly to do with Kiéri.

Another method of which I learned is to charge someone before Kiéri. Briefly stated, this is how it is done:

Make an arrow out of carrizo and paint it with a mixture of indigo and resin. Then stick five beads on the shaft with beeswax. On a small piece of cardboard outline a human form with beads and tie it to the arrow. Place the arrow at the root of a Kiéri tree and pray: "The person in this picture has done such and such a wrong to me. I am helpless. So please make me at ease with your power. I offer you this arrow." The individual so charged falls ill, and no mara'akáme can heal him.

Again, as plant, Kiéri does not participate in these methods. However, there is one case in which a person did appear to be harmed by Kiéri's pharmacological effects. It was recounted to Benítez in 1967 by the aforementioned José Carillo:

When he was not yet ten, José Carillo followed the deer hunters to Lechuguilla. Though five deer were spotted, they all escaped because no one could shoot an arrow. Then one of the hunters said, "We must offer a manda to the plant in Airiukarie. Otherwise, every deer will escape." There is a big rock at the foot of the Lechuguilla hill, and in the middle of it grows a Kiéri tree. This man tied his arrow to a branch of the tree. José was watching the man when he found yellow fruits on the tree. He opened the fruit and put the powder inside onto his palm. Then the powder disappeared. Startled, José involuntarily put his hand over his face. By the time the deer hunt was resumed, José was completely intoxicated. The sun looked like the moon, and this moon was circling around a human being. José was screaming, but the hunters mistook it for the cry of a deer caught in a trap. It looked as if water was gushing out of the soil. Everything around him appeared to be spinning. When he was trying to go toward the cliff, one of the hunters grabbed José's arm and asked what was going on. José came to, and repeatedly vomited up a yellow powdery substance. The mara'akáme removed the powder from his head using a *muviéri* (a feathered arrow used for ceremonial purposes). A grain of powder fell to the ground from the mara'akáme's hand.

The whirlwind that befell José is called Kiéri Taweakáme. Not all Kiéris are kakauyári. In order to avoid such harm, a ceremonial arrow, two candles and a votive bowl with the image of a deer drawn in beeswax and beads must be offered before the deer hunt at a special place like Airiukarie (Benítez 1968:280-281).

José Carrillo was the son of Hilario, the mara'akáme previously mentioned, and was working in San Andrés as a grade school teacher employed as an educational *promotor* by the Instituto Nacional Indigenista. He died about twenty years ago and so it is not possible to ascertain a more detailed account of the incident.

Of course, children might approach Kiéri out of curiosity and become intoxicated just by sipping the dew that collects in the flowers, thinking they are drinking nectar, or by licking the pollen. But there is no mention of José ingesting anything. Instead, the seeds or the powder they contain got on his hands when he broke open a fruit capsule. In this case, the Kiéri might be *Brugmansia*, or floripondio, because *Solandra* does not bear fruit. Inasmuch as the seed is the part of the plant containing the highest concentration of scopolamine, it is possible to become disoriented and delirious if fifteen to twenty seeds are consumed. Yet, in José's case the powder had disappeared from his hand. Despite this, he felt everything revolving around him, and that is a clear sign of disorientation. Moreover, seeing water gush forth from the soil is a hallucination related to the toxic symptom of dryness of the mouth. The mara'akáme treated José by brushing the powder off his head with a ceremonial arrow. Though no parts of the plant were ingested, the incident depicts the typical toxic effects of excessive ingestion of the Kiéri plant. And that is quite puzzling.[7,8]

The story does, however, provide a clue to the understanding of the collective symbolism, or common cognition, of Huichol Indians. Huichols agree that not all Kiéris are kakauyáris. In other words, the reason why José, who should have experienced very little pharmacological effects from his contact with Kiéri, was nevertheless victimized by Kiéri is not the Kiéri plant's pharmacology, but that conceptually this particular Kiéri was indeed kakauyári—Kiéri Taweakáme, the Kiéri who makes one drunk. In the mythology a kakauyári, having been defeated by the Sacred Deer Person Kauyumári, has transformed himself in a Kiéri tree. Thus, the term "Kiéri" may define both the plant itself and the Kiéri inhabited by the very powerful kakauyári. As a plant, the Kiéri does not harm humans so long as they do not intend to "utilize" it, that is, have no physical contact with it. But Kiéri Taweakáme, the Drunkard Kiéri, is dangerous. It is also called Kiéritáwe, the Drunken Kiéri, and as such it approaches us of its own volition.

Taweakáme, or Kiéritáwe, can also manifest itself as a small screaming bird at night, or as a tiny adult deer by day. It can, of course, appear in the form of a Kiéri plant. It stalks around, indifferent to where it is. If we encounter such a Kiéritáwe, it could take us away to some place on the wind, saying, "I like this man." For one or more months we would move about like sleepwalkers. We don't notice or remember what we eat during this time, but Kiéritáwe does not let us die of starvation. When the time is up, we are released. Here, José Carillo's experience illustrates the Huichols' belief that there are ordinary kiéris and Kiéri as Taweakáme or Kiéritáwe. Next, let us look further at encounters with Kiéri that cannot be considered as the effects of the plant itself.

LEOCADIO'S EXPERIENCE

When Leocadio López Carrillo, a Huichol friend of mine who was born in 1939, was twelve years old, Kiéritáwe tried to take him away.

Leocadio was helping his father cut trees for lumber on a hill in Tuxpan. On the rocky slope on the other side of the hill there was an old Kiéri tree. During the dry season it was just a trunk, but with the rainy season it started to sprout many branches that flowered with yellowish blossoms. At night, father and son camped by a brook at the foot of the hill. One night a man came to Leocadio when he was asleep.

"Wake up! It's time to go. What are you doing here? Let's go!"

"Yes, but I feel cold."

"We have a fire and tortillas there," the man replied.

"Then I will come," said Leocadio and began climbing up the hill. Just then his father shouted after him:

"Where are you going?"

"With this man to his house." Even as his father was shouting, the man kept urging: "Come on, come on. Let's go to my house."

"What are you dreaming, come back!" shouted his father. He caught up with Leocadio and refused to let him go.

What would have happened had Leocadio gone along with the man? Leocadio always answers that he would have come back, whether the next day, three days later, or after a month.

Although there was a flowering Kiéri tree (in this case, *Solandra*, or copa de oro) on the other side of the hill, it is most unlikely that the hallucination was caused by the perfume of the Kiéri flowers. There was just too much distance between them. It is possible for people suddenly to rise and wander about like sleepwalkers if more than a small quantity of *Solandra* is ingested. If addressed by others, they would answer, but what they say does not make sense. Afterwards, they would not remember what they had done or said. In the case of José Carrillo, other adults were unaffected, and both Leocadio and his father were physically too far distant from the Kiéri to absorb its pharmacological properties. Apparently, the father noticed before going to bed that his son was acting strangely. According to his father's diagnosis, Kiéritáwe had tried to take Leocadio away. It is possible to say that the reason for being called by Kiéri lay in the unusually sensitive nature of Leocadio.

What happened to Leocadio in August, 1986, provides another example:

He was invited to a ceremony at a rancho and brought a manda with him. His brother Fausto, who had served as governor of Tuxpan in 1982 and who is now a kawitéro, a member of the council of elders, was also invited. After drinking some *nawá* (the Huichol word for the fermented maize drink elsewhere called *tesguíno*) and talking with people, he suddenly felt ill. Leaving his brother, who planned to stay for two days, he started out for home by himself. His memory works up to the point where, intending to relieve himself, he tied his mule to a bush by the side of the trail. Then he passed out.

When he recovered consciousness, it was morning. He found himself sleeping on the rocky slope of a hill. Near him was a Kiéri tree. He had no memory, then or now, of when and how he climbed the hill. He staggered back down and found his mule grazing in a patch of weeds. After returning home, he went to bed feeling ill. Five days later the only female mara'akáme in Tuxpan came to his bedside.

"Here I am," she said. "I knew you were ill. Can you stand up? What a shame, I know what's wrong with you. Why did you go over there?"

"Oh no, I didn't go over there of my own free will," he told her. "I was just taken there. Because I don't remember anything at all."

"Nothing serious," she said. "You will soon be fine." And she gave him some instructions.

And indeed, the following day he woke up feeling fine. So, in accordance with the female mara'akáme's instructions, a few days later he took a jícara, a votive gourd, as an offering to the rocky slope of the hill. Leocadio himself does not believe that spending the night unknowingly on the hill was caused by the Kiéri's psychotropic and anesthetic properties. Rather, he believes that it was caused by the power of a supernatural being called Kiéritáwe.

I, too, do not think the Kiéri plant had any part in this, at least not directly. Leocadio had been invited to a fiesta, and given maize beer to drink. Perhaps having had too much to drink made him ill and he left for home in the evening. He awakened at dawn, having spent the night on a hill where there just happened to be a Kiéri tree. Does it follow that he was summoned there by Kiéritáwe? He was making his way home drunk on muleback through the desolate highlands of the Huichol mountains. He had no light to guide him. August falls in the rainy season. Though it was not raining, the night sky was starless and it was pitch dark. Without a point of reference in such a sensory-deprived environment he must have lost his sense of direction. Then the hypnotic state induced by sensory deprivation gradually deepened and he must have fallen asleep almost as soon as he came to a stop. He was lucky, for there are occasionally accidents thought to be caused by drinking and hallucinations in the deep darkness of the night.

Is it coincidence, then, that upon awakening he found himself face to face with a Kiéri tree? The woman mara'akáme seemed not to think so, for she asked him, "Why did you go over there?" She apparently sensed that Leocadio's problem lay in his having been called by the Kiéri. And in the final analysis what counts is not how we intellectualize it but how it is perceived by Huichols.

Leocadio is under an obligation to carry out the manda of his late grandfather. His grandfather did not complete his vow to go on five pilgrimages to the sacred land of Wirikúta, the home of the peyote. His parents and uncles all passed away before completing the grandfather's manda, as custom demands. While working as an agricultural instructor for the Instituto Nacional Indigenista in 1983, he was stung by a scorpion and for some days hovered between life and death. The mara'akáme who treated him on that occasion told him that the ancestor deity he had offended expected him to make a pilgrimage to Wirikúta. Since then he has gone there three times, leaving only two more to fulfill his obligation.

What worries him is that since he quit his job with INI in March of 1986 and returned to his native Tuxpan, various reasons have prevented him from going on another pilgrimage. In the meantime, since he went to Wirikúta for the first time in 1983, he has vowed to become a mara'akáme and continue to teach himself as a trainee. A person can learn the history of the ancestor deities, the kakauyáris, in Wirikúta during his peyote-induced dream state. This direct communication with the gods through the medium of peyote is of enormous significance, and there remain for him two more of these experiences before he completes himself as a mara'akáme.

Now, what about the possibility of Leocadio completing his vow to become a shaman through Kiéri right there near his home, without having to do two more of those arduous and time-consuming pilgrimages? As noted earlier, one may circumvent the need for peyote pilgrimages and become a shaman faster by taking a vow with Kiéri. In terms of ascetic practice, carrying out this vow and, at the same time, fulfilling his grandfather's manda, may be the same. But the kakauyáris who dwell in Wirikúta and the Kiéri who is a kakauyári are supernatural beings of a very different order, and one must not take on obligations to two such fundamentally different supernatural beings simultaneously. A person cannot wish two things to two beings at the same time. Thus, in the final analysis Leocadio's obligation is to complete the five pilgrimages to Wirikúta.

Leocadio also came across a small Kiéri when he was living in San Andrés. It was only about a foot and a half in height and had small yellow flowers that smelled good. While greeting it he touched it with his hand but left it in place. That night a man appeared in his dream and invited him to come to his house, but Leocadio refused. The next morning he went where the little Kiéri had been the day before, but there was not a trace of it. He was told by a mara'akáme that had he picked the flowers or gone along with the man, he would have gone wandering off in the mountains with no awareness. This small Kiéri looked outwardly like a plant, but was in fact Kiéritáwe.

The fact that in shamanism a dream is one of the principal forms of communication with the deities or supernatural beings is well known (Anzures and Bolaños 1987). It is true as well for the Huichols. We can say that Leocadio, too, is gifted in the shamanistic ability of dreaming. As a kawitéro, his younger brother Fausto consults dreams on important matters affecting the comunidad. Both Huichol culture and Leocadio's particular family environment seem to exert an influence here. Although the pilgrimages to Wirikúta should have been considered as his first obligation, on his way home from the fiesta he was drawn towards a Kiéri. The woman mara'akáme sensed an impatience on Leocadio's part in the fact that he had gone beneath a Kiéri, and scolded him for it.

Since then the Kiéri has appeared to Leocadio one more time. At the ceremony of the changing of the staffs of the community's governing officials in 1987, he was asked to treat an illness suffered by a man called Agustín, who was an assistant to a kawitéro. About a year earlier, when Agustín was on his way with his wife to a ceremony to which he had been invited, he had met a Kiéri and had taken a vow to him. He had asked it to give him more knowledge, a reasonable request for him to make as a kawitéro's assistant. His wish was granted, but his hands and feet became paralyzed. Other shamans would not treat him, so he asked Leocadio. Leocadio, too, refused, saying, "I am not a mara'akáme." That night a child appeared to Leocadio in his dream and said, "Do not touch him, for he has broken his vow. But if you want to help him, you can. Treat him well, then what he has already gained will be your's. But if you do not keep your promise, a bad thing would happen not to Agustín, but to you. Here is the promise. Eat these."

The child showed Leocadio what looked like five tablets. They signified five months of abstinence. Since he was under obligation to carry out the other manda, he flatly refused to take on two things at once. He did so because there was something he needed to do, and not because it was risky to make a vow with Kiéri. He no longer hesitated. It turned out to have been Kiéritáwe with whom Agustín had taken a vow.

Fortunately or unfortunately, the Kiéris have never appeared in my own dreams, even though I regularly collect them. Is this because these plants were not Kiéritáwe? It would seem so. It is said that a shaman named Eusébio, from the San José district of the comunidad of San Andrés, acquired more knowledge and power after he became a mara'akáme when he encountered a Kiéritáwe and put the pollen of the Kiéritáwe flowers on his cheeks. Though still a young man, he became the Tsaurixika, the chief mara'akáme, of the tuki, the indigenous community temple, of San José.

Although Leocadio touched his diminutive Kiéritáwe, there are very few people who have had physical contact with such a plant. Yet there is a surprising number of Huichols of my acquaintance who claim to have seen a small childlike Kiéri between a foot and a foot-and-a-half in height. Out of fear and respect they come no closer than ten feet or so, remaining rooted to the ground while staring at the Kiéri they describe as looking like a child dressed in the characteristic Huichol hat and outfit. There are cases where a person fell asleep while looking at such a Kiéri and was given knowledge in his dream.

In any event, to Huichols the Kiéritáwe is not an ordinary plant but a kakauyári that moves about in the form of a small human. Is it possible to identify this Kiéritáwe botanically? I do not necessarily assume it to be simply people's illusion. For the witnesses to its existence are not always limited just to shamans who can come and go between the world of "extraordinary" experiences and the world of "ordinary" ones. The circumstances and localities of such sightings are quite concrete. Also, people say, it is easier to observe the Kiéritáwe during the dry season than the wet. I have therefore not given up my hope of actually collecting a specimen of the diminutive Kiéri.

In fact, in August, 1992, I encountered the diminutive Kiéri jutting out from a precipitous cliffside near one of the ranchos in the district of San Andrés. Regrettably, I was unable to collect it because climbing down the sheer cliff proved impossible. The Huichol friend accompanying me at the time said, "It is a true Kiéri, not a Kiérinánari." That suggests that the diminutive Kiéri, which many Huichols think of as the "true Kiéri," might actually be just a young Kiéri (*Solandra*). But until we have a specimen in hand for botanical study we cannot be sure.

THE TUTAHURI

In looking back over the foregoing, there is no doubt that pharmacological knowledge of the Kiéri plant (*Datura*, *Solandra* and *Brugmansia*) is incorporated into the collective symbolism of Kiéri. Yet it is also clear that Taweakáme (i.e. Kiéritáwe), who appears sometimes as a bird, a deer, or a Kiéri plant, is not the plant as such. Taweakáme is the one who causes whirlwinds that may carry people far away or drive them insane. But the problem is even more complex, for there is still another manifestation of the Kiéri, or, rather, of Kiéri as Taweakáme.

Taweakáme, I learned, is also called *tutahuri*. Tutahuri is the source of a special power some shamans seek to acquire. That a tutahuri is not the Kiéri plant itself is apparent, since Kiéri plants do not necessarily grow where the trainee shamans visit in hopes of receiving the tutahuri's power. It is said that candidate shamans, as well as those who have already "completed" and are functioning as mara'akámes, seek a tutahuri in hopes of obtaining even more power. Just as do those who are training themselves as mara'akámes, they spend the night atop a huge rock. Psychotropic plants, such as peyote or Kiéri, are not employed in this vision quest. Candidate mara'akámes meditate as they wait for the sacred Deer Person Kauyumári to manifest himself, and those seeking tutahuri continue to do so until they "feel" the abnormal power. When they have experienced it, they become aware of a strange entity having taken up residence in their physical beings.

Obtained in this way it may be described as some sort of indeterminate "power," rather than as a guardian spirit. If a seeker did not feel the power of tutahuri, it merely signifies his having spent a fruitless night. But if after feeling the power he was unable to endure it, he would lose consciousness and later find himself in an entirely different place. Those who have caught a tutahuri must observe a period of sexual abstinence and fasting—that is, go without salt. Otherwise, death would ensue. The illness from a tutahuri is not susceptible to treatment by a mara'akáme. Moreover, the power thus obtained can be used for good as well as evil. Unbeknownst to others, one may practice sorcery, called *i'ikewári*, and gain fame as a mara'akáme. But Huichols think that those who practice sorcery must sooner or later pay the gods for it.

In contrast, no candidate shaman who fails to encounter Kauyumári (who is comparable to a guardian spirit), or who does not keep a specified period of abstinence, would go mad. All that would happen is that all his previous training becomes invalid and he is disqualified from becoming a mara'akáme.

Conclusion

To sum up, the pharmacological effects of Kiéri as plant are recognized among Huichols. Yet the root of its power—in other words, that which is most feared—is not the Kiéri itself. Rather, it is a form of supernatural power, somewhat, but not exactly, comparable to mana. This power is variously called Taweakáme, Kiéritáwe, or Tutahuri. The boundary between personified power and impersonal power is not clear, but it may be said that as transformations of one of the kakauyáris, the divine ancestors or ancestor gods, Taweakáme and Kiéritáwe are personified powers, while Tutahuri shades from personal into impersonal power.

NOTES

1. The national census of 1990 gives the number of Huichol-speakers over the age of five as just over 19,000, some 7,000 more than the highest estimates of just a few years ago.(—Eds.)

2. The Huichol term *e'éka*, "wind" or "airs," is so close to *ehécatl*, the Nahuatl (Aztec) term for wind, that T. J. Knab (personal communication) considers it to be one of the Nahuatl borrowings that came into the Huichol language via the Nahuatl-speaking Tlaxcalans and other Central Mexicans whom the Spaniards transplanted to the western frontier. Also according to Knab, the Huichols have a well-developed vocabulary for describing the stages of inebriation with peyote, which, he says, conceivably extends to Kiéri. One of these stages is called *e'eka-xuri*, meaning flowery wind or wind of flowers, *xuri* being derived from the Nahuatl *xochi*, flower. (The indigenous Huichol term is *tutu*). The Aztecs also associated wind, or *aires*, with illness, as do their modern descendants and rural Mexicans generally.(—Eds.)

3. I have previously explained that it is difficult to decide which, among various versions of the same myth, is the "right" one, because all of them may be "right" (Yasumoto 1989c). So far as Kiéri is concerned, in the myths collected by Zingg (1938) and Furst and Myerhoff (1966), this particular Kiéri was a sorcerer who was killed by Kauyumári. In the explanations of yarn paintings collected by Negrín, Kiéri was a sacred deer, "Our Brother with White Antlers," transformed into the Kiéri and given power by the gods. Negrín states, however, that a Kiéri is generally associated with witchcraft and sorcery.

4. *Datura tatula* L. may be the so-called "lost narcotic plant" used by the Shawnees of Ohio and Indiana for its narcotic and analgesic properties (Tyler 1990). Despite the purple flowers and stem of *Datura tatula* L., some taxonomists do not consider the differences between it and *D. stramonium* L., whose flowers are white, to be sufficiently significant to classify it as a separate species of the genus, and customarily classify them as one (Tyler, Brady and Robbers 1988). However, as Tyler (1992) points out, there is one "appreciable difference," and that is origin: whereas *D. stramonium* is thought by some authorities to have been introduced into North America from Asia, *D. tatula* "apparently originated in the American tropics and became naturalized throughout this continent and Asia as well" (Tyler 1992:40-42). According to Schultes and Hofmann (1979:41), however, "modern opinion" favors a New World origin for *D. stramonium* as well. (—P.T.F.)

5. El Cerro de Saucillo is called "Kiéri-tsa-ta," to indicate that it is a place where there are various Kiéris. Kiéri-tsa is literally the plural of Kiéri. Ta is the suffix meaning place. On the summit of Saucillo are various kinds of Kiéri of the kind identified as copa de oro (*Solandra*) or toloache (*Datura*), and there is also a xiriki, or god house, for Kiéri. This Kiéri has five sons, one each on the five different hills located in the community of Tuxpan. From any of these hills one can see the summit of Saucillo. As might be expected, the Kiéri on Saucillo is the most powerful.

6. In a recent paper entitled, "A Synoptic Revision of *Solandra* (Solanaceae)," Bernadello and Hunziker (1987) write that they examined the Kiéri specimen deposited by John C. Lilly Jr. in the Departmento Botánico of the Universidad Autónoma Nacional de México in 1971, and reported by Knab in his 1977 paper on *Solandra* among the Huichols, and identified it as *Solandra guttata* rather than *S. brevicalyx*. They also note that the names for *S. guttata* in Mexico include "kiéri, *floripondio* and *floripondio del monte*, and that for the present at least only *S. guttata*, *S. guerrerensis* and *S. maxima*, and not *S. brevicalyx*, can be identified with the *tecomaxochitl* described by Hernández in 1651.(—P.T.F.)

7. This is not to suggest that nothing happens if lesser amounts are taken. I cannot warn often enough that *any* amount is extremely dangerous.

8. Various psychotropic substances, including tropane alkaloids and nicotine, the potent chemical contained in *Nicotiana* (tobacco), another member of the Solanaceae, are easily absorbed through the skin. As Wilbert has shown in his path-breaking study of tobacco and shamanism in South America, application of tobacco to the skin is widely practiced among South American Indians. Clinical studies, he writes, have confirmed that nicotine readily penetrates the skin "and percutaneous absorption of the alkaloid in amounts large enough to cause severe and even fatal poisoning in humans has variously been effected by the application to the skin of tobacco, tobacco leaves, infusions or decoctions" (Wilbert 1989:143). Even the smoke of tobacco of the species *Nicotiana rustica* is said to be capable of penetrating the body not only through the sensitive mucous membranes but the skin (ibid., pp. 189-190). Percutaneous application of *Datura* was also practiced by Aztec healers.(—P.T.F.)

INTRODUCTION TO CHAPTER 9

By far the most esoteric variant of Huichol shamanism is that of identification with wolves and the wolf as primary source of spirit power. In fact, this phenomenon presents a vexing culture historical problem. Why are wolves so prominent in one area of Huichol shamanic myth and practice (Figure 55) when they seem to have played little or no comparable role anywhere else in Mesoamerica, past and present? Why, indeed, do the closest analogies to Huichol wolf shamanism and transformation appear to be not in Mexico but in North America? And, finally, why does the primary symbolic and practical association of wolf shamanism seem to be less with peyote than with the solanaceous Kiéri plant? Is the story of the first people as wolves and their hunt for the deer just another example of the multiplicity of Huichol origin mythology, reflecting heterogeneous historical origins, or does it, as Preuss thought, translate real events in the sky into the language of myth and natural history?

These remain open questions. But others are answered for the first time in the following chapter. That a woman ethnographer, Susana Eger Valadez, was able to gain intimate entry into a belief system that is little known not just to outsiders, but even to most Huichols, is due to her long professional involvement with a Huichol shaman-artist named Santos in Spanish, and Ulu Temay (*ul, ur* = arrow, *tema* = young person) in Huichol.

Her intellectual association with this gifted and knowledgeable man had its inception in the mid-1970s during her field work in San Andrés. At that time he was still a young apprentice shaman, and she was just beginning to study the arts of women, particularly the complex and colorful embroideries with which they embellish their own and their men's clothing.

In *Mirrors of the God*, a 1989 publication that accompanied an exhibition of Huichol art she and her Huichol artist-husband Mariano Valadez curated for the San Diego Museum of Man, she has told the history of a most uncommon collaboration. When she first met Ulu Temay, she writes, people had another name for him, "Rot Arm." This not very flattering nickname came from the fact that he was then suffering from a seriously infected squirrel bite that appeared literally to be rotting his right arm away.

FIGURE 55. Huichol Wolf Shaman with His Wolf Allies. (*Yarn painting by Mariano Valadez.*)

The affliction did not respond to the ministrations either of the local shamans, or the medical doctors whose help he sought on an emergency flight to the city. The shamans consulted the gods and told him his sickness was due to his having violated the taboo against extramarital sex while studying to be a shaman. There was talk that the gods were punishing him and though he was clearly suffering and had even spoken of suicide, there was little sympathy for him among the people.

Susana, who had been bringing medicines to San Andrés for some time, would not accept this and convinced him to let her photograph his arm and take the pictures to specialists in tropical medicine back home in the UCLA School of Medicine. Two weeks later she returned to San Andrés with their diagnosis: the bite had introduced a dangerous and tenacious spore that really was eating away his tissue. She brought back with her several bottles of potassium iodine, an extremely bitter medicine the doctors were reasonably certain would cure the infection. But it had to be administered orally with great care over a three-month period.

So here she was, a "gringa" bearing some miracle western medicine that was supposed to do what all the shamans and the doctors in Tepic had been unable to accomplish. Even the patient's father, himself a well-known shaman, was dubious, informing her firmly that her medicine would do no good because the Huichol gods were determined to punish his son for his transgression.

But the following morning brought an astonishing turn-around. There was a knock on her door and there stood young Rot Arm/Ulu Temay and his shaman father, who now told her that he had a prophetic dream during the night in which he was taken to a faraway place in the north that was filled with light, and that although the gods there addressed him in English, he could understand their words. What these gods of the north told him was that it had been they who had sent a foreign woman with a foreign medicine to treat his son and show the Huichols how to use new cures in addition to their own, and that these gods of the north would instruct them in how to combat and heal the illnesses that had come to them in recent times.

Ulu Temay's father then conducted a purification ritual for the medicine bottles, using the feathers of his *muviéri* to cleanse and put the power of the Huichol deities and ancestors into the medicine. He also purified her. That done, he allowed her to administer the medicine without ill consequences, and his son to begin the treatments, with the stipulation that he would renew his shamanic vow and make restitution to assuage the displeasure of the gods.

Ulu Temay responded well to her treatments, and by way of physical therapy to restore the use of his arm, she gave him felt-tip pens and paper on which to draw. The first of his colored drawings depicted his peyote visions, for each of which he provided Susana with a detailed explanation. As time went by and he completed his training as a shaman, he continued—as he did to his untimely recent death—not only to produce his vivid illustrations of the ever more complex knowledge he was acquiring as a shaman of the metaphysical and natural realms, but to elucidate them in meticulous detail in repeated marathon interviews.

By the time of his death in 1994 this unique collection had grown into the many hundreds. The uncommon cooperation between a Huichol philosopher-artist and practitioner of the sacred, and an American woman who came to the Huichols intending only to record and preserve traditional women's art for an M.A. thesis, but stayed to render practical assistance, first to the women in her Sierra community, and then to Huichol migrant farm workers, endured for over twenty years. Her intervention may have saved his life, but without the long-term relationship of mutual respect and trust between them that developed from this fortunate encounter in the course of these two decades, the in-depth glimpse we are here being given into a branch of Huichol shamanism so esoteric that even few Huichols, much less foreigners, have any but the most superficial knowledge of it, would have been unthinkable.

Stacy B. Schaefer

9 : WOLF POWER AND INTERSPECIES

COMMUNICATION IN HUICHOL SHAMANISM

SUSANA EGER VALADEZ

Author's Note: The ethnographic literature on the Huichols contains a good deal of information on the "archaic" practices of shamanism that persist to this day among these still very traditional Mexican Indian people. But little has been published about one evidently very old shamanic phenomenon, or skill, that survives to this day within the Huichol form of shamanism: a close association, indeed, qualitative identification, of certain shamans with wolves. Every now and then one hears talk of Huichol shamans who transform themselves into wolves. This is a rare and secretive power, mastered by only a few outstanding individuals. For the most part, it has, until very recently, remained an enigma to researchers. Much of it still does.

There are numerous Old World legends about people who transform into wolves or who are wolf and human at the same time, a phenomenon known as lycanthropy. In the Indian Americas, too, there are numerous tales of people who can take the form of spirit animals with which they have formed special "shape-shifting" relationships. In Mexico this phenomenon has been called nagualism, from the Nahuatl (Aztec) nahualli, meaning "something hidden." In Aztec culture, according to the sixteenth century cleric Diego Durán (1971:68), nagualism was a basic aspect of the ancient religion. The god Tezcatlipoca, Smoking Mirror, for example, was renowned for his ability to assume the forms of a wide variety of animals (Brundage 1979:82). As we shall see, those few Huichols who have succeeded at this special skill attain, in the eyes of their fellows, an exalted esoteric level of shamanic completion. They also function as guardians of a vast body of knowledge about a phenomenon that must have impressed and astounded ordinary folk since the days of the paleo-hunters.

While it is common knowledge among Huichols that there are among them certain shamans who transcend the boundaries of the physical realm and metamorphose into wolf-people, most Huichols are either too uninformed, or too afraid, to discuss the subject openly. Almost every-thing the ordinary person knows of the phenomenon is hearsay, and unless he or she has close family members involved in the practice, or has had occasion to witness it, the average Huichol is not privy to the details of this "cult." That could explain why so little has actually been documented about what is an important, if hidden, aspect of Huichol shamanism.

Another reason for the reluctance to discuss it openly, especially with outsiders, is the erroneous but widespread association of wolf-people with sorcery. Living as they do in a Catholic country intolerant of "pagan" survivals would naturally predispose even those who know very well that wolf shamanism has no more to do with sorcery than ordinary shamanism to evade the issue. Indian people still consider the missionaries and their zeal a threat to the continuation of their ancestral traditions, and therefore think twice before revealing information that might well lead to a witch-hunt among them. Precisely because there is little agreement about just what "nagualism" really is, and because of the negative connotations of brujería, witchcraft or sorcery, that have come to be attached to the term nagual,[1] I believe it to be more appropriate to speak of "wolf power" and "wolf shamanism," meaning the ability of a certain class of shamans to communicate with, obtain spirit power from, and transform into, wolves, than to speak of "wolf nagualism."[2]

For whatever reason, then, the suppression of knowledge about wolves as sources of shamanic power and wolf shamanism has shrouded this topic with negative connotations. Both within Huichol culture and among the vecinos, their mestizo neighbors, there are all manner of misconceptions about werewolves, black magic, and malevolence. In this essay I will try to correct some of these false impressions and shed light on the truly awesome system of beliefs and practices of an aspect of Huichol shamanism that may well be among the most ancient. Placed in its proper perspective, wolf shamanism among the Huichols can then be seen as a blueprint for the reestablishment of what Mircea Eliade has described as "the situation that existed in illo tempore, in mystical times, when the divorce between man and the animal world had not yet occurred" (Eliade 1964:94).

Much of the information to be presented below was provided to me by an old friend and trusted consultant, Santos Aguilar Carrillo, whose Huichol name is Ulu Temay, Young Arrow Person. This Huichol shaman, from the indigenous comunidad of San Andrés Cohamiata, Jalisco, has for several years been drawing on his own personal experience to create a pictorial narrative of his six-year apprenticeship as a wolf shaman. He and I have worked together for nearly a dozen years, systematically documenting the Huichol magico-religious belief system, by utilizing his drawings as a basis for interpreting his cultural knowledge (cf. Eger-Valadez 1987 and 1990 for details of the methodology employed). His drawings give a very personal, inside view of the profound experiences he underwent as an active participant in this esoteric realm of Huichol shamans. The explanations that accompany his drawings reveal much about the reasons why Huichols undertake the long and arduous apprenticeships that are a precondition for full acceptance by the wolves and learning their great secrets.

As will be seen, Ulu Temay's descriptions of the wolves endow them with superhuman characteristics and telepathic powers that help us to understand why he insists that his experiences are real and true. Throughout his explanations of his drawings, his attention to detail has been so meticulous as to make it unlikely that he invented anything. In any event, believe him or *not, his personal insights into the mysteries of the wolf shaman are, to say the least, thought provoking.*

I am here presenting his information in a format that preserves his own words and his own interpretations. The commentary I offer, and documentation from other sources, are meant only to highlight certain aspects of his unique view of Huichol spiritual life. While most of the information in these pages is drawn from long taping sessions with Ulu Temay, other Huichols, including my artist-husband Mariano, and knowledgeable individuals from different communities, were also consulted.

The scarcity of published information on this topic, and the well-known idiosyncratic nature of esoteric knowledge among the Huichols, makes it difficult to verify Ulu Temay's story in each and every detail. Still, published confirmation of the existence of wolf shamanism and wolf transformation among the Huichols can be found in Lumholtz's pioneering work (1902), in Zingg (1938), and in Vol. 2 of Fernando Benítez's Los Indios de México (1968).

Finally, I want to affirm that throughout our continuing association, Ulu Temay has been fully aware that his drawings and the accompanying information were intended for eventual publication. It is with his knowledge and approval that they are being brought to light in their present form.

At the dawn of Huichol history, according to one creation myth related by Ulu Temay, the first people were half human, half wolf. Before the Great Flood, and for a time after, these wolf-people lived in darkness, in the coastal region near San Blas, Nayarit, which is the homeland of the Wolf People, the Kumuketai, as the wolves of myth are called. The wolf-people, that is, people who could exchange their outer form with wolves at will, were like helpless little children, living in a cold world where there was no sun, no rain, no maize, and little to eat.

The wolf shamans of these ancient ones anointed their offerings with lizard and grasshopper blood, because they had never hunted deer, and had not yet discovered the power of deer blood. The wolf people still did not know about deer hunting, which is why, as they were to discover, there was no rain. It was only the magic of deer blood that would make the votive offerings come alive and nourish the Rain Mothers and the Sun God, who would then permit the maize to grow.

But the wolf people soon learned about the deer. That was when a Deer Person, Maxa Tewíyari (*maxa* = deer, *tewíyari* = person), the human form of Kauyumári, who came from the land of the Sun and the peyote desert in the east, allowed himself to be hunted by the Father of the Wolves, Kumukemai. While being devoured by the wolves, the Deer Person magically transformed into peyote. The wolves ate the deer's heart, which, because the deer itself was peyote, was also the heart of the peyote, and attained great wisdom in all things. In the words of Ulu Temay:

> The man-wolf-god, whose name was Kumukemai, lived on the coast near San Blas and left from there to hunt the Deer Person. He followed the Deer Person to the

mountain in the peyote desert where the sun was born. The wolves that now live on this high mountain are the Samalówe, the descendants of the Father of the Wolves, Kumukemai. Every year the people from the temples still have to visit the birthplace of the sun on the high mountain in the peyote desert where the Samalówe live, and bring them offerings.[3]

Since the Wolf God Kumukemai was one of the original ancestors who went to the peyote desert, where the sun was born and where the deer he hunted turned into peyote, he was ordered to return to his family to teach them to do the same. He went back to his people and made a temple so that the people from many different regions could have a temple from which to make the journey to the peyote desert. In every temple, every year, someone assumes the role of the original wolf ancestor Kumukemai and goes to the peyote desert to leave offerings to his descendants, the wolf hunters we call the Samalówe.

Once the wolf people learned about deer hunting, rain making, healing, and all the infinite knowledge of the peyote given to Kumukemai by his cohort Kauyumári, they moved out of the darkness and into the light. They followed the deer out of the "dark," "nocturnal" coastal lands (west) into the mountains and *barrancas* of their present homeland, and went as far east as the peyote desert. When the wolf people saw the sun emerge from its volcanic birthplace in the peyote desert, they were given the chance to choose whether to change into humans or to remain wolves.

The Father of the Wolves, Kumukemai, took human form and was instructed by the hunting deities to build the first of many Huichol temples. According to Ulu Temay, this *tuki* was located in the Sierras in a place called Tuxupa, near San Miguel Huastita. Kumukemai was told to make the temple so that the gods and goddesses could now be properly cared for and compensated with the life-giving magical properties of ritually hunted deer blood. In exchange for the blood offerings, the Huichol shamans were given the power to become rain makers. Ulu Temay continues:

Because the Father of the Wolves was the first hunter of the deer, he was also the first to receive directions to construct the temple. He placed the fire inside and surrounded it with the special offerings: the stone disk, *tepári*, that bears the symbol of the tuki; the staff of Takutsi Nakawé, Grandmother Growth; the round gable stone, *nearíka*, for the door, which would allow him to be in contact with all of his descendants, once they had moved and spread out to the peyote desert, the Sierras, and the coast; the "arrow of the wolves," *Kumukemai uruyare*, so that the people could always communicate with the wolves; and, finally, a candle with a viney plant (representing long life and soul for the people, so that many people would continue to be born and grow and have more children). These and other offerings would appear in all future temples.

In addition, when he made the first tuki, the Father of the Wolves planted the five colors of maize, in the five directions, outside the temple. He learned to call the rain and asked that it should rain the entire season, so that the maize would grow and would never be lost. After they planted the maize they went deer hunting and killed the deer and anointed the maize with the blood.

They now had a temple to keep all the objects that would be anointed with deer blood, and where the stewards of the votive objects, the "cargo holders," could guard their offerings for the deer hunt, and for the annual journeys to the peyote desert and the birthplace of the sun.

Ulu Temay's description of the relationship of reciprocity between wolves and deer, hunter and hunted, illustrates why the Huichols have such esteem for their "Elder Brothers," the wolves. The wolf ancestors possessed the hunting prowess needed to kill the mystical deer, the messenger of peyote knowledge, who willingly gave his life so that his blood could be used to propitiate the deities. This primordial sacrifice of the Deer Person, and the subsequent rituals of atonement, initiated by the Wolf Father once he obtained enlightenment from peyote, was the genesis of Huichol religion. From the death of the deer came the life of the Huichols. The rain, the maize, the discovery of the birthplace of the sun in the peyote desert, and the new horticultural way of life, all came to be because of the symbiotic relationship between the ancestral wolves and the valiant sacrificed deer.

Much of Huichol ceremonial life revolves around rituals of compensation, on the order of those established for the martyred deer by the wolf hunters in primordial times. All the peyote hunting rituals and numerous temple traditions relate back to this creation myth. The rituals ensure that the Huichols, the human counterparts of the predatory wolves, ceremoniously thank the deer for giving their lives and blood to "pay" the agricultural deities for providing life and abundance. Moreover, the observances guarantee that the Huichol hunters collectively express their gratitude to the souls of their victims, so that the Father of the Deer, or Master of the Deer Species, may have no qualms about sending more of his children into the hunters' traps.

The mutual exchange of "favors" between predator and prey is again illustrated in another of Ulu Temay's narratives, this one about five ancestor deities sent by the Earth Mother, or Grandmother Growth, Takutsi Yurameka, to teach the first people how to hunt deer. She, too, was hungry for offerings of deer blood and tired of nurturing the people living on her body without ever receiving anything in return. So she created five ancestors out of sea foam to teach the people to hunt the deer.

Since no one had ever seen a deer or knew what they looked like, the hunters had to experience much trial and error in order to find them. But Grandmother Growth's magical staff, wherein remained her heart when she died, eventually taught the Huichol ancestors all the rituals they would have to perform in order to locate where the deer were hiding.

The five hunter-messengers found the deer locked up in a pen that was guarded by a person half human, half deer. He had deer antlers and could understand deer language. He had locked up the deer because he knew the hunters were after them. In Ulu Temay's words:

The five hunters left their arrows behind and took their feathered wands and flowers to the Owner of the Deer. They didn't want to scare him, and they gave him the flowers. He threw the flowers into the pen. The hunters had hoped that the deer would eat the flowers, but they did not. They only got scared and ran to the other side.

The Owner of the Deer told the five hunters that if they wanted to talk to the deer they would have to do it through the wolves. "The wolves know how to hunt the deer and will talk to the deer for you if you make a special arrow and place it by the deer pen at sunup. The name of the arrow pertaining to the wolves was 'Arrow of the First Hunters.' The arrow will call the wolves, and the wolves will arrange things with the deer," is what he told the hunters.

So the following day the leader of the five hunters, whose name was Kauyumári, took the arrow and colors of five flowers to the pen to call the wolves (Figure 56). The wolves did not appear in the corral, because had they done so they would have scared the deer. Instead, they spoke to the deer through their intermediary, the arrow, and encouraged them to leave the enclosure.

The leading hunter threw the flowers into the pen and the deer ate them. When the sun came up, the deer started to run and jump and go crazy because the flowers made them "drunk." The flowers were like Kiéri (see Yasumoto, Chapter 8) and made the deer feel happy but confused, so they all jumped out. Once the deer were freed, the wolves spied on them so that they wouldn't run far away. The wolves turned into people so that they could watch over the deer and make certain that they ran into the deer traps. They hid in the brush where the traps were, and waited for the deer to be chased into the traps so they could be the ones to teach humans to kill deer. These wolf-people guardians were called Awatámete. The five hunters asked the Awatámete for their help, because they were wolves and already had the knowledge of hunting the deer and because they could run fast.

The great respect in which Huichols hold wolves and other members of the canine family extends into the celestial realm, where the Awatámete now reside. Every time Huichols look up into the evening sky they see the five wolf constellations accompanied by a human hunter and a dog chasing a deer constellation through the heavens. These stars represent the Awatámete, the original wolf hunters, who, when asked by shamans, send luck and hunting skill to the Huichols.

Wolves, then, play the role of culture heroes for Huichols. Humans and wolves share the characteristics of social carnivores and they embody traits toward which Huichol hunters aspire. They are swift runners, they cooperate in the hunt, and they are heirs

FIGURE 56. "The Leader of the Five Hunters Took the Arrow and Colors of Five Flowers to Call the Wolves." (*Drawing by Ulu Temay, Huichol Shaman.*)

to the great wisdom of the peyote-deer that was hunted and eaten by the Wolf Father Kumukemai.

Thus, wolves are considered teachers and role models. For when the wolves consumed the "heart of peyote," they formed a mystical link with the deer-peyote spirit, Kauyumári, and obtained the shamanic skills needed for communicating with the non-human world. Through Kauyumári, the wolves and their human shaman counterparts acquire a guide and messenger to the otherwise undecipherable realm of the gods. As Ulu Temay puts it:

> If I desire to communicate with the spirit animals and gods and goddesses, I cannot speak with them directly. Over there are pure lines and rays and symbols I do not understand. There are many eyes and tongues and I do not know what they say. But I have a spirit in my medicine basket who does understand. He translates for me and is my messenger. His name is Tamatsi Kauyumári, Elder Brother Deer Spirit.
>
> Other people do not see him, only I. I turn my head to listen to my *muviéris* (arrow-shaped feathered shaman's wands) where he speaks to me. I see him and I hear him, and the people around me listen to what he says through me.

The Rules and Regulations of Wolf Shaman Apprenticeship

Considering the above, it is little wonder that certain candidate shamans aspire toward uniting in mind, body, and spirit with their mystical mentors, the omnipotent wolves, and seek to acquire the extraordinary powers Huichols ascribe to this species as a whole. The unquestioning affirmation of the extraordinary power of wolves is well in keeping with the veneration other native peoples hold towards animals, in some instances especially wolves. Joseph Campbell's explanation as to why Indians hold animals in such high regard, a quality that some non-Indians would regard as outlandish, should also be kept in mind when evaluating the assertions Huichols and other nature-religion–based peoples make about what he calls "the way of the animal powers":

> The Indian relationship to animals is in contrast to our relationship with animals, where we see animals as a lower form of life. In the Bible we are told that we are the masters. For hunting people . . . the animal is in many ways a superior. A Pawnee Indian said, "In the beginning of all things, wisdom and knowledge were with the animal. For Tirawa, the One Above, did not speak directly to man. He sent certain animals to tell mankind that he showed himself through the beast. And that from them, and from the stars and the sun and the moon, man should learn." (Campbell 1988:79)

To continue with Ulu Temay:

> When I was young, my grandfather, my father's father, used to bring the wolves home with him. When I got bigger I wanted to know about them. He told me that his father, my great-grandfather, taught him how to change into a wolf and to talk to them. And I didn't believe it. How could it be true that animals can communicate with people? It's not true, I thought. But later on I found out that it was true. I had to suffer a great deal in my youth to find out what I learned, but I earned it.

Wolf shamanism, in fact, has traveled through the paternal line of Ulu Temay's family for as long as anyone can remember. His grandfather and father began teaching him as a boy, just as he is presently teaching his own seven-year-old son. While anyone, of any age, male or female, is free to embark on this shamanistic quest, it is considered advantageous to begin as a youngster under the tutelage of an older family member.

Most often, Huichols undertake this course of study of their own free will. However, Ulu Temay did mention that some people are, so to speak, drafted into service with the wolves to replace older family members, usually a parent or grandparent, who, for some reason, made their vows but failed to complete them. Under the informal rules of Huichol shamanism, descendants can be punished for errors committed by their forefathers. Thus, after someone has been repeatedly visited by illness or some other misfortune, the shaman called to perform the cure may eventually inform the patient that the root of his or her problem may lie in a debt another family member owes to the wolves.

Of course, not every candidate shaman pledges to the wolves. But regardless of whether one vows to "complete" with the wolves, with the sea, with the peyote desert, with the Kiéri plant, with the old fire god, Tatewarí (Our Grandfather), the Sun god, or any one of the divine beings that inhabit the innumerable sacred places of the Huichol universe, the rules for completion are virtually the same: one has to make a commitment for a certain period, usually five or ten years, to fulfill the requirements of apprenticeship. Failure to do so may result in life-threatening consequences.

The most essential requisite for the successful completion of the shamanic curriculum, but especially so in relation to the wolves and the Kiéri plant spirit, is a vow of sexual fidelity for a specified number of years. Many researchers have commented on this, the first among them being Carl Lumholtz (1898) who, in observing the sexual taboo among the peyote initiates, attributed it, perhaps mistakenly, to the negative effects of peyote on the libido:

> It is important to note that a marked effect of the plant is to take away all sexual desire, this no doubt being the cause of the Indians imposing, by a curious aboriginal mode of reasoning, abstinence from sexual intercourse as a necessary part of the *hikuli* (peyote) cult. (Lumholtz 1898)

The restriction is not quite as stringent as Lumholtz thought, however, celibacy being required of the future shaman only at certain times during the apprenticeship. For the future wolf shaman, however, sexual fidelity is required at *all* times. According to Huichols with whom I have discussed this, the sexual prohibitions are applied not so much because of a lack of desire but because sex is a terrestrial characteristic, which is left in the world of humans when one embarks on the path of the gods. Sexual fidelity to one's spouse is imposed in order to ensure that the apprentices are not distracted from their ascent by corporeal concerns. This may present the polygynous, and often promiscuous, Huichols with a difficult obstacle to overcome. But, even though the Huichols have several rituals by which sexual transgressions can be obliterated and purity restored, in this instance the rule would seem to be unbending.[4] This is what Ulu Temay has to say on the subject:

> If a person was not married when they began the apprenticeship, then they are permitted to marry during their training. A man and his new wife will make a special round disk, nearíka, with wax and beaded figures on it and take it to the wolf shrine and give it to the wolves. They will remain the whole night, and confess to the wolves to ask their forgiveness. They do this so that the wolves won't get mad and punish them. There is no escape for people who were already married when they began and then had sex with another. If a person does this bad thing he is no longer admitted

entry into the wolf shrine. The wolves will tear at him and kill him. They will devour him because he betrayed them and will punish him so their secret doesn't get out.

I would suggest two other reasons why the wolves won't tolerate taking a lover or another spouse once one has begun the wolf-shaman apprenticeship. Deservedly or not, wolves have the reputation of being monogamous and remaining faithful to one mate throughout their lives. If so, this would be one of many adaptive habits shared by wolves and many humans, though not necessarily by all Huichols, a number of whom, shamans included, have more than one wife at a time, and among whom desertion and extra-marital affairs are not uncommon. In other words, human wolf shamans are supposed to emulate the social behavior of the species from which they seek power and knowledge, and if one violates this rule, he is immediately disqualified. The same restriction also deters the human wolf shaman from taking a wolf spirit wife. Indeed, in the belief of some Huichols, taking a wolf wife would cause a wolf shaman to lose his ability to regain his human form.[5]

The second reason for the difficult sexual sanctions has to do with the compact between husbands and wives, who serve the apprenticeship together. When married people undertake an agreement with the wolves, both spouses are automatically committed. Most often the husband is the active partner, and the one to undergo the transformation. But the wife is silently supportive of all his endeavors, making votive and power objects on his behalf and keeping vigil for him while he travels to sacred places. This mutual cooperation between couples engaged in wolf shamanism (but also in other forms of Huichol shamanism) is described as follows by Ulu Temay:

> The woman may accompany the man to all of the places he has to visit over the course of the five years while he is in training with the wolves. Or he may go alone. If she does not go with him, she will make a beaded gourd bowl into which she has placed figures, and send it with him. He also has to make different things. All the family makes things and sends them with him. If they have a baby, they have to make a figure in the bowl to represent the baby, too, because they all go in the bowl now.
>
> Another offering the man and woman make together is a special nieríka, a disk made out of stone, paper, or yarn. They will take this disk to where the wolves live. The woman often accompanies the man, and she helps him make these offerings so that he will return safely, so that they will always be together. This is so he won't get sick while with the wolves, and so that they don't harm him.
>
> If the woman does not go with her husband, she will stay home and protect him from harm by doing rituals in the family god house (xiriki). She lights a fire and candle for him at dawn and dusk, and uses her special seed maize (the male and female sacred maize kernels that came from the mother plant in her fields) in her rituals. She does this for the entire time that he is away.

The women who support their husbands by performing sympathetic magic to ensure their safe return share similar characteristics with women temple officers who emulate the role of the first female ancestor after the great flood, the Dog-Woman who had the name of Yokawima. The temple women who take on the identity of this deified being, who in addition to being the Mother of the Huichol race is also the Mother of the Deer and the Rabbits, symbolize the dogs the Huichol hunters use to help run the deer into traps.

Whether in deer hunting or in shamanic apprenticeship, these examples illustrate how important women are to the successful outcome of various endeavors. Women play an indispensable role in ensuring that both the deer and their husbands return from their missions to the sacred realm. The women who perform vigils for their husbands in the privacy of their household shrines are not called Yokawime, the name of the Black Dog progenetrix in the temple, but their function is virtually identical. They are completing their obligations that fall upon all Huichol women married to men who faithfully practice traditional Huichol religion.

The men perform the external, overt functions of running down the deer and killing it in the sacred hunt, or traveling to distant shrines in perilous places to deliver votive objects in fulfillment of vows taken by both partners. The men also risk their lives by undergoing physical transformation into wolves. The women provide invisible protection through psychic interactions with the spirit world, which guarantee that the couple will obtain what is sought. They hold their men in the light of their candles and fires, and remain celibate while they are away. The man and wife are a team, and their dependence on one another in mutually meeting the challenges for the five-year apprenticeship must never be undermined.

Sacred Shrines of Wolf Power

What follows is Ulu Temay's explication of the drawings that depict the circuit of places the initiates must visit over the course of five to ten years. The offerings they make for each of these places, and the rituals they perform there, will be described later.

This is how one asks to become a wolf shaman (Figure 57). There are five places to go to learn to transform into a wolf. All of the wolf shrines are in an area called Kumukita, named after the Father of the Wolves who came from the coast to teach his descendants, the wolves, and wolves who took human form, how to be in contact with the old ones. Some of the places are close, and others are far away, but each apprentice has to go to all of them in the course of five years.

Each shrine is inhabited by a wolf of a different color, red, yellow, white, blue, and multicolored, just like the five colors of maize. The colors of the wolves and the shrines they inhabit pertain to their position in the hierarchy of power. The grey or multicolored wolves are the highest, and the red wolves are the lowest.

FIGURE 57. "There Are Five Places You Go to Learn to Transform into a Wolf." (*Drawing by Ulu Temay, Huichol Shaman.*)

The names of the five wolf places are Turikíye, Turiamukamai, Paritsikatsiya, Kuyetuaripa, and Muxia Uxiye. One visits those locales in that order. The minor places of power are first, and the others follow. One begins with the red wolves at Turikíye, which means "Place of the Children." The name refers to the wolf children descendants of Kumukemai, and to the initiates, who are "like children."

The places that one goes to for the first three years are like the "children" of the powerful places the apprentices go to in the fifth and sixth years. These "parent" places are Kuyeturpa ("Place of the Stacked Trees"), which is considered female and married to the male place, Muxia Uxiye ("Where the Sheep Lay"), where the main house of the wolves is, and where the highest ranking multicolored ones (Ulowe-Noitze) live.

So one begins the first year at the "Place of the Children," with the red wolves, and then one goes the next year to where the yellow wolves are, in Turiamukamay ("Hill of the Deer and Wolves"). From there one goes to the white wolves, in Paritsikatsiya. After one circulates in these three minor places for the first three to five years, then they go on to the blue wolves in Kuyetuaripa, and finally to the grey wolves, the most intelligent, wise, and powerful of them all, in Muxa Uxiye. These last two places are where one learns how to do the transformation into wolf form, once they have proven to the wolves that they have tried hard and will complete all the tests the wolves give them.

Ritual Paraphernalia Required for Wolf Transformation

Thus, during the first five years of apprenticeship, the wolves get to know the candidate, and test him to see if he will make good on his promise to bring them offerings every year. He and his wife make a variety of objects, especially different types of arrows, and on the full moon of the same month of every year take these offerings to the wolf shrines. Ulu Temay:

> One has to go to each place and bring prayer arrows, feathered wands (*muviéri*), medicine baskets (*takwátsi*), candles, votive gourd bowls, and other things. One has to be fasting when they go to leave the offerings there. One prays for what one is asking for, to be a shaman, and to learn how to turn into a wolf. The wolves tell him in his dreams what other objects he needs to make in order to complete himself and turn into a wolf. He makes what they tell him to.

Under the tutelage of the Tsamalówi, the wolf descendants of Kumukemai, the apprentices ascend the shamanic ladder. Little by little the wolves begin confiding in their trainees. By the end of the fifth year there will have been numerous exchanges between the initiates (who by now are recognized as "completed" shamans) and their wolf teachers. After "graduation," or "completion," the wolves trust their human protégés enough to reveal to them the secret knowledge of the transformer.

There are two categories of offerings the apprentice learns to make over the five-year period. The first group pertains to the shamanic paraphernalia they will accumulate for routine healing and singing as public and private shamans. The second group pertains to objects that will defend the shaman in the mysterious realm of his animal ally, where many dangers lie. The initiates acquire all the tools of their trade by going to the sacred places and soliciting the wolves to provide them with instructions in their dreams.

Some of the objects the initiates create or acquire as a part of their shamanic apprenticeship into the wolf "cult" are similar to those obtained by apprentices in other branches of Huichol shamanism. During the first three to five years, the initiates bring feathered shaman's wands, or muviéris, that in form closely resemble votive arrows with pendant feathers at the butt, or nock, end. For these, the feathers of hawks or eagles are preferred. The feathers they take with them have now been empowered, and from then on will be a permanent fixture in the shaman's medicine basket (cf. Eger Valadez 1986:35 for other examples of this ritual for empowering objects).

During the early stages, the initiates make many different types of nieríkas. In addition to the above-mentioned disks, one made by husbands and wives as prayers for a safe return, and the other to petition for forgiveness for sexual transgressions, there are many other nieríkas that communicate the desires and intentions of the initiates to the wolves.

These disks are routinely left at the wolf shrines. One common type, cut from white tufa, a soft volcanic stone, is decorated with incised images of different deities in their animal forms, including rain serpents, deer, eagles, and wolves. These are deposited each year outside shrines of lesser importance. Another disk that pertains particularly to wolf apprenticeship consists of a circular piece of wood decorated with wax and wool yarn images of male and female wolves, with an eagle at the top and representations of the initiate and his wife at the bottom. In the center there is a round mirror, symbolizing the power of shamans to "see" into the spirit world and communicate with their teachers. This mirror disk, called Tsamalowi nieríka, wolf "image" or disk, is left together with an arrow called Kauyumari Ulu ayeh, Arrow of the Deer Spirit, a kind of votive or power arrow made by apprentices in all branches of Huichol shamanism.

The symbolic attachments on this arrow, which represent the prayers of the initiates for empowerment, include a miniature shaman's chair, to help the supplicant to learn to sing or chant the sacred poetry and to cure; a pair of paper cutout sandals for the initiate to use when he "walks" the sacred landscape; and a miniature deer snare or trap, to be used by the initiate to "trap" his luck. These objects, complemented by feathered wands and candles with ribbons attached represent payments to the gods; as the Huichols put it, they function as "signatures" of the petitioners in settling their "annual debts" to their wolf benefactors.

To mark the completion of five such annual "payments," the apprentices make a special commemorative arrow with many attachments, as here described by Ulu Temay (Figure 58):

> When the initiate has completed five years he will make an arrow called Tsamalo-wete á Ulu, Arrow of the Wolves. Again he will dream of what he has to attach to the arrow, and what other offerings he had to make. He attaches the following things to it: a heart, so that he can think well; a drum that he will use in his ceremonies; a shaman's wand; a shaman's chair; a nieríka symbolizing the one he will use to diagnose illness; and a *yakwé*, the tobacco gourd, which symbolizes the *peyoteros* and also Tatewarí, Grandfather Fire.

This arrow will be left with the wolves at the "Place of the Children," where the initiate began five years earlier. Upon receiving this payment, the wolves will in turn grant all his wishes.

Once this Arrow of Completion has been made, it acts as an intermediary between the now "completed" initiates and the wolves. The special wolf arrow made by the initiates serves to place them in contact with the original wolf arrow in the temple of Kumukemai, the first tuki, or temple, made by the Wolf Father, located far away, and with all the wolf mentors who inhabit the shrines they have visited. The arrows serve

FIGURE 58. Arrow of the Wolves. (*Drawing by Ulu Temay, Huichol Shaman.*)

in the manner of relays that allow the wolves and humans to communicate in other ways than only in their dreams. Penetrating the language barrier between species, these arrows act in the same manner as those mentioned at the beginning of this essay; as may be recalled, the first hunters used an arrow to talk to the wolves, and they, in turn, used the arrow to convince the deer to jump out of their pens.

Again and again, then, we perceive the old hunting ideology and hunting weapons at the heart of Huichol religious culture: in this instance, as in the primordial past, the same compound arrows that slay the game function as a means of communication between species. In the same way arrows, or the shaman's muviéris, which are constructed like compound arrows, facilitate communication between humans and the gods. No wonder that arrows form such an indispensable part of the initiate's collection of power objects, be he a wolf shaman or any other kind! Here Ulu Temay speaks of another kind of arrow (Figure 59), which not only communicates with the wolves in all the world directions but also serves a protective function:

These are arrows with holes in them that are made for the wind. He makes these so that when he runs real fast with the wolves he won't be harmed by the wind and the air. The arrows are attached to an object in the middle that is called "horns of the wolves." This refers to the horns the wolves blow when they howl, like the horns the peyoteros blow. On the bottom he will attach a round nieríka with five holes. These

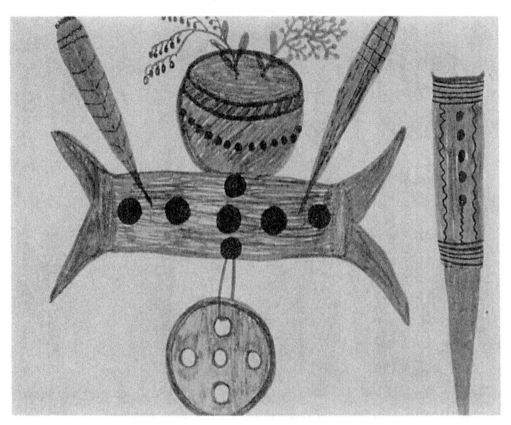

FIGURE 59. Wolf Shaman's Power Objects. (*Drawing by Ulu Temay, Huichol Shaman.*)

represent the four directions and the center. This disk will allow the initiate to be always in contact with the different colored wolves that inhabit the five places where he studied. He will never lose sight of them and will always be able to communicate with the five locations. He will leave this offering in the head shrine, at Kuyetuaripa, the female place of great power.

Now that the initiate has embarked on the most important and dangerous year of his quest, the sixth year, there are more offerings to be made that pertain to his protection while in the process of what we might call a "transcorporeal being." One of the most complex of these is a disk of paper or wood with wooden wolf claws attached (Figure 60). Also tied to this nieríka are the feathers of a bird called Awatz tzai (the San Blas blue jay, *Cissilopha sanblasiana*), which is believed to have the power of keeping people from "becoming lost" while under the influence of peyote or kiéri. Ulu Temay referred to this jay many times. In this context it, and another bird called Hu tai, are believed to protect the candidate from becoming disoriented in the realm of the wolves. According to Ulu Temay, this type of nieríka is deposited at the shrine of the red wolves in the "Place of the Children" at the beginning of the sixth year:

One makes this offering as a prayer so that when one turns into a wolf one will be able to return to his normal state at will, so that the wolves don't become contagious

FIGURE 60. Wooden Niérika with Attachments of Wolf Claw and Feathers of the Blue Jay. (*Drawing by Ulu Temay, Huichol Shaman.*)

to him, and so that he does not remain a wolf forever. The design on the center of the disk represents the two worlds, the human and the wolf world, and serves as a reminder to him to return to his race and never to lose sight of his family.

After acquiring and making everything he needs to become a wolf shaman, the initiate is now ready to perform the ceremonies that will generate the power needed to go through physical transformation. His medicine basket is complete, his guitar and violin have been blessed with the ability to play wolf songs, the special seed corn from the Mother Plant in the field has been consecrated at the wolf shrines, his hunter's bow and arrows have been empowered, and the candles with the ribbons and paper flowers attached, called *xu-tule*, are now ready to be used in a crucial upcoming ceremony. The transformation rituals to follow will prime him to undertake the crowning achievement of his career as what Eliade has called "technician of the sacred."

Transformation Rituals

In the sixth year he is a shaman and can cure and sing. He now has to make a ceremony of completion, which is called Kumukíta Waitowe, the "ceremony of the wolves." He will make this ceremony at the wolf shrine at the Place of the Children, where he began his apprenticeship. He has to sacrifice a bull, or a cow, or a sheep, because he is now completing. He will use the blood to anoint the five candles with ribbons and paper flowers attached, which represent the five places where he asked for his luck. The candles also represent the sun, and will be lit at midday during the ceremony he will take the candles and leave them at the different places where he studied. (Ulu Temay)

The initiate now has to make a circuit of all five places, approaching each to see where he will find his luck. First he goes to a minor shrine, to wait and see what will happen:

He sits with his medicine basket in front of him, waiting. At first a rattlesnake comes to him. Then a rat looks at him. Many animals jump out and try to scare him, to see if he is courageous enough to withstand the fear of turning into a wolf. The wolves are watching him to see if he will run away. But he does not run away, because he wants to see what happens. If he doesn't turn into a wolf at this place, he will go to the other places, until finally it happens.

The initiates prove to the Master Wolves at the minor shrines that they will endure the shock of transformation. The red, yellow, and white wolves at the less powerful locations assess whether or not the initiate deserves to receive partial power from a minor shrine, or full power from a major one:

If the wolves think that one day I am going to fail, then I am not given the biggest power. I get the power from the lesser places. But if they see that I have a good, strong heart, and that I can bear what they are going to do to me, then they give me the big power in the big places.

The initiates who are granted power at the smaller places never learn the secrets of transformation, but they do become very powerful shaman singers and healers as a sort of "consolation prize."[6]

Those who do make it to the top of the hierarchy enjoy the fruits of knowledge they have gained through competence and bravery. But even when one ascends to the top, the greatest obstacles still remain to be overcome. Because if and when the candidate makes it to the two places that rule over the wolf kingdom, Muxia Uxiye and Kuyetua-ripa, they will have their first encounter with real wolves, rather than the wolf spirits with whom they have been dealing at the minor locations. Ulu Temay describes what happens at Muxia Uxiye, the male shrine of the multicolored wolves (Figure 61):

It is the night of the full moon and he sits outside the shrine with his feathered wands in front of him. He has also brought with him offerings of copal incense (*putse*), ground maize meal (*tumale*), maize beer (*nawá*), and chocolate water. All these offerings are used in every ceremony. In addition to these, he has a gourd bowl in front of him filled with special plants that the wolves like to eat, in order to make

FIGURE 61. Male Shrine of the Multi-Colored Wolves. (*Drawing by Ulu Temay, Huichol Shaman.*)

friends with them. He places all the offerings in front of the shrine, and stays awake all night.

The man has found his luck there, because the wolves come to this place at midnight. They howl at him and he passes out with fear. He falls off his shaman's chair. He drops the candle and his medicine basket and his feathered wands. While he is unconscious the wolves speak to him in his dreams. They make it as if he has eaten peyote, so they can talk to him. He feels as if he is awake, but he is sleeping.

The wolves circle around him and urinate on him and lick him, and they give him their power in his hand, head, and feet. They are "arranging" him so that he will be able to turn into a wolf (Figure 62). He is dreaming.

Thus we see the wolves signalling their acceptance of the initiate by urinating on him — that is, by staking their "claim" — and licking him, a gesture taken as one of purification and acceptance. The following night, again on the full moon, the wolves who have claimed the initiate will take him into their den. This time he will be under the influence of the powerful wolf-kiéri plant* he encountered in Kuyetuaripa, the gov-

* *Solandra guttata.* (—Eds.)

FIGURE 62. The Shaman Dreaming and the Wolves Preparing Him for Transformation. (*Drawing by Ulu Temay, Huichol Shaman.*)

erning shrine that is considered the "female" of the two-parent wolf locations. Arrow Man describes how the potent effects of the wolf-kiéri induce visions that prepare the initiate for the portentous events to follow (Figure 63):

He leaves his medicine basket and feathered wands in the shrine below. Then he climbs up to the mountain top on the other side of the shrine to where the wolf-kiéri plant is. He deposits other offerings at the base of the plant: a nearíka, a red arrow which represents him, and a blue arrow for his wife, and some feathered wands. He will leave the wands there and take with him some that were left there before by another person, in the same way as he did at the other wolf shrines with those arrows of his that are feathered with hawk and eagle feathers.

He takes his new wands down with him and enters the shrine. It is now very late at night. He sits in front of a stone disk made by the wolf gods long ago with designs of wolves carved into it. His hunting bow and arrow are on one side of him. Now he is "drunk" with the effects of the kiéri flower that he ate on the top of the mountain. He is seeing many visions of snakes biting him and the wolves dancing and jumping all around him.

When the wolves enter the shrine he loses consciousness, like the night before. The wolves, led by the multicolored number one wolf, whose name is Ulowe-noitze,

FIGURE 63. The Shaman Climbing Up the Mountain to Where the Wolf-Kiéri Is. (*Drawing by Ulu Temay, Huichol Shaman.*)

want to take him to their den to see if he will like it. He is seeing many things now, but he is not asleep. He feels like he is one of them now. They speak to him and he answers, because he is like one of them now and understands them. But he is still in human form, and afraid, and he holds onto the wolf disk and does not get up.

In his vision the wolves take him to their den and "fix him up," so that he will no longer be afraid of them. The next night he goes out with them again to their den, this time not in a dream but for real, but he is not afraid of them any more. This is the night they will teach him to change into a wolf.

Recalling Lumholtz's reference (1902:206) to the singing shamans who would eat *yerba de lobo* five times to transform themselves into wolves, I asked Ulu Temay if it was necessary to visit the wolf-kiéri every time a person wants to talk to the wolves or transform into one. Could Lumholtz have been talking about the wolf-kiéri? Is the unidentified "yerba de lobo" *Solandra*? Ulu Temay's revealing reply:

One eats the wolf-kiéri in order to have an exhibition, a vision, of what it will be like to become a wolf. One usually eats the kiéri one time, unless for some reason he doesn't understand or "see" well. Then he will take it another time, until he learns how to do everything. There are only two kiéri plants that teach people

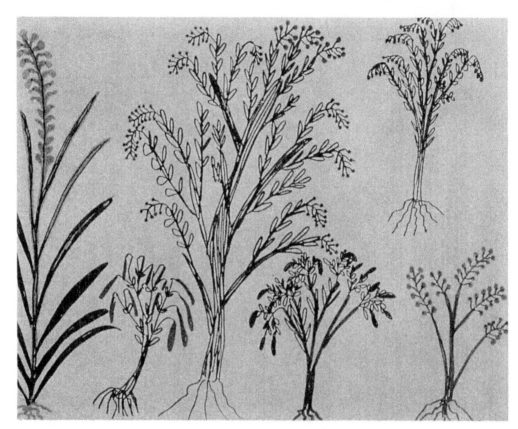

FIGURE 64. The Wolves Testing Him with Wolf Plants, for If the Shaman Is to Turn into à Wolf He Has to Eat Like One. (*Drawing by Ulu Temay, Huichol Shaman.*)

about becoming wolves. The one in Kuyetuaripa and another one not far from there, in Nalatawoatua. But many people eat peyote when they want to become wolves, because the peyote provides the strength and energy one needs to run and keep up with them.

Ulu Temay talks about other, non-psychotropic, plants that are collected for the wolves by the initiates. The wolves require the candidates to bring them these plants so that they may undergo one more test before being allowed to metamorphose into wolf form. The following is Ulu Temay's explanation for his drawing of this event (Figure 64):

> Here the initiate is about to become able to turn into a wolf, so he leaves these plants as offerings. There are three types of berries, called *upa pali*, *tsoka tsana leke*, and *xake xa*. The other plants are called *maxa telutsi*, *hale-uke*, and *xuave tecuculi*, which are very bitter. The wolves give these plants to the man so he can taste them to see if he likes them, and to see whether or not these wolf plants do him any harm. If he is to turn into a wolf, he must eat like one.

It is with the tasting of these plants that all the criteria for wolf transformation have been met. Thus, by the beginning of his sixth year, the novice wolf shaman has mastered the five tests the wolves have placed before him. The first was to make a circuit of the five locations to "find his luck." In the second, fearsome creatures tried to scare him off. The third entailed maintaining his composure while being terrified by the wolves in his kiéri visions. The fourth consisted of accompanying the wolves to their den without fear. And the fifth was to eat the bitter plants. But there still remains a sixth test, and this is the biggest of them all.

The Ultimate Esoteric Challenge

Fifteen days pass and it is now the time of the new moon. On the new moon the wolves will make their final preparations for the profound changes their pupil will undergo when the next full moon shines above. Here is Ulu Temay's description of what occurs on the new and the full moon:

> When the moon is born, he (the initiate) gets together with the wolves. He is not afraid, nor does he any longer lose consciousness. He is now going to dance with the wolves so that he can change his thoughts. He runs with them to where they live, and they circle round and round.
>
> The next day at dawn the wolves come out of their cave. They tell the man to bathe with a plant called *jamol* in Spanish. The wolves tell him they will meet him after he bathes, that they will be waiting for him on the path. When the sun sets the wolves leave their den and go to meet him. He follows the wolves and follows where they go. They tell him that when the moon is full he is to return to this place.
>
> In two weeks, on the full moon, he remembers where the wolves told him to go. It is on a steep hill in the wolf territory called Cerro de Kumutemai (Wolf Mountain). He goes there and hides his clothes in a cave. He will then begin to do five somersaults, one in each direction, to see if he will turn into a wolf or not. He does five turns, and he turns into a wolf (Figure 65).[7] His wolf friends greet him and welcome him to be their companion, and then they take him to their den. Now he will really be put to the test when they take him deer hunting.

Five Days in the Life of a Wolf Shaman

Now that the shaman has triumphed over his greatest challenge, he will have five days to complete the final phases of his entry into the "wolf cult." By this time it is assumed that the initiate can no longer fail. But there still remain obstacles to overcome. The first requirement for the wolf transformer to complete is the ritual deer hunt, which he must undertake that very night, followed by a bull sacrifice the next night. Ulu Temay explains why these are necessary:

> At midnight they go out to hunt the deer, and he is tested to see if he can keep up with the wolves, if he can run and get a deer. He needs to do this in order to leave

FIGURE 65. Five Somersaults, One in Each Direction, Will Turn Him into a Wolf. (*Drawing by Ulu Temay, Huichol Shaman.*)

deer blood as an offering he is required to make. They found one and killed it and he has to eat the meat raw like the wolves show him (Figure 66).

That same night they have to take the deer's heart out and run the heart and all the meat to the shrine of Grandfather Fire, Tatewarí, in Teakáta. The man-wolf has to take the heart there to pay for the initiation that he is now completing, and so that he won't be harmed by eating raw meat. The wolves help him with this obligation, and they are there with him and pray with him (Figure 67).

When the deer sacrifice is over they are going to look for a bull or cow and run it down and kill it. They do the same with the bull as they did with the deer: they skin it, eat a little of the raw meat and blood, take out the heart, and bring it to Tatewarí, Grandfather Fire. Now he has completed, and will never have to perform these ceremonies again. From then on he is free to roam with the wolves whenever he wants.

Recalling that in his book on the Huichols, Fernando Benítez (1968:327) mentioned that two men were seen turning into wolves on their way to the shrine of Tatewarí, Our Grandfather, the aged fire god, located in Teakáta, the most sacred place in the Huichol country. I asked Ulu Temay to expand on the association between the wolf hunters and this, the oldest principal male deity. He explained that it was important for the wolf hunters to go and visit this deity for a number of reasons.

FIGURE 66. Day One in the Life of a Wolf Shaman. As a wolf, he must run down a deer and eat the meat raw as wolves do. (*Drawing by Ulu Temay, Huichol Shaman.*)

There is first of all the requirement that the wolf transformer has to obtain forgiveness and permission from the old fire god in order to drink the blood and eat the raw flesh of the deer. This relates back to the time when the first wolf hunters killed Kauyumári, the Deer Person, who thereupon transformed into peyote. It will be recalled that it was the peyote heart of Deer Person that taught the wolf people ancestors to become shamans, to sing and hear by contacting him in his peyote spirit form, Kauyumari. The only way for shamans to activate the powers of this deer messenger to the spirit world is to obtain permission from the fire god, Tatewarí, the wise old Master Mara'akáme who is the divine patron of the shamanic arts and of success in the hunting of the deer.

In addition to his role as the facilitator of the relationship between Huichol shamans and the divine beings of the spirit realm, Tatewarí is also considered to be the "Great Transformer," he who changes cold to heat, raw to cooked, darkness to light, solid to ash, and, with the old earth goddess Takutsi Nakawé, whom Lumholtz aptly characterized as "Grandmother Growth," the tired, depleted earth to fertile fields. The obligation for the wolf transformer to make amends with Tatewarí so that the raw meat will not cause him harm, suggests that the latter's intervention is essential to

FIGURE 67. So That the Raw Meat Will Not Harm Him, the Wolf-Man Must Offer the Deer's Heart as Payment to the Shrine of Grandfather Fire. (*Drawing by Ulu Temay, Huichol Shaman.*)

bring about the changes the metamorphosing shaman undergoes when he does his somersaults in the five directions. This might explain why the nocturnal wolves, who are normally afraid of fire, nevertheless come to honor the old fire god Tatewarí, the "Great Transformer." Inasmuch as, according to Ulu Temay, the wolves, for their part, are able to transform themselves into humans, this would presumably place them under the tutelage of Tatewarí, the great primordial transforming shaman.

Not only shamans but also Huichols from all walks of life periodically visit the complex of sacred shrines dedicated to different deities at Teakáta, to bring various kinds of offerings, including animal meat and blood, as payment to Kauyumári, the Deer Person and messenger to the gods, who assists the divine Mara'akáme, Tatewarí, and his human counterparts in curing and conducting the ceremonies, to Takutsi Nakawé, and, of course, the Wolf Father Kumukemai. These rituals are meant to ensure that the souls of the sacrificed animals are propitiated and transformed back into the realm of the gods.

In the peyote pilgrimage, the participants are considered to be the "children of the Fire," and as such are constantly in touch with their guardian, Tatewarí, the old fire god and First Shaman personified by the leader of the pilgrims to Wirikúta (cf. Furst,

1972, 1976; Myerhoff 1974; Schaefer 1990). The pilgrims are obligated to go to Teakáta every year, just as are the deer hunters, the apprentice shamans, and the wolves. The yellow face paint (*uxa*) the peyote pilgrims wear is said by some Huichols to represent sparks from the fire, thus helping to merge the peyoteros with the ancestor gods they represent on the sacred journey. The *yakwé* (tobacco gourd) that is one of the distinguishing characteristics of the Huichol peyotero, is also the attribute of Tatewarí, and is responsible for the peyoteros being conceived as in a "delicate," "sacred," and "untouchable" state.

Ulu Temay's mention of the wolves who assist the initiate in his performance of his ceremony at Teakáta, and Benítez' mention of wolf transformation on a pilgrimage to Teakáta, led me to ask whether wolves travel to any other sacred locales. Ulu Temay's reply, taken from his own firsthand experience, reveals more of the relationship wolves are thought to have to Wirikúta, the sacred desert where Huichols go to find peyote, and where, according to him, the wolves, as "original peyoteros," still go on their own pilgrimages. Ulu Temay asserts that when the wolves make these journeys they turn themselves into human beings. The reasons given for the visits by the wolves to the sacred locations, and for the rituals they perform there, provide an insight into the deeper levels of the personal rapport between certain Huichols and their wolf-spirit tutelaries.

The Ceremonial Life of Wolves

According to Ulu Temay, the wolves follow an annual ceremonial circuit from the sea, where the Wolf Father Kumukemai started on his pursuit of Deer Person, to Wirikúta, where Deer Person was sacrificed on the summit of Paritekua, so that the wolves might obtain enlightenment by means of peyote, and to Teakáta, where both humans and wolves perform rituals of atonement for the slain deer. Here is his account:

The Samalówe are the descendants of the Wolf Father Kumukemai, who originated in San Blas, Nayarit. Some of his descendants now live in the Sierras, but they come to the ocean every year to visit him. The Wolf Father from San Blas, whose complete name is Kumukemai Muyu-e ("Black Wolf"), ordered his descendants, sons of Kumukemai Noítze ("Multi-Colored Wolf"), to go to the sea and take the sacred water back to the Sierras with them, so that they can bless their children and families. They make ceremonies, just as we do, and they need the sacred water of the sea, just as people do.

Wolves from the Sierras also go to Wirikúta to visit their relatives, the Samalówe, who live there on the high mountain. The wolves were the first ones to take their votive arrows to the mountain, and the peyoteros follow what the wolf ancestors did. That is why every temple peyote group has a role for the person who assumes the identity of the Wolf Father Kumukemai.

FIGURE 68. Peyoteros Depositing Offerings at Wakuli Kiteni, the "Doorway" to Wirikuta. For a discussion of the meaning of the name and the symbolism of this sacred passage see chapter 1, fn. 5. (*Photograph by Stacy B. Schaefer, 1987.*)

The wolves that live on the mountain above the peyote are there together with the coyotes, the Yauwitutsi. These are the coyotes that have the "key" and open the door for the peyoteros who want to enter Wirikúta. When the Huichols want to enter, they pray to the coyote and sing to him so that he will open the door for them. He is the "doorman" of Wakuli kitene (Figure 68) and he is associated with the wolves over there. The wolves pertain to the mountain, and the coyotes pertain to the peyote desert below. The two understand each other, and they communicate with one another. The coyotes protect the door, they open it when the peyoteros enter, and close it when they leave.

So the two groups of wolves lived in separate locations long ago and they traveled all over and got to know each other, and that was how their custom began, how they began to exchange knowledge, and why they still make ceremonies.

This last point, about the wolves making ceremonies, just like human beings, is significant, especially in light of the similarities Ulu Temay observed between the behavior of wolves and humans, their common survival strategies, and the level of interaction the transforming shaman may achieve with his wolf hosts during the five days in which he is their guest. Ulu Temay again:

Wolves are people, like us, which is why they need to make ceremonies. They have their customs also. They go to Wirikúta, to Haramara (the sea), and Teakáta, and they come home and they do the peyote ceremony, the drum ceremony, and the rain-making ceremonies. I have been to several of their ceremonies. They have to go deer hunting first, but since they don't have fire, they have to eat the meat raw.

They do the ceremonies different than we do them, in their minds. I was at one of their peyote ceremonies in September, and they do the five steps and turn around and come back, just like Huichol shamans do in their ceremonies. They have a mara'akáme on each side, and they sit and howl. They howl five times, and at about four in the morning they howl again, five times. Meanwhile, they sit there, all projecting their visions to one another, doing the ceremony. Some sit and some lie down, all speaking to one another and envisioning the actions in their minds. If they can't make the journeys to the different places, like the sea, they will go in their minds and bring the water back.

When I am with the wolves I can speak to them with my thoughts and they understand and I understand them. They speak like we do, in their language, but they do not speak like we are speaking, with words, only with their thoughts. You don't hear them speaking, but when you are together with them we understand one another, as if we were speaking over the telephone. When people speak on the telephone they don't see each other. That is how it is when talking to the wolves: pure thoughts, but we understand one another.

Did these telepathic powers he ascribed to the wolves result from their eating peyote? Did they use it in their ceremonies? Ulu Temay's reply contained an unexpected bonus that goes beyond wolf ceremonialism into a longstanding problem: whether or not Mexican Indian people knew of and utilized not just the different species of *Psilocybe* mushrooms but perhaps also the spectacular fly-agaric, *Amanita muscaria*, the "magic mushroom" of Siberian shamanism and, according to R. Gordon Wasson (1968), the mysterious plant deity known to the ancient Indo-Europeans as *Soma*.[8] Judging from Ulu Temay's description, the answer is yes:

No, they do not eat peyote. They eat their own plants that make them feel as though they had eaten peyote. They bring mushrooms which they eat. This is a red mushroom with white spots. They use these mushrooms in all of their ceremonies. They say this is their peyote, but it is not their peyote. I tried some of it, just a little bit. It didn't feel like peyote, it felt different. It felt like I was off the ground, like I was in a gentle wind that lifted me off the ground. When I eat peyote I can touch the ground, but with this I couldn't. I didn't eat more of it because I did not know what would happen to me.

It seems to me inescapable that Ulu Temay's description of a red mushroom with white dots refers to the fly-agaric, *Amanita muscaria*, the intoxicating mushroom of Siberian shamans.* Of course, we are talking here of a very remote past, and of peoples many thousands of miles removed from the Huichols, but there is an interesting analogy between early ethnographic descriptions of Siberian hunters waiting until reindeer browsing on fly-agaric become so inebriated they are easily caught, whereupon the hunters intoxicated themselves on the contents of the animals' stomachs, and, presumably their bladders (Wasson 1968; Furst 1976), and the story of the first Huichol deer that were kept in a pen and fed flowers that made them "drunk." When the intoxicated deer jumped out (at the urging of the wolves, who communicated with them through their magic arrows), they tried to flee but were run into traps. We recall that the traps were guarded by the Awatámete, wolves that transformed into people, hiding in the bush and waiting to eat the peyote heart of the deer and acquire shamanic knowledge. As to the inebriating "flowers," these could have been the spectacular yellow, *Datura*-like blossoms of kiéri, i.e. *Solandra*, the more so in that Benítez (1968:280–81) reported that on the ritual deer hunt the yellow pollen of the kiéri plant is, or was, used to confuse and entrance the deer.

Clearly Huichol beliefs and behavior here raise a great many ethnological and historical questions.

Changing Back Into Human Form

In Ulu Temay's drawings he represents the being into which he, as wolf shaman, transformed as a blue composite creature, neither quite wolf nor quite man, but more like the latter than the former (Figure 69). I asked him to tell me more about the actual physical changes experienced by him when he turns into a wolf, and how he changes back into human form. His answer:

> My body does not change at all, my ears remain the same, and everything. When I look at myself, I appear to myself to be the same, but when other people look at me, I look like a wolf to them. To other people I look like a wolf, but to me I am the same. I won't have a tail, or long ears, or hair on my body. But I am naked with them, and I'm going to feel a lot stronger, my hands and feet, because I am going to run and jump with them, and I won't be able to stand on my two feet. I have to walk with them, on all fours.
>
> If someone I know meets up with me when I am like this, now they aren't going to recognize me. They are going to think I am the same with the wolves. They are having the vision that I am a wolf—that's how they see me. It's a projection. It is the same when wolves turn into humans. One can be walking down the path and meet up with an old man with feathered arrows in his hat. They greet people and talk to

---

*For a yarn painting and a reference to the use of such a mushroom from another source two decades earlier, see Figure 71. (—Eds.)

FIGURE 69. Tail-less and hairless, the Transformed Wolf-Man Traveling with His Allies and Companions. (*Drawing by Ulu Temay, Huichol Shaman.*)

them and try to see if anyone will recognize them, but no one ever does, because they look exactly like humans. They are intelligent and wonderful and speak any human language they want to.

Also while I am in my human form, both the wolves, and other Huichol wolf-shamans, can recognize me as one of them. They recognize me because I now have the wolf sign on my face and wrists, which tells any wolf who I am, and how far I have gone. For example, when I go to the peyote desert and climb the mountain where the wolves are, they can recognize which of the peyoteros are wolf shamans. They recognize their human friends who know about them—they try to follow the people. That is one of the reasons why we leave [votive] arrows to the wolves in Wirikúta, so that the wolves will leave us alone when we go there in our peyotero group. We are very special at that time, very delicate because we are sacred and blessed and have a lot of work to do. It would be distracting if the wolves were to follow us, which is why we leave the arrow there, to calm them down.

Once a person knows how to turn into a wolf, the wolves will always be at his beck and call. I can howl to them in their den when I am in the woods, and they will come to me. If I go to a zoo and call to them, they will recognize me and come up to me and greet me. I can also arrange to meet the wolves any time I wish, by talking to them through my dreams and setting a time and place. I will meet them and I will take off my clothes and hide them, and I go with them, to go play, or they accompany me when I have to walk far away to go and heal someone.

Ulu Temay's description of transformation from human to wolf and vice versa suggests that in Huichol belief there is no actual change in the body's appearance; rather, the shaman has command of a kind of psychic transformation that breaks through visual and language barriers. The shaman experiences himself as looking the same but walking on all fours and having greater agility. The wolves who take human form, in turn, are said to be able to "project" as human beings to people they meet on the trail, which gives them the reputation of great trickster-transformers. What counts, of course, is that those who believe themselves to have such special skills, the power to transcend the limitations of their physical selves and the physical world around them, are also so regarded by their fellows. The master shaman's ability to achieve complete identification with the mystical essence of his spirit animal empowers him to project its outer physical and mental form. As Ulu Temay points out, traces of these transformations remain forever etched on the faces and wrists of transforming wolf shamans, who, he says, can instantly recognize one another, and may be recognized by other wolves. They are all now members of the same belief system.

Here is how Ulu Temay describes the technique used by wolf shamans to transform back into human beings (Figure 70):

The person may remain a wolf for five days and nights, but on the sixth day he must change back. On the morning of the sixth day the sun comes up and the wolves go to sleep. The man has to return to the same place where he bathed, and now he must dive into the pond. He is still a wolf when he jumps in, and he swims below, below, below. When he comes up, he will be a person again. Now he will go to his house.

When he was a wolf, they gave him various things to eat, which he left with his hidden clothing, thinking that he would take these foods with him when he returned home. But now that he was in his human form again, he saw that the wolves played a trick on him. They gave him plants that wolves eat, and pine sap. They told him that cow pies were cheese, and gave him rock tortillas. He realized that he couldn't eat these things, or take them home with him, so he took the wolf food to the wolf shrine where he began his apprenticeship.

He goes home after that and makes a fire. Then he makes a special arrow and

FIGURE 70. The Wolf-Man Diving into the Magical Pond to Change Back into Human Shape. When he comes up, he will again look like a man.

brings all of his family members together and blesses them with it. He tells his family all about what he did. Then he makes crossed sticks out of branches with thorns that he will take outside and place on all of the trails that lead to his house. He puts the thorny crosses to block the paths and to calm the wolves if they follow him home and come near his house, so that they won't bother his wife and children. If the wolves wish to see him, they can howl at him from far away, but they won't scare the family by coming close. He also places a magic cross above his door.

If the shaman doesn't wish to accompany the wolves again, he still has to remember to bring them offerings every year. Even if he doesn't go out with them any more, he must still bring them blood from the ceremonies, arrows, plumed muviéris, and go to talk with them. He must never forget his wolf friends, and they will never forget him.

Fikes (1985:325) reported that the way the transformed "nahual" returns to his human form is by rolling around in the five cardinal directions, just as he did to become a wolf. He also mentions wolf foods and rock tortillas, that, if consumed, would cause a person to remain a wolf forever. Ulu Temay seemed cautious in discussing them, but gave the distinct impression that he ate them anyway, once, as his final test as an apprentice wolf shaman, and again while participating in the wolf peyote ceremonies, when he readily tasted the mushrooms he called "wolf peyote."

FIGURE 71. Yarn Painting of "Ancient Hewi Sorcerers." In the summer of 1970, Ramón Medina, who had not previously spoken of wolves or mushrooms, surprised Furst with this yarn painting, which he said depicted "ancient Hewi sorcerers" gathering red mushrooms they ate to transform themselves into wolves and foxes. The red cap and white stipe with its ringlike remnants of the veil leave little doubt that the mushroom involved is the fly agaric, *Amanita muscaria*. Ramón also identified the flowers as Kiéri. (*Yarn painting by Ramón Medina. Southwest Museum, Los Angeles.*)

He never mentioned that eating wolf food would cause him to remain a wolf forever. Rather, he said that one sees the wolf food as though it were real food, rock tortillas and all, and eats it as such. He did mention being embarrassed one time when the wolves tricked him by calling cow pads "cheese." But since wolves are peyoteros, who, like Huichol peyoteros, commonly use reversals in talking of things or people (cf. Myerhoff 1974; Furst 1972, 1976), he could appreciate the tradition that lay behind the joke the wolves played on him. Wolves, like peyote pilgrims, delight in their reputation as tricksters.

In any event, eating wolf food was not something Ulu Temay stressed when talking about taboos whose violation would result in not being able to change back into human form. According to him, rather, the one thing that would prevent a wolf shaman from getting back his human shape was mating with a female wolf:

It is forbidden for us to have sex with them. If you have sex with them you can never change back into a person. They offer you their females, and since you are a wolf, you think about marrying a female wolf, but if you do that you never return home again to your wife.

Conclusions

Ulu Temay's is the "inside view" of a participant in a little-known aspect of Huichol shamanism. His revealing descriptions of Huichol wolf shamanism and transformation have added, I feel, much to the ethnographic record. I feel, too, that the information he provides may help move us toward a better relationship and attitude toward the animal and vegetable species with whom we share the earth. It is sad, and injurious to us as a species, that with all the strides we have made in science and technology, we remain largely ignorant of the natural phenomena that for people like the Huichols are an integral and accepted part of everyday life. The invisible world of the wolf shaman may not be quantified, qualified, or measured, but its existence is, for the Huichol, second nature. Ulu Temay and his ancestors have dedicated their lives to the study of these mysteries and the penetration of the barriers to a sacred realm of knowledge that is not accessible to ordinary people. Once on the other side, they seek answers to questions all human beings ask: Where did I come from? Why am I alive? Where am I going? How will I get there?

Ulu Temay's inside view of the Huichol wolf-shaman cult seems to me to have provided one example of how humans, plants, and animals may share and exchange information and gain access to reservoirs of survival knowledge nature provides for all of us. This idea is epitomized in the Huichol tradition that the first people, half wolf, half human, obtained the knowledge to hunt, grow maize, and perform rituals to connect them to the metaphysical realm only after eating the peyote heart of the deer. From that day on, the Huichols acquired new mentors, the peyote and the kiéri. These plant teachers gave the ancestors the visions that taught them how to transcend the human condition, to penetrate the barriers to the unknown, invisible world. The enlightened wolves became the guardians for generations to come.

The revelations that Huichols believe come to them while under the influence of peyote and kiéri inspire deep religious feelings, enlightening them to the reality of what the ethnobotanist Terence McKenna has called the "mind behind nature." McKenna suggests that the plants we label as "hallucinogens" actually function as "inter-species chemical messengers," communicating information from the plant kingdom (the realm of "solid state" entities) to the animate world of human beings: "If hallucinogens are operating as exo-pheromones, that is, inter-species chemical messengers, then the dynamic relationship between primate and hallucinogenic plant is actually a transfer of information from one species to another" (McKenna 1993:5).

McKenna and his colleagues have proposed that psychotropic plants may have functioned as "causal agents in the appearance of spiritually aware human beings and the genesis of religion" (ibid.) Something like that certainly seems to be the case among the Huichols, whose plant-induced visions help them to better adapt to their environment and evolve to its spiritual apex. In this sense, could not wolf transformation among the Huichols be seen as a manifestation of the evolution of the human psyche? Does the "inter-species communication" Huichols insist takes place between themselves, the wolves, and the sacred psychoactive plants represent a kind of breakthrough in human understanding of the ways nature provides its multiplicity of life forms a way of sharing in what might be called a "meeting of the minds"?

Inter-species communication provides adaptive benefits for all involved in it. In the case of Huichol wolf shamanism, it appears that the population benefits by collectively tapping into ways of not just adapting to, but flourishing, in a harsh environment. Even though the Mexican wolf is nearly extinct, wolves are revered—universally and not just by specialists in wolf shamanism—for their knowledge, and protected as though they were indeed the "Elder Brothers" of the Huichol people. People really believe that if a Huichol were to kill a wolf, even accidentally, he will most probably be punished by other wolves and even die shortly thereafter. The benefits deer receive from inter-species unity is a recognition of their function as intermediaries in the spirit realm. While they are seen as willing sacrificial victims in the physical world, their exalted role in the transcendental realm as messenger and mentor endows them with the greatest consideration and reverential treatment by the other species, especially human beings. Finally, the last group of beneficiaries from inter-species communication are the members of the plant kingdom, who share the earth with human cultivators whose behavior insures that the sacred plants will flourish.

From Ulu Temay's descriptions it appears that animals, too, receive knowledge and ways to adapt to the environment through the use of the sacred psychoactive plants. The wolves used them in their ceremonies just as do human beings, and, in another instance, fed the deer the flowers that made them "drunk." The numinous experiences induced by these natural substances in people, wolves, and deer, experiences that include metamorphosis, the ability to speak and understand each others' languages, travel to distant places in one's thoughts and dreams, and "telepathic" group projections, are all part of the knowledge the Huichols believe the sacred plants communicate to those who use them for spiritual purposes.

As the natural habitats and numbers of wolves continue to be depleted at an alarming rate and modern humanity continues "to eliminate the panoply of life" by "elbowing species off the planet" (Myers 1984:158), we may be cutting off the possibility of any further evolution of human consciousness. Instead of recognizing and respecting the wisdom of those who, like the Huichols, have pioneered the hidden realms of nature, we have dismissed their beliefs and practices as superstition or even witchcraft. Such attitudes have given license to the elimination of all that we should be sworn to preserve—sacred plants, forests, wetlands, wolves, Indians, and anything else that competes with us for space to inhabit or exploit.

The Huichols and their shamans, those who, like Ulu Temay, gain their power from the wolves, and those who attain it through other means, have much to teach us. All we have to do is learn to listen.

NOTES

1. At the 47th International Congress of Americanists in New Orleans in 1991, the German ethnologist Ulrich Köhler suggested, on the basis of recent ethnographic research, a modification of the traditional negative association of "nagualism" with malevolent witchcraft to include belief in, and practice of, transformation into their companion spirits by curers for the benefit of their patients or social group (Mullenax 1994:19). But the association and shared destiny with companion spirits commences at birth and the individual has no choice over their identity, which may be determined by the newborn's father or grandfather from some visible sign, such as animal tracks near the house. In Huichol wolf transformation, however, there is no indication of wolves as predestined companion spirits of this kind.

In the Huichol case, the adult individual selects the wolves to be his power source, or to accept their offer to serve as such, and to learn from them how to join them temporarily in shape and behavior and for a time even participate in their lives. Huichol wolf transformation is surely related to what has been understood by "nagualism." But as the author learned from her consultant, there is in the Huichol case, among other crucial differences, a process of learning, in a lengthy and arduous apprenticeship, that is entirely absent from the shared fate from birth to death between an individual and his or her companion spirit. That alone would require seeing the phenomenon on its own terms, as she has through the eyes and personal experiences of her Huichol friend.(— Eds.)

2. "Wolf nahualism" is the term Fikes (1985) used in an unpublished doctoral dissertation. His description corroborates much of what Ulu Temay has been relating over the past dozen years or so in our taping sessions. The information Fikes collected is extensive and useful, but it does not include details of the long and hard road the future wolf shaman has to travel toward completion, nor does he touch upon the question of "inter-species communication" between wolves and humans that figures so prominently in Ulu Temay's accounts. Both topics are crucial to an understanding of the phenomenon as a whole, and to the specific focus of this essay, which is to explore the question of how and why some Huichols come to assume the spiritual identities and physical forms of their "Elder Brothers, the Wolves." An earlier major published source that treats wolf transformation among the Huichols in considerable detail is Vol. 2 of Fernando Benítez's five-volume popular ethnography, *Los Indios de México* (1968-1980).

3. This is only one of several versions of the origins of the peyote pilgrimage. In other myths the first people, who had both human and animal form, were not necessarily wolves; in fact, there is mention of other species. In any event, Preuss, a follower of the astral school of myth interpretation, would have read myths such as that in which the wolf people of the pre-Deluge

First World, after living in darkness in the coastal lowlands in the west (where the Huichols locate the entrance to the underworld), pursue the celestial deer to the land of sun and light in the east, not as indicating historical origins or migrations, but as metaphors for observable phenomena in the night sky.(—Eds.)

4. Perhaps not quite so absolutely, apparently, because Ulu Temay also told me that a serious illness with which he was afflicted did not yield to treatment until some shamans diagnosed the cause as divine punishment for a transgression of the sexual taboo. To pay for this offense and regain his health, he had to sacrifice a bull. Once he had done so, he recovered. On this same subject, Fikes (1985:267) quotes an informant as follows:

> The man who wishes to become a wolf must practice sexual fidelity. Sexual involvement with anyone other than one's spouse prevents one from changing into a wolf. To achieve this metamorphosis both husband and wife must be sexually pure. This study puts one's family and livestock in danger. It is very serious. The wolves may eat a person who fails in this endeavor. Or the rattlesnake or puma may attack him.

5. Whereas Ulu Temay insists that marrying a wolf woman while being married to a human spouse would preclude the transformed wolf shaman from ever returning to his human form or going home to his human wife, Fikes (1985:323) quotes his informant as telling him that, though married to a human wife, he not only married a wolf woman but had twin children with her, and yet returned to human form and resumed life with his human wife.

Such discrepancies are an instructive example of the many variations in Huichol sacred beliefs, and also of how knowledge about the wolf cult is often incomplete or contradictory. The scarcity of informed people willing to discuss wolf transformation openly, and thereby help clear up such inconsistencies, makes it difficult to determine what the truth is—in the unlikely event that there is only one truth.

6. This practice was also reported by Fikes (1985:216).

7. Somersaulting as a technique of shamanic transformation is not limited to Huichols. For some South American examples, see Karin Hissink (1961) on the Tacana of Bolivia. Her consultants told her of several instances of shamans transforming themselves into jaguars by somersaulting.

In a conversation one of us (P.T.F.) had on August 8, 1993, with Guadalupe de la Cruz Ríos, the widow of Ramón Medina (see Chapter 6), she related a story about wolf shamans she remembered hearing as a child from her paternal grandfather, who had been a highly respected shaman-singer in Santa Catarína before the family relocated to San Miguel de Zapota in the Sierra de Nayar, where she herself was born. (Her maternal grandfather had also been a shaman, she explained, "but he was not of the first class," like her other *abuelito*.)

She remembered having been very frightened by her grandfather's wolf people stories. One time he told her and the other children about a man who knew the secrets of the wolves and who took offerings of votive arrows, food, and other gifts to their house, which was a cave in the Sierra de Nayar. After waiting five days, the wolves appeared to him. To become a wolf just like them he made five somersaults, one in each of the four cardinal directions, and then a fifth one in place, in the center. When he made this fifth somersault, "he got up as a wolf." When he wanted to turn back into his human form, Lupe quoted her *abuelito*, he made somersaults in the opposite direction. Her grandfather also told her about a man who always had great wealth in deer meat. The people were surprised that he was always so well supplied with venison and they asked him where he got it. He told them to follow him next time he went hunting and see for themselves. They followed him and when they came upon a herd of deer, they saw that it was really a wolf that was killing many deer. But then the wolf went down to a barranca to kill sheep and goats. So they hunted the wolf and when the wolf died, so did the man who had so much deer meat.(—Eds.)

8. Wasson's case for *soma* as *Amanita muscaria* is not without its critics. Several alternatives have been proposed. Perhaps the strongest argument is one that Flattery and Schwartz (1989) make for *Peganum harmala*, wild rue or harmel, a woody perennial native to Central Asia and Iran, whose psychoactive constituents, harmaline, harmine, and tetrahydroharmine, are also found in *Banisteriopsis caapi*, the tropical forest vine that is the source of the hallucinogenic drink known as *yajé* to the Tukano of the Upper Amazon and *ayahuasca* to Quechua-speakers (Schultes and Hofmann 1979:53, 76-77; Rudgley 1993:56-62).(—Eds.)

INTRODUCTION TO CHAPTER 10

The meaning to Huichols of each of the three components—deer, peyote, and maize—that fuse into what since Lumholtz has been recognized as a unified symbol complex can properly be understood only in relation to the others. As the French ethnographer Dennis Lemaistre observes in the following chapter, this ideological triad is really a "circle of metamorphoses," in which each constituent part is perceived to be at one and the same time each of the other two. In other words, while each has its specific roles in Huichol physical and metaphysical existence, in the spiritual sense deer, peyote, and maize are not completely discrete categories. Rather, in Lemaistre's words, each "is the creator of the others at the same time as it is created by them." Thus, maize is the "child" of peyote, and to hunt peyote is to hunt deer (and vice versa). That is why peyoteros say "Our game bags are full" when they consider the number of the potent little psychoactive succulents they have "hunted" to be sufficient to cover their needs in the coming year. It is also why, to this day, they string peyotes on cactus fiber cords as though they were pieces of deer meat, exactly as we know—from archaeological remains in northeastern Coahuila—it was done by Desert Culture hunter-gatherers a millennium and more ago. Conversely, according to Zingg (1938:490-91), pieces of deer loin and steak strung on cords and boiled into deer meat soup at the ceremonies are referred to as "peyotes."

If Huichols go to hunt peyote "to find their life," it is conversely true that, peyote being a manifestation of deer, the ceremonial deer hunt is likewise an imperative for the reaffirmation of their life as Huichols. It is thus impossible to overstate the crucial role of the deer hunt in Huichol religious ideology and ritual. Lemaistre's chapter provides the deeper meaning behind Zingg's description of the deer hunting rites that are tied to the "First Fruits" ceremony (1938:490-500). As Zingg noted, like the hunt itself, the elaborate preparations, which include the planting by the deer hunters of numerous hunting arrows in the ground beside the altar, and their subsequent transformation into magical messengers to the master or guardian of the deer species and the gods by the shaman, by means of tying eagle or hawk feathers to them, have their charter in the Huichol origin myths. In his chant, the shaman magically dispatches these arrow messengers to Wirikúta, the home of Kauyumári, the sacred Deer Person and culture hero, and to other sacred places to notify the divine ancestors, the master of the species, and the other extra-human powers of the urgent need to hunt deer, and to request their cooperation in providing a sufficient number. This kind of shamanic behavior relating to the hunt and the spirit owners or masters and mistresses of game is very familiar to us from other parts of the Americas and elsewhere.

In Zingg's time, sixty years ago, the Huichols still caught deer by means of nets, thereby assuring, as Lemaistre observes, the preservation of ecological balance. Even today, deer are still occasionally—very occasionally—run down and captured by hand, the idea being to preserve every last bit of the precious blood for anointing ceremonial objects, the images of deities, and the cultigens, led by the sacred maize. But nowadays deer are mainly hunted with firearms. And so, just as the Huichol territory has been shrinking, so has the deer population, which has suffered from both loss of habitat and increasing reliance on the gun. Deer have thus become very scarce in and around the Huichol country, and hunting outside the limits of the community is dangerous. The animal that is so important to Huichol spirituality is the common white-tailed, or Virginia, deer, *Odocoileus virginianus*, which is found all over North America—in the absence of natural predators often in such numbers as to constitute a real pest. In the country of the Huichols, meanwhile, this graceful animal has virtually disappeared.

There is now real fear among the Huichols that, along with his species, Tamáts Kauyumári, the culture hero as sacred deer, himself may disappear. That, as Lemaistre writes, would be a great spiritual calamity. But it is one that can be avoided, be it by restocking or some other workable solution in which the Huichols themselves need to be given a decisive voice.

More than just a study of the profound spiritual meaning of deer and deer hunting in one small corner of the Indian Americas, then, there is surely a message here for deeper dimensions to the restoration of ecological balance beyond the obvious ones of conservation and the preservation of species diversity.

Peter T. Furst

10 : THE DEER THAT IS PEYOTE AND

THE DEER THAT IS MAIZE

The Hunt in the Huichol "Trinity"

DENIS LEMAISTRE

Translated from the French by KARIN SIMONEAU

In company with the peyote cactus and maize, the deer is one of the three emblematic figures in Huichol mythological thought (Figure 72).[1] The Norwegian ethnographer-traveler Carl Lumholtz, to whom we owe the discovery of this ideological triad, saw in it the synthesis of the three economic stages of the tribe: hunting, gathering, and agriculture. But the neatness of this division should not obscure the essential: their role, here and now, in the social, ceremonial, and cognitive life of the Huichol people.

Peyote, deer, and maize are united by a network of close correspondences. Myth and ritual present to us a circle of metamorphoses in which each figure is the creator of the others at the same time as it is created by them, like vessels open to infinity. The identity of each figure is defined by its fluidity, the degree to which it is permeable by the others. One may speak of a "plural identity": maize is also the blood of the deer; peyote, as we shall see, is also the powder from the deer's antlers; and maize, Niwétsika, is the "very child" of the peyote.

The Deer in Huichol Mythological Thought

In the endlessly repeated cycle of the renewal of life the Huichol deer hunt can be seen as a significant ritual, included among other rituals that inevitably define it and that in turn are defined by it. Thus, it is possible to place the hunt diachronically, as an identifiable sequence in the festive and cognitive cycle, but also synchronically, for the elements in the triad mentioned above are inseparable, and at any ritually charged

FIGURE 72. Yarn Painting of the Sacred Triad of Deer, Maize, and Peyote. (*Yarn painting by Chavélo González de la Cruz.*)

moment each figure engenders the others and takes on their external characteristics. According to one Huichol myth, the Great Deer Paritzika, the most elaborate embodiment of Maxa Mateáwa, The Great Deer with the Wise Antlers, ate his own horns. But he left a piece in the shape of a peyote rib, and from it seven "flowers," seven *hículis* (peyotes), were quickly born (Benítez 1968:228).[2] In a related myth, the little maize girl weeps like a fawn when her first minuscule leaves emerge, for like the fawn she grows during the rainy season. And do the women not grind the peyote on the metate as if it were maize?

The three figures relate to one another in innumerable ways that would require a very complex study. They are reflected in the *nieríka*, "the power of the supernatural vision" (Negrín 1986; Furst 1978:30–32),[3] and they complete one another in a dynamic, kaleidoscopic unity. But they are also opposites: the deer and the peyote, joined in a solar circularity connoting masculinity, here differ somewhat from the maize—perhaps we should say the "she-maize"—which clearly has a strong feminine connotation and whose entire life cycle is limited to the rainy season.

To mitigate this opposition between deer and peyote, on the one hand, and maize on the other, the mythology has created Niwétsika, the "very child," which, according to all Huichol testimony, is both peyote and maize. But the maize is also the child of the peyote, which brings us a bit closer to the logic of Lumholtz's periodization mentioned earlier.

Still, there remains a non-concordance between the life cycle of the deer, which reaches maturity only after several years, and the reproductive cycle of the maize, which is limited to four or five months during the rainy season. Then we understand the full significance of the remark made by a *mara'akáme* (shaman) from Ocóta who one sunny August day confided to me: "At that time it is night for the deer." Literally and symbolically, it is during the rainy season that the deer loses its antlers, also called its "staffs of power" (*muviéris* in Huichol),[4] similar to those of the shaman. The deer that "knows" loses its power temporarily while the maize grows. This is no doubt one of the reasons for their intense interrelationship in symbolic and ritual practice. To give an obvious example: shortly before the harvest festival (Namáwita), significantly also called the Farewell Festival (because it is the last festival before the dry season), the authorities of the community "return the benches" to the *casa de las autoridades* and wash them. This act of inversion and purification marks the halt of all official political and judicial activity. Any current matters will now be handled inside the office, in the dark, and no longer in public.

However, Huichol mythology teaches us that the political authorities have their power from the sun and its messengers, the deer. The authorities will thus ritually accompany the sun-star and its agents during their subterranean journey, until October 4 (the day of San Francisco), when the inverse ceremony takes place. This ceremony is held at Teúpa, a mass of dark rocks, where, in the myth of the origin of the sun, the child-sun threw itself into the fire, only to reappear "five steps later," at Reunar, the extinct volcano that dominates the peyote country, about 300 miles to the east in the north-central desert of San Luis Potosí (Figure 73). Only after the ceremony at Teúpa can the last series of festivals be celebrated, in particular the harvest festival.

Thus the sun, the deer, and the peyote are here seen as the opposites of the night, of growth, and of maize, just as, more abstractly, the lucidity of knowledge is the opposite of the mystery of life. For what unites the peyote and the deer, the assistants of the mara'akáme, is the fact that they are two elements in the speculative knowledge possessed by the latter, each reflected in the other. Let us give a few examples of this, taken not from mythology in the strict sense (which would require much more profound study), but rather from the behavior of the deer as described by Huichols.

The deer is always alert, watchful and listening, attentive to the smallest tremor. Thus it is not enough to say, as Lumholtz does, that the Huichols have sanctified the

FIGURE 73. View from the Foot of Rau'unár the Sacred Mountain in Wirikúta from Which the Sun Was Born. (*Photograph by Stacy B. Schaefer, 1987.*)

deer because it is "the emblem of sustenance and fertility" (Lumholtz 1902:43), unless we understand that it is also a founding ancestor and a model for knowledge. This shamanic society, which has a very definite conception of the gradual communication with the infra- or extrasensory world, has not failed to be impressed by, for example, the animal's antlers: "Deer possess the virtues of the mara'akáme. According to the Indians, they acquire these virtues by eating the 'powder' of their own antlers after rubbing them against the trees. This powder has the same powers as the *híkuri*, which is the peyote itself" (Benzi 1977:252). The entire mythology confirms it for us: the deer (which at that time was also a man) carried the peyote inside its horns (Figure 74), so that in order to give it to human beings it had to somehow devour itself.

From this came its lucidity, but also the danger of approaching it without extreme prior purification: the deer is delicado.[5] The mara'akáme, the emissary of the culture hero, the Deer Person Kauyumári,[6] who is himself an emissary of the great founding ancestors, is all the more aware that his own power lies in the feathers of his muviéri, just as the power of the deer lies within its antlers.

One might wonder why the deer is not taboo and its consumption forbidden. The deer itself provides the answer: in order to give human beings peyote it has committed the act of partially devouring itself. Its flesh—especially in its hardened form, the antlers—is peyote, and thus the ritual of the hunt and of consuming the flesh follows inevitably.

FIGURE 74. Yarn Painting of the Birth of Peyote from the Antlers and Body of the Great Deer in Wirikúta. From its tail, of which the deified shaman-chief, Maxa Kwaxí, is the namesake. The artist identified the rectangular striped object at top right as a *namá*, from *namá*, to cover sacred objects woven of sticks and yarn with geometric or naturalistic representations of deer, snakes, rain clouds, peyote, and other designs and that are prominent in the array of votive objects offered to the deities. (*Yarn painting by Chavelo González de la Cruz.*)

If it were necessary to emphasize once more the nearly absolute equivalence of deer and peyote it would be enough just to look at a *rancho* in the sierra: smoked pieces of venison are hung to dry on strings in the same way as the peyote is, to the point where an inexperienced eye has some difficulty in distinguishing between them (Lumholtz 1902:135; Myerhoff 1974:162–163; Furst 1976:124).[7] And not very long ago the deer was "gathered" in a net (Figure 75), while peyote was symbolically "hunted" with two crossed arrows (Lumholtz 1902:134; Furst 1976:124). Thus, the rituals of hunting and of gathering exchange characteristics.

FIGURE 75. Yarn painting Illustrating a Deer Hunt. This painting shows how, before the advent of the rifle, deer were run down and driven into nets or string traps made of *ixtle*, cord made from agave cactus fibers. (*Yarn painting by Ramón Medina. Fowler Museum of Cultural History, University of California at Los Angeles.*)

As we have seen, there is no identification between deer and maize, only a recognizable parallelism between the growth of the young maize and the growth of the fawn during the rainy season. Still, the two "nourish" each other. The great festivals of the agricultural cycle, whether they precede the planting or the harvest, are inconceivable without the sanctification of the maize by the blood of the deer and the communion of the people in the *caldo* (meat broth).

Conversely, the dead deer is offered *tostadas* (toasted tortillas) and balls of maize paste along with chocolate, which, as among the Aztecs, is a food of the gods. Finally, the deer "masks" and the antlers will reinforce the power of the *tuki* (the circular community temple), the prestige of the mara'akáme, and the fertility of the *coamil* (milpa, maize field).

Thus we see to what degree the three fundamental figures in Huichol subsistence and culture are dialectically linked, so that the disappearance of one would, in the long term, bring about the disappearance of the other two as the tribe's emblems of identification and integration.

But right now, let us follow the men from the temple district of San José-Hayucarita (Where the Water Grows), a part of the community of San Andrés Cohamiata, as they go on the deer hunt.

The Ritual Practice of the Hunt

A MYTHICAL GEOGRAPHY

The hunting grounds encompass a much more extensive area than the communal land, and lie beyond it. There are no longer any deer in the communal territory. The reasons for their disappearance are political: the area occupied by the community has been considerably reduced by the pressure of the mestizo *ejídos*,[8] especially during the last forty years. But over-hunting also plays a part: the now widespread use of rifles, even revolvers, is upsetting the demographic balance of the deer population. Thus, the practice of the hunt is becoming more and more problematic. In the final section of this essay I shall discuss the reasons for this further. On the other hand, Huichol spatial mythology, which suffuses the entire hunting ritual, describes a territory extending like a star toward large parts of the states of Jalisco, Zacatecas, and Durango. It shows us a vast occupation of physical space before the Spanish conquest, particularly prior to the last forty years.

Thus, mythical consciousness contradicts administrative reality: the caves, mountaintops, and water holes of the hunting area, which are linked with the most ancient myths of this people, are so numerous that in order to give up hunting in these places the Huichols would really have to ignore their historical awareness. Moreover, every area inhabited by the deer has a "door" (*kiteniye*), made of rocks that bear carvings connected with the sun and peyote.

The choice of territory is determined by political, financial, and religious parameters. The hunters avoid camping too close to the ejídos, and discuss the fare to be arranged with the truck driver, which depends directly on the distance of the territory chosen.

The chosen area can also indicate the preference of the group, or of the mara'akáme: a certain place may be richer in clan mythology or may better reflect the mara'akáme's nocturnal dreams. This is why the group from the tuki of San José feels itself strongly linked to the entire hunting ground around the cave of Ututáwita. Here the ancient shaman-chief Maxa Kwaxí, Deer Tail, kept watch with his companions in those distant and difficult times when the Huichols had neither peyote nor maize. It is said that there Maxa Kwaxí's two sisters, "caught in a whirlwind," left for the land of the peyote. The younger sister remained there, feeling "cold." The older, after a journey of initiation, brought back the first peyotes with which Maxa Kwaxí was able to chant and hunt the first deer.

The area of Ututáwita is thus rich in the joint presence of the two great figures that are emblematic of knowledge. The cave itself is located in the nearly vertical side of a cliff, on top of which a large deer is said to sometimes stand with head held erect. A bit farther down, a huge rock with a flat top emerges from the mass of stones, Tatewarisíe, "Up there where Our Grandfather (Fire) is." At its foot grows a special flower, shaped like an elongated cup, yellowish white with some touches of light brown, the bloom of a kind of knotty root of black and mournful wood which grows horizontally inside the cracks in the rock. "Whatever you do, don't cut it! Don't touch it!" This is the kiéri plant (*Solandra* spp.), formerly the enemy of the peyote and then defeated by it. It contains a yellow pollen somewhat similar to the powder from the deer's horns, but this kind can cause madness; only certain mara'akáte (pl. of mara'akáme) may use it.

A bit higher up on the rocky wall the mara'akáme will travel alone with some *jica-reros* (Guardians of the Votive Bowls) toward Wawatsáta, the cave of the great deer Wawatsári (Benítez 1968:567; Furst 1976:120).[9] Across, on the other side of the valley, two hills can be distinguished, Aituníta (Round Mountain) and Yuramáka (Mountain of the Budding). Farther to the left is Maxa Manáka (Where the Deer Rests), and to the right, Waxa Manáka (the resting place of Waxáa 'uimári, Young Maize Field, Maxa Kwaxí's sister who brought peyote). Witnesses of stone and water to ancient Huichol history surround us on all sides.

RITUAL PREPARATIONS FOR THE HUNT

A hunt usually lasts for five days, five being a sacred number (the four cardinal points and the center). But when it is unsuccessful it can be extended long beyond this and can then become exhausting. For the gods decide when the hunt is over, not man: "They always get the deer, because, as they say, the shaman prays to the fire until the fire says: 'Yes'" (Lumholtz 1902:155).

The fire, and also the *vainúri*.[10] The vainúri is a feathered arrow with a string nieríka (see note 3) symbolizing the "trap" set for the deer (Figure 76), and it also has attached to it a small bag containing tobacco. Every family group represented in the hunt carries a vainúri, the symbol of its shamanic belonging to fire, for tobacco is the special food of fire. The tuki is also represented by a vainúri. The hunters must catch as many deer as there are vainúri, and so the nocturnal chants multiply: the representative of each rancho, of each family, must sing all night when his turn comes, for the following day "his" deer will be hunted.

Sometimes the mara'akáme suggests that the hunt be extended according to a very strict rule: if the hunt was supposed to last for five days it will be extended by as many days.

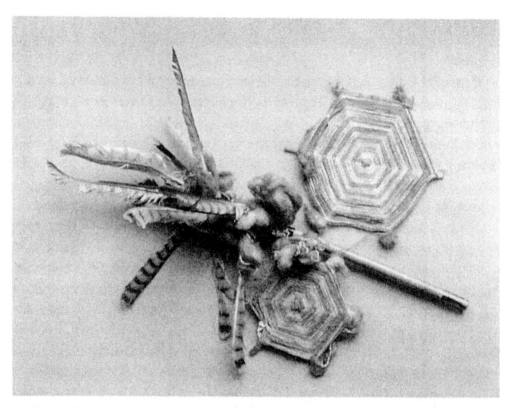

FIGURE 76. Prayer Arrow with Niérikas Symbolizing the Nets Used in the Traditional Deer Hunt. Although nets or noose traps have not been used for this purpose for a long time, the symbolism persists. Huichols still reproduce them in miniature on prayer arrows for boys, matched by small weavings and embroideries for girls. (*Collected by Konrad Theodor Preuss in 1907 in Cora territory. Museum für Völkerkunde, Preussischer Kulturbesitz, Berlin-Dahlem.*)

The Offerings. At dawn, before breakfast, the men set off from a small mestizo village on what used to be Huichol territory. They halt in the middle of a pasture ground around a small heap of burned sticks; this is Maxa Kwaxí Matiniéri, where their ancestors used to rest during their search for fire. There they leave votive gourd cups (*xukúri*) decorated with wax figures of deer, crosses, snakes, scorpions, children, representing prayers for fertility, health, and wealth (Figure 77). The men also offer up small bamboo arrows painted with red, blue, and black symbolic and geometric motifs, and maize flour, salt, and chocolate that is scattered to the four winds. Their prayers have a curious, discordant rhythm, each person praying for himself even though the prayer is collective. Then, leaving a hamlet of small wooden houses, they gather around a hole with brackish water; this is Hauríta, Where the Candle Is. It is not purity the pilgrims are searching for, but the permanence that also underlies their constant return to the path where their ancestors used to halt. They place another set of offerings there. The mara'akáme blesses each person with his muviéri, and the men drink the water from their cupped hands and rub it energetically over their faces and on one another.

The path continues, steeper and steeper, toward the heart of a mighty cliff: Ututá-

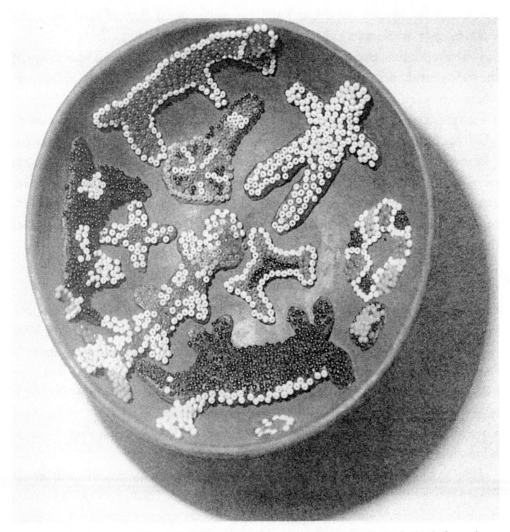

FIGURE 77. Votive Gourd Bowl. Xukúri in Huichol, *jícara* in Mexican Spanish (both from the Nahuatl *xicalli*), this votive gourd bowl is decorated with beeswax and bead images as visual prayers. (*Museo Nacional de Antropología y Historia, Mexico City.*)

wita, an obligatory stop before they look for Tamáts, Our Elder Brother, the Deer. It is also the last sacred place visited by the men from San José before the approaching great festival in the tuki. They have already gone to Teakáta in the east, "the Huichol Mecca," as Lumholtz calls it[11]; then to Haramára (the Pacific Ocean) in the west from where everything living came; then to Xapawiyemeta by Lake Chapala in the south. Now, here is the north, Ututáwita. Before pressing on, the whole group sits down at the edge of a forest in order to make offerings, which will have all the more power for being new and fresh.

The mara'akáme cuts a leaf in the form of a slender palm, bends it into a circle, and sews some blue thread around it, creating in a couple of minutes a very pretty bracelet. A *jicarero* (Guardian of the Votive Gourds) makes a miniature rifle from a small piece of wood. Another, gluing wax on a piece of cardboard, designs a *nama*[12] representing a blue deer inside a red tail (Maxa Yuávi, the metaphorical form of Kauyumári, the shamans' deer-interlocutor), and a nieríka (see note 3), also red.

Now the pilgrims ascend along the rock wall, led by the *urukuakáme*, the carrier of the staffs of authority (*'urú*, arrow). At last Ututáwita appears, a great fault in the rock, where erosion has created a high, jagged double arcade, accentuating the similarity to a natural temple. The wall is covered with ferns beaded with drops of spring water, which the people call Waxa Kupáya, The Hair of Waxaa 'Uimári, Maxa Kwaxí's sister. The cliff rises in a series of steps toward the dark interior, ending in a kind of altar on which lie innumerable old offerings: arrows inserted even among the ferns; votive cups of all sizes; arrows bearing namas embroidered with colored thread; nieríkas with radiating spokes forming a wheel; *tablas* (miniature yarn paintings) representing deer (blue, red, yellow); a tiny color print of the apostle St. James; white flowers.

Then the candles are lit and the prayers begin. The men sprinkle sacred water over themselves and fill their bottles with this eternal water, which they will later use in all their ceremonies (baptisms, healing rituals, communal feasts). But in this place where the dangerous kiéri plant embraces the stone in which Tatewarí, Grandfather Fire, lives, it is scarcely surprising to find indications of sorcery. Two objects, carefully wrapped in cloth and cotton, are well hidden in the mass of vegetation. In one someone discovers hair, apparently from an old person, in the other, a snake skin. "Bad," they say. As it might be dangerous to undo what has been done, the man replaces the two packages among the plants. At no time has he touched them with his hands, only with the tip of his machete.

Later in the afternoon, bringing arrows and votive gourd cups, the men will set out toward two natural springs known collectively as Aicutsíta. The second spring consists of a nearly 10-meter-high crevice dug vertically into the rock and crowned by an enormous stone. As at Ututáwita, the water drips incessantly over the moss. At the bottom there is a small arcade in the form of a nearly perfect oval so that the offerings can be left inside, to be blessed every second by the cool drops falling from the top. This small cathedral in the depths of the cliff seems to harbor a secret going back to the youth of humankind. "Bathe well," orders the mara'akáme.

The Chants. A man sits down cross-legged, and falls silent. Soon his hunting companions will fall asleep around the fire. He looks at the flames, still in silence. They are like the antlers of the deer; they are the muviéri of the fire, its feathered sticks. He, too, is holding his muviéri in his hand; he is the spokesman for the group of hunters. Then a sort of humming sound escapes him, and gradually changes: the long nocturnal chant begins.

It is said in the chant:

> Where the votive cup shows us
> Where our arrow shows us
> For alone we cannot.

The song is like this cup, like this arrow: it seeks to capture knowledge through the conscious perception of energy flows. Like the antlers of the deer the singer's muviéris show him whether he is following the right path. Later in the night his voice will become slow and solemn:

> Yes, indeed, the song of the flowers,
> the song of the deer approaches and is
> transmitted in the muviéri.[13]

By quoting these few elements of the chant recorded by me I only want to show that the *cantador* (Sp. "singer," another name for the mara'akáme, or shaman) has a well-defined objective in mind—the hunt for the deer the next day—as he tries to capture knowledge, realizing that he will remain ineffective if he cannot communicate concretely with the symbols of power as represented by the muviéri. "Alone, we cannot"; this bleak statement recurs in a number of songs.

This acknowledged powerlessness is partially mitigated by the practice of the *costumbre*[14]; the song says so expressly. The costumbre is sacrifice: the shaman often begins his statement to the ancestors with a detailed account of all the recent animal offerings. The fresh blood is also a message. The costumbre is memory: the hunting chant searches the cultural model, looking for traces of it in the nieríka (see note 3), which will yield more and more information "around two o'clock in the morning," say the Huichol, referring to the hour which they call *pari*[15] and which marks the point, the spark, that unites night with day.

The cultural model appears in the primordial principle of knowledge: fire. It is the intermediary, the messenger—"the blue deer," Kauyumári, "the yellow fawn of the sun" (Negrín n.d.):

> Over there, the hooves of the blue deer clattered
> We hear it.

Kauyumári, Tamátzika, Our Elder Brother, is not perfect. He is someone the Huichol projects himself onto and identifies with. He, too, has known temptation and error, to the point where the singer sometimes calls him "The Deceiver." Still, he was successful, through his "double," Maxa Kwaxí, who overcame all difficulties and eventually conquered the peyote and the deer. The entire song seeks to retrace this path with its crossroads, doubling back, then advancing toward the final goal. "They took another step," says the song. The singer, who calls himself "your descendant," sometimes comments: "For them it was not so difficult."

Kauyumári is perhaps above all the word, or rather what has emerged from all the paradigms of the word, namely song.[16] More than anyone else Maxa Kwaxí, Kauyumári's active double, knew how to turn the word into action, and then into ritual.

All the same, the test of the mara'akáme's chant will be the hunt the following day. All his talent consists of gathering concrete information: Where are the deer hiding?

Who are they? Are they female, or male? In the latter case, do they have large antlers? He is not alone; he is accountable to the group of hunters, and shortly before dawn he will have to "translate" to them what he has found out while straining all night to understand the lesson of the somewhat labyrinthine path of the ancestors.[17]

Here is an example of the concrete knowledge obtained after the long nocturnal dialogue: the mara'akáme has seen a *namakáme*.

In the old days the namakáme was "the mother of the peyote"[18] who would try to trap and test the first hunters of "the little rose."[19] But more generally the namakáme (*namá* = to hide, to cover), somewhat like a mask, denotes an identity which hides another within it. If the singer sees a namakáme within the framework of the hunt, it means that he sees a deer and predicts the arrival of another. A young deer without horns appears first. The mara'akáme then understands that this is, so to speak, the messenger of a deer with large antlers, a *maxa mateáwa* (*maxa* = deer, *máte* = to know, *awa* = horn, antler), of which the most marvelous is Paritsika, the Great Deer, the wisest one, the one who gave peyote to human beings. From this moment, the mara'akáme can decide to let the hunt last until Paritsika has been caught. This is an important element in understanding the Huichol custom of prolonged and excessive hunting that so infuriates the *téiwarí* ("neighbors," the foreigners): as long as reality does not conform to the vision, the hunters continue to kill more deer. The prestige, the renewal of the power of the mara'akáme, depends on this concordance. If the hunt is fruitless, it is primarily he who will be indirectly held responsible. Furthermore, his chant must be a subtle combination of his mythological knowledge, his ecological familiarity with the place where he is hunting, and his own níeríka, his vision. Then he can sing:

> Rise up, you who are hiding, and have no fear,
> Rise up, my elder brothers, rise up,
> Beings of knowledge, my masters,
> Rise up from behind the hill!

RITUALS DURING AND AFTER THE HUNT

The ritual of the hunting days is highly codified: nothing affecting the success of the enterprise can be left to chance. The women who have remained in the village are restricted by food and sex taboos, and try to communicate with the distant hunters through prayer and sacrifice.

As for the hunters, they can be divided into three categories, according to the role assigned to them:

1. The *xaurishikáme* is the foremost of the jicareros (see definition below) and is somewhat apart, in the sense that he must be the thinker, the organizer, and thus the principal singer of the hunt. However, on occasion the xaurishikáme may be judged to be wanting or ineffectual as a singer, and then he is replaced by another of the principal jicareros.

2. The *jicareros*, that is, the carriers or guardians of the jícaras, votive gourd cups (*xukúri* in Huichol).[20] This office within the tuki of San José must be held for a period of five years. Each office holder is responsible for a xukúri dedicated to a particular ancestor, purificatory water, or place. Every decision of a political or religious nature is debated by the group of jicareros. Being a jicarero is not a restful job; it is a demanding duty and increasingly burdensome, requiring animal sacrifices, expenses for festivities, and numerous journeys to often distant religious sites. The institution of the jicarero demonstrates the separation of economic and political power in traditional communal thought.

There are at least thirty-odd jicareros in each *tukípa*. We shall mention only those who appeared to us to be the ones principally in charge of ritual activity.

- The xauríshikáme, mentioned earlier.
- The urukuakáme, "the Carrier of Arrows," a term that includes the *varas*, the staffs of authority made of brazilwood. This jicarero often walks at the head of the group during the search and hunt for the peyote. With some simplification one might call him the political guide of the group, the religious guide being the xaurishikáme (saulítsika).
- Tatewarí, representing fire, the "prince" of shamanism. This is nearly always a man of some experience who has already held most of the other offices. He will be designated to aid the xaurishikáme in case of failure.
- Naurratáme, also an experienced man, responsible in particular for hearing the "confessions" of the participants in the peyote pilgrimage, and for throwing into the fire the small knotted strings representing sexual transgressions.
- Niwétsika, the maize-peyote. He is expected to sing in secret occasionally, parallel with the principal chant.
- 'Utuanáka, a jicarero representing the earth moistened by water and personified as a female deity, Tatéi (Our Mother) 'Utuanáka. In his breast he carries the principle of the maize.
- Wérika (werikúa) "the solitary eagle," the sun. This is often a young man, resembling the youth who threw himself into the fire to be transformed into the primordial sun.
- Maxa Kwaxí, who represents the first guide on the first journey undertaken by the ancestors.[21]
- Paritsika, whose role during the hunt is important because he personifies the Great Deer-Peyote of the mythology.
- Haramára, representing the Pacific Ocean as the mother from whom all life has issued.

A complete list of jicareros would require an entire paper. We shall merely note that each one is obliged to watch over his jícara: one slip, one oversight might bring punishment down on the whole group, it is said.

3. The third function-defined group in the distribution of tasks is made up of the

young people. They are not yet jicareros but are considered apprentices and are placed in charge of domestic duties: keeping the camp in order, gathering firewood, cutting up sacrificial animals, and carving the meat. Being an ethnographer I joined this active group; indeed I was encouraged to do so by the jicareros.

When a deer has been killed it must be received and ritually transferred from its "delicate" condition (see note 7) to a state where it is fit to be appropriated and eaten. The intensity and level of detail of the ritual vary according to the power of the animal, its age, and sex, but for all there are expressions of respect and tenderness. The deer is placed in front of the improvised small table on which rest the varas, the staffs of authority, the special symbols of the prestige of the tuki, and of the different ranchos represented. Usually the head faces east, toward Wirikúta, the land of the peyote and of the ancestor-deer. They are graceful animals, with a soft, greyish brown coat, long, slender legs ("the peyote, barely distinguishable in the desert of Wirikúta, is like the light tracks of the deer," it is said), and a small rhomboid tail which will soon decorate the effigies of power, the beams of the tuki, and, on occasion, the hats of the hunters and the peyoteros. The face of the xaurishikáme, who has remained in the camp, gently lights up and a tender smile passes over his lips. He speaks to his victim while caressing first its head and tail (the attributes of power and knowledge), then the entire length of the spine.

The few women in the group sprinkle small flowers between the horns and place *tostadas* (toasted tortillas), fruits, and cakes near the mouth. If the animal is a large male, the staffs of authority are placed on its spine.

Then all the hunters gather around the fire with the xaurishikáme in the center, and they light candles, symbols of "soul,"[22] of life, of metamorphosis. It is a collective prayer, thanking the deer for having come and the ancestors for having responded.

Urgently, each person dips his arrows in the bottles of purifying water and moistens first the "staffs of authority," to which the vainúri have been attached, then the ears of maize of each color,[23] the xukúri, or votive gourd cups, and finally his own wool or string bag (*kutsiuri*). They spread the water using both the muviéri and irises. All these symbols of power also receive the blood of the deer and some chocolate. Everything is done with an almost obsessive attention to detail. Finally, they also sprinkle water and blood on the guns, and on the hunters' wrists and cheeks.

The deer has been given two peyotes, which are placed over its eyes. At last its "soul" can free itself and travel toward the east. In Huichol thought the deer is not dead, only *enfriádo*, "cool," like the great ancestors who are "cooling" in the caves in the form of solid rocks.[24]

The jicareros energetically rub peyote cactuses over the animal's eyes, muzzle, horns, everything by which it lived, sensed, and knew. In particular they rub its mouth, so that its "breath" will reenforce the power of the peyote (and, conversely, so that the sacred plant will help the "soul" on its great journey).[25]

But only a mara'akáme may perform another act over the deer, an act that allows no mediators: inhaling its breath mouth to mouth in the hope of receiving the *urukáme* (also called *tewarí*, Grandfather), a small stone that is the concrete manifestation of an ancestor's "soul," like a part of eternity offered to the most highly initiated (see Perrin, Chapter 14). However, it should be noted that the urukáme can equally be drawn from the breath of a sacrificed bull, and besides, the breath of the deer can be offered at the beginning of a mara'akáme's initiation (with no need to acquire the stone). This is what a mara'akáme from another community told me: "Tatéi Wérika 'Uimári (Our Mother Young Eagle Girl)[26] sent me a dream, and I met a deer beside a spring. It showed no fear, and let me approach. I drank and swallowed the foam which it had on both sides of its mouth, each being of a different color."[27] Later, in the mountains, the peyote will make him encounter deer that will transform into a crowd of men, women, and children.

Thus ends the consecration of the "soul" of the deer. Certain jicareros gently pull out a few hairs from the tail and place them in their *takwátsi* (a plaited, oblong, covered basket containing all one's shamanic objects). Then everyone shares a modest meal of tostadas, taking care first to give some to the fire and the deer. Now the young people can begin to prepare and cook the deer. After very carefully removing the skin (it is left to dry for about twenty-four hours), they dig one or several pits, depending on the numbers of animals caught, and light a fire within each which they cover with stones. When the stones are red hot the meat is placed on top, with a protective covering of aromatic herbs. Then everything is covered with earth.

Other young people wash the intestines. The heart is reserved for the most highly initiated, thus generally for the adults. They ingest part of the blood from that organ, leaving the rest for upcoming feasts.

Then an interminable chore begins: threading little pieces of meat onto strong *ixtle* (agave cactus) fiber strings in order to dry them. When they are very dry these pieces will bear an uncanny resemblance to the strings of dried peyote, thus reenforcing the symbolic equivalence.

THE RITUAL FULFILLMENT OF THE HUNT: THE "BAPTISM" OF THE *TEKWARI*

The equivalence just referred to is also found in a ritual act common to both the hunt and the peyote pilgrimage: the choosing of a new name. No ritual more resembles a game; none is merrier. Beneath the laughter and the jokes lies the idea of returning to one's origins: in order to find the peyote, to encounter the deer, one must have a pure heart (in particular, free from sexual preoccupations), returning to that state of innocence and openness that characterized most of the great ancestors.

All Huichol mythology considers birth and naming as identical: neither fire nor the sun could warm and light up the world before the people (animals in those days) had been given their names. Every year the hunters revive this principle, as do the peyoteros.

The hunters suggest names for each person, and a discussion ensues. For certain participants up to five names are sometimes proposed before one is agreed upon, which causes great hilarity. The newly baptized person must stand up, with an arrow in his hand. He must dip the arrow in a bottle of purificatory water, turn toward the fire, and sprinkle the water in the four directions. During the journey to the peyote, following the confession, a companion shakes each peyotero over the fire "so that his old name will burn and Grandfather Fire will protect them both" (Benítez 1968:83). In both cases fire, who is the first shaman, has accepted the new name by erasing the old.

Here are some of the names: Waxa Yuri (Maize Field), the name given the xarishi-káme during the present hunt; Muti Werúku for the jicarero of the *namakáte* (difficult to translate; an allusion to the vulture, a bird without feathers, for the man's pants are in shreds!); Muviéri Yuávi (Muviéri with Blue Feathers) for another; Muku Yuávi Muyéika Awatúsa for the mara'akáme's brother-in-law (White Antlers that Travel in the Blue Hill).

As for this Frenchman, he already has three names. No matter what these names may mean in the ironic spirit of the Huichol I am pleased, for to name someone is to cause him to be born, to renew one's knowledge of him. In the village a mischievous old man calls me Werúku Tupíya, Vulture Bow. Do they think I am too thin? Or am I considered a shameless observer who lives only on dead flesh? I found out later that I was mistaken.

During the hunt my companions named me Wérika Niuquiári, The Word of the Solitary Eagle. I swaggered a bit, cooing: "Oh, let's not exaggerate now!" Then a companion explained to me: "You've got *tumíni*,[28] lots and lots of money, many coins. On our coins there's an eagle that swoops down on a snake. We glue them on crosses and votive cups to offer them to the 'gods.'[29] They are like words that we address to the 'gods,' like prayers."

But the name claimed most often by the Frenchman was a common one, Teukári, meaning both Grandfather and Grandson.[30]

Thus the hunting companions and the companions on the hunt for the peyote challenge one another. It is a strong, though provisional, alliance.

Political Problems of the Hunt

These hills where the Huichols hunt, these caves and springs which the ancestors visited in search of fire and knowledge, no longer belong to them. They are part of the land that the Huichol communities have lost, especially during the last forty years. The

Indians have become visitors there, seldom welcome, for when they hunt they do so in contravention of the game protection laws, and they cause inconvenience to the mestizo ranchers and farmers of the neighboring villages. To the latter, the Huichol hunters are nothing but poachers. With the help of the police and the local mestizo authorities, and sometimes also the army, they make the hunters pay dearly for their ritual need for the deer. The groups of hunters know that they must conclude agreements with the mestizo authorities of the villages. They must present themselves, promise not to hunt for more than a couple of days, and only a few animals, and assure that they will pay in case a livestock animal is killed. *Tepe*, a potent, locally brewed agave alcohol, is exchanged to seal the contract. But how much longer can this kind of agreement continue? The mestizo village leaders are afraid of the army (which takes advantage of the marijuana traffic to arrest the hunters and confiscate their guns; this is how little the government still trusts the Indians) and are increasingly reluctant to grant their permission. If the xaurishikáme of the group to which I have devoted the major part of this paper did receive permission, it was because he had a long-standing acquaintance with the mestizo authorities, because he never forgot to offer them part of the meat, and because he did business with them. They even suggested to him that he accept a trade of a two-ton pickup truck for fifteen stud bulls. The deal would principally benefit the mestizos: the bulls would increase in value, whereas the truck, which was not quite new, would quickly depreciate. Still, the offer was a tempting one, and the people of the village knew it. Since the hunters do not have a vehicle they must rent one to get to their destination (about eight hours over unpaved roads). This time they paid 300,000 (old) pesos, which represented one month's wages for an agricultural worker in the region. The costumbre is troublesome, the Huichol often say. Troublesome and expensive, in fact more and more expensive; as we have already said, having political responsibilities is the traditional way to gain prestige while losing money.

In spite of these expenses the hunt went well, thanks to the diplomatic skills of the mara'akáme, and there will be a lot of venison to share for the upcoming Híkuri Néixa feast (the Dance of the Peyote). But how many other hunters will be ejected or imprisoned because they preferred to hide from the mestizo village authorities? These hunters, with some justification, think they are still on their own land. (For ten years now, by presidential decree, there has existed a territory recognized as Huichol, although the "invaders" never bother to worry about it one way or the other.) They consider that the deer are there for them and that they are accountable to no one. Moreover, with the number of deer declining and army repression increasing, fierce competition has been created between indigenous hunting groups. Did not another Huichol group from another community, with the apparent aim of discrediting their competitors, inform the authorities that our group had killed seven deer?

Thus, the Huichols are seen as intruders on this land that has called to them for centuries. But despite the great expenses incurred over the hunt, despite the military repression that extends all the way to San Andrés, in the very heart of the community,[31] the Huichols have such a strong ritual need for deer that they keep returning to these ancestral lands.

Still, one may legitimately wonder whether the deer hunt is not ultimately doomed. Like the territory of the Huichol, the deer have grown scarce. From the earliest colonial days the pasture grounds of the Spaniards have been encroaching on the forests, and thus also on the habitat of the deer. Today, the generalized use of the gun, which has increasingly replaced the net, represents a danger to the reproduction of the species, in that pregnant females are often killed. The ecological balance, which only a few decades ago was still assured, is being upset. The deer must be hunted farther and farther away, and the Huichols are being faced with this dilemma: in order to find their "life" they must hunt the deer, but today the hunt risks the destruction of the very animal that is the source of their joy and their power.

Some people, among them the medical doctor now practicing in the community of San Andrés, look for a provisional solution in rebuilding the deer population in the Sierra Huichol, which might perhaps ultimately eliminate the need to hunt on "foreign" lands. In any event, some sort of regulation seems necessary, but taking the Huichols into account, and not excluding them, as is still too often the case. That way, perhaps the disappearance of Tamáts, Our Elder Brother, can be avoided.[32]

NOTES

1. The Huichol word for deer is *maxa*. Pronunciation varies in different regions from *masha* to *marrsha*. The scientific name is *Odocoileus virginianus*, that is, the white-tailed Virginia deer (Grimes 1981:68).

2. Is it coincidence that the ritual name for the deer among the Aztecs was Chicome-Xochitl, Seven-Flowers?

3. The nieríka ("in which one can see," the idea of the mirror) is at one and the same time a concept and an object. As a concept it is "the power of the supernatural vision" (Negrín 1986; Furst 1978:30–33). As an object it may be of the architectural order—lintels of baked clay, pierced by a central hole and placed near the roof of the *tuki*, the circular communal temple, or the small family temples, *xiriki*, whose high reliefs, carved on both sides of the hole, represent mythological beings. Or it may be of the "artisan" order, although with a religious purpose, consisting of a small bamboo circle from which spokes radiate, like a wheel, with inner circles of yarn or thread. It may also be a mirror or a piece of a mirror. The idea underlying all these forms is that of the hole through which both the ancestors and the shaman can "see."

4. The *muviéri*, a feathered staff in the form of a compound, wooden-tipped arrow with pendant feathers at the nock end, is no doubt the most frequently used of all shamanic objects. Every shaman has several. Covered at one end with pigeon, vulture, or more rarely parrot, falcon, or eagle feathers, such a wand represents at the same time the shamanic dream and the reality of the power it contains, for it is believed to move only when the shaman has been able to "capture" its energy with his chant.

5. The Spanish adjective *delicado* is frequently used by the Huichols to designate everything

that has magical, thus potentially dangerous, power, and which has to be "delicately" rendered harmless by means of the appropriate ritual. (See also, p. 241 this volume.)

6. Kauyumári: the spirit of the deer, and the shaman's favored interlocutor during his nocturnal chant. This is an extremely rich and complex character, as this paper tends to demonstrate. In more classical ethnological terms he would correspond to the trickster-culture hero or hero-deceiver in many North and South American Indian tales.

7. The oldest known example of a Huichol-like "peyote necklace," excavated from a Desert Culture rock shelter site in the Cuatro Ciénegas Basin in northeastern Coahuila, Mexico, has been dated by the Smithsonian Institution between A.D. 810 and A.D. 1070 (Adovasio and Fry 1976:95). Known as CM 79, the site is one of numerous caves and rock shelters occupied by Desert Culture hunter-gatherers on both sides of the Rio Grande and in the Trans-Pecos area of Texas from ca. 11,000 B.C. to ca. A.D. 1000. A surface find of a similar "peyote necklace" was recently reported from an area not far from Rio Grande City, Texas, where adherents of the Native American Church gather peyote for their ceremonies. Its discoverer told one of the editors (S.S.) that it "looked very old" to him. These finds suggest that stringing peyote like deer meat on a fiber cord is an old desert hunter-gatherer custom.(—Eds.)

8. The ejído is defined legislatively in the revolutionary Constitution of 1917. The term refers to non-transferable land, collectively farmed, and held by the peasants in usufruct. In the framework of this constitution an "indigenous community" is defined only as a particular type of ejído.

9. Tamáts Wawatsári: a stag whose antlers have eight tines (Benítez 1968:567). See also Furst 1976:120. Furst's informant, Ramón Medina Silva, identified Elder Brother Wawatsári as the "Principal Deer" and the animal manifestation of the sacred peyote cactus.

10. In spite of my efforts I have not yet found the etymological meaning of this word. However, I hypothesize that there is a connection with *vai*, meat. (—D.L.)

(For more information on the vainuri, see Schaefer (1990: 268-284. [—Eds.])

11. Teakáta, located in a deep gorge only about three or four miles, but many hours' hard walking, west of the ceremonial center of the *comunidad* of Santa Catarina, is rightly described by Lumholtz (1902:169) as "the most sacred locality in the entire Huichol country." It is full of natural caverns and shrines, among which the cave of Great-grandmother Nakawé (Lumholtz's "Grandmother Growth") with its holy spring, and the cave shrine of Grandfather Fire, are the most sacred (Lumholtz 1902:157-179). It was on this exhausting expedition that Lumholtz put the reputation of peyote as a restorative to a test: "Under ordinary circumstances," he writes (p. 177), the plant was nauseating to me; but now, when I was thirsty and tired, I could, rather to my surprise, swallow the cool, slightly acid cuts without difficulty. I found them not only refreshing, quenching thirst and allaying hunger, but also capable, at least for the moment, of taking away any sense of fatigue, and I felt stimulated, as if I had some strong drink." According to T. J. Knab (personal communication), who visited Teakáta in the company of a shaman in the early 1970s, some Huichols are convinced that one of the many caves contains the mummified remains of the deified shaman-chief Maxa Kwaxí.(—Eds.)

12. The traditional *nama* (from the verb *namá*, to cover, to hide) is a rectangular piece of cloth, embroidered with cross-stitch, which is hung on the arrows being offered. Again, Lumholtz has analyzed with great insight Huichol religious art from the beginning of the century (when it was apparently richer than it is today) (Lumholtz 1900:138; Zingg 1938:620-628; Furst 1978:32).

13. The extracts quoted here were taped by myself in the community of San Andrés. Some of them were translated for me by a Huichol *maestro* living in the town of Tepic. Our collaboration continues, but remains insufficient. More than ever the ethnologist needs the linguist in order to disentangle grammatical and syntactic problems that at first seem insurmountable.

14. This Spanish term conveys infinitely more than what is meant in French and English by "custom" or "tradition," and so I have preferred to leave it in Spanish. The Huichol word is *yeiyári*, "the very way."

15. *Pari:* this term would merit study all by itself, for it seems to designate sometimes light, or dawn, sometimes night.

16. The idea that Kauyumári is the word itself was also suggested to me by Juan Negrín.

17. The mara'akáme is not blindly trusted by his companions, and it happens fairly often that someone throws a sarcastic comment at him, such as: "All that is nonsense!" as a preamble to the discussion which is to follow.

18. Information from a mara'akáme from San José.

19. "The little rose," "*la rosita*," is what the Huichol's mestizo neighbors call the peyote, perhaps because of its small, faintly pink flowers. But this is also the translation of the affective word which the Huichol themselves use to denote the "head," the ball which is ready to be eaten: the *tutu*, "the flower itself."

20. The decorated votive bowls, "the most beautiful things that the Huichols make with which to regale their gods" (Zingg 1938:632), both embody the gods and are sacred to them. They are "particularly fitting as an offering to the rain-goddesses," writes Zingg (ibid., p. 635), because the old earth and creator goddess Nakawé caused the bowls to fill with rain. The other deities, too, have their votive gourd bowls. They are clearly among the most important of the sacred paraphernalia. They have the power of communication with, and between, the gods and, says Zingg (p. 635), their great beauty exemplifies Huichols' "emphasis on art in the service of the gods."(—Eds.)

21. In some versions of the tradition of the primordial peyote hunt the guide and singer of the divine ancestor-peyoteros was called Maxa Kwaxí, Deer Tail, in another it was the old fire god, Tatewarí, Our Grandfather.

22. The analysis and understanding of the Huichol conception of the "soul" would clearly require an entire paper, if not a book. As its semantic field differs profoundly from the associations carried by this word in English and French, I have preferred to place it in quotes. See also Perrin's chapter in this volume and P. T. Furst's 1966 essay, "Huichol Conceptions of the Soul."

23. Five being the Huichol's most significant number, the maize has five "official" colors: white, yellow, blue, red, and *pinto*, multicolored. Blue is the most sacred. In actuality, there is also "black" maize.

24. The mara'akáte (the plural form of mara'akáme) believe that they can transform themselves into deer after death. One of them said to me with a smile: "Perhaps my own people will kill me. But my 'soul' won't die!"

25. This replicates a ritual in Wirikúta in which the leading shaman touches the forehead, eyes, cheeks, lips, and throat with the sacred cactus.(—Eds.)

26. *Ta*, our; *téi*, mother (lit. "aunt"), *wérika*, solitary eagle, *'uimari*, young girl. This is a complex being who well illustrates the subtlety of Huichol syncretism, itself very rare. Indeed, it demonstrates masculine (the eagle) and feminine properties simultaneously and mixes indigenous and Christian attributes, for it denotes both the mother of the sun and the Mexican Virgin

par excellence, the "Guadalupana." It is also said that it is the eagle that holds the world in its talons, thus presiding over life and death.

27. According to Zingg (1982, vol. 2:77), the foam on one side was the peyote.

28. *Tumini* is the Wixárika (Huichol) word for money. It is derived from the name of an old Spanish coin and was most likely introduced into the sierra with the arrival of the first settlers and Franciscan missionaries at the beginning of the eighteenth century.

29. Since the abstraction denoted by this word does not exist in the vernacular I have placed it in quotes.

30. Teukári can also mean "godchild." However, in ritual thought and practice there is an obvious reciprocity between grandfather and grandson, indicating a theory of preferential inheritance.

Teukári is also the reciprocal address used among all the participants in a peyote pilgrimage who journeyed together to Wirikúta, which may explain why Lemaistre himself was addressed as teukári. My own fellow peyoteros still affectionately call or refer to me as neteukari. (—S.B.S.)

31. In 1988 twenty-eight rifles ("twenty-two long rifles") were requisitioned by the army and handed over after "payment." This intervention by the army (at the beginning of 1988) led to an official complaint by the community of San Andrés, denouncing the theft, as well as the theft and slaughter of cattle.

32. Some projects along these lines have been initiated in Santa Catarina and San Andrés by the Asociación Jalisciense de Apoyos a Grupos Indígenas (AJAGI). A moratorium, or at least a limit, on hunting deer is said to be under way in Santa Catarina. A sizeable protective corral has been established below the western side of the mesa of San Andrés, stocked with deer brought into the Sierra in the summer of 1993 by AJAGI. The logistics were impressive: the deer were transported in large crates on a DC-3 to the San Andrés airstrip and from there transferred— still in their crates—by an ingenious pulley-tram system down the sheer drop from the mesa to the corral. Huichols often come to the overlook to watch the deer, although the animals, being well-camouflaged, are hard to spot. Huichol women told me they had never seen live deer so close up. (—S.B.S.)

INTRODUCTION TO CHAPTER 11

As noted in Chapter 2, the first written account of inhabitants of the Sierra Madre Occidental identifiable as Huichols is that of Fray Alonso Ponce, dating to 1587. Neither in his report nor in those of later travellers in the colonial period do we find any mention of the large, steep-roofed, circular communal temples found by pioneer ethnographers like Lumholtz, Diguet, and Preuss in all the major indigenous settlements. The Huichol word for the temple is *tuki;* when speaking Spanish to outsiders Huichols commonly call their temple *calihuey,* and inversion of the Nahuatl (Aztec) *uey calli,* big house, which the friars and their Central Mexican vassals introduced into the Sierra languages in the early eighteenth century. The exact meaning of tuki is uncertain, although *ki* by itself means house, as it does in a number of languages that, like Huichol, belong to the Greater Nahua, or Uto-Aztecan, family.

That Spanish descriptions of the subjugation of the Huichol and Cora regions in 1722 mention calihueys, that is, native temples, only for the Cora but not the Huichol area, does not, of course, mean that none existed at that time in the latter even before the founding by the Spanish authorities of the *comunidades indígenas* that together form the present-day Huichol territory. Nor does it mean that prior to 1722 religious activity among the Huichols was limited solely to the extended family rancho or larger ranchería, rather than extending outward into the larger community. Huichol ranchos and rancherías all have their own *xiriki,* the Huichol name for the structure set aside for domestic ritual, ceremonial paraphernalia, representations of different ancestor deities, and above all, as the dwelling of the family guardian spirits called *urukáte* (sing. *urukáme*) (see Chapter 14).

There is reason to believe that like the tuki, the xiriki, now generally rectangular, was formerly round. In fact, the author of this chapter, Stacy Schaefer, reports that she has seen two circular xirikis, one in a ranchería in Las Guayabas, the other on the San Andrés mesa at a rancho where the former rectangular xiriki was torn down and a larger circular one was being constructed in its place. It is perhaps not too much to say, then, that the tuki may be seen as the xiriki writ large. Ruins of circular ceremonial structures exist elsewhere in western Mexico, including the Bolaños valley in northern

Jalisco, and at Ixtlan del Río, Nayarit. The ancient Anasazi kivas were round, and the floor plans of those in New Mexico's Chaco Canyon bear a remarkable resemblance to that of the tuki. Circular ceremonial structures were a hallmark of prehispanic Huastec architecture, and they are visible above ground today even in and near the peyote country in San Luis Potosí to which the Huichols make their sacred pilgrimages. Whether, or how, any of these might relate—other than ideologically—to the circular Huichol temple is unknown.

Admittedly, direct evidence for great time depth for the Huichol temple is scant to non-existent. Zingg (n.d., pp. 68–87) recorded a myth in which the first tuki was constructed in the midst of a smallpox epidemic at the behest of the Sun Father, who threatened to kill all the Huichol children if his command was not obeyed. In some of the myths, smallpox was a disease that originated with the Sun; in fact, this terrible Old World scourge, to which Indian peoples in North and South America fell victim in the hundreds of thousands, if not millions, was introduced in the sixteenth century as a deadly by-product of the European invasion. If there is a historical basis for the Huichol myth of the construction of the first temple, then, it would date its origin no earlier than the colonial era.

Be that as it may, as the following chapter demonstrates, the tuki embraces many meanings and purposes, not least that of solar and lunar observatory. This suggests a long evolution and, perhaps, influences also from outside sources. But more to the point, like sacred architecture in all religions, like the ancient and modern kivas of the Puebloan Southwest, the tuki is above all the architectural model, the physical manifestation, of the Huichols' own vision of the cosmos, and as such grew organically out of their own spiritual and social matrix.

Spanish silence on the subject notwithstanding, the sacred microcosm that is the Huichol temple is deeply embedded and enmeshed in indigenous religious and social consciousness and organization. Thus, whenever it might have come into existence as we see it today, we have to assume centuries of development for the tuki's remarkable ideological complexity and sophistication, much of it hitherto unsuspected, its function as the focus of community and ethnic consciousness and cohesion—in short, its manifold spiritual, symbolic, social, and economic ramification, as these were observed and laid out for the author of the following chapter by her long-time Huichol friends.

Peter T. Furst

11 : THE COSMOS CONTAINED

The Temple Where Sun and Moon Meet

STACY B. SCHAEFER

San Andrés Cohamiata, Jalisco

It was near the time of the total solar eclipse, a celestial drama scheduled to occur around noon on July 11, 1991. Suddenly western Mexico, especially the states of Nayarit and Jalisco, had moved to center stage, for it was this general area that was about to experience the longest period of total darkness—almost seven full minutes. Northwestern Mexico was crowded with tourists and astronomers who had come solely to observe the eclipse.

My own reasons for spending the summer in San Andrés went beyond sky watching. But they did relate to what Huichols see in the heavens, in particular their tracking of the movements of the Sun, and the part—if any—the *tuki*,[1] the circular, thatch-roofed temple of aboriginal Huichol religion (Figure 78) plays in these observations. The Sun is conceived as male, one of the four most important deities in the crowded aboriginal pantheon. The others are Tatewarí, Our Grandfather, the old fire god and, for many Huichols, the premier *mara'akáme* (shaman-singer); the ancient white-haired earth mother and creator goddess, Takutsi Nakawé, and Tatutsi Maxa Kwaxí, Great-grandfather Deer Tail. All figure in major ways in temple symbolism and ceremonial. But the Sun god and his positions in the sky occupy a unique place.

I was again living in the extended family rancho that has been my home over many seasons of field work among the Huichols. Needless to say, the eclipse was much on my mind, and to be able to hear firsthand from my Huichol friends about how they experienced and interpreted it gave it a special dimension. What would be their reactions? How did they explain it? Did they know of it beforehand?

I did not have to wait long for answers. Before I even had the chance to broach the subject with my Huichol family, they brought it up themselves. Was I aware, they asked, of the predictions that a great eclipse would happen very soon? I said yes, I was indeed. But how had they learned of it? The radio, of course. There was much

FIGURE 78. The Temple in the Ceremonial Center of San Andrés, 1967, Framed by Its Associated Xirikis (God Houses). (*Photograph by Peter T. Furst.*)

talk of it over the air, they said. Portable radio cassette players are prized possessions and each rancho usually has at least one in working order. When not playing Mexican cassettes of *corridos, cumbias, mariachis,* or *norteños,* all of which enjoy great popularity among the Huichols (without, however, having affected the indigenous musical style), or their own recordings of traditional Huichol music, the radio is tuned to a favorite Spanish-speaking station, Radio Monterrey.

And there had also been much talk about it among foreigners living in the Sierra, and among the *téiwari* (Sp. *vecinos*, "neighbors," the term by which the indigenous people generally refer to mestizos or non-Indians). The ceremonial and civic center of San Andrés now has a community clinic, with a resident Mexican doctor. The *medico*, I was told, was distributing information on how to protect yourself, especially your eyes, during the eclipse.

I asked my Huichol family if they knew of anyone who remembered past solar eclipses and how the shamans interpreted these events in the sky. One of my compadres, Tukíya, who is close to thirty years old, could not remember any previous eclipse. But he said that the shamans did, and that elders before them had also passed down accounts of earlier eclipses. Tukíya told me that, according to the shamans, Sun, Tau, is a man and Moon, Metsa, a woman. When there is a solar eclipse it is because the sun and the moon are making love. It is a dangerous time, because their lovemaking heats up the earth, crops can dry up, cattle and other animals can die, and the fruit on the trees can spoil.

It appeared, then, that most people in San Andrés knew about the coming eclipse, and that not a few were worried about it. In fact, several people told me afterwards that while it was in progress they had been so alarmed they remained in their houses, making sure their children did not wander out until the sun and moon had finished their union. Several complained of feeling dizzy, and told me of all the roosters that started crowing, and of a dark foreboding wind that came up at that time. There was talk in the countryside surrounding the *mesa* on which the ceremonial center is situated that those who had planted before the eclipse would lose their crops.

Well, I asked, what did the shamans do, did they sing in the tuki? No, Tukíya replied. Most of the temple shamans were not even in San Andrés, because the governor of Nayarit had invited them to Mexcaltitan. Airplanes had come to fly them from the San Andrés airstrip to Tepic, the state capital. From there they were taken by bus to Mexcaltitan, an island entirely covered by a circular town in the lagoon of San Pedro, in the middle of an estuary that feeds into the Pacific Ocean. Here, in Mexcaltitan, a place that some people have—improbably—proposed as the legendary Aztlán, the birthplace of the Aztecs, the eclipse would last the longest. Tourists from around the world had crowded onto the island to witness the eclipse, and the governor, who has been very friendly toward the Huichols, had made them, especially the shamans, the guests of honor.

The eclipse itself was an incredible experience, not least because when the sun began to disappear and the sky became dark, all the domestic animals and the birds started behaving as though night was falling. Before the light returned the roosters really did start to crow, as they usually do before the sun comes up. And there was a strong and sudden wind. As to people's fears of possible doom, I was told that when it was all over and everyone had returned to their Sierra communities to settle down to the numerous tasks of the rainy season, people found that the maize of those who did plant before the eclipse, the tender young seedlings that had just begun to emerge from the earth, was being ravaged by worms. In fact, every day following the eclipse members from different ranchos would come to our rancho and the ceremonial center, terribly upset because their maize crop was being destroyed. From all appearances, the plague had reached epidemic proportions, both on the mesa and in the *barrancas*. As I was getting ready to leave San Andrés, the last I heard was that the shaman in charge of the San Andrés tuki was going to conduct a ceremony in the temple, to sing to the gods and seek their counsel and guidance in divining why the worms had come, and what people had to do to resolve this great calamity.

The above sets the stage for getting some grasp on Huichol culture at the beginning of the 1990s, and Huichol philosophy about the nature of life, or at least as much understanding as I have been able to achieve during field research that has now extended over a dozen years (and that I fully intend will continue into the indefinite future). The major beliefs and practices that constitute the foundation for Huichol culture and identity, past and present, are laid out not only in the rich oral traditions, the ancestral myths the Huichols call, in Spanish, their *historias*, and in the rituals, but within their tukis. The intertwining of ancient knowledge and modern technology, of multicultural boundaries with sacred time and space, of Huichol traditions and western ways, are pervasive paradoxes in contemporary Huichol culture.

Balancing such extremes requires a strong sense of cultural identity that comes from experiencing, from learning the beliefs and practices that are the essence of Huichol culture. According to Huichol cosmology, the center of the universe, the navel from which life enters the world, lies within the tuki, the temple. Its interior arrangement, vertical and horizontal, mirrors the indigenous cosmos and, in turn, is its model. Contained within the physical structure of this microcosm lies the social structure of the lives of the temple members, past and present, linking them to the deities and the other worlds. Much like the kiva in the Puebloan Southwest, the tuki, then, becomes a kind of terrestrial/celestial stage where the ancient customs and beliefs are constantly re-kindled, are brought to life by means of the major rituals of the annual ceremonial cycle, in order to meet the needs of the contemporary participants and deal with the challenges they may have to face in the future. I should mention that here in San Andrés, in contrast to some other parts of the Huichol territory, the religious, ceremonial, and social structure of the native temples, and their crucial functions in the maintenance of the indigenous ideology and identity, have survived fundamentally intact. Change is inevitable, and there are signs and portents of it all around, even in the kin-based temple cargo system. But as of now, at least in San Andrés, there is reason to hope that the vitality of the native temples and the religion and world view they represent will not soon succumb.

When referring to the entire temple compound, including the sacred ground occupied by the tuki itself, the ceremonial space surrounding it, and the several *xiriki*, small family temples or oratories, or, to use Lumholtz's term, "god houses," that are usually associated with a tuki (Figure 79), Huichols use the term *tukipa*. One or more of the small ancestor god houses, rectangular now but reported to have been oval or round in times past, are also an essential feature of most of the widely scattered extended family ranchos and larger rancherías that characterize the Huichol settlement pattern (Figure 93). The xirikis may be dedicated to particular deities and/or to ancestor spirits, who, in their physical manifestations as unworked rock crystals or small colored stones, are revered as *urukáme*, from *'uru*, arrow. The name derives from the fact that the miniature sacred bundle containing the ancestor stone is attached to a compound bamboo and hardwood prayer arrow modeled on the hunting arrow (see Perrin, Chapter 14, this volume).[2]

God houses that function in association with tuki ceremonies may or may not be kept in good repair during ordinary times, and some have a decidedly temporary look.

GOD HOUSES

FIGURE 79. Artist's View of the San Andrés Temple Layout. (*Drawing by Nancy Moyer.*)

Occasionally, they may even be without walls. On the ranchos, however, the xirikis are constructed of the same materials as the ordinary nuclear family dwellings, and, except for certain special features not immediately apparent to the outsider, such as animal designs scratched into or modeled onto an adobe brick or a gable stone with an entry and exit hole for the gods in its center, are outwardly often indistinguishable from them. In any event, these ancestor-god houses are of central importance to Huichol ceremonial life, playing the same role on the extended family, or rancho, level as do the tukis for the temple district. Indeed, where the wider temple organization has disintegrated and/or the tukis have fallen into disuse, or are not readily accessible to a local group (especially those that have moved outside the Huichol territory proper), it is the xirikis that function in their place as sacred spaces to convoke all the deities to come and participate in the ritual event.

Tukis and tukipas, the indigenous temples and their surrounding sacred grounds and associated god houses, are scattered throughout the Huichol part of the Sierra Madre Occidental. Some have even sprung up in recent years outside the Huichol region proper to serve the needs of people who have emigrated from the Sierra communities and are making their lives in rural or urban settings. There are some Catholic mission churches, too, but tukis continue to function as major ceremonial centers for the various family lineages residing in the region. Interestingly enough, certain crucial features of the tuki interior, such as a center emergence hole dedicated to native deities and filled with prayer arrows and other offerings, have been added to some of the old churches, in an effort to assimilate them to Huichol cosmology.

There are five major functioning tuki compounds in the San Andrés region. The temple of San Andrés is located in the ceremonial center itself. Huichols know it as the tukipa of Tunuaméi, the Morning Star. To the west lies the temple of Las Guayabas, the tuki of the rain serpent, Kuyuwananéime. Cohamiáta (a modified Nahuatl place name dating from the early eighteenth century, when this and the other *comunidades indígenas* were established, probably from pre-existing temple district communities made up of clans), is located to the east and is called Tseriakáme, tuki of the rattlesnake. To the south is Las Pitáyas, which Huichol call Ulu (Uru) tzutúa, the place where the first brazil trees, and the ceremonial arrows and the governing staffs made from their red-colored wood, appeared. According to the myth, these trees rose from the blood of the old earth and creator goddess Takutsi Nakawé when, in the mythological First Times, she—herself a great transforming shaman—went underground to escape being killed by male shamans intent on appropriating her great powers. The tuki of San José, Ta Werikua, named after the Sun's bird, the eagle, and known as the temple of the sun, is located north of San Andrés.

The San José tuki is where, over a period of five years, I participated in many of the temple ceremonies. This included accompanying the members of this tuki on their peyote pilgrimage to Wirikúta. Although each temple has its own distinct characteristics, in construction as well as the performance of ceremonies, San José is the most unique of all the temple districts, for there are actually two temples here, one for the Hikuri Neixa (Dance of the Peyote) ceremony, held in May or June (Figures 80, 81), the other, smaller one, for Tatéi Neixa, Dance of Our Mother.[3] The latter, usually observed around October, is focused on the children up to the age of five, whom the officiating shaman magically transforms into little birds and leads, in chant and to the beat of his drum, to the Land of Dawn and the deer/peyote in the east. These youngest Huichols are represented by the first squashes and other new fruits of the fields.[4]

Not far away from San José lies a major complex of shrines for the gods, Taupa, from *tau*, sun, so called because this is the sun's birthplace in the Sierra. All the temple members go there to leave offerings to calm the sun when the rainy season is upon them. The Sun god also has a very sacred birthplace in Wirikúta, the consecrated land of the peyote three hundred miles to the east. This, the Land of Dawn, is where, ac-

FIGURE 80. Larger of the Pair of Temples at San José. (*Photograph by Stacy B. Schaefer.*)

FIGURE 81. Hikuri Neixa, the Peyote Dance, in Front of the San José Temple, 1986.
(*Photograph by Stacy B. Schaefer.*)

cording to the solar myth, the Sun, having sacrificed himself as a young boy in the west, traveled underground from the western side of the world to the east, to be reborn in a fiery eruption from a now extinct volcano, known in Huichol as Rau'unár and in Spanish as Cerro Quemado, Burned Mountain.[5]

Over the years I have been most involved in the San José temple group, where my weaving teacher and her husband, who are also my *compadres*, were fulfilling the cargo of Uru Kuakáme, the Keeper of the Temple. But I have also participated in ceremonies at the temples of San Andrés, Cohamiáta, and Guayabas.

Together with their families, the most knowledgeable women and men who befriended me and agreed to share their knowledge have been involved in the San Andrés temple for many generations. They include one family in which the father is a *kawitéro*.[6] Ideally, the kawitéro is an elder renowned for esoteric knowledge, wisdom, and experience accumulated over time; in most cases, but not all, kawitéros are also shamans. Nowadays, however, younger men of special qualities may also become kawitéros.

This kawitéro's wife, his eldest daughter, herself a shaman, and his younger daughter Kuka helped orient me to the multiple dimensions that make the tuki what it is. Another compadre of mine, who has completed not just one but several five-year temple cargos, answered many of my questions by means of diagrams he drew on the ground. With his mother, my compadre Tukíya (who was himself fulfilling the cargo once held by his father, Kewimúka) patiently explained the complexities and meanings associated with the temple traditions in conversations that extended over a period of four years. Tukíya's mother is also a shaman and singer of the sacred chants.

According to the origin myths — and there are several versions of each of these — construction of the first tuki required the cooperation of all the gods. The temple myth collected by Zingg (n.d., p. 70) relates how the first tuki was to be constructed. In the first times the Huichols traveled to the western ocean to learn the will of the mighty gods. The people called the greatest shaman-singer, Grandfather Fire, Tatewarí, to advise them. He emerged

> from the fire, blazing in all of his pomp of costume and feathers. Then he sat in the shaman's chair and drank sacred water. This calmed him. After singing all night he revealed what the gods had said to him as he sang. "If you do not accept the command of Father Sun, your children, crops, animals, and everything will die." The people retorted, "This command is very harsh." They had to discuss it among themselves. They decided that they would have to accept the command of the Sun father. So they began to fulfill his desires. They cleared a dancing-patio, and in this erected a dwelling for the Sun father and for Grandfather Fire.

The myth goes on to relate how Kauyumári, the culture hero, chief assistant to Tatewarí (and, by extension, to all shaman-singers when they officiate at the ceremonies) and divine messenger between the gods and the people, was asked to oversee the construction of the first temple, using the feather wands of Tatewarí to communicate with the fire god and the Sun Father:

> (The people) dug and took out building stones with which to make the walls of the temple. Others were sent to kill deer and javelinas (peccary).[7] Still others, at the command of the Sun, had to offer sheep. Others had to collect twenty-eight votive bowls. And others, twenty-eight ceremonial arrows and front and back shields, etc., for hanging on the arrows.
>
> The earth goddess, Utuanáka, ordered cavities to be made in the walls for all of the gods, and in the cavities, offerings of an arrow and votive bowl for each specific god were to be placed so that all the gods "could look out on the world" and "listen."[8]

Although Huichol temples are focused primarily on Fire and Sun, as sacred spaces they welcome all of the gods and, through the shaman-singer, call upon them for help and guidance. Tukis are rebuilt every five years, from the ground up. Each time this is done, the new cargo holders of the temple recreate the original temple as it is laid out in the origin myths, thus establishing anew the ordering of the cosmos, the deities, and the newly initiated temple members. The leading shaman of the temple and the kawitéros sing and dream who will be the new temple members to take over the next five-year religious cargos. The selection of people for these positions is largely determined by the cargos held by past family members. Huichols firmly believe that it is up to the living to continue the religious responsibilities their kin have completed generation after generation.

In March 1987 I was present for the rebuilding of the new temple of San Andrés. Coinciding as it does with the initiation of the new temple cycle of all the temple districts belonging to this community, the event also marks a major turnover in the powers of those who would lead the ceremonies for the next five-year cycle. In the past, San Andrés itself was essentially just a ceremonial center, largely deserted except for the times when Huichols came to perform ceremonies related to the temple, the community at large, the annual changing of the staffs and the government offices they stand for, or the major Catholic ceremonies introduced in the colonial era. Over the past decade or two, however, the center of San Andrés has gradually taken on the appearance of a pueblo. More and more Huichols from the San Andrés area are building adobe or brick houses around the traditional government houses near the main dirt plaza, and reside there for months at a time, rather than only on ceremonial occasions. Stores are also cropping up, but only a few of these are open regularly on a daily basis. As the community continues to grow, the former distance between the temple and the residential structures is diminishing. Because of this, the ceremonies at the San Andrés temple are usually well attended by those who have cargo as well as those who do not.

The ritual was essentially the same for each temple membership. Before the new temple members could begin their cargos, the roof of the tuki, which measured between thirty and forty feet across, was removed and the soaring roof support posts and adobe walls were torn down. After the temple had been reduced to a circle of jumbled stones and adobe bricks, various animals were sacrificed and there was a ritual exchange of food, the native maize beer called *nawá* (elsewhere known by the Nahuatl-derived term *tesgüíno* or *tejüíno*), distilled alcohol, tobacco, and offerings passed from the old temple members to the new. All the feasting was done within the circle of the crumbling wall.

The newly appointed shaman in charge, called Saulízika, gathered his congregation together, as he does for all the major ceremonies.[9] In his chant he called upon his spirit helper, Kauyumári, to help oversee the construction and the proper placement of the new temple in the center of the three worlds of the Huichol universe, divide the temple into two halves to establish the rainy and dry seasons, and unite the four other temple groups within the cardinal directions in the interior of the sacred circle of the temple. To me, the division of the temple interior into dry and rainy season halves strongly suggests a former moiety system in Huichol social organization.[10]

To properly measure off the three layers of the Huichol universe, Saulízika now sings to Kauyumári to help him locate the sacred trees, usually, though not always, pines. These will, in the manner of the cosmic axis, hold up the roof, which is the metaphorical upperworld. The temple group leaves for the woods, ritually cuts the designated trees, and carves them into two tall posts and a cross beam. With these preparations complete, the builders can begin the construction of their microcosm.

Hixuápa: The Middle World

The middle world, the world of the living, is laid out in a circle with large unworked stones that serve as base for the adobe brick wall. In reconstructing the walls, the cargo members spatially arrange their places within the temple according to the order of the deities in the Huichol pantheon. Every temple cargo holder has charge of a particular deity and must care for him or her during the entire five-year period. Each deity has his or her special place in the temple, and just as it was done in the temple origin myth, cargo holders carve out crypts or niches and bury within the interior wall a votive arrow, a decorated gourd bowl, a carved image of maize, and a stone that is the deity itself.[11]

In contrast to all the other offerings, which are made anew for every five-year cycle, these stones, which Huichols consider to be the gods, are passed down from cargo holder to cargo holder. My friend and consultant Kuka told me about the origin of one of these divine stones. In times past in the rainy season there was a period when the rain did not want to fall, threatening the community with drought and famine. It was already August and sometimes more than three weeks would go by without a drop of rain. Then her great grandfather, Juan Carrillo, a leading mara'akáme who has become a legend in the region,[12] looked to see what could be done to make it rain, so that the *milpa* would not dry up.

"For me it was an incredible thing," Kuka said. "My grandfather concentrated all of his faith and power and from far away clouds came rushing in and it began to rain very hard. And when he concentrated his power in his *muviéri*, lightning struck and a rock appeared. It was the rain god Nu'ariwamei. This is the stone, and it is still in the tuki, the one that my great grandfather caught."[13]

The muviéri, I should explain, is a specialized shaman's wand or power stick, consisting of a compound arrow with a bundle of feathers attached to the neck end, which the shaman holds by the long, slender point of dark red brazil wood.

Inside the temple, the location of each god is marked with deer antlers that protrude from the wall. During the ceremonies, which often last several days or longer, every cargo holder and the members of his family reside under the antlers signifying the deity whom they represent.

Along the west side of the interior wall, a new ceremonial shelf or altar, known in Huichol as *niwetári*, has to be made. I have seen two kinds of these altars. One consists of long, flat pieces of cane (*Arundo donax*) that are tied together with fibers and raised off the ground by wooden posts, forming a *mesa*, or table. The altar in the San Andrés temple was made of rocks and mortar. It started from the ground and reached upward in several successive tiers, rather like a stepped pyramid. According to Tukíya, this is a more ancient style, and functions in the manner of a stairway up to the sky. This stairway in the temple, he said, is the stairway that the sun climbs on it's journey across the sky (for a small wooden model of a stepped, pyramidlike "stairway of the Sun" that was once part of a prayer offering deposited at Teakáta, see Figure 15).[14]

Taheitüa: The Underworld

Just as it is in the Hopi or Anasazi kiva, the world below is linked to the middle world through openings dug into the dirt floor. But where the kiva has one central emergence hole, called *sipapú* in Hopi, the tuki has several (Figure 82). Beneath the altar is a hollowed-out cavity that, I was told, is meant for the deity of the western sea, Tatéi (Our Mother) Haramára, who receives the setting sun. During the ceremonies, the two men who have the cargo of musicians will sit beneath the altar and play their violin and guitar. Their music supplements certain parts of the shaman's song after he has finished a cycle and the cargo members circle the temple and temple compound. According to Tukíya, when Saulízika is singing and the musicians answer him back with the same melody and rhythm, they do so because through their music they have the same capacity to "guide" the sacred fire, Tatewarí, as Saulízika himself (Figure 83). Dancing often accompanies the music, especially during the ceremony called Hikuri

TEMPLE - INTERIOR VIEW

FIGURE 82. Artist's Rendering of the Principal Shaman, His Assistants, and Musicians Conducting a Ceremony. In front of the shaman is the sacred hole that, like the shaman himself on such occasions, is called Tunuamei (Venus). The emergence hole of Tatewarí, Grandfather Fire, is located beneath the hearth. (*Drawing by Nancy Moyer.*)

Neixa (*híkuri*, peyote, *Lophophora williamsii*; *neixa*, dance, fiesta), whose purpose it is to prepare the soil for planting and to call upon the rain.

In front of the altar and the musicians is a squared-off and hollowed-out wooden bench, like a long and narrow trough turned upside down. This is the *taríma*, a kind of foot drum, upon which the temple members step and literally dance out a syncopated beat to accompany the musicians.[15] In three of the temples where I have participated in the Hikuri Neixa ceremony I've noticed that there are always some temple members who take the dancing especially to heart, leading and encouraging others to give their utmost to the dance. After all, as Kuka pointed out to me, the foot stamping dance is done for the benefit of the gods, to awaken them so that they may come and participate and answer the prayers of the temple members.

FIGURE 83. Musicians Playing in Their Customary Place Beneath the Niwetári (Altar) during the Peyote Ceremony, Hikuri Neixa, in the San José Temple. (*Photograph by Stacy B. Schaefer, June 1988.*)

In front of the wooden foot drum, between the twin axis mundi that holds up the roof, is another sacred hole (Figure 84). Known as Tunuamei, it is named after the shaman in charge of the ceremonies. Although the cargo for this shaman is called Saulízika, when he chants for the ceremonies there is a change of names. He becomes Tunuamei, the name that is also applied to the planet Venus. Assisted by two other men who sit at either side and repeat the verses of his song, the shaman-singer is guided through his nocturnal vigil into the other world by Venus. Tunuamei sings directly into the hole at his feet as he follows the Sun god on his nocturnal journey from west to east through the underworld.

Residing in this cavity are some three-dimensional images that are specially made for this purpose. During one of the temple ceremonies I had the opportunity of getting a good look at one of them, because a child from my family's rancho had taken it out to play with. The image was a simple wooden carving of Takutsi Nakawé, the old earth and creator goddess, recognizably female and wearing a miniature skirt. When the participants in the ceremony saw the little image among the children, Saulízika, the presiding shaman, gently took it from them and, chuckling to himself, put it back in the hole. (I could not help but note, on this as on other ceremonial occasions, the good-natured tolerance and good humor of Huichols toward behavior that in our own culture would be considered sacrilege). Other images deposited in the cavity are of

FIGURE 84. José Carrillo, a San Andrés Huichol. Employed by the Instituto Nacional Indigenista as grade school teacher, he (*standing left*) explains the symbolism of the sacred hole for Tunuamei (Venus, covered by stone disk), into which the premier temple shaman, in his role as the Morning Star, narrates in song the Sun's nocturnal journey through the Underworld. (*Photograph by Peter T. Furst, 1967.*)

Tatewarí, the personified fire; Paritsika, who is associated with the birth of the sun and deer hunting, and who generally functions as the spirit master of game; and Kariwarí, a deity of water and rain. When not in use, the hole is covered with a circular disk of volcanic tufa. This disk, called *tepári*, is decorated with incised deer and eagle images, the insignia of Saulízika.[16]

A third sacred, sipapu-like hole, for Tatewarí, is located beneath the central hearth, which consists of a circular bed of dirt and ashes raised half a foot from the floor (Figure 84, lower left). This hole, *mawatisawa*, is quite deep, around eighteen inches. It is difficult to spot because it is covered not only with another stone disk but with ashes from the fire. Tatewarí's hole contains offerings of wooden or clay figurines of deer, cattle, and other animals, made by individual cargo holders to represent the property of their families and their prayers for successful deer hunts. Decorated with snake designs, Tatewarí's tepári is only removed every five years, when the temple roles change, and the contents made by the old cargo members are replaced with those of the new, to rest within the hole beneath the sacred fire throughout the new five-year cargo cycle. Tukíya and his mother explained all this to me, adding that "when one eats peyote, he or she will look where the fire is, will look where Saulízika's hole is, and will see the clay figurines as if they were alive, dancing between the flames or in the flickering shadows of the fire in front of Saulízika. The fire is no longer fire, it is Tewátzi, which is the animal form of Tatewarí that watches over all of the animals." Here, then, it is Tatewarí, the old fire god and First Shaman-Singer, who, manifesting himself in animal form, is the Owner and Guardian of animal species, a familiar figure in the religions of hunting societies.

Tahéima: The Upper World

The world below the floor is connected to the upper world by the two large, freshly cut pine logs that, standing at either side and slightly back of the central fireplace, support the solid crossbeam (Figure 85). Pine trees are trees of the rain gods. Because of their height, in a thunderstorm they are some of the first to be struck by lightning. Not surprisingly, then, these posts are associated with rain and conceived as lightning rods to bring down the much desired rain. In the temple they represent the major rain gods Nu'ariwaméi and Kevimúka.

Facing into the temple, the post on the left is Nu'ariwaméi, the god of lightning and thunder who comes from the east. Facing out, toward the east and the rising sun, as the shaman and his assistants do when conducting the ceremonies, this post is of course on the right. According to a Huichol myth, Nu'ariwaméi was once a young boy who was always cranky and getting into trouble. His mother finally had enough and angrily yelled at him to get out of the house. Nu'ariwaméi was hurt and greatly saddened by his mother's treatment. Through his tearful wanderings, he ended up near Tatéi Matiniéri, Where Our Mothers Dwell, the sacred water holes that are one of the last, and most

FIGURE 85. Divine Male and Female Balance in Temple Architecture. The two tall pine posts support the roof beam of the San Andrés tuki. Seen from the doorway the post at left (but to the right when facing east from the shaman's position in the interior) is male, representing the god of thunder and lightning, Nu'ariwaméi, who lives in the east. The one to the right is the rain goddess, Kewimúka, who comes from the west. (*Photograph by Peter T. Furst, Spring 1967.*)

important, of the stopping places on the way to the peyote country. Here he decided to remain. Meanwhile, his mother became very worried and sent Nu'ariwaméi's brother, Waxa Temaikü, to search for him. At last he came upon his sibling in Tatéi Matiniéri and convinced him to return home. Nu'ariwaméi, however, was still very angry at his treatment and determined to exact vengeance. He insisted that before he would agree to return home, his brother had first to go home himself and plant a pine and four other kinds of trees. Five days later Nu'ariwaméi followed, by way of the sky with thunder and lightning bolts, which he shot down with his bow and arrows and spat from his mouth. He struck the pine and other trees. When his mother saw him coming in this terrible way she ran to take cover. But Nu'ariwaméi struck her with his fury. As the story goes, whenever the rainy season begins, Nu'ariwaméi is one of the first to arrive with his thunder and lightning (for another version, recorded in 1907 by Preuss, see Chapter 4, this volume).

The post on the right side, facing in, is Kewimúka, a rain goddess who lives in the west. She has a much gentler temperament and brings steady rain. When Tukíya had the five-year cargo of this goddess, he told me, he had visited her on several occasions in her sacred place, which is on the Nayarit side of the Sierra, near the Cora com-

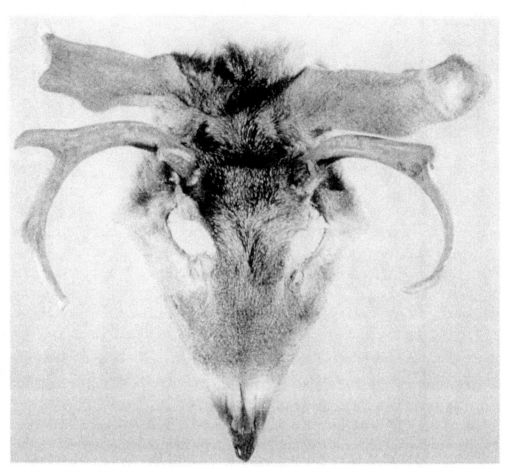

FIGURE 86. Deer Mask. Huichols place deer masks inside the temple as prayer offerings for luck in hunting and rain, and to confirm the presence of the sacred deer at the temple ceremonies. (*Photograph by Peter T. Furst.*)

munity of Mesa de Nayar. There he left offerings in behalf of all the cargo members, along with those Saulízika had instructed him to make for himself. These included small carved pieces of wood decorated with colored wool yarn and pieces of cotton to represent rainbows. However pretty these may appear, Huichols do not look favorably upon rainbows or consider them beneficial, because they signify that the sun is keeping back the rain to nourish their crops. Also according to Tukíya, the two posts take on the appearance of snakes, the animal form of the rain goddesses, and, according to Tukíya, that is how they appear to people whenever they eat peyote in the temple. Kewimúka becomes the rattlesnake, *raye*, which represents the dry season. Nu'ariwaméi turns into the benevolent blue corn snake, the *haiku* of the rainy season.

Tied around these posts are numerous dried deer masks that reflect successful hunts of the temple members. The presence of the deer masks enables the souls of the deer to be present for the ceremonies (Figure 86). They also serve as offerings by the cargo holders for luck in deer hunting and in bringing the rain. Farther up the pine posts notches are carved to sustain the center beam, which, placed crosswise, serves as the apex of the building. Between the two posts, which are secured in place with long sections of reed, is the center of the frame of the roof. Long poles that form a circle radiate out from this center point and slope down to touch the top of the temple walls. The spokelike arrangement of the poles is mirrored in the central hearth below, in the way the logs are placed for the ceremonial fire.

Reeds are crossed over the poles and secured in place. The roof itself is made of dry grass. Rebuilding and thatching are community efforts. When the time comes for the thatching, the cargo holders arrive from distant locations, carrying large bundles of dried grass across their backs or on the backs of their mules and donkeys. Climbing up the open framework of the roof and standing side by side they pass the long reeds through and then, beginning at the bottom and ending at the top, tie the grass in bunches, overlapping like shingles until every inch of the framework is covered.

Laying the Cardinal Directions: Social Bonding Among the Tukis

Once the roof is finished, the recently chosen temple members from the four other major temples come to participate in the inauguration of each new temple and its cargo members.

In the inauguration of the central tuki, each temple group places its gifts and the prayers represented by the offerings within the interior thatch of the roof on the side corresponding to the geographical location of its own temple. The offerings from Las Guayabas are placed in the western portion of the roof, Cohamiáta in the eastern part, Las Pitayas in the south, and San José in the north. The fifth direction, the center, is reserved for the San Andrés temple itself. The offerings consist of five special kinds of plants. Palm fronds, pine branches, a special grass used as a bed to receive the body of recently killed deer and also newborn Huichol children, and the branches of a plant called *háisi*, are hung in the roof. The fifth plant, *taukawuwu*, is a species of vine said to represent the souls of the cargo holders. Added to these plants are a votive gourd bowl, arrow, and candle, indicating the five directions of the temples and of the world.[17] All five plants are bound together with two ropes made of twisted palm fiber that run the length and width of the roof and intersect in the center (Figure 87).[18]

The uniting of the ropes also signifies the uniting of the temple members, and when everything has been placed securely in the roof, everybody prays while circling the temple with candles to the sound of violin and guitar music. The women circle first, carrying their votive bowls of the gods, for which they are caretakers. Their husbands, in turn, carry the prayer arrows. The men also make special arrows to which they tie bundles of the powerful sacred tobacco (*Nicotiana rustica*). A kind of throwing contest takes place in which temple members throw the arrows into the air toward the roof, while their counterparts on the other side are expected to catch them. After the to-

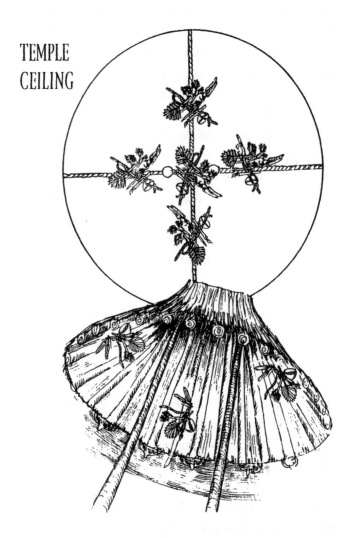

TEMPLE CEILING

FIGURE 87. Artist's Rendering of Offerings of Five Sacred Plants. Tied beneath the interior roof, each plant has its own symbolic and directional associations to the cardinal points and the sacred center. The plants are bound together with two palm fiber ropes that mark off the world quarters. (*Drawing by Nancy Moyer.*)

bacco and arrows are tossed, balls of maize flour, tortillas, and tamales are tossed across the opposite cardinal points, a ritual that cannot help but recall the ritual ball games of North and Middle America.

While all the temples are ritually united within the interior of the roof of each temple, the bonding goes much deeper, for it is also the joining together of all of the temple members who have the same five-year cargo. Saulízika and his wife from San Andrés are ritually tied with the Saulízikas and their wives from the four other temples. The cargo holder who plays the violin is bonded with the violin playing cargo members of the other temples. The same holds true for the temple member who plays the guitar, and all of the others holding temple cargos. They cement these ties with their counterparts from the other temples by the ceremonial exchange of food, nawá (the native maize beer), and distilled alcohol.

Throughout the five-year period they use the Spanish term *compañero* when referring to their counterparts, as well as when they address them directly. Literally, the term means "companion," but used in this ritual way it has deeper connotations, something on the order of "soul mate," or "soul brother."

The bonding between the cargo holders that is symbolized by tying the rope together in the temple roof, or the exchanging of food and drink, has a more profound dimension: not only the cargos and their holders are intimately bound together but the very soul stuff of the temple members and their counterparts is linked in a metaphysical compact of shared destiny. Thus, if some illness or other misfortune befalls one of the cargo holders, his or her corresponding compañeros from the other temples are subject to the same danger.[19] That the individuals concerned treat this concept of shared destiny with their counterparts with extreme seriousness is illustrated by the following incident:

In 1988, the Cohamiáta temple member with the cargo of Uru Kuakáme, the keeper of the temple and the sacred offerings, suddenly died two days after returning from the deer hunt in which he and his temple members had participated. Word spread that he had accidently shot a wolf, and that this wolf came back to take revenge and killed him. The husband of my weaving teacher, Utsíma, had the same cargo in the San José temple. He, and his counterparts in the San Andrés, Las Pitayas, and Las Guayabas temples, were extremely worried for their own welfare after the death of their compañero from Cohamiáta, because they themselves were about to set out on the deer hunt for their own temple group, and feared that the wolf would come for them just as he had done for their compañero from Cohamiáta (for Huichol conceptions of the wolf as shamanic power source, see Eger Valadez, Chapter 9, this volume).

Compañeros: The Rainy and Dry Season Families

The cargo members, like their counterparts in the other temples, are organized in the same manner within their perspective temples. Their positions are defined according to the gods for whom they are caretakers. The major cargo temple members must fulfill is the one their parents, grandparents, and lineage ancestors held and passed down through the family line. So, for example, a temple member fulfilling the above-mentioned cargo of Uru Kuakáme is chosen for this duty because his or her parents completed the same religious obligation in the past. Temple cargos, then, are kin-based. Families associated with a particular temple pass down the cargo roles from one generation to the next. In the majority of cases, those who are completing temple cargos for their family were once playmates during the ceremonies, and helped their parents or other close kin complete the same cargo they now hold.[20]

Just as temple members are organized on a temporal level, so, too, are they arranged

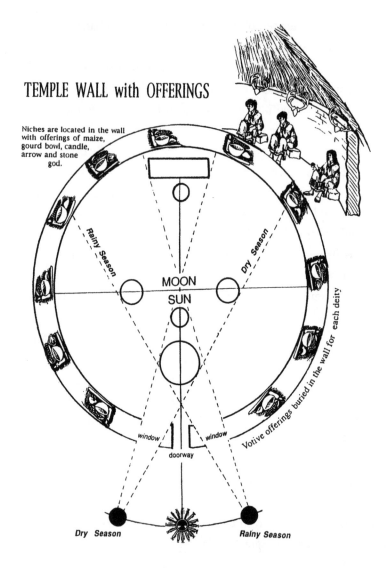

TEMPLE WALL with OFFERINGS

Niches are located in the wall
with offerings of maize,
gourd bowl, candle,
arrow and stone
god.

Rainy Season

Dry Season

MOON
SUN

Votive offerings buried in the wall for each deity

window   window
doorway

Dry Season   Rainy Season

FIGURE 88. Circular Floorplan with Niches along Interior Wall with Offerings to the Deities.
The two halves "belong" to Sun and Moon. The east-west axis separates the temple into rainy
season, *left*, and dry season, *right*. (*Drawing by Nancy Moyer.*)

spatially. This is reflected inside the temple in their physical placement along the circular temple wall (Figure 88). The individual cargo members and their families take their places beneath the deer antlers that mark the spot of the respective deity of whose care they have charge. In the past, cargo holders would also indicate their designated places by making designs in the wall that represent their specific gods. A bull, for example, was the insignia for Ta Werikúa, the sun god, pine tree designs marked the locations of Kewimúka and Nu'ariwaméi, the rain deities. In the San José temple, during the five-year cargo cycle in which I participated, I stayed in the temple with Utsima and her husband, who had the cargo of Uru Kuakáme. They were the only cargo members who had carved designs in the adobe walls. The drawings were of deer and stick figure hunters. These simple but powerful designs by twentieth century Indian people could not help but remind one of those made fifteen and more thousand years ago by people who might have been similarly motivated by the spiritual forces at work when hunter and prey confront one another.

The temple members are arranged in the temple into two groups, the dividing line being the east-west axis between the doorway, which always faces east, and the altar. According to Tukíya's mother, the two major deities presiding over the right-hand sphere are Paritzika, the god of the hunt and spirit guardian of animals, and Haramára, the goddess of the ocean. Other deities with important roles are Tatewarí, Grandfather Fire; 'Utuanáka, the goddess of the earth-ready-for-planting; Ta Werikúa, the sun god; Eka Tewari, the wind god; and Xuxu Weri, who along with Eka Tewari is in charge of the fire during the ceremonies. On this side of the temple stands the pine post of Kewimúka, the rain deity of the west. The two major cargo holders who orchestrate the other members on this side are Saulízika, the shaman-singer of the temple, and Uru Kuakáme, the primary caretaker of the temple and the sacred offerings. All of the gods and their corresponding temple members on this side represent the dry season.

I became aware of this ordering of status when a conflict arose during the Semana Santa (Holy Week) ceremony in the center of San Andrés. The individual who held the cargo El Segundo, the second to the governor in the hierarchical community government, was angry because outsiders had gone on the pilgrimage with one of the temple groups, especially, one photographer. In the middle of the Holy Week ceremonies, when the temple members known in Spanish as the *peyoteros*—those who have gone on the peyote hunt—presented themselves and a sacred candle to the tribal government, the Segundo suddenly stopped their ritual and demanded that the *topiles* (bailiffs, from the Nahuatl *topilli*, Sp. *alguaciles*) arrest the peyoteros who had assumed the identity of Uru Kuakáme and Saulízika, and the photographer. They were duly taken into custody, and all were forced to spend time in the community jail. Like the other cargos of the civil-religious hierarchy, from the governor on down, the topiles, who, as they did in this instance, function as a native police force, date back to the Spanish colonial era.

After the dry season comes the rainy season, the other half of the yearly cycle. The rainy season is represented by the deities and their cargo holders on the left side of the temple. The two prominent gods in the temple for the rainy season, according to Tukíya's mother, are Tatutsi Maxa Kwaxí, Great-grandfather Deer Tail (whom some Huichols consider to have been the first singing shaman in the Huichol world, while others assign that role to Tatewarí), and Tunuaméi, the planet Venus. Other major ancestor deities on this side include Takutsi, the Great-grandmother and goddess of creation; Xapauviyéme, the goddess of Lake Chapala; and Itsu wa'uiya, literally meaning the wife tied to the staff of power. This is the caretaker of the temple's own brazilwood staff of power in the community government. Then there are Ha Keli, the messenger god who is often represented by a young child wearing a muviéri tied to his or her head with a woven belt, and Kariwarí, the rain goddess who manifests herself in "S"-shaped currents of rain brought on by the wind.

As mentioned above, the pine post on this side of the temple is Nu'ariwaméi, the little boy who brings the thunder and lightning. The presiding cargo holders in this half of the temple are Tatatári, the counterpart to Saulízika, and Uru Kuakáme of the rainy season. I have recently noted that the names of most of these major deities, and the time of year when they are most powerful, appear to be linked to the stars and celestial constellations Huichols consider to be important. Near the time of the summer solstice, and the beginning of the rainy season, three distinct stars are the first to rise in the western sky and shine the brightest. The three were identified to me as Tunuaméi, Maxa Kwaxí, and Ha Keli, three of the major deities of the rainy season.

The division of the temple into two halves, the rainy and dry seasons, is mirrored in the outside patio directly in front of the temple. Here, two god houses are constructed. The god house on the right is for Paritsika, the principal deity of the dry season; the house on the left is for Maxa Kwaxí. The temple thus divides its membership physically, socially, and symbolically into rainy and dry season families.

To repeat, ideally the tuki structure is based on kinship. However, past disruptions in the region have caused kin groups to become fragmented and there is an insufficient number of related people to fulfill all the cargos. At present, there is also a drop in the number of Huichols who actively participate in the cargo cycle, some because they have lost interest in keeping up the family traditions, others because they want to avoid the economic hardships imposed by the religious obligation. Because of this, an individual may now receive a cargo that had not previously been held in the family.[21] Oftentimes these cargos are given to young children who have nearly died, but were miraculously cured by the healing powers of a shaman. I am familiar with two families whose children were given the important cargo of Maxa Kwaxí, the great shaman-singer of the remote ancestral past.

Although the cargo system in the temple has thus been undergoing some alteration, the organization of the temple members and their families strongly points to an old moiety and clan system whose members derive their descent from common, though not necessarily human, ancestors. Whether actual or mythical, the common ancestors from which the two groups, the dry season families and the wet season families, claim descent are the deities Paritsika for the dry season kin, and Maxa Kwaxí for the rainy season kin.

Each clan member has a counterpart. Saulízika's counterpart is Tatatári, Kewimúka's counterpart is Nu'ariwaméi. The Uru Kuakáme of the rainy season and the Uru Kuakáme for the dry season are counterparts, one giving, the other receiving.[22] Their places in the temple are located directly opposite each other. The two different clan members ritually bind their relationship through the exchange of food and drink. They refer to each other as compañero, and will dance together in the ceremonies.

Despite the fragmentation in the old kinship structure, there are still some families that hold on strongly to the old temple traditions, and in every five-year cycle are involved with the cargo of their kin, either dry or wet. The dual opposition of kin members is reciprocal and essential, for the members of each group bear the major ritual responsibilities during the time represented by their families, and the presence and participation of the cargo holders from both sides of the temple are necessary to complete the annual ceremonial cycle.

The rainy season kin are in charge of the ceremonies during the rains, from around May to October. One of the major ceremonies during this season is Hikuri Neixa, the peyote dance, which combines the last peyote ceremony of the year with a ceremony for rain-making and a ceremony for planting. From around November to April, the dry season kin take charge of the ceremonial cycle. The major ritual focus for this time of the year is on Tatéi Neixa, Dance of Our Mother, the harvest ceremony for the children under five that inaugurates the deer hunting ceremonies and the peyote pilgrimage.

The Tuki As Solar Calendar

Anyone familiar with the layout of the circular kivas of the archaeological Southwest, particularly those at Chaco Canyon, will have noted the several correspondences between the interior arrangement of the Huichol tuki and the ceremonial structures of the Anasazi. These may be fortuitous, derived less from historical contacts than from similarities in conceptions of the cosmos, on which both are modeled. Nevertheless, the fact remains that the round-house architecture, fireplaces, emergence holes of the gods, a low bench circling the interior, niches or crypts whose number may or may not correspond to the lunar cycle and that hold offerings to the deities, even the foot drum, are among the characteristics found in both areas. There are similarities also in their respective origin myths.[23]

What only became clear to me in the past two seasons—and only because of close personal relationships extending over many years with people privy to special knowledge—is that like at least some of the archaeological kivas, especially those in Chaco Canyon, all five of the major tukis in the San Andrés region are solar temples, oriented toward the annual cycle of the sun, used as solar observatories, and literally permeated by solar symbolism and associations (Figure 89). (Presumably, the same holds true of the other tukis in the Sierra as well, but I have personal knowledge only of those in this comunidad.)

The temple members keep track of time and the ceremonial calendar by watching the sun and how it shines into the temple. The doorway, which, as noted, faces east to greet the rising sun, is located between 70 to 80 degrees NE. In addition, some of the temples have two small openings placed at either side of the doorway, while others have one. In the Cohamiáta temple the one window next to the doorway is situated at 90 degrees NE. Rays of sunlight enter the dark temple through these openings. The illumination cast by the sun rays is measured on the floor of the temple and on the section of the wall that is bathed in light.

HUICHOL TEMPLE

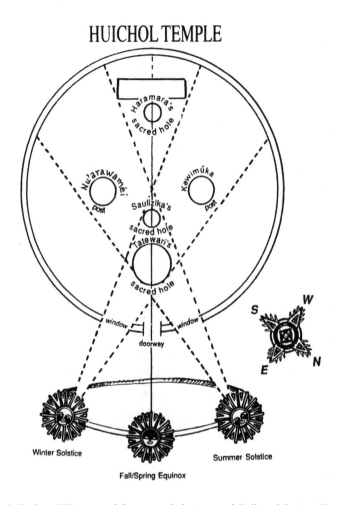

FIGURE 89. Sun's Path at Winter and Summer Solstices and Fall and Spring Equinox. (*Drawing by Nancy Moyer.*)

In September, at the time of the fall equinox, the sun shines straight into the temple. In the tuki of San Andrés, as the sun ascends, it climbs the stairway of the altar in the back of the temple. From there, the sun will gradually travel south. Its penetrating rays enter towards the left of the doorway and fall upon the wall where Uru Kuakáme and other dry-season cargo holders are situated. When this time approaches, the temple group starts making plans for the ceremonies of the upcoming harvest, deer hunting, and the peyote pilgrimage. During this time span, the sun also touches the pine post of the rain god, Kevimuka.

By the time of the winter solstice in December, the sun has reached its southern-most position in the sky. Sacred maize is brought for Niwétsika, the maize goddess, and placed upon the altar to greet the sun. The path of the sun returns the way it had begun and shines directly in to climb the altar during the spring equinox in March.

From there it travels north and shines into the temple along the wall at the place of Uru Kuakáme, the temple caretaker of the rainy season. Along with the rest of their group, Uru Kuakáme and Tatatári, the counterparts of the shaman-singer, commence planning for the ceremonies of the rainy season. During this time, the sun touches the pine post of the rain god Nu'ariwaméi. In June, around the time of the summer solstice, the sacred maize for Niwétsika is removed from the altar, and by July the male maize will be burned at the planting ceremony, called Nawárixa.

It is toward the end of August, when the food plants are growing in the fields and young and tender cobs appear on the stalks, that the Huichol new year begins. All of the temple members bring the decorated votive gourd bowls of the deities for whom each is caretaker. The bowls are ritually washed, and the cleansing reunites both the rainy and dry season temple groups. September comes along and the sun's annual journey is repeated once again.

The xirikis, or ancestor-god houses, that stand outside the tuki in the sacred patio — particularly those for Paritzika and Maxa Kwaxí, which are situated directly in front of the entrance to the temple — are likewise oriented towards the annual cycle of the sun. Each god house has its tepári, the circular stone disk, which is placed just below the roof in the wall above the shrine. This kind of tepári differs from those made to cover the holes in the temple floor, the cavity below the fire, Saulízika's hole, and that of the musicians. Its center is perforated, and with this hole it becomes the "niérika of the sun," niérika having the meaning of aspect, face, or sight or view into the other world (Figure 92). In the temple myth he collected about the making of the god houses, Zingg (n.d.:15) describes these tepáris as follows:

> The Sun also commanded that there be a tepári as a god disc for the god-chair of the sun. . . . In the middle of the tepári a hole should be cut . . . at midnight, while they slept, the people dreamed where to find the stone suitable for the tepári of the Sun. It was cut round and a small hole was drilled through it. This hole is for seeing, since the tepári is the "vista" (Sp., sight or view) of the god. It must be there to permit him to see.

When the rainy season has come, the sun shines on the god house for Maxa Kwaxí and through the niérika of the stone tepári disk, thus giving "sight" to this major rainy season deity. The location of the sun changes from the gable of one god house along with the movement of the sun to the other. The same solstitial event occurs for the dry season, when Paritzika gains sight from the sun ray that filters through the niérika in the center of his tepári.

The daily path of the sun is also charted inside the temple. As the sun creeps up to the mesa tops and then ascends in the direction of the western side of the barrancas, rays from the morning light enter the temple close to ground level. By midday, when the sun is directly overhead, it will shine down through an opening in the roof and illuminate the dirt floor around one of the pine posts or directly onto the fire. Depending upon the time of the year, the sun shines around the post of Nu'arewaméi during the rainy season, and lights up the post of Kewimúka during the dry time. In the back of the temple, along the west side, is another window opening. This one is located in the wall above the altar, and as the sun begins to set, the late afternoon rays shine back into the temple from the west. Having descended into the underworld in the west, at night the sun travels back toward the east, the Land of Dawn. Saulízika follows the sun's perilous path through the hole into which he sings. People say that the sun is down there, traveling below the earth, through the world of darkness, from west to east, just as it did on its first journey in the time of the remotest ancestors. Every time it reaches a certain location in the lower world, the temple members mark its stopping point with a ritual circuit with their offerings around the temple and then in the cardinal directions around the patio.

Just before the breaking of dawn, the sun finally arrives at Táupa, where it was first born, and then travels to Rau 'Unar, the now inactive volcano just east of Wirikúta, the sacred peyote desert in San Luis Potosí. At the precise moment when the first shades of dawn light the eastern horizon, Saulízika sings a special song to greet the sun. There is a stirring among the temple members as they prepare for the meeting with the sun. Candles are lit, and food is warmed and served as offerings to the deities, to thank them for coming, and for sharing their presence in the temple.

The Sun's Compañera, The Moon

The sun, whether it be passing through the rainy or the dry seasons, through the upper- or the underworld, reflects the dual structure of the temple, the kin members, and the Huichol cosmos. The sun itself has a compañero, or, rather, a compañera, because the male sun's counterpart is the moon, and the moon is female. Both have their places marked within the temple. While the boundary for the dry and rainy seasons runs east and west, the dividing line for the sun and moon runs from north to south along the middle of the tuki (Figure 90). The sun's place is in the front half of the temple, while the rear half belongs to the moon's sphere. As we shall see, the gender relations between the male sun and the female moon are also reflected in the social, ritual, and physical lives of the men and women of the community.

The paths of the sun and moon run in opposite directions, hence the concern among the Huichols about solar as well as lunar eclipses. The luminous paths of these two heavenly bodies are mirrored inside the temple. On one night of the full moon in late June 1991, I attended a ceremony in the tuki of San Andrés. The night was unusually clear for early summer and I was able to follow the moon's nocturnal path, which she cast as a silvery beam of light upon the temple floor. At this time of year, the moon entered the temple through the opening in the southern side of the roof shortly before midnight. The next day, the sun mirrored the moon's position on the opposite side of

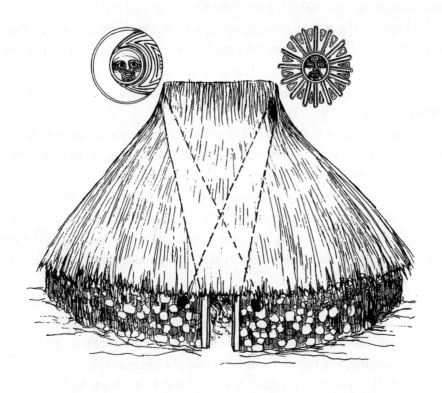

TEMPLE - PATHS of SUN and MOON

FIGURE 90. San Andrés Temple with Paths of Male Sun and Female Moon. (*Drawing by Nancy Moyer.*)

the roof. At midday the sun shone into the temple through the northern opening in the roof.

Huichol mythology relates that the moon was actually the first sun, but that she was not bright and warm enough for the purposes of the creator gods. The deities tried to make a brighter sun that would radiate more heat and light. They chose a Huichol boy to become the sun, and he sacrificed himself in the fire. From the great flames of the funerary pyre the boy descended into the underworld and burst forth into the world from Rau'unár. To this day he endlessly repeats the same cyclical journey, year after year after year, from the place of his descent in the west to his rebirth in the east, the Land of Dawn in the sacred geography of the Huichols.

In everyday language the name for the sun is *táu*, because that was the name the turkey gave him when he first appeared, crying, "tau-tau-tau-tau." In a ceremonial context, the name of the sun is Werikúa, meaning eagle. Werikúa is the bird of the sun because, like the sun, it travels high up in the sky.

In daily speech the moon is called *metsa*, a word closely related to the Nahuatl (Aztec) *metztli*. Huichol women are very much aware of the moon and its relationship to them, because their own menstrual cycle corresponds to that of metsa's own cycle. Huichol shamans who act as midwives are especially attuned to the moon in relation to fertility and pregnancy.

When I asked Tukíya if the moon had another name, he said, no, it is just called metsa. This puzzled me, for, after all, the sun has two names, an ordinary one, táu, and a ceremonial one, werikúa. Why not the moon? Tukíya's mother, who as a female shaman specializes in fertility and birthing, corrected her son: just like the sun, she said, metsa does indeed have a ceremonial name, and it is Tukári. Tukári means day, but even more it means life. Breaking the noun down, *tuka* means spider, and *ri* indicates the state of becoming. In other words, Tukári, the moon goddess, is in the state of becoming spider.

Aerial web-spinning spiders are much respected by Huichols for their ability to spin thread from the very substance of their bodies, an action Huichol equate with spinning the thread of life. But Huichols also have great regard for spiders that make their homes below ground, and this too is directly related to Metsa/Tukári.

It goes without saying that Huichols have their own ideas about the different phases through which the moon passes in the course of the month. When a cycle is complete, three days elapse before the new moon rises. I asked Tukíya's mother whether there was also another name for the moon during this period of darkness in the night sky. Yes, she replied, the moon goes underground into darkness and becomes Tukakáme. In contrast to Tukári, meaning becoming spider, Tukakáme translates into one who *is* spider. When the moon is Tukakáme in the underworld, she transforms into a kind of human ogre who is a death goddess. Tukíya's mother describes her as a large woman who comes to devour humans. She wears the bones of the people she has devoured as her prized jewels, and people know when she is coming because they hear the rattling of the bones adorning her body.[24]

There is clearly a relationship between this imagery of the spider and the moon descending below the earth and, on the one hand, a Huichol narrative published by Furst (1975) about a large, hairy subterranean spider called Utsa, who functions as undertaker for the first people in the world, and, on the other, with the well-known Spider Grandmother of the Southwestern Pueblos, who is sometimes creator, sometimes ogre. In the story collected by Furst, the ancient people Huichols called Héwi consult Utsa about what to do with their dead. Utsa digs out a burial room, weaves a blanket in which to wrap the corpse, and later sings the deceased back to life with her magical song. Furst suggests that the mythological Utsa is, like the Puebloan Spider Grandmother, none other than the trapdoor spider, a large earth spider resembling the tarantula that builds tubular silk-lined subterranean nests with an ingeniously constructed and carefully camouflaged trap door, through which it emerges at dusk to lie in wait for passing insects and small creatures. These she kills by leaping upon them and injecting them with her venom through needle-sharp vertical fangs. Then she devours her prey, leaving only the indigestible exoskeleton behind. Both Tukakáme, the moon as death goddess, and the terrestrial spider emerge from their underground homes and devour the flesh of their victims. There is a striking similarity in imagery between the exoskeleton discarded by the trapdoor spider and the bones left over from Tukakáme's cannibalistic meal. The natural history and ecology of the terrestrial spider thus provides the model for her supernatural counterpart, Tukakáme, the one who is both spider and moon during the brief period of darkness between the moon's death and rebirth. After several nights of gorging herself on flesh, Tukakáme goes back down below, into the earth. When the new moon rises, she is once again Tukári. Tukári, the goddess of life, rises to bring light into the night sky. And just as the sun has the eagle for his animal companion, so the moon's own animal is the rabbit. Huichols say that when Metsa is full, that is, at her most fertile, you can clearly see the rabbit in the moon.

The complementarity of male and female principles is an essential aspect of Huichol intellectual culture. The male association with the sun, and that of the female with the moon, reflect themselves in the temple members themselves. In order to complete a temple cargo well, it is of great importance, indeed vital, that the cargo holders be married couples. Several divorced women have told me that it is very difficult to complete the temple cargo if one is without a husband. The same holds true for men lacking wives. This is the reason why single adults are frequently not the first choices for fulfilling temple cargos. Men and women have their specific, complementary roles in the ceremonies: for example, while the men are the hunters of deer, the women care for the animals' souls. Men plow the furrows or make the holes in the ground with a digging stick, women follow behind sowing the seeds. Male and female maize are equally sacred. Before planting the sacred family maize, it must be danced by the couple to ensure fertility for the crops and the family. Even the major offerings are made so as to symbolize the importance of male and female counterparts. Women make the votive gourd bowls that, on the esoteric level, are their wombs. The votive arrows, made by the men, have phallic attributes. Both the phallic votive arrows and the uterine gourds are essential to fulfilling the needs of the deities.

The same male-female imagery extends into the temple itself. When Tukíya's mother saw from my line of questioning that I was beginning to grasp these primal concepts in the temple lore, she simply said that yes, the temple itself is also a woman's womb. As she explained it, the sun's ray, called *tau'uru*, meaning arrow of the sun, enters the womb of the tuki to impregnate her and bring fertility throughout the daily, as well as the annual, cycle for all the temple members.

The Temple as Matrix for Social Networks

The lives of Huichols living in the Sierra revolve around the temple ceremonies, and their survival depends on a keen attunement to nature and the natural elements. The Huichol ceremonial calendar corresponds to the seasons of the year, fusing sustenance and spirituality together in their lives. Dry season ceremonies emphasize deer and peyote hunting, while abundant rain and fertile crops are of primary concern during the wet season. In fulfilling temple cargo, the members take on the personae and responsibilities of the gods they represent, all of whom are themselves reflections of the natural elements that surround them in their environment.

The Huichol temple is also a center where, in completing ceremonial responsibilities, social networks are generated, creating a cohesive matrix made up of family, kin, and community. As noted, temple cargos are usually passed down generation after generation within the family. Every time an individual receives cargo, he or she completes this role for the welfare of the entire family, both living and deceased. In the performance of these ceremonies, cargo holders give special attention to family ancestors and living relatives and acknowledge them in particular votive offerings brought for the occasion. Prayer arrows and gourd bowls adorned with miniature representations of family members in wax and beads, thread crosses (Lumholtz's "god eyes") to protect children, and rock crystals that hold the heart memory, or crystallized life force, of family ancestors are some examples in material form of the depth of family involvement in these ritual obligations.

Families in the temple work together to perform the ceremonies and properly attend to the gods. They become a communal work force that not only hunts deer and fishes together, and helps work the land, plant, tend, and harvest each other's crops used for daily sustenance, but ceremonially tends the temple-owned crops grown specifically to feed everyone during the ritual events.[25] Women comprise an important part of the work force. The bountiful quantities of food and drink prepared at these times require great cooperation among the women in the group. In the beginning of the Hikuri Neixa ceremony this is ritualized by the female temple members, who carry a *costal* (sack or bag) with special tamales in a circle around the inside of the temple. They stop in front of Saulízika, who blesses them. Then the women feed each other tamales until they are full. The two women who share the cargo of Uru Kuakáme with their husbands are responsible for overseeing the work and organizing the women into an efficient work group. In addition to the main fire in the temple, which is for Tatewarí, two cooking hearths are built, one for the dry season cargo members, the other for the rainy. Although the food preparations are a major part of their temple responsibilities during the ceremonies, women also participate in caring for crops, the deer that have been hunted, the dancing, and the making of offerings.

These cargo responsibilities place a huge burden on the individual's economic means. All the temple members incur massive debts in order to sponsor the ceremonies. Money is needed to pay for the food at all temple ceremonies. Oftentimes the quantity of harvested maize is not sufficient to feed everyone, including the guests. Additional maize beer, distilled alcohol, candles, and ribbons need to be purchased. The greatest expenses come when bulls, cows, sheep, and goats are required as sacrifices for the ceremonies. Which cargo members are to provide and sacrifice animals is revealed to Saulízika in his songs with the gods. These costs, as well as those incurred in transportation, food, and lodging on pilgrimages, can force cargo holders to seek out temple members, kin, and others with whom they have ritual ties, to borrow money to cover their immediate financial needs. Those selected by Saulízika to fulfill the wishes of the deities have to comply in order to ensure the health and life of all temple members. The repeated, and unavoidable, need to provide ceremonial goods requires that temple members maintain a steady reciprocal network not only for social but economic needs as well.[26]

In addition, some families go to work on the coast under extremely adverse conditions to earn money to sustain these religious observances. Others sell artwork to help offset the costs. Regardless of the manner in which money is earned, or the amount, in the course of the five-year cargo period temple members go into massive debt, and will drain their social networks within the family, temple group, and beyond to cover the costs. On the other hand, notwithstanding the economic hardships, there are social and religious rewards for holding temple cargo. In fulfilling their share of cargo goods and responsibilities, temple members can raise their social status. Holding successive cargos enables families to achieve a higher political standing in the decision-making and ritual roles in temple activities and, in the community at large, in the tribal government. Not to be overlooked is also the spiritual dimension. Couples well established in the temple continually evolve through their experiences in their own spirituality and understanding of the traditions and become the knowledgeable ones who lead the rest of the members through the ceremonies.

For five years as the temple congregation, members unite in enduring hardships, joy, sadness, triumphs, births, and deaths within the families. They are bonded together. The interlinking of the group is perhaps best demonstrated in the ritual relationships they have among one another. In the physical structure of the temple, they and their animals are united under the fireplace of Tatewarí. They are joined together on the peyote pilgrimage, each a vital part of the whole. This is symbolically illustrated in the knotted cord that binds them together on the journey and the sacred woven tobacco pouch that contains all of their souls.

For me, personally, the most profound illustration of this unity came on a peyote pilgrimage in which I participated with a temple group. I have told the story briefly elsewhere (Chapter 5), but it is worth recounting in more detail in the present context. One member family in the peyotero group had an infant daughter who had fallen deathly ill. The medical doctor in the clinic at San Andrés supplied the family with a glucose solution to administer orally, but to me he expressed his doubts that the young peyotero had much of a chance to survive. The child was terribly dehydrated and because the mother was fasting, her milk had dried up. As we traveled down out of the Sierra and reached Zacatecas, the child was near death and we stopped in the emergency room of the hospital. The doctors there insisted that the little girl remain in the hospital under medical care. The mother should also stay with her. The shamans and various temple members talked it out in lengthy dialogues, and Saulízika, along with the child's father, were adamant that we all stay together. Our souls were linked at this point and they had to come along, otherwise, they said, we would not be properly following the traditions. The doctors in Zacatecas prescribed antibiotics for the little girl and powdered milk formula to give her every couple of hours. At every sacred place we stopped in the desert, mother, child, and medicine were blessed by Saulízika. Against all odds, not least of them the freezing cold winter nights in this barren high desert, the child made it through and, as I write this, is now a healthy eleven year-old.

In other rituals, such as the initiation of the new year in August, all of the members come together to wash the votive gourd bowls of the gods for whom they are the care-takers in the temple. The intertwining of wet- and dry-season cargo holders through the ceremonies and the ritual relationships as compañeros, fuses the group together into a single entity, the temple with which they are affiliated.

The social networks stemming from temple cargo memberships spirals outwards to encompass the major temples and link the members together. The compañero relationships established between all the members of the temples holding the same cargo provide even more extensive links in the chain of religious, social, and economic relationships. These relationships are always reciprocal, whereby the temple congregations in turn invite the other temple groups to participate as guests in their ceremonies. A ritual exchange of food and drink reestablishes the ties between the various cargo holders of the temples every time a ceremony is performed. This balanced reciprocity is taken quite seriously. I could not help but note the great care my Huichol companions with temple cargos took with their food offerings and nawá—a term meaning maize beer—for their compañeros. Oftentimes they would seek out special delicacies to enhance the gifts of food—bananas, oranges, apples, mangos, papayas, plums, cookies. The presentation of the food is also important, some being extremely elaborate, with tamales and fruit strung on fiber around various sized gourds that hold the fermented maize drink. Beans, rice, pasta, egg, and nopal dishes, and tortillas and tamales accompany the maize beverage. I have heard some women speak especially highly of their compañeros if their gifts of food were particularly generous. On the other hand, they will not hesitate to criticize a compañero if the gift exchange is considered miserly and not well presented.

When cargo members have completed their five-year commitment, they will almost certainly continue to be involved in temple activities. These will most likely be in the temple with which they have been associated, but also in other temples where family members have cargo. Tukíya told me that even though he has completed his five-year cargo as Kewimúka, he still has to leave offerings in the temple, and should continue to do so all his life. "That's the way it is," he said. "For example, when it is the time of the Hikuri Neixa ceremony, I also have to bring my son, my children. So that they can participate in the ceremony of the drum. Even though I no longer have cargo, I can make *tejüino* (nawá). I have already completed my cargo and now all of my children are united there in the tuki."

Although the cargo positions change after the cycle has been completed, many Huichols are given continuous five-year cargos indefinitely, until they can no longer fulfill them and family members take on the responsibility. Those who have a break from these obligations will help kin complete their temple cargos. Many will also leave the Sierra for extended periods to earn money to repay the debts incurred in serving their cargos and accumulate additional revenue to be able to afford the next cargo they are given. Even some Huichols who are in the middle of their cargo term will seek work outside the Sierra, but cargo holders usually do not remain absent from the Sierra for long periods of time. The money earned is earmarked for special ceremonial purposes, and families try to refrain from spending all of it on the consumption of luxury items and alcohol. Whenever a substantial amount has been earned, the gods are always thanked in prayers and offerings for the help they gave in making these economic gains. Nevertheless, there are times when, due to unforeseen circumstances, cargo members will return late or not at all to complete the upcoming ceremonies.

Tuki Traditions in a National and International Setting

Because of this extensive traveling, there is an intricate communication network between Huichols in and outside of the Sierra. Indeed, Huichols who are heavily involved with carrying out the temple traditions are not cut off from interaction with the world outside their homelands. Nor, conversely, are Huichol emigrants, permanent or temporary, necessarily divorced from the temples and their ceremonies in their former communities. With the scarcity of deer, they must travel farther and farther into neighboring areas for the hunt. Pilgrimages to sacred places such as the peyote desert, the Pacific coast, and Lake Chapala, involve contact and interaction with the larger Mexican culture, as well as with Huichols who have left their mountain communities and settled in rural or urban communities.[27]

Whether Huichols are visited by outsiders, or are themselves visitors outside their home community, they are continuously faced with cultural differences that force them to examine their own identities, and the beliefs and values that go hand and hand with this identification. Perhaps more so now than ever in the past, Huichols are having to define who they are and the importance and meaning of their cultural traditions, especially when it comes to communication and exchange with the many non-Huichols with whom they are in contact. An increasing number of outsiders eager to observe and experience their ceremonies have brought about an ironic twist in intracultural relations. While some Huichols perceive these outsiders as intruders, for others their presence reaffirms the pride and self-assurance they feel as Huichols.

Through the temple ceremonies, Huichols maintain a secure social base where individuality and group affiliation are recognized and reinforced. Within the context of these temple traditions, Huichols are able to gain a strong sense of personal and cultural identity, and a deep understanding of their place in the world. This, in turn, has an influence on how elements from the outside world are integrated into the value system and world view of Huichol culture. The western technology they have adopted or adapted provides some useful examples. Violins and guitars were copied early on from instruments introduced by Spanish settlers and missionaries, and they, and "Huicholized" forms of old Spanish round dances, have been indispensable to Huichol ceremonial life for centuries. So have metal tools. As noted above, in the last two or three decades tape recorders have become highly valued, and once ritually cleansed, are frequently employed to record the shamans' song in the ceremonies. Rifles have also been incorporated into the ritual paraphernalia of temple members. These rest upon the altar, or among the bags of offerings, and are painted with the same sacred yellow paint from a desert root that peyoteros use to paint their faces. Vehicles that are used to take pilgrims on their journeys must be purified, and in some situations, miniature representations of these are left in sacred places along the way as prayers for a safe journey. There is sufficient flexibility and elasticity within Huichol cultural traditions, temple cargos, and even sacred ritual to enable members who have a strong sense of personal and cultural identity to consistently modify and incorporate change in such a way that change appears not to bring with it the sorts of disastrous acculturative consequences we have seen among many other indigenous groups.

I would not want to leave the impression that what I have described for the tukis with which I am most familiar applies across the board to the entire Huichol region. In fact, there are marked differences between temple traditions in different parts of the Huichol homeland. In some places, missionary influence and the intrusion of outsiders, especially mestizos who have usurped Huichol land, have been more severe and lasting than in others, bringing about erosion and even disintegration of these traditions. Communities that have felt the effects the most no longer even have tukis, and ceremonies formerly associated with the temple are either no longer practiced, are greatly altered, or have retreated to the rancho level, with the xiriki, or god-house, functioning in the manner of the tuki. In other situations, past wars, especially the troubles of the Mexican Revolution and the Cristero revolt in the early part of the twentieth century, have forced Huichols to leave the Sierras and eke out a living near Mexican towns and cities.

Still, because there exists such a strong network between Huichol kin in the Sierra and in the cities, some Huichols who have lived for years in or near the urban world have still maintained, if not the kinship basis of the temple traditions, at least the fundamental ideological foundations, as a source of ethnic identity, affiliation, and pride. In Nayarit, this phenomenon has recently had not only a religious, but a political impact as well on Huichol relations with the state government and the non-Indian population.

In Tepic, the capital of Nayarit, a kind of Huichol revitalization movement has been under way, triggered by the founding of a Huichol temple within the city limits on land that, though eyed eagerly by developers, was presented to the Huichol community by the state governor. This unusual development has been studied by two investigators from the Universidad Autónoma de Nayarit, Lic. Lourdes Pachecho and a student, Nestor Gómez, and what follows is based on information they generously shared with me.

Tepic, where the Instituto Nacional Indigenista has had its center for the Huichol region since the 1960s, has for years been home to a scattered community of Huichols who had settled in the city to try and better their economic lives. These Huichols united to try and find a place where they might establish a cohesive settlement for all the Huichols and families who were living dispersed throughout the city, many in conditions of great poverty. This group called upon a mara'akáme, a shaman-singer, to sing for them to ask the gods for a sign where they should establish themselves. Guided by Tatewarí, Our Grandfather Fire, this mara'akáme identified the destined location as a hill above the Mololóa river, overlooking downtown Tepic. Here, the gods had marked the exact location with a large rock in the shape of a sheep's head (Figure 121). This, the mara'akáme said, was where the temple should be built. Although this particular piece of prime real estate had already been divided into lots for a future mestizo *colonia*, one of the leaders of the group, the well-known Huichol artist José Benítez Sánchez, talked to governor, Sr. Celso Delgado, and convinced him to set this land aside for the Huichol temple and settlement. The 2nd of October, 1988, marked the commencement of the construction of the temple on the sacred land, known to these Huichols as Zitakua, meaning the tender part of the maize. A circular temple was built, complete with patio and god houses. The tuki, a modified version of the traditional temple, is made from bricks covered with a smooth facade. When not in use, the doorway is closed up with a wrought iron door and lock.

Since its inauguration, the temple has been a major place for ceremonial meetings. In the spring of 1990, Gov. Celso Delgado and his wife attended, as honored guests, the ceremony to greet the temple cargo holders who had just returned from their peyote pilgrimage to the sacred desert of San Luis Potosí. The fact that here in Zitakua, the solar eclipse was also observed brings us full circle back to my introduction to this essay, for while the temple shamans from the San Andrés region had gone down to Mexcaltitan and were calming the potential danger from the union of the sun and moon in the presence of the tourists, the astronomers, and the local inhabitants, the temple members and the shamans in Zitakua were similarly occupied in ritual undertakings related to this remarkable celestial event. As reported by Lic. Lourdes Pacheco, in their temple patio on a hill above the bustle of the city of Tepic, they watched the merging of sun and moon. As the sky became dark, the people sacrificed a goat, because, though not indigenous, it is an animal of the land. Next, they sacrificed a turkey, which is indigenous and one of the birds of the male sun. Then, a rabbit, the animal companion of the female moon, was offered to the gods in hopes of balancing the two forces and restoring equilibrium to the world.

It was all happening not in the traditional setting of a Sierra community, but in the city, and it was certainly different in detail, but in its own way it did what the temple traditions have done for centuries: provide the means by which Huichols are constantly involved in maintaining balance in social, religious, economic, and political affairs. The temple system continues to have a major presence in Huichol life.

Conclusion

Whether in the Sierras, or outside of the Huichol homeland, Huichols continue to keep the traditions alive, creating and recreating social networks of cargo holders who together play an active part in keeping the cosmos in balance. Participation in the ceremonies and the temple cargos enable Huichols to maintain a strong sense of cultural identity. While Huichols see themselves as culturally distinct from the larger world around them, the ceremonies they perform are not meant just for their own benefit. In the perceptions of many Huichols they are also done to insure harmony and well-being for everyone. Amidst the ever increasing changes brought about by development and modernization, the tuki remains, emotionally and physically, the strong house, the keystone of Huichol culture. Their physical, cultural, and spiritual survival lies in the temple, the place where the sun and the moon meet. The tuki encompasses within its walls and roof and the foundations upon which it stands, the Huichol universe. And the continuation of the traditions related to this microcosm, in whatever manner, balances the world without.

POSTSCRIPT

For some time, with my colleague Peter T. Furst and others, I have been convinced that the Huichol tuki, its architecture, and the niches that line the inner wall, must have had important lunar as well as solar associations. After this chapter was completed and with the book about to go to press, I came across a fascinating missionary document (written in 1843 by a Franciscan priest) describing the Huichol temple and a reference to its relationship to the moon in Beatriz Rojas's *Los Huicholes: Documentos Históricos* (1992). Like all the clergy of his time, the priest condemns the tuki, which he calls "Caliguey," and all traditional religious practices as pagan. The document mentions that almost every time there was a full moon the Huichols conducted ceremonies inside the temple: "Por lo común en cada lleno de la Luna tienen fiesta en el Caliguei o templo de los idolos, presidiéndola los viejos. El ella se cometen mil exesos tanto de impureza como de embriaguez" (ibid., p. 150). ("Usually every full moon they have a ceremony in the calihuey or temple of the idols, presided over by the elders. In the temples they commit a thousand sinful crimes, such as becoming intoxicated.")

Though short on description, the document verifies that even as late as the mid-nineteenth century, Huichols were conducting ceremonies in honor of the moon in the tuki, which could, in fact, have been just as much a lunar as a solar observatory.

NOTES

1. When speaking Spanish to outsiders, Huichols often refer to the tuki as *calihuey*, which some students of the Huichol have erroneously taken to be a Huichol word. In actuality, calihuey derives from the Nahuatl (Aztec) *calli*, house, and *uei*, large. It is one of the Nahuatl borrowings that came into the Sierra during the colonial era with the friars and the Nahuatl-speaking Central Mexicans whom the Spanish transplanted to the western frontier.

2. For discussions of the role and meaning of the urukáme in Huichol religion, see Perrin, this volume, and Furst 1967:39–106. Weigand (1972:25) writes that the ancestor god house "is the most observable monument to the ancestor orientation of much of Huichol rancho-based ceremonialism."

3. At some time during the five years in which I participated in ceremonies with the San José temple group, the smaller tuki had burned to the ground, and all ceremonies took place in the larger temple compound. In the fifth year, during May and June of 1990, the second tuki was rebuilt during the ceremonial exchange, when the completing cargo holders pass their cargos on to the new members. This twin tuki complex may have had greater importance in the past, for the area surrounding it has a high concentration of obsidian, and obsidian tools, of uncertain age, have been found here. The San José temple group passed over the cargos one year later than the other temples.

4. cf. Furst and Anguiano 1976:95–181 on this ceremony.

5. See Lumholtz (1900:11), Furst and Anguiano (1977:116–117), and Negrín (1975:50–52) for variants of the solar origin myth.

6. The kawitéros have responsibility not only in the naming of the new cargo holders in the indigenous temple organization but also in the naming of the officials of the hierarchical community government imposed on the Indians by the Spanish. Fikes (1985) also discusses the role of kawitéros in his doctoral dissertation.
Considering the importance of kawitéros both in relation to the aboriginal temple and the government of the comunidad, it is interesting that, as my co-editor has pointed out, the term kawitéro appears not to be Huichol but a neologism combining a Nahuatl word with a Spanish suffix. If so, like other neologisms and modifications of Nahuatl and Spanish words in Huichol, it dates back only to the early eighteenth century. Whether or not the office had pre-contact antecedents is not known.

7. Although dwindling in numbers, peccary are still ritually hunted. Sometimes, if a peccary is the first animal to be killed on the ceremonial deer hunt, the head is dried and a sacred tobacco pouch is tied to the animal's forehead. The peccary is also the animal form, and the companion animal, of the earth and creator goddess Great-grandmother Nakawé. It is interesting that one of the epithets of Xmucane, the female half of the primordial aged creator pair in the *Popol Vuh*, the sacred history of the Quiche Maya of highland Guatemala, is Great White Peccary (Tedlock 1985:71, 369).

8. The relative importance of certain of the leading deities varies from temple to temple.

Lumholz (1900:10) counted forty-seven gods, but he notes the difficulty of arriving at a definitive number because each principal one has as many as eight to ten names. One myth recorded by Zingg (n.d.:76) mentions twenty-five chief temple cargo holders, each in charge of a particular deity. The legend, recorded by Diguet, credits Majakuagy (Maxa Kwaxí) with having introduced a pantheon of thirty-seven principal deities (see Chapter 2).

9. I have noticed over the years that Huichols do not necessarily begin their temple ceremonies at the time appointed by Saulízika. In fact, quite often they don't. Usually, this is due to the widely-dispersed settlement pattern, which makes it difficult to gather the major temple members together on time. Weather conditions may also impinge on the scheduling of the ceremonies. For example, if there has been no rain, the planting ceremony cannot commence. Also, there are always exceptions to the usual way of conducting ceremonies. In fact, each religious performançe, regardless of how many times it may have been done before, is different and unique. Much, though clearly not all, of this variation has to do with the leading shaman, Saulízika, and the messages he receives from the deities as to how to proceed.

10. There is a good chance that prior to the assumption of formal control over the Sierra Indians by the Spanish in 1722, Huichol society and the settlement pattern may have been clan-based, a possibility that has also been discussed by Weigand (1972, 1976) and Negrín (1985). In any event, the Huichol kinship system and social structure have hardly remained static from pre-Hispanic, or even colonial, times but have undergone various modifications at different points in time, as they do even today. Missionary influence, disruptions, and temporary depopulation of entire communities caused by the Mexican Revolution and its bloody aftermath, the Cristero rebellion, invasion and alienation of traditional lands by mestizo settlers and cattlemen, and out-migration and resettlement outside the Huichol homeland have all contributed to the fragmentation of family lines. Nevertheless, as I was able to observe in San Andrés, in some of the indigenous communities the temple districts still maintain a strong orientation to lineages and at least a semblance of former clans.

11. Wall crypts or niches containing offerings are also a common feature of the Great Kivas of Chaco Canyon (Vivian and Reiter 1960). In some cases, for example, at Casa Rinconada, the number of these niches, like that I observed in the San Andrés tuki, corresponds, or is close, to the moon cycle.

12. The vocation of shaman tends to run in families, and the Carrillo family line of San Andrés produced quite a number of particularly prestigious specialists in the sacred, whose renown, like that of Kuka's grandfather Juan, or the late Nicholas Carrillo de la Cruz (see Chapter 15), extended well beyond their own communities.

13. As Furst has suggested to me, just as the tuki is the ancestor-god house writ large, so the "god stones" that are placed in the tuki wall replicate on a larger scale the urukámes, the small colored stones or crystals that, tied to arrows and stuck into the walls of the xirikis, represent— indeed, from the native point of view *are*—deified ancestors.

14. Since this was written, the new five-year temple cargo holders made a new bamboo mesa-type altar. Lumholtz (1900:62) discusses a miniature staircase carved of stone he found in the San Sebastián-Santa Catarína region. The staircase, he writes, symbolizes the journey from the coast to the Sierra. See also Schaefer (1989) for Huichol conceptions of the embodiment of the sun's path in the symbolism of the backstrap loom.

15. Masonry pits thought to be the foundations of wooden foot drums are also a feature of the Great Kivas at Chaco and elsewhere in the Southwest. The same kind of foot drum is employed

to this day in some kiva ceremonies. One, at Acoma, the "Sky City," was described as follows by Stirling (1942:19):

> In front of the fireplace is tsiwaimituma (another-altar-placed-under). It is a hollow place in the floor in which an altar . . . is kept. It is covered with a board. The chianyi are the only ones who are allowed to dance on it. It gives out a hollow sound. . . . whenever a medicine man wanted to get more superhuman power for himself he has to dance and roll over his altar.

16. Lumholtz collected numerous tepári, which he published in 1900 (pp. 25–68), as did Preuss in 1906/07. The Lumholtz collection is in the American Museum of Natural History, Preuss's in the Museum für Völkerkunde in Berlin-Dahlem. See also Furst 1978:32–33.

17. My consultants say that certain colors are associated with the cardinal points: red is east, black west, green north, blue south. The center is yellow and above white.

18. Lumholtz (1903:149) and Zingg (1939:179) describe a cord made from bark fiber running beneath the roof toward the cardinal points, crossing each other in the center. In the myth of the first tuki recorded by Zingg (ibid.), the Sun commanded that this cord be made to secure the sacred house against wind and lightning.

19. P. T. Furst (personal communication) notes that this cannot help but recall the widespread Mesoamerican concept that each person has a companion animal, commonly known as a *nagual* (derived from the Nahuatl [Aztec] *nahualli*, transforming shaman, sorcerer, magician), with which he or she shares a common destiny. If the animal falls ill or dies, so does its human counterpart. That the belief in the nagual predates the Spanish invasion is clear not only from the accounts of the Spanish chroniclers, who reported on it in the sixteenth and seventeenth century, but from the art of the Maya and other pre-Columbian cultures. There is, of course, this difference: human beings are thought to enter into a community of fate with a companion animal at birth, and to retain it through life. Huichol "cargo nagualism," in contrast, begins and ends with the five-year temple cargo.

20. During the several years in which I attended temple ceremonies, the leading shaman of the San José tuki was fulfilling the cargo of his long-deceased maternal grandfather. His father had refused to take on this major cargo, so it fell upon him to complete the responsibility. In his dissertation, Fikes (1985) provides interesting details about the temple organization in Santa Catarína, but oddly enough writes (p. 73) that, rather than the kawitéros dreaming who will fulfill the next five-year temple cargo, the "officers simply select their replacements." Further, he cites his informant, a kawitéro, to the effect that the "selection of temple officers is unrelated to one's gender or kinship status" (ibid.:72). If correct, this would suggest much more advanced disintegration of the traditional kin-based tuki cargo system in Santa Catarína than I have found it to be the case in San Andrés. It is also at odds with Negrín's statement that in Santa Catarína the tukis are organized around families on a clan level (Negrín 1985:16) (cf. Note 10).

21. I know of several instances of Huichols being given cargos which neither their parents nor any other members of their families ever served. Among these was a temple member who had the cargo of Tekuamana. He claimed he was given this cargo twice and that when he finished with the temple cycle in progress, he would have completed ten years with this cargo.

22. That unforeseen circumstances can compel the merging of these complementary opposites in one and the same cargo holder is shown by what happened to Utsíma's husband. Already burdened with the cargo of one of the two Uru Kuakáme in the temple, he had to take on the additional religious and economic responsibilities of the other Uru Kuakáme in the same tuki. His counterpart had a son who was dying of cancer and was caught up in the cities going

from clinic to clinic and hospital to hospital in a desperate try to save his boy. Needless to say, the five year cargo Utsíma and her husband already shared was extremely time consuming and demanding in physical and financial terms.

23. Weigand, who has published a survey of some of the remains of circular ceremonial structures in different parts of West Mexico (Weigand 1976), has proposed that these—particularly such sites in the upper Bolaños valley as Totoáte (first described, and partially excavated, by Hrdlička [1903]—"served as models from which the *kalihuey* religious compound of the Huichols was developed" (Weigand 1978:101).

24. Lumholtz [1902] and Zingg [1938:365–366] both discuss this death deity. In 1966 Ramón Medina also dictated a similar tradition to P.T. Furst and illustrated it with a yarn painting. The descriptions they recorded are very similar to the one I acquired, but they did not mention an association with Tukakáme as the moon.

25. Each temple group has a plot of communal land, which surrounds the temple, for planting. These fields are alternated with others to allow the soil to rest and recuperate its strength. When the land lies fallow, the temple group will communally plant on land set aside by one of the members for this purpose. Weigand (1972) devotes a monograph to the organization of Huichol work groups for communal hunting, fishing, and agriculture, but only in relation to everyday subsistence, without reference to the ceremonial, sacred side of communal cultivation on the temple-owned lands.

26. The kinds of social and economic networks established through kin, ceremonial, and ritual ties is extremely complex. Future research may reveal that this complex scheme of redistribution of goods and services, and the meaning which arises from these relationships, shares similar qualities with the exchange system of the Nuyootecos of Oaxaca reported by Monaghan (1990).

27. Huichols in rural and urban areas outside of the Sierra are discussed by Valadez (1986), Weigand (1978, 1981) and Nahmad (1995 and this volume). One problem is that some of these studies tend to treat Huichols who have moved into urban or rural areas outside their home territory as a static, permanent phenomenon, when in fact it has always been a fluid one, with some people returning to their old life in the Sierra after years of exile. Over the last four years I have even noticed an acceleration in this process of reintegration. Even some Huichols who left the Sierra long ago to reside in the cities are returning to their old communities. Many say that because of the economic crisis in Mexico, they can no longer sustain themselves. Others are simply homesick and miss the rich ceremonial life. Upon returning to the Sierras they are usually given cargo roles, regardless of how long they have been away. It is also interesting to note that some bilingual Huichols employed by the Instituto Nacional Indigenísta, Secretaria de Educación Pública, and Sistema para el Desarrollo Integral de la Familia as schoolteachers or *promotores* of other aspects of modernization, such as public health, also fulfill these cargos if they are working in their family's community.

ACKNOWLEDGMENTS

The many years of fieldwork that went into this research would not have been possible without the generous assistance of the following organizations and individuals: Fulbright Fellowship, OAS Fellowship, UCLA Program on Mexico Research Grant, Denwar Craft Studio Scholarship, Vernon and Elizabeth Anderson, and Faculty Research Grants from the University of Texas-Pan American. I am also grateful to

Anthony Aveni for his interest and comments on the draft of this chapter, as well as Johannes Wilbert, who encouraged me to examine the importance of the tuki on all cultural levels. Over the course of several years, he spent endless hours orienting me to astronomical phenomena in relation to traditional long- or roundhouse structures (see Wilbert 1981) and discussing the complex symbolism that accompanies any traditional model of the cosmos.

INTRODUCTION TO CHAPTERS 12, 13, AND 14

Among the indigenous peoples of the Sierra Madre Occidental, a story is told of an Indian who missed his dead wife so much that he decided to go looking for her, however far from his home it might take him. He walked and walked in the direction of the setting sun, to see if he could find the land of the dead and there look for his beloved spouse. After arriving at the opening to the netherworld, he begged those who were guarding it to allow him to enter and search for his dead mate. He wept and pleaded so piteously that, although properly only the deceased and shamans can come into the land of the dead, the people in charge relented and permitted him inside. Looking about him in the land of the dead, which appeared to him to be just like that of the living, he saw his wife among her relatives. She told him that she was happy here, but also how pleased she was to see him. He told her how much he and her relatives in that other life had missed her, and he begged her to return with him to their village. She said that even though she was very satisfied with her new life, she too had missed him and her old home, and would gladly return there with him. But those people who guard the land of the dead would not at first permit this. Husband and wife pleaded with them to let her go, until at last they agreed.

"We allow you to go," they told her. "But there is a condition. When you arrive at your former home in that other life, your relatives will be happy to see you. They have missed you and wept at your death, and they will greet you with great joy and invite you to celebrate your homecoming with them. But you must not laugh with them, and you must not dance. If you do not obey our instructions, if you laugh and drink and dance with your husband and your relatives, your time with them will at once come to an end, and you will return here forever."

Harsh as it seemed, for Indian people enjoy dancing and singing and celebrating their rituals, husband and wife agreed to this condition. Thereupon the guardians of the land of the dead changed the woman into a small luminous fly. They instructed the husband to place the little fly who was his wife inside a hollow reed and seal the ends with wild cotton from a tree. His wife thus secured for the journey, he, overjoyed at the prospect of resuming life with her, made his way back to the place where he had first climbed down into the land of the dead. When they reached the upperworld, he unplugged the reed and his wife appeared in her former human form. Together they walked back to the village, where the relatives were as happy at her return as they had been sad at her death. They offered her maize beer and peyote and invited her to dance with them in celebration of her return to the village of her relatives.

Remembering the condition set by the guardians of the land of the dead, and afraid of losing her again, this time forever, the husband tried to stop his wife. But she, filled with happiness at seeing her relatives again, dismissed the warning from her mind. Laughing with pleasure, she joined in the dancing, singing, and drinking, and urged her husband to do the same. But he stood there, unable to move, full of fear and foreboding. And as his wife joined in the festivities, laughing and dancing with her relatives, he saw her begin to recede before his eyes, her voice growing fainter and fainter, until at last all trace of her was gone.

It will not have escaped the reader that this story is nothing less than an indigenous West Mexican equivalent of the familiar Greek tale of Orpheus and Euridice. A version that was probably Cora was reported by a Spanish priest shortly after the conquest of the Sierra de Nayar in 1722. But it also occurs among their neighbors, including the Huichols, and, farther away, among other indigenous peoples that likewise have never heard of anyone called Orpheus (for a survey of the Orpheus motif among North American Indians see Hultkrantz 1955).

As Jill L. McKeever Furst, who has worked on other Native North American and Mesoamerican forms of this myth, and on Aztec conceptions of the soul and death and the afterlife, has pointed out to us, the indigenous West Mexican variant is actually far more profound than its classic Greek counterpart. The Greek story, as McKeever Furst interprets it, is essentially about human frailty, the inability to keep faith with the gods. We don't know whether the gods indeed intended to trick Orpheus, she says, or whether they would really have given her back. It was Orpheus who doubted at the last minute and turned around. And why? Because he did not hear Euridice behind him, for shades make no footfall.

The Sierra Madre story, McKeever Furst suggests, speaks instead about what constitutes a real human life. Once you have passed over, even if the gods let you return, you can no longer do the things that give a human being joy—singing, laughing, dancing, full ritual participation. In other words, everything that makes you a true Indian person. So what is the point of being here?

What the indigenous story does do is provide a mythological framework for the final stage in the drama of separation, the Huichol mortuary ritual, that last brief moment for the departed to return in spirit form and savor the gifts and the familiar ceremonial foods, before the limits the gods have set catch up with you and you are made to take your final, irrevocable leave.

The following three essays all deal with different aspects, and from different viewpoints, of the same theme: the journey of the soul after death. The first, by the Mexican anthropologist Marina Anguiano, sets the stage with a description of the ceremony, called *Müüqui Cuevixa*, "time to bid the dead farewell," in which the spirit of the recently deceased is summoned from the afterworld for one last reunion with its grieving relatives. The second is an "inside view"—Ramón Medina's version of the journey of the soul to the village of the ancient, ancient ancestors, the *hewixi*, ending with its capture by the shaman and his helper Kauyumári for its final farewell visit to its former home. It is excerpted here from a much more extensive discussion, long out of print, of Huichol conceptions of the soul by one of the editors (P.T.F.) that appeared nearly thirty years ago in *Folklore Americas*, a semiannual journal that specialized in Hispanic and Latin American folklore and that unfortunately long ago ceased publication.

Just as it leads naturally into the third and last of the essays, a consideration of the soul of the deceased in a new and positive materialization, there is a good fit between Ramón's narrative and Anguiano's descriptive account. Without it we would not understand, for example, why the shaman's array of sacred objects for the ceremony in Anguiano's list has to include a thorny branch of an acacia shrub or tree, or that the food offerings the spirit takes on his journey are not necessarily just intended to feed himself but are needed to placate an angry guardian of the path.

The third essay is a reconsideration of the complex symbolism of the *urukáme*, a topic on which Ramón Medina expounded at some length almost thirty years ago for one of the editors (Furst 1967). The urukáme (from *uru* = arrow) is the spirit of a deceased individual, usually a wise elder or a shaman, who has returned from the afterworld to take up residence in his or her former *rancho* as family guardian spirit. In its material form this semi-divine guardian and advisor to the family headman or shaman is a small rock crystal or colored stone that is placed, like the dead wife in the story, inside a hollow reed that is kept in a special covered votive gourd or, more commonly, tied to an arrow with a hardwood point. Lumholtz (1900, 1902), Preuss (1907), Zingg (1938) and P. T. Furst (1967) have all discussed its symbolism and significance, but it remains for Michel Perrin, a French anthropologist with a strong interest in the religious ideology of South American and Mexican Indians, to provide the most thorough analysis to date of what is probably a very ancient, and a typically shamanic, phenomenon in Huichol religion.

Peter T. Furst

12 : *MÜÜQUI CUEVIXA:*

"TIME TO BID THE DEAD FAREWELL"

MARINA ANGUIANO FERNÁNDEZ

Translated from the Spanish by MARIBEL CARRIZALES

The time for this part of the great universal drama of separation as it plays itself out among the Huichols is the night of the fifth day after death, after the officiating *mara'akáme*, the shaman-singer, and his assistants, the *cuinaopuvamete*, have, in their chants, narrated every step in the long and arduous journey of the soul to the nether-world, conducted dialogues with the deceased, and, in behalf of the surviving relatives, inquired about his or her welfare.

The place in this instance is Santa Catarína, the specific locale, the ceremonial space in front of a *xiriki*, the ancestor god-house or temple hut of the *rancho* in which the deceased had made his home. The participants are, in addition to the shaman-singer and his two helpers, the extended family of the deceased and other relatives and friends from nearby settlements.

As always in Huichol ceremonial, the most important participant, though, the one who truly guards and oversees the proceedings, is Tatewarí, Our Grandfather, the aged fire god and patron of shamans, who is present in the blazing hearth in the center of the patio, and who is himself assisted by the Deer Person Kauyumári. Kauyumári is the principal helper of Tatewarí and of the officiating shaman. He is also the divine messenger between the Huichol people and their many deities. In fact, rather than the shaman-singer himself traveling in his chant to the land of the dead to call the deceased for one final visit to his home before taking his leave forever, it is usual for the shaman-singer to ask Kauyumári to do so on his behalf.

Close by, on the left side of the entrance to the xiriki, is a low rectangular altar constructed of poles and branches. This is called *müüquitapestiéva*, the "altar, or plat-form, of death" (*müüqui* = death, *tapesti* = altar.)[1] If this is its usual location in the ceremonies, that is, to the left of the xiriki and the ceremonial hearth, this may well be significant, for many people consider the left side to be the side of death and misfortune. The tapesti is constructed of four forked uprights and four horizontal poles, forming a square. Laid on top of this are numerous branches, and it is on these that the property of the deceased is placed, along with food offerings from family and friends for the spirit to dine on before taking his final leave. If the relatives have some disposable wealth, a cow is sacrificed and its hide placed beneath, and the horns on top of, the tapesti. The personal belongings of the deceased that are displayed on the altar include clothing, sandals, and working tools, along with gourd bowls, plates, and other small receptacles filled with different foods. Foodstuffs dedicated to the deceased include soup made from the meat of a sacrificed bull (or other sacrificed animal, as one always is for the ceremony), tamales, gorditas, deer meat, cooked maize and squash, as well as little tortillas, *tortillitas* in Spanish.[2] Among the beverages are jugs of maize beer, *nawá* in Huichol and *tesgüino* or *tejüino* elsewhere; cups of chocolate; and bottled distilled alcohol. The gorditas and tamales are placed on platters with lighted candles. The meat broth is served in gourd bowls.

Suspended from the tapesti is a pair of much-used shoulder bags containing food and various sacred objects, such as votive arrows, ears of maize that have been spattered with deer's blood, a deer's head, candles, and containers with sacred water collected at various springs. These include the water holes called Tatéimatiniéri, Where Our Mothers Dwell, which are visited by Huichol *peyoteros* on their way to Wirikúta, the sacred peyote country near Real de Catorce, in the desert of San Luis Potosí (Figure 91).

The mara'akáme and his helpers are seated, facing east and the blazing fire—that is, Tatewarí—on low chairs and footstools. Directly in front of them is what one might call a kind of ground altar, consisting of a plaited mat on which the different ritual objects to be used during the night are placed, along with the alcohol, tobacco, and peyote they will consume throughout the night. These include:

1. a *takwátsi*, the Huichol name for the elongated plaited and tightly lidded basket in which shamans and other ritual specialists keep their votive arrows, *muviéris*, and other power objects;
2. several *muviéris*;
3. *urutexi*, votive arrows;
4. a *catira* (from the Spanish *candela*), or candle;
5. a *xikiri*, a magical mirror that makes the secrets of the deities visible to the shaman;
6. a votive gourd bowl, *xukúri tumine ayamaniti*, containing money;
7. a *xukúri yayatsáme*, votive gourd bowl containing tobacco (*yá* = tobacco, *Nicotiana rustica*);
8. *xama*, dried corn husks for rolling ritual cigarettes with *N. rustica* tobacco;
9. a *quizasuri nawa ayamati*, bottle gourd with maize beer;

FIGURE 91. Peyotero Couple Whose Child Almost Died. This family is at the sacred water holes called Tatéi Matiniéri, Where Our Mother Dwells, near Wirikúta. See Chapters 5 and 11. (*Photograph by Stacy B. Schaefer, 1987.*)

10. *tuchi*, a potent alcohol distilled from the *sotol* cactus (in an earthen still of the Filipino type);
11. plenty of *hikuri*, or peyote.

In addition, there are two stones to the left of the three singers on which the five crosses made of pitch pine, a branch of *huisache* (acacia), and a plant called *tuxu*, rest until they are used.[3] Two lighted candles and a bowl of the black pigment called *tuxári* are placed next to the stones.

As in all other rancho-based ceremonies, the xiriki plays a vital role, for it is in this ceremonial house, the rancho temple, that not only the material form of the family guardian spirits called *urukáme*, but many different male and female deities, are located, along with numerous ceremonial paraphernalia. It is worth enumerating everything of a material nature that goes into the making and the symbolism of a typical xiriki.

First, it must be understood that everything, including the architecture and the materials of which the xiriki is constructed, as well as its contents, is symbolic. Except for its (usually) slightly larger size, to the naked eye the xirirki differs little from the ordinary nuclear family dwelling, with this exception—and it is an important one: in some xiriki, two gable stones with a hole in the center are set into the wall in front and back

FIGURE 92. Tepári for the Sun in the Wall of Xiriki on the Rancho of the Great Mara'akáme Nicholas de la Cruz at San Andrés. See Chapter 11. (*Photograph by Peter T. Furst.*)

just below the peak of the roof. Some are round, others rectangular but with a circular design (Figure 92). Of these stones, called *tepári*, the one in the back wall represents the east, or sunrise, the one in front the west, sunset. Just as it does in the much larger *tuki*, the community temple, the space between the stones marks the trajectory of the sun during the day (Figure 93) (see Schaefer, Chapter 11). The perforations in the tepári are used by the deities to see the offerings that are inside the xiriki. If they find them pleasurable, they will enter the temple through these openings in order to enjoy the gifts.

Huichol offerings to the deities consist of both foods and certain ritual objects. The latter include votive arrows; feather wands or staffs; votive gourds; the thread crosses called *tsikuri* in Huichol and "eyes of god" by Lumholtz (Figure 94); images for "seeing" called *niérika*; wooden miniatures of various animals; deer heads; deer tails; chocolate; miniature and full-size bows, deerskin quivers, and compound arrows with hardwood tips; and miniature replicas of *uwéni*, the woven, high-backed chair with a deerskin border on the seat on which shamans and elders sit during ceremonies (Figures 95 and 96). The food and beverages offered to the nature deities are the same the Huichols themselves prepare and consume during the festivals. Some meals, however, are specific to the ceremony in which they are served.

As noted, the xiriki is used for all the ceremonies conducted on the rancho level,

FIGURE 93. Circular Adobe Brick Xiriki under Construction on a San Andrés Rancho. See Chapter 11. (*Photograph by Stacy B. Schaefer, July 1994.*)

including that of calling the dead. On the particular occasion described here, the following ritual objects were observed inside:

1. Two *uwéni tiritsi*, miniature chairs for the gods who enter at midnight to rest and enjoy the gifts (Figure 95);
2. five *catira*, wax candles, one each for the four cardinal points and the sacred center;
3. a *takwátsi*, the plaited oblong basket in which the shamans keep their muviéris and other power objects;
4. five *hayuríme*, bottles containing sacred water from the peyote pilgrimage; the ocean; the sacred place of the old fire god, called Tatewarita; Lake Chapala; and the lake the Huichols call Takutsita (from Takutsi [Great Grandmother] Nakawé, the white-haired old earth and creator goddess);
5. a full-size *uwéni*, or shaman's chair (Figure 96);
6. a *mitsi*, or ceremonial mat;
7. maize of five sacred colors—red, yellow, white, black and pinto;
8. numerous *muviérite* (pl. of muviéri), arrow-shaped power staffs with a bundle of hawk feathers at the butt end;
9. two *putsi*, or copal incense burners;
10. a small *tapesti*, or platform, to support the miniature god chairs;
11. a *caitsa*, or gourd rattle;

FIGURE 94. Tsikuris. Huichols use tsikuris, mistakenly translated as "eyes of god" by Lumholtz, for two purposes, with very different meanings. The main use of these thread crosses, which serve as amulets for many peoples, past and present, is to protect and pray for children under five. However, objects of identical construction are set up in death ceremonies as spirit traps to entangle the dead attempting to return to the rancho outside the proper ritual context. In this context they are called *tüwe*, jaguar. Modern versions are much more colorful. (*Collected by Konrad Theodor Preuss in 1907 in San Andrés, at Los Baños, and along the Río Chapalagana. Museum für Völkerkunde, Berlin-Dahlem.*)

12. numerous *xukúri* (votive gourd bowls) containing cookies, chocolate, tamales, tortillas, beans, and pumpkin seeds;
13. several tobacco gourds;
14. a box for tobacco snuff powder;
15. *caapura aguaya*, the sheep horns used as musical instruments by peyoteros;
16. an animal skull, or *calavina* (from the Spanish *calavera*);
17. several baskets of *tsamurite*;
18. tamales, *tetsu* in Huichol;
19. thread crosses, *tsikúri* (Lumholtz's "eyes of god");
20. large clay pots, *olla* in Spanish, *xaríte* in Huichol, for the fermented maize beer (Figure 97);
21. a carrying bag;
22. a mirror, *xiquiri* in Huichol, used by shamans to "see" into the Otherworld.

The actual ceremony of raising, or calling, the deceased begins at approximately 9 p.m. Gesturing with their muviéris, the singers chant their invocations of the deities of the

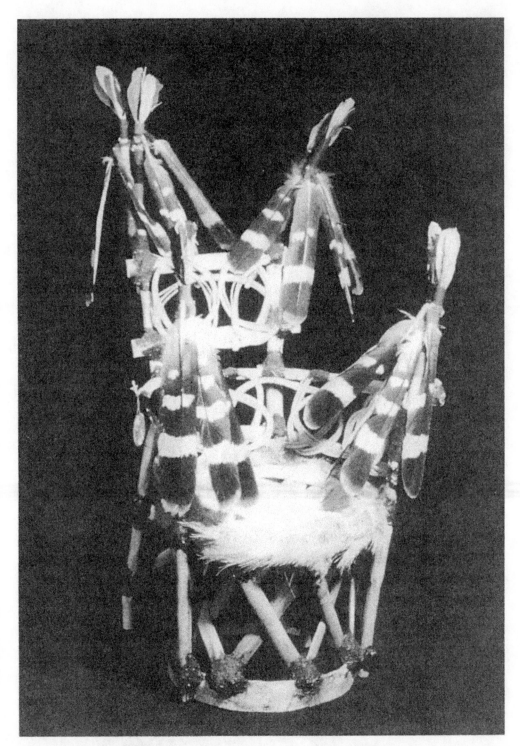

FIGURE 95. Small "God Chair" with Prayer Arrows. In the solar myth, the first god chair was made on the orders of Tatewarí, Grandfather Fire, to keep the young Sun, exhausted from his perilous subterranean journey from the west to his place of rebirth in Wirikúta, from sinking down and burning up the earth. (*God Chair by Ramón Medina. Fowler Museum of Cultural History, University of California at Los Angeles.*)

FIGURE 96. Uwéni, the Special Chair Reserved for Shamans and Elders. Though seemingly of simple construction, all parts and materials, including the deer hide that borders the seat, are

FIGURE 97. Stirring the Fermented Ceremonial Maize Beer Huichols Call *Nawá*, San Andrés, June 1991. (*Photograph by Stacy B. Schaefer.*)

imbued with complex symbolism emphasizing balance. According to Ramón Medina, who made this chair for his own use in the rituals leading up to the 1968 peyote pilgrimage, the designs woven into the backrest represent peyote and are meant to protect the shaman-singer against sorcerers' attacks from the rear. (*Chair by Ramón Medina, Southwest Museum, Los Angeles.*)

four directions and the center. The women prepare food around a small hearth. The five above-mentioned pitch pine crosses, resembling the Christian symbol but here representing the world directions, the *huisache* (acacia) branch, and the tuxu *Artemesia mexicana* plant, are presented to the mara'akáme, who proceeds to set the crosses afire on three of their sides, the ashes being carefully collected. The shaman-singer extinguishes the flames and hands the half-burned crosses to four young men, who take them a distance of about 300 feet in the four world directions, with the fifth cross placed directly in front of the mara'akáme.[4] The ashes are then divided among all the participants. Each mixes his portion with saliva and smears the resulting black paste, *tuxári*, around his or her abdomen. The objective of this ritual is prophylactic: to prevent the spirit of the deceased from bringing them harm at the moment he, or, as the case may be, she, is instructed to say goodbye. The stomach is said to be especially vulnerable to a spirit sickness called, in Spanish, *peque dolor de estomago*.

The mara'akáme and his helpers sing incessantly to the soul of the deceased, and in turn listen intently to, and repeat, its replies, all the while consuming small amounts of peyote and such alcoholic beverages as fermented maize beer and *tepe*, a potent distillate which the Huichols get from the Tepehuanes. Tatewarí, meanwhile, is continuously fed his "food," in the form of firewood. About midnight, the singing ceases for a short while. Some participants sleep or rest, while others socialize.

The four half-burnt crosses that the young men had deposited at a considerable distance from the singers are now put in front of them. The mara'akáme lights numerous candles that have been sanctified with the blood of sacrificial deer or cattle, and hands them to a group of women who have formed a circle to the right of the ceremonial hearth, that is, to the right of Tatewarí, and are now serving a beef broth made from a sacrificed bull, gorditas and tamales in gourd bowls, cups, and other containers. A chocolate drink prepared by a relative of the deceased is served to the men in gourd bowls. Food and burning candles having been distributed all around, both men and women rise with their rations of food in their hands and form a circle around the blazing fire, joining in the singing and invoking Tatewarí by sobbing, singing, and offering soup, tamales, and pieces of gorditas to the old fire god. There is also a young girl, who is carrying soap and a purple cloth—objects used, along with others, to "clean" Tatewarí.

This portion of the ceremony completed, the guests are directed to the xiriki. The mara'akáme enters by himself, followed by his assistants, the cuinapuvamete, the mother and sister of the deceased, the young girl carrying the soap and cloth, and some women holding lighted candles. Everyone, inside and outside the xiriki, now prays and weeps. If the deceased received Christian baptism, there is a special ritual inside the xirirki: the mara'akáme takes the soap and cloth from the young girl and with them wipes a crucifix, a ritual Huichols call *tatata*. Like baptism, this act is meant to purify everything, because everything has come to an end, and everything is now clean.

The party then exits from the xiriki to assemble again, all the while chanting and weeping, at the tapesti with the belongings of the deceased and the offerings for the spirit. With their muviéri the singers—the mara'akáme and his assistants—call upon the deities who were present at the birth of the deceased, as well as to the spirit. Of course, only the mara'akáme can see the deceased. Some people in Santa Catarína told me the spirit of the dead person at this point appears to him in the form of a small cloud; others in this community, and also in San Andrés Cohamiata, described it as a luminous fly.[5]

The soul of the deceased has now come to rest on the muviéri of the shaman, and from its perch addresses its relatives as follows: "I can no longer arrive as I had done before, I am no longer corporeal, it is better that you forget about me." As only the mara'akáme can see the spirit, so it is he alone who can hear his voice, and it also is he who transmits its sad message to the living. Hearing its voice through the shaman, all the relatives and friends weep disconsolately while offering the deceased a final meal by placing their gifts of food on the tapesti.

Once more now, the friends and family of the deceased return to the xiriki, where the mara'akáme picks the soul up on his muviéri to carry it to the house in which it resided during life so it can say goodbye. The mara'akáme then places the spirit on a mule that had belonged to it in life so it can start on its voyage, leaving its earthly belongings behind to its relatives. Since this is the final farewell, everyone cries with much grief, praying also for the mule's safe return.

But this by no means puts an end to the ceremony, for soon afterwards the participants assemble once more before the ceremonial hearth to pray to Tatewarí. From there, they make a ceremonial circuit past the elevated granary and through the patio to the house of the progeny of the deceased, to offer prayers to the Huichol deities for their welfare, and back again to the sacred space in front of the xiriki. Here the singers once again take their seats, facing the blazing fire, Tatewarí, and singing non-stop. The five crosses are now burnt completely in front of the tapesti and the ashes mixed with water to create a black paste similar to the tuxári the participants had earlier smeared on their abdomens to ward of spirit illness.

Around 6 a.m., with the first light of day, commences the part of the mortuary ceremony called *teúte tauteúni táuxi*, "the placement of black molars," from the image of a small black molar that is painted on the right cheek, wrist, and ankle of all the participants after they ritually washed their faces and hands.

According to what I was told by the Huichols, the act of washing signifies the removal of any memory they might have of the deceased: since he no longer exists, there is no reason to remember him. The cheek is painted in black because that is what people saw when they looked at the deceased; the wrist is painted because it was by a handshake that he greeted them; and the ankle because that was what he used to move close to them. With this same black paste, they also draw crosses on the house doors, the cooking shed, and the xiriki, as well as their furnishings, in order to stop the soul of the deceased from haunting these areas.

According to Lumholtz, at one time the Huichols hung crosses made of the tuxu plant in the house in order to keep the spirits of the dead away from the pots containing the fermenting maize beer because they might spoil the drink. They also hung branches from the zapote tree (*sapodilla*) around the area were the ceremonial maize beer was fermenting and covered the pots with them to keep the spirits out. According to Lumholtz, when a Huichol goes to fill his first gourd bowl with maize beer or tepe, he first puts a finger inside the gourd and flings a few drops from side to side as an offering to any spirits of the dead that might be present. Were he to neglect this ritual, his body would swell up with the first taste of the drink.

Now, at long last, the *müüqui cuevixa*, the raising of the dead, concludes with the shamans blessing the ears of maize, candles, and their own feathered staffs of power, which they moisten in the cold meat soup and the chocolate. With full light the guests are served gorditas, tamales, bull meat soup, cooked squash, cheese, fruit, maize beer, and chocolate, but of each dish in turn they must offer a small part to Tatewarí.

What all this signifies is the ambivalent attitude Huichols have toward the dead. On the one hand, death is an occasion for sadness and mourning. On the other, the spirits of the dead are feared because of the harm they can bring. Huichol society is watched over not only by the many deities, most of them manifestations of natural forces and phenomena, but also by the ancestors, and supernatural sanctions are employed as a form of social control against individuals who break the moral code. It is important to understand also that other than bidding farewell to the deceased, the ceremony of "calling the dead" for one final time is also an important social occasion.

The closeness people feel at the time of a death in the family affirms and reinforces group cohesion and maintains the traditions and customs that constitute Huichol culture. On traditional communal occasions such as this, no less than individually within the family from parent or grandparent to child, these traditions and customs are transmitted to the new generation, thereby guaranteeing the continued existence of the Huichols as a distinctive indigenous society.

NOTES

1. As Alan Sandstrom has pointed out to us, this is clearly derived from the Nahuatl *tlapextli* = bed.(—Eds.)

2. This is a special treat that, as seen in the next chapter, is not meant as food for the deceased but as payment for passage to the dog that guards the trail to the Otherworld.

3. Acacia thorns are used symbolically by the shaman to pierce a male soul's foot to interrupt its dancing so it can be captured for the farewell ceremony. See Ramón Medina's text and yarn painting, Chapter 13.(—Eds.)

4. This places him and the celebrants symbolically in the center of the universe.(—Eds.)

5. In Ramón Medina's narrative, the spirit of the dead person starts out as a little cloud or puff of air and later manifests itself as a luminous insect, presumably a firefly (see Chapter 13).(—Eds.)

13 : A HUICHOL SOUL TRAVELS TO THE

LAND OF THE DEAD

RAMÓN MEDINA SILVA

Editor's Note: There is an intriguing sexual aspect to Ramón Medina's narrative of the journey of the soul after death that was surprising enough to make me wonder, when I first heard it nearly thirty years ago, whether it was truly aboriginal. I need not have worried. First, I was to hear more or less the same thing a year or so later from another Huichol, a native of the comunidad indígena of Guadalupe Ocotán. Second, and this was more surprising, it turns out that it is shared also by the Hopis, a thousand miles to the north.

This, in brief, is how I first heard it from Ramón: On its long and arduous journey to the land of the dead in the west, each soul, man or woman, bears the burden of every sexual encounter its owner had in life, in the form of the sexual organs of the opposite sex. The female soul carries with it all the penises that ever pleasured its owner, the male soul all the vaginas. Promiscuity not being unknown among the Huichols, the burden can be a heavy one. Not surprisingly, at various stopping points along the trail, the soul attempts to rid itself of the evidence of its sexuality. But the ancient ones will not permit this, for, as we shall see, it takes the physical evidence of sexuality to assure food and plenty of fermented drink for a proper welcome for the newly arrived soul. The operative principal here seems to be not punishment but fertility and interdependence between the living and those who came before, though in Ramón's narrative these are both deceased relatives, former lovers, and Héwis, an ancient race that, except for one man and his female dog companion, Huichols say perished in the watery cataclysm that drowned a previous creation. The little dog, in turn, transformed into a young woman by taking off her pelt, to become the genetrix of a new human race (Furst 1993:303-323).

When I first heard Ramón tell of the wandering soul's unusual burden, I considered briefly whether this might not be Ramón, who on occasion waxed eloquently about the proper way of "being Huichol," doing some creative philosophizing. All doubt about the authenticity of the story vanished a year later in San Andrés Cohamiata, when I asked the Huichol husband of our Indian (but non-Huichol) cook to tell me and the students in our medical-anthropological summer field research project about the soul and what happened to it after death. The man's name was *Jesús* and he was very much the traditionalist, as convinced as was Ramón of the superiority of Huichol religion over any other. Earlier, he had told us that he was originally from Guadalupe Ocotán and had to flee to San Andrés when his life was threatened by the same group of fanatical converts who had burned down the tuki, the circular "pagan" temple that the traditionalists there had constructed for their aboriginal ceremonies in the face of strong opposition from the church and its adherents.

Jesús was reluctant at first to talk about the journey of the soul. Certain things in the story, he allowed, were not proper for the ears of women. What finally convinced him to tell it uncensored was that our women students seemed more like men in the kind of work they did. Nevertheless, he was careful to refer to the sexual organs only as "cosas de mujer" and "cosas de hombre," "women's things" and "men's things."

Having had this aspect of Ramón's narrative confirmed by another Huichol living, unlike Ramón, in one of the traditional Sierra communities, was welcome. But the really startling thing came in 1989, when the Mexican journal Tlalocan, having finally reappeared after a hiatus of several years following the death of its longtime editor, the very able Nahuatl scholar Fernando Horcasitas, published a Hopi text of a visit a young man named Honanyestiwa made to the beyond in the company of the Sun god. The narrative is one of many collected by Edward Kennard in 1934–35 and 1938–39 in the Hopi villages on Second Mesa, Arizona, but that had remained unpublished. It tells of a brother and sister who once lived at Oraibi. They preferred their own company to that of others, and neither liked to participate in the social dances. Instead, the brother would go running by himself and take lone ritual baths. But what he really yearned for was finding out about the land of the dead, and he prayed to the Sun god to help him. The Sun Father agreed, instructing him to make many prayer sticks for the journey with his father while smoking the ritual tobacco, and to go to sleep on the night of the fifth day without telling anyone but his sister what he planned to do (Kennard 1989:151–171).

The story of his journey in the company of the Sun is long and there is not space here to do it justice. Suffice it to say that at different points along the way our hero encounters many people, women and men, who are also trying to reach the land of the dead. They have difficulty doing so, however, because, like the souls in the Huichol narrative, they are burdened with the sexual organs of the opposite gender:

> Continuing like that, they came to Awatovi. They climbed up there. "All right, you must look. They are coming along," he (the Sun god) said to him.
> He looked out. A big cloud was approaching. Once more he advised him.
> "Again you must not say anything to them (the dead)."
> They came up to them. There were women who had no clothes. Some had carrying baskets on their backs, and others were carrying penises on their backs. Women who had husbands from men already married were carrying baskets. They held up their carrying baskets with the string wrapped around their hair. . . . And others as many women as had intercourse

with married men were carrying penises on their backs. Whoever she wanted very badly, that one was hanging in front from her forehead . . .

"All right. You will look again. Over there again. Those are the men," he (the Sun) said to him.

Continuing that way, they came up to them, too. They went the same way, too. Boys who had married women for wives had carrying baskets on their backs. And the men, however many girls they had, also had their vulvas similarly carried on their backs. . . . (Kennard 1989:159–161)

The Hopi variant contains more the flavor of punishment for moral infractions than does the Huichol tale, because, unlike their Huichol counterparts, who are no less burdened with the physical evidence of illicit sexual activities on their way to the underworld, the Hopi men and women have difficulty making it to their destination. Also, there is no mention here of a useful role for the disembodied organs. But then, of course, we do not know how much might have dropped out of the Hopi tale by the time it was recorded by Kennard.

In Ramón's narrative, after reliving all its life experiences, which the officiating mara'akáme narrates in the memorial chant at the ceremony of calling back the dead, the soul begins its actual journey at "The Place of the Black Stones," a kind of foot drum of ringing stones on which it stomps to signal its impending arrival to those awaiting it in the afterworld.[1] Soon, it comes to a fork in the road (Figure 98). One path leads to the left, the other to the right. The former, lined with numerous painful ordeals, is for people who have committed incest or who have had intercourse with a non-Huichol, the latter is for those who "had a Huichol heart," in other words, behaved according to the unwritten code. The former road ends in a corral full of mules, who stomp on the soul of the offender (Figure 99). There is no permanent punishment, however; like this one, the successive ordeals inflicted on transgressors are only temporary, and even Huichols who have committed the most serious breaches will be permitted to trace their way back to the black stones and take the right-hand trail, which leads to a place where the souls of long-dead people are waiting to welcome them with a great festivity, with much dancing and drinking.

On both paths, however, the soul carries a heavy burden. As Ramón says of the male soul:

He is walking there, carrying many vaginas in his arms, all those he enjoyed in life. All those vaginas one has been inside, these one carries in one's arms. The soul carries all that and he is very tired.

The female soul is similarly loaded down with "men's things." The following text continues Ramón's narrative, beginning about half-way between the black stones and the soul's destination.

P.T.F.

FIGURE 98. The Bifurcated Path in Huichol Eschatology. The left fork is for transgressors against incest taboos and other offenses; the right is for Huichols who follow the rules of life. But both are fraught with tests, like the opossum, crow, and dog mentioned in the narrative. (*Yarn painting by Ramón Medina. Fowler Museum of Cultural History, University of California at Los Angeles.*)

First, one comes to where there is a dog. It is a male dog, it is black, that little dog, with a white spot on its throat. It stands there, that dog, as if it is tied up. It is barking there. It is as if it wants to bite that soul as it tries to pass. One asks permission of that dog to pass, because there is a water over there. One must pass through that water. And that little dog says to that soul, "Oh, I am so hungry. Why were you mean to me over there? You did not feed me well. You would eat in front of me. You would let me be hungry as you ate your tortillas, as you ate your maize. As you ate your beans you would let me starve. And now you want me to open this way for you? How can you

FIGURE 99. The Soul of an Offender against Huichol Mores. Temporarily in a corral with mules, the offender's soul is trampled and left for dead. The symbolism of the mule is double-barrelled: mules, introduced by foreigners, are alien as well as barren, as Huichol are said to become if they have sex with non-Indians. Because eternal punishment is not part of the Huichol belief system, the trampled soul picks itself up, retraces its steps, and continues on the right-hand path in search of its waiting relatives. (*Yarn painting by Ramón Medina. Fowler Museum of Cultural History, University of California at Los Angeles.*)

expect such a thing? You would throw stones at me. You would beat me. Oh no, I shall not make way for you. On the contrary, I shall perhaps bite you."

That is why, when one of us dies, we make little tortillas for him to take along, little thick tortillas. They are put in a bag, he puts them in a bag which he carries. So that he can feed that dog. Be it a man or a woman, that soul brings those tortillas to feed that dog. Because the dog says to that soul, "Give me something to eat now, so that I may let you pass."

And that soul takes out some of this food and gives it to the dog. Because that poor little dog is hungry. It is from ancient times, when it died, that little dog. It died and then it remained there, to stand watch on that road. Then the man or the woman, the life of the man or the woman who died, takes the tortillas out of the bag. Five little tortillas, made of the five colors of maize. The soul takes out this food and gives it to the little dog.

The dog is busy eating and right away that soul leaves. Right away, as that dog is busy eating, that soul can pass and it keeps on walking.

He walks there, that soul, and he comes to where the crow is. That is the crow that roams our fields when we are ready to pick the maize. That crow wants to steal our maize and we are angry at him for this. For this reason we have someone who waits there in the field, so that he can chase the crow away. We say, "You ugly crow, only doing damage." So we speak in this world, not knowing that it is over there that one has to pay. That is why the crow sits there, eating in front of us. He sits there eating well, that crow. His tortillas, his beans, his chile made in a bowl which is especially for that purpose. Eating there very peacefully, very contented, belching.

And we walking there with hunger, carrying that load. That soul asks the crow for some food but the crow tells him, "No, I won't give you any. You see, you did not feed me over there, you would not let me eat. You said I was a thief, that I stole things from your field. You said I was damaging your maize. You said this, that and the other. Now I will not feed you, as you did not feed me over there. I will not give you tortillas or anything."

So the soul says, "Very well, if that is how it is." The soul tells that crow, "If that is how you are, very well, don't give me anything." And the soul keeps on walking, carrying all those things, all those vaginas, all those things of the man, whichever it may be. All those things one has enjoyed over there.

Then he comes to where there is the Opossum. He arrives there and Opossum says, "Open your mouth." He says to that soul, "Let me see now, didn't you eat me?" And there where he arrives, he opens his mouth and sees whether he has been eaten by that man, by that woman. Those dead ones. Opossum says, "If you have eaten me over there, I am going to put you in a trap."

Opossum has a trap there, a big stone, a flat one, very heavy. That stone is held up by a small stick, to catch the one who has eaten his meat. But when one has not eaten the meat of the opossum, nothing happens to him. He passes through that trap, safely.

Do you know why Opossum defends himself in this manner? Because he is sacred. It is he who obtained Tatewarí (fire) for everyone.[2] It is because of this that we live. That is why he defends his rights.

In this manner Opossum punishes those who have eaten his meat. He has his trap there, on that path where the soul travels. That one who ate Opossum's meat, he walks there and then the stone falls on him. It presses down on that person, hard. Opossum lets it fall. And that life says, "Oh, oh, this hurts much." And Opossum says, "That is the way it hurt me when you were eating me. Every time you bit into my meat, it hurt me. It hurts you now? Well, it hurt me, too." So Opossum advises him.

But as many have never eaten Opossum's meat, many pass through there without harm. But some remain there a while. Because one must not eat Opossum's meat. It is sacred.

Then that soul goes walking and walking. Very tired, very tired. Carrying all those things of the woman, all those things of the man, whichever it may be.

Let us say it is a woman. Well then, a woman is born. She is a little girl and one sees her with much affection. All love her for the reason that she will be good for man, to grind the maize, to make his tortillas. To do for him all his life as he does for her. And then, when she begins to walk it is she who does her parents' bidding. It is the same for the boy. Be it a girl or a boy, it is the same. Well, then they take good care of her so that she will not fail in one manner or another. So that she will not commit some errors. So that she will not do these things with some boy when she is too young.

But then, as one says, their custom comes to them. They are transformed. And then they begin to dream things. In this manner things come to their minds and one watches them much. The Moon comes to them, as one says. Well, then she begins to do these things with some man. She takes pleasure with this man and that, even when she is married. This happens. These things are transgressions but there are many women who get crazy notions. They do these things very much. I tell these things to you because all this comes back to them when they die. It is that when they die, when she is going to die, that woman remains there without speaking. Many hours, sometimes twenty-four hours. Just breathing a little in the heart. Because she has committed many errors with those different persons. The woman should take care of herself as it is said. . . .

. . . Well, when they die, whoever brought them into this world, those great ones, they say to her, "Look, why did you want so many of the men's thing?" And then that Old One puts out his arms, or if it is one of Our Mothers, she puts out her arms, and they show the amount of men's things she has taken pleasure with. To commit so many errors! And the poor woman has to carry all that. The poor woman, the life of that woman, goes tired, tired, saying, "Oh, how tired I am, having to carry so many things." And they say to her, "Well, that is your pleasure. That is what you wanted to do over there where you lived." They say, "Well, look, why did you want so many things? You kept at it, you kept at it. Now you must take the whole bunch."

That is how they speak to her. They say to her, "You used to say over there that you were never going to get tired of men's things. So that is your pleasure now. There goes that poor woman's life, carrying all that. And the mara'akáme, he follows her. So that he can catch that soul.

It is all the same, for the woman and for the man. They have to carry all the things they took pleasure with. They walk and walk, carrying it all. If it is a woman, she arrives there at the place of the black rocks. She arrives very tired. And she gathers together a bunch and throws them down there. But they tell her not to throw them away. If it is a man, he tries to throw it all away, just like the woman. But they tell him, "No, do not throw that away. It was your pleasure, gather them up." So they gather them up. That woman picks them up one by one. She puts them in her cape. It is the cape which Huichol women wear. Thirsty, hungry, they have to carry these things until they arrive over there.

Well, the life of the man walks there with all those vaginas. All those women he has enjoyed. And the woman walks there with all those penises. All those that they have taken pleasure with her . . .

Well, that life goes on walking, thirsty, tired, very thirsty, very tired. Very hungry. If it is a woman, always with her hands full of those things, those men's things she carries. And with the man it is the same.

Well, that life comes over there where they are waiting for them. And he yells, that life, he yells and he calls out to those others who have died before him. That is where the tree is, that large tree, that which is called *xápa*. It is the wild fig tree. They are *héwixi*, ancient, ancient people. They are waiting there for that life. They have souls just as we have but they are the ancient ones, those that have gone over there before. They are as they are. That is what they are there for, waiting there to make those ceremonies with that life.

So that life calls out, "Brothers, sisters, I, too, am coming where you are. I am going over there." Then those others there become happy. They say, "Oh, fine, here comes my brother. My brother is coming." And they say, "Ah, it is my sister who is coming." Whichever it may be, that is how they call out: "My brother, my sister, they are coming."

They are shouting, "Ah, now we are going to eat! Ah, now we are going to eat those fruits that are on that tree!"

Then someone plays his violin, if he has such a thing. He plays this song that those others over there can hear it. They hear and they say, "Oh, he is coming now. Now let us go and eat. We are very hungry. Surely he is coming, surely we are going to eat now."

Very well. Then after taking five steps he comes to the tree which is a large wild fig tree. Then that man who is carrying the vaginas of the women he enjoyed tells his brothers, "Yes, my brothers, now we are going to eat." If it is three women he enjoyed in his life, or four, or five, however many it may be, he has these things with him. He carries them all in his hand. He says, "Yes, my brothers, now I am going to throw these women's things into the tree." He says to them all, "I am going to throw them as one throws a stone. I will throw one up there to see how many of those fruits will fall down from that tree."

So he speaks. He says to them, "Ah yes, now I do have something to throw at those fruit, something I can throw up there." And then he throws those things at the fruit. He strikes the tree with those vaginas and then they start to fall (Figure 100). Many fruit fall down there. After throwing the first vaginas, he throws the rest to one side. He leaves them there, all in one heap. There where the others have thrown them, those

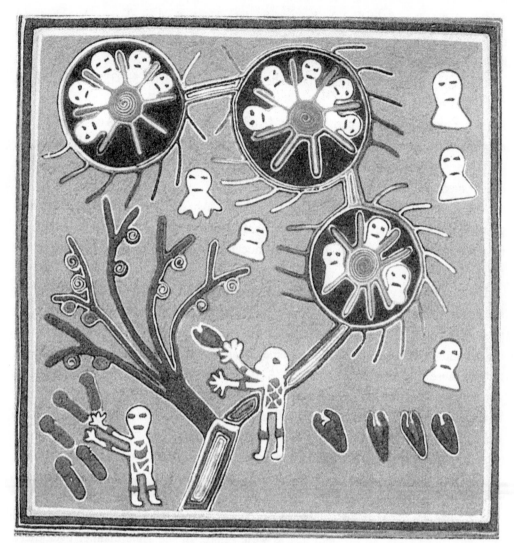

FIGURE 100. Yarn painting of Tree of Life with Gathering of Souls. Burdened with the evidence of an active sexual life—disembodied vaginas for the man and penises for the woman—the soul finally arrives at a great tree of life, heavy with ripe fruit, around which the souls of the ancient Héwi wait to entertain it with food and drink after the newcomer knocks the fruits down with the sexual organs flung into the branches. This is followed by spirited round dances. (*Yarn painting by Ramón Medina. Fowler Museum of Cultural History, University of California at Los Angeles.*)

that came before. There is a pile of them there, some dressed, some without a thing on, some well covered—well, there is this pile of vaginas. He leaves them there, lying where he threw them down.

Well, that woman, the life of that woman, she arrives there in the same manner. There where the tree is, where they are waiting. It is very large, that tree, very high, with five branches and five roots. It has many fruits, that tree. There where she arrives, that woman's life makes a sound. It is a sound like that made by the dove. She calls out,

"Kukurukú, kukurukú!" And the boys with whom she had taken pleasure hear her and they clap their hands and say, "She has come now." All those that are over there hear her and they say, "Ah, our sister, she has come."

Then she takes the man's thing and she throws it at the tree. She throws it at those fruits and as the thing is very big, many fruits fall down. She says, "Ah, this was good. It throws down much." Then she says, "And here is another one. And another and another." Five throws with strong sticks, those men's things. The woman throws them up there. And the others she throws away. They remain there. There is that pile, that pile of men's things. Where the tree is.

And all those who are waiting there, they shout, "Ah, now we are going to eat!" And they eat there, they eat those fruits which have fallen down from the tree. The life of that man, and of that woman, they have knocked down those fruits. Now they all eat there together.

Well, then. They arrive where they are dancing, those who have died before. They are dancing there to the music of the Huichol violin. He arrives and there are many pretty Huichol girls there, fully adorned, very well painted on their faces. All are dancing around Tatewarí, some drinking, some already drunk. Some are already wanting to fight because they have drunk so much. And the one who is playing for them, his hand almost breaking from playing so much. And the one who is singing there, drunk from having drunk so much, he is close to Tatewarí, very close, because he does not know where he is going from having drunk so much.

And that life arrives over there, and his brothers embrace him. They say to him, "Come, brother, let us go dance, let us follow the dancing." So he gives five turns around the fire, dancing there in a circle around the fire as one does on this earth.

And that woman, that girl, in the same manner. She arrives and all embrace her, her brothers, her sisters, all of them just as we do here. In the same manner over there. She asks, "You there, did you come first?" He says, "Well, yes." She says, "Come and embrace me. You know I am yours and you are mine." And he says, "Well, then, if that is how it is." And he says, "Come let us go dance." They go dancing, dancing, dancing, to the music of the Huichol violin. It is exactly as it is with the man.

Then they go on, first to this ceremony, then to that. It is that they are going to the ceremonies of the Héwixi, who came before. All those dances are the same, only they are ancient. He goes to the ceremony of the parched maize, where they are around Tatewarí. Again he gives five turns around the fire. There they eat peyote. They grind the peyote and they mix it with water. They grind it in a special way and they mix it and then they drink it. They eat and they drink it. And they drink the nawá, they drink and drink and drink. And they sing their song, "Ah, our brother, now you have arrived and here we are dancing, dancing well." So they sing and give five turns around Tatewarí.

Then he travels again, walking, walking. He comes to the ceremony which is called the Dance of the Spindle-whorls. There one drinks much nawá again, nawá, nawá,

nawá, as one does over here. They are singing, "Dance, dance, dance, you spindle-whorls." This is danced in a quarry of stones, the stones from which one makes the tepári [stone disks] of Tatewarí. He makes another five turns there. He drinks nawá. He eats fish soup with those others. He eats deer soup with those others. And the same with the woman.

And they go to the place where they are dancing the dance of the *nanáwata*, which is like the fifth place where they dance. One, two, three, four, five—all those ancient ceremonies. There they dance the nanáwata, there they throw the balls of yarn. It is very ancient, this dance. That is why we still have this ceremony, because it comes down from ancient times.

He gives five turns, dancing the nanáwata. He continues there, dancing and dancing. They are all together there, throwing those balls of yarn back and forth. And he is drinking there, drinking the nawá as one does.

And they drink *tsinári* of maize of five colors, drinking a drink made from chocolate. He is going to and fro, very drunk. One of them speaks to him, saying, "Ah, my brother, why have you taken so long, why have you not come before?" And he says, "Well, it is this way and that, that is why."

And the same with the woman. They say to her, "Ah, my sister, we waited and waited and you did not come. Now you have come at last." And she says, "Yes, I have come at last."

Well, then the mara'akáme and the soul catcher, that one we call Waxíewe, they are waiting there, trying to catch that life. Ah, he is ready to fall down as he dances there with those others. He says to them, "My brothers, I am enjoying myself very much." He says this to them as he dances there with a pretty girl at his side. And that woman also, she is enjoying all that, dancing with all those boys who have gone before.

Then the mara'akáme speaks to the soul catcher, "Now is the time." They are ready to catch him. All this the mara'akáme sees, all this he tells the relatives as they wait there for that life.

And if that life is a man, the mara'akáme says to those relatives, "Have you brought the five thorns of which I told you, those five thorns of the acacia?" And if it is a woman, he says, "Have you brought me those five burrs of which I spoke? Because it is time now." And they say to him, "Yes, mara'akáme, we have brought those things as you asked."

And with that he takes those five thorns, or those five burrs, whichever it may be, and he throws them there at the feet of the one who is dancing down there.

That one dances and dances and then he jumps. He jumps up and down—ah, one pierces his foot! He cries out, "A thorn has pierced my foot! A thorn has pricked me. Let go of me, let go of me." And those girls who are holding hands, they let loose. He says, "My brothers, my sisters, come and help me, something is stuck in my foot."

The girls let go of him and he sits down there to take that out of his foot. And if it is a woman, she sits there to take away those burrs the mara'akáme threw there at her. It is then that the mara'akáme says, "Waxíwie, it is time for that thing as it was arranged." And Waxíewe, the one who is helping the mara'akáme down there, he throws his noose, catching that soul.

All this the mara'akáme tells them, as they wait up there. He describes it well, as it happens. The mara'akáme and the soul catcher, they secure the noose around that life. With his power, with his arrows [muviéri], with his colors, they blur the vision of that soul so that it cannot see well. He has that power, because it has been given to him by Tatewarí, by Kauyumári.

Then he calls a wasp, a black wasp. It is like the wasp we have in this world. He calls this wasp so that with the help of his feathers it can pick up the life of that man, if it be a man, or that woman, if that is what it is. There are five of these wasps, in five colors, red, blue, white, yellow, and black.

In Ramón's narrative, the soul is reluctant to leave the dancing and singing and drinking and the shaman-singer has to coax him:

Well, that wasp lifts him. With the help of the plumes of the mara'akáme, that life is lifted up from there. It has been purified of everything. He arrives pure. Then the mara'akáme says to him, "Now we are taking you there where you lived in this world so that your relatives can see you. They need you. Even though you are not as alive as you were before, your relatives are waiting for you. They want to see you. They have food for you. They have killed a cow. They have fish, and a hen. They have brought you much to eat. They have sugar cane there, and coffee. They have meat for you, turkey, maize, many things. They have nawá for you because they are waiting there for you. Why don't you go?" The mara'akáme speaks to that life over there, so that all can hear him. But he does not want to come (Figure 101).

Then the mara'akáme speaks to the Sun. He says, "You with your power, he does not want to come." And that life says to them, "No, I do not want to go there. My brothers did not love me over there where I was. My wife would quarrel with me. My sisters, they quarreled with me. Therefore I will not go."

At this point the shaman-singer informs the waiting relatives that the soul of the departed is reluctant to appear, and all weep. But, he says, possibly it might be persuaded if it were offered a small drink of nawá. In Ramón's words:

The relatives give some of the nawá in a gourd bowl and using his plumes he gives it to that soul. Ah, with that nawá he begins to change his mind. Drinking some of that nawá he begins to waver.

FIGURE 101. Yarn Painting of Funerary Ceremony. In the final act, the shaman, who narrates the path of the soul at the funerary ceremony, catches hold of the soul with the help of Kauyumári and a wasp (*lower left*), transforms it into a firefly and returns it on the tips of his muviéri feathers to the relatives waiting at the mortuary altar. After a final tearful farewell, he sends the soul on its way to Wirikúta. (*Yarn painting by Ramón Medina. Fowler Museum of Cultural History, University of California at Los Angeles.*)

Kauyumári aids all that with his power. He throws many colors at the soul so that it will change its mind. He erases all that which troubles the soul, so that it will agree to appear there before everyone, so that all can greet it there, so that it will leave from there as it should (in its manifestation as a luminous fly).

NOTES

1. Many of the elements in Ramón Medina's text of the post-mortem journey of the soul, first published by Furst in English in 1967 and in Spanish in 1972, and excerpted in these pages, also appear, or are alluded to, in a funeral oration from Santa Catarina published by Fikes (1993:120–

148). His narrative follows the path of the soul of a woman who died by suicide. However, unlike Ramón, who resolutely rejected anything that to him smacked of Christianity. Fikes's source, whom he describes as a renowned singer and healer, not only held the position of chief custodian of the Catholic Church in Santa Catarina but had clearly absorbed not a little of the Church's teachings. An example of this is the refusal of the higher powers, early on in his narration, to admit the woman's soul into heaven because she had died by her own hand. This is a deadly sin in the eyes of the Church but not of the Huichols. Huichols accept suicide, which is not uncommon among them (especially by hanging), as a regrettable but perfectly acceptable way of ending one's life. "Heaven," too, is not indigenous but Christian. There is not complete agreement on the ultimate destination of what we would call the soul, but the general idea is that it goes to Wirikúta, the peyote country, where at least those of shamans, elders, and other meritorious persons rise into the sky with the Sun Father and, until they return as *urukáte* (see following chapter), join him on his daily round.

2. Opossum was the animal person who volunteered to steal fire from its guardians after several other animals of higher prestige had tried and failed. Opossum succeeds by tricking the fire guardians and with his prehensile tail sneaks a bit of live coal from the fire. Hiding it in his pouch he makes his escape, but when he cannot resist taunting his adversaries with his success, they catch up with him and cut him up into little pieces. But in myth time nothing ever dies completely, and after a while he picks himself up, puts himself back together again, and climbs to the fifth and final level to share his booty with his companions. And that is how Tatewarí came into the Middle World, to light up the night, keep the people warm, and enable them to cook food they formerly had to eat raw.

Ever since Opossum has been sacred and his meat taboo.

ACKNOWLEDGEMENTS

A word of thanks is due to Jill L. McKeever Furst, who discovered the intriguing parallel to the Huichol tradition in Kennard's Hopi text while doing research into Uto-Aztecan eschatology for a book (McKeever Furst, 1995) on the natural history basis of Aztec conceptions of the soul.(—Eds.)

14 : THE *URUKÁME,*

A CRYSTALLIZATION OF THE SOUL

Death And Memory

MICHEL PERRIN

Translated from the French by KARIN SIMONEAU

San Andrés Cohamiata, Jalisco.

A. C. has carefully untied a strange package made of five different small pieces of cloth rolled up and tied together with a cloth string. He unrolls the first piece, saying: "Look, here are your grandfather and your grandmother." Playing on the ground in front of the little straw-roofed house, his little boy tries to pick up two small, transparent stones glued to the fibers of a piece of cotton (Figures 102, 103). I would not have seen them had A. C. not made an effort to pull them away from their strange bed. "They are glued to it," he explains to me, "for every time there is a festival they are given food: we place some deer blood and deer broth on top of them, some ox blood and beef broth, and some fish blood and fish broth."

A. C. picks up another piece of cloth, unrolls it, and places it near the first one after indicating with a gesture the two stones which it sheltered, one on each side. Slowly and solemnly he identifies them: "This one is my wife's maternal aunt, who has been dead for a long time; next to her is her husband, my wife's uncle, who died only little over a year ago." Carefully he folds the cloth again and unfolds the next one. Its stones are a bit larger, one transparent, the other black. "This is my grandmother, my mother's mother," he says of the black stone. "The other is her husband. They used to live here; they died long ago."

A. C. opens the last three packages and then closes them again after pointing out some more strange couples: "My wife's paternal grandparents, long dead; one of my sisters and her husband, who are still living; my father and my other mother—my father had two wives—both dead. Well, now you have seen all our *urukáte,*" he says. After

FIGURES 102, 103. Urukáme Bundle Unwrapped. This little bundle, measuring $2\frac{5}{8}''$, consists of a short length of bamboo containing a tiny rock crystal—the crystallized "heart soul" of a deceased shaman or elder—wrapped in cotton from the cottonwood tree, and an embroidered cloth as outer covering. Urukámes can be replaced, or, more accurately, replace themselves, which is why, much to the astonishment of outsiders, Huichols will sometimes readily part with such a potent relic after several years of use. (*Collected by Carl Lumholtz in the 1890s. American Museum of Natural History, New York. Photographs by Peter T. Furst.*)

showing me the last couple, he quickly ties the five packages together again and replaces the strange bundle inside the dark interior of a halved gourd. The container is decorated with three wax figures, their shapes roughly outlined by a few brightly colored beads. One represents a deer, another a peyote cactus, the third an ear of maize: the famous "Huichol trinity."

Associated with the dead and with those living persons who have "accumulated a lot of tradition," these modest and touching objects occupy the center stage in Huichol thought and ritual. They participate in a life cycle, tied to the sun, which gives death meaning and assures the perpetuation of human society. They are at the center of a kind of cult that establishes special relations between the community of the living and that of the dead, between the shamans and the other members of society, and between the children and the old people, a cult which also ties the health of the children to the social value attached to respect for tradition. Finally, they reveal a particular con-

FIGURE 104. Urukáme Bundle Attached to the Hunting Arrow from Which It Gets Its Name. (*Collected by Carl Lumholtz a century ago. American Museum of Natural History, New York. Photograph by Peter T. Furst.*)

ception of memory and of the mourning process, as well as the existence of cycles of degradation and regeneration of human and cosmic energy.

The word *urukáme* (from *uru*, arrow, pl. *urukáte*) or *uruteru* denotes a small stone with an average length and diameter of between one-half and one centimeter, that is, the size of a bean that is usually tied in a bundle to an arrow (Figure 104). But the term also designates the person from whom this stone emanates. The urukáme comes from a natural splinter of rock crystal, quartz or amethyst, or from stones with translucent or mirrorlike qualities, stones which the Huichol know as *te'ka*. The urukáme is a *tekari tshimé'pepe*, literally "a small te'ka stone."

When they are not gathered together and placed in a votive gourd—a *xukúli* (alt. xukúri)[1]—as described above, each small cloth "bed," called *kau'xe*, is attached to a ceremonial arrow. This is their most typical arrangement. The word urukáme is formed from *'urú*, "arrow" (used either for hunting or votive purposes), and -*káme*, a suffix denoting belonging, support, content.[2]

The pieces of cloth in which the urukáte are wrapped and the gourd or the arrows which hold them are kept inside the house in the *takwátsi*, a small oblong box made of plaited fibers in which votive objects (arrows, feathers, candles, etc.) are placed, or inside a small "altar" or oratory known as *urukáte wa'riliki*, "house of the urukáme." During the collective festivals the urukáte are taken to the *tuki*, the circular communal ceremonial house, or temple, where they will be "fed."

The Huichol Self

"*Ne'jeetsia mie'me, puutaine ulukame:*
The urukáme is part of me when it speaks." (X.B. 1989)

"The urukáme is itself; it is part of everybody.
It forms a crystal, like a ball,
a ball which is dangerous for the family." (J.L. 1989)

According to what the Huichol themselves say, the urukáme is connected with the concept of the self, and many associate it with the soul, even though others consider them two separate things. "*Neiyári urukáme,*" or "*Neurukame iyári,*" "My urukáme is my soul," I was told many a time. This point forces us to digress briefly in order to discuss the indigenous concepts of *iyári* and *kupüri*, two basic elements of the self which many Huichols confuse, especially since bilingual speakers often translate the two words as the Spanish *alma*, soul, and in quoting their informants anthropologists frequently repeat this equation.[3] However, my own field work[4] has shown me that in many cases we must distinguish between these two concepts if we want to recognize the coherence of indigenous thought.

Kupüri corresponds to what is usually called "vital principle." The Huichols locate it at the top of the head at the level of the tonsure, or "in the hair in this part of the head," adding that "if even a single hair is taken from you" you will become weak, ill, indeed even condemned to die. The kupüri, "which comes with life," disappears at the time of death, it is often said. *Pukulipi'ya* can be translated as "being without life." The more commonly used word for life is *tukaále*, a third concept which is sometimes confused with the other two and which is associated with destiny, the process of living, the passage of a life through time.

The word kupüri is also used to refer to a sacred and beneficial water sometimes known as *kuutsala*. A bilingual man translated "*Eeki peunétse haniliene kupürine'tulitsie-meme*—literally "Bring some sacred water (kupüri) for my children"—as "Bring me life for my children (*Tráigame vida para mis hijos*)." Finally, kupüri denotes the stigmata on the ear of maize (more specifically called *kupáya*), and, according to some, it also refers to the down that covers the nodes on the lower part of the peyote, more commonly known as *híkuli kariuyaale*. This is also the name for a plant described as "a small herb as bitter as the peyote," found near Wirikúta, the end destination of the pilgrimage during which the well-known hallucinogenic cactus is gathered. When the pilgrims return, their wives chew it, using the juice thus extracted to moisten their husbands' kupüri in order to assure them of a long life.

Iyári denotes what is classically called the "soul": an entity capable of detaching itself from the body and existing independently of it. This term also refers to the heart, the supposed seat of the soul. Dreaming is conceived of as a journey on the part of the iyári, and death as its wandering without end. "The iyári goes off during the night," a shaman explained to me, "and if it meets anyone or anything the person will dream." Then one must search for it. Five days after the death of someone, it is also the shaman who departs to search for the iyári, in an impressive nocturnal ceremony during which he evokes the life of the deceased in his chant and locates the iyári to predict its future. And it is the shaman who encourages the journey by the still frail souls of young children to Paliatsi, a place along the road to Wirikúta, during a ceremony called *wima'kuara*, which is part of the great Tatéi Néixa autumn festival. Guided by the shaman's chant, the children's souls ask for their life (*tukaále*), in this case good health (cf. Anguiano and Furst 1978).

The iyári is sometimes likened to the mobile shadow (*etuli*) associated with each living creature, as opposed to the nearly static shadow of plants or objects called *atupa*. Like the etuli, the human soul disappears at death, having lost its support.

The iyári is also associated with thought and understanding. Bilingual speakers translate *iyaritsíye* as "through his thought," and *iya' wa'uka pukayári* as "having a lot of experience," meaning reflection. *Iya' neukauka ayári* means "having one's head in the clouds," "unreflecting."

But "the kupüri is necessary to the iyári," and without it neither thought nor personality can develop:

> "The kupüri grows from your childhood.
> The soul, life, depend on it.
> When you die you lose your kupüri; it disappears.
> Then the soul leaves like a bird . . ." (J.B. 1990)

> "The kupüri is what makes our thoughts move;
> it is what causes the iyári to roam.
> At death, the iyári and the kupüri join together and
>   wander.
> When we celebrate the feast for the souls of the dead
>   the kupüri becomes fixed.
> Then it can no longer move about freely;

it remains in the cemetery where the dead body lies.
Otherwise the kupüri would continue as if it were still
   alive . . ." (H.C. 1990, Santa Catarina)

In certain contexts kupüri and iyári are confused and thus become interchangeable, with some people claiming that after death the kupüri or the iyári join the urukáme and go together to the heavens (*yutsi te'akua*). It is also said that sorcerer-shamans can steal the kupüri, in the same way that they can seize the iyári, or even both at the same time. Envoys or spirit helpers of evil chanters, such as the *itáuki*, know how to take away the kupüri or "gnaw" at the iyári, some also claim.[5] The serious illness which follows is called *pukupuripi'en*, or *pukupuripi'ya*, "taking away the kupüri," or "his kupüri has been taken."

The iyári·is also associated with memory. This refers not only to the individual memory but to the collective memory as well, the accumulated knowledge. According to a debatable claim, the iyári makes it possible to "enter into contact with the vast 'pan-genetic' memory stored among those whom the Huichol call Our Ancestors or Our Great-Grandparents (Nuestros Bisabuelos)" (Negrín 1985:41).[6] Kinsmen are supposed to originate from a single heart, *ta iyariyári*, their blood flowing from body to body as the rivers flow toward the sea (Negrín 1985:30). This statement must have come from José Benítez, the well-known maker of yarn paintings, who told me in 1990:

> "*Taiyari puyu'revi, ne'iwa'ma re iyári:*
> Our whole family has a single heart, a single thought."

The power or weakness of the soul reflects the character of its owner. But each individual can build himself or herself a strong soul by accumulating "tradition"—*yereeya*, *irua'lali-takiekari*, "the feast." One's soul gains continuously through activity, provided one accepts tradition, directs sufficient offerings and sacrifices to the other world, and participates actively in the multiple ceremonies which punctuate Huichol life. Thus, the soul gains in power and consequence, to the point where it becomes burdensome and pathogenic.

> "The urukáme is the soul coagulating,
> like blood that dries and hardens . . ." (J.B. 1990)

> "The urukáme is a person's heart, his iyári.
> For when we die our iyári goes far away,
> up there, into the sky . . ." (J.L. 1990)

> "The iyári dries like rain and the urukáme appears;
> it is of the same substance as the dead,
> as the iyári which issues from the dead person." (The shaman D. 1990)

The urukáme is thus a part of the self associated with the soul, which can finally be materialized, and thus neutralized. It is also a condition. A Huichol will say: "*Ne nepe'reya urukame*," "I have an urukáme," or "*neu'urukame*," "I am an urukáme." The urukáme is the concretization of a strong soul into the form of a rock crystal. Thus, there is a sort of consubstantiation between the soul and the urukáme.[7] And those from whom an urukáme must be "extracted" are said to be pathogenic, or to cause bad dreams, indirect proof of the excessive mobility of their souls:

> "The urukáme is dangerous when it has not yet been extracted.
> At night it injures the family . . ." (J.L. 1989)

> ". . . (The) soul of an old man projects a mysterious and uncontrollable power. . . . For instance, if an old man who has reached the state of urukáme dreams that he strikes a child or that he throws stones at an animal, the next morning the child will wake up with marks from blows, and the animal will be injured." (Benzi 1972:167)

Urukáte and Kakauyári

The urukáme can also be seen as a link in a chain that goes from human beings to the gods, connecting this world with the other world. It is, in fact, comparable—and often compared—to other, larger stone objects which represent the *kakauyári*, an intermediate, localized, and weaker form of the gods. These "god-rock crystals," as they are sometimes called, come from sacred beings whose mobility has negative effects. They are therefore neutralized by shamans who materialize their "heart" (iyári) in the form of rock crystals, also referred to by some as urukáme or urukáme kakauyári, even though others believe that only humans have urukáte.

The following story, told to Lumholtz, illustrates the way in which priest-shamans "capture" these stones, which come from Sun and which belong to the category of god-crystals:

> About thirty years ago, so an Indian told me, a shaman near Santa Catarina informed the people that the Sun wished to visit the place. A great many people gathered, and the women brought many ceremonial "beds" for the use of the distinguished visitor. My informant averred that he would not have thought it possible for such a thing to happen as he saw on that occasion. Three boys and two girls, holding votive bowls, stood outside the temple beside the shaman. He had been singing all night with his people, and held his plumes in one hand and a votive bowl in the other, ready to receive the Sun when he came down (Figure 105). After a while the man began to reel, put his plumes into the bowl, and fell to the ground. . . . As soon as he regained his senses, he asked for his bowl. "Let me see it," he exclaimed, and to the astonishment of the multitude he produced from it a small stone, very hard and red (probably a rose quartz). This stone, which was more intensely red on the inside

FIGURE 105. Urukámes. The crystallized souls of dead relatives, urukámes travel with the rays of the rising or setting Sun and are metaphorically "caught" by the shaman on the feathers of his muviéri and lowered into the waiting votive gourd bowl, as the great shaman of San Andrés, Nicholas Carrillo de la Cruz, is doing here at sunrise during a parched maize ceremony on his rancho in May 1967. (*Photograph by Peter T. Furst.*)

than on the outside, was afterward very carefully kept in one of the god-houses of the temple at Santa Catarina. (Lumholtz 1902:197)[8]

A few years after death the "degraded" or "discharged" urukáte go to join the kakauyári in the caves where the latter have been placed directly. There is a kind of symmetry in this: it is as if the small stones that represent the urukáte of men who have accumulated tradition and who therefore are dangerous, were to the human community what the larger stones representing the kakauyári are to the community of the gods. In fact, this kind of correspondence recurs frequently in Huichol thought: the same relationships—between gods or between places, for example—are reproduced on different scales. Finally, another consubstantiation is thus suggested: that of gods and men. For they are materialized in comparable form, a process which, in both cases, temporarily paralyzes their power and at the same time proves the power of the shamans who know how to bring about their crystallization. In any case, we see two trajectories, each ending in a materialization that signifies evolution and neutralization. The latter is the more important, for the crystal, whether it comes from human beings or the gods, can be mastered once it has taken material form: one can worship it, watch over it, and place it in a cave when it is "discharged," like an electric battery. This is an important point for someone who spends a lot of time communicating with the other world, using objects as intermediaries, calling upon it, constantly directing tokens of good will toward it.

Urukáte and Sun

The urukáte, though they emanate from the human soul, are also connected with the cosmos:

> "The urukáte come with Sun and Tatewarí, Fire.
> They join together over there; they are caught in the sun . . .
>   Some emerge in the blood of a cow;
> others emerge from Sun. . ." (A.X.C. 1990)

> "(The urukáte) seem to be with Sun.
> There they are taken away; the snake *ra'inu* catches them.
> They are stuck to a rock next to Sun.
> Paritsika removes them,
> or perhaps Kauyumári, the Deer, who is the best of all. . .
> It is a rock belonging to the sun, a place he passes by.
> For the sun never stops moving. . .
> We go there when we die. . ." (J.R.M. 1990)

FIGURE 106. Ramón Medina's Visualization of the Shaman's Quest for an Urukáme. The shaman's path is along a trail lined with brilliant marigolds and marked, as in the old codices, by his footprints. Revealing itself to him like a shiny star, the urukáme is concealed behind a fiery curtain of solar rays, which the shaman, pictured in x-ray style, with power arrows stuck in his headband to simulate deer antlers, must penetrate to reach his goal.

"The urukáte hide behind the sun.
There the shamans find them.
They pull them out to come here,
tawalita: they take them from behind the sun. . ." (J.L. 1990)

"The urukáme presents itself to Tatetemawejetsu,
where the sun and the clouds are.
The urukáte join the sun and they watch over us;
along with Sun they look after us and take care of us. . ." (B.H. 1990)

"The urukáte accompany the sun;
they are near him; they help him. . ." (X.H. 1989)

The urukáte are associated with the rays of the rising or setting sun and, more generally, with Sun himself, an important mythical personage. The shamans are said to find him during a journey in or behind the sun (Figure 106):

"Our life, our soul, is attached to the sun; it goes with him. When someone dies, his soul is cut away from the sun the way a piece of string is cut from the ball. Detached from the sun, the soul hardens and turns into stone. Once cut, it can never return. ('So the sun is forever losing some of its substance?') Yes, all the substance of those who have become urukáte. After death, the soul, the iyári, goes to the sky. But it no longer travels with the sun. . ." (J.B. 1990)

As we listen to these words, two opposing hypotheses become evident. According to one, the sun is a sort of fluid in motion, capturing the wandering souls of the dead in the same way as it checks the excessive mobility of the souls of the living in exchange for the inert material from which the urukáte are made. From this point of view, the operating principle is one of conservation of energy and substance. According to another point of view, Sun gives but gets nothing in return, thus inexorably losing its own substance. But only the arguments of a single person support this second hypothesis, which in fact reflects the classical ideas of the societies of ancient Mexico.

The "Precipitation" of the Urukáme

The urukáme is rendered concrete by a shaman:

> "Only the great shamans can catch the urukáte.
> One must be strong, for they are dangerous.
> They create dust when they come.
> They make people faint. . ." (J.B. 1990)

> "The shamans know the chants for the urukáte.
> They are the ones who get them to move.
> They stir up all the urukáte they want. . ." (J.L. 1990)

> ('Where do the urukáte that we see here come from?')
> "Some come from the blood of a cow,
> others were caught in the maize as they came from the sun.
> Sometimes they emerge from the 'barra' of the governor.
> They can also come out of the ears of a deer
> or from some beef broth,
> or from all these things at once: the horn of a deer
> or a cow, 'barra'. . ." (A.X.C. 1990)

This concretization of the urukáte underlies an ambiguous conception. Borrowing from the language of chemistry, there is a "precipitation" leading to neutralization. But the urukáme also has to be hunted, or extracted. On the one hand, the soul is said to coagulate; on the other, it is claimed that the shaman must catch it (*nuwoltiviya urukate*), master it, tame it, (*mansarlo*, in Spanish), place it in a small gourd, and offer it to someone in the family so that the sick family members will be able to get well (Figure 105).

> "The shamans know how to catch the urukáte.
> They first learn what is happening through a dream.
> 'You, his relatives, will become sick
> if you do not make urukáme', they say.
> That is what they said about my grandfather who
> recently died.
>
> My father has his urukáme in his house.
> I remember when it was 'tamed.'
> We went over there, to the mountain across from here,
> myself, my father, Pablo, and his wife.
> It was over there, at night, that a shaman caught his urukáme.
> It looked like a stone.
> When daylight came it seemed to be a stone, not a person.
> Sometimes this is done in the ceremonial house, the tuki.
> Whenever a person dies his urukáme must be caught,
> otherwise the children become sick." (N.J. 1989)

"During the night, while the old man sleeps, the mara'akáme keeps up a dialogue with his soul in order to ascertain its condition. If the old man is in fact urukáme, the sacrifice of an animal becomes obligatory, demanded by the soul itself in return for letting itself be 'tamed'. The sacred crystal is generally found in the blood of the deer or bull that has been killed for this purpose . . .

At the set date, the sons lead their father to the oratory of the rancho, make him sit down near the altar, place eagle feathers over both his ears, and offer him maize beer so he will become intoxicated. . . . The shaman chants, and at the precise moment when he pronounces the words 'The urukáme has come!' the oldest son, who is standing in the yard ready to sacrifice the bull, plunges the blade into the animal's neck. . . . Assistants catch the first blood that spurts out in a votive bowl and place it on the altar, covering it with *muviéri* feathers. The shaman continues to chant until dawn. Then he orders the bowl to be brought and, dipping his hands in the blood, he pulls out the crystalline stone." (Benzi 1972:167)

The bull, of course, is a substitution for the indigenous deer, and, indeed, in another version, related by Furst (1967:87–88), it is a deer that is ritually hunted and sacrificed, rather than a bull. In this case, the votive gourd in which the rock crystal comes to rest contains *nawá* (the ceremonial maize beer called *tejuíno* in Tarahumara). The deer is ritually fed some of the nawá, after which the participants touch the deer all over and rub "part of that" (presumably the deer's blood) on their chests. Then what remains of the sacred maize drink is given to the "owner of the deer," that is, the hunter in whose snare it was caught, who drinks it down. Inasmuch as in the aforementioned "holy trinity" of the Huichols deer is not only peyote but also maize, one can assume that an equation exists here between the sacred beverage made of fermented maize and deer blood.

Thus, the ceremony implies a certain logic of sacrifice: the urukáme, which has emerged from the soul of its "owner" and/or from some place near the sun, needs the mediation of the body (and blood) of an animal in order finally to become concretized. There may also be an appeal to another intermediary whose presence confirms the association of the urukáme with the concept of the life cycle: a child, known as *hakéri* (*hakiru*), who can be said to represent the souls of children. For if the urukáte are connected with the power of tradition and with death, they are also associated with children, whom they protect from misfortune. They attend the arrival from the sun of the souls of young children and their subsequent settlement, as well as their taming and their departure at the time of death.

Age Class and Urukate

As suggested by an expression such as "I am urukáme," the urukáme defines an age class for men and denotes the power associated with it. The age of the urukáme follows the age of the hunt. In fact the two are interdependent and complementary:

> —Will you be urukáme one day?
> "I don't know yet, not before the age of thirty-five . . .
>
> If I continue to hunt deer,
> if I worship the gods ('si yo cumplo con los dioses'),
> then maybe I will . . ." (B.H. 1990).

> "Someone who is urukáme doesn't hunt deer any more.
> But if his son goes deer hunting,
> when he returns he will kill a cow,
> he will do everything to satisfy his father's urukáme."
>   (B., about 25 years old, 1990).

> "I wanted to hunt deer, but I wasn't able to kill one.
> 'You can't kill a deer for you are urukáme,' they said to me . . ."
>   (J.C.B., about 40 years old, 1990)

> "We who live here in the city have no urukáme,
> but we have to find deer to feed the urukáte.
> I don't go hunting, but I give cartridges,

or money to buy some. . . . If one went hunting
without offering anything to the urukáte,
a deer would never die.
The urukáme would make a sort of trap.
But if one makes the necessary offerings,
the deer will die . . ." (H.C., from Santa Catarina
    but living in Mexico City, 1989)

"You take the urukáte along into the mountains to hunt deer,
in their gourd or in a small cloth bag,
and you put them there with their arrows . . .
Then, when you go hunting, you will kill the deer.
You bring it back here; you cut it up,
and you give some of its blood to the urukáte.
For they helped us find the deer . . ." (A.X.C. 1990)

Thus it is not good to hunt without an urukáme. Some also claim that one can no longer hunt when one is urukáme. In any case, in order to become urukáme one must first have been a successful deer hunter and respected tradition. In fact, the "precipitation" of the urukáme frequently takes place during a hunting expedition:

"The first time, the urukáme emerges in the tuki.
But there are urukáte which only appear in the bush.
Many even appear while the hunt is going on.
If it doesn't happen during the hunt it will be in the tuki, the communal house . . ."
    (J.L. 1990)

The age at which someone reaches the state of urukáme is highly variable—some say thirty-five, others sixty—and depends on one's connection with tradition and ritual:

"Those who die young never have urukáme, even after death.
You must have traveled through this world in order to be urukáme.
You must have followed the tradition.
You must have gone to the sacred places.
You must have participated in the festivals.
Then the gods will transform you into an urukáme;
then your family will remember you
and everyone will contribute,
everyone will pay to transform your soul into stone . . ." (J.B. 1990)

To some people, a significant number of urukáte, never more than five, is the mark of shamans, a sort of material manifestation of their spirit helpers, or at least their power. But, it is also said, every living person who has accumulated "tradition" can have urukáte, especially if he has often participated in the deer hunt (or the hunt for the peccary, *jabalí* in Spanish, I was told in Tuxpan), or in fishing. "Those who know how to take care," men or women, can also have some. But the more exemplary one's behavior, the sooner one will be urukáme.

The urukáte emphasize the interdependence of the old and the young. By "extracting" the urukáte from their fathers, the men of the hunter class take care of the fathers and venerate them. At the same time they push them toward the grave . . .

A Double Social Control: Urukate and Children's Diseases

Under the pretext of protecting the health of a family, the precipitation of an urukáme can be imposed, indeed prescribed, by a shaman. For usually the urukáme first manifests itself by its pathogenic effects; in fact, it comprises an actual nosological category, generally called *neptikuuye urukame'ku*, "urukáme sickness":

> "*Iya' ptikuuye ulukáte meupteyuulie,*
> *wapa'pama meupteyuulie:*
> This (child) is sick because of the urukáte;
> his relatives are harming him . . .
> *Netikuuyee urukame'neyemu'utu:*
> I am sick because I am urukáme." (J.L. 1990)

> "All those who die
> are later caught through their urukáte.
> For after their death their relatives become sick." (V.C. 1989)

> "When people die their children and grandchildren are left behind,
> and some of them become sick.
> For each dead person becomes urukáme.
> Then the chanter will say: 'Kill a cow;
> we are going to catch the urukáme, *nuvoltiviya urukame.*'
> It is the one who is sick who has it.
> The shaman brings it out into a gourd and gives it to him
> so that he can keep it with him . . .
> Afterward all the sick people in the family get better,
> but for that they must remain together . . ." (Ch. 1989)

> "After someone has died,
> if a child in the family becomes sick once more
> that means the dead person's urukáme has to be caught again.
> For that is what is shooting the children with its arrows,

bringing the bites of scorpions or snakes.
Five times the urukáme must be caught . . ." (J.B. 1990)

After examining sick children, who are often the victims of scorpion bites (these animals are considered messengers of the urukáte), a shaman will one day announce that the problem is an urukáme, especially when several people, children and sometimes adults, are affected within the same family.[9]

The shaman is thus master of the game. By attributing a child's sickness to a certain soul that is too powerful, he forces the family of the "guilty" party to organize a ceremony to "precipitate" the urukáme. This is how he singles out the individual he has fixed upon, whether that person is reaching the state of urukáme for the first time or whether he is a repeat offender, thus proving that he has accumulated more tradition. The shamans can also indirectly accuse the owners of urukáte of negligence by attributing illnesses to a lack of attention toward these demanding objects.

"If one does not observe tradition
the urukáte will make the children sick.
They can die quickly." (B.C. 1990)

"The urukáte must be fed;
that way they won't cause sickness.
Otherwise they will make the children ill,
and scorpions will bite them . . ." (J.L. 1989)

The urukáte are charms against misfortune. Well fed, respected, revered, they will serve their owners well, but mistreated, they become pathogenic. Power and honor are not without their counterpart!

In any event, by means of the urukáme the shamans can implicitly establish a scale of worth by attributing several urukáte to certain people, living or dead, and by denying them to others, or making them wait long. The crystallization of the urukáte is thus an important element in Huichol shamanic power.

Protective But Demanding Ancestors

"Every year one makes an arrow for the urukáme,
or an illness might strike.
If a kinsman goes hunting he takes these arrows with him.
Each urukáme has its own arrow.
Near the hunting ground the people gather,
men and women, and the shaman chants . . .
During the day they will hunt deer.
If they find one it will be killed easily.

This means that the urukáte bring good luck;
they are extremely important . . .
That way the whole family is assured of a good life:
airu tinteo'eiriaka tanaitu; tuukale temere'iane.
Otherwise there will be bad luck: *meukatenake . . .*"

(A.X.C., about 30 years old, 1990)

In other communities the urukáme is more generally called *tewarí* (*te'valí*, according to Lumholtz). The same word is used for "grandfather," an ancestor, and for the old Fire God, who is addressed as *Tatewarí*, Our Grandfather.[10] The word tewarí, a kinship term which is also applied to the urukáte, denotes the gods as well, I have been told, or the rock crystals that are associated with them. In any case, this term is used to express the distance between two generations (from grandfather to grandson, or vice versa).

Be that as it may, the urukáte require the observance of tradition. They transmit the words of the dead. And the more tradition one tries to accumulate, the more demanding the urukáte become:

"If someone is very wise
he can visit the gods ('los dioses') and ask them for life,
or the power to heal.
Then he must accept everything the gods say.
If he refuses, members of his family will die, his son, his daughter . . .
The gods demand to be brought offerings in exchange . . .
If a father has had power and he dies,
his children must provide what is demanded;
they must pay for him.
They must pay five times . . ." (H.C. 1990)

The urukáme wants to return to his relatives;
he wants to be there, in the *riliki* (*xiriki*) to be with them.
That is why he makes the children sick.
'He has not been fed for years,' says the shaman.
If one does not listen, if one does not arrange a feast,
then another child will become ill . . ." (J.R.M. 1990)

"The urukáte are like ancestors (*uki'raatsi*).
The family feeds the urukáme.
He lives in the house, in a small *riliki* (*xiriki*) altar.
Otherwise the children will get sick . . ." (J.L. 1990)

But the words supposedly voiced by the ancestors are heard and recast by the shamans, who filter them:

"The urukáte speak in the wind.
The shamans hear them when they chant.
If we don't do what the urukáte want,
we will get sick . . ." (B.J. 1989)

" 'Do this, do that . . .
You haven't gone to the cave by the sea with offerings,
or the cave at Chapala, or the one at Wirikuta.'
If you follow the tradition nothing will happen . . .
If the family does what the urukáte have asked,
then the shaman can't say anything . . ." (J.L. 1990)

The urukáte collected in the caves when they are "worn out" are venerated and receive offerings in the same way as the kakauyári, the crystallizations of the gods mentioned above. Strictly speaking it is not an ancestor cult, for the urukáte that have been gathered in this way are anonymous and, so to speak, "discharged." What we see here is a very Amerindian conception of ancestrality: grouping together certain elements associated with the dead, evoking a sort of common substance which is shared and shareable, indicates the power of the kin group, as does the belief that relatives share one iyári, one soul, one thought. From this point of view, the urukáte serve as a reminder not only of the merit of a living person but also of the memory of a deceased, and, when they have finally been gathered together, they recall the "substance" of the family, an important matter in a society where the kinship system is undifferentiated.

The Urukate and the Family Guardian Spirit[11]

The sum of the urukáte, some of which will be stored in a cave, is in a way a concrete manifestation of the heart or soul of the family, the sum of individual souls. From this point of view, it is essential that it is always someone other than the affected person who demands the extraction of the urukáme. The urukáte are at the center of a family cult; they must be fed on every special occasion and at each of the great collective festivals. The person who makes the pilgrimage to Wirikúta often finds himself entrusted with them.

There are hierarchies and orders of distribution, and there are individuals who determine when a crystallization will occur. When someone dies, his or her urukáte are divided up: the urukáme is a reminder of the limits of the family in the strict sense, the principals, the "base," and the obligations associated with it. Every person must think of extracting the urukáte of those who precede him, or there will be lacunae; the continuity will be broken. From this perspective a systematic study should be made concerning the division, transmission, and inheritance of the urukáte, and of their "disappearance." Such a study would certainly provide precious information on the definition, function, and limits of the Huichol family.

Indeed, if one has no family, if one is single, one has no urukáme:

> "If I have a wife, and if we have neither a son nor a daughter,
> which can happen,
> then there will be no one to remove the urukáte from us.
> But if I were ill because of that,
> I would summon a shaman . . .
> He would say to me: 'You are hurting yourself.
> It is because you have no family.
> There is no one who can extract the urukáme from your body.
> So you must arrange a feast . . .'
> That is how the shaman can remove the urukáme from an old man . . .
> It is he, the shaman, who will paint him with blood every year,
> and the old man will pay him for that . . ." (J.L. 1990)

> "A son removes the urukáte from his parents.
> Each person has his family, people whom he owes this duty.
> It falls only to close (direct) relatives.
> Each person has his children who will do it for him . . .
> *muka aetsie mieme*, 'it is not a duty';
> *tita munejetsie mieme*, 'it is my duty'." (J.B. 1990)

And the urukáte are associated with a new life (*tukaale*) for the family:

> "The family gathers;
> they are going hunting, taking the urukáte along.
> They eat; they talk.
> A shaman chants . . ." (J.L. 1990)

The Urukáme and Relations between Men and Women

The urukáte are nearly always presented and extracted by "conjugal pairs," thus conforming to a Huichol concept according to which completeness is the addition or juxtaposition of masculine and feminine principles, of man and woman.

There seems to be equality and symmetry. All the urukáte that I saw were couples:

> "We all have urukáte, men as well as women.
> Only the young do not have them.
> It is only the older people . . ." (A.X.C. 1990)

"If the wife of the old man is also urukáme, the priest extracts the two 'spirits', then raises them to his ear and proclaims: 'This one is his grandfather; that one his grandmother. . . .'" (Benzi 1972:168)

Indeed the woman's urukáme follows automatically. But when people say that an urukáme has been extracted from a woman, are they not always referring to a dead person? At least that is what the men insinuate, even though many among them also say that in this respect there is no difference between men and women:

"When one is called, the other comes . . .
The wife is caught at the same time as her husband . . ." (J.B. 1990)

"Shikuri became sick. . . . The shaman diagnosed the cause of the illness: 'It is the soul of your (dead) mother which is urukáme and which is traveling with the sun. It will emerge in the mouth of a deer.'. . . (He) advised going on a ritual hunt." (Benzi 1972:168)

The couple is connected with the Huichol concept of totality, but in ritual as well as daily life the women seem to be subordinate to the men.

Huichol Totality: Continuity and Discontinuity

The number five and the male-female couple are the two complementary marks of Huichol totality. Five means closure; six means a new beginning. The urukáte also serve the function of constantly restating the properties and limits of this totality:

"Five times a living person is caught.
I have been caught four times.
One more is needed; it will come when the time is right . . ."
(The shaman D., 1990)

"After five or six years one has to start over again.
The old stone will be kept by one of my children;
the new one will go to another son.
If I don't have any I can keep it myself . . .
The last urukáme to emerge
will be fed three times a year.
Then five years will pass, and another will be caught.
Five times, that means twenty-five years . . .
After that it is all over:
they go to the sun . . ." (A.X.C. 1990)

"The shaman chants to call the urukáte.
There are five chants: the chant of the peyote, the chant of the drum,

the chant of the deer, the chant of the bull,
and the chant of the urukáte.
Every year the shaman also chants five chants about them:
the chants of the maize, the deer, the peyote, the sun,
and the chant of the urukáte . . .
Every five years urukáte can be extracted.
When a new one comes out, the old one is taken to a cave.
After five years nothing can be done.
But if the family is a large one they do it:
'It is his turn to do it;
he should pay for it,' they say . . ." (J.L. 1990)

"No more than five urukáte can emerge from one person,
five during his lifetime and five after death . . ." (H.C. 1990)

The urukáte are a way of denying the discontinuity between life and death, creating a neutral zone.

The urukáte also establish a sort of continuity since "the time of the original ancestors." But it is a continuity made up of a succession of short periods. Five or six times one can extract urukáte from a living person, and then five or six times after his death. Finally, all these stones will be gathered together in the caves. But already another living member of the family, a descendant of the previous person, has taken up the relay: an illness has served as a pretext, or his children have contacted a shaman who has made him urukáme one, two, three times. And so it continues.

Compensation for Old Age; Memory and Oblivion

A person who becomes urukáme acquires prestige, but he also becomes more fragile. Each new "precipitation" brings him closer to death:

"If a stone is extracted from someone he will soon die." (J.R. 1990)

"I can be urukáme if relatives of mine ask me to,
relatives who want to have their urukáme.
('But won't that make you die?')
If I were old, yes, that would make me die . . ." (J.L. 1990)

"Someone from whom an urukáme has been taken out dies afterward.
If one is taken from me when I am old I will die . . ." (B.H. 1990)

"I am already urukáme, but I am alive.
If they took my urukáme I would die.
I would have to die in order for them to get it . . ." (J.R.M. 1990)

What is needed is the neutralization of an excessive energy which, like the soul of a dead person that still wanders close to the living, has to be restrained periodically, and temporarily "frozen" in the form of an urukáme. Thus, its pathogenic mobility is checked. As the urukáme is added to the substance of the community, it is slowly "discharged"; it "hardens," "cools," and becomes anonymous:

> "The stones grow old; they deteriorate,
> until they are nothing but shells . . ." (J.R. 1990)

> "After five years the soul has left the urukáme.
> Then the urukáme counts for nothing;
> it can no longer speak; it is finished, pure garbage . . .
> It must be renewed;
> a new urukáme must be caught:
> *rakali, kanayai muku urukame. . . .*" (J.R.M. 1990)

The soul, on the other hand, recovers its vigor and mobility, until a new urukáme must be extracted.

The souls of the dead are active until they finally disappear, caught by Sun where, according to some, they regenerate matter. In a parallel fashion, the urukáte, now anonymous, are accumulated in the caves. It is the end.

The urukáte and the rituals associated with them are thus equally ambivalent: the former, if well treated, are pathogenic before the precipitation and curative after; the latter, at first an act of social recognition, end up as a ritual of oblivion. The Huichol bury their dead quickly, and only once. But by renewing the process of crystallization periodically and almost at will, Huichol shamans recall the mourning and the memory, as opposed to other societies, for example, the Guajiro, who have only two formalized rituals for the ordinary dead: the primary and secondary burials (Perrin 1976, 1991).

Urukáte and Acculturation

Finally, it should be pointed out that all individuals, if they live long enough, will one day become urukáme—unless they have partly broken with tradition. Not having an urukáme thus indicates that one has abandoned the tradition, and is a sign of acculturation:

> "All the old people are urukáte.
> All, except for some, who wander around just any place.
> They haven't been on a deer hunt;
> they are like you whites . . ." (B. 1990)

> "There are some who don't have urukáte.
> They are the ones who don't have any 'life.'

It doesn't interest them.

They don't believe in it;

they just want to wander, to run around . . ." (H.C. 1990)

Conclusions

Privileged mediators between the visible and the invisible, between this world and the other one, between life and death, the urukáte and the rituals associated with them are among the most important elements underpinning and justifying Huichol tradition. They enforce it in two ways: at the moment of crystallization, in order to cure sick people, and afterward, so that they will not turn pathogenic toward close relatives. The urukáme is a powerful agent: it is an object loaded with symbolic values, a social marker, and an amulet for good or bad luck. Both an emanation from the human being and a fragment torn from the cosmos, it establishes primary connections between the body and the object, between self and substance, between man and the other world. It certainly also testifies to an ambivalent cultural position. Indeed, the data analyzed and the hypotheses set forth above suggest that the Huichols, who have a hunter ideology but who subsist as agriculturalists, belong to two culture areas: the Southwest, because of their belief in the logic of sacrifice, and Mesoamerica, because they conceive of gradually degrading energies. But the synthesis they have arrived at seems to be unique, which complicates the task of those who want to place them in one category or the other at any cost. In any event, let us hope that this modest study, which in order to make its point has gone beyond conventional anthropological theory with regard to these two culture areas, will stimulate further research and fruitful discussion.

NOTES

1. *Jícara* in Mexican Spanish. *Jícara*, derived from the Nahuatl *xicolli*, is one of a number of "Aztecisms" in Mexican Spanish; thus the term would not be understood in other Spanish-speaking countries, where the word for gourd bowl is *calabasa*.(—Eds.)

2. According to Lumholtz (1904:98) *ulu'-ukámi* means "the one for whom it is necessary to make an arrow," for, he says, "its owner is obliged to make ceremonial arrows for his *te'vali*," that is, his ancestor.

Twenty-five years ago, Furst (1967:39-106) published an essay on Huichol conceptions of the human soul that included a discussion of the urukáme and its function as family guardian spirit. This essay was published in Mexico in 1972 in Spanish translation by the Instituto Nacional Indigenista. It was the latter version that I had at hand during my own studies of the urukáme, with the goal of unravelling some of its deeper meanings.

3. In the course of conversations about the Huichol conceptualization of the human "soul"—more accurately the essential life force or life essence—Ramón repeatedly called the soul *kupúri*, thus using the same term for it which he had earlier employed for the fontanelle. Occasionally, he also called it *kupúri iyári*, which could be translated freely as "heart and soul," since *iyári* literally means "heart" (according to Grimes, less in the sense of the actual organ than as an identification of self in relation to others (Furst 1967:40).

Significantly, Furst speaks of kupüri variously as "the life essence," "the life of the soul" or "vital essence" (1967:51–53), or, in the Spanish version, as "vida del alma" (1972:17, 29, 30), "alma o fuerza vital" (1972, plate 5, ill. 9), "vida o alma" (1972:36, 75), "alma, o esencia de la vida" (1972:38), "el alma, esa vida" (1972:39), and, as though conscious that rendered into Spanish the two could be confused, "la vida . . . el alma" (1972:18, 41). Furst rightly proposes translating kupüri as "esencia vital" (1972:31), "fuerza vital" (1972:42), or even "vida," as his informant does (1972:32, 72, 73). He is thus moved to resort to such concepts as "la fuerza esencial de la vida, o alma" (1972:75) and is obliged to translate iyári as "corazón o esencia" (1972:75), which could lead to a sort of inversion of the respective meanings of iyári and kupüri when these are rendered into Spanish or English. Quoting the linguist Joseph E. Grimes, Furst (1967:41; 1972) notes that iyári means heart "less in the sense of the actual organ than as an identification of self in relation to others."

Negrín (1985:26) writes: "Lo que el huichol anhela . . . es constituirse un corazón, *iyári*, fuerte y sano para alimentar la vida espiritual, *cupuri* (alma), más importante que la vida física." Though Negrín makes an effort not to confuse *iyári* and *kupüri* (*cupuri*), he actually inverts their meaning, or chooses the easy way out by emphasizing an ambiguity indeed shared by many Huichols: ". . . saber algo del *iyari*, del *cupuri* (alma) . . ." (1985:32). He renders kupüri as "alma" (1985:25, 32, 55) and repeats, or adapts, the comments made to him by the yarn painter José Benítez Sánchez, according to whom the kupüri is "the collective soul" issued from the center of the world (1985:61), "which belongs to all and which makes us speak, live, and think," for "without the *kupuri* we would neither be able to think nor live" (1985:61). However, further on, realizing there is a problem, Negrín says that "en el *cupuri* se puso a pensar un *iyari*," that is to say, he concludes, "from the *cupuri* come the thoughts, the 'memory,' of Our Ancestor, called *iyari*, the heart" (1985:61). He translates iyári as "corazón" (1985:26) or "corazón limpido" (1985:35), and rightly defines it as "corazón, pensamientos y memoria inmanentes" (1985:64) and as "a true being, the source of identity and the seat of the individual spirit" ("verdadero ser . . . fuente de identidad y albergue del genio personal") (1985:27), something "que nace de la disciplina" (del huichol) (1985:26). Negrín (1985:35) speaks of the inner power of the iyári ("fuerza interior del iyári"), which knows how to hide behind a mask.

4. The data analyzed here were gathered in the course of three visits to the Huichol country, the longest of which took place in the region of San Andrés Cohamiata (1989, 1990). Some data also derive from Santa Catarína (1990), San Miguel (1990), and Tuxpan de Bolaños (1988).

The Huichols like to say that they know little, or that knowledge is reserved for certain specialists who keep it a secret. In fact, there exists a shared knowledge, and that is precisely what I was interested in. This knowledge is extensive with regard to the urukáte, a subject which everyone enters upon easily and often passionately.

5. *Rewitu mara'akáme nétsi uunanai mave piné tsiukupuli pive* (N.J. 1989): literally, "a shaman may take away my kupüri."

6. Also according to Negrín, the iyári is a "memory-heart" (1985:37), something upon which each person's spiritual experiences are carved (1985:40), but it is also a common memory ("los corazones, la memoria conjunta, *waiyari*, de Nuestros Bisabuelos") (1985:55). From this, he derives the basic idea of a possible accumulation of individual elements into a collective whole, which is necessary for the hypothesis of a crystallization (". . . les prestan nuevas fuerzas al *iyari* y les refrescan el alma *cupuri* con rocio") (1985:29).

7. Furst (1967:81–82) reproduces his informant's narrative describing the reconstitution of

the deceased's animate bones, or skeletal soul, into a rock crystal, "very pretty, shining with colors, very transparent." Furst thus speaks rightly of "alma cristalizada" (1972, plate 2, ill. 3), a characterization reiterated by Furst and Anguiano (1976:136), who, in another context, define the urukáme as "the crystallized skeletal soul of a deceased shaman or other person of superior knowledge" (in the Spanish version [Anguiano and Furst 1978], this reads, "alma esquelética cristalizada de un chaman fallecido o de alguna otra persona de sabiduría superior" [p. 59]).

Speaking of the destiny of the soul after death, Zingg (1938:299) makes the same point, but in the manner of a caricature. He evokes the ritual in which five days after someone's death the shaman searches for the soul of the deceased, often causing it to appear in the form of a large fly (*rayu*) before he concretizes it in the urukáme. Then he says: ". . . the soul becomes completely sacred or untouchable in the process of transforming into a fly or a bird, and finally sheds all the attributes of its human personality in the form of a quartz or a rock crystal. . ."

Furst's informant, Ramón Medina Silva, described the soul in its insect manifestation as a "luminous fly," a kind of firefly, giving it the Huichol designation *xáipi'iyári* (*xáipi* = flying insect, *iyári* = essence, or "heart") (Furst 1967:80).

8. Lumholtz (1904:196) has also written that "after death, deer hunters become *tevali'r* and accompany the sun on his journeys. They live in a place called Hai (clouds) Tono'lipa (rising up, liberating oneself), where the sun goes up. . . ." Citing Furst (1967:85), Anguiano and Furst also state that the urukáme "es recuperado en el viaje del chaman detrás del sol," and Benzi (1972:165) confirms this. In a note (p. 166), the same author adds: "According to our informants from San Andrés, urukáme means . . . God's (Sun's) arrow. The reference is to the *'urú*, arrow, of the Sun Father, for, as the Indians say, 'the souls of the mara'akáme become the arrows of Tau. . . .'"

According to Fernando Benítez (1968:591), the urukáme, or at least those from whom it originates, later joins the Sun in order to accompany him. Several of my informants confirmed this claim.

9. See also Furst (1967:82–84) for a discussion of "urukáme illness."

10. Three terms denote grandparents: *akutsi* (grandmother, in the proper sense; ancestor); *teukali* (grandfather, in the proper sense; baptismal godfather); and *tewarí* (grandfather, grand-uncle, and reciprocally, grandson, grandnephew, ego being masculine; for a feminine ego the corresponding term for grandmother or grandniece is *miitali*).

> "*Ne nepu'ulukameli*:
> I am a grandfather; I am an ancestor." (J.R.M. 1988)

The kin term tewarí should not be confused with *téiwari*, literally "neighbor," the term by which Huichols refer to mestizos, whites and others who speak only Spanish—in other words, foreigners.

11. Cf. also Furst 1967:89, 100 on this aspect.

INTRODUCTION TO CHAPTER 15

What strikes one immediately upon entering the office of the Director General of the Instituto Nacional Indigenista on Avenida Revolución in Mexico City is a large framed color photograph of a Huichol *mara'akáme* named Nicholas Carrillo de la Cruz (Figure 107). 'Colas, as he was known to one and all, was one of the truly great shaman-singers, an elderly Huichol of quiet dignity, wisdom, and knowledge whose prestige extended far beyond the boundaries of Tatéi Ki'ye, meaning Place of Our Mother, the indigenous Huichol name for the ceremonial center the Spaniards christened San Andrés Cohamiata when they established it in the early eighteenth century. 'Colas was nearly ninety years old when he died in 1974. It is appropriate that his portrait should hang here, as a constant reminder that this office, this federal Mexican agency, represents for many Mexican Indians, as it did for 'Colas, their last best hope—not always realized—for the defense and preservation of the indigenous peoples, their lands, their culture, and their religions. For the current director,[1] Maestro Guillermo Espinosa Velasco, the photograph also has a very personal meaning. For it was 'Colas who, in the last three years of his life, befriended him, and vice versa. As it turned out, that friendship also profoundly affected the direction Espinosa's professional life was to take.

To hear Espinosa tell of 'Colas brought back many memories. For I, too, once had the benefit of the good humor, generosity of spirit, open-heartedness, and sagacity of this great shaman and *kawitéro*, one of the wise old leaders of the entire community, though on a smaller scale and over a much briefer time. Nearly thirty years ago I was invited by Salomón Nahmad Sittón, an anthropologist who had recently assumed the directorship of INI's Cora-Huichol Coordinating Center in Tepic, to accompany him on a visit to San Andrés. As I remember it, Salomón intended to ask 'Colas how he and the elders felt about having a gasoline-powered generator installed by INI. 'Colas said he would think about it and, after deliberating with his fellow kawitéros, key players in the civil-religious hierarchy that has governed the *comunidades* since the Spanish assumed formal control over the Sierra Indians, he would give Salomón his, and their, decision. As it turned out, 'Colas and the council of elders politely declined the offer of a generator. 'Colas told Salomón, we Huichols thank you, but it is better to listen

FIGURE 107. 'Colas, as Family Shaman, Conducting the Parching of the Maize Ceremony. *Right*, 'Colas' wife, holding a newborn grandchild, whom 'Colas will present to the Sun and to whom he will give its first name. Assisting 'Colas is one of his sons. (*Photograph by Peter T. Furst, May 1967.*)

to the voices of the birds and the other animals, and to the crackling of Tatewarí (Our Grandfather, the old fire god) as he eats his food, which is the firewood, than to the din of a generator. Or words to that effect.

Nevertheless, 'Colas made us feel welcome, less the unwanted, intrusive, and ignorant strangers we truly must have seemed, than guests, even family. He invited us to his *rancho*, (Figure 108), some distance from the San Andrés ceremonial center with its government buildings, its eighteenth-century Catholic church, and its *tuki*, the indigenous temple. When we arrived, all the members of his substantial extended family, down to the small children, were engaged in preparations for the ceremony of the Parching, or Popping, of the Maize. In part this is a rain-making ritual, the last of the round of dry season, peyote-related ceremonies before the onset of the rains. The purpose of parching the maize on the griddle is symbolic and ritual, but the technique is also the simplest of the several kitchen technologies the Huichols had to learn along with the technology of cultivation in order to make the harvested kernels edible.[2] Ordinarily, the shelled kernels have first to be soaked in water with the addition of ashes or lime to make *nixtamal* (from the Nahuatl *nextli* = ashes, and *tamalli* = tamale) for processing into tamales, tortillas, and the various other forms in which maize is eaten or drunk.

FIGURE 108. The Extended Family Rancho of 'Colas in San Andrés, Summer 1967. (*Photograph by Peter T. Furst.*)

But, of course, in this ceremony the parched maize was not meant to be eaten, at least not by human beings.

'Colas's parching ceremony would be held in the patio of his extended family rancho, in front of the *xiriki*, the ancestor god house, and it would last through the night, the following day, and well into another night, in the course of which everyone, not excluding the foreign visitors, was expected to remain awake.

I also had a specific purpose in coming to San Andrés at this time: to get permission to bring a group of graduate students from the UCLA School of Public Health and the Anthropology Department to San Andrés for a summer field school in native medicine and governmental health care. 'Colas agreed, and so did INI. I served as co-field director (with my partner, a medical doctor), although it seems to me in retrospect that I spent almost as much time with 'Colas on his rancho and wandering through the woods with him hunting for wild mushrooms (the edible, not the psychedelic, kind) as I did with the students.

Espinosa tells how 'Colas used to come to the INI boarding school where he had his room, just to talk; 'Colas was in his late eighties then, and with his home some distance away, once he had made the effort, he liked to stay and converse with the much younger man over many cups of strong coffee. Because the school was closed for the summer, we too were quartered there, and there were mornings when 'Colas would appear just after sunup to invite me to come mushroom hunting with him. Sometimes he had already been out in the woods and then his shoulder bag was stuffed with the big yellow tasty fungi he knew I liked and which, with the eggs shipped up to us on the weekly plane from Tepic, we made into breakfast omelettes. 'Colas never took payment for his gifts of wild mushrooms. But he appreciated small presents like coffee or cigarettes, accepting them matter-of-factly, and in silence. With reciprocity their guiding principle, the Huichols have no indigenous word for "thank you," although they have huicholized the Spanish *gracias a Díos*, thanks be to God, into something like *pampayutsi*.

In the recollections that follow there is mention of the murder of 'Colas's son and how deeply his death affected the old man. It was the start of a long depression and apparently also affected his physical health. I remember the son well. Unlike most other Huichol men, he wore his hair uncut (his grey-haired father sported a sort of bowl cut, similar to that seen in Amazonia). One day during our summer program he arrived with his leg bleeding profusely from a deep machete cut. Our medical students were delighted: here was their first real live "patient," and there were obviously none of the restrictions that inhibited a medical student from treating patients at home. Three of them converged to clean the wound, sprinkle it with sulphur powder, and swaddle the injured leg with a large, impressive bandage. The victim, meanwhile, sat patiently and somewhat bemused at all the fuss, puffing away on a cigarette. Father and son conversed briefly, and then 'Colas told us that his son wanted us to know that his wound was punishment for his having neglected to feed his machete at the last ceremony of the feeding of the tools. Tools are sentient, like people and animals and plants, and they must be properly honored, lest they take revenge on their owners for their thoughtlessness.

There was also a practical object lesson in this for our students, who were given a brief taste of the efficacy of native medicine and Huichol knowledge of healing herbs. As per instructions, their patient returned after three days for a change of bandage. When the now very dirty gauze wrapping was unwound and 'Colas's son saw that his wound was, though evidently improved, still partly open and oozing, he pulled back his sleeve and, with obvious relish, showed the foreign "doctors" another cut—clearly also recent but nicely healed over, the scar tissue a healthy pink. He explained that the machete had also cut him on the arm when it struck a hidden stone and flew from his hand. But how had it healed so quickly when the leg wound was still open? Reaching into his shoulder bag the son brought out a fistful of leaves that were slightly the worse for wear and pressed them like a poultice on the cut on his arm.

Dr. Armando Casillas Romo, the Mexican physician who has contributed his own study of Huichol herbal medicine to this volume, would not have been surprised. But for our own young future doctors from up north, supremely confident in the superiority of western, "scientific," medicine, it was a humbling experience that made a first small dent in that abiding faith. One hopes it was remembered.

Peter T. Furst

15 : MEMORIES OF TATEWARÍ

GUILLERMO ESPINOSA VELASCO

One night not long ago I answered a knock on my front door and there stood Pablo Carrillo. Pablo is my friend from Tatéi Ki'ye, Place of Our Mother, which is what the people taught me they call San Andrés Cohamiata. So there he was, from the sierra of the Huicholes. "I have come to tell you that now I am a *kawitéro*," Pablo said, with a broad smile on his face. "For the next five years," he said, "I am a kawitéro. And I have come to visit my friend."

Pablo's unexpected visit took me back to 1974 and the last time I saw 'Colas alive, and what the old man said to me on that final morning. 'Colas is what everyone called Nicholas Carrillo de la Cruz. He was a great man, a wise man, the most important *mara'akáme* (shaman-singer) in San Andrés. He was also a loving grandfather and great-grandfather, who always made time for the children and told them wonderful stories (Figures 109–111). He was my friend and mentor and I miss him. 'Colas had been very ill, and he had come to Mexico City at my urging because I wanted to take him to see some specialists to find out what was wrong with him. And to see if perhaps they could do something for him.

On that last morning, before returning to his *rancho*, he suddenly said to me, "Look, I have this for you." And he handed me his *takwátsi* (the oblong plaited basket in which Huichol shamans and elders keep their sacred paraphernalia and power objects).

I was very moved. I sensed that this was something special. I admired the gift in the proper manner, complementing him on how well it was made, how fine, how tightly woven. All the while he was peering at me intently and I realized he wanted me to open it. So I pried the lid off the takwátsi, and still he never took his eyes off me. And there inside was a *muviéri* (shaman's arrow, or wand). I saw at once that this was not just any muviéri, but his own. Had he perhaps forgotten that it was in there? I said, "Oh, look, 'Colas, you have left your muviéri here." "No, no," he said, "that is what I am giving to you, the muviéri there inside the takwátsi."

And suddenly it came to me what he was doing. He was going to die and he was

FIGURES 109, 110, 111. The Shaman as Grandfather. (*Photographs by Peter T. Furst.*)

giving me his magical arrow, his feathered shaman's wand. I was very moved and expressed my appreciation. 'Colas smiled with evident satisfaction. Then he pulled several small tobacco gourds from his shoulder bag and added them to the gift. These were the *yakwé* peyote pilgrims carry when they go to Wirikúta. Suddenly, I felt very heavy and sad and at the same time grateful.

Then 'Colas said, "My friend, I want you to be in charge of Pablo Carrillo."

I did not know Pablo Carrillo. But I said, "Yes? Sure, I will do as you ask." And 'Colas said, "Good. I will be dead before the rainy season begins. Now I go. I am going to gather some money for my wife and to see that everything is taken care of."

That was the last time we were together, the last day. In that same year, 1974, precisely at the time he had said he would die, before the coming of the rains, he died.

Some time passed and one day there was a knock on the door of our apartment. And there stood a young Huichol, perhaps 25 or 26 years old. "I am Pablo Carrillo," he said. We did not know each other, but there he was. We talked for a long time. Pablo told me that although he had been going on the peyote pilgrimage to Wirikúta many more times than he needed to become a full-fledged mara'akáme, he did not yet consider himself to be completed, because he had not yet learned to cure. "I have gone many, many times," he said. "I am young but I have gone to Wirikúta almost as many times as 'Colas himself. But I do not feel myself to have the power to cure, I do not have that special power yet. That is why I am not yet a mara'akáme."

I suppose he will consider himself to be completed as a mara'akáme one of these days, when he feels himself to be ready. Because now he is already a kawitéro, perhaps not yet a shaman in his own eyes, but a kawitéro.

Since that first visit Pablo has come many times to my house in Mexico City. He really didn't need looking after, but we kept in touch. I had made my promise to 'Colas and I could not do otherwise. Pablo knows that I have 'Colas's muviéri and he thinks of me as a man of knowledge. For myself, I do not think one can be a man of knowledge, in the Huichol sense, unless one is trained from the very beginning of his life in that tradition.

I was twenty-four years old when I first became conscious of the Huichols. This was in 1971 and I was attending the University of Wisconsin, taking graduate courses in computer sciences, with a minor in mathematical sciences. The academic year ended, summer came, and I went back to Mexico to spend my vacation when I saw Fernando Benítez's books on the Huichols (1968a, 1968b). I became fascinated. What an interesting people! I knew nothing about that part of our country, and so I decided to visit them and see things for myself. How could an indigenous culture have survived like that, I thought, with all their ancient beliefs, their gods, their old rituals, still so intact?

So I went to Tepic (the capital of Nayarit) and talked with the people at the Cora-Huichol Center of the Instituto Nacional Indigenista. Diego Vázquez Juárez was then in charge of education in the Sierra. He suggested I go to San Andrés and ask the INI teacher in charge of the boarding school up there to give me a place to sleep and see about solving the problem of where and how I might get my meals. Early the next day I flew to the Sierra. Our little plane set down on the dirt strip and as we came to a bumpy stop I saw this Huichol man standing beside the runway, obviously waiting to be taken out on the very same aircraft. I introduced myself and told him the INI people in Tepic had recommended that I go and see the teacher and ask him for help in locating a place to stay and get my meals. Where could I find this teacher? "I am the teacher in charge," he said. "and I would help you, but now I must go to Tepic." With that he left.

What to do? I decided to go and find the INI school by myself and see if there was somebody, another teacher perhaps, whom I might ask about getting settled. Luckily, I met a party of Huichol men who said they had been hired by the Secretaría de Obras Públicas (the federal Ministry of Public Works) to repair the airstrip. They invited me to stay with them until the teacher returned, or I could find more permanent quarters in some other way, perhaps at the boarding school. They gave me my first opportunity to stay and talk for several days with real Wixarika (the name by which the Huichols call themselves).

I knew nothing of their language. But I loved literature and appreciated the art of speaking, and I sensed somehow that, strange and unfamiliar as were the words and the manner in which they were strung together into complicated sentences, and non-literate though my hosts obviously were, when conversing with one another and telling stories they were using the native tongue in a wonderfully expressive and even poetic way. One could see the pleasure in their faces as they reacted to the words of their fellows.

I was terribly frustrated by my cultural and linguistic ignorance. But there was also in me a growing conviction that there was so much to be done here, that there seemed to be no true dialogue between the Indians and the government. With the conceit of the young, I thought that perhaps I might serve as a sort of mediator between these people and ourselves, a kind of cultural broker. When one is as young as I was, one has that sort of certainty.

I decided to stay, not go back either to Mexico City, or the United States to resume my studies at the University of Wisconsin. And I remained in the Sierra for the next year and a half. In that short space of time I had the opportunity to learn so much—more, I like to think, than I had ever learned in all my life, or ever would have in a college classroom. But I had to justify my presence. I wanted to find an occupation that would explain to the Indian people why I was there, why I wanted to live among them.

The one thing I did not want to do in those days was write, even to make notes. I did not want to collect data and write it up like an anthropologist. And, in fact, this is really the first time I am actually putting some of my experiences together in a coherent way. Twenty years ago I refused to do so, to write anything down, because that was not my main purpose. My reason for being there was to gain some knowledge, an understanding of their culture. I could say that to them, and I thought they understood, because they were quite familiar with others who had come with a similar purpose. But in the past these visitors had stayed only a short time, not as long as I hoped to do. And I also felt a strong responsibility not just to live there but to find something to do that would be of benefit to them.

I chose arts and crafts, for which they have long been famous and which I felt could, if properly organized, become a ready and much-needed source of cash income for them. Huichol artisans who had left the Sierra had been doing relatively well with their handiwork, there had been Huichol exhibitions in the United States and in Mexico, and I saw no reason why the economic benefits of their artistry should not also extend into the Sierra itself. But the materials they required—wool yarn, glass beads, cloth, needles, plywood, masonite—were all expensive, especially in the haphazard way they were buying them and marketing the finished product. In those days, they had little understanding of pricing structures. So I began a regular program of buying materials wholesale in Mexico City and Guadalajara and bringing them up the Sierra. Then I would take what they did with these materials, the weavings and beadwork and other products of their artistic and technical skill, back to the outside world to dispose of for fairer prices than they had been getting on their own. In their eyes that gave me a valid reason for being there. At the same time, I was trying to convince them that they could do this on their own, by going themselves to Guadalajara and even to Mexico City, to purchase the raw materials in large quantities much cheaper than the prices they were being charged by itinerant merchants. And they could make contacts and perhaps establish a permanent market.

Much of my free time was occupied working on translating from Huichol to Spanish with one of the boys at the school, and one of the women teachers. But I also did a great deal of traveling in and out of the Sierra in this way. On several of these occasions I took a few Huichols with me, to introduce them to the ways of the city and the dominant culture. Once I had the idea of taking three of the boys from the INI boarding school with me to Mexico City. I thought it would be a great experience for them. But it turned out to be even more instructive for me. To see their reactions was worth all the expense. In our own culture we are impressed with size: tall buildings, big cars, big crowds, large sums of money, wide boulevards, huge supermarkets and department stores. But that was not at all what impressed these young Huichols; quite the contrary. For example, more than anything else, they were taken by our little Volkswagen Beetle, precisely because it was so small and agile that it could beat our crazy traffic and almost always find a parking space just big enough to squeeze into, when the drivers of larger cars were completely frustrated. That is what impressed them: whatever gave you independence from restrictions, whatever facilitated things you wanted to do. They liked the fact that trolley buses were much quieter and less smelly than those powered by gasoline. But what they liked even more was that our little car could travel independently instead of being chained to overhead cables!

Another thing that was uncanny was their sense of orientation. Sometimes my three young Huichol friends would simply leave and go off on their own. I was worried for them because I would not hear from them for hours. Where were they? Were they lost? Were they safe? What if they became confused by the immense urban sprawl of the capital? Well, I needn't have been concerned, because after some anxious hours on my part there they were again at my front door, having unerringly found their way back to my house. No printed map, which they could not have read in any event, just the subjective map they had imprinted on their own minds while walking the streets and driving with me in their favorite conveyance, my little Volkswagen.

It was during one of those visits to Mexico City early on during my residence in San Andrés that I met Marina Anguiano. Marina was a talented and sensitive young Mexican anthropologist who had worked with Huichols in the Sierra and in the colony founded in the 1930s along the lower Río Lerma by families fleeing from the Cristero troubles in the Sierra. I told Marina that I had settled down in San Andrés, and she said that in that case I absolutely had to meet a very great mara'akáme, one of the truly great Huichol men of knowledge. His name was Nicholas Carrillo de la Cruz, she said, and he lived on his rancho not far from the ceremonial center. His Huichol name was 'U Temay, but everybody called him 'Colas. All I had to do was ask for 'Colas, and people would take me to him.

I was a little intimidated by what Marina told me about this man's prestige and spiritual power and I thought and thought what kind of gift I might take to the Sierra to introduce myself to him. I knew how much Huichols love the violin and had many times heard the wonderful music they make on the primitive little instruments they construct for themselves from local materials. They play their violins in all the ceremonies, and they admire anyone who is a proficient player. And so I went to a music store and purchased a small-sized violin to take to 'Colas.

As I had hoped, he expressed great pleasure at my gift, admiring the fine wood varnished and polished to a brilliant shine, the beautiful grain, and the melodious, clear tones the bow produced on the strings. The funny thing is that much as he appeared to like it, I never saw that violin again, neither in his or anyone else's hands, or hanging in his house.

If the gift itself vanished from sight, the bond that grew between us from that day on did not. Always he was in charge of me, of that there was never any doubt. Unasked, he accepted responsibility for me, for my physical welfare, for my state of mind, for learning about the Huichols, for everything.

In those early days I was not yet married. One day 'Colas came to Mexico City and visited my mother. They talked for a time in Spanish—his Spanish was not fluent but quite adequate for conversation—and he said to her, "For sure, when Guillermo goes to the Sierra, you are worried for him, no?" "Yes," my mother said, "I worry very much for him." And 'Colas said, "Well, do not worry for him, because when he comes to San Andrés he is in my house. When he is in San Andrés Cohamiata, he is truly in my house."

Strictly speaking, I never actually slept or even ate in the house of 'Colas, meaning in his rancho. But Tatéi Ki'ye, The House of Our Mother, the ceremonial center of San Andrés Cohamiata, that really was also the house of 'Colas. That is what he meant by coming to "my house." Because in Tatéi Ki'ye, in his place, he had influence not only over the social and ceremonial life of the community and relations between individuals, but over the whole environment, religious, social, and natural. And so all the time I was in San Andrés I was in "his house," in the shelter of this great man.

On several occasions he made this clear to others. As I said, I was then just twenty-four years old. Often he would walk from his rancho to the INI boarding school and visit with me in the little room in which I had my cot. Everyone, teachers and boys, saw how we sat together and talked and talked. I was in daily touch with all those boys and girls of all ages who were enrolled in the school. And they always took me with them to the ceremonies in their own ranchos. It was an incredible opportunity to see so many things and to think about them, because being in such intimate touch with Indian people is to me something like social therapy, in which one starts to question and challenge one's own cultural assumptions and attitudes.

And then I would talk it all out with 'Colas, try to get him to explain what this and that meant and how it fit into the larger scheme of things. I was much in awe of the knowledge, the spiritual power, and also the practicality, that lay behind his quiet and modest demeanor. With him I had the opportunity of talking out what I was seeing and absorbing, in long, slow, patient conversation. I learned to appreciate his experience and great wisdom, and his quiet dignity. That was why it was not such a surprise later on when I heard the wisest among them say that 'Colas was Tatewarí, that in 'Colas they had Tatewarí himself living right their in their midst. That is why they felt them-selves to be secure and living in a special place, because with 'Colas they were always in the physical and spiritual presence of Tatewarí.

One day when I was living in San Andrés something very sad happened. A Huichol man had hanged himself from a tree and when 'Colas came to the school that morning I asked him if he knew why this man had decided to take his own life.

"Well, you know," he said, "this man was very sensitive. And he felt ashamed."

I asked him why the man felt so ashamed that he no longer wanted to live, and 'Colas told me that the man's wife had refused to continue to prepare his meals for him, that she had decided that she no longer wanted to feed him. And he was very sensitive and felt very badly and decided that he had better hang himself.

"But 'Colas," I asked, "is that the right thing to do? Did he do the right thing to hang himself, to take his own life, over something like that?"

"No," said 'Colas, "he was wrong to hang himself for such a reason. But it is also true that his wife should have been sensitive enough to understand his sensitivity, to know that her action would make him very ashamed before others. She should have realized that her duty was to prepare the meals for him and that he would be very ashamed if she did not."

We talked back and forth in this way for a while, and then we went to the tree from which the man had hanged himself. We cut him down and took his body to the old Franciscan church. Inside we found the widow and some of the couple's relatives. I watched 'Colas as he started to speak with her. His words were soft and gentle, for he never overtly displayed his position of moral authority. He did not berate her or thunder at her or express outrage. He spoke very softly and she listened closely to his words. When I asked him later what he had said to her, he said he had told her that she had been wrong to refuse to cook for her husband. This made her partly responsible for her husband's death, he told her. Not completely responsible, because her husband should not have hanged himself for such a reason. He told her that the decision to do so had been his own. But she should have been more sensitive to his feelings and his needs.

It was impressive to me to see him exercise his wisdom and authority at this difficult moment for the survivors, to see him tell her gently, yet firmly, that she bore a part of the responsibility, but not the whole. In that moment, I understood something I had not known before, that for Huichols suicide is neither strange nor an unusual response to stress.

I regretted very much that I could not converse with 'Colas in his own language. But we could always speak together in Spanish. He was not fluent but he was able to communicate all his thoughts very well. Once, when Scott Robinson (an American anthropologist living in Mexico) had filmed a peyote pilgrimage from San Andrés to Wirikúta, and we were trying to get some mara'akámes to do the commentary in Spanish, 'Colas said, "Oh, I wish I could do that, but in my own language." We planned to have him to do it at some time in the future. Unfortunately, he died before we could get around to it.

One day 'Colas and I were talking about punishment, about how the Huichols decide to mete out punishment for this and that transgression. "The Mexicans are much more cruel than we," 'Colas said. "Look, you put people in prison for years, and that is very hard and cruel for a man. But it is even worse for his children. It makes it very difficult for his children. Because they are deprived of the stories he can tell them, and the teaching he could have given them. So we think it is better for a man to be beaten if he does something wrong, to receive a certain number of blows, than it is to put him in prison. That is why we take them to the stocks for just a few hours.

"No one is allowed to get away free with the fault he has committed," he said, "but none of our children are deprived of their father and teacher."

These conversations with 'Colas, my life with the people—they gave me the opportunity to hear and see many things and think about them, because being in such close touch with the Indians was for me something like social therapy. You might almost call it cultural psychoanalysis. One sees how they order their lives, how they see themselves in the universe. And as I said, one begins to question one's own culture and values and attitudes.

I thought a great deal about the wisdom of 'Colas even after I left the Sierra to resume my studies—not any longer at the University of Wisconsin but at our own national university (UNAM, the Universidad Nacional Autónoma de México). And then one day in 1974, three years after I first went to San Andrés, a friend who was working on a film in the Sierra called me. "I have a message for you from 'Colas. He says he is going to die and he wants you to come to the Sierra right away to see him."

In less than three days my wife Lilia—I was now married—and I were back in San

Andrés and in the rancho of 'Colas. Perhaps, you remember, from the day his son was murdered in his sleep, 'Colas had begun to decline. And now I found him very, very ill. You remember that the people who sneaked into his house and shot his son thought they were killing 'Colas. And after his son's death 'Colas's spirit began to decline and he began to look really old.

I did not know his son, but according to what I heard about him he was a very deep and sensitive man who was being trained by 'Colas to be a mara'akáme like himself, not necessarily to be his successor but someone who acquires, and is the repository of, knowledge.

And so now here we were, Lilia and I, and we found 'Colas lying on his cot. He was very sick. We talked about many things, but his sickness was never mentioned. Nor was there talk of his being near to death. We stayed with him all afternoon, and the following day we came back, and again he never mentioned the reason for which he had called me to come to the Sierra.

We had made arrangements for the plane to pick us up the next day, and when I told 'Colas that we were going to leave the following day, he said, "I want to go to Mexico (City)." "Fine," I said, "why don't you pick up your things and tomorrow we go together to Mexico." Even though he had said nothing at all about his illness, or about how he felt, I saw this as an opportunity to take him to see some specialists. "No," he said, "I will come later." "When?" I asked, and he said, "In February, perhaps the fifteenth of February." And I said, "Well, fine, but how will you find me? How will I meet you? Do you know where I live and how to get there?"

"No, no," he said, "you just pick me up at the bus station."

And there we left it. The next day the plane came for us and we returned to Mexico City. The day mentioned by 'Colas for his visit approached and I was wondering how I would locate a Huichol Indian who was then almost ninety years of age amid all those buses arriving and departing and in all those crowds. On February 15 I went to the big new Mexico City bus station and sat there watching the buses arriving and people pouring out of them. And I wondered, how, with all this traffic and with so many people, will I even see him? I was really worrying, when a bus came and pulled to a stop right in front of me. People got off with their belongings and the last to emerge was 'Colas.

He was not at all surprised to see me there. Very simply and directly he said, "Here I am. I came already." He was wearing Huichol clothes. He was carrying his takwátsi and he was wearing his hat with all the feathers. I took him to stay with us in our house, and he said, "I want to eat some fish." 'Colas was a great lover of fish, he always wanted to eat fish. And of course we went to buy him fish.

Then I made arrangements to take him to different doctors to determine just what he was suffering from. We thought it might be a recurrence of prostate cancer, for which he had been operated on several years before in Guadalajara. I was anxious to find a doctor who had respect for Indian culture and was sensitive to Indian attitudes, and who would treat this wonderful old man with dignity and appreciation for what he was, in the proper manner.

I have a good friend, a well known pathologist named Ruy Pérez Tamáyo. When I was still living in San Andrés, whenever I came back to the city I always made a point of going to see him, because he, and also his wife and children, could never get enough of hearing about the Indian people among whom I was living, their culture, and the conditions under which they were existing in the Sierra. It was always good for me to talk to him, and now, with 'Colas so ill, it was more important than ever. I told Ruy we needed to see a specialist, and how important it was that he have the same sensitivity to Indian culture and Indian attitudes as he had himself, someone who would treat 'Colas with the dignity and regard he deserved. Ruy said yes, he knew just such a doctor. He recommended Dr. Ignacio Purpon, and when 'Colas and I came to see him, the doctor was open and friendly and at the same time showed great respect. They consulted together for quite some time, the doctor asking questions, not only about his health but about his culture and his life, and listening with the interest and attention he would have shown a learned colleague who had his respect. And they conversed in this way for quite some time, these two specialists, the Mexican physician and the Huichol shaman.

Ruy had also recommended a gastroenterologist. He was another man who respected Indian people, and it was from these doctors that I finally got the diagnosis I had feared. They agreed that it was not 'Colas's prostrate acting up again but that there were other internal problems of great seriousness, especially for a man of his age. There were several alternatives, the doctors told me, but to determine which, there was common agreement that he would have to be operated on before they could be sure.

With this verdict we returned to Ruy Pérez Tamáyo. 'Colas said he would wait downstairs in the car while I went upstairs to talk to my doctor friend. It was Ruy's recommendation that 'Colas should not be operated on in Mexico City. He was very old and even if the operation succeeded in prolonging his life somewhat, he would have to spend his last weeks in a city hospital, where he would be treated as just an ignorant Indian and not as the great man of knowledge that he was. And he would probably die there. So it was his recommendation that 'Colas should go home. Probably he would die soon, perhaps in a few weeks or months, but he would die as the great mara'akáme he was in his own country, not as an unknown Indian here in the city. Ruy took me into his library and with his medical books showed me what the specialists were recommending. This was to make sure I understood, and would be able to convey to 'Colas that, according to the doctors, to have some possibility of additional life, from now on to his death he would have to live in a hospital here in the capital. That was not what he would advise, Ruy told me. His advice was that 'Colas should return to the Sierra.

Ruy had yet to meet 'Colas, but he had heard me talk about him many times. And he said, "I would like to meet your Huichol friend." I said, "Well, he is downstairs in the Combi." "So let's go," he said, and on the way down he suddenly stopped and said,

"I don't want you to think of me as a *cuervo*, as one of those black crows." I said I didn't understand, what did he mean by "black crows"? And he explained it by telling me the story of one of the Greek gods who, upon hearing from a crow that his son was going to die, became so angry that he turned the crow black. That's how Greek mythology accounted for crows being black. He knew that it would be very hard for me to think of 'Colas dying and he worried that perhaps I would hold it against him that he was a messenger of death. "Don't worry," I said, "I would never think of you in that way, as the bringer of bad tidings. You have meant too much to me for that." And, in fact, we have remained close right up to the present day.

Well, they had their meeting, he and 'Colas. Ruy Pérez Tamáyo is one of the great pathologists, famous not just in Mexico but also abroad, and here I was in the presence of these two men who, each in his own way and by his own tradition, were the repositories of wisdom, of knowledge. It is a picture I have carried with me ever since, the Huichol doctor of the soul and the Mexican doctor of the body. It gave me enormous satisfaction. When Ruy said goodbye to 'Colas he did it in the knowledge that he was bidding farewell forever to a man of dignity whose accumulated knowledge would go with him when he died. A whole generation, a whole history, would be gone when 'Colas himself went.

I got in the car and 'Colas and I drove back to my house. On the way I started explaining everything to him, the diagnosis of the doctors, their plans to operate, and, if that was his choice, the need for him to remain in the hospital for many weeks. I did not tell him what Ruy had said, that he personally was opposed to 'Colas undergoing an operation that would be chancy at best, just to have his life prolonged for no more than a few weeks, in the end to die in a hospital among strangers, among people who had no appreciation of his culture and his knowledge.

But I didn't have to. "No," said 'Colas firmly, "no, I will go back to the Sierra." Without knowing that this had been Ruy Tamáyo's advice all along, 'Colas had made the decision for himself: "I will go back to the Sierra, to Tatéi Ki'ye. I will die in my own rancho."

But there were things he wanted to do right now. He said, "I want to see Salomón Nahmad." 'Colas had known Salomón for many years, since he became director of the INI Center in Tepic. Salomón used to come to San Andrés to visit and talk with him. He event spent some of his holidays there, with his wife and two little boys. "And then I want to see President Echeverría," 'Colas said. "And after him I want to see Fernando Benítez."

I tried to make the arrangements, but neither the President of Mexico nor the author of *Los Indios de México* was available. The president was otherwise occupied and Benítez was in Japan.

But Salomón Nahmad was in his office. He said that, of course we could come and see him at any time, that he would be happy to greet his old friend 'Colas. He was then director of indigenous education in the Secretaría de Educación Pública. And that is how I myself finally got to meet Salomón. We drove to the Ministry of Public Education and Salomón and 'Colas had their reunion.

As I sat watching them talk with such great animation, about San Andrés and its beauty and many other things, it suddenly came to me why 'Colas had come to Mexico City. Not to learn about his illness, how serious it was, or that he would die of it. These things he already knew. Nor had he come to be operated on. He had come to say goodbye to his friends, to people he had met, people he had befriended or who had befriended him. Not in so many words, perhaps, but that was clearly what he had in mind. That, and also to get some financial support, a little money, to give to his elderly wife to live on when he was gone. He didn't have to tell Salomón this. Salomón understood without the necessity for words, and gave 'Colas a gift of money for his wife.

At 'Colas's request we also went to see Osvaldo Ramos Vasconzelos, whom everybody knew as El Teniente (the Lieutenant), even though he was actually a lieutenant colonel. This military man was very much taken with the Huichols and their traditional culture, and in the past had given assistance to them and to 'Colas personally. Again I was impressed with the ease with which my old shaman friend from the Sierra and the Mexican officer bridged the cultural gulf between them. They talked and talked, and even though there was this undertone of a final farewell, they clearly gave each other pleasure.

It was after this that 'Colas gave me his shaman's basket with his own muviéri inside, together with the cargo, the obligation, of seeing that the young Pablo Carrillo was all right. And predicted the time of his death.

'Colas died precisely when he said he would, just before the onset of the rainy season in the year 1974. It was after his death that I began to hear of many things he had been doing in the Sierra in the days before he succumbed to his final illness. He made the rounds of his relatives and many other people, to make certain everyone know that he was going to die. He collected money for his wife to live on. He ordered his coffin to be built and how it should look. Most important, he chose the place in which he was to be interred. This was a house he himself had built but that was now inhabited by some mestizos. He walked in on them and announced, "I am going to be buried here." I can imagine the horror and fear on the faces of those mestizos when they heard 'Colas tell them that he would be buried right there, in the floor of this very house!

In the Huichol way, a death is followed by a ceremony lasting several days in which a mara'akáme guides the soul to the afterworld. And so it was with 'Colas. On the day of his death the most important mara'akámes held a council to consider who among them should conduct the ceremony. The one they selected declined, because, he said, "'Colas himself made all the preparations for his death and he did not say a word to me about wanting me to do this for him. So I do not think I am the one."

And all of them were of the same opinion: 'Colas had not specifically asked for them and they did not feel that he had wanted them to carry out this important ritual.

Just then an old mara'akáme who had his rancho at the very foot of the *barranca* came climbing up to the San Andrés plateau to announce that he was supposed to conduct the ceremony of taking 'Colas's soul to the other world. And so he did. Later I heard that two years later this mara'akáme was shot to death. I cannot help but think that somehow there was a plot afoot to kill those who were distinguished mara'akámes in this part of the Sierra. I cannot prove the existence of such a plot, but I would not be surprised.

'Colas had not only left instructions that he was to be buried inside the house, but also that after five years his body should be taken out of the floor and moved from the house to the cemetery of San Andrés. Every time I have gone back to San Andrés and brought it up, I was told that yes, those were the instructions 'Colas left. I suppose for this, too, there was a specific mara'akáme whom 'Colas had instructed to conduct the ceremony of moving his remains from one place to the other.

Years passed, I completed my studies at the University, and then one day in March of 1989, Arturo Warmann, the Director General of the Instituto Nacional Indigenista, called to offer me the position of head of the INI legal department. I thought to myself, well, perhaps this is the real cargo 'Colas gave me on that final day with the gift of his muviéri, implicitly, if not in so many words. Thinking of 'Colas and his gift is what made me decide to accept the job.

Soon after I joined the Instituto I returned to the Sierra with my wife to explain to the kawitéros that I was now working with the INI, and that I wanted to learn from them what they might wish me to do in my new position. I told them that to know this was important to me, because I felt that helping them in some manner was the cargo 'Colas had entrusted to me when he gave me his muviéri.

I showed them 'Colas's takwátsi, and the muviéri inside it, and said, "I have come to listen to your advice." When they had satisfied themselves that the takwátsi and the muviéri really were those of 'Colas, they said, "Well, you know that now that 'Colas is dead he is one of our gods. He is Tatewarí.

"And for us this is very important, for our life, for our survival. And it is very important to us that you have come here to show us the takwátsi and the muviéri of 'Colas."

And then they said, "Well, why don't you just go around and visit your friends here in San Andrés? Because we are going to have a council in our own language, and you will not understand what we are saying. And when you have visited your friends, you will come back and we will explain to you what we have decided."

So I went to visit the widow of 'Colas, and then I went to the INI boarding school where I had lived so many years ago, to visit with the teachers and the children. Some of those teachers were themselves boys enrolled at the school when I first came to the Sierra, and so I knew them well.

Some hours passed in this way and I decided that perhaps it was time now to meet once again with the kawitéros. And this is what they told me:

"We have decided that you will take two cargos that were the cargos of 'Colas. One of these two cargos was to defend our lands. And the second cargo was to defend *la costumbre*, our customs, our religion."

Of course I was surprised and I said, "Well, I just came to see you and tell you in a very humble way that I am now working for the INI, and to see what you might want me to do to help you."

And they said, "There is no arguing about this. The kawitéros have decided. These were the two cargos of 'Colas and now they are yours. These are the cargos we want you to accept: to defend our lands, and to defend our customs."

And now I sit here in this office, in this position of Director General of the INI, with the picture of 'Colas on the wall. Who knows—perhaps that was why I was asked to succeed Arturo Warmann as Director, when he was appointed to administer the privatization of *ejído* land under the new agrarian law. Perhaps so. Of course I still have in my possession 'Colas's takwátsi, and 'Colas's muviéri, the takwátsi and the muviéri of Tatewarí. Sometimes I wonder if I should be holding on to these sacred things, or whether I should pass them on to someone in the Sierra. That is one of the mysteries left to me by 'Colas.

NOTES

1. Until 1995.
2. I am grateful to T. J. Knab for pointing this out. (—P.T.F.)

INTRODUCTION TO CHAPTER 16

That Konrad Theodor Preuss entitled his first report from the field about his stay among the Huichols "The Marriage of Maize and other Traditions of the Huichol Indians" (Chapter 3) is more than just a mark of the fascination this particular origin story of the sacred staple has had for him and other foreign investigators for more than a century. What interested Preuss especially is that he found virtually the identical story also among the Coras, neighbors and cultural and linguistic cousins of the Huichols, and, perhaps most significantly, among the Indians of San Pedro Jícora, Durango, who spoke a Nahua dialect closely related to Nahuatl. These Nahua-speakers, who, since Preuss's time, increasingly lost their native tongue, are assumed by some historians to be descended from Nahuatl-speaking Central Mexicans the Spanish settled on the northwestern frontier to guard against Chichimec incursions. Along with the fact, already mentioned elsewhere, that many Huichol terms connected with maize agriculture are borrowings from the Nahuatl, the virtual identity of the Huichol–Cora maize origin tale with that recorded by Preuss at San Pedro Jícora raises the question with whom the story, which is sung in sacred chant form at Huichol ceremonies connected with maize, originated in the first place. The kitchen technology required for the processing of maize into the different foods made from it is no simple matter, and that of the Huichols closely resembles that of the Central Mexicans. Who borrowed what from whom? The story is the charter for how the divinities wish the sacred maize to be treated, if the collapse of the harvest and famine are to be averted.

Here as elsewhere the successful integration of a new food into an established indigenous economy as grounded in religion as is that of the Huichols presupposes that it be validated by a sacred story and its associated complex of rituals, because unless the religious specialists know its sacred origins and to whom to address their petitions for its well-being, whom to thank, it will not flourish. There will be too much rain, or not enough, too much sun, or not enough, or pests will devour the plants. If the story came from the Central Mexican immigrants, might it have been they from whom the Huichols adopted maize as their principal sustenance, along with the myth accounting for its origin and proper treatment? Why is Niwétsika, the young maize goddess, called "the very child" of peyote, and why, in one version of the maize origin myth, does she explicitly return to Wirikúta, the sacred peyote desert in the east, because she was not treated with respect by her young husband's mother?

Scant though it is, on the early archival evidence the sierra Huichols were not then full-time sedentary maize farmers. Had they been, it is unlikely that the Spanish invaders would have succeeded in recruiting numerous Huichols to serve as a frontier militia of *flecheros* (archers)—a service for which the Huichols were later exempted from onerous taxation. In 1587, Commissioner-General Fray Alonso Ponce reported that the sierra Huichols he had visited grew little food of their own, relying for subsistence mainly on hunting and gathering. That Huichols were still traveling outside their territory for maize as late as the end of the eighteenth century emerges clearly from the proceeding—recently discovered in the Jalisco state library by anthropologist William L. Merrill of the Smithsonian Institution*—of an Inquisition trial in July and August 1786 of several Cora Indians for "idolatry and superstition." The Indians were arrested and tried for having secretly obtained forbidden "idols" and other outlawed ceremonial objects from members of the "Huizola nation." In exchange the Huichols, who had traveled from San Andrés Cohamiata to the Cora center, asked for maize. The smuggled "idolatrous" objects the Huichols had brought to Jesús María included images of native deities, among them a "mother goddess," "feathers of many birds," and a ceremonial *jícara* (gourd bowl) decorated (as they still are today) with "many strings of glass beads on the inside stuck together with wax and in the center a large stone or bead of turquoise." The accused Cora had secreted the illicit objects in their homes and caves and employed them in clandestine *mitotes* (dance ceremonies) for rain and curing. For their part the Huichols had gathered the then rare and expensive glass beads from several of their mission towns, including San Andrés, San Sebastián, and Santa Catarina, to offer their Cora neighbors for the maize.

How does all this fit with that curious tale, cited in the chapter by Dr. Casillas Romo, that connects the coming of the first maize with the appearance of foreign epidemic diseases, such as smallpox, which the myth says came to the Huichols from Central Mexico? Admittedly, against these speculations we have others according to which Huichols have been practicing their technologically simple slash-and-burn maize agriculture for more than a thousand years before the coming of the Spanish and their Nahuatl-speaking protegés, clearing brush and planting their crops on steep hillsides, without the benefit of the kind of terracing one sees in other parts of Mexico with a long pre-Conquest agricultural history (Figure 112). This theory, however, bases itself almost entirely on very thin and purely circumstantial evidence: the discovery of a few

---

*who shared it with the author of this chapter and he, in turn, with the editors. We are grateful to him, to University of Pennsylvania historian Nancy Ferris for transcribing the lengthy handwritten document into the computer, and to Julie Goodson-Lawes for assisting in the translation.

FIGURE 112. Steep Slope Planted with Maize Near Las Guayabas, Jalisco. It is typical of Huichol slash-and-burn digging stick agriculture. Huichols call such fields *coamil*, a term derived from the Nahuatl. (*Photograph by James A. Bauml.*)

ancient maize cobs in a series of rock shelters — not in Huichol country but considerably to the north, fifty miles northwest of Durango city (Cutler, 1978: 186–189).

No definitive answer as to when the Huichols first started cultivating maize, or when maize became their most important staple, is possible with the present state of our knowledge. In any event, wild and other cultivated foodstuffs, including amaranth, formed an important part of Huichol sustenance in the past, and do so now. What is beyond dispute is that maize as the most important and most sacred staple has helped sustain the Huichols physically and metaphysically for a considerable time — long enough, in any event, to have become securely associated with the ancestors, and tied to peyote in a spiritual as well as blood kin relationship and an inextricable conjunction of belief, symbol, and ritual. In the following chapter, the English ethnologist Anthony A. Shelton employs the basic origin myth as a starting point for a consideration of the potentially serious conflict that will inevitably follow governmental projects for agricultural change if they fail to take into account, and are carried out in accordance with, Huichol sensitivities and sacred histories regarding their beloved maize.

Peter T. Furst

16 : THE GIRL WHO GROUND HERSELF

Huichol Attitudes toward Maize

ANTHONY A. SHELTON

Opinion has been divided on the extent of Huichol acculturation. Early researchers, such as Preuss and Zingg, following the lead of Seler (1901), emphasized the cultural conservatism of the peoples of the Sierra Madre Occidental and stressed the importance of ethnographic inquiry as a means of reconstructing ancient patterns of Uto-Aztecan belief, ritual, social organization, and so forth. More recent ethnographers, including Furst (1968, 1972, 1976), Myerhoff (1974), and Schaefer (1990) have likewise focused on the survival of aboriginal religion, myth, and ritual among the Huichols. Others, such as Reed (1972), Nahmad (1981), Weigand (1981) and Gonzalez (1987), have concentrated on culture change. Drawing on both these traditions, this essay looks at development projects the federal and state governments have tried to impose over the region, and offers an assessment of their chances of success and an explanation of their shortfalls by examining their confrontation with indigenous conceptual categories. My argument will give particular attention to agricultural innovation and ideas surrounding the importance of maize.

Although I will be principally concerned with Huichol attitudes toward maize, I would suggest that certain of the themes, if not always the structures, of their conceptualization of this basic, and to them very sacred, crop have dense historical precedents and a wider geographical distribution. It will be argued that any attempt to introduce new crops into an area as part of a regional development plan must be predicated on thoroughgoing and sympathetic knowledge of a people's classificatory structures that determine the value and significance of different forms of vegetation.

Significance of Maize in Huichol Culture and Ideology

From primitive beginnings, maize has been cultivated in Mesoamerica for some 5,000 to 7,000 years, in the course of which it became the basic foodstuff for the Maya, Zapotec, Teotihuacan, and Classic Veracruz civilizations, and, later, the Aztec state society. There is much evidence that its cultivation was accompanied by a cycle of ritual, from the preparation of seed for sowing, to the clearing of the fields, harvesting, storing, and its transformation into food and drink. More than that, the growth of the plant, from its first emergence from the earth to the ripening of the ears, was celebrated at each of its distinct phases, and appropriate offerings were made that in the final analysis were intended to placate the anger of its spirit at being "killed" during the harvest. That Aztec maize beliefs and rituals survive to the present day among Nahua-speakers is clear from such recent ethnographies as Alan Sandstrom's *Corn is our Blood* (1991).

The Huichols identify five varieties of maize according to the color of the kernels (Figures 112, 113). On this, all versions of the maize origin myth agree. In the tradition I recorded, each color is considered to be a maize girl descended from the union of Watemukáme with a female rain mother, sometimes identified as Tatéi (Our Mother) Haramara, the deified Pacific Ocean. The five maidens are:

1. Tuzáme, White Maize Girl
2. Taurawime, Red Maize Girl
3. Tashawime, Yellow Maize Girl
4. Chichiwime, Mottled Maize Girl
5. Yoáwime, Blue Maize Girl

According to this version of the story, maize was given to the Huichols by Watemukáme, who took pity on a poor, starving old woman who, with great difficulty, traveled to his house to beseech him to ease her and her adopted boy's hunger.

Watemukáme told the old woman that he would have to consult his wife and daughters. But in the meantime he presented her with a bowl of maize to take back to her home. Although there seemed to be very little maize in the bowl he gave her, the old woman and her boy found that no matter how much they ate, the bowl never became empty but continued to replenish itself. When the old woman returned to Watemukáme five days later, he had still not made up his mind how he might best answer her needs, but instructed her to return in another five days.

After a series of similarly unsuccessful journeys, Watemukáme inquired of his daughters which of them would be prepared to leave his house and accompany the woman to her home. All protested that they did not wish to go, weeping copious tears. But finally Yoáwime, Blue Maize Girl, agreed to go with the old lady. Before they set off, Watemukáme warned the old woman that his daughter must not be made to do hard work, because she was sacred and this would harm her. The woman agreed and took Blue Maize Girl home.

FIGURE 113. The Five Colors of Maize. As in the United States Southwest, blue maize (*left*), *yoáwima* in Huichol, is the most sacred. (*Photograph by James A. Bauml.*)

The old lady's adopted son liked Blue Maize Girl very much and they soon took to sleeping together in the maize house he had constructed for her. She taught him how to prepare the soil for seed, but in the meantime, while they were awaiting the first harvest, maize in abundance accumulated in the maize house. This was because the girl's brother came each night to make certain that his sister was well and being looked after. Each night on his arrival he caused a rain of maize to fall from the rafters and accumulate on the floor. By the fifth night, the house was full.

Every day now the girl's husband would leave the rancho to attend the fields, as he had been instructed by his wife. In his absence, the old woman soon tired of the girl, complaining that she did not help her with the domestic chores. Blue Maize Girl was saddened by this and agreed to help the widow by grinding maize on the stone metate. Now sooner had she thus begun her chores, her arms became ground up into a bloody pulp. By grinding the maize she was grinding herself.

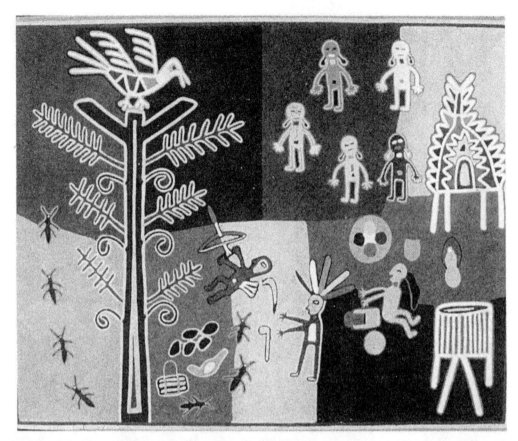

FIGURE 114. Narrative Yarn Painting Illustrating the Story of the Origin of Maize. *Left*, the Ant People, whom the hero trusted to take him to find maize, proved themselves to be thieves who gnawed him naked and hairless. At the top of the pine tree rests the dove who, as the hungry hero aimed his arrow at her, revealed herself as the divine Mother of Maize. She leads him to her rancho, *right*, where he gets no maize but meets her daughters, the Maize Maidens. One, Blue Maize, agrees to accompany him to his rancho as his wife. The circles within the circle below them represent a gourd bowl with five tortillas the Maize Mother gives him to still his hunger and that magically replenish themselves as he eats. *Lower right*, the yarn painting shows the elevated granary the hero builds for Blue Maize on her mother's instructions and, next to it, his young maize wife as she, shamed by her mother-in-law, begins to grind herself into bloody tortilla dough. (*Yarn painting by Ramón Medina.*)

When Watemukáme heard that the family had broken its vows he commanded his daughter to return home. Her husband, angry at what had happened, exiled the old woman from the house and went to plead with Watemukáme to let his wife return. Finally, after long pleading, her father agreed, but ordered that people should no longer have such easy access to maize. From now on they would have to observe a long ceremonial cycle on which the propagation of the plant would depend. Instead of the crop maturing in five days, it would now require much longer, and whereas previously precious little physical work was required, the labor would now be exhausting.

Another version, similar in many respects to that above and also to a variant re-

FIGURE 115. Young Huichol Girls Sweeping. An important instruction by the Maize Mother of mythology was to sweep everything clean in preparation for Blue Maize Girl's arrival. Huichols, from the youngest girls to aged grandmothers, still do this at maize harvest time. (*Photograph by Stacy B. Schaefer.*)

corded by Preuss in 1907 (cf. Chapter 3), was performed and illustrated for Furst and Myerhoff in 1966 by Ramón Medina Silva in a series of yarn paintings (Figure 114).[1] Myerhoff (1974:210–213) published this myth in shortened form. Ramón added his own thoughts to the conclusion of this sad tale, which never fails to move the Huichol audience to tears:

> Our Mother spoke to us like that. As she said it, some of us have maize, others have not. They did not take care of it. They did not adore it. That is why the spirit prefers to leave the place, back to its Mother, where there is no danger. Only the shell is left, rotten. That is why this is such a sacred story among us. It is very sad, very hard, this story. Maize is our nourishment. We must work it by ourselves, we must obtain it from the earth. We must treat it well, as a sacred thing. So that it does not leave us. (Myerhoff 1974:213)

Maize is thus a gift to the Huichols from the ancestral deities. It is anthropomorphized as a young girl descended from, and entering, a sacred union not unlike that of the Huichol nuclear family and occupying a similar type of household. There is a homophily between the family, descent, and residence patterns of Maize Girl and those of the people themselves. Even the frequent strain between mother-in-law and son's wife residing in the same household are replicated in the myth: it is because of the former's resentment and jealousy that Huichols must work so hard for their nourishment. Like Maize Girl, who annually prepares to sacrifice herself for them, the Huichols have to sacrifice themselves through hard work: that the sacrifice is as great for the Huichols, that the work is so laborious, is the punishment they must endure because the old woman mistreated her daughter-in-law.

Maize thus appears to be conceptualized as having an isomorphous type of relationship with problems similar to those found within the wider social structure. But as we shall see, the significance of the sacred food is greater still. To demonstrate this requires the excavation of a literal pile of superimposed metaphors heavily stacked around the conception of the food plant.

In primordial times, before the events recounted in the narrative of the origin of maize, it is said that maize was originally a deer, and that, like peyote, it grew from the footsteps left by the animal. Maize is planted by means of digging sticks that are pointed at one end. The holes made by the digging stick are sometimes referred to as deer tracks, and there is much sexual joking about the act of thrusting the stick downward into the earth and dropping the seeds into the hole. Huichols make no bones about the sexual symbolism: planting maize is like impregnating a woman. Earth is a woman, the digging stick is the phallus, and the hole it makes is the womb. Hence the joking. Moreover, the boy who becomes the mythical father of maize could also assume the form of a deer. The thrust of the digging stick that makes the womblike hole reenacts the mythical union between him and his Maize Girl wife to produce their daughter maize. But maize has a dual sexual identity—the maize plant is female but the ear is male. Nor is it accidental that the boy's mother, whatever her name in the different versions of the myth, is always associated with water, when she is not actually identified as Tatéi Yurianaka, Our Mother the Earth-Moistened-for-Planting.

Thus, the procreation of maize through the union of male and female categories resembles that of human beings. It takes place in the earth, conceptualized as the womb of Tatéi Yurianaka.

From sowing to maturation minute attention is given to the plant. A certain degree of deer symbolism persists throughout this process. When the first shoot breaks the soil, it is described as the small antler of a young deer. When the stalks have reached their full height, they are said to be the many-branched antlers of an old deer. Each stage in the maize plant's growth is the subject of much talk and expectation. There exist at least fourteen terms to describe the different stages of its history, which by tradition are also used as names for Huichol women at the different stages of their life.

The ceremonial cycle connected with the rainy season orchestrates a series of *rites de passage* that mark the major stages of the plant's origin and development: sowing, Tatéi

Híkuri (Our Mother Peyote); the supplication of the rains, Mawarixi; the weeding of the fields, Itsanaxa; the maturation of the maize, Tatéi Neixa (Dance of Our Mother); and the harvest, Eachakiute. These ceremonies mark the act of conception, birth and baptism, childhood, and maturity, when she is cut down and, having first been offered to the deities, is consumed by the Huichols.

Each of these ceremonies also prescribes a particular type of behavior appropriate to the plant at that particular stage of its life history. During Tatéi Híkuri, the ritual concerned with clearing the field of brush implores the earth womb to be fertile. Offerings are made and placed in a cavity at the center of the field before it is cultivated. These offerings correspond to those required of Tatéi Yurianaka, Our Mother the Earth made ready for planting by the first rains, with a prosperous harvest. This principle of reciprocity that governs relations between deities and human beings is well expressed in the words of one Huichol: "As the earth gives us to eat, so we feed her." The clearing of the field, then, is tantamount to preparing the womb of the earth mother, Tatéi Yurianaka, for conception, and all behavior is directed toward that end.

This ceremony is followed by Mowarixi, a supplication for the rains, that may be repeated as often as necessary to ensure abundant downpour. The Rain Mothers stand as sisters to the earth, and are thus the aunts of Maize Girl. Relations between sisters and their children are ideally close and warm. The advent of the rain, brought about by the sacrifice of a bull and other offerings to these deities, ensures their complicity in helping their sister with the birth of her daughter, and their continued assistance in nurturing after birth.

It is also in this ceremony that the children in a household group may be given ties of spiritual kinship. The episode, which includes a baptismal ceremony directed toward this end, parallels the first use of the name of the Maize Girl in other episodes of the same ceremony. The naming of Maize Girl—her removal from nature and incorporation into a supernaturally constituted domestic unit—parallels a similar transition that is carried out for the human child.

The next ceremony, Itsanaxa, like certain others, takes the form of a communal feast that concentrates a sufficient number of people to assist in the second clearing of the fields. The participants nourish the Maize Girl by giving her offerings of chocolate and the mild maize beer the Huichols call *nawá*, elsewhere known as *tesgüino*. She is addressed and reassured by the participants, who rid the field of the weeds that try to choke her. Led by the shaman-priest, the participants express their appreciation toward Maize Girl for the travails she endures and the transgressions against her dignity she tolerates for the Huichol people.

Irony is the strongest element of the harvest ceremony that marks the closing of the rainy season, irony expressed by the joy over the bountiful harvest, which, however, implies at the same time the imminent death of Maize Girl. This is what happens:

The ears of maize from the center of the field are cut and carried to the *xiriki*, the household temple by the rancho elder's wife. The Maize Child is placed on the altar and, after having received offerings, is welcomed and thanked for her presence. Prayers and dances are held in her honor. In his chant the shaman who officiates at the ceremony describes the weeping of the Maize Child as she beseeches her Mother to save her from the ritual parching that will constitute the culminating episode of the ceremony. The shaman asks her pardon for the atrocities they must inflict on her, and, once he has obtained permission from her parents, proceeds to reassure her and calm her fears at being burned on the fire. When the parching is completed, and after the kernels have been offered to the deities of the five sacred regions—the cardinal points and the center—the maize may be harvested and eaten.

The life history of the Huichol is directly comparable to that of the maize. The ceremonies of birth, baptism, maturation, and death parallel one another. Even life itself is similar, establishing the maize family as a metaphor for the Huichol family.

The shaman attempts to ease the suffering of the maize as she is parched by sprinkling her with water and, in the version of the chant that names Tatéi Haramara, the Pacific Ocean, as the female rain mother who gave birth to Maize Girl, telling her that her non-material aspect will soon return to the western sea so that she can join her mother. Much the same happens to the Huichol. After death, the bones are taken by the chthonic deity to be guarded below the earth, while the soul travels to the entrance to the underworld in the west to celebrate with the waiting relatives below, before commencing the journey that takes it to the ancestors in the celestial realm (cf. Chapter 12). The only difference between the life history of the maize and that of the Huichol is that the former ends with a ritual sacrifice and the pseudo-anthropophagous consumption of the maize, which is said to return to life each year.

The behavior of the maize cultivator to the sacred plant is also similar to that which a human child receives from its mother and father. It is given favors and taught its obligations. And it is soothed and reassured. In fact, there is another maize myth, also dictated by Ramón Medina to Furst and Myerhoff, that explicitly identifies the human infant with the young maize:

"When maize was born it was a small baby, very small. It crawled there on the ground, in the house, outside the house. And it soiled itself very often. And because of this, the father and mother became tired. At last the father tells his wife, 'It is enough. I do not want this child here, let us throw it out.' The mother felt much pity. She said, 'We cannot do this thing. It must be planted well, no matter what . . .'"

But the father insists and the baby is thrown out. It is lonely and cries and cries, until the Mother of Maize, Tatéi Kukurukú Uimari, hears it. She comes to take it home to her rancho, and where the baby left its trail she plants beautiful flowers. After a while the parents miss the child and go looking for it. But it has disappeared and they follow its trail of flowers to the home of the Maize Mother. They beg her to let them take Maize Baby home but are refused. They try to take hold of it but it drops from their hands: "It unraveled in their hands, like pretty wool. They would take it up and try to put it over their shoulder but it would slide down again, like drops of water, like little kernels of hail." Now they realize that they have lost Maize Baby forever.

Disconsolate they return home. When they had left, the house had been full of maize; now they find it empty. "Nothing had been left," Myerhoff (1974:214) quotes the narrator. "Because they had not raised it as it should be. They rejected it and threw it out.

"All that happened because they had scorned the life that was to have been theirs. This is the story as the mara'akáme (shaman) sings it, the story of the little baby that was maize when it came into this world."

Here again the moral is obvious. Finally, as noted earlier, the names bestowed upon the maize at its different stages from birth to maturation are also bestowed on girl children. It is the paternal grandfather who gives the child its name, which has been supernaturally communicated to him by Great-grandmother Nakawé, the old goddess of the earth and of growth, or by one of the rain mothers, or, perhaps, Tatewarí, the aged fire god and First Shaman. A girl may also be named for the time of year in which she was born, more often than not the wet season. Then, too, the child's name may be taken from the type of cloud formation seen in the sky at the time of birth, but this too is conceptually related to the stages in the plant's maturation. But maize names are not limited only to children, for women, too, may be given a maize name.

A compulsive metaphorical relationship thus exists between maize and women. The birth and maturation of the plant follows similar paths and is accompanied by similar processes as those of human beings, especially women. The process unfolds in a family and home environment constituted by similar relations and according to the same protocols. Maize thus appears as a metaphor in which Huichol identity is rooted.

One of the principal criteria by which the Huichols identify themselves as distinct from other ethnic groups is the ceremonies they offer to their deities. The most important of these is surely the harvest ceremony, Tatéi Neixa, at which the new maize is roasted and offered to the deities before it is deemed to be fit for human consumption. There is, of course, much more to this complex ceremony, which has been well described in the ethnographic literature, but this aspect of giving the gods to eat of the first fruits so that they may reciprocally sanction its consumption by human beings is without doubt central.

There is some convergence here between the Christian cycle of rituals and myths and traditional Huichol thought. According to one version of the story, the Huichols recognize five different races, each descended from five members of an ancestral, pre-Huichol race called the Hewixi, the plural form of Hewi. Originally, all five were equal, but according to this Indianized Christian narrative, after Jesucristo had taught both the Mexican and the Huichol the art of cultivation and the necessary agricultural rituals, the Mexicans forgot to observe the appropriate ceremonies. Jesucristo grew angry with the Mexicans and punished them by giving them inferior maize, so that they had to grow alternative crops. But because the Huichols have always observed the ways of the deities, they have always had prosperous harvests. This narrative ploy inverts the normative relationship as defined by the dominant society by making the Mexicans moral inferiors to the Huichols.

This sojourn from metaphor to reason finally arrives at its destination in the postulate that certain foods are appropriate to certain types of people. The metaphors encode the significance of these associations by distributing human and plant categories, what is edible and inedible, along the vectors of the ethical and unethical. Mexicans eat wheat-based products, potatoes, tomatoes, onions, and only inferior strains of maize as a punishment for their sin of forgetting the deities, while the Huichols are able to enjoy their maize-based diet because of their special relationship to their gods. And this is precisely where problems arise in attempts at guided culture change, specifically development plans aimed at transforming the economic base of the area in which the Huichols and their Indian neighbors make their homes. The fact is that the proposition of these plans have come into conflict with the beliefs just described, without the planners even being aware of the reasons.

Before we look at the objectives of these development plans, it is necessary to summarize the material and geographic conditions under which the Huichols live, for in addition to the traditional emotional and economic attachment to maize as sacred sustenance, politics and ecology also play a role.

Rural Development and Agricultural Innovation in the Huichol Heartland

The absence of a centralized political authority among the Huichols and the apportionment of their *comunidades* to four different Mexican municipalities (Mezquitic, Bolaños, Huajimic, and Huejuquilla el Alto) effectively disenfranchise them from political power and influence. Not only are they politically fragmented at the local and municipal level, but communally held territories are split between different states: San Andrés is partitioned between the states of Jalisco, Nayarit, and Zacatecas; Guadalupe Ocotán, San Sebastián, and Tuxpan de Bolaños are divided between Jalisco and Nayarit, and Santa Catarina between Jalisco and Zacatecas. There are Huichol rancherías also within the state of Durango. As a result, the Huichols are subject to different and often contradictory policies from different directions, ranging from benevolent to indifferent, from developmental to isolationist, and that frequently exploit the antagonism between Huichols and mestizos for the benefit of their contending political and territorial interests.

The five Huichol communities incorporate approximately 404 rancherías that are dispersed over an area of 4,107 square kilometers (SEP-INI 1971:27). In 1970 the Instituto Nacional Indigenista estimated the total number of inhabitants of the area at 4,441, for a density of only 1.1 inhabitant per square kilometer. Even then, however, the actual number should have been about double this figure, and the population density adjusted accordingly.[2] An idea of their wide dispersion and isolation in the Sierra itself can be derived from the settlement pattern recorded for a total area of 4,959 square kilometers, including the heart of the Huichol country in Jalisco and adjacent non-Huichol lands. Of 412 population nuclei within this region, 88.4 percent were composed of fewer than 100 residents, 10 percent had between 100–500 people, and only 0.7 percent had 500–2,500 inhabitants (Plan Huicot 1971:95). Between 1960 and 1970, the area lost 21 percent of its economically active work force and registered an overall population decline of 10 percent (Plan Huicot 1971: 95).

Inaccessible terrain, the lack of essential services, and poor to nonexistent health and educational facilities, at least in the recent past, have contributed to its extreme marginalization. Poor soils and unpredictable rains have encouraged the Huichols to migrate and engage in seasonal work on the coastal tobacco and citrus plantations in Nayarit during the dry season, while many of their dependents remain in the Sierra, where they suffer malnutrition and ill health.

The recent penetration of the Sierra by federal government agencies and private enterprise can be divided into three periods: (1) from 1960 to 1970, when the Instituto Nacional Indigenista established its Cora–Huichol Center in Tepic, the capital of Nayarit, to coordinate services and integrate the area into the Mexican nation-state; (2) from the institution of the regional development plan known as Plan Huicot (for Huichol-Cora-Tepehuan) in 1970 to its cancellation four years later; and (3) from 1976 to the present, when a separate INI-sponsored Huichol center was created with responsibility for those parts of the communities that lie within the state of Jalisco. Because most of the land of Guadalupe Ocotán is situated in the state of Nayarit, it falls within the purview of the INI Cora Center in Tepic, whereas Huichol rancherías in the states of Durango and Zacatecas remain isolated from the development strategies affecting other areas in their comunidades.

FIRST PHASE: INITIAL STAGE OF INI INFLUENCE, 1960–1970

The characteristics, resources, and problems of the area were defined and evaluated, and policies formulated for implementation later in this period. Huichol agriculture was considered inefficient, because it relied on one main staple, maize, and favored the traditional system of slash-and-burn cultivation with the digging stick on relatively steep mountain slopes subject to erosion and was practiced in ignorance of proper scientific techniques and lacked modern tools and machinery. Such problems were compounded by difficult terrain, poor soils, and capricious climatic conditions (SEP-INI 1971:46). INI formulated a policy intended to modify traditional agricultural practices by demonstrating the advantages of diversifying crops, introducing more resistant strains of maize that withstand sharp fluctuations in temperature and mature more rapidly, and using fertilizers, insecticides, and herbicides (SEP-INI 1971:49). Similar methods of demonstration were used to improve animal husbandry, and a program was developed to vaccinate cattle and substitute better breeds for those held by the Huichols. Nurseries were also introduced during this period to provide fruit trees for orchards that were planted near newly developed boarding schools.

Perhaps the project with the greatest long-term impact, however, was the construction of an educational center in Mezquitic to train young Huichols and Coras in modern agriculture, animal husbandry, and fisheries. The intention at the time of its opening was to enroll thirty students for a two-year course that would equip them to carry out INI's agricultural and livestock programs and encourage their adoption throughout the Sierra. Two generations of *promotores* were educated before the center was closed after four years of operation (Gonzalez 1987:25-26).

SECOND PHASE: PLAN HUICOT, 1970–1974

Plan Huicot shared many of its aims with the program initiated by INI. The ideal was the systematic transformation of an area that would include the Huichol and adjacent indigenous territories, in concert with the social and economic integration of a wider region. The total area consisted of 2,700,000 hectares in the states of Jalisco, Nayarit, Durango, and Zacatecas, with a total population of 70,000 belonging to five different ethnic groups (Plan Huicot 1971:30). Responsibility for the coordination of the plan was given to INI. The first phase of the agricultural and fisheries program had begun in San Andrés Cohamiata during the previous period, including a 100-hectare demonstration plot on the mesa near the community center, and an animal husbandry facility. At the bottom of the valley below San Andrés, a second demonstration plot was planted at the important ranchería of Las Guayabas.

Boarding schools offering primary education were constructed in San Andrés, Guadalupe Ocotán, Santa Terésa, Tuxpan, Ocóta de la Sierra, San Sebastián, and Nueva Colonia. The growth of educational installations encouraged the spread of orchards throughout the area.

The project included plans to open and equip government-subsidized stores (Conosupo) selling basic foodstuffs at low prices. However, by 1979 the Conosupo store in San Andrés, which had been operating since the mid-1960s, was closed, and others suffered from irregular deliveries and were not well patronized by the people they were intended to serve.

From 1973, beginning in San Sebastián and later spreading to other areas, credit began to be obtained from outside sources for the financing of small agricultural development projects supervised by INI. Along with agricultural development and the establishment of primary schools, there emerged an ambitious plan to create access to outside markets by constructing two roads that would penetrate the region and relieve it from dependence on expensive air transport (cf. Reed 1972:73-75). Construction was focused on efforts to complete the Tepic–Zacatecas road and shorter dirt roads linking the Huichol centers of San Andrés and Tuxpan with the mestizo towns of Santa

Lucía and Bolaños. Significantly, no attempts were made to improve communications between the Huichol communities that might have stimulated greater ethnic cohesion between them.

Preparations were also made for the construction of three medical centers (SEP–INI 1971:87), but lack of personnel and essential supplies prevented them from providing regular services to the region.

In 1974 Plan Huicot was suspended by presidential decree and the powers invested in INI as the federal coordinating agency for the area were returned to the different state governments. Although Zacatecas withdrew its support for a coordinating body for indigenous affairs, the other three state governments cooperated in the establishment of separate branches of INI to deal with their respective Indian populations (Gonzalez 1987:31).

THIRD PHASE: INI CENTRO COORDINADOR HUICHOL, 1976–1984

The INI Huichol Center was established in 1976 with a much reduced area of jurisdiction that was limited to the community lands within the state of Jalisco. The San Andrés mesa continued to be the focus for pilot projects and provided the community with a surplus source of maize during periods of scarcity. While orchards were extended and fruit trees spread to many rancherías, new crops such as potatoes, onions, and tomatoes, which INI had tried to introduce, were rejected by the Huichols and abandoned. The four years from 1978 to 1982 saw the opening of fourteen fisheries that were meant, like the original idea behind the cultivation of orchards, to supplement the diet of enrollees in the boarding schools.

Marked improvements in cattle breeds and other domesticated animals created larger holdings and widened discrepancies between wealthy and poor Huichols. However, because of the difficulty of transporting animals to external markets, there was little possibility of converting cattle into money. Cattle wealth remained only a symbolic reference to status. That, however, might well change rapidly with the completion of the Tepic-Zacatecas road.

Throughout this period there was a growth of credit facilities for Huichol farming that were accepted through the urging of INI and implemented through promotores trained by that agency. By 1983 the amount of credit extended by outside financial institutions reached 449,181,000 pesos (Gonzalez 1987:32), effectively integrating the Huichols into the money economy.

How the newly implemented agrarian law providing for the privatization of communal lands will affect the Huichols (and other indigenous communities throughout Mexico) is anybody's guess, but there is much fear among anthropologists that it has the potential of disaster for the Indian peoples.

Development and Resistance

Any evaluation of the twenty-four years during which the Instituto Nacional Indigenista worked in the Sierra must recognize their uneven success in integrating the Huichol country into the national political and economic system. In some measure, this may be attributed to the lack of continuity in implementing programs uniformly over the area originally designated for development. Many of INI's projects were met with sustained opposition from outside vested interests, and INI personnel have had to devote much time and resources in attempting to alleviate conflicts over land ownership and related judicial matters. On the Huichol side, the different historical experiences of the various comunidades have shaped their receptivity to change and also created obstacles to the efforts of development agencies. Another and more general and pervasive explanation, however, can be found in the clash of two only marginally reconcilable conceptual systems—the one striving to maintain its dominion over a world made increasingly precarious through almost five hundred years of foreign domination, the other seeking to extend its sovereignty to overcome the last vestiges of "exotic" thought that questions its symbolic mastery of "practical knowledge."

Although the Instituto Nacional Indigenista emphasized its respect for local traditions and political organizations—many of its workers were, after all, anthropologists—the presuppositions and implementation of the development plan were, in the last analysis, incompatible with the ethos of the communities it was designed to help. INI workers assumed the existence of a common rationality shared between themselves and the local culture in which they were operating. They believed, therefore, that once the social and economic benefits of the program had been demonstrated, innovations would automatically be emulated. What was wrong was that the plan, formulated and instigated by agencies of the dominant society, ignored the indigenous meanings and significance of agriculture and sustenance, and failed to recognize that practical techniques are matrixed in their own cultural logic.

The Huichol response and adaptation to INI's program of agricultural change can be summarized and explained by reference to three different but related contortions in their semantic field:

1. Those changes that were most readily accepted, such as the introduction of fruit trees, and the improvement of cattle breeds and other domestic animals, were supplementary to the cultivation of maize. Consequently, they do not receive the same amount of conceptual elaboration in indigenous ideology as surrounds primary activities such as those related to maize activities. Because these secondary activities are recognized as traditional categories, and therefore legitimate, and because of their relative cultural fluidity (in the sense that the practices associated with them are only vaguely determined by local cultural

values), there need not necessarily be any conflict between indigenous conceptualizations and those originating from the model of the developers.

2. It is precisely those categories that are both viewed as legitimate, and most deeply matrixed in a cultural logic, that are the most resistant to external change. As we have seen, the significance of maize is deeply embedded in Huichol culture and is the subject of an elaborate body of myths and rituals that define its relation to the divinities and to human beings and teach the correct manner for its cultivation (for an example, see pp. 191-93 in this volume). The ceremonial practices based on privileged religious knowledge are an integral part of the Huichols' technical manipulation of their environment, on which the growth of the plant depends. The ceremonies and their associated knowledge partly provide the justification for the shaman-priests who officiate over them, and since, traditionally, Huichol society has otherwise been undifferentiated, these help uphold authority based on religious understanding and the prerogative of seniority. Furthermore, it is the performance of the maize ceremonies that tie individual Huichol rancherías to a district organization, centered on the *tuki*, the sacred house or temple of the indigenous religion, that integrates the extended families with their larger comunidad and provides cooperative work forces needed to clear the fields and plant and harvest the crops. Maize is the very foundation of the Huichol social contract, and the ideas that have evolved around it over the centuries are an important part of their ethnic identity.

   The Huichols initially responded to the INI demonstration plots by rejecting any idea that maize could be successfully raised without performing the correct round of ceremonies. Some thought that the plant would become diseased and, if it did survive, would be unfit for human consumption. Its eventual maturation did not challenge their view that proper ritual prescriptions had to be followed for successful cultivation. On the contrary, some shaman-priests claimed that it had been raised by sorcery and would cause illness to those who ate it. Others argued that such a manner of cultivation might be appropriate for Mexican maize, but for the Huichols to respect their obligations to their deities they must continue to perform their traditional ceremonies or risk courting divine retribution. Eventually, however, improved strains of maize allowing two harvests annually were accepted for cultivation on family land holdings.

3. Changes that were unconditionally rejected by the Huichols were often the result of attempts to introduce new categories of produce into the area that were either not recognized in traditional conceptual classifications, or that were valued negatively.

   I do not wish to suggest that traditional conceptual classifications, and the significance that distinct cultural logics apply to their subject, entirely determine what outside changes are acceptable and what are not, but in the case discussed they have clearly limited and constrained the acceptance of new foodstuffs.

Change can also be expected to come about through structural contradictions, such as when a marginalized population accepts certain aspects of change that later necessitate other transformations formerly considered unacceptable. An example of such change might be long-term repercussions of the spread of credit, such as the need to generate a means of repayment. That, in turn, may lead to commercial agriculture, in contradiction to Huichol egalitarian and religious ideals. In fact, up to now much of the new wealth from the sale of crafts and cattle has been used to make interpersonal loans and in elaborating traditional religious ceremonies (Weigand 1981:17). Nevertheless, once these areas become saturated and unable to absorb further surplus, the contradictions between production for an external market and the internal mechanisms for consumption and circulation may cause severe disruptions. Together with the growing necessity of providing an increasing number of overseers for the growing size of cattle herds, which may exaggerate social differentiation, the new prosperity is based on powerful mechanisms that threaten the wholesale transformation of Huichol society and culture and its absorption into the Mexican peasantry.

Despite claims that the Huichols are now able to produce sufficient quantities of maize for their own needs and even on occasion create a surplus for use as cattle fodder, the average yield of maize reported in 1987 of 300–400 kilograms per hectare (Gonzalez 1987:15) is identical to that reported in 1971 in another official publication that judged such an amount to be insufficient for subsistence (SEP–INI 1971:47). The same source also quotes identical average yields of beans over the same sixteen-year period. Statistics such as these are perhaps the best indication of the value and worth of development plans that are instituted in terms of external western perceptions of foreign conditions and social institutions and that pay insufficient attention to indigenous conceptualizations and thought.

Conclusion

I have tried to describe the complex and strong warp and weft of Huichol ideas about maize in order to emphasize the pervasiveness and depth of the indigenous conceptual system that any external development plan must confront. Such systems cannot simply be ignored or belittled as remnants of exotic or "prerational" modes of thinking that will crumble under the power of reasoned demonstration.

When extensive, long-term development projects, such as that described here, are undertaken among peoples with distinct and vigorous cultural identities, change may be more easily stimulated by working within the parameters of the semantic space defined and regulated by indigenous classifications. There is little evidence that development policies formulated and implemented "from above" achieve, from the point of view of the local communities, any more positive than negative results.

NOTES

1. For Huichol, Cora, and Nahua variants of the Maize Maiden myth, see Furst's essay in the *Journal of Latin American Indian Literature*, Vol. 10, No. 2, 1994.(—Eds.)

2. As noted elsewhere, the 1990 national census gives the unexpectedly high number of more than 19,000 speakers of Huichol over the age of five, including those in and around the Huichol territory itself and those who have migrated out.

INTRODUCTION TO CHAPTER 17

In the final chapter, the Mexican social anthropologist Salomón Nahmad Sittón shares thoughts on the impact on the Huichols of the dominant society and their chances for survival as bearers of a long and proud indigenous cultural and religious tradi-

FIGURE 116. Anthropologist Salomón Nahmad, Director of the INI Center for the Cora-Huichol region. Nahmad, *left*, was frequently called to the different sierra communities, to help solve, as on this occasion in San Andrés, perennial problems like food shortages or invasions of Huichol lands by mestizo-owned cattle. (*Photograph by Peter T. Furst, August 1967.*)

FIGURE 117. Twin-Engine Beechcraft Bonanza on the Dirt Strip at San Andrés in the Spring of 1967. Before the recent construction of dirt roads linking sierra communities with each other and the outside world, single-engine Cessnas and the occasional Beechcraft were the only means of transport. In this photograph, INI's Nahmad supervises the unloading of basic foodstuffs for CONASUPO, the government store. (*Photograph by Peter T. Furst.*)

tion. These thoughts are the fruit of more than thirty years of close professional and personal involvement in virtually all aspects of official and unofficial policies and programs directed at Indian peoples that had its start, in the 1960s, among the Huichols themselves (Figures 116, 117). These have ranged from numerous visits to Indian communities for face-to-face meetings with indigenous authorities, to basic education and language instruction, to improvements in the food supply, hygiene, agriculture, cattle raising, health, and technical and economic assistance, to Indian relations with the governmental bureaucracy and complaints against mestizo neighbors greedy for Indian lands, to participant-observation of Indian ceremonial life, including, in the Huichol case, their most sacred ritual, the peyote pilgrimage (Figure 118), and, most recently, to providing the necessary environment and support, including computers, for native intellectuals from different language groups to become their own linguists and ethnographers. Beginning in the 1960s, when, after the obligatory social service with Indians in Veracruz, he was made director of the Cora-Huichol Coordinating Center of the Instituto Nacional Indigenista in Tepic, Nayarit, and continuing over the past several decades, Nahmad has served as director of indigenous education in the federal Secretaría de Educación Pública, as director general of INI, and, after settling in Oaxaca,

FIGURE 118. Salomón Nahmad with Ramón Medin on a Peyote Pilgrimage in Wirikúta, December 1968. Ever the applied anthropologist, Nahmad counted participant observation and recording of Huichol ritual in the face of pressures for change as a prime duty of the regional INI director. (*Photograph by Peter T. Furst.*)

the state with the greatest number of different indigenous language groups, as a senior investigator of CIESAS (Centro de Investigaciones y Estudios Superiores en Antropología Social). As a consultant anthropologist to the giant Aguamilpas Dam in Nayarit, whose construction and operation as a major source of electricity directly and indirectly affects thousands of Huichols, he has come full circle back to his beginnings in applying anthropology not only to assist Indian people in dealing with massive change but, as important, in helping those who bring that change avoid mistakes borne not of ill will but of cultural ignorance.

Peter T. Furst

17 : HUICHOL RELIGION AND THE MEXICAN STATE

Reflections on Ethnocide and Cultural Survival

SALOMÓN NAHMAD SITTÓN

Translated from the Spanish by BONNIE GLASS-COFFIN

I.

From my first contact with the Wixarika (which is what the Huichols call themselves), I was struck by the vast gulf between the image the indigenous people of the Sierra Madre have of the state and the Mexican nation, and that held by the surrounding mestizo or "criollo" population.

This sharp contradiction is immediately apparent in the differing concepts of land and territory, of the natural world in general, and especially of the person, the human being. For the Huichols, the idea of "territory" encompasses not just the communal or ethnic space. Rather, it extends from certain sacred places on the Pacific coast across mountains, lakes, springs, and rivers into the north-central high desert, all the way to the sacred land of the new sun and the divine peyote cactus. On Mexican maps, this ideological oasis in the desert just north and south of the Tropic of Cancer is the old Spanish silver mining district of Real de Catorce, in the state of San Luis Potosí. For the Huichols, it is Wirikúta, or alternatively, Paritsikiye, the place of dawn.

In contrast, so far as the national society is concerned, the Huichol territory is fragmented and divided into different *ejídos*, communally held lands that lie within the jurisdictions of three different states of the Federal Republic of Mexico—Nayarit, Jalisco, and Durango. The ejídos and indigenous communities, in turn, belong administratively to the jurisdictions of various municipalities. This, then, is the political and economic reality: the Indians see themselves as independent, self-governing in their own *comunidades indígenas*, and having full charge of their own lives. In truth, they are both economically and politically under the control of Mexican municipalities, three federal states and, ultimately, the nation.

FIGURE 119. Change in One Direction: the Graduating Sixth Grade Class of 1987, San Andrés Cohamiata. (*Photograph by Stacy B. Schaefer.*)

Then, there is the Catholic church and its far-ranging interests in the affairs of the indigenous peoples of the Sierra. The Franciscan mission in Zapópan, on the outskirts of Guadalajara, has charge of the evangelization of the Huichols and their neighbors and cultural cousins, the Coras, with headquarters in Jesús María, the political and religious center of the Cora people in the municipality of Nayar. Finally, there is a new problem: the increasing activities of fundamentalist evangelical missionaries, who operate among the Huichols, as among other native peoples, with financial support from north of the border, and their converts. In some places, this has been very disruptive, not only at the larger community level but even within families; at the very least, it is responsible for aggravating factionalism.

Given these realities, religious and ideological resistance to acculturation and assimilation, tempered by accommodation, is a prime characteristic of both the Huichols and their Cora neighbors (Figures 119, 120). During the entire colonial period, relationships between Indian and Catholic religion were marked by tension and conflict. It was especially among the Huichols that all efforts at evangelization and the imposition of Christian-Catholic concepts were consistently frustrated by a whole series of conscious and unconscious defense mechanisms. One of the most important of these strategies has been for Huichols to increase their physical distance from the missions by moving their extended family ranchos ever deeper into less accessible regions of the Sierra.

A salient characteristic of traditional Huichol religious ideology is an almost endless multiplicity of male and female deities, many of whom personify natural forces

FIGURE 120. Change in the Other Direction: Sacred Hole with Offerings for the Huichol Gods Dug into the Floor of the Franciscan Church in San Andrés. (*Photograph by Peter T. Furst, Spring 1967.*)

and phenomena. In the centuries of direct and indirect contact following the Spanish invasion, the Huichols, while strenuously holding on to their own gods, adopted some Christian personages and rituals, recasting and reformulating them so as to fit them more easily into their ample native pantheon and ceremonial cycle. They were even perfectly ready to lay claim to being "Christian" or Catholic themselves, even while thoroughly "Huicholizing" the newly introduced gods, saints, rites, and symbols. They might even claim, as many do, that some of these symbols were stolen from them by the "Spaniards," that the Virgin of Guadalupe was a Huichol woman seduced by drunken Spanish soldiers, that the cross was Huichol before it was Christian, and that the foreigners appropriated Tatéi Kukurukú 'Uimári, the dove form of the Mother of Maize, and made her into their Holy Ghost. All this has to do with the profound openness of Huichol ideology, as a social system, to the ways of other peoples, in contrast to the religious ideology of the dominant society, which is rigidly closed to the beliefs and thoughts of the native population.

This dichotomy extends from the religious and ideological realms into the modern political systems and a national economy that is predominantly capitalist. Mestizo peoples—the poor peasant farmers (*campesinos*) and ranchers (*vaqueros charros*)—are conjoined in rural civil societies that became petrified in the colonial era, in a system of production in which the land and the territory are treated as objects of exploitation and despoliation. In this system, the predominant values are those the church and the colonial authorities disseminated among the non-Indian populations of Jalisco, Nayarit, Zacatecas, and Durango.

These conflicts in world view, together with the opposition between the indigenous juridical structure and that of the nation-state and the Catholic church, are what the Huichols must confront each and every day, for both state and church in their own ways deny and interfere with the Huichols' rights to their own ethic and to those religious beliefs and practices by which they define their identity as Wixarika, the true people.

The state, by means of its judicial organs and the organization of the national society, assumes the right to enforce acculturation and assimilation, without granting Indian governmental institutions equal rights. For its part, the church, with some few exceptions on the part of individual priests, considers all Mesoamerican indigenous religions and all surviving native rituals to be "pagan," and hence beyond the pale. This applies above all to the Huichols, as the largest surviving native population in Mexico with its aboriginal religious and ritual system still relatively intact.

In fact, the Huichol population is clearly growing: the latest national census, conducted in 1990, gives the number of Huichols over the age of five as 19,363, of whom 9,753 are female and an almost equal number, 9,610, male. With an estimated 4,000 children aged one through four, that makes for a total of nearly 24,000, compared with the most common estimates of ca. 12,000 in the late 1960s. Of the total, the 1990 census gives the number of bilinguals, that is, Huichols able to converse in Spanish as well as their own language, as 15,247, and only 3,250 as monolinguals, the majority of them women, with a smaller number, under 1,000, of indeterminate language status. I should note that the same census gives a substantially lower Cora population—11,923 above the age of five. There is some reason for questioning the accuracy of these population figures, but these are the latest official counts. The least that can be said is that the Huichols have substantially increased their numbers since my own everyday association with them in the 1960s.

What we have, then, is a very traditional indigenous people that, largely due to improved medical care, is increasing in numbers at a much faster rate than is sustainable with the agricultural potential of their homeland, and, at the same time, a movement of more or less coercive acculturation that is directed, in informal alliance with the state, toward dismantling and demolishing the ideological and juridical structure and the cultural ethos of the Huichol people, or that, at the very least, has these effects.

It is for these reasons that some of us, as Mexican anthropologists concerned with the preservation of native cultures, see relations between indigenous religion and indigenous government on the one side, and the Catholic church and the Mexican government on the other, as totally asymmetrical and unequal, to the point where they give the appearance of internal colonialism within Mexican society.

In contrast, relations and attitudes among the indigenous peoples of the Sierra Madre, the Huichols, Coras, and Tepehuanos, are ideologically symmetrical; indeed, because of similarities in religion, ritual, and oral literature they consider themselves related. On the other hand, all three see themselves as distanced from, and alien to, the mestizo population and the national society. I have the feeling that this kind of symmetrical and egalitarian relationship between diverse ethnic populations in Meso-america goes back a long way, to pre-Hispanic times, when different variants based on common ancestral forms arose in different regions in response to different social and natural environments.

In other words, there was a natural evolution here, favoring cultural adaptation to external influences and an open religious ideology. One people did not impose its religion on another by force; rather, there was borrowing and interchange as gods and rituals became "naturalized" in the course of time. What a contrast to what happened after the Spanish conquest of the Sierra Madre, when the religion of the invaders and colonizers was proclaimed to be the only valid ethic, one to be imposed by force and persuasion on the newly subjugated populations!

II.

As noted, the indigenous peoples of the Sierra Madre Occidental, and especially the Huichols, have in the course of time generated numerous subtle strategies and techniques to resist evangelization and integration into the dominant Mexican society. Such resistance, conscious and unconscious, was necessitated by what happened not only during the period of the Spanish colony but after independence from Spain in the first quarter of the nineteenth century.

Ideally, the newly established Mexican nation-state should have been one whose structure and laws reflected its ethnic diversity, the existence of numerous distinct native peoples and languages, each with its own cultural traditions. Unfortunately, the early period of independence actually aggravated the tensions of the colonial period, with the new state persisting in the program of westernizing and Christianizing the indigenous peoples of the Sierra Madre Occidental. Colonization was promoted and stimulated as mestizo settlers were given political, military, judicial, economic, and religious power to expand the boundaries of the state ever deeper into what had traditionally been indigenous territories.

Toward the middle of the last century, the law that released the lands of the indigenous populations from inalienable ownership, or mortmain, severely impacted the region, sparking armed resistance throughout the mountains of the territory of Nayarit. At the end of the nineteenth century, the region of Nayar was separated from the state of Jalisco and converted into a federal territory, the purpose being to maintain central control and military and legal authority over the Indian inhabitants.

The Coras managed to limit the national program to disrupt the unity of the villages. But with a reorganization of municipalities in northern Jalisco during the reign of Porfirio Díaz, the indigenous communities here found themselves fragmented. The Huichol comunidades of San Andrés Cohamiata, Guadalupe Ocotán, and Santa Catarína were folded into the municipality of Mezquitic, while the municipality of Bolaños was created out of the comunidades of San Sebastián Teponahuaxtlán and Tuxpan de Bolaños. Subsequently, with the creation of the state of Nayarit in 1917, the boundary between it and Jalisco was arbitrarily drawn through Huichol country, and various villages and hamlets became assigned to the municipality of La Yesca. But they never received their grants, nor were they enabled to maintain their own geopolitical unity.

Thus, both the era of the colony and of the newly created republic during the nineteenth century were a time of open or covert war against indigenous social units that had maintained their own lifestyles. State and church in unison were determined to "civilize" and "de-paganize" native peoples viewed essentially as savages and primitives. National and state legislation tried to break up and dissolve the Huichols' social and political norms, while the church focused on liquidating the traditions and rituals of Huichol religion.

Beginning with the Mexican Revolution, the region was also drawn into agrarian struggles and conflicts within a divided mestizo population that participated either with or against the revolutionary leadership. These internecine struggles set the region on fire, involving the Huichols themselves in the war of the Cristeros, who hid out in Huichol communities that now, in turn, received the brunt of the Catholic fanaticism that predominated in the *Altos*, the highlands, of Jalisco. Once again the Huichols resisted, gradually expelling the invaders and driving them into the periphery of the native territory. But in the process whole regions, especially in San Sebastián, were depopulated of Indians, to be replaced, in part, by mestizo settlers.

III.

From the last decade of the nineteenth century on, the Huichols, as a major indigenous group in the region that preserved very old traditions of religion, cultural norms and social organization with singular purity, have been the object of special attention from ethnographers, who, beginning with Lumholtz, could not help but note their profound pride in their own culture, their deep spirituality, and their determination to repel attempts, from whatever source, to meddle in and damage their traditional way of life.

For Mexicans in general, and especially for city dwellers living in the area around the territory of the Huichols, these Indians have long posed a great many questions. How do they live? Why do they dress differently? Why do they insist on speaking a different language? Why do they prefer to keep themselves apart? Why do they take peyote? And who are they, anyway?

Beneath the distinctive Huichol dress, the ceremonial costumes of both men and women dazzling with brilliant embroideries, is the beat of a culture that represents, in a very real sense, the historic past, perhaps the deepest core, of our multicultural nation. And yet, for lack of objective information, the nations's growing mestizo population, which shares so many common problems, all too often holds, and acts on, negative attitudes and prejudices—sometimes to the point of absurdity—against the very people in whose continued existence, in the face of all adversity, it should take pride.

I well remember one such absurdity from my own experience as director, from 1967 to 1969, of the Cora–Huichol Coordinating Center of the Instituto Nacional Indigenista in Tepic, Nayarit, a time during which I shared, on a daily basis, the problems of Huichol men, women, and children and, indeed, entire communities. In December 1968, during a peyote pilgrimage in which our INI Center's medical officer, Dr. Enrique Campos, and I had been invited to participate, we stopped at a small rural *tienda* in the Zacatecas countryside to purchase some bread, cheese, and oranges for ourselves (our Huichol companions were ritually enjoined from eating anything but dry tortillas for the duration of the pilgrimage). Seeing one of the Indians and recognizing him as a Huichol, the mestizo woman who owned the little store inquired, *sotto voce*, whether "those Indians" were with us. Told that it was really the other way around, that we were their companions, not they ours, she whispered urgently to take much care, because it was well known that they were "cannibals." Our Huichol friends, cannibals! That is precisely how sixteenth-century Spanish colonial maps of western Mexico defined parts of the then still unconquered Sierra Madre: *terra incognita* inhabited by "*antropófagos*," eaters of men. Thus endure the calumnies of the conquerors into the last part of the twentieth century.

IV.

For a long time—in fact, until very recently—the rugged topography of the Sierra ruled out the construction and year-round maintenance of all-weather roads to and from any of the major Huichol ceremonial centers. For that reason, the Huichol region to this day remains one of the most isolated of Mexico: in the 1960s and '70s, unless one wanted to go on foot or muleback, as Lumholtz and Preuss did in the last decade of the nineteenth and first decade of the twentieth century, respectively, and as Zingg was still forced to do in the 1930s, the only way to get in and out was by small plane.

The Huichol region corresponds, as already noted, to four states: Jalisco, Nayarit, Zacatecas, and Durango. The indigenous communities maintain ceremonial centers in close to ten municipalities. In other words, the Huichols are separated into distinct entities, a situation exacerbated by the traditional pattern of widely dispersed settlements.

The mountainous region inhabited by Huichols covers close to 10,000 square kilometers, although there are also numerous Huichol speakers who live outside the Sierra Huichol proper. The country is traversed by several major rivers that cut through deep gorges, forming small islands of one or more related extended families enclosed, and separated from their nearest neighbors, by steep mountains and rapidly flowing waters that become especially dangerous, if not impossible, to cross during the rainy season. Only for the most important ceremonies, especially those of Christian origin introduced during the colonial period, but radically reformulated by the Huichols, do they come together with other residents of the comunidad.

Because of the above-mentioned characteristics of the Huichol homeland, time in the mountains seems almost at a standstill: except for the transistor radio, many people still live out their lives in virtual isolation from the outside world, their days occupied in agricultural and herding activities but, above all, in a plethora of ritual and ceremony—the peyote pilgrimage and its attendant rituals; the festival of the toasting of the maize; Holy Week; pilgrimages to San Blas to visit Tatéi Haramára, the Pacific Ocean personified as a water goddess, or south to Lake Chapala, or to the numerous landmarks sanctified by the ancestors. In other words, cultural patterns and tradition complement the geographical framework.

In my time with them as an INI administrator, among the 10,000–15,000 Huichol-speakers who then inhabited this extensive physical and mental territory and its environs, continued monolingualism, especially among the women, was one of the indicators that social and cultural change remained limited. As a rule, it was then mostly the men, many of whom traveled each year to labor in the tobacco plantations and maize fields on the coast, who spoke a limited "ranchero Spanish," enough, at any rate, to make themselves understood. The organizers and leaders of these migrations generally had a better command of the language of the dominant society, although they, too, could, and still can, neither read nor write. Even today, of course, when the majority of men and women have become bilingual, their Spanish is hardly that of the educated city dweller but remains a form of "ranchero Spanish" without much regard for the finer points of grammar and syntax.

It is only when they speak the language of the dominant society that they refer to themselves as "Huicholes"; within their own culture, they continue to speak of themselves as Wixarika, and to identify those who do not belong to their ethnic group as *téiwari* in Huichol and *vecíno* in Spanish. Literally, these terms translate as the neutral "neighbor," but the Huichols are often anything but neutral when they use it. Depending on context, it can even be an insult, one way of countering the humiliating way in which mestizos often address them by the familiar "*tú*" rather than the more distant and respectful "*ustéd*," or refer to them condescendingly as "Huicholitos," our little Huichols. It is from this kind of thing, no less than more determined assaults on their culture, that Huichols, including many of those who have physically moved into mestizo surroundings, seek refuge in their mythic world, in their legends and the traditional rituals.

V.

On the surface, the Huichols are resistant to change and reject it. But one should see them climb, with complete ease, into a plane, clutching a transistor radio under one arm, or see them opening and downing cans of beer by the score on feast days! That is to say, those things of foreign origin that interest them and they can use they adopt and quickly integrate into their lives. But change in their traditional systems, such as agricultural technology, or ways of managing their livestock, they are much slower to accept. That applies even more to their world view, their way of conceiving the universe and themselves within it, their religious schema, their whole interpretation of life. For here attempts to get them to accept alien ideas run up against a brick wall. Just as an example, to change one's mode of dressing signifies for a Huichol the abandonment of the symbols—the embroidered scorpions or deer or birds and plants, especially the sacred peyote cactus—that protect his or her body.

Similarly, although there are exceptions, to marry a *téiwari*, a white person or a mestizo, means to lose one's group identity; half-Huichols tend not to be accepted precisely because they represent a threat to the unity and cohesion of the group. This aversion to miscenegation also governs Huichol ideas of what happens when a man or woman who has had sexual relations with a non-Huichol dies and his or her soul is on its way to meet the ancestors. The soul of such a one, I was told by one Huichol shaman, has to pass through a corral full of mules that stomp on it until it is in pieces. Only after this painful ordeal is it permitted to put itself back together again and continue on its way to the home of the ancestors.

I recall a case of the representative of the communal lands from Guadalupe Ocotán, who felt himself closer to his mestizo father, a rancher who had moved into the comunidad from Zacatecas, than to his Huichol mother. Because of this, he was able to persuade only a few of the residents to follow him, being scorned by the rest, no less than for having turned Guadalupe Ocotán lands over to Huajimic than for his mixed parentage.

Even those Huichol families who long ago settled on the banks of the Río Lerma de Santiago and who, to the uninformed outsider, might seem to be more acculturated for having, during the last forty or so years, abandoned their remote ranchos in the Sierra to live closer to their seasonal sources of modest cash income on the coast, have not accepted, and do not now tolerate, basic changes in their ethnic norms and cultural patterns. This can be seen in what happened when, during my tenure as INI director in Tepic, a member of the Río Lerma community returned from the coast with a mestizo wife. She, the daughter of a coastal *campesino*, no doubt saw no problems living with a Huichol husband in a Huichol community—in fact, I have heard rural women on the Huichol periphery express a preference for Huichol husbands over mestizo ones, because the former have a reputation of treating their wives, with some exceptions, with greater respect. But his indigenous neighbors in the Lerma settlement would have none of her: rejected and shunned by all but her husband, and excluded from any participation in group social and religious life, she despaired and finally abandoned her Huichol mate and the community to return to her old life on the coast.

VI.

The programs of economic and social development which the Mexican government and its organs have enacted at various times in the Huichol region were all founded on theories of assimilation and national integration, always with the intention of modifying the traditional lifeways and creating new ones that would make "real Mexicans" out of the Indian people. Here one remembers the old slogan from the time of Beníto Juárez: "*No hay Indios en México, somos todos Mexicanos:* ("There are no Indians in Mexico, we are all Mexicans"). And yet Juárez himself was a full-blooded Zapotec.

Recently, the indigenist theories and practices formulated by social science specialists, particularly by anthropologists, have become the subject of constant, and sometimes very spirited, debate, both within academic circles and within the indigenous movement. Here it is important to point out that criticism of the Mexican Revolution, considered static by some and "ex-revolution" by others, has also been renewed. There is no doubt that the often very nasty criticism leveled at applied anthropology, at *indigenísmo*, and at the revolutionary movement of 1910, is closely linked to the rise of Mexican indigenísmo, which reached its greatest heights between 1935 and 1955. It was this period that saw the crystallization of the idea that, with effective action programs and a revolutionary spirit, the indigenous communities and even the most isolated regions of the country could be, indeed would be, transformed and integrated.

This attitude changed radically in the decade of the 1980s, for during that time the most conservative forces in the country were able to assail ethnic groups with impunity, formulating programs to free hitherto protected communal lands from inalienable indigenous ownership—putting these lands up for individual sale, or putting the Indians into a new and supposedly fruitful association with private capital. The indigenous peoples, their natural resources, and their labor would supposedly thus be placed in a "just" association that would be of real benefit to the individual landowners!

Indigenist theory was originally formulated and developed for two basic reasons:

1. The felt need of political leaders to identify the means and methods for the application of programs that would serve to integrate and shape our multiethnic country into a real nation.

2. The need to improve the unsatisfactory economic and social conditions of life endured by millions of native people living in precarious economies and subject to colonial-type exploitation, particularly so in such cultural refuge areas as the Sierra Madre Occidental. This was becoming all the more urgent as exploitation became refined with modern capitalist development and new means were found to maintain the indigenous population in conditions of subordination.

The indigenist ideals that appeared, in the first instance, following the ideas of the anthropologist Manuel Gamio, and in the second, implementing the vigorous reformist impulse of President Lazaro Cárdenas, represented an advance in the development of the Revolution. That is to say, it was hoped that within this framework of development the contradictions between indigenous groups, on the one hand, and a growing industrial and urban society stratified into social classes with antagonistic interests, on the other, would be quickly resolved.

So here, now, were ethnic groups like the Huichols, persisting within their own traditional territory, yet marginalized from national life in terms of their cultural values, languages, traditions, dress, etc. But now they were facing a new and unfamiliar phenomenon in their very midst: new forces that sought to capitalize in new ways on human and natural resources, not for the good of the native peoples, however, but for the benefit of a small non-Indian minority that had managed to come to terms with the revolutionary structure, using it as a means of extending their involvement into the remote regions where most of these ethnic groups lived.

It is, in fact, not unusual to find, tied into Huichol community life, prosperous urban businessmen, politicians, and even some priests intent on drawing the "Coritas" (the diminutive of Cora, a term which mestizos employ for the native peoples of the Sierra, regardless of whether they are Cora, Huichol, or Tepehuan), out of the Sierra for the bean or maize harvest or for threading tobacco leaves on the rich coast of Nayarit. Conversely, there are the invasions of the Sierra by those intent on placing their cattle on native pastures, leaving the Huichols to watch over, fatten, and otherwise stimulate the growth of herds that belong not to themselves but to the wealthy members of the Regional Livestock Union. Then, also, there is the flourishing itinerant trade in radios, firearms, and alcoholic beverages in and out of the Huichol country. Its practitioners, merchants residing in Mezquitic, Bolaños, Acaponeta, Ruíz, or Tepic, entrepreneurs with the right political connections, call this to "huicholear." In my experience, to "huicholear" almost always ends up to the detriment of their Indians customers in the Sierra.

As I mentioned earlier, in the past it was mostly Huichol men who went down to the coast to work in the harvest. But more and more now it is whole families, hundreds of them, that are forced by economic conditions in the Sierra to descend from their beloved mountains and mesas to travel to the coast for the maize, bean, and tobacco harvest. The conditions under which they have to sell their labor are generally terrible.

Without protection they do the spraying with poisonous chemicals, without protection they handle tobacco leaves that have been soaked with pesticides and insecticides, they sleep under trees or the stars or in shelters they construct of these self-same leaves, sanitation is virtually nonexistent and promiscuity rampant, they get sick with malaria and tuberculosis and chemical poisoning with God knows what future consequences. And they have no security of employment. So they make a few pesos with which to buy a few kilograms of maize and pay their passage back to their isolated ranchos on planes they share with livestock owned by mestizos.

VII.

I ponder what has happened that is good for the Huichols—or, conversely, bad—sixty years after the beginning of Mexico's indigenist policy. What are the levels of acculturation and what are the social changes that have resulted from the political development of the states of Jalisco and Nayarit during this period? What are the changes brought about by more than twenty years of the new Christian evangelization, and by more than ten years of the anthropological program of the Instituto Nacional Indigenista? What are the directions and the expectations of the Huichols themselves?

There can be no doubt that the Mexican Revolution achieved fundamental changes in many parts of the country. But in the case of the Huichols, even if their ancient problems were not aggravated by the Revolution, many of them persist and have become more complicated with time. Take, for example, the situation of the communal lands. The fact is that communal land holdings are protected far more in theory than in practice. Mestizos constantly jail and even assassinate native people in order to force them off their land. Bribery is commonly used to corrupt native leaders and get them to collude in the alienation of land. The Cora community of Jesús María saw most of its land holdings evaporate; 30,000 hectares were taken from the indigenous community of San Andrés Cohamiata, allegedly to form a new indigenous community, Santa Rosa. In fact, the new community was formed by a mestizo, who during the years he served as secretary to the Huichol governor of San Andrés amassed a personal herd of more than 2,000 cattle. And again and again one hears of valiant leaders of the Huichols thrown into jail on trumped-up charges for fighting against these injustices. One example that I have never been able to get out my head was the rape of the eleven-year-old niece of an INI worker, a Huichol, by a mestizo cattleman who with his friends had occupied some lands belonging to San Andrés. The crime had nothing to do with sex: the mestizos wanted the Indians out and the rape was done solely as a show of power and intimidation. When the Huichol police arrived to arrest the culprits, they were disarmed by a unit of the state police, whose chief, it turned out, was the rapist's brother.

I should add, however, that the man who is governor of the state of Nayarit as this is being written has shown himself to be a friend to the Huichols. But what happens after the next election? And the next?[1]

VIII.

Every society has its system to regulate and control the conduct of its members. Culture, history, environment, contact with other groups, all these play their part in determining what a society regards as antisocial behavior and how it is to be dealt with. In the Huichol case, the individuals socially recognized as having the authority and the obligation to apprehend the accused are those who hold the top cargos in a rotating system of local government that was introduced by the Spaniards when they took control of the Sierra in the eighteenth century. It is they—the governor, the judge, or the captain—who send the *tupiles*, the police, to bring the wrongdoer in, peaceably or, if the crime is serious enough or he resists, tied up.

Let's see just what kinds of offenses are considered serious and how the indigenous authorities of one comunidad, Tuxpan de Bolaños, deals with them.

1. *Homicide*. The authorities, acting together with the Council of Elders, place the delinquent in a room with a *cepo*, a kind of pillory, consisting of a horizontal beam with holes in it that was introduced by the colonial power. Depending on the seriousness of the crime, the defendant may have both feet placed in the stocks, or only one. After twenty-four hours, the maximum time allowed for *cepo* punishment, the accused is taken out and hung up by his wrists outside, the idea being to bring his crime to public knowledge. Once he has thus been punished within the indigenous system, he is turned over to the authorities of the state.

2. *Flagrant adultery*. Here the authorities decree that the accused be brought in tied up and naked, the objective being public shame and a vow that he not repeat the same offense again.

3. *Cattle rustling*. One so accused is detained for investigation to determine whether he is actually guilty as charged. If found guilty, he is obliged to pay the owner of the stolen cattle double the value of what he took.

4. *Witchcraft*. A person who feels him- or herself to have been bewitched can seek redress from the Council of Elders and civil authorities, who have the power to compel the accused sorcerer to cure the victim. Refusal justifies severe punishment. The victim can, of course, also engage the services of a shaman to return the witchcraft to its source and visit an injury or illness on the perpetrator from afar with a magical "arrow of sickness."

Other kinds of minor offenses include drunkenness, public scandal, doing injury to another, and so forth. In such cases the governor and the tupiles are empowered to detain the offender in the pillory for a day, or even two, depending on the seriousness of the crime, without food.

In the formal system of justice, in contrast, a Huichol accused of a crime is judged in Spanish, by rules which he did not make and which he does not understand. That is to say, the indigenous community is not aware of the contents of governmental decrees such as the penal code. Thus, what for us might be a crime, is probably not one for them. For example, it is a serious crime against the national drug laws for members of the dominant society to consume hallucinogenic mushrooms or peyote. Under current laws, such a person would be arrested and tried for taking dangerous drugs. But for indigenous peoples, mushrooms, peyote and other plant hallucinogens are taken in a sacred context that has nothing whatever to do with drug use in the western sense. Indeed, the plants themselves are sacred and thus not even thought of as "drugs," in our terminology. In the United States, years of constitutional argument and education by anthropologists, lawyers, and indigenous people have brought about the legalization, however limited, of peyote use within the Native American Church. In Mexican law as it has functioned up to the present, on the other hand, a Mazatec or Mixe taking sacred mushrooms in religious and divinatory ritual, or a Huichol using the divine cactus *hikuri* (peyote) that for him is equivalent to the sacred deer, is committing a criminal act, even though there is not a shred of scientific evidence to support the state's argument that these are "dangerous drugs" from which people need to be protected "for their own good." It would seem obvious that to subject a native person to a law over which he has had no say, and in whose framing, passage, and application no one sought his or her opinion, and to thereby restrict his or her religious freedom, is obviously to commit a gross injustice, an act that violates cultural traditions built many centuries ago. So there is obviously a conflict between the customary rights of the indigenous inhabitants and the legal rights assumed by the Mexican state.

The problems are exacerbated by the political division of the Huichol country between three federal states, inasmuch as one community is located in Durango, four in Jalisco, and two, plus a number of Huichol ejídos, in Nayarit. Huichol participation in municipal policy is very limited, the lives of the Indians, their very existence, even, being given virtually no consideration when decisions are made that affect the entire territory. Generally speaking, the native peoples see themselves as completely apart from, and hence indifferent to, political positions of a statewide or national character. Without understanding how all these economic and political forces work, they know only that they are always supposed to acquiesce to the decisions and actions of the téiwari, for it is they who have the law and power on their side.

Typically (there are, of course, some exceptions), relationships between mestizos— the téiwari—and the Indians are reduced to minimal economic transactions, and even in these the native people have a deep fear when it comes to demanding their rights. Of course, there have been confrontations, through the law or by violence, but never without tremendous anxiety for having finally to face down people whose customary behavior toward them has been scorn, aggression, or theft. To the Huichols, the norms and the values of the téiwaris are strange and incomprehensible. But they respect their own authorities and their decisions to the point of reverence, preferring the governor's justice to resolve their problems to anything they might get from the state, whether in questions of inheritance or any other civil matter, and, of course, they prefer their own traditional forms of marriage to those the state or church devoutly wish them to follow.

For more than forty years, there have been attempts at formal education. Nationally trained teachers have tried as hard as they could to impart to their Huichol pupils not only the elementary skills of reading and writing, but also a rudimentary knowledge of Mexico as a nation and an accompanying national ideology. It hasn't worked, or it has worked only to a minimal degree.

IX.

THE NEW EVANGELIZATION

The year 1953 saw the renewal of evangelizing efforts that had been abandoned with the 1767 expulsion of the Jesuits, whose order established the first missions in the Sierra. With church support, and a firm resolve to finally achieve goals that had not been attained in so many centuries, the Franciscans took charge of the Christianization of the Huichols, Coras, and Tepehuanes.

Evangelistic action has embraced every means to get the Indians to accept Christianity and abandon their own beliefs and rites, ranging from apparently purely pre-Hispanic rituals to those that might be termed crudely syncretistic and therefore essentially "pagan." That these efforts have largely failed, that the Huichols, especially, continue to reject the missionaries, as individuals and as a group, reflects the fact that as in the past they see no need to transform their rituals and their own forms of religious life. Put simply, they are just not interested.

That is not to say that evangelization has not resulted in some serious disruptions on the local level, or exacerbated the factionalism and frictions that plague most native societies.

After establishing themselves in the community of Guadalupe Ocotán, for example, missionaries succeeded in attracting the community leader, who, assisted by a small group of followers, burned down the *tuki*, or, to use the Nahuatl term for the native temples introduced in the eighteenth century, the *calihuey*. For the next ten years the traditional Huichols, under constant threat from that particular official and his relatives, were forced back onto their ranchos for the rituals of the annual ceremonial round.

Not only was the Huichol temple destroyed, but the Catholic priests also took action to do away with the long-accustomed Huichol use of their own votive objects and sacrificial animal blood in the veneration of the Virgen de Guadalupe in the local church.

During Holy Week and other Catholic observances that the Spaniards had introduced into the Sierra communities in the early eighteenth century, the Huichols customarily offered *muviéris* (sacred arrows), *tsikúris* (thread crosses), decorated votive *jícaras* (Huichol: *xukúri*), and above all the blood of a deer or bull, which was sprinkled on the altar before the statue of the Virgin. To put a stop to these "pagan" practices the priests removed the old statue, carved of wood and dating at least to the early nineteenth century, if not before, and replaced it with a brand new one, at the same time forbidding the Indians to place any offerings before it, much less sacrifice animals in the Virgin's honor. Also prohibited within the church was the customary lighting of a fire representing Tatewarí, the old fire god and patron god of the shamans.

It is not surprising that the "theft" of a sacred statue that the Huichols considered their very own stirred up a great deal of anger. In fact, there were so many rumors of an impending uprising that the priests grew fearful that the Indians would try to burn down the mission. That, in fact, had happened once before—in San Andrés Cohamiata. Instead of turning to violence, however, the Indians petitioned the Mexican authorities to intervene and compel the priests to return the "stolen" image to the community. The substitute had no power, they complained, and would answer no petitions. Only their own Virgin was the real one, only she could be venerated. And, they said, if the priests did not want the true Huichol image in their church, they were prepared to construct a small chapel for her where she could be placed and properly honored.

Tensions built up to the point where it required the intervention of the bishop, who calmed the Huichols down by promising to return their old image to them. So the priests had no choice but to give it back, to be venerated as the Huichols pleased. The substitute remained in the church, however, so that from then on two different "Guadalupanas," with differential powers, were venerated in Guadalupe Ocotán.

The foregoing gives some inkling of Huichol reaction to attempts to intervene or transform their customs. For their part, the Huichols of Tuxpan de Bolaños, San Sebastián, and Santa Catarína have steadfastly opposed mission activity within their communities.[2] The Coras, though on the surface far more acculturated to the ways of the dominant society and the Catholic church, are not all that different either. In Jesús María, for example, even during the Holy Week observances, neither the bishop nor the priests are allowed to participate in the ceremonies. Religion, in the view of the Indians, is solely in the hands of their own indigenous specialists in the sacred, and Christian ceremonies have nothing to do with their own traditional customs. The missionaries, needless to say, look upon the native ritual system as little more than paganism thinly disguised.

X

PROTESTANT EVANGELISM

A new phenomenon is Protestant evangelism, and it has exploded with a vengeance. Twenty-five years ago, when I was INI director in Tepic, we had one or two Protestant linguist-missionaries from the Summer Institute of Linguistics in the Sierra. The best-known and best-informed was Dr. Joseph E. Grimes, who with his wife Barbara studied the Huichol language in Guadalupe Ocotán for, as I remember, a dozen years. His plan was to translate the New Testament into Huichol. He had his regular informants, people he worked with closely year after year on the difficult native language. He also had great respect for the Huichol way, and I do not recall him ever saying that he had converted anybody to his own religion.

It is very different now. Starting about ten years ago, Protestant *evangelistas*, Americans from California, have had some success both in the Sierra and in the Huichol colony on the Lower Santiago in Nayarit. In the capital, Tepic, there are also quite a number of Protestant converts among the Huichols. These new Protestant missionaries have a great deal of money, at least in terms of the Huichol subsistence economy, and they come with gifts of food, cash, clothing, and tools. They have 24-hour radio programs, too, broadcasting their message day and night. Despite a certain amount of accommodation and assimilation, most Huichols living in Playa de la Golondrina and Colorado de la Mora, two of the larger Huichol communities in this colony, remain traditionalists. Yet, of the three-hundred people living in Colorado de la Mora, some 25 percent have become "*aleluyas.*" About the same percentage has converted in Golondrina. You find a similar division between a majority of traditionalists and a minority of aleluyas in Tepic, and also in the smaller Huichol settlements on the Lower Santiago. At La Mera Cortina, you had seven Huichol families, of which four are staunch followers of the old Huichol religion and three have converted to Protestantism. Eventually, the converts left and settled in a mestizo village by the side of the road to Tepic.

Inevitably, there is a certain tension, although most people seem to be tolerant and continue to go their own way. At Colorado de la Mora, when the Protestants built themselves a church, the traditionalists countered by building a tuki. The problem is that the evangelists won't stand for the traditional fiestas, or at least most of those that, like the fiesta of the peyote, are really crucial, and they will not allow their converts to have a *xiriki*, the small rancho temples for the ancestor deities that are, on the level of the extended family, the center of the traditional religion. All the traditionalist extended families have their xirikis, which here are often round, like the tukis in the Sierra. In the traditional ranchos, here as in the Sierra, the nuclear family houses are grouped around the xiriki. Not so where the missionaries have control, for here the emphasis is on isolation, each family to itself.

Sometimes the religious split between traditionalists and converts occurs within the same family. There was one Huichol, himself a mara'akáme, who also left the Lerma colony and settled in a sizable mestizo pueblo lining the Tepic road. But while his daughter did the unusual thing of marrying a mestizo, the father not only remained traditional but built himself a xiriki, an ancestor house, and practices his vocation of shaman right there in the midst of his mestizo neighbors!

Much as one might deplore the factionalism and tensions and breakdown in the old ways that have occurred, or been exacerbated, by the activities of the Protestants, there is another side to it. The big problem among the Huichols is alcohol, as it is in the indigenous villages all over the country. The Protestants bring down the rate of alcoholism, which is why they are more accepted by the women—understandably so, because it is women who always suffer the greatest consequences, physically and economically, of addiction to alcohol among their men.

XI.

THE HUICHOLS AND THE AGUAMILPAS HYDROELECTRIC DAM

As I write down these observations, the Huichols and the Coras are suddenly faced with an entirely new situation: the near-completion of the huge new hydroelectric dam in the basins of the Huaynamota and Santiago Rivers in central Nayarit. The billion-dollar dam and the waters rising behind it directly affect Huichol communities and, less directly, the entire Cora–Huichol territory and conceivably even other regions of the state of Nayarit.

The Huichols most immediately affected are those that moved out of the Sierra proper two or so generations ago to form these new communities on the lower Río Lerma de Santiago. Actually, twenty-eight inhabited places will feel, or have already felt, the effect of the hydroelectric project. Of these, six are Huichol: El Embarcadero, Las Cuevas, Playa de las Golondrinas, Paso de los Reyes, Colorado de la Mora, and El Carrizal. As I write this (in 1991), their inhabitants have already been relocated.

Actually, although about a thousand Huichols are directly affected, only a few hundred have had their lands flooded and have been moved to higher ground. INI has been overseeing this, with a group of anthropologists in Tepic who are looking out for the interests of the Indians. This dam project is truly gigantic: at La Cortina alone there are now some 5,000 workers. And before the monstrous size of the hydroelectric dam and all the problems entailed in its construction, the question of Indians is minuscule. They are building a proverbial mountain here, a real monster of a dam. So who cares about a handful of Indians? Well, the Indians do, and the anthropologists, and that is why we are there as outside advisors.

It is not that the engineers or the agronomists and all the other university-educated professionals working for the Comisión Federal de la Electricidad have bad intentions in their dealings with the Indians. It is that they know nothing of the culture. And so, mistakes are made, with the anthropologists left to pick up the pieces. That is what happened when the engineers laid out wonderful plans for a new village with brand-new houses for the Huichols from Colorado de la Mora who were scheduled to move to higher ground. The plan was all drawn up—a rectangular village with one-family houses and nice streets between them. No Huichol had ever been consulted, and neither had the anthropologists. What the planners failed to take into consideration was anything of the traditional culture, the Huichols' own ideas of how they wanted to live. We, the anthropological advisors, and the Huichols themselves, took one look at this marvelous plan and unanimously declared it null and void. The Huichols said the way the engineers had laid it out was exactly the way the missionaries wanted them to live—in isolation, each family by itself, and with the church as the focal point. The Huichols told the engineers that what they wanted instead was terraces along the new lake—three, four, five or more terraces, one for each extended family, with nuclear family houses grouped around the xiriki.

The situation at Playa de las Golondrinas was exactly the same. The original plan was scrapped and a new one drawn up under the supervision of the Huichol elders and the anthropologists. Now, the new houses follow the traditional plan, and so do the xirikis. The architecture is strictly traditional, the only difference being that the Indians were given adobe bricks and decent roofing, building materials far superior to the poles and thatch they were used to. Of course, both at Colorado de la Mora and at Playa de las Golondrina, as at the other resettlements, not only the houses of the Huichols were affected, but also their lands. For the latter they were paid—two to three million dollars in all, at the current exchange rate—and, except for sums spent to buy some trucks and motor launches to take produce and cattle to market, it is invested and is drawing interest for these communities.

One other thing occurs to me in connection with the Aguamilpas project. In advance of the construction of the dam and the attendant relocation of Huichols living in the area scheduled for flooding, Mexican archaeologists carried out an extensive survey of the entire region on both sides of the Río Lerma, or Santiago Bajo. They located several old shrines that, on the basis of the offerings, could be securely identified as of Huichol origin. On the other hand, no evidence was found to indicate that this region was ever settled by people of greater socioeconomic complexity than that typical of hunter-gatherers and incipient agriculturalists.

XII.

Curiously, there is little published information about the total ethnic population living in the four municipalities that make up the region of the Aguamilpa project, and little is known also about the origins of the Huichol colony. There is a tremendous amount of misinformation and misinterpretation of the actual situation. Some foreign anthropologists who have never visited the area simply assumed that it was heavily acculturated and hence not worth their time. In fact, as Fernando Benítez was able to affirm during his visit there in 1967, many people were as traditionalist as their relatives in the Sierra. They remain so now, and have also not lost contact with the Sierra.

So, apart from the interesting phenomenon of religious continuity, there are numerous historical as well as practical socioeconomic questions: When were these communities and ranchos actually established? What were the reasons why they were founded outside the area that Macías (1988) has defined as the "Huichol territory" proper? How did they manage to establish themselves so formally in the Aguamilpa zone? How did they achieve access to and control of arable land? Why are there two types of land tenure here, ejído and communal, the latter an extension of the characteristic Huichol pattern in the Sierra?

References to Colorado de la Mora are found in my own writings (e.g., Nahmad 1972) and in Karen Reed's study of the relationship between the Huichols and the Instituto Nacional Indigenista (Reed 1972). And it is this colony on which I will concentrate in these paragraphs.

There have long been two hypotheses to account for indigenous migration out of the Huichol territory into the central area of Nayarit. One is the need to take advantage of the job market for unskilled agricultural jobs, meaning the coastal region of the state that annually absorbs a great amount of labor in commercial agriculture, notably in tobacco, sugar, coffee, and maize. The second suggested reason is the scarcity of arable land in the traditional territory for people with an intense attachment to the soil, thus forcing them out to find land elsewhere on which to grow their sacred, and economically absolutely essential, crops. There is a third reason: the disruptions and bloodshed in the aftermath of the Mexican Revolution and the Cristero Revolt that followed it, and the concurrent takeover by mestizos of indigenous ranchos and lands whose proper owners had fled for their lives, especially in the community of San Sebastián.

However these figure into the picture, the fact is that, as I wrote twenty years ago, Huichols have been abandoning their territory, settling on the banks of the Santiago and seasonally migrating to the coast, while at the same time resisting and resenting changes in their ethnic norms and cultural patterns.

In this connection, Macías (1988:123) has stressed the constant invasion of Huichol territory by mestizos, that is, the forcible reduction of "traditional" Indian lands, as a factor in the increasing land hunger in the Sierra. Against these unceasing land grabs, which have enjoyed the support of *caciques* and local power groups, the Indians have had no recourse other than out-migration, or pushing beyond their own community boundaries into the lands of neighboring Huichol comunidades, thereby exacerbating already existing tensions and conflicts between them.[3]

Unlike the situation in the traditional Huichol country in the Sierra, the Huichol communities and extended family ranchos in the Río Lerma/Santiago colony share the same land-holding system and coexist in close proximity with mestizo communities (e.g., Los Sabinos with Huaynamota, or Playa de las Golondrinas, whose lands are held in the ejído system, with the mestizo communities of Paso de Ahomas and El Cruelar). Thus, there is more interaction between mestizos and Huichols than in the Sierra, not only because of work-related migration but also because both groups co-exist permanently. Not surprisingly, this sometimes causes friction. One example that comes to mind is the community of Zoquipan, whose permanent population is almost completely Huichol. The two mestizo families with which we had frequent contact at the INI Center in Tepic exhibited the attitude of superiority toward the Indians that is so typical of mestizos. But in spite of their certainty that they were in every respect "better" than "those indios," they complained of feeling excluded from decisions affecting all the residents of the community because they could not participate in the monthly meetings in which the predominant language was not Spanish but Huichol.

Another question: How is it that the prevalent system of land tenure includes both these otherwise very distinctive groups? What type of coexistence occurs between them? What are the implications of this closer coexistence between mestizos and Huichols? Do the Huichols maintain their independence because they have preserved their traditional pattern of widely scattered settlement?

The fact is that work-related migration toward the coastal area involves not only the Huichol population of both the Sierra and the Río Lerma de Santiago but also the mestizo population of the latter area. According to Ladrón de Guevara (1977) and Serrat (1979), the principal commercial product of the state of Nayarit is tobacco. According to the former, by 1977 there were no less than one hundred tobacco-growing ejídos in Nayarit, with production localized in nine of the nineteen municipalities of the state. At that time, two-thirds of the 42,000 hectares of tobacco in the nation as a whole were concentrated in Nayarit.

More recently, tobacco production has suffered serious reversals. In some parts of the country, tobacco farming has come at least temporarily to a complete halt, in others it has been restricted. Tobacco growing in Nayarit has not been completely interrupted, but it is passing through a crisis. All this, of course, affects those Huichols whose main cash income, however modest, has been from the harvesting and threading of tobacco. There are, of course, other agricultural products, such as sugar cane, chile, beans, peanuts, and coffee, to mention a few of those that consume the labor of the population of the area of the Aguamilpa dam project. For example, Huichol families from Colorado de la Mora are hired for the harvesting of coffee and sugar and the harvesting and threading of tobacco leaves, while those from other communities and ranchos have been engaged in the harvesting of maize and peanuts.

Considering all this, how much have the dam-zone colonists been influenced by wage labor, inasmuch as this has brought about increased coexistence with the mestizo population? Could they have developed, as a way of preserving their own cultural and religious identity, a strategy of "double identity," one of apparent acculturation on the outside, while on the inside preserving cultural patterns similar to those prevailing in the traditional territory in the Sierra? That seems to be the case.

According to Macías (1988), Huichols who went to work in the mines at Bolaños would dress in *pantalones de mezcilla* (trousers) and shirts, in other words, non-Indian clothing, in order to go to work, but immediately upon returning to their ranchos and home communities go back to dressing in traditional costume and participating fully in the indigenous ceremonies and rituals.

With respect to the Huichols living in the Aguamilpas zone, one could imagine that they laid aside those cultural patterns they found to be incompatible with, or even detrimental to, their new reality. The fact is, however, that whenever they face greater pressure of the larger society on their daily lives, they go right back to patterns that they had apparently—and I stress apparently—cast off completely. This retrieval of religious practices then becomes a strategy for preserving their unity and their identity when confronted by the larger, and politically and economically more powerful, society threatening them with disintegration as a group.

Then there is the question to what degree the Huichols of the dam zone have preserved relationships with the ceremonial centers in the Huichol territory proper. This is a question that has not been previously asked. Fernando Benítez, for example, in his Huichol volume published in 1968, assumed that in the absence of access to the temples and temple organizations in the Sierra, religious and ritual life had become exclusively concentrated on the extended family ranchos. But according to the assessment of more recent investigators, at the very least the Huichols of the dam zone do in fact maintain emotional and kinship ties with families that participate regularly in the community ceremonies in the Sierra, and even trek back into the mountains to attend, among other major rites, the traditional change-of-office the Huichols call, in Spanish, *cambio de las varas*, the changing of the staffs of authority. There is, finally, also this interesting but little-known fact: there has been a real tuki in the Río Lerma colony since the 1970s. Smaller than those of the Sierra, it is nevertheless a real temple, constructed in the old style, and used as of old, with the financial assistance of the well-known Huichol artist and religious specialist José Benítez Sánchez.

XIII.

ACCULTURATION, ASSIMILATION, OR ACCOMMODATION?

Openness to the ways and beliefs of others may be typical of the Huichol way, but not always and not everywhere, even outside the Huichol country proper, and most certainly not vis-à-vis the other religions or the mestizos at Playa de las Golondrinas, Colorado de la Mora, and the other Huichol enclaves along the lower Santiago. On the contrary, here they are very much more closed when faced with "the other" than even the traditional communities in the Sierra proper. That has been their salvation as Huichols, this shutting themselves off from outsiders and resisting their influence. It is ironic that these people living outside the traditional territory should have protected

FIGURE 121. The Sacred Rock at Zitakua, the Hill above Tepic, the Capital of Nayarit. The Huichols, acting on divine inspiration, selected this place to construct their own tuki, the traditional circular temple. See Chapter 11. (*Photograph by Lourdes Pacheco.*)

their beliefs and rituals and lifeways more forcefully than even their relatives in the Sierra.

This is a phenomenon you see also in urban areas, among many of the so-called "urban Huichols." I have long been convinced that this is, in any event, a false category, because all that is "urban" about them is that they make their lives in an urban environment—but as Huichols, not as acculturated, or even acculturating, people trying to become mestizo. Look at Tepic, for example. There is a sizable colony there now of *puros Huicholes*, as they say of themselves, and they hold on as hard as they can to their fiestas and their ceremonies (Figure 121). They even have their own tuki, also built with the help of José Benítez Sánchez. This artist is himself an example of this trend to become more Huichol, not less, in the face of the larger society. The same thing was true three decades ago of Ramón Medina, but that artist-shaman's physical and emotional distance from the traditional Huichol lifeway was then much shorter than that of José Benítez, who grew up urban. To me, this is enormously significant, something anthropologists are going to have to learn to understand. All the old assumptions about how acculturation proceeds, and all the old categories, fall by the wayside, because they just do not work anymore.

In actuality, they never did, because what we see now, far more clearly than before, is that it is precisely those Huichols who have moved into urban environments, with greater opportunities and access to knowledge and economic means, who have the greatest motivation for remaining Huichol. In my experience, it is actually precisely these, who have more money in their pockets and who are in daily contact with the larger society, rather than those who are poor and isolated, that have greater recourse to ways of developing and maintaining resistance to acculturative pressures, and a greater consciousness and respect for their own parental culture. This is ironic and it requires serious study to understand the psychological processes involved. And you see it not only with Huichols but also with other indigenous peoples, especially the Indian intellectuals who are now developing their own knowledge and understanding, who are recording their languages and their myths and their own inside view of their religion by means of computers. These Indian intellectuals, who are working right now with different centers, are not less Indian than when they still lived in the mountains, but more Indian, more conscious of their own traditions, and more ready to defend these against the pressures of other religions and economic and sociopolitical forces.

I do not know whether anyone in the United States is working on this phenomenon. But it is necessary to develop a new science of acculturation that does away with outmoded ideas. Is it not obvious that the poorer and more isolated people are, the more vulnerable they are to outside influences? You see the same thing in non-Indian situations. Mexicans who migrate to the United States, or Mexicans living across the border from the United States, do not become less Mexican but more so, more conscious of their Mexicanness. In contrast, here in Mexico proper you have people who desperately want to become *norteamericanos*, who copy everything North Americans do and say. And it's almost pathetic. But then look at Ramón Medina and his wife Lupe. When they moved to Guadalajara from Paso de los Muertos in the early 1960s, what did they do? They did not try to melt into the mestizo society, they looked for land and when they found it, they planted their *coamil* and built their little hut in the middle of that coamil, and tried to live as much like Huichols as they had always lived. And when they were thrown off that land, they resisted even more and stayed Huichol. Their identity vis-a-vis the Mexican state was: I am Huichol. I am better than you. At least, I am as good.

The Huichols are very open, permitting the whole world to come in, and for the most part they keep little of their religion secret from outsiders. The great curiosity is that at Colorado de la Mora, to take one case, the fact that a part of the community converted did not weaken the determination of the majority to hold fast to the old traditions. It even strengthened it. In this community, being confronted every day with the presence of the other religion gave the Huichol tradition more force, more validity, not less. It is the same thing on the individual level, where, with some exceptions, Huichols who moved closer to, or even into, the cities tended not to become less Huichol but more, more aggressively determined to hold on to and defend their religion, their way of thinking, and their Huichol identity. The reality of the mestizo world had been around them for a long time, but while its influence made some people fall away, it failed to affect the majority. And now with the aleluyas in their own midst, that majority, the traditionalists, became even more Huichol, more determined to remain Huichol and be identified as Huichol people by the outside world. These are aspects of acculturation and adaptation that many anthropologists have not understood, and for which, because they failed to understand it, they have invented false categories.

For me, as an anthropologist, it has been an extraordinary experience to see Indians, first Huichols and now other peoples in Oaxaca, the state with the greatest number of surviving Indian language groups, move into the capitalist economy in the city without becoming less "Indian." The impressive thing in Oaxaca is seeing Indian people actually coming away from the experience of higher education with an increased Indian consciousness, not less, fending off with greater awareness even subtle inroads into their ancestral Indian cultures. In contrast, when you go into the mountain villages, isolated from the mainstream and poor, what you see is people, ignorant of the corrosive effects of the dominant culture on their own, trying to surrender or deny their Indianness because they are daily made to feel ashamed of not being "progressive." Unless, of course, they come under the influence of a charismatic individual, who knows about his or her own traditional culture and can pull people along.

This latter is an extremely interesting and significant phenomenon that is occurring not only with Huichols or, as in Oaxaca, Mixes or Zapotecs, among others, but in many other places. And you see it not just with Indians but with non-Indian Mexicans, or Guatemalan refugees, who migrate to the United States. Of course, some—many, even—become submerged in the dominant culture. But those Highland Maya, Quiche, Cakchiquel, Tzutujil, and others, who fled across the border into Mexico from the terror of the Guatemalan police, the army, and the death squads, did not lose their Maya identity, even if sometimes they tried to hide it. It is instructive to see the evolution here. At first, they sometimes exchanged their distinctive national clothing, their *traje*, for western dress so as to submerge and hide. But many did not, and once they felt relatively safe, some of the others returned to their old way of dressing. So now you see Maya women right here in the market in Oaxaca, or in Mitla, wearing their wraparound homespun skirts and their beautiful *huipiles* and speaking Maya. They may live and work in Mexico, but they proclaim themselves as Maya from the Guatemalan highlands.

In the Huichol country, meanwhile, the important development has been that the Huichol maestros, the literate teachers employed by the government, are now writing down their own culture, their own knowledge, the myths, and what happens in the rituals. They are writing it down in the Huichol language—not in Spanish but in Huichol—and they are teaching the information to the children. That has never happened before. The teaching *promotores* we had in the sixties—intelligent men like the late José Carrillo—had been taught the basics, reading and writing in Spanish, and arithmetic, and they passed these subjects on in the classroom. But they did not themselves write down the things that made them Huichols, so that they could in turn transmit their knowledge. Now they are doing just that. They are doing it in the Huichol comunidades in the Sierra and they are doing it in Tepic and in Colorado de la Mora and the other settlements on the Santiago. My old organization, the Instituto Nacional Indigenista, is helping a great deal in this. The INI workers are encouraging the maestros and the mara'akámes, the shamans, to teach and transmit the culture. They are working to see that the peyote pilgrimages are not interfered with but protected as a religious journey with all the rights of freedom of religion accorded to the observances of the majority religion and the Protestants, that the ancient right to collect and use peyote in their ceremonies not be thwarted by government persecution, and that Tatéi Matiniéri, the sacred springs, be protected as a sacred place for the observance of Huichol religion and open to Huichol pilgrims. I remember in December 1968, when we went to Wiri-kúta with Ramón Medina, all that area was still wide open, and the Huichols could reach the sacred springs without having to crawl through barbed-wire fences and risk being penalized for following their ancient ways or be driven off, as Huichol pilgrims have to do today because technically, if not in their own minds, they are trespassing on private land.

As a worldwide movement among indigenous people, ethnicity is extremely strong, for better or worse, and it is strong also in Mexico. In Oaxaca there is demographic reinforcement for this, because there you are dealing not with small groups living in relative isolation but with hundreds of thousands of Indians who still know and converse in their own languages. What is badly needed among the Huichols is more teachers with fluency, and literacy, in both languages, that of the dominant society and their own native tongue, to give the Huichols better access to dealing with the forces of change.

One great problem that worries all of us who have worked with the Huichols is the new agrarian law, under which communal lands are to be, or can be, privatized. How is this going to affect the Huichols? How is it going to affect all the Indian peoples who hold land in common, as common property? How are they to be protected from victimization, exploitation, and ruin? This is a grave concern. Take the Huichols of Colorado de la Mora. What if under the new law one group wants to sell its land, or associate itself with some rich mestizo cattleman? What if the aleluyas, the evangelicals, are talked into selling, and the traditionalists resist? It is not a new problem, but it is aggravated and legitimized by the new law, which some of us regard as the most anti-Indian law Mexico has seen in a century. At the present time Arturo Warmann, an anthropologist who understands the problems of Indian people and who is determined to protect their rights, is the Procurador Agrario. But what happens when he is out? As I write, the present government has only another two years left in office, and when there is a change of presidents, Warmann will probably be out as well. And then who will protect the Indian people?

All the Indians of Mexico are affected and threatened, every Zapotec village, every Mixtec village, speakers of Nahua, Mixe, Zapotecs, Mazatecs, Huichols, Coras, Mayo, Tepehuanes, Tzeltal, Yucatec, and other Maya tongues — anyone with agricultural land, or grazing land, or forests. In northwestern Mexico the Tepehuanes have been struggling with this problem for years against one of the largest logging companies. It is Mexican-owned, but the multinationals are not far behind. In the United States and Canada, they have virtually denuded huge areas of the Pacific Northwest and now they are eyeing the Indian forest lands in Mexico that will fall under privatization. The Indians are offered what to them look like huge sums of money, but when the money is gone — and it will be gone quickly — they will be left with nothing — exactly as happened in the United States under the Dawes Act. They will be landless Indian peasants, not very different from the bad old days of the Spanish colony.

The Huichols and Coras surely have natural resources that are not now being exploited and on which the big Mexican companies and the multinationals have their eye. These are delicate and difficult problems that affect the very survival of the indigenous peoples. What I said earlier — that Huichols, when they migrate out and find themselves confronted with other religions and other cultures in the cities, often tend not to become less Huichol but more so, more convinced of the superiority of their own old lifeways and the beauty of their homeland — is true. But this is closely tied to the concept of land as a sacred heritage. It is only natural that in retrospect everything becomes idealized and the problems that drove them to seek a life elsewhere tend to be forgotten. Nevertheless, a key to their survival as Indian people is the certainty that they have their homeland, their own lands and fields and forests and mountains. If they lose these in the rush to privatization, if they no longer have that emotional focal point, I am not so sure they can survive as Huichols, any more than can other Indian people. It is not just this dam or that, but the exploitation of the other resources, the forests, minerals, grasslands, rivers. These are the problems that will confront the Huichols and the other indigenous populations of Mexico in the coming century.

The last census of 1990 gives the number of Indians in Mexico above the age of five as 5,500,000, or a little under 8,000,000 if children under five are counted. According to the census, then, seven or eight million Mexicans are legally recognized as Indians. With other Mexican anthropologists, I believe the reality is considerably greater, because there are hundreds of thousands, even millions, living in the cities who, though clearly Indian, are not officially recognized as such, or who might not declare themselves as Indians to the census takers for fear of discrimination. If you add these numbers you arrive, in my opinion, at something like ten to fifteen million whom anthropologists would regard as Indians and who regard themselves as Indians, even if they do not proclaim themselves as such to the census people, and even if they have given up their distinctive dress. There are old Zapotec towns and barrios in Oaxaca— I live in one, the barrio of San Felipe—where no one dresses as an Indian and no one, except perhaps a few old folk, even remembers the native language. But the people are Zapotec nonetheless, in their way of thinking, their view of the world and themselves in it—all this is pure Zapotec. And there are millions like them in Mexico, people who once spoke their own languages but who are now monolingual in Spanish, the language of the dominant society, and who yet remain conscious of their Indian ethnicity.

So where does this leave us in terms of acculturation? It was Melville Herskovitz who wrote the bible on that subject in the 1930s, and our own leaders in applied anthropology, like Gonzalo Aguirre Beltrán and Julio de la Fuente, by and large followed the ideas he formulated. It was they who developed the theory, dominant for a long time in Mexican social policy, that Indians who become educated and leave their home communities lose their Indianness. In the nearly three decades in which I have worked on these problems, I have become convinced that, notwithstanding their great intellectual contributions, on this they were fundamentally in error.

As anthropologists we are facing a crisis, and a severe one. We have to decide where we stand, whether we wish to hold on to outmoded categories that have no reality in the real world and that serve only the interests of the dominant society, or whether to learn to appreciate the reality of the Indian intellectual and the other Indian people who, while assimilating or adapting to aspects of the dominant society without, nevertheless do not surrender ethnic consciousness. I happen to be Mexican, and the Mexican reality is what concerns me first of all. But it is not exclusively a Mexican problem. It is a worldwide phenomenon that people want to maintain their ethnic identity, for better or worse, and sometimes even in very violent and bloody ways.

XIV.

SOME THOUGHTS ON INDIGENOUS SELF-DETERMINATION

Where are the Huichols headed? This is a complex question and the answers are far from clear.

The pressures, direct and indirect in form and method, exerted on the Indians by the dominant societies are obviously increasing at an accelerating rate. Thus, the Indians, feeling themselves ever more disarmed in the face of overwhelming economic and political power, are again resorting to dispersion to less accessible reaches of their mountainous homeland, where they find themselves increasingly fenced in. In order not to lose their cohesion and their ethnic identity, they flee; should this avenue of escape be closed off, they become alienated in certain critical ways. To quote Bonfils (1970), the Indian communities have their own culture, but it is the culture of a dominated minority and, therefore, it is oppressed, defensive, and isolating. Unlike the situation of the exploited within the dominant system, which is also an oppressed culture, but which only has alternatives within the national system, the indigenous cultures have alternatives outside the national system, because their legitimacy is not founded in terms of the national culture, but rather in their own distinctive past. "It is precisely the fact of their having been exploited as natives," Bonfils writes, "that has permitted the survival of their own distinct cultures."

The problem indigenous communities like the Huichols face is the need to organize and determine their own destiny, within a national society that is more just, that gives them political participation and that respects their traditional ways and values, so that they may achieve their own development in terms of their own internal contradictions, not those of the larger society. The Huichols need bilingual professionals. They need teachers and they need their shamans who understand the Huichol universe and the universe beyond the Huichol boundaries, who can be leaders because they know the outside world and can stand back from their own culture so as to be more aggressive in the defense of the Indians.

It is not that the Huichols and comparable indigenous societies exist statically, isolated, and that they do not contain within themselves the seeds of movement. It is, rather, that being on the defensive allows for no internal movement toward change or development. Whether they intend, or even wish, to or not, they are increasingly being drawn into the larger economic system, into the system of *tiendas* and markets. Already there is a road into San Andrés, another into Santa Catarína, and a third into Tuxpan de Bolaños. Soon there will be roads and road traffic into and between all the comunidades. Of course, travel by land is still, and will continue to be, difficult; the roads are narrow and in the rainy season they can become impassable. But the effect of these roads is immediately apparent. Back in the 1960s the only way I or our INI doctor could get in and out of San Andrés was by single-engine Cessna or a rickety old twin-engine Beechcraft Bonzanza whose brakes were rarely in working order. On a recent visit to the same community, I saw twenty trucks there, and a great deal of beer. So, change is occurring at an ever faster rate. Yet, based on past experience and history, I believe that the Huichols are going to find ways of defending their integrity, no matter what.

Somewhat unexpectedly—because they are supposed to be so much more "acculturated"—that applies even more to the Coras, the closest cultural relatives of the Huichols. It has been my experience that notwithstanding their apparently greater assimilation, in comparison to the far more "traditional" Huichols, the Coras tend to be more closed and to maintain a more solid resistance. In fact, they sometimes amaze me in their determination to keep outsiders at bay, no matter how powerful. In 1991 President Salinas de Gortari himself had that experience when he went to visit the

Cora community of Jesús María. There was supposed to be a meeting in the Casa Reál between the Cora governor and the elders and the President of the Republic. But the Coras informed the president's party that only he was allowed to enter—no retinue, no bodyguards, no military. For a time, there was a real standoff, because the president's aides did not want to let him go into the building without any protection. But the Coras were adamant: only the president could come in because he was the only one in authority, and he was therefore on exactly the same level of power and prestige as their own Indian governor. Hence, the two could meet as equals, but nobody else, and no protection was necessary. And, in the end, they won.

The Huichols are very different. They tell the world to come in as it pleases—not always and everywhere, and not in every instance, but openness has pretty much been the Huichol way. The experience of the President of the Republic among the Coras would be inconceivable among the Huichols. Yet, at the same time, there is this marvelous determination to defend themselves in order to live.

In general, however, whenever the Huichols have tried to organize themselves, they have had to face total opposition in the municipalities to which they are subject, as well as the state capitals and the capital of the republic, for all these structures are ultimately linked. There are, to be sure, some bright spots on an otherwise gloomy horizon. There are moves one can only hope will be successful. One is the possibility of laws establishing once and for all the legitimacy of peyote in the context of Huichol religion and ritual, replacing the chaotic present situation in which the Huichols are as subject to stringent "anti-drug" laws as any other Mexican citizen—quite unlike the United States, where peyote use has been legalized in most places for adherents of the Native American Church. There is a move toward making Wirikúta, the sacred land of the peyote, a national monument freely accessible to Huichols for their sacred peyote hunts. There was the recent success of the Coras of Jesús María in forcing the governing party, the PRI, to accept the candidate favored by the traditional governors as president of the municipality of El Nayar, in place of an old-style cacique the party establishment had tried to impose.

There have been other movements in the right direction. To mention one, on December 10, 1990, the Official Gazette of the state of Nayarit published a decree by the governor, Lic. Celso Humberto Delgado Ramírez, establishing a substantial portion of the island called Isla del Rey in the municipality of San Blas, on the Pacific coast, as a cultural monument reserved for Huichols who come to the sea to make offerings and pray. According to Huichol tradition, this island, which had been a prime target for large-scale private development, was the gateway through which some of the ancient gods emerged from the sea.

It is significant that the decree, recognizing that the Huichols are culturally situated in two eras, "el tiempo sagrado y el tiempo profano" (sacred time and profane time), actually based itself on a Huichol version of their own mythological history as it pertains to the island and the places on and around it that are sacred to the Indians. Sacred time is represented by their origin myths, according to which the entrance of the gods of the First World is located in what is now the municipality of San Blas, and according to which La Piedra Blanca, the White Rock, is the personification of Tatéi Haramára, the goddess of the Pacific Ocean, and that the two white rocks are the gateway to the Second World, which the gods closed off just in time to prevent entry of the malignant forces. So far as I know, this is the first time that a state government has actually expressed such unreserved respect for the religious beliefs of its inhabitants. Nor has this ever been done in the United States, where similar efforts have, for the most part, been thwarted by powerful private interests. The Nayarit law even codifies that, based on their origin myths, the Huichols to this day make long and arduous journeys to the sea to conduct ceremonies essential to the agricultural cycle, the curing of the sick, and other "activities that sustain the life of the Huichol people."

Dare one hope that even Wirikúta, the sacred desert country of the Deer-Peyote, the land of dawn where the Sun was born, and the home of the kakauyaríte, the Huichols ancestor gods personified by hills and mountains, might one day soon also be declared a cultural monument reserved for Huichols and other Indian people and closed off to casual thrillseekers no less than to mestizo cattle interests and other would-be despoliators of the desert?* And might one also hope that Mexico may finally point the way in liberating the Huichols and other Indian peoples from oppressive drug laws that fail to differentiate between addictive and dangerous narcotics and a little cactus and other intoxicating plants that do no harm to the body, that grow freely in nature, that are sacred to the Indians because they make the world of the gods accessible, and that for hundreds, even thousands, of years have been integral to the religious and therapeutic rituals of the original stewards of the Mexican earth?

NOTES

1. This pinpoints precisely the problem with Indian policy on both the national and the state level. INI policies tend to fluctuate, positively and negatively, with every presidential change, the election of a new President every six years being followed by the replacement of the responsible officials in every federal ministry and agency. The process is replicated on the state level with the election of a new governor. (—Eds.)

2. In late October 1995 word reached us from the Sierra of moves by some Huichol authorities in San Andrés Cohamiata and other places to put an end to the Franciscan missions and expel all friars and nuns. Whether these moves are purely "nativistic" and indigenous, or in some part a consequence of the rise of Protestant evangelism, is at this point unknown. In fairness to the Franciscans we should note, however, that, while their ultimate purpose is obviously Catholic instruction and, where possible, conversion, and while the Church has consistently sought to undermine the prestige and authority of the shamans and other traditional community leaders, some priests and nuns have also sought to protect the Indians against the worst injustices and have frequently taken their side in disputes with the outside world. Whatever the reasons and the

*On recent developments in this regard, see "Conclusion."

perceived benefits, wholesale expulsion will thus also remove some of this protection, however limited. (—Eds.)

3. This is precisely what has happened between San Andrés Cohamiata, the comunidad in which I have been working for many years, and its neighbor Santa Catarína. The boundary between them used to be the Chapalagana River, but recently Santa Catarína has moved beyond the river into lands owned by San Andrés, to the point where San Andrés Huichols coming down to the river to visit their old sacred sites or to hunt on their own traditional lands, are sometimes arrested and thrown in jail as trespassers by the Santa Catarína authorities. (—S.B.S.)

CONCLUSION

PEYOTE PILGRIMS AND DON JUAN SEEKERS

Huichol Indians in a Multicultural World

PETER T. FURST & STACY B. SCHAEFER

From all that has been said in these pages, it is self-evident that, old theories to the contrary notwithstanding, Huichols do not live isolated in time and space, and never did. The book provides a diachronic picture of Huichols as a persevering people, maintaining rich cultural traditions rooted in pre-Hispanic times even as they must daily come to terms with accelerating change. To a certain degree, entirely unintended, their very autonomy has brought them now face to face with the problem of avoiding dilution of their culture, if not of ethnocide. For, to a large degree, it is their uniqueness that has drawn the outside world into their midst. More than that of any of their contemporaries in Indian Mexico, their spectacular art—even that produced for sale—reflects and embodies their religious beliefs. And more than most, they have succeeded in maintaining the integrity of these religious traditions, at the center of which stands peyote as the unifying element of their traditional world view.

Although there are obviously differences, the Huichols today face many of the same problems that broke into the open in Chiapas with such dramatic urgency on the very day that the North American Free Trade Agreement came into force, and that so many of Mexico's twelve million surviving Indian people face. Chiapas, a small state in the far south with only three million inhabitants, more than half of them Maya, has become the operative metaphor for much that is wrong in Mexico between rich and poor, especially the condition in which Indians find themselves nearly five centuries after the European invasion, for "poor" all too often equates with "Indian." Like the Maya, the Huichols are trying to recover control of their forest resources from outside commercial interests, as well as agricultural and grazing lands that mestizo neighbors usurped by the tens of thousands of acres, often with the active or tacit complicity of corrupt, biased, or complaisant government officials. The problem of grazing versus agriculture is shared by Huichols and Maya alike, the more so in that most of the cattle that have invaded traditional Indian lands are owned by outside cattle interests allied with political bosses. It is in large measure the alienation of so much of their arable land (of which, in any event, there is little enough) in the face of a rapidly expanding population, that has been forcing so many of them to seek seasonal employment in the tobacco plantations of the hot and humid coastal lowlands, while comparable conditions froze the Maya into lives of deprivation, poverty, and such overt discrimination that as recently as thirty years ago an Indian had to yield the sidewalk to mestizos and whites. Although formal recognition and legal title to their lands was guaranteed to them generations ago, the Huichols, like the Maya, are still waiting for that recognition, and now must contend with the uncertainty of the effect on them of the new Article 27 of the Mexican Constitution that authorizes the privatization of ejídos and communal lands. Again like the Maya, the Huichols were caught in the middle between the contending sides in the Mexican Revolution and its bloody aftermath, and they are still paying the price today. And, like the Maya, they are treated like pawns in the increasingly contentious politics of modern Mexico. Finally, like other Indians the Huichols demand recognition, respect, and equality, not merely on paper, or as colorful bait for the tourist industry, but in the real world, as indigenous people who have chosen to remain Indian in a modernizing multicultural nation. At the same time, more Huichols than ever have become familiar with the world beyond their borders, and more of them are aware that to control their own present and future, they need to be active players in relations with the dominant society, and to make common cause with other Indian peoples facing similar problems.

We see three major threats to the Huichols today: they are threats to the integrity of their traditional lands, to the integrity of their cultural traditions and of their religion, and to the integrity of their physical well-being. This last is so serious, so immediate, and so little known to the outside world and even to the Huichols themselves, that it will be a major focus of this final section of this book.

Don Juan Seekers, Peyote Pilgrims, and Other Strangers

Other than the long-standing problem of land theft and lack of legal title, the Huichols are faced with a more subtle assault on their spiritual equilibrium. Unwittingly, they have become the matrix in which other people who have lost their spiritual center seek sustenance for their souls. This is an entirely new experience with foreigners, whose unfortunate byproducts are both a degree of social disruption and unwelcome attention from authorities evidently more concerned with pleasing the giant to the north than safeguarding the religious traditions of their own people—even when their drug laws and the fears that inspired them, like those in the United States, fly in the face of all the scientific evidence.

Foreigners seeking solace and safety in the far reaches of the rugged Huichol country are not a new phenomenon. In addition to Tlaxcalans and other Nahuatl-speakers who first arrived with the invading army of the unspeakable Nuño de Guzmán, some of whom undoubtedly escaped into the mountains, and others whom the Spaniards settled on the edges of the Sierra to guard the frontier against the Chichimecs, a wide variety of other peoples sought refuge in the Sierra in the sixteenth and seventeenth centuries: Indians, escaped African slaves, disaffected mestizos, and apparently even some Filipinos who deserted the Manila galleons when they put into port on the Pacific coast. The Franciscans, who already by the sixteenth century were in charge of evangelizing this part of the Sierra, became serious about it in the early eighteenth century, after the Spaniards finally succeeded in establishing some measure of political and military control over the Sierra Madre Occidental and its peoples. The existence of present-day *comunidades* and their form of rotating indigenous civil-religious government headed by a *gobernador* date from this period. Intensive Spanish influence in the Sierra declined after Mexican Independence, and by 1860, virtually all missionaries had abandoned their churches and missions. In the succeeding decades, the Huichol mountains once again became a refuge for bandits and all manner of revolutionaries, including Villistas and Carranzistas during the Mexican Revolution, and federal troops and fanatical partisans of the Catholic Church in the Revolution's bloody aftermath, the so-called Christero Revolt.

Other outsiders of a very different type, and from even more distant places, had appeared in the Huichol country even before these events. At the end of the nineteenth century and in the first decade of the twentieth, came the pioneer ethnographers, Norwegian, French, and German, respectively, whose objective was not to change the Huichols, or to rediscover among them their own spiritual equilibrium, but to document their unique lifeway, their rich oral literature, and their religious traditions. These were followed in the 1930s by several American students of their culture, notably Robert M. Zingg, as well as Otto Klineberg and Donald and Dorothy Cordry.

In between, however, other Americans with less benign intent also appeared in their midst. These were the prospectors and miners, who came scouring Huichol lands for silver and other precious metals, and whose activities for many years to come were to bring every other foreigner under suspicion. As Klineberg, a psychologist, wrote in 1934 after a stay of several months in San Sebastián and nearby settlements:

> It can hardly be said that the Huichols were pleased with our visit. They have little liking for Mexicans (whom they call vecinos or neighbors), and much less for North Americans, who are all potentially, if not actually, miners coveting Huichol land for its silver. There are silver mines controlled by Americans at Bolaños, at the edge of the Sierra, and the Huichols cannot understand anyone's making the difficult trip into the mountains without having interests in that direction. They have not forgotten the American who about twenty years ago arranged with the gobernador

in San Sebastian for a fifty year's lease of a large area, and began the work of looking for silver until under cover of a revolutionary skirmish both he and the gobernador were killed. The suspicion that we were also miners clung to us most of the summer, and even though our own host at the Ciudad became progressively more amiable, there were a great many others who remained hostile. (Klineberg 1934:446–447)

All during this time, the Huichols remained fairly isolated, living in areas inaccessible to outsiders. Most of the arts and crafts that had been collected by ethnologists—Lumholtz, Diguet, Preuss, Zingg, the Cordrys—remained housed in museum basements beyond the reach of the general public. Publications about the culture enjoyed, for the most part, only a small circulation within academic circles. In the 1950s, however, the situation began to change dramatically. The Catholic Church once again began to make inroads into Huichol communities, constructing airstrips and missions, and reactivating churches that since their earlier abandonment had become thoroughly "Huicholized." (Most recently, Huichol religion has come under sustained, and invariably divisive, assault by U.S.-based fundamentalist Protestant denominations, resulting in a brand new phenomenon, the Christian converts Huichols call by the unflattering name "Aleluyas.") Even greater changes came in the 1960s, when, under then-President Luís Echeverría, the National Indian Institute (INI) promoted an ambitious regional development program known as Plan HUICOT (for Cora-Huichol-Tepehuan). Its, and INI's, projects were designed to integrate Huichols into the mainstream of Mexican national culture. Agricultural and livestock improvement projects were introduced along with medical clinics and schools. Perhaps the greatest irreversible economic change was brought about by the construction of numerous airstrips and some roads linking isolated communities to the outside world for the first time.

Whether or not the majority of Huichols were in favor of these projects is debatable. What they created, however, was an open doorway that could no longer be shut. At about this time, too, there was renewed ethnological interest in the Huichols, and, with it, popular interest as well. Mexicans learned a great deal about Huichol culture and the peyote pilgrimage in 1968, when the prominent journalist-historian Fernando Benítez published *En La Tierra Magica del Peyote* and *Los Huicholes*, the latter as Volume 2 of his five-volume work, *Los Indios de México*. (The former, a firsthand account of a peyote pilgrimage and its mythological and ceremonial context, was published in the United States in 1975 as *In the Magic Land of Peyote*.) In the mid-sixties, too, came other ethnographers from the United States. One was the co-editor of this book, who with the late Barbara G. Myerhoff began to document Huichol intellectual culture, including the arts, elements of the rich mythology, and the peyote pilgrimage. A number of publications (Furst and Myerhoff 1966; Furst 1967, 1968, 1969, 1972, 1976) resulted from these efforts, as well as a documentary film by Furst of a *rancho*-based peyote pilgrimage he accompanied in 1968. Myerhoff published a study of the maize-deer-peyote symbol complex, *The Peyote Hunt: The Sacred Journey of the Huichol Indians*, in

1974. Intended primarily for an academic audience, these writings, like those of Benítez, presented the Huichols as a compassionate, artistically gifted, intelligent, knowledgeable, and resilient people, whose unique culture, still relatively unaffected by religious acculturation, and including the peyote traditions, is an important part of Mexico's cultural heritage. In the meantime, another ethnographer, Phil C. Weigand (1972), had studied the organization of cooperative work parties and agricultural technology in the *comunidad* of San Sebastián, filling in a niche left empty by the concentration of other scholars on religion, ritual, art, and mythology.

But something else was going on in the same decade. There developed a burgeoning interest, mainly among young people, and not only in the United States, in exploring "inner worlds" and "alternate realities" through the use of psychedelic substances. Scientists were discovering and studying these substances in the laboratory as well as in the natural environment. Others documented the use of these wondrous plants among living peoples. Still others found evidence for the long-time use of psychedelics in the historic literature, not least in the accounts of sixteenth century Spanish chroniclers in Mexico. It is difficult to pinpoint where it all started. Certainly not in the '60s and not with Timothy Leary, for scientific interest in hallucinogens was much older than that. The German psychopharmacologist Louis Lewin published on peyote as early as 1888, and his classic work, *Phantastica*, appeared in 1924. The first edition of Weston La Barre's *The Peyote Cult* appeared in 1938. The University of Chicago's Heinrich Klüver published *Mescal: The Divine Plant and its Psychological Effects* in 1928. Aldous Huxley's *The Doors of Perception* appeared in 1954. The Swiss chemist Albert Hofmann unknowingly created a revolution with his discovery of LSD way back in 1938, and there were numerous articles about its effects during the 1950s. R. Gordon Wasson "rediscovered" the magic mushrooms of Mexico in a 1955 issue of *Life*, and he and his wife Valentina published their first book, on the Siberian fly agaric cult, in 1956. *The Peyote Religion* by J. S. Slotkin, a prominent anthropologist who joined the Native American Church and even became its secretary, came out in a commercial edition in 1956. Richard Evans Schultes, director of the Harvard Botanical Museum and the ranking authority on New World "hallucinogens," published numerous papers on peyote in the 1930s and '40s, and his pathbreaking study of *ololiuhqui*, the Nahuatl name for the inebriating seeds of a common morning glory, *Rivea corymbosa* (now *Turbina corymbosa*), dates to 1941. And on and on.

Still, it was in the '60s, at a time when, not coincidentally, America was losing an innocence it may never have possessed but which many people had bought into, by involving itself in what was to become its most divisive and unpopular war, that the inner journey and the search for instant chemical Nirvanas became a growth industry. Whatever the intent of scholars, news of the Huichols and their peyote-centered religion fit right into that. And then, finally, toward the end of that turbulent decade came Carlos Castaneda with his *The Teachings of Don Juan: A Yaqui Way of Knowledge* (1968). To everyone's—including Castaneda's—surprise, the book became an almost instant bestseller. Of course, Castaneda's book was not about Huichols (as it turned out, it was not about Yaquis, either, but that is another story). But it was largely Castaneda's kind of "popular" anthropology that created a great demand for shamans, or what were fondly imagined to be shamans, especially those practitioners versed in the mysteries of the psychoactive flora and its marvelous effects. And the Castaneda tradition persists. Nearly two decades after psychologist Richard de Mille debunked Castaneda's books in two carefully researched and reasoned studies (1976, 1980/1990), as fiction, and not a new kind of ethnography, they continue to sell in the many thousands in the United States and abroad.

Not surprisingly, the Huichols and their art achieved a growing popularity around this time, although for the most part both were still admired from a distance. People were content to view their artwork in private galleries and at exhibitions mounted by such public institutions as the Los Angeles County Museum of Natural History, which held the first exhibition of Huichol art in 1969. In the 1970s several filmmakers, including John Lilly, Jr., Kal Muller, and the anthropologist Scott Robinson, made documentary films on the Huichols and the peyote pilgrimage, but none of these was widely circulated. Japanese, Mexican, Canadian, and French films soon followed. Most recently, the peyote hunt appeared on television as part of the *Millennium* series on the Public Broadcasting System. This past year, another film, produced by a woman who has long befriended individual Huichols as well as guiding Americans on "spiritual" tours to meet Huichols in Mexico and participate in a peyote hunt, was advertised as showing "that people now come from around the world to join the pilgrimage and learn from the Indians' sacred tradition." Flyers and advertisements in *Shaman's Drum* and other New Age journals invite seekers of spiritual highs, if not in so many words, to partake—for a hefty fee, of course—of a unique opportunity to sit at a real-life Huichol shaman's feet and listen to "teachings" allegedly as old as the human race. The latest work to come out on the Huichol peyote pilgrimage, *El Venado Azul* (*The Blue Deer*), is composed in true Castanedaesque tradition by a Mexican author, who describes alleged mystical experiences that he claims cured him of cancer. People are so hungry for what they take to be the Indian peoples' special access to some eternal wisdom that, notwithstanding its obvious lack of credibility, the book has caused a minor sensation in Mexico and will no doubt inspire even more efforts to partake of such a magical, and health-restoring, experience. And there's the rub.

We personally have no objection to people trying almost anything to recover their spiritual selves, especially if they do so by reaching back to their own cultural roots, but also, if they want to take the time and trouble, by reintegrating into their own lives something of the shamanic world view and ecological wisdom of Native Americans, including the Huichols. At the same time, it must be stressed that native peoples are maintaining that wisdom at some political cost to their very existence, and that their "spirituality" is an inextricable component of their physical and social environment. In other words, the so-called "spiritual teachings" for which white people are so hungry did not develop, and do not persist, in a vacuum, but are part of an all-inclusive matrix.

This does not mean that Indian people do not have something to teach whites. We appreciate the objections some traditional North American Indian elders have to what they regard as another form of the white man's theft of what properly belongs to Indian people, and its commercialization. Yet, one could also see it as borrowing, which people have always done, not only in material culture but in the realm of ideas. And shamanism, after all, is as close to a pan-human "*Ur*-religion" as we can hope to come.

And if some Huichols want to travel to the United States to acquaint sympathetic individuals and larger audiences with their art, their history, their songs, their knowledge of how to bring body and soul into reasonable internal and external balance, who are we, as white anthropologists, to object? They are not children, and the Huichol country is not an ethnological zoo, with fences to keep them in and outsiders out. And Indians have been exploited long enough—so let them do some exploiting back. Clearly, Huichols like to travel, and have been doing so since far in their past, when their ancestors traded peyote for salt and other necessities. Most recently, some Huichols have participated in pan-Indian pow-wows in Oklahoma and the northern Plains, as well as joining in other gatherings in Mexico and the United States that bring Native Americans together from many parts of the Americas. Some Huichols have visited Rio Grande pueblos in New Mexico as guests of their elders, and then traveled all the way to Cree villages in northern Quebec. In one pueblo, back in 1988, the Governor was so impressed with his indigenous visitors from Mexico he invited them to participate in the dances and the feast that followed—a singular honor—and even displayed sacred objects from the kiva for the Huichol party that no outsider had ever been permitted to see. The formal invitation the elders of a Canadian Cree community transmitted to an extended family of Huichol artists that happened to be visiting the Southwest asked them to please come north and perform their ceremonies in their beautiful costumes, so that the community's own young people might be made to forget about drugs and alcohol and learn how Indian people in a faraway country keep to the old ways. In the past ten years, Huichol artisans and artists have also traveled to the United States, Europe, and Japan to participate in public exhibitions and demonstrate their skills to museumgoers, and although that might not have been their main intent, they have thereby won new friends and admirers for their culture and, coincidentally, expanded the market for their creations. That, of course, is all to the good, especially in a time when the Huichols are being more and more drawn into the market economy. But it needs also to be emphasized that the only way Huichols can do these things is with the help of sympathetic outsiders, for otherwise they would have no papers and would fare no better when they arrived at the U.S. border than do other "illegals."

There is also little doubt that seeing their knowledge, their art, and their sacred ways so respected and desired by outsiders strengthens their own determination to keep on being Huichols, a point that the Mexican anthropologist Salomón Nahmad makes so well in the final chapter of this book. But physical intrusion into their most sacred rituals on the pretense—and for a foreigner it always has to be a pretense, however well intentioned, and whether consciously or not—of active, believing participation, in the hope of receiving some sort of revelation or salvation in another people's historic experience, that is not merely naive but highway robbery. It is worse than highway robbery, because it exposes the hosts to real danger. So why do Huichols let them? For the most part, the answer is economics: to organize and participate in a peyote pilgrimage is expensive, and many people who feel a need to go cannot afford to do so. The money foreigners offer to contribute makes it possible, and in recent years Huichols have even relied on INI and other agencies to help them defray expenses.

It occurs to us that beyond economic benefits, their Huichol hosts may even see some good in having outsiders along as fellow pilgrims, precisely because such people so often make fools of themselves. Watching a foreign participant in distress, or drunk out of his mind on alcohol he brought along—as has actually happened on peyote pilgrimages that graciously, or out of economic necessity, allowed foreigners in as more than observers—may reinforce the Huichol's own sense of identity, even superiority. But that is surely a minor benefit, and Huichols say it is more than offset by the disruptions and violations of established norms of behavior by foreigners of which many Huichols have long complained, not to mention the risk of official interference.

Foreign "seekers," though disillusioned with, and alienated from, their own society, its religions, its customs and traditions, its faith in technology, come with their own histories and goals that have been shaped by *their* culture, not that of the Huichols. They seek out the Indians in hopes that they will help them come closer, find community, perhaps even become part of the sacred realm. Incredibly, there is more than one documented case where a foreigner who should have known better went to the Huichols in the vain hope of remaking himself into a full-fledged "Huichol shaman," someone initiated into the techniques, the knowledge, the experiences, and the practice of the indigenous specialist in the sacred. But what most outsiders fail to appreciate is that Huichols, no matter how outwardly hospitable, make a sharp distinction between themselves and non-Huichols. As a rule, those not born Huichol can never become Huichol. No matter how sincere, how respectful, how eager to be taught, they cannot become Huichol shamans, and they will not learn from the peyote what it has to teach Huichols. To reemphasize what has been said elsewhere in these pages, peyote is not just a means, through its complex chemistry, of transcending, temporarily, the limitations of the human condition, but serves in a very practical way as an enculturating force, echoing religious tenets in recurring themes that are transcended to visions, the spoken word through myths and songs, actions in rituals and ceremonies, and beliefs that permeate all levels of individual and collective Huichol consciousness. How can a westerner ever hope to penetrate into, and participate in, such a complex and age-old system, one that grew over centuries, even millennia, out of native soil?

One Huichol named Tukía, whose mother is a shaman, said this to Stacy Schaefer about an outsider who joined a temple group on the pilgrimage in the hope of gaining access to some ancient wisdom:

> Who knows what these people think, but for us it is very bad. They say it (the peyote) is very beautiful and that they know because they have an honest heart. . . so they also want to learn like how the Huichol learns. They go on the pilgrimage and it doesn't turn out the same. For example, I just had a temple cargo and this time an outsider accompanied us. And later he ate peyote, but our gods got him lost because he did not complete the same rituals that they told us to do. He was doing it in his own way. He never left offerings in the sacred places. Yes, he carried a candle, but he did not leave it in the sacred place like we did.

This outsider ended up wandering lost in the desert looking for water. The Huichols were concerned that if he died they would be blamed for it. They went looking for him and finally found him, extremely dehydrated and suffering from heat exhaustion. When he recovered, he harangued the Huichols about what a powerful shaman he was, even more powerful than any Huichol shaman. Another example: one time a foreigner arrived in the community where Stacy Schaefer has been working since 1977, this one an Italian, looking for a shaman to whom to apprentice himself, á la Castaneda and "don Juán." He acquired some peyote and started consuming it in the government center during a community ceremony. When the complex chemistry of the cactus started taking effect, he walked through the central plaza, criss-crossing it diagonally, creating consternation and chaos by grabbing the shoulder bags of the women as he went along. The Huichol authorities quickly cornered him and threw him into the flea-infested jail, where he remained until hours later, when he had "come down" from the peyote experience.

Rather than continue with a litany of horror stories about "bad trips" and other negative experiences by individual "Don Juan seekers," let us say that the converging of outsiders on the Huichols, especially American tour groups that go on pilgrimages, whatever their immediate economic benefits (which more often than not are disappointingly meager for the Huichols concerned), has brought upon them unwelcome attention from decidedly unsympathetic local law enforcement officials. The general attitude these officers have towards young "New Age" Americans or Mexicans has become increasingly negative, especially during the decade of the Reagan-Bush "War on Drugs." Sad to say, these hostile attitudes have spilled over to those Huichols who tolerate foreign participation in the peyote rites, the more so in that they dovetail with racist stereotypes about Indians that are still all too common among mestizos and whites.

Since possession of peyote is illegal in Mexico, at this writing technically even for Huichols, Americans and other outsiders who accompany them make the peyoteros easy prey for Mexican narcotics agents, both locally, and, because they cross several states in the course of a pilgrimage, on the state and federal level. And although some local agencies do not enforce the law against Huichols (and there are moves afoot to guarantee the Huichols their legal rights to the peyote pilgrimage, unrestricted access to Wirikúta, and the transporting and use of peyote in the ceremonies), we know of instances when Huichols were arrested for possessing "dangerous drugs"—that is, peyote. Thus, one Huichol woman of Stacy Schaefer's acquaintance told her that some seven years before, she and all the pilgrims from the temple group to which she belonged were arrested on their return for "transporting peyote," and were held in jail for over a month. And this—a clear violation of what Indian people have always considered their sacred right, not to say duty—even in the absence of any outsiders!

With all that, let it also be said that the inconveniences and other problems Huichols have suffered because of outsiders pale beside those that befell the Mazatec Indians in the mountains of Oaxaca after the "rediscovery" of their traditional use of the sacred mushrooms in divination and curing. "The profanation of the mushroom cult did not stop with the scientific investigations," writes Albert Hofmann, the Swiss chemist who discovered LSD and later identified the alkaloids in morning glory seeds as lysergic acid derivatives closely allied to LSD. "The publication about the magic mushrooms unleashed an invasion of hippies and drug seekers into the Mazatec country, many of whom behaved badly, some even criminally. Another undesirable consequence was the beginning of true tourism in Huautla de Jiménez, whereby the originality of the place was eradicated (Hofmann 1980:143)."

Perhaps the Huichols should count themselves lucky that peyote does not grow naturally in the Sierra Madre Occidental, as the *Psilocybe* mushrooms do in Oaxaca, or their communities, however hard to reach, might likewise have been inundated with unwanted visitors.

Professional Intruders: Anthropologists and Medical Doctors

This whole problem of the effects of outsiders also raises another question—that of the role, negative or positive, we as anthropologists play, both in drawing attention to the Huichols through our writings, and, however unintended, in introducing or accelerating change. The idea that the anthropologist is merely a benign and neutral observer whose presence will leave no residue once he or she has completed and published the research, is a naive conceit. Apart from the inevitability of publicizing the people about whom we write, even in the field there are problems. Take the issue of what used to be called "informants," a term with unfortunate connotations that we hope can be dropped in favor of "consultants." More often than not, those willing to talk to us may be, to one degree or another, themselves marginalized in their own society. We recall one American researcher, for example, who, having congratulated himself for having almost immediately found a knowledgeable and cooperative individual in a highland Guatemalan Maya village, went on to discover that his would-be collaborator was regarded by everyone else as a malevolent witch! Even where there is no such problem, just seeming to favor some individuals over others as consultants can cause envy and friction. Or a source might be suspected of having revealed too much, or of using his or her good relations with a foreigner for gain at the expense of others.

The possibilities of unintended harm, subtle or even major, even before the anthropologist leaves, are thus clearly many. On the other hand, the foreign researcher can also have a positive effect. In the Huichol case, the arts, which play such a prominent role (inspiring Zingg to give his 1938 ethnography the title, *The Huichols, Primitive Artists*), provide one such case, especially because it is through their artistic talents that many Huichols have achieved a moderate measure of economic security, unknown before anthropologists and collectors of folk art helped create a foreign market for their productions. During her two-year residence in San Andrés in the 1970s Susana Eger Valadez established an archive of traditional embroidery designs that was accessible to every woman in the community, as well as providing the materials to keep the craft alive. Her continued encouragement and promotion ever since of the traditional arts, through exhibitions, lectures, and a Huichol cultural center near the Pacific coast of Nayarit and in the town of Huejuquilla, at the entrance to the Huichol Sierra, have certainly helped preserve the crafts internally and publicized Huichol art in Mexico and abroad, as have the efforts of the several Mexican government agencies specifically set up to encourage folk arts and crafts. Stacy Schaefer's learning to become a weaver in the Huichol tradition as the woman's path in Huichol culture had the unintended, but positive, effect of renewing the interest of some young Huichol girls in San Andrés in acquiring the skill and its spiritual dimension, in which they had previously shown little interest, or which they did not consider important. Her co-editor had something to do with the evolution of the yarn painting—today the most prominent and internationally popular Huichol folk art, and one that counts among its practitioners artists who have achieved wide recognition—from mere *adorno*, decoration, into a graphic device for recording their mythic histories in a style reminiscent of the codices. It was, in fact, Furst's and Myerhoff's principal consultant, the late artist-shaman Ramón Medina, who pioneered the storytelling yarn art in the 1960s, and drew others, in the first place his wife Guadalupe, into what was to become a lasting tradition and a major source of cash income for many families.

Among the diverse foreign intruders into the culture whose potential effect can be either very bad or very good, perhaps we should close with the western-trained medical worker. Huichols, like all the native peoples of the Americas, have a long tradition of effective therapy for physical and emotional ills, including an extensive inventory of medicinal plants, both in the Sierra and in the distant peyote desert. But the European invaders in the sixteenth century, and later on, the processes of modernization, brought with them disastrous afflictions for which their shamans had, and have, no remedies. So Indians died by the millions. However, the aspect of the shaman as curer, while clearly important, is not the be-all and end-all of his role, which is why, however well-intentioned, government-mandated efforts in the 1960s and '70s to discredit them as ineffectual and even dangerous quacks and replacing them with western-trained, non-Indian medical personnel were potentially disastrous for the well-being of Huichol society. Shamans are preeminently the repositories of esoteric knowledge and the guardians of the equilibrium of their societies. More often than not, the fatal weakening of their roles and their prestige was followed by the disintegration of their societies. Fortunately, some of the doctors and nurses that were sent into the Huichol country from the 1960s on saw the potential harm of such policies and proceeded to do just the opposite. Among them were Enrique Campos, M.D., who on his first visit to San Andrés back in the sixties called on a mara'akáme to make his vaccines effective by putting the power of the Sun into his instruments, and whom the shaman, the famous Nicholas Carrillo de la Cruz of San Andrés, in turn named, only half-jokingly, "mara'akáme chico," little shaman. Then there was a whole series of medical workers, including doctors and nurses, who each laid the foundations for his or her successor in providing medical care in which they enlisted the local shamans as respected collaborators.

One medical team, Armando Casillas Romo, M.D. (see Chapter 6) and his coworker Carlos Chávez, deserve to be singled out because they worked with shamans in San Andrés to revitalize indigenous medical ethnobotany, record the names of medicinal plants and the illnesses for which they are used, establish medicinal garden plots, and integrate western medical knowledge and practice with traditional shamanic experience and techniques. Most important, their project involved the shamans as equal participants. And it was Dr. Casillas Romo's successor as medical officer doing his social service in the Sierra, Dr. Silviano Camberos Sánchez, who since the 1980s has become committed to the detection and combatting of the physiological effects of pesticide intoxication among Huichols who hire themselves out for the tobacco harvest in the hot and humid coastal lowlands, and among those in the Sierra who have chosen paraquat and 2,4-D over machete and ax in the clearing of land for subsistence crops. (Add to this another blessing of modernization: in ignorance of its inherent dangers, some Huichol women have been replacing their customary metal *comales* with sheets of asbestos for heating tortillas and other foods.)

The Greatest Threat: Pesticides

As already noted, it is the increasing contact of the Indians with dangerous pesticides that poses the greatest threat, graver and more lasting than the theft of land or all the Don Juan seekers in the world. Land can be recovered. Don Juan seekers can be sent packing. What the Huichols are facing now is irreversible: a silent assault on their health, their genes, and their very lives. And because the poisons do not discriminate, and entire families participate in the tobacco harvest, and organophosphate-contaminated runoff from tick baths for livestock seeps into the subterranean springs from which the Sierra Indians get their drinking water, not just men but women and children and pregnant mothers are at risk. And, thus, not only the present generation is threatened, but, through contaminated mother's milk and damaged genes, future ones as well.

The story of this environmental disaster has been gradually surfacing in Mexico, thanks largely to the efforts since 1986 of an independent investigator named Patricia Díaz Romo and her colleagues, who have exposed it in the press and in a devastating videotape entitled *Huicholes y Plaguicidas* (*Huichols and Pesticides*) (1994), and the Mexican medical workers most directly involved in dealing with its immediate consequences, the doctors and nurses of the clinic in Santiago Ixcuintla, Nayarit, in the heart of the tobacco country. That this is not a case of crying wolf, or of isolated cases sounding the alarm, but an unfolding tragedy of massive proportions can be seen from a single statistic: according to Ignacio Cano Hernández, M.D., director of the clinic of the Instituto Mexicano del Seguro Social (IMSS) in Santiago Ixcuintla, Nayarit, in the center of the tobacco plantations, in 1991 alone he and his staff treated 480 cases of organophosphate poisoning among Indians, most of them Huichols and others employed in the tobacco harvest (Díaz Romo and Schneider 1993:6). Compare that with just under 200 cases of pesticide poisoning reported in 1982 among *all* farm workers, including applicators, in the state of California (Harte et al. 1991:122) and one gets an idea of the extent of the problem facing the Huichols and others—Indians and mestizos—employed in harvesting tobacco.

A chart of thirty-nine pesticides to which Huichols are regularly exposed in the tobacco fields and in the Sierra was published in the October 11, 1993 issue of the Mexico City periodical *Macrópolis*. Of these, twenty-three are classified as "extremely toxic" or "highly toxic," eight as "moderately toxic," six as "slightly toxic," and only one, the antibiotic streptomycin, manufactured by Chevron and sold in Mexico as an agricultural fungicide under the trade name Agrimycin 100, as nontoxic. It is significant that several of the most toxic of the pesticides with which Huichols have had direct contact since the 1980s, and from which they are in acute danger of poisoning, are restricted or even banned in the United States; in fact, the General Accounting Office "estimates that 25% or more of the pesticides exported from the United States cannot be used domestically" (Harte 1991:126).

To single out just a few of the most toxic of the pesticides to which Huichols are now exposed by name, the published list includes Aldicarb; 2,4-D; DDT, Azinophos-Methyl; Carbaryl; Diazinon; Paraquat; and Parathion and Methyl-Parathion. To give an idea of what is involved, here is what Harte et al. say about just one of these, Aldicarb, in their authoritative book, *Toxins A to Z: A Guide to Everyday Pollution Hazards*:

> Aldicarb is one of the most toxic pesticides in use today. Registered for use in 1970, it is a *carbamate* insecticide, effective against not only a variety of insects but also mites and roundworms. It functions as a *systemic* poison, meaning that it is taken up by a plant's roots or leaves and circulated throughout the plant, making it

available to sucking and chewing pests. Unlike many of its relatives, aldicarb is an acutely poisonous pesticide and is therefore not registered for home or garden use. (1991:205)

As for health effects, they continue, extremely small doses are lethal, and in 1985 several hundred people were poisoned by eating watermelons containing a residue of the insecticide. It is readily absorbed through the skin, "a factor that raises concern for fieldworkers who might be exposed to high levels of residues after crops are treated" (p. 206). The problem here is, of course, that Huichol farm workers are not exposed only *after* treatment of the tobacco plants, but *during*, because it is they themselves who do the application. "Signs of poisoning in humans include dizziness, muscle weakness, stomach cramping, diarrhea, excessive sweating, nausea, vomiting, blurred vision, and convulsions" (ibid., p. 206). In addition, there is evidence that aldicarb poisoning affects the immune system, that there is a link to such reproductive effects as spontaneous abortions, and that, like certain other carbamates, aldicarb "can be transformed to a carcinogenic nitrous derivative under the acidic conditions of the stomach" (ibid., 205–206).

What makes the danger to the Huichols all the greater is that they lack the training and other protections that are mandated in the United States by the Environmental Protection Agency. Although monitoring and enforcement are haphazard even in the United States, and compliance inconsistent, at least on paper the people mixing and applying dangerous pesticides are supposed to be trained and certified, and for the most toxic chemicals, protective clothing and special equipment such as long-sleeved shirts, long pants, boots, gloves, masks or respirators, and enclosed cabs are required (Harte et al. 1991:122). Paper mandates might also be the case in Mexico, but in practice the situation is very different. As Patricia Díaz Romo points out, even if protective clothing were at hand, with temperatures in the hot and humid coastal lowlands where tobacco is grown reaching as high as 42 degrees centigrade, it is practically impossible to use clothing and protective equipment to avoid direct contact of the insecticides with the skin, or to avoid inhaling them, the two principal avenues of intoxication. A third is in its way even more scary: unaware that even minute residues of the toxins are dangerous in the short as well as the long term, Huichols fill the empty pesticide containers with drinking water (Figure 122).

True, other Indians and mestizos are also seasonally employed in the tobacco harvest, but it is the Huichols who are most exposed. As another Mexican doctor, hematologist Esperanza Barrera, M.D., put it, because of chronic malnutrition, the Huichol farm workers are particularly vulnerable to aplastic anemia, which manifests itself through bleeding from the nose and ears, as well as the digestive and urinary tracts, processes that are greatly speeded up by dietary deficiency.

Mexicans rightly resent preaching and interference from foreigners. Clearly, as

FIGURE 122. Stringing Pesticide-Soaked Tobacco Leaves. In the coastal lowlands near Santiago Ixcuintla, Nayarit, this Huichol woman works in a toxic environment without protective clothing or masks. (*Photograph by Susana Valadez.*)

North Americans it is beyond us to protect Huichol lands from invasion and theft, or even demand that the Mexican government protect the Huichols against antidrug zealotry. These are Mexican problems and they must be solved by Mexicans, including the Indians themselves. In these matters, all we can reasonably do, indeed, must do, as anthropologists who owe our careers to the generosity, openness, or forbearance of native peoples, is lend support to those Mexican organizations and individuals working in behalf of the religious rights of indigenous groups, such as the Huichols, and these peoples' efforts to obtain legal title to their lands and the preservation of sacred sites. Nor is it our business to dictate to Huichols how to conduct their affairs or whom they should invite or keep out of their ceremonies, any more than whom to befriend or where they should travel.

But it is quite another matter when U.S. and multinational chemical corporations flood the Third World with pesticides so toxic that their use is outlawed in this country, and when Huichols, who have with such singular success preserved their minds and their rich intellectual heritage against ideological contamination, are now being exposed beyond repair to physical contamination. That is, indeed, our business.

Postscript

Shortly after the final draft of this book was completed and delivered to the University of New Mexico Press, word reached us from Mexico City of the success of long-standing efforts by the Instituto Nacional Indigenista to have Wirikúta and associated sites sacred to the Huichols officially declared a protected ecological and cultural sanctuary. A decree to that effect, guaranteeing Huichols unrestricted access and religious rights to sacred places and a sacred territory comprising approximately 182,108 acres in the state of San Luis Potosí, for the purpose of conducting their ceremonies and gathering peyote, and preserving it from overexploitation by non-Huichols, was signed on September 19, 1994 by the Governor of San Luis Potosí, Sr. Horacio Sánchez Unzueta. Though not quite as sweeping as a decree with the same aims proposed in May 1993 by the Eduard Seler Foundation for Archaeological and Ethnohistoric Research in San Luis Potosí, the wording of the new decree is similar, both having had the benefit of input by Huichol community leaders themselves. In fact, because some sacred places in and around Wirikúta may be specific to one comunidad or group of peyoteros and not another, INI (then headed by Guillermo Espinosa Velasquez, one of the contributors to this volume) brought Huichol elders and shamans from different parts of the Sierra to San Luis Potosí to pinpoint sites their people consider especially sacred and wished to have named in the law.

Past experience with other ecological and cultural zones protected on paper—the Lacondón rain forest comes to mind—suggests a degree of caution. Nevertheless, there is no question that, explicit as the decree is on the rights of the Wixárika (Huichols) to conduct their sacred ceremonies in a territory they—to quote from the preamble—"consider as sacred and as a part of their cultural and historical patrimony," this represents, for the Huichols and for the preservation of the natural and cultural environment in and around the peyote desert, truly a giant step forward.

Article 1 declares the peyote pilgrimage route traversing the municipalities of Villa de Ramos, Charcas, and Catorce in the state of San Luis Potosí, and the sacred sites located along it, to be part of Huichol historical and cultural heritage, and hence subject to ecological and cultural protection and preservation. Article 2 divides the protected region in which Huichols can freely conduct their rituals and collect local resources into two zones: (1) a "nuclear area" with seven named sacred sites within the municipalities of Charcas and Catorce, including the springs called Tatéi Matiniéri ("Where Our Mother Lives"); Kauyumári's Hill (see Schaefer, Chapter 5, for description); and two mountains that share the name Cerro Quemado in Spanish and Reunar (Rau'Unar) in Huichol and that are venerated as the eastern birthplace of the Sun, and (2) an "Intermediate Area," that is, the peyote desert itself.

Article 3 gives preferential rights of access to Huichols and limits construction (such as fences) exclusively to that required for the protection of sacred objects and natural resources. Articles 4 and 5 recognize peyote as the motivating force of the pilgrimage, call for measures to protect the plant and its continued well-being and propagation, including limitations on the exploitation of natural resources that pose risks to the present and future of the sacred cactus, enjoins non-Huichols who make their livelihood in the region to do so in accordance with this decree and state and federal laws for the protection of the environment and its natural resources.

While the new law only pertains to the Huichol peyoteros so long as they are within the territory of the state of San Luis Potosí, there is reason to hope that eventually they might enjoy the same rights—if only on paper—all along the entire length of the traditional pilgrimage routes.

Coincidentally, at almost the same time, the U.S. Congress passed, and President Bill Clinton signed into law, a Bill to amend the American Indian Religious Freedom Act of 1978 to provide for the traditional use of peyote by Indians "for religious purposes, and for other purposes." Introduced in the Congress by Rep. Bill Richardson (D., New Mexico) and in the Senate by Sen. Daniel Inouye (D., Hawaii), the bill, which became law on October 6, 1994, affirms Congress's finding that the traditional use of peyote "has for many centuries been integral" to the way of life of many Indian people and significant in the perpetuation of their tribes and cultures, and that although twenty-eight states are in conformance with federal regulations that permit peyote use by Indian religious practitioners, twenty-two are not, a lack of uniformity that has "created hardship for Indian people who participate in such religious ceremonies." By way of example, the new law makes reference to a 1990 Supreme Court ruling in the case of Employment Division v. Smith, originating in Oregon, which held that the First Amendment does not protect Indian people "who use peyote in religious ceremonies" and also raised uncertainty "whether this religious practice would be protected under the compelling State interest standard."

As it happens, that ruling had already been rendered mute in 1993 by the passage, and signing into law by President Clinton, of the Religious Freedom Restitution Act. Welcome though it was as a reaffirmation of religious freedom for Indians under the First Amendment, that Act did not, however, do away with remaining ambiguities regarding the right of Indians to peyote use, regardless of the laws of any particular state. Public Law 103-344, as the new amendment is known, recognized that the lack of explicit legal protection for the religious use of peyote by Indians "may serve to stigmatize and marginalize Indian tribes and cultures, and increase the risk that they will be exposed to discriminatory treatment."

With the new law, Indian people now have precisely this explicit legal protection:

Notwithstanding any other provision of law, the use, possession, or transportation of peyote by an Indian for bona fide traditional ceremonial purposes in connection with the practice of a traditional Indian religion is lawful, and shall not be prohibited by the United States or any State. No Indian shall be penalized or discriminated against on the basis of such use, possession or transportation, including, but not limited to, denial of otherwise applicable benefits under public assistance programs.

This last phrase again refers back to the Smith case, which had its genesis in the denial of unemployment benefits to two Navajos dismissed from state employment in Oregon for having used peyote in a ceremony of the Native American Church. The new law does not prohibit "reasonable regulation and registration" by the Drug Enforcement Administration of people who cultivate, harvest, or distribute peyote for religious use by Indians, or the placing of "reasonable limitations" on peyote use prior to such critical activities as driving or operating dangerous machinery, or to conform to international law or the laws of other countries. But it assures that any and all such restrictions shall be adopted not at the sole discretion of the authorities, but only after "consultation with representatives of traditional Indian religions for which the sacramental use of peyote is integral to their practice," and in accordance with the "balancing test" set forth in the Religious Freedom Restoration Act of 1993.

The new law specifies the meaning of "Indian" as a member of any tribe, pueblo, or community of Indians or Alaskan Natives, and of "Indian religion" as any religion practiced by Indians, the origin and interpretation of which "is from within a traditional Indian culture or community." As for Indians in federal or state prison, whether to prohibit or allow them access to peyote for religious purposes is left up to the prison authorities.

All in all, then, the fall of 1994 saw a considerable advance in Indian religious rights, both in Mexico and the United States. Interesting to see will be just how United States authorities will try to reconcile fully legalizing peyote for Indian people and, on the grounds that it is a drug as dangerous as addictive narcotics, strictly prohibiting its use by anyone else. As for the situation in Mexico, on first consideration, removal of the last barriers to unhindered religious peyote use by Indian people north of the border has little to do with what Huichols face on the peyote pilgrimage. In fact however, there is a connection. Interference with peyote pilgrimages and the collecting, transporting, and ingesting of peyote by Huichols, to which Schaefer refers in Chapter 5, and Nahmad in Chapter 17, is a recent phenomenon that can at least in part be seen as fallout from the "war on drugs" in the United States, in which peyote, along with other members of the plant kingdom with similar non-addictive psychoactive properties, continues to be, against all the evidence—pharmacological, historic, and cultural—treated as equivalent to heroin or cocaine. In Mexico, where twenty years ago herbalists in the public markets used to display peyote along with their other medicinal plants, policy soon followed suit.

San Luis Potosí has done its part in removing the threat of persecution from the Huichol pilgrims once they have entered the state and reached their goal. One can only hope that the new federal law finally guaranteeing Indian people north of the border unrestricted religious rights to the sacred cactus will have positive effects south of the border as well. As inheritors of a millennia-old religious tradition, the Huichols deserve to be as safe from persecution by antidrug zealotry on their way to the sacred peyote desert in San Luis Potosí, and after they depart for their homes, as they now are while engaged on the hunt for the divine succulent.

GLOSSARY

This glossary is a compilation of the majority of Huichol, and some Spanish, terms found throughout the chapters. Each author has his or her own way of transcribing Huichol words, and since it is technically an unwritten language, with several local dialects and pronunciations, there are numerous variances in the orthographies employed, even among trained linguists. To compound the problem, in a volume of this kind, with an international group of contributors whose first language may be one of the following— Spanish, English, French, German, Japanese, or Huichol—there are bound to be discrepancies not only in how each author pronounces or transcribes the words, but also in how she or he hears them. The phonemes [l] and [r] and how they are transcribed is one example; another is the variation found among the authors in the transcription of the phonemes [u] and [ü]. In order to preserve the integrity of each contributor's work, in most instances we have not attempted to standardize the Huichol terms. Wherever possible, alternate spellings are noted. (S.B.S.)

acuitsi (acuichi, ha cuitsi): diarrhea

acuitsi-huayéya: plant (*Helianthemum glomeratrum*, Cistaceae family) used to cure diarrhea

akutsi: grandmother in the proper sense, ancestor

ai (hai): cloud

Aicutsíta: two natural springs

aikutsi: barrel cactus, possibly *Echinocactus visnaya*

Aituníta: sacred hill (Round Mountain), across from the hill Yuranáka

aixiya: digestive tract disorder

aixíya-huayéya: plant (*Ipomoea* spp., Convolvulaceae family) used to treat aixíya illness

Arawá mata: sacred place near Santa Catarina

arecú: (harecú) nematode worm (*Ascaris lumbricoides*)

arecúxi: digestive tract disorder related to arecú

atacuai: small lizard

atacuaixíya: illness with symptoms of fatigue, diarrhea, dehydration, malnutrition and possible addition of gastrointestinal infection

até (atétsi pl.): louse

atupa: static shadow

Autarika: sacred mountain near Mesa de Nayar, Nayarit

aüxiya-wequíxa: root of *Odontrichum pachyphyllum*, Compositae family, used to cure stomach ache

awatam'te (awatámete): wolf-people guardians

awatz tzai: San Blas blue jay (*Cissilopha sanblasiana*)

caapura aguaya: sheep horns used as musical instruments

caitsa: gourd rattle

caniwewe: female infertility

canuaríve: male infertility

cariu: walnut tree (*Julgans regia*, Junglandaceae family), used medicinally to treat dandruff

catira: candle

cauxi: fox

Chichiwime: Mottled Maize Girl

Chinamekuta: sacred place

cuaxuari: plant (*Erythrina leguminosa* or *E. corraloides*) used to cure dysentery cucu: small chili pepper

cucuiniya: pain

cucuiniya yuriépa: stomach ache

cuinaopuvamete: assistants of shaman singer

cuquiya-huayéya: medicinal plant to cure cough

cuitapuri: large green flying beetle (Nahuatl *mayatl*; *Hallorina dugesii*)

cuitapuríxiyá: epilepsy

cuitayári: stool

cuítsi (cuíchi): pinworm

cuitsi-huayéya: plant (*Antigonum reptopus*, Polygonaceae family) used to cure pinworms

cuitseri-huayéya: plant (*Calea* spp., Compositae family), used medicinally to treat venereal diseases

cuitsiteri (or cuisteri): venereal disease of any kind

cuquíya: cough

cuumu: "to have a dream"

cúuri (kúuri, kúri, cúuli): elder sister (see *wakúri'kitene*)

eachakiute: the harvest

E'éka Taweakáme: whirlwind that transforms everyone into a drunkard

etsá: smallpox

etuli: mobile shadow

Hai mutiyo: place in Wirikúta where white peyote grows

Hai Tono'lipa: place called Clouds Rising Up

haiku: blue corn snake

haikuri: puff of air

haisi: plant, branches hung in temple and xiriki roof

Haixaripá: sacred place on the slopes of Popocatépetl, the great snow-covered volcano near Mexico City

haiya: skin disease that appears in large lumps

Hakayuka: mythical monster that lives in the sea

hakéli (hakéri, hakiru): child who represents the souls of children

hale-uke: bitter plant used in wolf shamanism

Haramára (Aramara): the Pacific Ocean

harápai: small aquatic animal, role of man who carries drum and accompanies shaman-singer

haríme: brief chant

harrits: long white ceremonial grass

haüri: tree (*Brossimum alicastrum*); bark used as medicinal remedy

hawíme: drenched or soaked

Hauríta: Where the Candle Is

Háutsitámi: Boy of the Falling Dew

haxári: ceremonial maize cake in the form of a rooster atop a mountain

Haxári Kuáixa: ceremony in June, eating of maize cakes before sowing ritual

Hayucarita: community of San José

hayuráme: bottles containing sacred water

heüyá: fever

Hewásiixe: the last, the sowing ritual

héwi (héweixi; héwixi pl.): ancient one

híkuli kariuyaale: down that covers the nodes on the lower part of the peyote

híkuri (híkuli, hiculi, hiculis, hikuris pl.): peyote (*Lophophora williamsii*)

Híkuri Néixa: ceremony, Dance of the Peyote

hikuricuiniya: disorder related to the ingestion of too much peyote during pregnancy

hixuapa: the Middle World

huave: amaranth (also called *wave* or *uáute*)

Hu tai: bird believed to protect apprentice from disorientation in the realm of the wolves

húna: man who steadies sacred post from falling over

huriécate: arthritic, rheumatic ailments and paralysis

icú (iku): maize

icú pepáyeyetsá (or icuxiya): digestive tract disorder caused by maize

i'ikewári: sorcery

ipaü: uterus

ipaüxíya: uterine prolapse, possibly cystocele,

rectocele, and/or enterocele

ipinári: chant which refers to the post that "reaches to the sky"

irücáriyá (or irüváriya): whooping cough; plant (*Triumfetta* spp.) used medicinally to treat whooping cough

irüváriya-huayéya: succulent (*Euphorbia* spp., Euphorbiaceae family) used medicinally to cure whooping cough

Itsanaxa: ceremony of the second clearing of fields

itári: bed

itáuki: envoys of the evil chanters, small malevolent animal visible only to shamans

itéüri: big ceremonial candle

itéüxiya: digestive tract disorder related to itéüri

ixitári: kidney stones; terminal part of deer intestine

iya' neukauka ayári: having one's head in the clouds, unreflecting

iya' wa' uka pukayári: having a lot of experience

iyári: heart-memory

iyaritsíye: through one's thought

kakaí: sandals

Kakauyaríte: ancestor dieties; the mountains and sacred stones as ancestors of the people

kaliwey (calihuey): temple (word borrowed from Nahuatl *calli* = house, *uey* = large, great; used by Huichols when speaking Spanish

Karatsíki: song that accompanies deer hunt ceremony

Karuánime: feast in June of the esquite

karwánime: ceremonial maize cake

Kariwari: deity of water and rain

Katsi: bat deity

kau'xe: cloth bed for sacred offering

Kauyumári: Deer Person, Huichol culture hero

Kauyumári Ulu ayeh—arrow of the deer spirit, power arrow made by all Huichol shaman apprentices

Kauyumaritzie: hill in middle of Wirikúta, home to Kauyumári

kawitéro (kahuitero; kahuiteros pl.): wise elder

Kewimúka (Kiewimúka): rain goddess who lives in the west

kiéri: Solandra spp.

kiéri-nanári: root of kieri

Kiéri Tewíyari: the personification of kiéri

Kieritáwe: the drunken Kieri person

kiéri-tsa: "similar to Kieri"; (also used for *Datura inoxia*)

kieríxiyá: possession by kiéri

kiliwei: woven baskets used to collect and transport peyote

kiiteniye (kitene, quiitenye): doorway, entry

Kuanameyéipa: place in Wirikúta where blue peyote grows

Kúkatámi: Bead Boy, Vulture

Kukatawíye: sacred place—cliff on southwestern plateau of San Andrés

Kumukemai: Father of the Wolves

Kumukemai Muyu-e: Black Wolf, Wolf Father from San Blas

Kumukemai Noít-tse: Multicolored Wolf, descendents of Black Wolf

Kumukemai uruyare: arrow of the wolves

Kumuketai: place near San Blas coast where wolf people lived in darkness

Kumukíta: area of all the wolf shrines

Kumutemai: Wolf Mountain, where an individual transforms into a wolf

kupá: hair

kupáixa: corn silk on young ears of corn

kupáya: stigmata on the ear of maize

küpiéri: tree trunk used to feed the ceremonial fire

küpierixíya: urinary infection

küpúri (cupuri): vital principle of the self located at the top of the head at the level of the tonsure or anterior fontanelle

kupüripiya (or kupüricuíniya): soul loss, i.e., when the küpuri of a person is stolen by an itáuki kutsiuri: woven or embroidered bag

kuutsala: sacred, beneficial water

Kuyetuaripa: Place of the Stacked Trees; power place of the blue wolves, considered female and married to the male place, Muxía uxíye, where there are kíeri plants that teach people how to become wolves

küxauri nánari: plant (*Lagenaria siceria*, Cucurbitaceae family), used to treat burns

Kuyuwananeime: temple of the rain serpent in Las Guayabas

kwíxu: hawk, raptor

mái: century plant (*Agave* spp.)

maixíya: severe malnutrition; may be associated with intestinal worms

makuche (macuche, makutse): tobacco (*Nicotina rustica*)

mara'akáme (mara'akáte pl.): shaman

maára: cactus (*Cereus*) used medicinally to treat kidney stones

matsi: elder brother

mawatisawa: sacred hole underneath the fire in the center of the temple

maxa: deer

Maxa Kwaxí: Deer Tail, shaman chief and ancestor deity

Maxa Kwaxí Matiniéri: where the ancestors led by Great-grandfather Maxa Kwaxí rested while searching for fire

Maxa Manáka: Where the Deer Rests, sacred place

Maxa Mateáwa: The Great Deer with the Wise Antlers

Maxa Teiwíyari: Deer Person

Maxa Yuávi: Blue Deer, metaphorical form of Kauyumári

maxaxiyá: deer disease, kwashiorkor

maye: feline

mayordomo: cargo member in charge of Catholic church and icons

métsa: moon

metsáxiyá: menstruation (also called *puxúre*)

meukatenake: bad luck

miküri: owl

miitali: reciprocal term for grandmother, great aunt, granddaughter or grandniece for a feminine ego

mitsi: ceremonial mat

Mowarixi: rain ceremony

Muequi (Müüqui) Cuevixa: ceremony to call the dead

Muku Yuávi Muyíka Awatúsa: White Antlers Which Travel in the Blue Hill

Muiníma: House of Their Mother

Muti Weúku: vulturelike bird without feathers

mu-u: head

mu-úcuiniya: headache

müüqui: death

müüquitapestiéva: mortuary altar

muviéri: shaman's plumed wand of power

Muviéri Yuávi: feathered wand with blue feathers

Muxía Uxíye: Place Where the Sheep Lay, main house of the wolves where the highest ranking multicolored wolves (Ulowe-Noitze) live

náite (náitu): all

Nakawé: name of Tatutsi, Great-grandmother—the old goddess of the earth and growth

nakawé-küye: tree (*Ptelea trifoliata*, Rutaceae family) used to treat tawaiya disease

Nalatawoatua: place where people eat kiéri to learn about becoming wolves

nama: to obstruct, to close or hide

namakáme: an identity that hides another within it

Namáwita: harvest festival

namáxiya: digestive disorder

nanaimari: female infertility

nanáwata: ceremonial dance, named after a pre-deluge people

nari muxa: plant (*Triumfetta* spp.) used to treat whooping cough

Nariwamei: goddess of water, also responsible for epilepsy

natikari: the god's night

natüárica: tuberculosis

Nauku: Our Elder Grandmother, rain goddess

Naurratáme (Nauzra): man responsible for hearing the confessions of the peyoteros

nauxi: flower (*Macrosiphonia hypoleuca*, Aposynaceae family) used medicinally to cure cough

Nauzra (Naurratame): keeper of the peyote, cargo

nawá: maize beer, fermented drink

naxi: white ash

naxipúri: root of plant (*Senecio* spp., Compositae family) used medicinally to treat urinary disorder related to naxi

naxixíya: urinary disorder

neptikuuye urukame'ku: urukáme sickness

nerüitsi: scabies

netü: that which sprouts or gushes

netüáricá: digestive tract disorder that is from that which sprouts or gushes

netüáricá-huayéya: generic name for two kinds of plants to heal the disorder netüáricá

neu' urukáme: I am an urukáme

niérika: portal to the other world

niérikáxiyá: disease of the niérika, depression, paranoia

niwemama mepucaxüri: falling and hitting the head causing disharmony of the life force of a person's küpúri

niwetári (tapesti): altar

Niwétsika (Nivétsika, Niuetsika): maize goddess, the cargo holder of the maize-peyote who is expected to sing inaudibly in parallel with the principal shaman-singer

Nu'ariwaméi (Nariwamei): rain god of the east

nuwoltiviya urukáte: to catch, master, and tame the urukáme

pari: hour that unites night with day

Paliatsi: place along the road to Wirikúta

pampayutsi (pampariós): Huicholized

Spanish for *gracias a díos*, "thanks be to God"

panacaxüni (panacayüna): dehydration

panyé-iwetsi: miscarriage, premature birth

Párikuta Muyéka: he who wanders about at the end of the night, i.e., the Morning Star

Paritsika: great deer

Paritsika Manáve: place in Wirikúta where yellow peyote grows

Paritsikatsiya: place where the white wolves live

Paritsikiye: the place of the dawn, Wirikúta

Paríyakutsie: the end of the night

paye-ucá: pregnancy

piwáme: falcon

Pukulipi'ya: being without life

pukupuripi'ya: taking away the kupüri

puta-eva: vomiting

putse: copal incense

putsi: squash stem

puxure: menstruation (also called *metsáxiyá*), from *metsa* = moon

quetsü (ketsu): fish

quetsüxíya: illness called "fish disease," may be tuberculosis

quiitenyi (kiitenyi): doorway, entry

quizasuri nava ayamati: bottle gourd with maize beer

Rau'unár (Reunar): sacred extinct volcano in Wirikúta

raye: rattlesnake

rayu: large fly

Sakaimúka: western solar deity

Samalowe (Samalovi): descendents of the Father of the Wolves, Kumukemai

Samalowe nearíka: wolf image or disk offering

Samalowete á Ulu: arrow of the wolves

San Andrés Cohamiata: community (Huichol name = Tatéi Kí'ye, House of Our Mother)

San José: community (Huichol name = Hayucarita [Ayukarita], Where the Water Grows)

San Miguel Huastista: community in the jurisdiction of San Andrés Cohamiata

San Sebastián Teponahuaxtlan: community of San Sebastián

Santa Catarína: Tuapuri

Saurizika: (Saulizika, Saurixika, Tsaurrika, Xaurixikáme) chief mara'akáme of the indigenous community temple

Seriekáme Maxa Kwaxí: Great Grandfather Deer Tail

sikuáki: clown

situi (tsitui): small bird

sumé (chumé): mucus

taatsi: sweet cane similar to sorghum

tacuache: opossum (Nahuatl) (see Huichol *yauúxu*)

taheitüa: the underworld (also *tapiápa*, according to Preuss)

tai: fire

Takutsi Nakawé: Our Great Grandmother of Growth and Generation

Takutsi Yurameka: another name for Grandmother Growth

takwátsi: plaited, oblong covered basket containing all one's shamanic objects, also called takwátsi Kauyumári

Tamáts Haiwiyéme: Our Elder Brother the Rain-giving Cloud

Tamátsi, Tamátzika: Our Elder Brother Deer

Tamátsi Wawatsári: a stag whose antlers have eight tines, the "principal deer" or master of the species

Tamátsi Ékatewári: Our Elder Brother Wind

Tamátsi Kauyumári: Our Elder Brother Kauyumári, the culture hero, Deer Person, divine messenger and principal spirit ally of Tatewarí and the mara'akáme (shaman-singer)

tamé: tooth

tamé-cuiniya: toothache

tamíwari: large ceremonial maize cake

tápa: either side of the thorax

tápacuíniya: pneumonia

tapesti (niwetári): altar

taríma: foot drum

Tashawime: Yellow Maize Girl

Tatata: Christ figure, crucifix

Tatatári: singing cargo counterpoint to Saulizika

Tatéi Haramára: Our Mother the Pacific Ocean

Tatéi Híkuri: Our Mother Peyote

Tatéi Ki'ye: Place (House) of our Mother (San Andrés Cohamiata)

Tatéi Kukurukú 'Uimari: Our Mother Dove Girl, the maize goddess

Tatéi Matiniéri: Where Our Mother Is, sacred springs on pilgrimage to Wirikúta

Tatéi Nariwáme: Our Mother Who Lives in the East (also *Naariwáme*, according to Preuss) (see also *Nu'Ariwamei*)

Tatéi Neixa (Tatéi Neizra, Tatéi Néirra): Dance of Our Mother, autumn ceremony

Tatéi Wérika 'Uimári: Our Mother Young Eagle Girl

Tatéi Xapawiyemáka: Our Mother the Rain-giving Zalate Tree

Tatéi Yurianáka: Our Mother the Earth Moistened-for-Planting

Tatewarí: Our Grandfather (Fire)

Tatewarisíe: sacred place; "up there where our Grandfather (Fire) is"

tatewarixíya: urinary disorder related to Tatewarí

tátsiu: rabbit

tatuani (tatoani): govenor (an honorific, of Nahuatl origin)

Tatutsi Mazra Kwazí (Maxa Kwaxí): Great-grandfather Deer Tail

Tau: the sun

tauka: the soul that remained in the earth at birth

Taupa (Teupa): Where the Son Was Born, sacred place near San Jose

táuri: maize dough balls ritually fed to the fire

Taurúnita: the land of light

tau'uru: sun's ray, arrow of the sun

taukawuwu: vine hung from temple roof, represents souls of cargo holders

Taurawime: Red Maize Girl

tawiya (tawaiya): bubonic plaque, disease that comes from the sun

Taweakáme (Tawekáme): drunk, alcoholism, god of drunkeness

Ta Werikua: temple in San Jose, named after the eagle

Tayaupá: Our Father the Sun

te iyariyári: to originate from a single heart

Teakáta: sacred area with complex of caves and unusual geological formations near Santa Catarína, called the Huichol Mecca by Lumholtz

teaku (tekü): squirrel

téiwari (téwari): neighbor, mestizo, whites and others who speak only Spanish, foreigner; Sp. vecino

te'ka: stone

temu: toad

temuitsi: impetigo

temuxíya: severe malnutrition accompanied with anorexia and severe diarrhea

temuxíya-huayeyári: plant used to treat temuxíya illness

tepári: circular stone disk carved with sacred symbols

teparíxiya (or teparicuíniya): disease caused by a tepári

teparíxiya huayéya: that which cures tepári sickness

tepe: potent, locally brewed agave alcohol

Tepecano (Tepehuan): indigenous neighbors of the Huichols speaking a Piman language

Tetamuyéwie: Where the Stone Hangs, sacred place south of the Huichol community of Guadalupe Ocotán

tétsu: tamale

tetsuxíya: severe malnutrition, may be associated with intestinal worms

teuainuríxe (tevainuríxe): young maize cobs, name given to young children in the first fruits ceremony

teukali: grandfather in the literal sense, baptismal godfather

teukári: grandparent, grandchild

Teúpa: sacred area near San José, "Where the Sun Was Born"

teute tauteuni tauxi: part of mortuary ceremony called the placement of black molars

tevali'r: deceased deer hunters

tewainuríxe: young ears of maize

tewarí (te'vali): grandfather, grand uncle, and, reciprocally, grandson, grand nephew, ego being masculine; generic term for urukáme

Tewarí Yuráme: Jesucristo, Christ

tewátzi: animal form of the aged fire god Tatewarí

tewíyari: person

teyupani: church

tikaripa (tukaripa): in the night, in the rainy season

Timuxáwe: fire spirit who planted the first milpa

toloatzin (toloache): Nahuatl name for several species of *Datura*

tolohuaxihuitl: Nahuatl name for several species of *Datura*

Tseriakáme: temple of the rattlesnakes in Cohamiáta

tsikári: short chant when ceremonial cakes are eaten at noon; thorn or spine

Tsikúri temai: Thorn Boy

tsikúri: thread crosses, God's eye

tsinári: maize beverage made with maize smut

tsipüriquiyá: rubella

tsipüriquiyá-huayéya: root (*Kosteletzya tubiflora*, Malraceae family) used medicinally to treat rubella

tsítsicayacuai: plant used medicinally to treat urinary disorder

tsoka tsana leke: berry used in wolf shamanism

tsucáxiyá: respiratory tract illness related to mucus

tsuwíri: false peyote (*Ariocarpus retusus*)

Tuapuri: community of Santa Catarina

tuchi: potent distilled alcohol from sotol cactus

tuka: spider

Tukakáme (Tutákame): god of death, death goddess, counterpart to moon goddess

tukari: (tukaále)—life; moon goddess

tuki: circular community temple

tuíxu: peccary, animal spirit companion of Takutsi Nakawé

tumári (tumále): maize meal mixed with water

tumíni: money

Tumuánita: At the Place of Dust

Tumuxávi: mythical person; also name of bird

Tunuamei: the morning star; also name of temple in San Andrés, and name of Saulizika when he is singing in the temple

tupiles: police in the traditional community government (borrowed from the Nahuatl *topilli; topileque* pl.)

tüpina ukí: plant (*Loeselia mexicana*, Polemoneacae family) used to treat headaches

Turiamukamai: Hill of the Deer and Wolves, place where the yellow wolves live

Turikíye: Place of the Children, home of the red wolves

tutahuri: source of special power sought by some shamans that involves psychotropic plants and vision quests

tutu: flower, often used as verbal and pictorial metaphor for peyote

tutú-yuyuavi: flower (*Cuphea* sp., Lytracea family) used to treat conjunctivitis

tutuwári: flower (*Zinnia augustifolia*) used medicinally for fever

tutuwi: parrot

tuxári: black pigment

tuxaríya: dandruff

tuxu: plant used for funerary ceremony

Tuzáme: White Maize Girl

Uaínu: name of litle bird with yellow feathers that lives near the coast, appears as shaman's helper

uáute: amaranth (also called *wave* or *huave*)

Uaxa Kupáya: sacred place, "The Hair of Uaxa 'uimári"

Uaxa 'uimári: Maxa Kwaxí's sister

uki'raatsi: ancestors

ukiwákame: companions of Thorn Boy, leaders of the hunt on the right and the left

uíwa: woven belt used in ceremony for new fruits

Ulowe-Noitze: highest ranking multicolored wolves

ulu (ülü, uru, ürü): arrow

Ulu Temay: personal name meaning arrow man, arrow youth, or newly made arrow

ulu'-uámi: the one for whom it is necessary to make an arrow

Ulu tzutúa: temple of the staffs of power in Las Pitayas

umé-manumuri: bone fracture

Upayaküha: sacred rocky area near Chapalagana River, where whooping cough illness emerged

üpá: skunk

üqui: sweet maize cane

üquixiya: digestive tract illness believing to come from maize

Üra: roadrunner (*Geococcyx californianus*), name of deity and disease

üracuiniya: disease caused by üra

uráwee: wolf

urú (ürü, ulu, ülü): arrow

urú muxáure: yellow arrow

urukáme (ürükáme, urukáte or ututeru pl.): stone or rock crystal; manifestation of living person's or ancestor's soul

urukáte wa'riliki (wa'xiriki): house of the urukáme, the ancestor god house found on most ranchos

urukuakáme (Uru Kuakáme): carrier of the staffs of authority; keeper of the temple urutexi: votive arrows

uruxiya: disease caused by the urukáme

utsa (ütsa): tree (*Haemotoxilon brasiletto*), "brasil tree" whose red wood is used for power objects and medicinally to treat pneumonia

utsa: hairy subterranean spider, probably trapdoor spider, also called "bear of the earth"

utú uxavi: plant used to cure dysentery

Utuanáka: Our Mother Moist Earth, cargo holder representing 'Utuanáka

Ututáwita: name of a sacred cave

uupári: small shrub with berries whose leaves are favored by deer

uwéni tiritsi: miniature chairs for the gods

uxa: yellow root used to make face paint

üxi: eye

üxicuiníya: conjunctivitis

vainúri (wainúri): miniature woven sacred tobacco bag

waiyari: the heart memory of our Great Grandparents

Wakuri'kitene: doorway or gateway of cuuri, elder sister (the Mother Peyote); place name of the entrance to Wirikúta

Wakúritsie: mountain at the edge of the peyote country, meaning uncertain but Huichols say it means "On their Peyote," where he/she manifests him/herself

Watákame: Clearer of Fields, the only man to survive the great flood that destroyed a previous world (also called *Watemukáme*)

wave: amaranth, alternate name for Watákame (also called *huave*, or *uáute*)

wavezríya: kwashiorkor

Wawatsáta: cave of the great deer Wawatsári

Waxa Manáka: the resting place of Waxáa 'uimari

Waxáa 'uimári: Young Maize Field, Maxa Kwaxí's sister who brought the peyote

Waxa Yui: Maize Field

Waxe Uimi: Our Mother (the beautiful maiden)

Waxíwie: mara'akáme's helper

Waxa Temaikü: Nu'Ariwamei's brother

wekiüxi: tail motion of a fish

wekiüxíya: digestive tract disorder said to resemble tail motion of fish

wequíxa: plant root used to heal namáxiya illness

Wérika (Werikua): the solitary eagle; the sun; red-tailed hawk

Wérika Niuquiári: the Word of the Solitary Eagle

Wérika 'uimári: Eagle Girl

Werikáme: Eagle Person

weriya-huayéya: plant used to treat arecüxi, nematode worms

Werúku Tupíya: Vulture Bow

weyéiya: medicine for, that which heals

wima' kuara: part of the Tatei Néirra ceremony

Wirikúta: sared land of the peyote

Wixárika: term Huichols use to refer to themselves, meaning uncertain but possibly "the people" or "true people"

xáipi 'iyari: luminous fly, firefly; manifestation of the soul of deceased

xama: dried corn husks

Xapawiyemeta: Lake Chapala

xápa: wild fig tree

xaquí: esquite, parched maize

xari (xarite): large clay pot used to ferment maize beer

xaurixikáme (Saurizaka, Sauüzika, Tsaurrika): organizer and principal singer of the deer hunt

xarixíyá: illness that may be kwashiorkor

Ximuánita: Place Where There Are Small Stones

xiquiri: mirror used by shamans

xiri: mouse

xiriki (riliki): household temple or ancestor god house

xiwerika tuxa: species of falcon

xrake xra: berries used in wolf shamanism

xruáve tecuculi: bitter plant used in wolf shamanism

xucúri tumíne ayamaniti: votive gourd containing coin offering

xucúri yayatásme: votive gourd containing tobacco offering

xukúri (xukúli, xucúri, xucúrii): votive gourd bowl (Nahuatl *xicalli*; Mex. Sp. *jícara*)

Xuráwetamai: Star Boy

xuriya cuitayári huayéya: plant (*Vernonia steetzil*, var. *aristifera*, Compositae family) used medicinally to cure dysentery

xuriya-cuitayári: dysentery

xürixíya (rrürixiya): high temperature in a specific part of the body

xüye: armadillo

xru-tule: prayer candle with ribbons and flower attached

ya: tobacco (*Nicotiana rustica*)

yakuaixiya (yakuarriya): urinary disorder

Yakwawáme: name for Thorn Boy, leader of the hunt and representative of the fire god

yakwé (yakwei): small wart gourd for the tobacco used for deer hunting and peyote pilgrimage

Yauvitutsi: coyotes who have the "key" to open the door for the peyoteros who want to enter Wirikúta

yáwe hikuri: peyote of Kauyumari and wolves and coyotes

yeeri: wild edible tuber

yeiyári (yereeya): custom, tradition, "the very way"

yeuca: avocado

yeuca xavari: leaves from the avocado tree (*Persea americana*, Lauraceae family) used medicinally to treat headaches

Yoáwime: Blue Maize Girl

Yokawima: Dog-Woman, the first female ancestor after the great flood

yuaitsu: blue staff

yucamá-peyemíe: breech delivery

yuhunáme: role of old man who acts out sexual intercourse with dancers disguised as women

Yuramáka: Mountain of the Budding

yuriépa: stomach

yutsi te'akua: the heavens

yuwíme: drenched or soaked

Zrapauviyéme (Xapauviyéme): female water deity in Lake Chapala

Compiled by Stacy B. Schaefer

BIBLIOGRAPHY

Adovasio, J. M., and G. F. Fry

    1976   Prehistoric Psychotropic Drug Use in Northeastern Mexico and Trans-Pecos Texas. *Economic Botany* 30:94–96.

Aguirre Beltran, Gonzalo

    1963   *Medicina y Magia.* Instituto Nacional Indigenista, México, D.F.

    1967   *Regiones de Refugio.* Instituto Nacional Indigenista, México, D.F.

    1970   *El Proceso de Aculturación y el Cambio Socio-Cultural en México.* Universidad Iberoamericana, México, D.F.

Amador, Elias

    1892   *Bosquejo Historico de Zacatecas.* 2 vols. Escuela de Artes y Oficios, Zacatecas. (Reprinted 1943.)

Anderson, Edward

    1969   The Biogeography, Ecology, and Taxonomy of Lophophora (Cactacea). *Brittonia* 21:4:299–310.

    1980   *Peyote: The Divine Cactus.* The University of Arizona Press, Tucson.

Anguiano Fernández, Marina

    1976   *Nayarit: Costa y Altiplano en el Momento del Contacto.* Escuela Nacional de Antropología e Historia, México, D.F.

Anguiano, Marina, and Peter T. Furst

    1978   *La endoculturación entre los Huicholes,* 2nd ed. Instituto Nacional Indigenista, México, D.F.

(Anon.)

    1871   *Memoria Presentada por el Ejecutivo del Estado del Zacatecas a la Honorable Legislatura Sobre los Actos de su Administración.* Imp. de Mariano Mariscal, Zacatecas.

(Anon.)

    1952   *Relaccion de los Pueblos du su Majestad de Reyno de Nueva Galicia y de los Tributarios que en Ellos Hay: Minas de Tepeque y Otros Pueblos.* Vargas Rea, México, D.F.

(Anon.)

    1959   *Relacion de Nuestra Señora de Zacatecas.* Porrua, México, D.F.

(Anon.)

    1968   Viajes de Fray Alonso Ponce al Occidente de México. Seminaria de Cultura Mexicana, Guadalajara.

Anzures y Bolaños, María del Carmen

    1987   La curación y los 'sueños.' In *Historia de la religión en Mesoamérica y Areas Afines,* ed. by B. Dahlgren, pp. 21–31. I Coloquio, Universidad Autónoma Nacional de México, México, D.F.

Arlegui, José

    1737   *Crónica de la Provincia de S. Francisco de Zacatecas.* Hogel, México.

Arregui, Domingo Lazaro

    1946   *Descripción de la Nueva Galicia.* Padua, Seville.

Bakewell, Peter J.

    1971   *Silver Mining and Society: Zacatecas 1546–1700.* Cambridge University Press, Cambridge.

Barth, Fredrik, ed.

    1969   *Ethnic Groups and Boundaries*. Little Brown, Boston.

Bauml, James A.

    1989   A Review of Huichol Indian Ethnobotany. In *Mirrors of the Gods, Proceedings on the Huichol Indians*, ed. by Susan Bernstein, pp. 1–10. San Diego Museum of Man Papers No. 25, San Diego.

    1994   Ethnobotany of the Huichol People of Mexico. Ph.D. dissertation in Botany, Claremont Graduate School.

Bauml, James A., Gilbert Voss, and Peter Collings

    1990   Short Communications, '*Uxa* identified. *Journal of Ethnobiology* 10:99–101.

Benítez, Fernando

    1968a   *En la Tierra Magica del Peyote*. Ediciones ERA, México, D.F.

    1968b   *Los Indios de México*, vol. 2. Ediciones ERA, México, D.F.

    1975   *In the Magic Land of Peyote*. The University of Texas Press, Austin.

Benzi, Marino

    1972   *Les Derniers Adorateurs du Peyotl*. Editions Gallinard, Paris.

Bernadello, Luis M., and Armando Hunziker

    1987   A Synoptic Revision of Solandra (Solanaceae). *Nordic Journal of Botany* 7:639–652.

Beutelspacher, Ludwig

    1991   Proyecto Arcqueológico Aguamilpa. *El Nayar* 4:21–27.

Bohannon, Paul, and Fred Plog, eds.

    1967   *Beyond the Frontier: Social Process and Cultural Change*. Natural History Press, Garden City, N.J.

Boke, Norman H., and Edward F. Anderson

    1970   Structure, Development, and Taxonomy in the Genus *Lophophora*. *American Journal of Botany* 57(5):569–578.

Bonfils Batalla, Guillermo

    1970   Del indigenismo de la revolución a la antropología crítica. In *De eso que llaman Antropología Mexicana?*, ed. by Arturo Warmann et al. Comité de Publicaciones de la Escuela Nacional de Antropología e Historia, México, D.F.

Brand, Donald D.

    1971   Ethnohistoric Synthesis of Western Mexico. In *Handbook of Middle American Indians*, vol. 11, ed. by Gordon Ekholm and Ignacio Bernal, pp. 632–656. University of Texas Press, Austin.

Cabrera Ipiña, Octaviano

    1991   La fantástica Cuenca del Río Verde de San Luis Potosí. Guia arqueológica. In *Arqueología de San Luis Potosí*, ed. by Patricio Dávila Cabrera and Diana Zaragoza Ocaña, pp. 31–78. Instituto Nacional de Antropología e Historia, México, D.F.

Campbell, Lyle

    1979   Middle American Languages. In *The Languages of Native America: Historial and Comparative Assessment*, ed. by Lyle Campbell and Marianne Mithun, pp. 902–1000. The University of Texas Press, Austin.

Casillas Romo, Armando

    1990   *Nosología mitica de un pueblo: Medicina tradicional Huichola*. Editorial de Universidad de Guadalajara, Guadalajara.

Ciudad Real, A. de

    1873   *Relación breve y verdadera de algunas cosas de las muchas cosas que sucedieron al Padre Fray Alonso Ponce en las provincias de Nueva España*. 2 vols. Madrid.

Corona Nuñez, José

1953   Relaciones Arqueológicas entre las Huastecas y Regiones al Poniente. In *Huastecos, Totonacos y sus Vecinos*, ed. by Ignacio Bernal and Eusebio Dávalos Hurtado, pp. 475–482. Revista Mexicana de Antropología, México, D.F.

Cutler, Hugh

1978   A Cultural Sequence from the Sierra Madre of Durango, Mexico. In *Across the Chichimec Sea, Papers in Honor of J. Charles Kelley*, ed. by Carroll L. Riley and Basil C. Hedrick, pp. 186–189. University of Southern Illinois Press, Carbondale.

Davila Garibi, J. Ignacio

1927   *Breves Apuntos Acerca de los Chimalhuacanos: Civilización y Costumbres de los Mismos.* Sainz, Guadalajara.

de la Mota y Escobar, Alonso

1968   *Descripción Geográfica de los Reinos de Nueva Galicia, Nueva Viscaya, y Nuevo León.* Instituto Jalisciense de Antropología y Historia, Guadalajara.

de Vos, George, and Lola Romanucci-Ross, eds.

1975   *Ethnic Identity: Cultural Continuities and Change.* Mayfield Publishing, Palo Alto, Calif.

del Hoyo, Eugenio

1949   *Jerez, el de López Velarde.* Grafica Panamericana, México, D.F.

Diaz, José Luis

1986   Plantas magicas y sagrados de la medicina indígena. *México Indígena* 9:26–29.

Diguet, Léon

1899   Contribution a l'Etude Ethnographiques des Races Primitives au Mexique. La Sierra de Nayarit et ses Indigènes. In *Nouvelles Archives des Missions Scientifiques et Litteraires*, vol. 9, pp. 571–630. Paris.

1907   Le 'peyote' et son usage rituel chez les Indiens de Nayarit. *Journal de la Societé des Americanistes de Paris* 4:21–29.

1911   Idiome Huichol. Contribution a l'Etude des Langues Mexicaines. *Journal de la Societé des Americanistes de Paris* 8:23–54, n.s.

1992   *Por Tierras Occidentales entre Sierras y Barrancas*, ed. by Jesús Jáuregui and Jean Meyer. Centro de Estudios Mexicanos y Centroamericanos de la Embajada de Francia en México and the Instituto Nacional Indigenísta, México, D.F.

Eger, Susan (Valadez)

1978   Huichol Women's Art. In *Art of the Huichol Indians*, ed. by Kathleen Berrin, pp. 35–53. Fine Arts Museums of San Francisco/ Harry N. Abrams, New York.

Eliade, Mircea

1964   *Shamanism: Archaic Techniques of Ecstasy.* Pantheon Books, New York.

Evans, Susan T.

1990   The Productivity of Maguey Terrace Agriculture in Central Mexico during the Aztec Period. *Latin American Antiquity* 1(2):117–132.

Fikes, Jay Courtney

1985   Huichol Identity and Adaptation. Unpublished Ph.D. Dissertation, Department of Anthropology, University Microfilms, University of Michigan. Ann Arbor.

1993   To Be or Not to Be: Suicide and Sexuality in Huichol Funeral-Ritual Oratory. In *New Voices in Native American Literary Criticism*, ed. by Arnold Krupat, pp. 120–148. Smithsonian Institution Press, Washington, D.C.

Flattery, D. S. and M. Schwartz

1989   *Haoma and Harmaline: The Botanical Identity of the Indo-Iranian Sacred Hallucinogen "Soma" and Its Legacy in Religion, Language, and Middle Eastern Folklore.* University of California Press, Berkeley.

Furst, Jill Leslie (McKeever)

1989 The Horned Rabbit: Natural History and Myth in West Mexico. *Journal of Latin American Lore* 15(1):137-149.

Furst, Peter T.

1967 Huichol Conceptions of the Soul. *Folklore Americas* 27:39-106.

1968 *The Parching of the Maize: An Essay on the Survival of Huichol Ritual.* Acta Etnographica et Linguistica 14, Vienna.

1969 Myth in Art: A Huichol Depicts His Reality. *The Quarterly* 7(3):16-26, publication of the Los Angeles County Museum of Natural History.

1972 To Find Our Life: Peyote among the Huichol Indians of Mexico. In *Flesh of the Gods: The Ritual Use of Hallucinogens,* ed. by Peter T. Furst, pp. 184-236. Praeger Publishers, New York.

1974 The Thread of Life: Some Parallels in the Symbolism of Aztec, Huichol and Pueblo Earth Mother Goddesses. In *Prospectos y Balance de la Antropología Mexicana,* pp. 235-245. Sociedad Mexicana de Antropología, XIII Mesa Redonda, México, D.F.

1974 Kunst der Klassischen und Nach-Klassischen Periode in West-México. In *Propyläen-Kunstgeschichte,* vol. 18: *Das Alte Amerika,* ed. by Gordon R. Willey, pp. 193-201 and plates 122-137. Propyläen-Verlag, Berlin.

1976 *Hallucinogens and Culture.* Chandler and Sharp, San Francisco.

1978 The Art of 'Being Huichol.' In *Art of the Huichol Indians,* ed. by Kathleen Berrin, pp. 18-34. The Fine Arts Museums of San Francisco/Harry N. Abrams Inc., New York.

1989a Review of *Peyote Religion: A History,* by Omer C. Stewart. *American Ethnologist* 16(2):386-387.

1989 The Life and Death of the Crazy Kiéri: Natural and Cultural History of a Huichol Myth. *Journal of Latin American Lore* 15(2):155-179.

1993 Huichol Cosmogony: How the World was Destroyed by a Flood and Dog-Woman Gave Birth to the Human Race. In *South and Meso-American Spirituality,* ed. by Gary H. Gossen, in collaboration with Miguel León-Portilla, pp. 303-323. Crossroad, New York.

1994 The Maiden Who Ground Herself: Myths of the Origin of Maize from the Sierra Madre Occidental. *Latin American Indian Literatures Journal* 10(2):101-155.

Furst, Peter T., and Marina Anguiano

1976 'To Fly As Birds': Myth and Ritual As Agents of Enculturation Among the Huichol Indians of Mexico. In *Enculturation in Latin America: An Anthology,* ed. by Johannes Wilbert, pp. 95-181. UCLA Latin American Center Publications, Los Angeles.

Furst, Peter T., and Barbara G. Myerhoff

1966 Myth as History: The Jimson Weed Cycle of the Huichols of Mexico. *Antropológica* 17:3-39.

Furuno, K.

1967 Mekishiko shaman no dokutake genkaku (Hallucination by toxic mushrooms among Mexican shamans). In *Genshibunka noto (Notes on Primitive Cultures),* pp. 121-140. Kinokuniya Shinsho, Tokyo.

1973 Mikaijin no shukyo taiken (The religious experiences of primitive peoples). In *Genshi shukyono kozo to tenkai (Structure and development of primitive religions),* pp. 390-416. Sanichi Shobo, Tokyo.

Gerhard, Peter

1982   *The North Frontier of New Spain*. Princeton University Press, Princeton.

Gonzalez Martínez, J. M.

1987   *Los Huicholes Ganaderos Ricos de Jalisco*. Instituto Nacional Indigenista, México, D.F.

Grimes, Joseph E.

1961   Huichol Economics. *América Indígena XXI*, 4:281-306.

1981   *El Huichol. Apuntes Sobre el Léxico*. Department of Modern Languages and Linguistics, Cornell University, Ithaca, N.Y.

Grimes, Joseph E. and Thomas B. Hinton

1969   The Huichol and Cora. *Handbook of Middle American Indians*, vol. 8, part 2, ed. by Evon Z. Vogt, pp. 792-813. University of Texas Press, Austin.

Harner, Michael J.

1973a   The Sound of Rushing Water. In *Hallucinogens and Shamanism*, ed. by Michael J. Harner, pp. 28-33. Oxford University Press, New York.

1973b   The Role of Hallucinogenic Plants in European Witchcraft. In *Hallucinogens and Shamanism*, ed. by Michael J. Harner, pp. 15-27. Oxford University Press, New York.

Harte, John, et al

1991   *Toxics A to Z: A Guide to Everyday Pollution Hazards*. University of California Press, Berkeley.

Hell, Christina

1988   *Hirsch, Mais und Peyote in der Konzeption der Huichol: Ursprung und Transformation eines Symbol-Komplexes*. Münchner Beiträge zur Amerikanistik, vol. 22. Klaus Renner Verlag, Hohenschäftlern, Bavaria.

Hendrick, Basil C., J. Charles Kelley, and Carroll L. Riley, eds.

1971   *The Northern Mexican Frontier*. Illinois University Press, Carbondale, Ill.

Hernández, Francisco

1651   *Nova Plantarum, Animalium et Mineralium Mexicanorum Historia. . . .* B. Deuersini et Z.Masotti, Rome.

Herskovits, J. Melville

1952   *El Hombre y sus Obras*. Editorial Fondo de Cultura Economica, México, D.F.

Hinton, Thomas B., ed.

1972   *Coras, Huicholes y Tepehuanos*. Instituto Nacional Indigenista, México, D.F.

Hrdlička, Aleš

1903   The Region of the Ancient "Chichimecs," with Notes on the Tepecanos and the Ruin of La Quemada, Mexico. *American Anthropologist* 5(3):385-440, n.s.

Jáuregui, Jesús

1992a   La antropología de Diguet sobre el Occidente de México. In *Por Tierras Occidentales entre Sierras y Barrancas*, by Léon Diguet, pp. 7-37, Jesús Jáuregui and Jean Meyer, eds. México, D.F.: Centro de Estudios Mexicanos y Centroamericanos, Instituto Nacional Indigenista y Embajada de Francia en México. México, D.F.

1992b   Tres Mariachis Jaliscienses olvidas en su Tierra. *Cuadernos de Estudios Jaliscienses* No. 9. *El Colégio de Jalisco*, Guadalajara.

1993   Un Siglo de Tradición Mariachero entre los Huicholes: La Familia Ríos. In *Musica y Danzas de Gran Nayar*, Jesús Jáuregui, ed. Centro de Estudios Mexicanos y Centroamericanos, Instituto Nacional Indigenista, México, D.F.

in press Como los Huicholes se hiciéron Mariacheros: El Mito e la Historia. In *Cultura y*

Comunicación: *Edmund Leach in Memoriam*, ed. by Jesús Jáuregui, Eugénia Olavarría y Victor Franco. Fondo de Cultura Económica, México, D.F.

Jiménez Moreno, Wigberto

    1943   Tribus e Idiomas del Norte de México. In *El Norte de México y el Sur de Estados Unidos: Tercera Reunión de Mesa Redonda sobre Problemas Antropológicos de México y Centro América*, pp. 121-133. Sociedad Mexicana de Antropología, México, D.F.

    1970   Nayarit: Etnohistoria y Arqueología. In *Historia y sociedad en el mundo de habla española, Homenaje a José Miranda*, ed. by Bernardo García Martínez et al., pp. 17-26. El Colegio de México, México, D.F.

Johnson, Frederick

    1940   The Linguistic Map of Mexico and Central America. In *The Maya and their Neighbors*, ed. by C. L. Hay et al., pp. 88-114. New York.

Kennard, Edward

    1989   Honanyestiwa and Honanyesnöma—A Visit to the Beyond (A Hopi Text). *Tlalocan* 11: 151-172.

Kimura, Y., and T. Kimura

    1981   *Genshoku nippon yakuyo shokobusto zukan* (An illustrated book of Japanese medicinal plants). Hoikusha, Tokyo.

Klüver, Heinrich

    1926   Mescal Visions and Eidetic Vision. *American Journal of Psychology* 37:502-515.

    1928   *Mescal: The "Divine Plant" and its Psychological Effects.* Kegan, Paul, Trench, Trubner, London.

    1942   Mechanisms of Hallucinations. In *Studies in Personality*, ed. by Q. McNemar and M. A. Merrill. McGraw-Hill, New York.

    1966   *Mescal and Mechanisms of Hallucinations.* University of Chicago Press, Chicago.

Knab, T. J.

    1976   Huichol Nahuatl Borrowings and their Implication in the Ethnohistory of the Region. *International Journal of American Linguistics*, 42:261-263.

    1977   Notes Concerning the Use of Solandra among the Huichol. *Economic Botany* 31(1):80-86.

    1979   Prestamos Linguisticos como Indicadores de Inter-cambios Culturales. *Actas de XVI Mesa Redonda de la Sociedad Mexicana de Antropología* 1:219-226. México, D.F.

Knoll, Max

    1958   Anregung geometrischer Figuren und anderer subjektiver Lichtmuster in elektrischen Feldern. *Zeitschrift für Psychologie* 17:110-126.

Knoll, M. and J. Kugler

    1959   Subjective Light Pattern Spectroscopy in the Encephalographic Frequency Range. *Nature* 184:1823-1824 (London).

Knoll, M., J. Kugler, O. Hofer, and S. D. Lawder

    1963   Effects of Chemical Stimulation of Electrically Induced Phosphenes on their Bandwidth, Shape, Number and Intensity. *Confinia Neurologica* 23:201-226.

Knoll, M., O. Hofer, S. D. Lawder, and U. M. Lawder

    1962   Die Reproduzierbarkeit von elektrisch angeregten Lichterscheinungen (Phosphene) bei zwei Versuchspersonen innerhalb von 6 Monaten. *Elektromedizin* 7(4):235-242.

Kroeber, Alfred L.

    1934   *Uto-Aztecan Languages of Mexico.* Iberoamericana 8. University of California Press, Berkeley.

La Barre, Weston

1970   Old and New World Narcotics: A Statistical Question and an Ethnological Reply. *Economic Botany* 24:368-373.

1974   *The Peyote Cult*. The Shoestring Press, Hamden, Conn.

Ladrón de Guevara, Eduardo

1977   *Importancia del Trabajo en el Estado de Nayarit*. Tésis de la Facultad de Economica de la Universidad de Guadalajara, Guadalajara, Jal.

Lewin, Louis

1888   Über Anhalonium lewinii. *Archiv für Experimentalen Pathologischen Pharmakologie* 24:401-411.

1924   *Phantastica—Die Betäubenden und erregenden Genussmittel*. G. Stilke, Berlin.

1964   Phantastica—Narcotic and Stimulating Drugs—Their Use and Abuse (English translation of above). Routledge & Kegan Paul, London.

López Austin, Alfredo

1991   The Myth of the Half Men who Descended from the Sky. In *To Change Place: Aztec Ceremonial Landscapes*, ed. by David Carrasco, pp. 152-157. University Press of Colorado, Boulder.

Lumholtz, Carl G.

1900   *Symbolism of the Huichol Indians*. Memoirs of The American Museum of Natural History 3(1), New York.

1902   *Unknown Mexico*, 2 vols. Scribner's and Sons, New York.

1904   *Decorative Arts of the Huichol Indians*. Memoirs of The American Museum of Natural History 3(3), New York.

1986   *El arte simbólico y decorativo de los huicholes*. Instituto Nacional Indigenista, México, D.F.

1988   *A Nation of Shamans: The Huichol Indians of the Sierra Madre*. Reprint edition of *Symbolic Art of the Huichol Indians*. Bruce I. Finson, Oakland, Calif.

Lyon, Capt. G. F.

1826   *Journal of a Residence in the Republic of Mexico in the Year 1826*. Murray, London.

Mandell, Arnold

1978   The Neurochemistry of Religious Insight and Ecstasy. In *Art of the Huichol Indians*, ed. by Kathleen Berrin, pp. 71-81. The Fine Arts Museums of San Francisco/Harry N. Abrams, New York.

Mason, J. Alden

1912   The Tepehuán Indians of Azqueltán. *Proceedings of the 18th International Congress of Americanists*, pp. 344-351. London.

1918   "Tepecano Prayers." *International Journal of American Linguistics*, 1: 91-153.

1924   *Use of Tobacco in Mexico and South America*. The Field Museum of Natural History, Leaflet 16, Chicago.

1936   The Classification of the Sonoran Languages. In *Essays in Anthropology in Honor of Alfred L. Kroeber*, pp. 183-198. University of California Press, Berkeley.

1948   The Tepehuan, and the other Aborigines of the Mexican Sierra Madre Occidental. *América Indígena* 8(4):289-299.

1950   *The Language of the Papago of Arizona*. Museum Monographs, The University Museum, University of Pennsylvania, Philadelphia.

1952   Notes and Observations on the Tepehuan. *América Indígena* 12(1):33-53.

Mason, J. Alden, and George Agogino

    1972   *The Ceremonialism of the Tepecan.* Eastern New Mexico University Contributions in Anthropology, vol. 4, no. 1, Portales.

Masuda, Y.

    1977   *Indio bunmei no kobo (Rise and fall of Indian Civilization)*, vol. 7. Sekai no rekishi (World History series). Kodansha, Tokyo.

Mata Torres, Ramón

    1976   *Los Peyoteros.* Guadaljara.

    1980   *La Vida de los Huicholes*, vol 1. Guadalajara.

Matute, Juan I.

    1885   *Noticia Geográfica, Estadistica del Partido de Sanchez Román, Estado de Zacatecas.* Guadalajara.

    1887   *Noticia Geográfica Estadistica del Partido Sanchez Román.* Perez Lete, Guadalajara.

McLeary, James A., Paul S. Sypherd, and David L. Walkington

    1960   "Antibiotic Activity of An Extract of Peyote *Lophophora Williamsii* (Lemaire) Coulter." *Economic Botany*, vol. 14, pp. 247-249.

McKeever Furst, Jill Leslie

    1995   *The Natural History of the Soul in Ancient Central Mexico.* Yale University Press, New Haven.

McKenna, Terence

    1992   *The Archaic Revival.* Harper, San Francisco.

    1992   *Food of the Gods.* Bantam Books, New York.

    1993   *True Hallucinations.* Harper, San Francisco.

Meade, Joaquín

    1942   *La Huasteca, época antigua.* Editorial Cossio, México, D.F.

    1953   Relaciones entre Las Huastecas y las Regiones al Poniente. In *Hustacos, Totonacos y su Vecinos*, ed. by Ignacio Bernal and Eusebio Dávalos Hurtado, pp. 475-483. Revista Mexicana de Estudios Antropológicos, México, D.F.

Mendizabal, Miguel Orthón de

    1943   Colonización del oriente de Jalisco y Zacatecas. In *El Norte de México y el Sur de Estados Unidos. Tercera Redonda sobre Problemas Antropológicas de México y Centro América*, pp. 40-49. Sociedad Mexicana de Antropología, México, D.F.

    1946/7   *Obras Completas*, vols. 1-6. México, D.F.

Miller, Wick R.

    1983   "Uto-Aztecan Languages." In *Handbook of Middle American Indians*, ed. by Alfonso Ortiz, pp. 113-124. Smithsonian Institution, Washington D.C.

Monaghan, John D.

    1990   "Reciprocity, Redistribution, and the Transaction of Value in the Mesoamerican Fiesta." *American Ethnologist*, vol. 17, No. 4, pp. 148-164.

Mullenax, Nancy A.

    1994   Languages of Heaven and Rituals of Earth: Interpretating Native American Religions. In *Five Hundred Years After Columbus: Proceedings of the 47th International Congress of Americanists*, comp. by E. Wyllys Andrews V and Elizabeth Oster Mozillo, pp. 18-20. Middle American Research Institute, Tulane University, New Orleans.

Myerhoff, Barbara G.

    1974   *Peyote Hunt: The Sacred Journey of the Huichol Indians.* Cornell University Press, Ithaca, N.Y.

    1978a   Return to Wirikuta: Ritual Reversal and Symbolic Continuity on the Peyote Hunt of the Huichol Indians. In *The World Upside Down: Studies in Symbolic Inversion*, ed. by Barbara Babcock. Cornell University Press, Ithaca, N.Y.

1978b   Peyote and the Mystic Vision. In *Art of the Huichol Indians*, ed. by Kathleen Berrin. The Fine Arts Museums of San Francisco/Harry N.Abrams, New York.

Nabokov, Peter, and Robert Easton

1989   *Native American Architecture*. Oxford University Press, New York.

Nahmad Sittón, Salomón

1981   Some Considerations of the Indirect and Controlled Acculturation in the Cora-Huichol Area. In *Themes of Indigenous Acculturation in Northwest Mexico*, ed. by Thomas B. Hinton and Phil C. Weigand, pp. 4–8. Anthropological Papers No. 38, University of Arizona Press, Tucson.

1982   Coras, Huicholes y Tepehuanes durante el periodo 1854–1895. In *Coras, Huicholes y Tepehuanes*, ed. by Thomas B. Hinton et al., pp.157–162. I.N.I. Serie de Antropología Social No. 11, México, D.F.

Negrín, Juan

1975   *The Huichol Creation of the World*. E. B. Crocker Art Gallery, Sacramento.

1977   *El Arte Contemporaneo de los Huicholes*. University of Guadalajara, Guadalajara, Mexico.

1985   *Acercamiento histórico y subjectivo al huichol*. University of Guadalajara, Guadalajara, Mexico.

n.d.   *Le chaman-artiste*. Embassy of Mexico, Paris.

Nuñez Franco, R., ed.

1982   *Canciones, mitos y fietsas huicholes*. CONAFE CULTURA/Secretaría de Educación Pública, México, D.F.

Oki, K.

1988   *Nonai mayaku to atama no kenko (The effect of narcotics on the brain and mental health)*. Kodansha Blue Backs Series, Tokyo.

Ortéga, José de

1754   *Apostolicos afanes de la Companía de Jesús en su Provincia de México*. P. Nadal, Barcelona.

1887   *Historia de Nayarit, Sonora, Sinaloa y ambas Californias*. México.

Oster, Gerald

1970   Phosphenes. *Scientific American* 222:83–87.

Ott, Jonathan

1979   *Hallucinogenic Plants of North America*. Wingbow Press, Berkeley, Calif.

1993   *Pharmacotheon: Entheogenic drugs, their plant sources and history*. Natural Products Co, Kennewick, Wash.

Palafox Vargas, M.

1985   *Violencia, drogas y sexo entre los Huicholes*. Instituto Nacional de Antropología e Historia, México, D.F.

Periodico Oficial del Estado de Nayarit

1990   Acuerdo del Lic. Celso Humberto Delgado Ramírez, Gobernador Constitional del Estado de Nayarit sobre La Declaratorio de Sitio de Patrimonio Cultural del Grupo Etnico Huichol, Ubicado en el Municipio de San Blas, Estado de Nayarit. Tepic, Nayarit, July 10, 1990.

Perrin, Michel

1976   *Le chemin des indiens morts. Mythes et symboles guajiro*. Payot, Paris. (Second edition, 1983.)

1986   *The Way of the Dead Indians*. (English edition of above.) The University of Texas Press, Austin.

1991   *Les patricien du reve. Un exemple de chamanisme*. PUF, Paris.

Plan Lerma Assistencia Tecnica

1966   *Operación Huicot*. Estados Unidos Mexicanos, Poder Ejecutivo Federal, Guadalajara.

Powell, Philip Wayne

1952   *Soldiers, Indians, and Silver.* University of California Press, Berkeley.

Ponce, Fray Alonso (see Ciudad Real, A. de)

Preuss, Konrad Theodor

1906   Reisebericht aus San Isidro. *Zeitschrift für Ethnologie* 38:955-966.

1907   Die Hochzeit des Maises und andere Geschichten der Huichol-Indianer. *Globus* 91:185-192.

1907   Ritte durch das Land der Huichol-Indianer in der mexikanischen Sierra Madre. *Globus* 92(10):167-171.

1908   Die religiösen Gesänge und Mythen einiger Stämme der mexikanischen Sierra Madre. *Archiv für Religionswissenschaft* 11:369-398.

1908   Reise zu den Stämmen der westlichen Sierra Madre in Mexiko. *Globus* 94:147-167.

1909   Dialoglieder der Rigveda im Lichte der religiösen Gesänge mexikanischer Indianer. *Globus* 95(3):41-46.

1912   *Die Nayarit-Expedition. Textaufnahmen und Beobachtungen unter mexikanischen Indianern. Vol. 1: Die Religion der Cora-Indianer.* B. G. Teubner, Leipzig.

1932   Au Sujet du Caractère des Mythes et des Chants Huichols. *Revista de Instituto de Etnología de Universidad Nacional de Tucuman* 2:445-457.

Reed, Karen B.

1972   *El INI y los Huicholes.* Colección de Antropología Social No. 10. Instituto Nacional Indigenista, México, D.F.

Reichel-Dolmatoff, Gerardo

1978   *Beyond the Milky Way: Hallucinatory Imagary of the Tukano Indians.* UCLA Latin American Studies, vol.42. Latin American Center Publications, University of California, Los Angeles.

Rendón, Francisco

1953   *La Provincia de Zacatecas en 1803.* Ed. by Beatriz Rojas. Zacatecas.

1992   *Los Huicholes: Documentos Históricos.* Bibliotéca Gonzalo Aguirre Beltrán, Instituto Nacional Indigenista/Centro de Investigaciones e Estudios Superiores en Antropología Social, México, D. F.

Rojas, Beatriz, ed.

1993   *Los Huicholes: Documentos Históricos.* Instituto Nacional Indigenista/Centro de Estudios Mexicanos y Centroamericanos, Colegio de Michoacán, México, D.F.

Romney, A. Kimball

1971   The Genetic Model and Uto-Aztecan Time Perspective. In *The North Mexican Frontier*, ed. by Basil Hedrick, J. Charles Kelley, and Carroll L. Riley, pp. 225-232. Southern Illinois University Press, Carbondale.

Rueking, Frederick

1953   Ceremonies of the Coahuiltecan Indians of Southern Texas and Northeastern Mexico. *The Texas Journal of Science* 3.

Rudgley, Richard

1993   *Essential Substances: a Cultural History of Intoxicants in Society.* Kodansha International, New York.

Ruiz de Alarcón, Hernando

1984   *The Treatise on the Heathen Superstitions that Today Live among the Indians Natives to this New Spain, 1629.* Trans. and ed. by J. Richard Andrews and Ross Hassig. University of Oklahoma Press, Tulsa.

Sahagún, Bernardino de

    1950–1969 *Florentine Codex: General History of the Things of New Spain*, 12 vols. Trans. by Charles E. Dibble and Arthur J. O. Anderson. The School of American Research and The University of Utah, Santa Fe, N.M.

Salinas de la Torre, Gabriel

    1946   *Testimonios de Zacatecas.* Imp. Universitaria, México, D.F.

Santoscoy, Alberto

    1899   *Nayarit.* Yguiniz, Guadalajara.

Sasaki, H.

    1980   *Shamanizumuu. ekusutashi to hyorei no bunka (Shamanism: the culture of ecstasy and the culture of spirit possession).* Chukoshinsho, Tokyo.

    1983   *Hyorei to shamanizumu (Spirit possession and shamanism).* Todai Shuppankai, Tokyo.

Sauer, Carl O.

    1934   *The Distribution of Aboriginal Tribes and Languages in Northwest Mexico.* Iberoamericana 5. University of California Press, Berkeley.

Schaefer, Stacy B.

    1989a   The Loom and Time in the Huichol World. *Journal of Latin American Lore* 15(2):179–194.

    1989b   Huichol Weaving: A Preliminary Report. In *Mirrors of the Gods, Proceedings on the Huichol Indians*, ed. by Susan Bernstein. San Diego Museum of Man Papers No. 25, San Diego. pp. 33–39.

    1990   *Becoming a Weaver: The Woman's Path in Huichol Culture.* Ph.D. dissertation in Anthropology, University of California at Los Angeles. Under contract to University of Utah Press.

    1993a   "The Loom as a Sacred Power Object." In *Art in Small Scale Societies, Contemporary Readings*, ed. by Richard Anderson and Karen Field. Prentice Hall, Englewood Cliffs, N.J.

    1993b   Huichol Indian Costumes: A Transforming Tradition. *Latin American Art* 5(1):70–73.

    1995a   The Crossing of the Souls: Peyote Perception and Meaning in Huichol Culture. *Integration* 5:35–40.

    1995b   Huichol: Becoming a Godmother. In *Portraits of Culture: Ethnographic Originals*, ed. by Melvin Ember, Carol Ember and Richard Levinson. Prentice Hall, Englewood, N.J.

    1996   The Huichol Indians. In *Encyclopedia of World Cultures*, vol. 8. Hall & Co., Boston.

Schneider, Pedro, with Patricia Díaz Romo

    1993   La Agonía del Pueblo Huichol. *Macrópolis* 2(82):6–19, Mexico.

Scholes, France V.

    1935   The First Decade of the Inquisition in New Mexico. *New Mexico Historical Review* 10:195–234.

Schultes, Richard Evans

    1972   An Overview of Hallucinogens in the Western Hemisphere. In *Flesh of the Gods: The Ritual Use of Hallucinogens*, ed. by Peter T. Furst, pp. 3–54. Praeger Publications, New York. (Revised edition 1990, Waveland Press, Prospect Heights, Ill.)

Schultes, Richard E., and Albert Hofmann

    1992   *Plants of the Gods.* Healing Arts Press, Rochester, Vt. (Originally published by McGraw-Hill, 1979).

Schultes, Richard Evans and Albert Hofmann

    1988   *Sekai dai hyakka jiten. (World Encyclopedia)*, vol. 28. Heibonsha, Tokyo.

Secretaría de Educación Publica-Instituto Nacional Indigenista (SEP-INI)

1971   *Acción Indigenista en la Zona Cora–Huichol*. Dirección General de Educación Extraescolar en el Medio Indígena, México, D.F.

Serret, Carolina

1979   *Estudio Economico del Tabaco en el Estado de Nayarit*. Tesis de Lic. en Geografía de la Universidad Autónoma Nacional de México, México, D.F.

Shelton, Anthony A.

1988   Los Huicholes en el Mundo de los Santos. *México Indígena* 22:48–50

Siegel, Ronald

1977   Hallucinations. *Scientific American* 4:132–140.

Siegel, Ronald, and Murray Jarvik

1975   Drug-Induced Hallucinations in Animals and Man. In *Hallucinations: Behavior, Experience and Theory*, ed. by Ronald Siegel and Louis West, pp. 81–161. John Wiley and Sons, New York.

Siegel, Ronald, Peter Collings, and José Luis Diaz

1977   On the Use of Tagetes lucida and Nicotiana rustica as a Huichol Smoking Mixture: The Aztec'Yahuatil' with Suggestive Hallucinogenic Effects. *Economic Botany* 31:16–23.

Simeon, Remi

1963   *Dictionnaire de la Langue Nahuatl ou Mexicaine*. Akademische Druck- u. Verlagsanstalt, Graz.

Sorenson, E. R., Kalman Muller, and Nicolas Vaczek

1976   The Context of Huichol Enculturation. In *Enculturation in Latin America. An Anthology*, ed. by Johannes Wilbert, pp. 183–190. Latin American Center Publications, University of California, Los Angeles.

Spicer, Edward H., ed.

1961   *Perspectives on American Indian Culture Change*. University of Chicago Press, Chicago.

Stirling, Matthew W.

1942   "Origin Myth of Acoma and Other Records." *Bureau of American Ethnology, Smithsonian Institution, Bulletin 135*. Washington, D.C.

Swadesh, Mauricio

1968   Las Lenguas Indígenas del noreste de México. *Anales de Antropología* 5:75–86. Universidad Nacional Autónoma de México, México, D.F.

Tello, Fray Antonio

1984   *Crónica Miscelanea de la Sancta Provincia de Xalisco, Libro Segundo*. Guadalajara.

Thomas, Cyrus

1911   *Indian Languages of Mexico and Central America*. Smithsonian Institution, Bureau of American Ethnology, Bulletin 44, Washington D.C.

Torres, Fray Francisco Mariano

n.d.   *Cronica Miscelanea de la Sancta Provincia de Xalisco*. Instituto Jalisciense de Antropología y Historia, Guadalajara.

Tyler, Hamilton A.

1975   *Pueblo Animals and Myths*. University of Oklahoma Press, Norman.

Tyler, V. E., R. Brady, and J. E. Robbers

1988   *Pharmacognosy*, 9th ed., pp. 197–199. Lea and Febiger, Philadelphia.

Tyler, Varro E.

1992   John Uri Lloyd and the Lost Narcotic Plants of the Shawnee. *Herbalgram* 27:40–42. American Botanical Council, Austin.

Valadez, Susana (Eger)

    1986a   Dreams and Visions From the Gods: An Interview with Ulu Temay, Huichol Shaman. *Shaman's Drum* 6:18-23.

    1986b   Mirrors of the Gods: The Huichol Shaman's Path of Completion. *Shaman's Drum* 6:29-39.

    1989   Problem Solving in a Threatened Culture. In *Mirrors of the Gods, Proceedings of a Symposium on the Huichol Indians*, ed. by Susan Bernstein. San Diego Museum of Man Papers No. 25, pp. 17-32.

Valadez, Susana, in collaboration with Mariano Valadez

    1992   *Huichol Sacred Rituals.* Dharma Enterprises, Oakland, Calif.

Vidal, Salvador

    1972   *Miscelanea: Datos de la Epoca Colonial Comprendidos en los Años 1578-1810.* Zacatecas.

Waitz, Theodor

    1858-72   *Anthropologie der Naturvölker.* 6 vols. Friedrich Fleischer, Leipzig.

Warmann, Arturo, A. M. Nolasco, G. Bonfil, M. Oliveira de Vázquez, and E. Valencia

    1970   *De eso que llaman Antropología Mexicana?* Comite de Publicaciones de la Escuela Nacional de Antropología e Historia, México, D.F.

Weigand, Phil C.

    1972   *Cooperative Labor Groups among the Huichol Indians in Jalisco, Mexico.* University of Southern Illinois Press, Carbondale.

    1979a   Considerations about the Archaeology and Ethnohistory of the Tepecanos, Huicholes, Coras, Tequales and Mexicaneros; with Notes on the Caxcanes. In *Anuario de Historia*, no. 2. Universidad Autónoma de Zacatecas. (Republished, 1985, in *Contributions to the Archaeology and Ethnohistory of Greater Mesoamerica*, ed. by William J. Folan, pp. 126-187. Southern Illinois University Press, Carbondale.

    1979b   Contemporary Social and Economic Structure. In *Art of the Huichol Indians*, ed. by Kathleen Berrin, pp. 101-115. The Fine Arts Museums of San Francisco/Harry N. Abrams, San Francisco, New York.

    1981   Differential Acculturation among the Huichol Indians. In *Themes of Indigenous Acculturation in Northwest Mexico*, ed. by Thomas B. Hinton and Phil C. Weigand, pp. 9-21. Anthropological Papers No. 38, University of Arizona Press, Tuscon.

Weil, Andrew

    1980   *The Marriage of the Sun and the Moon.* Houghton Mifflin Co., Boston. (Japanese edition: *Taiyo to tsuki no kekkon.* Trans. by K. Ueno. Nippon Kyobunsha, Tokyo 1986.)

Weil, Andrew, and Winifred Rosen

    1983   *Chocolate to Morphine: Understanding Mind-Active Drugs.* Houghton Mifflin, Boston. (Japanese edition: *Chokoreto kara heroin made [From chocolate to heroin]*, trans. by Y. Hamilton, Daisanshokan, Tokyo.)

Werner, D.

    1989   *Donde no hay doctor. Una guia para los campesinos que viven lejos de los centros medicos*, 20th edition. Pax-México, México, D.F.

West, George

    1934   *Tobacco Pipes and Smoking Customs of the American Indians.* Bulletin of the Museum of The City of Milwaukee, vol. 17, parts 1 and 2, Milwaukee.

West, Robert C., and John P. Augelli

    1976   *Middle America: Its Lands and Peoples.* Prentice-Hall, Englewood Cliffs, N.J.

Wilbert, Johannes

1972   Tobacco among the Warao Indians of Venezuela. In *Flesh of the Gods: The Ritual Use of Hallucinogens*, ed. by Peter T. Furst, pp. 55–83. Praeger Publishers, New York. (Revised edition 1990, Waveland Press, Prospect Park, Ill.)

1976   Introduction. In *Enculturation in Latin America, an Anthology*, ed. by Johannes Wilbert, pp. 1–27. UCLA Latin American Center Publications, Los Angeles.

1981   Warao Cosmology and Yekuana Roundhouse Symbolism. *Journal of Latin American Lore* 7(1):37–72.

1987   *Tobacco and Shamanism in South America*. Yale University Press, New Haven.

Wilson, Peter J.

1988   *The Domestication of the Human Species*. Yale University Press, New Haven.

Yamazaki, T.

1989   Nasuka (Solanaceous plants). In *Nippon no yasei shokobutso II* (*Wild plants of Japan II*). Heibonsha, Tokyo.

Yoshida, T.

1984   *Shukyo Zinruigaku* (*Religious Anthropology*). Todai Shuppankai, Tokyo.

Zingg, Robert M.

1938   *The Huichols, Primitive Artists*. G. E. Stechert, New York.

1982   *Los huicholes, una tribu de artistas*, 2 vols. (Spanish translation of above). Instituto Nacional Indigenista, México, D.F.

n.d.   *Huichol Mythology*. Unpubl. manuscript in the possession of the School of American Research, Santa Fe, N.M.

Editor's Note: The English translations of the following titles of essays on the Huichols by Professor Masaya Yasumoto, and of the Japanese publications in which they appeared, were provided by the author:

Yasumoto, Masaya

1985   Semana Santa—the festivals of the Huichol. In *Studies of Catholic Culture in Mexico Villages*, vol. 3, ed. by Nomura Nobukiyo, pp. 33–80. Faculty of Literature, Kyushu University, Fukuoka.

1986   Notes on Huichol Logic. *Anthropological Quarterly* 17(3):231–253. Kyoto University, Anthropological Studies, Kyoto.

1987a   Peregrination of Peyote (1). In *Studies of Catholics in Mexican Villages* (IV), ed. by Nomura Nobukiyo, pp. 231–253. Institute of Comparative Studies of International Cultures and Societies, Kurame.

1987b   The Peyote Pilgrimage—concerning the several analyses of the symbolic association among deer, maize and peyote. In *Bulletin of the Institute of Comparative Studies of International Cultures and Societies* 2, pp. 37–58.

1988   The conquest of Nayarit and the Huichol Indians." In *Bulletin of the Institute of Comparative Studies of International Cultures and Societies* 3, pp. 1–34.

1989a   The Peyote Pilgrimage of the Huichol. *Ethnology Quarterly* 13(1):84–93. National Museum of Ethnology, Tokyo.

1989b   Polygamous Marriage among the Huichol. In *Religion, Law and Reality in Mexican Villages*, ed. by Nomura Nobukiyo, pp. 83–100. Institute of Comparative Studies of International Cultures and Societies, Kurume.

1989c The myths of the Huichols. In *Bulletin of the Institute of Comparative Studies of International Cultures and Societies* 6, pp. 73–108.

1989d Possession and Shamanism. Comment 1. In *Bulletin of the Anthropological Association of Kyushu University.*

INDEX

Paritsika, as principal dry season deity, 354; gaining of sight by, 357

Pariyakutsie, place of dawn, lit. "end of night," 126

Path of Completion, 20

Pax Porfiriata, 82

Peccary, 13, 14, 124, 180, 209, 231, 369; as companion and alter ego of earth goddess, 13; in Popol Vuh, 14

Perganum harmala, 305

Pérez de la Torre, Diego, 67

Pérez Tamáyo, Ruy, M.D., 443

Perrin, Michel, xi, xiii

Pesticides, as environmental disaster, 514; lack of protection against, 482; threats by, to Huichol health, 514

Peyote, as ally and protector, 20; antibiotic activity of, 20, 21; appearance of, as deer, 128; appearance of, as rattlesnake, 145; ceremonial eating of, on "Hill of Kauyumári," 149; ceremony of (Hikuri Neixa), 122; chemistry of, 154; cloning by, from root stock, 146 (Fig. 25); conception of, as female, 36; consumption of, by children, 161; cultural history of, 141; dating of, by UCLA, 141; designs of, woven and embroidered by women, 143; discovery of, in Trans-Pecos Desert Culture sites, 141; distribution of, by shaman as Nauxa (Keeper of the Peyote), 152; grinding of, 151 (Fig. 29); depiction of, in weavings, 144 (Fig. 23), 145 (Fig. 24); drying of, 215 (Figs. 45-47); earliest radiocarbon dates for, 56; ethnobotanical knowledge of, by Huichols, 136; as facilitator of ecstatic trance, 20; as flesh of divine Deer, 24; as focus of religious emotion, 23; functions of, 20; generation of, from antlers and body of deer, 312 (Fig. 74); generative nature of, 144; illness ascribed to, 213; importance of flowers of, 147; in daily life and religion 23; in pre-Columbian art, 141; in shaman's universe, 20; indigenous ethnobotany of, 141-48; ingestion of, as stimulant, 151; Keeper of, 152; legitimization of, need for, 500; levels of meaning of, to Huichols, 161-64; liquification of, 151; magical origin of, in Maxa Kwaxí legend, 36; manifestation of, as deer 17; as medicine, 20; Mother of, 17; natural range of, 141; "necklaces" of, 24; offerings to, 146; pharmacological links of, with tobacco, 154; planting of, in Sierra, 136; practical knowledge of, 136; preparation and consumption of, 148-53; relation of, to fertility of crops and animals, 23; representation of, in pre-Columbian art, 142 (Fig. 22); reproduction from seeds of, 144; role of: in ceremonies 17, in enculturation of children, 162, in life and religion, 23; in dry-season ceremonies, 17; rubbing of, on slain deer, 322; as sacrament of Native American Church, 55; slices of, distributed by shaman on peyote hunt, 150; spread of, in western Mexico, 43; stringing of, 24, 150; technique of harvesting of, 148; trade of, by Huichols, 24, 509; use of: by Aztecs, 141, by "civilized castas," 75, by Mexica priests, shamans and doctors, 55, by Spaniards in northern New Mexico, 86, in Tepecano ceremonialism, 53; as unifying force, 162; as virtual panacea, 20; as visionary sacrament, 53; visions, descriptions of, by peyoteros, 156-59

Peyote flowers, color symbolism of, 147

Peyote hunt, description by Preuss of 128; documentary films of, 506, 508; narrative of, 128; reenactment of, 129; relationship to growth of maize, 238

Peyote Mother, 26

Peyote pilgrims, 127

Peyote ritual, origin of, in Desert Culture, 23; relation of, to pre-Hispanic ceremonies, 23

Peyoteros, treatment of wounds by, with peyote, 21

Peyote visions, structure of, 156-61

Peyutl, 141

Phenylethylamine, 154, 155

Phenylethylamine alkaloids, 142

Phosphene images, integration of, into worldview and art, 156

Phosphene patterns, relationship of, to geometry of eye, 156

Pilgrimage, to Wirikúta, by wolves and coyotes, 143

Pima-Papago, 47

Pima-Papago-Tepehuan, 47

Piman, 48

Pine posts, symbolism of, in temple, 346-48 (Fig. 85)

Pinole, 192

Pipil, 47

Place of the Children, in wolf apprenticeship, 283

Plague, effects of, on Indians, 31

Plan Huicot, 462, 463, 506

Plants, use of, in wolf shaman training, 288

Polygyny, practice of, among Huichols, 236

Ponce, Fray Alonso, 40, 60, 69, 330, 449

Popocatépetl, 207

Popol Vuh, 14

Preuss, Konrad Theodor, xi, xiii, 11, 33, 89, 90, 92, 169, 264, 303, 448, 451, 455, 477

Preuss, Werner, 91

Priests, shamans as, 20

Prieto, Alejandro, 204

Primary education, 462

Prophylactic ritual, in Calling of the Dead ceremony, 386

Prophylactics, magical, 134

Psilocybe mushrooms, 27, 54, 155, 295; employed by Mazatec curers 233; identification of, with Christ by Mazatecs, 233-34

Psilocin, 155

Psilocybin, 155

Psychedelic patterns, recording of in art, as duty to the gods, 157

Puberty, 11

Purpon, Ignacio, M.D., 443

Querétaro, 142

Quetzalcóatl, 39, 121

Rabbit, horned, 15, 130

Radin, Paul, 186

Raijsbaum, Ari, 168

Printed in the USA
CPSIA information can be obtained
at www.ICGtesting.com
CBHW060012210924
14734CB00007B/497